Adult Development and Aging

Adult Development and Aging

♦

SECOND EDITION

MARION PERLMUTTER
University of Michigan

ELIZABETH HALL

JOHN WILEY & SONS, INC.
New York / Chichester / Brisbane / Toronto / Singapore

ACQUISITIONS EDITOR	*Karen Dubno*
PRODUCTION MANAGER	*Joe Ford*
DESIGNER	*Ann Marie Renzi*
PRODUCTION SUPERVISOR	*Lucille Buonocore*
COPY EDITOR	*Elizabeth Swain*
PHOTO RESEARCHER	*Jennifer Atkins*
PHOTO RESEARCH MANAGER	*Stella Kupferberg*

COVER PHOTOGRAPH: STOCK BOSTON/Jeffry Myers

Library of Congress Cataloging in Publication Data:

Perlmutter, Marion.
  Adult development and aging / Marion Perlmutter, Elizabeth Hall.—2nd ed.
    p. cm.
  Includes bibliographical references and indexes.
    ISBN 0-471-51846-8 (cloth)
    1. Adulthood. 2. Aging. 3. Life cycle, Human. 4. Developmental
psychology. I. Hall, Elizabeth, 1929– . II. Title.
HQ799.95.P47 1992
305.26—dc20   91-30732
                                                                            CIP

Printed in the United States of America

10 9 8 7 6

Printed and bound by R.R. Donnelley & Sons, Inc.

Dedication

For my parents, Eleanor Lifschutz Perlmutter and Frank Perlmutter, whose lives have been my primary model of adulthood and whose continued growth and development I look forward to sharing.

MARION PERLMUTTER

For my grandfather, Robert Norman Hall, whose life made me question the stereotypes of aging, and for my husband, Scott O'Dell, whose example demolished them.

ELIZABETH HALL

◆ *Preface*

Since the first edition of this text appeared, adult development and aging have become even more central to the concerns of researchers and the general public. The change in the population balance in the United States and other technological societies has accelerated. Each year a new cohort of postwar baby boomers enters middle age, and fewer of their parents and grandparents follow a style of life that fits the cultural stereotypes of old age. Previous concepts of development no longer match the adult experience. It has become increasingly obvious that later life is not simply a time of decline, nor is early life exclusively a time of growth.

Continuing Features

The response to the first edition of *Adult Development and Aging* confirmed the need for a text that not only takes a life-span view of development but also draws on research in a variety of disciplines. The life-span view involves an awareness that development and aging have a biological basis but are open to cultural and environmental influence and that cohort and historical factors are partly responsible for differences between generations. Therefore, we stress development and aging at multiple levels: biological, psychological, sociological, anthropological, and historical.

The book has a topical organization. After establishing basic concepts of development and its study (Part One), we view adult development and aging at the level of biology and health (Part Two), move on to psychological functioning (Part Three), and close by considering the adult within a social context (Part Four). The discussions avoid compartmentalization of development by providing frequent examples of the ways in which various levels of development interact.

We also stress the plasticity of aging, emphasizing the fact that individuals and societies are flexible and possess the capacity to change. Our position is that few people function at the limits of their capacity and that much of the decline associated with aging is the result of particular life situations. Although we present a view of aging that suggests a more positive prospect than is often portrayed, we do not ignore the negative features of aging.

Unlike some books, which discuss aging primarily in terms of norms and assume that the process is similar for everyone, we stress the diversity of aging: in individuals, in women and men, in different ethnic groups, and in different cultures. We have provided material on sex differences in biological and health status (Part One), cognition and personality (Part Two), the way relationships within and outside the family are experienced (Part Three), and the course of career development (Part Four). Ethnic and cultural differences are noted throughout the book, with Chapter 16 devoted entirely to this topic. A student who reads this book will not fall into the trap of assuming that experimental gerontological studies of white, middle-class males tell us all we need to know about aging.

With a basic goal of promoting an understanding of adult development and of life in an aging society, we present (1) the facts about adult development, adult aging, and the aging society; (2) the issues that grow out of those facts; and (3) the implications, for both the individual and the society. For example, in Chapter 7 we devote considerable space to discussing the ramifications visual and auditory changes have on daily life. We also help students relate theory and research to reality through the presentation of people's actual experiences, which are found throughout the text.

The book's content and presentation are aimed at advanced undergraduate students and beginning graduate students, and the book is written with the goal of developing analytic skills in students that will allow them to interpret age differences. Although the ideal reader has completed an introductory course in one of the behavioral sciences, we have tried to write in a clear and interesting manner that can be grasped by a student without this background. We have targeted a spectrum of disciplines so that the text can be used in a class made up of students in psychology, social science, biomedical science (such as nurses and dentists), or social service delivery (such as social workers).

Changes in the New Edition

Instructors familiar with the previous edition will notice both major and minor changes. Chapter 1 has been thoroughly revised, with an expanded discussion of the life-span approach, the introduction of the major processes responsible for developmental change, and a consideration of the plasticity of adult development and its limits. Chapter 8 has been reorganized to explain hypotheses concerning age changes in learning and memory and to spotlight the various influences on these processes, whether inherent in the task, the person, or the situation. The new organization of Chapter 9 sets the development of intelligence in a historical context, then proposes a three-tiered model of cognition that will help students understand changes in intelligence across adulthood. The discussions of creativity and wisdom have been revised and expanded in response to recent theory and research.

Another major change has been to drop the final chapter on death, which seemed to send some students away from the course with a negative feeling that we believe was unwarranted. We have incorporated essential portions of that chapter into Chapter 4, where we discuss the dying process, implications of modern medical technology, and an "appropriate death." Chapter 10 includes a discussion of life review and preparation for death, and in Chapter 11 we discuss bereavement in the context of widowhood.

Because work and retirement occupy a major portion of adult life, we now devote an entire chapter (13) to these topics, which have become as great a concern to women as to men. With the popularity of early retirement, what adults do in their leisure time has become an important issue, and so in Chapter 14, we have drawn together the non-work pursuits that fill the rest of adult life: leisure, education, religion, and politics. An entire chapter (15) focuses on social issues and social support; this allows us to consider social services as well as legal issues, economics, housing, and institutionalization.

Among the minor changes are the additions of sections on the debate over the adaptiveness of aging (Chapter 3), how a sense of control affects health (Chapter 5), how the presence of a family member with Alzheimer's disease affects the family (Chapter 6), Carl Jung's theory of adult personality (Chapter 10), and aging in Asian-American families

(Chapter 16). In addition the discussion of sexuality has been moved from the chapter on biological changes to Chapter 11, where it is integrated into the coverage of marriage relationships. Finally, the discussion of the personality changes that may accompany parenthood has been moved from the chapter on parent–child relationships to Chapter 10, where it is woven into discussions of gender differences in personality.

Pedagogy

Each chapter also contains the following special features that we hope will ease the student's path:

- An outline showing the logical arrangement of the text.
- An opening anecdote about real people that is followed by a brief overview of material covered in the chapter.
- A box on adulthood in today's world that shows how an aspect of the text affects real people. The boxes cover a broad spectrum, including a 100-year-old environmental activist trying to save the Florida Everglades (Chapter 1), a middle-aged man taking charge of his health after a massive heart attack (Chapter 4); a major corporation that discovers older adults make the best employees (Chapter 13); and a black, middle-class couple who enter retirement (Chapter 16).
- A concluding narrative summary of the material covered, organized by major topics within the chapter.
- A listing of key terms introduced in the chapter that appear in the glossary.
- An end-of-the-book glossary defining the key terms used in the book.
- An extensive bibliograhy at the end of the book that enables students to explore any topic more deeply or instructors to expand course coverage.

A complete *Instructor's Manual* is also available for the text. This manual contains chapter outlines, discussion topics, activity suggestions, resources, test questions, and transparency masters.

Acknowledgments

Revising a textbook requires the support and advice of many people. Deborah Moore insisted that we begin the revision, and Karen Dubno saw that we completed it. Others whose assistance was vital included Lucille Buonocore, who supervised the book's production and Elizabeth Swain, our copy editor. The inviting appearance of the final volume is the work of Jennifer Atkins, who tracked down the photos, and Ann Marie Renzi who designed the book.

We would also like to thank the reviewers, who were enormously helpful in their comments on the first edition and on various drafts of this edition: Freda Blanchard-Fields, Louisiana State University; Cameron Camp, University of New Orleans-Lake Front;

Stephanie M. Clancy, Southern Illinois University-Carbondale; Debra Cowart-Steckler, Mary Washington College; Sandra Fiske, Onandaga Community College; Jeffrey Flatt, Westfield State University; Stephen Hoyer, Pittsburgh State University; Janet Johnson, University of Maryland; Justin Lucien, Christian Brothers University; Robert Maiden, Alfred University; Rosellen Rosich, University of Pittsburgh-Johnstown; Mark Smircins, Blackburn D College; James H. Thomas, Northern Kentucky University; Amy Warren-Leubecker, University of Tennessee; Nancy White, Youngstown State University.

♦ Contents

Part One

❖

❖

Introduction to the Study of Adult Development

Chapter 1

◆

The Concepts of
Development and Aging

◆

"To enter the country of age is a new experience, different from what you supposed it to be. Nobody, man or woman, knows the country until he has lived in it and taken out his citizenship papers," explained critic Malcolm Cowley in *The View from 80* (1980). Impatient with the descriptions of aging produced by those of us who had not even reached a comparatively youthful 70, Cowley described old age without sentiment, recounting its triumphs and sorrows.

A member of Harvard's class of 1919, Cowley recounted the activities of some of his octogenarian classmates. Most of them seemed active and busy. Some were still in the occupations they had pursued all their lives—journalism, the ministry, business. Others had started new businesses. One classmate was now manufacturing cross-country skis; another was running a gardening firm; yet another had begun a service to sell out-of-print books by mail. A retired banker had become a successful painter, exhibiting and selling his watercolors.

Harvard graduates are a privileged group, with incomes far above the national average, but these men, who were born in the nineteenth century, may give us a preview of what aging is likely to become for more and more people. A famous Spanish toast wishes us *salud y pesetas y tiempo para gastarlas:* health and money and the time to use them. As we will discover in this book, general improvements in health and increased income among older adults indicate that this prospect may now be within the grasp of many people.

Although physical aging may place some limits on our activities and economic constraints still hamper far too many of us, the reports from researchers who study adulthood and aging are much more encouraging than the stereotypes most of us hold. Their studies indicate that life in the country of age is closer to Cowley's picture than to the gloomy portrait that haunts some people, and they hold the promise of continued improvement.

We begin this chapter by examining the place of adulthood and aging in the human life cycle and the changing experience of adulthood in American society. This discussion leads us to consider various perspectives on aging, where we find that the traditional picture of inevitable, universal decline has given way to a more optimistic picture of old age. The processes of aging, we discover, produce gains as well as losses. After looking at the multiple influences that foster change, we ask just how much consistency we can expect to find in a person's life. This question is heightened by our exploration of differences between and within individuals and the possibility of continued growth and development during the last decades of life.   ◆

THE HUMAN LIFE CYCLE

Divisions of the life span are arbitrary. They differ from one society to the next, and they change from one time in history to another. There are no clear physical benchmarks that guide the Western division of life into the main phases of infancy, childhood, adolescence, and adulthood. For example, some people see infancy as ending at about one year, when the baby begins to walk. Others see it as lasting until two, when youngsters begin to put several words together to form sentences. The marker that sets off one stage in the life span from another may be biological (puberty), cognitive (acquisition of language), or social (retirement).

STAGES OF ADULTHOOD

Once people enter **adulthood,** that portion of the life span after physical maturity, they continue to change in ways that make it difficult to treat the period as a single stage of life. Our study of adult development may be less confusing if we divide adulthood, which covers three-fourths of the life span, into five different stages: **early adulthood** (18–30), **middle adulthood** (30–50), **later adulthood** (50–65), **young-old age** (65–80), and **old-old age** (>80).

Deciding just when a person enters early adulthood is difficult, but we have chosen 18, the typical age at high school graduation and the usual time when those who do not go on to college assume adult responsibilities. The border between early and middle adulthood is also fuzzy, but the age of 30 is an approximate marker. During the early adult years, many women and men are relative novices at their undertakings, but by the age of 30, they presumably have assumed their independence and taken up their work and family roles. During the years between 30 and 50, most adult lives are heavily focused on the demanding responsibilities of family and work, but sometime around the age of 50, the nature of adulthood changes. Later adulthood marks the period when many adults have assumed a senior status and have begun to think and plan for retirement and life after their children have left home.

Changes in the nature of aging make it necessary to further divide the last portion of life. The years between 65 and 80 are referred to as young-old age, a time when the majority of people are free of major family and work responsibilities, but are still healthy and vigorous. The years after 80 are called old-old age, a time when an increasing number of people are frail and ill. But **chronological age,** or the elapsed time since birth, is not an infallible guide to this division. Bernice Neugarten (Neugarten and Neugarten, 1986), who first suggested these terms, has stressed that physical and mental condition, not chronological age, determines whether a person is ''young-old'' or ''old-old.'' A vigorous, healthy 85 year old would still be young-old, and a frail 65 year old would already have joined the ranks of the old-old.

BENCHMARKS OF MATURITY

It seems appropriate to call a 20-year-old man or woman an adult, but deciding just when a person reaches maturity or adulthood depends on how we define the concept. Maturity has been described in biological, psychological, social, and legal terms, but none of these descriptions produces an entirely satisfactory definition. Trying to establish the markers of maturity within the confines of U.S. society shows the extent of the problem and may explain why, as we will see in Chapter 15, the benchmarks of maturity differ from one society to the next.

Biological benchmarks of maturity are the easiest to measure. We can say, for example, that people reach biological maturity when they are able to reproduce. Yet few would call a 13-year-old girl or a 15-year-old boy mature. Another biological benchmark is the completion of physical growth; for most of us, this comes between the ages of 18 and 21,

Social maturity generally comes after biological and legal maturity has been reached. For many people, social maturity is marked by marriage and parenthood.

although growth may be prolonged until the mid-twenties under conditions of chronic undernutrition and disease (Bogin, 1988). Attaining these biological benchmarks is a precondition of maturity, but biological maturity by itself does not constitute maturity.

Psychological benchmarks of maturity are linked to the attainment of certain mental and emotional levels. The adult can adapt to new situations, think about the future, and plan for it. On the emotional level, the adult can commit himself or herself to intimate relationships (Erikson, 1980). Another benchmark of psychological maturity is the inner sense that one is an adult. This inner sense of maturity is so subjective that each person's sense of having attained it is highly ambiguous. When measured by the psychological benchmarks of maturity, some people in their thirties would still be immature.

The social benchmarks of maturity involve the assumption of adult roles. Social maturity generally comes when a person leaves home, marries, establishes a family, and becomes self-supporting. If childhood is a time of dependence, adulthood is a time of responsibilities. Yet many 25-year-old graduate students are still financially dependent and have not yet assumed family or occupational responsibilities. Other social benchmarks are conferred by law: an adult can vote, drive a car, drink alcoholic beverages, or serve in the armed forces. The time a person reaches these benchmarks varies, depending on the right specified and the country—or even state—of residence.

None of these benchmarks produces a satisfactory definition of maturity, and for most of us each comes at a different time. American society recognizes this disparity in an unofficial way when it regards adolescents as sexually mature but socially and psychologically immature (Miller and Simon, 1980). The recognition has led to such practices as the states' establishment of legal ages for sexual consent and the attempts by some states to require reproductive health service clinics to notify the parents of adolescent women who request an abortion. When the government grants individuals the right to vote in national elections, it assumes that by the age of 18 people are psychologically mature. But the Constitution sets up a different standard of maturity; it withholds the right to represent other voters in the House of Representatives until the age of 25 and in the Senate until the age of 30, and the office of president is restricted to individuals who are at least 35.

BENCHMARKS OF OLD AGE

Whether a person is old depends on what aspect of life we consider. An Olympic-class gymnast is old by the mid-twenties, and a professional tennis player by the age of 35. A musician or a writer may not be old at 80. The benchmarks of old age are as broad and subjective as the benchmarks of maturity, and the time of onset varies even more widely. The markers of age also may be biological, psychological, or sociological.

A major benchmark of biological age is the loss of reproductive ability. This biological marker, in the form of menopause, comes to women when they are about 50, but may never come to some men. Gray hair is another benchmark of age, and it, too, may arrive early or late. Physical decline is a third biological benchmark. With old age, sight and hearing usually deteriorate, breath becomes short, reflexes slow, and balance may become impaired, but there are great individual differences in the time of onset, rate, and severity of these changes. Another benchmark is frequent or chronic illness. When illness becomes a part of daily life instead of a brief interruption in good health, a further sign of age has appeared.

A major psychological benchmark of old age is the sense of decline, an awareness that the body no longer moves smoothly and without effort. When a person must plan carefully in order to get out of a bathtub, the sense of decline has arrived. A more positive psychological benchmark is the attainment of wisdom. With age may come an understanding of the significance of what is known—a realization of life's conditions and limits (Dixon and Baltes, 1986; Meacham, 1983: Orwall and Perlmutter, 1990).

The arrival of age's social benchmarks is spread across decades. Becoming a grandparent is a traditional social benchmark of age, but one that comes at no predictable time. The average American woman becomes a grandmother between the age of 49 and 51 and the average American man, a grandfather between 51 and 53 (Tinsley and Parke, 1984). But grandparenthood arrives as early as 30 for some people, while for others it is delayed until the seventies or eighties. Another social benchmark is retirement, which traditionally comes at age 65 but which arrives at an earlier age for many of today's older Americans and much later—or never—for others. The loss of one's parents is another marker of old age, because it promotes a person into the oldest surviving generation. This benchmark arrives later today than it ever did in the past. A final social marker is the loss of independence. In fact, dependence is the classic benchmark of old-old age, and it is closely associated with physical decline and illness.

All these benchmarks of old age are highly correlated with age, but for each of us they arrive at different ages. One woman may become a grandmother at 35, and another not until she is 70. One man may show severe physical decline at 55, but another may be 90 before his sensory and motor abilities are noticeably impaired. The existence of such wide differences among individuals indicates that years since birth is not a reliable guide to either maturity or old age.

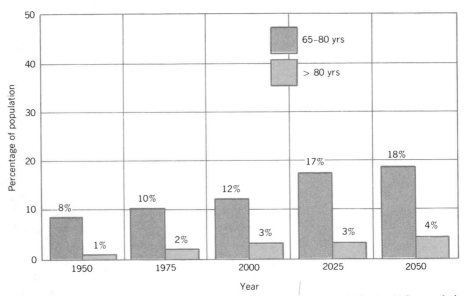

Figure 1.1   The graying of America. The percentage of older people in the U.S. population has increased steadily since 1950. By 2050, demographers expect the proportion of young-old adults to have increased by 225 percent and the proportion of old-old adults to have risen by 400 percent. *Source:* U.S. Senate, Select Committee on Aging, 1987–1988.

THE ADULT POPULATION

Not only do we have multiple definitions of maturity and old age, but over historical time the experience of adulthood has also changed. Two thousand years ago, half the Romans born in any year would be dead within 22 years; only a handful would live until their sixty-fifth birthday. By 1900, 4 out of every 100 Americans were 65 or older; half of those born during 1900 were dead within 49 years. Today 12 out of every 100 Americans are at least 65; by the year 2000, 13 out of every 100 may be that old, and by 2030 the proportion is likely to climb to 21 out of every 100 (U.S. Senate, Special Committee on Aging, 1987–1988) (see Figure 1.1). This dramatic change in survival rates has affected the structure of the population and the way individuals experience old age.

CHANGES IN THE AGE STRUCTURE OF THE POPULATION

The structure of a population is determined by two statistics: the rate of birth and the rate of death. When both birth rates and mortality are high, the population takes the shape of a pyramid, its broad base formed by infants and children and its narrow peak by old-old adults. In 1800, when more than half the population was younger than 16, the U.S. population formed such a triangle. Its base was massive and its sides rapidly narrowed to a long, sharp peak (see Figure 1.2). When mortality rates are low, the pyramid becomes increasingly rectangular. As each group of people born at the same time, known as a **cohort,** ages and moves up the pyramid, it loses fewer members until the peak becomes almost as broad as

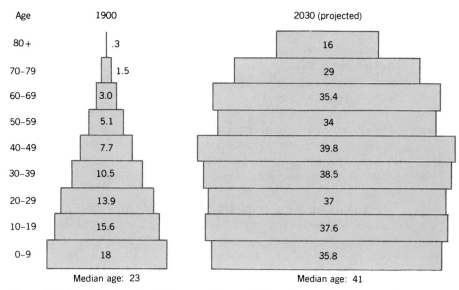

Figure 1.2   Squaring the triangle. Increased longevity has changed the structure of the U.S. population from a pyramid to a rectangle, as shown by contrasting the population (in millions) by decades in 1900 with the projected population in 2030. *Source:* Kotre and Hall, 1990, p. 349.

the base. Since 1800, something like that has been happening in the United States. But the trend has been accelerated in the past 25 years by declines in the birth rate (which shrinks the relative size of the pyramid's base) at the same time that more and more people began living into old age.

This combination of greater survival and reduced birth rate has changed the United States from a young society to an aging, even old, society. A fluctuating birth rate during the twentieth century has altered our population structure in an unusual way. Between 1946 and 1964, there was a sharp—and unexpected—upturn in American birth rates that created what has been called the "baby-boom" generation. As this cohort reaches each new stage of life, its effects transform society (Jones, 1980) (see Figure 1.3).

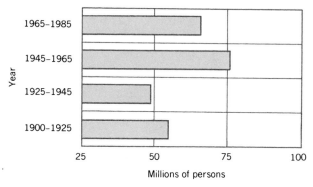

Figure 1.3   Size of birth cohorts across time. The size of a birth cohort affects all aspects of society, including job prospects, the demand for housing, and the consumption of resources.

When the baby-boom cohort was young, half the U.S. population was under 30. Babies were big business; homes for young, growing families were under construction. As members of the boom began leaving infancy, businesses that catered to infants and toddlers shrank, and businesses that catered to school-age children expanded. The educational system frantically built schools, only to see the classrooms empty and teachers lose their jobs as the shock of the boom moved on.

Most of the baby-boom generation has now entered middle adulthood; in fact, its first members turned 40 on January 1, 1986. As this cohort moves through later adulthood and old age, similar expansions and contractions will ripple through society. They will affect the sort of products that are available; the approach of advertising; the nature of housing; and the content of television, films, and other media. Just by being there, the baby boom has an enormous economic impact.

Meanwhile, the aging of the population already has changed society (Figure 1.4). Many high school classrooms are empty, and in some communities schools have been converted into centers for the aged; new houses have fewer bedrooms; retirement communities have sprung up across the land. Manufacturers of cars, appliances, furniture, fashions, cosmetics, and sporting equipment are more attentive to the wants and needs of middle-aged and old people. As the market for baseball bats shrinks, for example, the market for golf clubs and gardening equipment grows. As the cohort ages, we are likely to see fewer station wagons and vans on the highway and more full-size and luxury cars.

The aging of America has also spread to television. Networks that once insisted on youthful stars now find places in prime time for programs like ''The Golden Girls,'' ''Murder She Wrote,'' and ''Matlock,'' in which the leading characters have entered their sixties. In the future we can expect to see more advertising aimed toward people in the last part of their life span; for at least the last decade, people who are 65 or older have held about 30

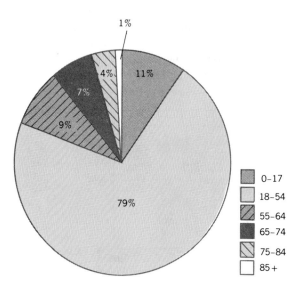

Figure 1.4   The United States today. The structure of the U.S. population in 1986 reflects the size of birth cohorts and increased longevity over the twentieth century.

percent of the discretionary spending power in the United States. As the baby boom surges into the retirement years, that proportion is likely to grow (Eisdorfer, 1983).

The shift in the structure of the population has other major implications for society. The looming increase in the number of retired people means a corresponding growth in the **old-age dependency ratio**—which is the number of people over 65 divided by the number between 20 and 64—the prime working years. Although many people over 65 are employed and a good many people over 20 are in school, this ratio is used as a guide to the number of workers whose Social Security contributions will be available to pay retirement benefits. In 1950 the ratio was 0.14; there were nearly 7 people of working age for each person who had reached the age of retirement. By 1984 the old-age dependency ratio had risen to 0.20; there were only 5 workers for each retiree. The ratio is expected to reach 0.38 by 2030, leaving only 2 1/2 workers to support each retired person (Palmer and Gould, 1986). Between 2025 and 2045, the baby boom will be turning 80. That means that the group of old-old people, those who are most likely to be frail and ill and so require social services, will expand dramatically, perhaps placing an enormous burden on the health care industry (Siegel and Taeuber, 1986).

CHANGES IN ADULTHOOD

Increased survival rates mean that most people can look forward to a longer adulthood. The great killers of nineteenth-century adults, such as tuberculosis, have almost been eliminated. Advances in the treatment of cancer and a better understanding of the relationship between life-style and heart disease have also reduced deaths among older people. As a result, Americans can expect to spend 50 to 60 years as adults. In the past, children and adolescents prepared for adulthood, but few adults prepared for an old age they doubted they would ever attain.

When we believe that we are likely to die young, physical risks may seem acceptable, and there may seem little need to save for the future. A Roman soldier who expected to die from cholera or dysentery may have found the risks of combat acceptable. The gladiator may have considered the financial reward that accompanied victory well worth the chance of dying in the Colosseum. But when we believe that we will still be alive at 80 or 90, we may become more cautious in all areas of life. Pensions become an important consideration to job applicants, physical risks become unacceptable, and health becomes a primary concern. Perhaps the popularity of physical fitness and attention to diet are partly attributable to the realization that our chances of living to a ripe old age have increased. As one octogenarian said, "If I had known I was going to be this old, I would have taken better care of myself."

Adulthood has changed in other ways as well. In 1900 a young couple could expect about 25 years of married life before tuberculosis, cholera, pneumonia, influenza, or accident ended the relationship. Today, unless they part voluntarily, a young couple can expect their marriage to last more than half a century. It has been suggested that the prospect of being married to the same person for 50 years may have contributed to the acceptance of divorce in American society (Erikson and Hall, 1987).

Over the past century, the amount of free time has increased. Working hours are shorter, vacations are longer, and automation and computers have made most jobs—whether in or out of the home—easier and faster. The 40-hour work week has become standard, and in some places flexible hours are resulting in a work week of four days. Throughout adulthood, we have more time to spend as we wish—in sports, travel, hobbies, or education; in cultural, political, religious, or civic activities; and in loafing or in front of the television set.

This increased freedom in the way we use our time has led to a corresponding increase in our potential for growth and fulfillment. Greater concern and more resources can be directed to enriching the years of adulthood. For some, of course, the new leisure of adulthood seems only a dream. As we will see in Chapter 12, the employed mother of small children may find that shorter working hours and automation have merely made it possible for her to take on twice as many responsibilities.

CHANGES IN THE STATUS OF THE OLD

The changes of adulthood have been matched by dramatic changes in the experience of being old. Today's older adults are more vigorous than the elderly of past generations. Sanitation, better nutrition, and medicine have combined to create a group of older Americans who are in relatively good health. Today's older adults are more likely to be active in political campaigns, civic groups, charitable organizations, out on the golf course, or attending college than sitting in a rocking chair. They are also better educated and in a far better economic position than their parents were. The elderly seem more youthful than they once did. When researchers interview older adults, 60 and 70 year olds often say, ''I am much younger than my mother—or my father—was at my age'' (Neugarten and Hall, 1987).

As more and more people live long enough to enter old age, age has become a time of leisure. Our great-grandparents, if they survived into old age, worked as long as they were physically able to do so; in 1890, 68 percent of all men 65 and older were gainfully employed (Zubin, 1973). There was no Social Security, and neither unions nor businesses provided pensions. A company's responsibility ended when it presented a gold watch to the employee who had—in the company's eyes—outlived any usefulness. In 1987, 16.3 percent of men and 7.4 percent of women 65 years of age or older were employed (U.S. Bureau of the Census, 1989). Most people retire by the time they are 65, their life savings bolstered by Social Security or pensions—or both.

Will this change in status of the old put an end to discrimination against older adults, known as **ageism?** Ageism develops when people apply the stereotype of aging to elderly people, seeing them all as unattractive, incompetent, feeble, sexless, and senile. Ageism still exists in employment practices, where it is illegal, and we will discuss its implications in Chapter 13. But attempts to uncover ageism among the general public have produced puzzling results.

In some studies, researchers have been unable to find a single, generalized view of old people. Instead, they have found that people hold a variety of beliefs about older people, which they use, depending on available information (Kite and Johnson, 1988). The less people know about an older person, the more likely they are to draw on stereotypes—but researchers have found that not all stereotypes are unfavorable. In one study, university students harbored at least a dozen stereotypes, some of them highly positive and others negative (Schmidt and Boland, 1986). The old ''sage,'' for example, is intelligent, interesting, loving, knows a great deal, is concerned about the future, and tells stories about the past, while the old "shrew/curmudgeon" is bitter, ill-tempered, demanding, complaining, selfish, humorless, prejudiced, and jealous of the young. Whether ageism entered into a student's treatment of older people may have depended on which stereotype the older adult most closely resembled.

A study of national newspapers indicated that the picture of aging presented in daily papers is generally favorable (Buchholz and Bynum, 1982). Older men and women in news stories are more likely to be active than passive and to be seen in a favorable light. Only 14 percent of the stories conveyed a negative image of old age.

Where then does ageism surface? Perhaps it is less visible in overt discrimination than in an attitude that dismisses old people or condescends to them. Often their attitudes are regarded as "cute," as when stories of 80-year-old lovers who finally marry or 75 year olds who run a marathon evoke the same kind of indulgent smile we give a 3 year old who dresses up in Mother's clothing and staggers through the house in her high-heeled shoes. Perhaps it also lies in the expectation of many aging people themselves, who assume that too many options are closed to them and that they are unable to learn new things. This sort of ageism is the hardest to dispel.

THE AGE-IRRELEVANT SOCIETY

Perhaps ageism will fade as changes in society make the concept of age steadily less useful. Neugarten (1975) has proposed that the United States is becoming an **age-irrelevant society,** in which chronological age, already a relatively poor predictor of the way an adult lives, is losing much of whatever meaning it once had. She has pointed out that there is no longer a particular decade in which a woman or man marries, has children, enters the labor market, or goes to school. Women, for example, are increasingly likely to have their first child either in their teenage years or after the age of 35. Extended education keeps some people out of the job market until they are 30, while others are supporting themselves before they leave their teens. College instructors expect to find students who are in middle and late adulthood in their classes. Sometimes it seems that the exception is becoming as common as the rule.

The public has responded to this spreading age-irrelevancy by shifting its own perceptions. When, in 1980, researchers repeated a 1960 survey concerning the "best" ages for major markers of adult life, they found that the unanimity of opinion that marked the original study had disappeared (Neugarten and Neugarten, 1986). In 1960, 90 percent of adults believed that women should marry between the ages of 19 and 24; in 1980, only 40 percent agreed. In 1960, "young man" referred to a male between the ages of 18 and 22; in 1980, that term described a male between 18 and 40.

PERSPECTIVES ON DEVELOPMENT AND AGING

Assumptions about development and aging affect the questions that researchers ask, the way they interpret their findings, and their conclusions about the nature of life in the later years (Kenyon, 1988). Is development after maturity a downhill course, in which aging means an escalating series of losses? Or do we get better as we get older, so that gains may balance losses? The answers to these questions are important, because views about the nature of old age determine our attitudes toward older adults and their place in society.

TRADITIONAL PERSPECTIVES ON DEVELOPMENT AND AGING

Thirty years ago, the answers to questions about the nature of aging were easy. Social scientists, zoologists, physicians, and the general public agreed that development was the province of the young. It consisted of age-related changes in body and behavior from conception to maturity (Harris, 1957). Development occurred in the fetus, infant, child, and adolescent. It was characterized by gains: structures grew, function improved, and the individual's adaptation to the environment steadily increased. Development was obviously a good thing.

For the most part, adults were not assumed to develop; they aged. Aging consisted of age-related changes in body and behavior after maturity. It was characterized by losses: structures decayed and function deteriorated, although the individual might, if lucky, compensate for some of that decay. Aging was obviously a bad thing, made up of wrinkles, falling hair, slowed movements, shortened breath, dimming vision, increasing deafness, and a failing memory. Yet it was an inevitable and universal biological process. Everyone in every society aged the same way, whether they lived in the fifteenth or the twentieth century.

These assumptions narrowed the focus of researchers. They assumed that development was aimed at the goal of maturity and that aging was aimed at the goal of death. And so they looked for gains among children and young people and for losses among older adults. Generally, they found what they were looking for (Uttal and Perlmutter, 1989).

LIFE-SPAN PERSPECTIVE ON DEVELOPMENT AND AGING

That old view of human development and aging is still held by many in the general public, but it is beginning to fade among researchers, whose studies of age-related change across the life span have refuted its assumptions. As more is discovered about growth before maturity, it becomes clear that aging, in the sense of loss or decay, can be found at any age. It begins before birth. For example, the fetal brain contains many more cells or neurons than it will ever use. As the brain develops, cells that do not make connections with other cells die. Even so, the cortex of the two year old has many more connections than it will ever need. During childhood, loss continues as unused connections gradually disappear when the overgrowth is pruned to increase the brain's efficiency (Goldman-Rakic, 1987).

Studies at the later end of the life span show that not all change after maturity involves decay or deterioration. Gains in some aspects of intelligence continue long into the second half of life (Sternberg and Wagner, 1986). Some of us will go on to make important contributions when we are well into old age. Few people realize that Tolstoy was in his seventies when he wrote *Resurrection,* that photographer Imogen Cunningham was doing important work when she was in her nineties, that Benjamin Franklin invented bifocals when he was 78, or that Pablo Picasso and Georgia O'Keeffe were still creating important works of art when they were in their eighties.

Researchers also discovered another fact of aging: different systems age at different rates, and the direction of development at any age may vary. Aging may involve stability, growth, or decline, depending on what function is studied. For example, an adult who shows gains in one facet of intelligence (expertise) may show losses in another facet (memory) (Baltes, 1987; Perlmutter, 1986).

Faced with a series of such findings, researchers revised their assumptions. They concluded that age-related changes before maturity are sometimes losses and fit the old defi-

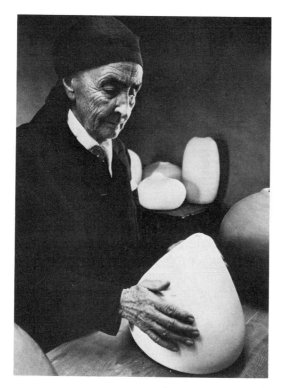

Many individuals continue to make creative contributions long after most people have retired. Artist Georgia O'Keeffe was still painting and scupting when she was well past 80.

nition of aging, whereas age-related changes after maturity are sometimes gains and fit the old definition of development. The old definition of development became unworkable. In the life-span developmental view, **development** is defined as any age-related change in body or behavior from conception to death. This change is not based solely in a biological process, but is also controlled by environmental, psychological, and social processes. Moreover, the direction of change can be positive (gains), negative (losses), or neutral (neither gains nor losses, but simply a difference).

Because development is a life-long process, it is no longer regarded as moving toward any goal (Baltes, 1987). And because, as we will see, development is heavily influenced by society, its nature may differ from one culture to another and from one historical period to the next.

EXTENDING THE LIFE-SPAN PERSPECTIVE

A further key to understanding development might be a shift in our perspective. We might learn more about the course of development if we no longer assume that the causes of gains and losses in structure and function—or even the direction of change—are necessarily tied to time of life (Uttal and Perlmutter, 1989). The tendency has been to assume that losses in early life are responses to gains (suppression) and that gains in later life are responses to loss (compensation). In the compensation model, older adults are assumed to compensate for age-related decline by refocusing their efforts and abilities in an attempt to maintain their functioning.

Yet in many cases there is actually no causal connection between gains and losses. Sometimes gains and losses that appear simultaneously are each the result of different, unrelated causes. Take the case of typing skill. When psychologist Timothy Salthouse (1984) studied typists of various ages, he found that older typists were just as fast as younger typists. Yet there were age differences in the various components of typing skill. Older typists were slower than younger typists, both in reaction time and in the speed at which they moved their fingers over the keys. However, they looked farther ahead in their copy. Salthouse concluded that this extensive preview by older typists was a compensation for a physiological slowdown. But it is just as likely that the gains and losses of older typists were unrelated (Uttal and Perlmutter, 1989). From their lengthy experience, older typists may have developed an expertise in typing that involved looking farther ahead. In that case, even though their extended preview developed independently from their loss of basic skills (reaction time and keystroke speed), it allowed them to maintain their overall speed.

Sometimes an apparent causal relation between gains and losses may be false for another reason: a third factor may be responsible for both the gain and the loss. As children learn to use advanced problem-solving strategies, for example, their use of simpler strategies declines. They often insist on using sophisticated strategies in situations where, because there is no perfect solution, a simple strategy produces higher payoffs (Weir, 1964). Traditionally, this change has been viewed as a gain (advanced strategies) causing a loss (suppression of simple strategies). But it is equally plausible that both changes are primarily the result of schooling, in which children are taught always to search for specific, perfect solutions (Uttal and Perlmutter, 1989).

During later adulthood, a similar loss of low-level strategies is typically interpreted in a quite different manner. When older adults give slow, thoughtful responses, for example, they are assumed to do so because they are unable to make a rapid response. But this may not be the case. It is equally plausible that a wise response can be produced only if a rapid response is suppressed.

ALTERNATIVE ASSUMPTIONS ABOUT AGING

Old age comes to all of us, and few find the prospect pleasing. Aging is often seen as a period of decline and depletion, a time of edging ever closer to death. In this view, we have aged successfully when we have inhibited the aging process. To do so, we must live in ways that allow us to escape chronic disease, so that we remain vigorous and active until we approach the limits of the life span (Fries, 1984). Even if we cannot inhibit biological aging, we can claim success if we arrange our lives by refusing to age in selective areas. We give up many activities and focus our remaining energies on only a few areas, where we can remain active and "young-old" (M. Baltes, 1987).

Some developmentalists feel that, instead of trying to stave off the aging process, we should welcome old age. According to David Gutmann (1987), successful aging is not a matter of adjusting to age-related losses, but of developing new capacities and seeking new challenges. Our bodies may age, but our mental and spiritual capacities ripen. Free of the responsibility for others, we can reclaim those aspects of ourselves that have been suppressed for decades.

At the age of 86, Malcolm Cowley (1986) gave us a final, brief report from the country of age that hints at this freedom. "The old, old man," he said, "can wake without apprehension, prepared for whatever the day might bring. He has earned for himself the privilege of surviving in this miraculous world as a free agent, not as a patient subject to regulations imposed by others."

MECHANISMS OF CHANGE IN DEVELOPMENT AND AGING

When we talk about development or aging, we are referring to change within the individual that results from some kind of interaction with the environment. Development and aging do not spring from some mysterious merger of person and environment, but are the result of specific individual processes, each related to the environment in a different way.

PROCESSES OF CHANGE IN DEVELOPMENT AND AGING

In the view of Dale Dannefer and Marion Perlmutter (1990), there are three processes of developmental change. The first is physical ontogeny, a process initiated by biology; the second is environmental habituation, a process initiated by the environment; and the third is cognitive generativity, a process generated by the self (see Figure 1.5).

Physical Ontogeny

Physical ontogeny is the process of biological regulation that accounts for regular, age-related changes in human physiology. (*Ontogeny* comes from the Greek words for "being" [*onto*] and "growth" [*geny*]; it describes the development of the individual.) Physical ontogeny is a highly programmed process that begins before birth. It directs brain maturation, physical growth, and such hormonally guided events as puberty. It may well be responsible for some of the changes associated with aging. Although physical ontogeny is primarily biological, both physical and social environments affect its course. Poor nutrition can restrict

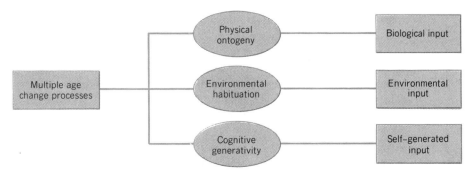

Figure 1.5 The processes of developmental change. Each of the processes of developmental change is related to the environment in a different way, and each has its strongest impact at a different point in the life span. *Source:* Dannefer and Perlmutter, in press.

programmed growth; inadequate visual and social stimulation can thwart the course of brain maturation; lack of exercise can hasten the physical deterioration associated with aging. Physical ontogeny is a relatively closed, or programmed, process, and it has its greatest impact early and late in life.

Environmental Habituation

Environmental habituation is the process of recording experience and developing more or less automatic responses. Habituation is the simplest kind of learning and can be found at every biological level, from the cell to the mind. Habituation refers to a reduction in response to a stimulus after repeated or continuous contact, so that we no longer actively notice it. Habituation is produced by the interaction of organism and environment, and—like physical ontogeny—it is underway before birth. It is both active and passive: active because we *impose* a learned conceptual framework on the stimulation we receive from the environment, and passive because it is largely reactive. Habituation is an essential developmental process, because it frees our attention from having to deal with unimportant, routine events, allowing us to notice and act on novel aspects of the environment. Habituation has its greatest impact during childhood, when we are learning to categorize the world and are developing ways of dealing with it. Because environmental habituation is not preprogrammed but is instead largely organized by the social world, it is a relatively open process.

Cognitive Generativity

The third developmental process, **cognitive generativity,** consists of cognitive awareness of self and world. It involves the conscious, intentional processing of experience, which means that it is self-generated. Whenever we reflect on our experiences, imagine something, exercise judgment, or formulate some intention, the process of cognitive generativity is at work. Cognitive generativity is the last process to affect development. It emerges only after a child is able to think about the past and the future and to form purposes and intentions. It grows out of the other two processes, for without the neocortex provided by physical ontogeny and the stable knowledge of the environment constructed through habituation, cognitive generativity could not develop. Cognitive generativity also depends on social input, because the self develops out of integration in a social world. Throughout the life span, cognitive generativity continually interacts with habituation, confirming, modifying, and reorganizing the framework developed through habituation. It does so by actively speculating about events, experimenting with various actions, and interpreting what it discovers. Of the three developmental processes, cognitive generativity is the most open and the least programmed. It is the basis for human intelligence, and it gives us some control over the construction of our self, our situation, and our social world. All of us have some degree of cognitive generativity and express it in our daily lives, while some of us, like Marjory Stoneman Douglas (see accompanying box, ''Still Going at the Century Mark'') show an exceptional amount.

The process of ontogeny works in similar ways in most human environments, and the changes it produces are predictable. But the changes wrought through habituation and cognitive generativity depend primarily on the nature of our environment—on our social, cultural, and economic circumstances.

✦ *Adulthood in Today's World*

STILL GOING AT THE CENTURY MARK

On April 7, 1990, Marjory Stoneman Douglas celebrated her one hundredth birthday by christening a new nature center on Key Biscayne in Miami, Florida. For 43 years, Douglas has been fighting to preserve the environment of the Florida Everglades, beginning the battle in 1947 with the publication of her book entitled *The Everglades: River of Grass.* At the age of 57, Douglas began to spread the word that drainage canals, commercial farming, and housing developments threatened the famous mosquito- and alligator-filled swamps. Her concern was not simply for the wildlife of the region, which abounded with ibises, roseate spoonbills, wood storks, manatees, panthers, and saltwater crocodiles. She was the first to realize that fresh water for all of southern Florida depended on the health of the saw grass swamps, which created, filtered, and retained the region's water. On her one hundredth birthday, Douglas, whose life demonstrates exceptional cognitive generativity, patiently explained the environmental cycle to a reporter, saying, ''Eighty percent of our rainfall depends on evaporation from the Everglades. If you don't have rain and water, South Florida will become a desert—it's as simple as that'' (LeMoyne, 1990, p. 20).

Through Douglas's writings and the unceasing efforts of Friends of the Everglades, an organization she founded, her once startling insight has become common wisdom. Much of the surviving Everglades have been preserved as a national park, and the government plans to bolster the Everglades' health by buying private land and restoring some of the original streams. Asked about whether she believes the program will be successful, Douglas replied, ''I am neither an optimist nor a pessimist. I say it's got to be done'' (LeMoyne, 1990, p. 20).

Marjory Douglas sees no reason to spend her remaining days rocking on the front porch of her English-style cottage. Although her eyesight is failing, this centenarian is hard at work on another book, this time a biography of the British naturalist and writer, W. H. Hudson, whose best known book is the fantasy *Green Mansions.*

MULTIPLE INFLUENCES ON DEVELOPMENT AND AGING

Developmental processes within the individual occur in the context of various influences that regulate the course of development. These influences operate throughout the life span, and they can be biological or social. They can be organized into three major types: age normative, history normative, and nonnormative (Baltes, 1987; Baltes and Reese, 1984). Each of these types of influence seems to follow a different course over the life span (see Figure 1.6).

Age-Normative Influences

Some influences affect almost every person in a particular culture at about the same time in their lives. These are known as **age-normative influences;** they are the most general

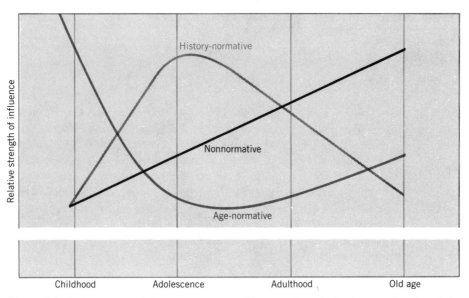

Figure 1.6   Developmental influences across the life span. The relative impact of various influences is believed to shift over the life span as shown in this hypothetical profile. Age-normative, history-normative, and nonnormative influences interact to produce age-related changes in development. *Source:* Baltes, Reese, and Lipsitt, 1980, p. 77.

factors in development, and they are highly correlated with age. Age-normative influences are the factors traditionally studied by developmentalists. Their onset, duration, and direction are fairly predictable. Walking, talking, puberty, and schooling are age-normative events encountered by almost every member of society. They change a person's capabilities and, therefore, result in differences between age groups. Marriage, parenthood, and retirement affect fewer people, but they are still so widespread as to be considered age-normative. Age-normative events that are social in nature involve roles, such as spouse, parent, or worker. Assuming the role of parent, for example, is likely to make a person feel more responsible and nurturant. The care of an infant demands changes in the person's priorities and behavior. The expectations of others about the behavior of parents also are part of such age-normative events.

Age-normative effects tend to increase similarities among people, although their intensity may depend on gender, social class, genetic background, and the like (Baltes and Reese, 1984). They appear to be strongest in childhood, although their influence may increase again in old-old age. The strength of age-normative effects during childhood is probably due to the relative power of physical ontogeny. Although the reason for their revived strength toward the end of life is not yet known, it may be the result of ontogeny—a genetic program that limits the life span.

History-Normative Influences

Some influences are the result of circumstances that exist at a particular historical moment. These influences are **history normative.** As they affect everyone who is alive at the time, they are not correlated with age. Although history-normative events have a fairly pervasive effect on all individuals living at the time the event occurs (whether the Great Depression of the 1930s, the Vietnam War, or the AIDS epidemic), the same event often has very different effects on people of different ages. No two birth cohorts experience the same set of events in the same way.

The computer, for example, is a history-normative influence that affects people of different ages in different ways. Eighty year olds who are approaching the end of the life span might find its influence slight, regard it as a nuisance, and never become comfortable with it. But 5 year olds will grow up in a world changed by computers and, as adults, will interact easily with them, finding it difficult to visualize a world without computers. Among other technological advances that have had history-normative effects on the present population are television and space exploration. For earlier generations, the automobile, the railroad, and the printing press were history-normative.

Medical events can also produce history-normative influences. AIDS, for example, is changing different generations in different ways. This disease, which effectively destroys the immune system's protective function, is often transmitted sexually. In its shadow, young adults find their sexual freedom curtailed and worry about past partners. Those who have entered the last decades of life are more likely to worry about their children's or grandchildren's exposure. But young children, who will grow up accustomed to the threat, may accept without question patterns of behavior that reduce their exposure. Other medical events with history-normative influences are the development of polio vaccine and antibiotics.

International events, such as wars or depressions, may lead to important history-normative changes in a population. The war in Vietnam is an example of a history-normative event with wide—and varying—effects on people's lives. Economic events can exert as powerful an influence. The Great Depression of the 1930s had an immediate and obvious impact on family relationships, the peer group, personality, motivation, and attitudes toward work. Researchers have discovered that the depression also had a lasting influence on those who lived through it. What is more, its lifelong effects on those who were children at the time were different from its effects on those who were adolescents or adults (Elder, 1974). History-normative influences seem to exert their greatest power on young adults who are making major decisions on career, desired style of life, and family, because these kinds of decisions are heavily influenced by social, cultural, and economic factors.

Nonnormative Influences

The developmental factors most restricted in scope are known as **nonnormative influences,** for they are specific to individuals. They do not affect all members of a society or all members of any cohort. Age bears little relation to their appearance. Winning the grand prize in a state lottery, for example, is clearly a nonnormative event. It happens to few people, but when it occurs, it can have a profound effect on the winner's life and development.

Some nonnormative influences are physical. Serious disease, such as diabetes, cancer, or Alzheimer's disease, is nonnormative, as is having a major accident. Losing a leg in a car crash, for example, can affect many areas of life. The threat of AIDS is a history-normative influence; contracting AIDS is a nonnormative influence. Other nonnormative influences are social: getting a divorce, losing a job, emigrating to another country, going to prison, winning a professional award. None of these things happen to most of us at a particular age, but any

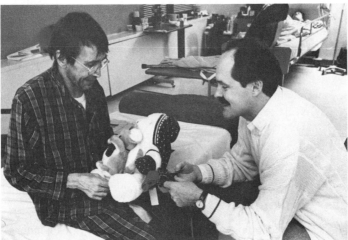

Nonnormative influences, which have little connection with age, can profoundly influence the course of a person's development. Winning an international contest can turn life in one direction, contracting AIDS turns it in another.

of them can have a significant effect on a person's life. Nonnormative events are most prevalent after people enter middle adulthood.

Each person's development is the result of interaction among the three classes of influence and processes within the individual. A question that immediately arises is whether the course and speed of development are fixed. Can we hasten the appearance of gains and postpone or at least slow inevitable losses? Is it possible to reverse the expected losses that accompany old age?

AGING: RIGID OR PLASTIC?

Buried within descriptions of ''typical aging'' is the unspoken assumption that aging is the result of physical ontogeny and that most people age in similar ways. If this were true, then age would tell us much about development, because age-related changes would be canalized. **Canalization** is a genetic predisposition that guides development in a direction that is difficult to deflect, because the predispositions are expressed in any natural human environment (Scarr, 1981). Among the young, many age-related changes *do* tend to be canalized. A 12 month old, for example, is likely to be learning to walk steadily; a 2 year old, to be acquiring language; a 15 year old, to be coming to terms with a developing body. Yet canalization is not entirely rigid. Instead, it provides a range of structure or function that results in substantial differences among individuals.

As we move through the life span, our development becomes less and less canalized; that is, it is less under the control of physical ontogeny. Environmental habituation and cognitive generativity become more important. That is why the information that a person is 65 tells us relatively little besides the fact that he or she has lived for 65 years. The fact of age is not very informative about a person's health, intellectual capacity, physiological functioning, economic and social resources, or life-style. Thus, the course of adult development is characterized by plasticity; it is not rigid, but flexible.

Not only are people very different from one another, but each person has some degree of control over the way he or she changes. Differences in patterns of change across individuals are known as **interindividual differences.** Changes within the individual, in which a person's behavior is compared with his or her own earlier behavior, are known as **intraindividual differences.**

INTERINDIVIDUAL DIFFERENCES

Human lives are like the spreading of a fan; the longer people live, the greater the differences between them (Neugarten and Hall, 1987). Some 55 year olds may already seem elderly, whereas some 90 year olds are vital and very much alive. During young-old and old-old age, changes among individuals tend to differ more than at any other time of life. In fact, differences *among* 65 to 90 year olds are often greater than differences *between* adults younger and older than 65 (Weg, 1983). The differences are so wide that focusing on typical characteristics and averages may distort the reality of aging (Dannefer, 1988).

The amount of interindividual difference in each cohort increases as the number of nonnormative experiences accumulates. Pleasant influences (inheriting a fortune, entering a happy marriage, earning professional distinction) increase the amount of interindividual difference just as unpleasant influences (disease, accident, divorce, loss of a job) do. Studies of older adults find wide individual differences in every aspect of life. These widening differences seem most closely related to interindividual differences in physical health and socioeconomic status. Some researchers have suggested that a major cause of this increasing divergence are the factors that produce social inequality (Dannefer, 1988).

Yet age-normative influences affect everyone in extreme old age, when they are unlikely to predominate until the life span is almost over. Because people die over such a wide span of ages (another interindividual difference), age-normative influences on a group of 70 year olds, for example, would affect mainly those likely to die in the near future. Those who will live until 80 or 90 or longer would not yet be strongly affected by any genetic program that limits the quality of the last portion of life or the life span itself.

INTRAINDIVIDUAL DIFFERENCES

Most of us expect people to change in minor ways, and we are not especially surprised to find that someone has a new job, a new house, a new hobby, or a new hair color. But we do not expect people to change in their personality, attitudes, beliefs, or intelligence. Many researchers have held the same view, assuming that human development is characterized by constancy and predictability, not change (Brim and Kagan, 1980). Childhood experiences are supposed to chart the course of adult development, and few of us are expected to stray from the charted path.

Some aspects of personality seem formed by middle childhood. Studies in which people have been followed from childhood through middle adulthood have shown that several areas of adult personality can be predicted from personality at about eight or ten years of age (Moss and Sussman, 1980). Researchers (McCrae and Costa, 1984) who tracked people throughout adulthood have found a similar stability. A good deal of this constancy lies in characteristics that have been encouraged by society. Achievement, generally regarded as a good thing, remains stable for both men and women. Other characteristics that depend on traditional sex roles show different patterns in women and men. Dependency, for example, has tended to be more stable in women, and aggression, more stable in men. Despite such predictability, people do change—more often than we might expect. Developmentalists emphasize that both constancy and change are present throughout life (Baltes and Goulet, 1970). When change appears, it may be predictable, or it may take a totally unexpected form.

When people take on new social roles, for example, they often change in predictable ways. They are plastic enough to adapt to the social demands of being a spouse, parent,

Therapy groups foster intraindividual change, helping people overcome the negative effects of non-normative events.

worker, grandparent, or retiree. Most are flexible enough to handle considerable stress. At the close of World War II, Germans faced massive social, political, and economic change. Studies showed that adults in middle and later adulthood adjusted to the new demands; had they not been able to change, they probably would not have survived (Thomae, 1979).

People may also change in unpredictable ways. Alcoholics stop drinking; teetotalers start to drink. Political liberals become conservative; conservatives become liberal. Agnostics embrace the church; religious zealots become agnostic. Convicted criminals lead exemplary lives; pillars of the community embezzle company funds. The existence of psychotherapy, organizations like Alcoholics Anonymous, halfway houses, drug education, occupational counseling, and affirmative action programs testifies to the possibility of change (Brim and Kagan, 1980). Such efforts are successful often enough to keep the organizations in business.

Cognitive functioning generally remains constant over most of the adult years. Between the ages of 25 and 60 mental abilities tend to remain on a plateau; some cognitive skills may decline slightly, but others may improve. Among people past the age of 60, researchers have found that some stay on the plateau, some show declines, and others show selective increases in functioning. Whether constancy or change prevails in cognitive functioning appears to be regulated by such factors as health, social roles, personality, attitudes, and life-style (Perlmutter, 1988).

TESTING THE LIMITS OF PLASTICITY

The connection between environmental influences and an individual's level of functioning suggests that much of the decline associated with aging may be the result of older adults' life situations. The lives of older adults may become so routine that they see little reason to learn new things or to exercise their imagination. Their undemanding, unchallenging existence results in the shutting down of large areas of their minds. Their level of habituation exceeds the range in which people function effectively, and they have, in effect, become hyperhabituated (Dannefer and Perlmutter, 1990).

People rarely function at the limits of their capacity. This notion has become commonplace among psychologists who study child development, and they often note that children's competence exceeds their performance. When they are placed in a situation that fosters or supports the use of a higher level skill, the skill is used, but they will not use it spontaneously (Flavell, 1985). Studies show that the performance of older adults in many areas of life is also below their actual level of competence. All people seem to have an unused reserve capacity that they fail to draw on because their situation does not require it (see Figure 1.7). This area of reserve capacity is known as the **zone of proximal development,** a term proposed by the Russian psychologist Lev Vygotsky (1978) to call attention to the fact that children were much more capable when guided by an adult than when acting on their own. Social guidance is effective with people of any age; with encouragement, training, or instruction from someone who already has mastered a skill, any of us can rise above our typical performance.

Operating on this assumption, researchers have demonstrated that healthy older adults, who usually perform well below the level of young adults on rote memory tasks, can learn to remember strings of nouns and digits at a level that far exceeds the performance of untrained young adults (Baltes and Kliegel, 1986). Other researchers have succeeded in *reversing* declines in intelligence test scores, so that after relatively modest training older adults' scores returned to the level at which they had tested 14 years earlier (Schaie and Willis, 1986).

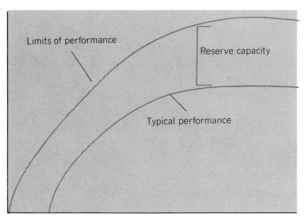

Age

Figure 1.7   Reserve capacity. Most people are more capable than they imagine; they rarely perform at the limits of their capacity because their situation does not require peak functioning.

Clearly, the human cognitive system is more plastic than has been assumed, and older adults are more capable than imagined by society—or themselves. In the next chapter, our exploration of the methods that have been devised to separate age-normative, history-normative, and nonnormative influences of development will suggest why it has taken so long for developmentalists to discover the capabilities of older adults.

SUMMARY

THE HUMAN LIFE CYCLE

Societies divide the life span in various ways. In the United States, life is seen as progressing through the stages of infancy, childhood, adolescence, and adulthood. **Adulthood** may be arbitrarily subdivided into **early adulthood** (18–30), **middle adulthood** (30–50), **later adulthood** (50–65), **young-old age** (65–80), and **old-old age** (>80). Although there are general patterns in the way people develop and age, knowing an adult's **chronological age** is not a very useful guide to that person's appearance, abilities, or status because individuals age at different rates. Maturity can be defined in terms of biological, psychological, or social benchmarks, as can old age. Most people attain these various benchmarks at different times.

THE ADULT POPULATION

As fewer members of each **cohort** succumb to accident or disease, the structure of the population changes, and those in old age make up an increasing proportion of the population. Changing mortality rates also change the **old-age dependency ratio,** leaving fewer workers to support each retired person. Today's longer adulthood may have made us more cautious about how we live our lives. It has increased the possible length of marriages, increased the potential for a long, healthy, vigorous old age, and made old age a time of leisure for an increasing number of people. As an increasingly **age-irrelevant society** develops, the concept of age steadily becomes less useful.

PERSPECTIVES ON DEVELOPMENT AND AGING

Development is any age-related change in body or behavior from conception to death. It can involve improved functioning, deterioration, or simply a difference. Although it was generally believed that gains dominate early life and losses dominate later life, this view has been refuted. Researchers have tended to believe that losses in early life are the result of suppression and gains in later life are the result of compensation, but there may be no causal connection between losses and gains at any stage.

THE MECHANISMS OF CHANGE IN DEVELOPMENT AND AGING

General processes of developmental change are **physical ontogeny,** a highly programmed process of biological regulation; **environmental habituation,** a relatively open environmental process that produces automatic responses requiring little or no attention; and **cognitive generativity,** a highly open, self-generated process that gives us some control over self, situation, and social world.

Developmental processes occur in the context of three major influences. **Age-normative influences,** which are strongest in childhood, affect almost every person in the culture at the same point in the life span. **History-normative influences,** which may have the greatest effect on young adults, affect every person in the culture at the same historical moment, although the nature of their effect differs for people at different points in the life span. **Nonnormative influences,** which increase in power over the life span, affect specific individuals with no regard to their age.

AGING: RIGID OR PLASTIC?

Canalization, a genetic predisposition that is difficult to deflect, guides development in childhood and again in advanced old age. As people grow older and nonnormative influences accumulate, **interindividual differences,** or differences among people, increase. **Intraindividual differences,** in which a person changes compared with his or her own earlier status, may be predictable, as when people take on new social roles, or unpredictable, as when life-style changes radically.

Most people have an unused reserve capacity, known as the **zone of proximal development.** With exertion or training, they can push their performance into this zone, exceeding their normal level of functioning.

KEY TERMS

adulthood

age-irrelevant society

ageism

age-normative influence

canalization

chronological age

cognitive generativity

cohort

development

early adulthood

environmental habituation

history-normative influence

interindividual differences

intraindividual differences

later adulthood

middle adulthood

nonnormative influence

old-age dependency ratio

old-old age

physical ontogeny

young-old age

zone of proximal development

Chapter 2

◆

Approaches and Methods in the Study of Adult Development and Aging

——— ◆ ———

ALTERNATIVE WORLD VIEWS
MECHANISTIC WORLD VIEW
ORGANISMIC WORLD VIEW   DIALECTIC WORLD VIEW

PERSPECTIVES ON DEVELOPMENT AND AGING
THE BIOLOGICAL PERSPECTIVE
THE PSYCHOLOGICAL PERSPECTIVE   THE SOCIOLOGICAL PERSPECTIVE
THE ANTHROPOLOGICAL PERSPECTIVE   THE HISTORICAL PERSPECTIVE

DEVELOPMENTAL DESIGNS
CROSS-SECTIONAL DESIGN   LONGITUDINAL DESIGN
◆
ADULTHOOD IN TODAY'S WORLD: THE BALTIMORE LONGITUDINAL STUDY
◆
TIME-LAG DESIGN   SEQUENTIAL DESIGN

RESEARCH ISSUES
SELECTING A SAMPLE   SELECTING A MEASURE
Reliability / Validity

SUMMARY

T here was once a city inhabited entirely by the blind. At its gates appeared an army headed by a king, who brought with him an enormous elephant. The elephant's sound struck fear into the people's hearts, and its mighty tread shook the ground beneath their feet.

The people wondered about this strange animal, and a group of men ran from the city gates to find out about it. They gathered around the beast, and each ran his hands over some portion of the elephant's body.

When the blind men returned to the city, their fellow citizens clustered around them, begging to be told of the awesome elephant. "What was it like?" they said.

The man who had felt the ear said, "It is simple; the elephant is like a great fan."

The man who had felt the tail said, "No, the elephant is like a tough rope."

The man who had grasped the trunk said, "You are both wrong; the elephant is like an enormous pipe."

"Never," said the man who had felt a leg. "The elephant is like a living pillar."

"Even you are mistaken," said the man who had touched its back, "the elephant is like an emperor's throne."

"You fools!" shouted the man who had touched a tusk. "The elephant is like a sharpened stick that will impale us all."

Each blind man had perceived a part of the elephant, but none had understood the entire animal. Their reliance on isolated information insured that everyone would be wrong (Shah, 1979).

This Afghan folk tale from the thirteenth century provides an apt analogy of any understanding of adulthood and aging that relies on the theories and findings of a single discipline. Most developmentalists, aware of the dangers of isolated information, draw on insights and research from several disciplines. Those who focus on the later part of the life span are engaged in **gerontology,** which is the scientific study of older organisms and the process of aging. Gerontology is different from **geriatrics,** which is a branch of medicine concerned with the study and treatment of disease among old persons.

As we will see in this chapter, the theories behind developmental research are shaped by researchers' assumptions about human nature and behavior. Research into adult development is carried out by biologists, psychologists, sociologists, anthropologists, and historians. In studying development, researchers rely on standard methods of studying people, but the nature of development has led to special research designs that take into account the time and cohort effects produced by history-normative events. ◆

ALTERNATIVE WORLD VIEWS

In their search for theories to explain the processes of development and aging, developmentalists have relied on various models of human nature and behavioral processes. Each model takes a different view of the world and uses a different analogy to represent development (see Table 2.1). The world view taken by developmentalists affects the way they define, study, and interpret various aspects of development. The dominant models are mech-

Table 2.1 DEVELOPMENTAL WORLD VIEWS

	Mechanistic	*Organismic*	*Dialectical*
Analogy	Machine	Organism	Orchestral music
Individual	Generally passive	Active	Interactive
Focus	Observable changes in behavior	Internal changes in structure	Relationship between individual and society
Type of change	Quantitative	Qualitative	Quantitative and qualitative

anistic, organismic, and dialectical. None of them is ''true'' or ''false,'' but each can be useful as a guide to understanding development (Baltes, Reese, and Nesselroade, 1977).

MECHANISTIC WORLD VIEW

In **mechanistic models,** the analogy is the machine. This view does not mean that people *are* machines; rather, it maintains that we can understand development better if we assume that it is the result of laws as regular as those that govern the functioning of machines. Because behavior is lawful, the mechanistic model assumes it can be studied in isolation. Combining knowledge of all types of behavior would allow us to understand development. Thus, in the mechanistic view, the whole equals the sum of its parts.

External forces are the dominant influence on development; the individual's behavior is shaped by past experiences and present situations. The feelings, thoughts, and actions of human beings change, but not their structure. For example, the cognitive structures of a 30 year old are no different from those of a 7 year old, but the 30 year old has developed more efficient strategies for dealing with information. In mechanistic models, the computer is a favorite metaphor for human cognition. In terms of this metaphor, the 30 year old's hardware is similar, but the data base and software (or computer program) are more sophisticated than the 7 year old's.

Because hardware does not change, any new capabilities that develop have been built into the machine. They appear when the program reaches the proper sequence, just as information appears on the terminal only when the computer reaches a statement in the program telling it to display data.

In the mechanistic model, behavior is the result of stimulation, so that human actions are often explained in terms of reactions to the environment (Perlmutter, 1988). A person becomes a lawyer, gets married, has children, goes to concerts, or roots for the Detroit Pistons because of the rewards connected with similar activities in the past. As rewards (or reinforcements) and punishments explain activity, the environment becomes all-powerful as a way of explaining behavior.

Learning theorists use a mechanistic orientation to explain behavior, and some cognitive theorists use it to explain intellectual functioning. This approach to human development originally portrayed human beings as passive. However, in **social cognitive theory,** a view that grew out of mechanistic models, the individual is seen as reasonably active, using rewards, punishments, and the example of others as information that forms the basis for beliefs about the self, goals, plans, and future actions (Bandura, 1986).

ORGANISMIC WORLD VIEW

In **organismic models,** people are seen as living organisms that are active and changing. As they interact with the environment, people change in basic ways. Any advancement in thought is not simply the result of new strategies and experience; instead, it reflects a biologically specified change in structure so that the cognitive processes of the 30 year old are different in quality from those of the 7 year old (Perlmutter, 1988).

Although experience in the world is necessary if development is to take place, that experience has meaning for the individual only after it has been incorporated into his or her understanding of the world. Identifying the external cause of behavior, then, is not the ultimate concern of investigators with an organismic orientation. They are interested in the goal of developmental change and in the way behavior is organized into systems. Their aim is to identify the rules of intraindividual change and to describe the entire system (Baltes, Reese, and Nesselroade, 1977).

In the organismic model, the individual is spontaneously active, and what gives rise to activity is often self-generated. Given this view of human beings, the search for laws of environmental effects on behavior cannot be entirely successful, and the study of isolated stimulus-response relationships is unlikely to advance greatly our understanding of development. A lack of total understanding is inevitable because the whole system is greater than the sum of its parts.

DIALECTIC WORLD VIEW

In the **dialectical approach,** people are assumed to interact with a continually changing environment, so that each generation within a society is assumed to reach a new level of functioning. As yet there is no generally accepted dialectical metaphor for development, although Klaus Riegel (1975) compared it to orchestral music. He viewed development as having biological, psychological, social, and physical dimensions that are never in perfect harmony. Development progresses through a series of small leaps as the individual resolves contradictions and conflicts that arise when one of the dimensions is out of step with the rest. In the orchestra model, the conflicts and their resolution are like musical counterpoint that is synchronized through harmonics or like the disharmonies of jazz that are synchronized through rhythm and beat.

The dialectical approach focuses on the relationship between the individual and society, who are engaged in a continuing "dialectic" in which both undergo change as a result of their interactions. The development of one depends on the development of the other (Buss, 1979). Much knowledge is regarded as social, which makes relationships a central part of development. In this view, individual development is heavily influenced by history-normative events. Because of this social influence, the development of people born in 1890 is likely to be different in many ways from that of people born in 1960.

Some developmentalists (Lerner, 1978) have suggested that the dialectic view is capable of integrating concepts from the mechanistic and organismic views. That is, development at the level of the organism is a synthesis of the sorts of quantitative development studied in the mechanistic approach with the qualitative change studied by organismic researchers. Once again, the whole system is greater than the sum of its parts.

The Preservation Jazz Band exemplifies the dialectic model of development because it synchronizes disharmonies through rhythm and beat.

PERSPECTIVES ON DEVELOPMENT AND AGING

Whatever their world view, developmentalists in all disciplines focus on age-related changes in behavior. However, the level of analysis varies from one discipline to the next. Some look at the biological bases of development; some at changes in individual function; others at social interaction and social roles; and still others at sociocultural forces. It is generally agreed that these four levels interact in their influence and that no one of them can by itself explain development (Table 2.2). Most developmentalists also agree that individuals are not

Table 2.2 **LEVELS OF DEVELOPMENT**

Discipline	Level of Study[a]
Biology	Cellular and anatomical function and change
Psychology	Individual function
	Social interaction
Sociology	Social roles
Anthropology	Cultural patterns
History	Social roles and cultural patterns across time

[a] Human development can be studied at various levels, each leading to a different way of understanding the process. For a complete understanding of development, all levels must be taken into consideration.

passive victims of biological forces; instead, each person is seen as an active force in his or her own development.

THE BIOLOGICAL PERSPECTIVE

Biologists focus on development at the cellular and anatomical level, studying biochemical and physiological changes across the life span of the organism. Development is viewed as an expression of a genetic program that interacts with the environment. Each of us has a general genetic program that reflects the evolution of the species and causes us to develop into human beings instead of chimpanzees, horses, or goats. We also have a specific program that reflects the characteristics of our own family; it determines such things as eye color and height range, and it may carry predispositions for a particular disease or temperament. Although the specific program can affect the length of an individual life, the upper limit of the human life span is believed to be set by the general program (Shock, 1977).

When researchers look at its biological base, they tend to study development either early or late in the life span. Some are interested primarily in fetal development; some in development until maturity; and others in the aging process. Although the realization that many age-related biological changes are actually caused by disease or the environment has led to some modification in their views, most developmental biologists still distinguish between development and aging in the traditional sense of the words, seeing them as opposing forces (Perlmutter, 1988). As a result, they have developed two relatively independent bodies of knowledge, which has impeded the creation of biological theories of development that apply to the entire life span (Baltes, Reese, and Lipsitt, 1980).

When studying adult development, biologists often focus on the effects of aging on body function or appearance. Because of the nature of the research, most biological studies are done with animals. Animals' genetic makeup can be controlled through breeding, and their environment can be controlled or manipulated in ways that are neither possible nor desirable with human beings. The short life spans of animals allow researchers to trace development and aging in months (as with rodents) or even days (as with fruit flies) instead of decades. The results of such studies cannot be directly applied to human development, but physiological functioning in people and in rats—a favorite experimental species—is often similar enough to provide insight into human development. Studies of pancreatic function in aging rats, for example, have given us clues to the development of diabetes in aging men and women, just as studies of reproduction in hamsters have produced insights into the relation between weight loss and infertility in female athletes, dancers, and women with eating disorders (Schneider and Wade, 1989).

Not all research is done on animals. For example, the skin is one of the first places where we notice the signs of aging, and research with human beings indicates that a change in the speed at which surface skin cells are replaced may explain why this is so. Investigators (Grove and Kligman, 1983) have found that, among adults ranging in age from 18 to 50, the rate of cell replacement is steady—in about 20 days, old cells have been shed and new ones are in place. After the age of 50, the replacement rate begins to drop, slowing to about 25 days among people in their fifties, to about 31 days among those in their sixties, and to about 37 days among those in their seventies. However, one of the oldest individuals studied had a replacement rate as rapid as that of young adults, and an adult in the early twenties had a replacement rate typical of a person well into the fifties. Such interindividual differences help to explain why some people appear comparatively youthful at 60, whereas others resemble 80 year olds.

Other biological researchers have examined changes in sleep patterns, sexual response, skeletal structure, the body's ability to regulate its internal temperature, brain structure or electrical activity, and so on. Some investigators study diseases that are prevalent during later adulthood and old age, hoping to find ways to postpone them or to prevent their occurrence.

Biologists study the aging process itself in the hope of discovering why people age at all, conducting research at the genetic, cellular, or physiological level. If these investigators are successful, they may be able to extend the human life span, devising methods that slow the natural aging process—or postpone it for several decades. Many biologists believe that the ultimate cause of aging will be found at the cellular or molecular level, but that understanding at the physiological level—the relationship among cells, tissues, and organs, is most likely to enable us to extend the life span (Shock, 1977).

THE PSYCHOLOGICAL PERSPECTIVE

Psychologists study development at two levels: individual function and social interaction. They are interested in how emotion, personality, cognition, and behavior change across the individual life span and in the way these changes affect a person's individual functioning and social interactions.

Looking at development in this way leads to the study of intraindividual changes and interindividual differences. As mentioned in Chapter 1, interindividual differences become progressively larger as the effects of nonnormative events pile up and age-normative influences decline. Because chronological age becomes an increasingly poorer guide to development, most psychological theories of adult development make little attempt to link changes to specific chronological age. Instead, they look at predictable sequences of development that may occur at somewhat different ages but that progress in the same order and in the same direction (Baltes and Willis, 1977).

Whether developmental psychologists take a mechanistic, organismic, or dialectical view of development, their basic concern is the same: individual function. Even when the object of study is social interaction or social roles, the focus is on the individual, not on the wider society. In approaching the study of development in this way, however, psychologists need to take into account both biological and social influences on behavior (Featherman, 1981).

Psychologists may study any aspect of adult development. For example, one aspect of aging that has received a good deal of attention is memory. When adults are brought into the laboratory and asked to memorize material, such as a list of words, older adults generally remember less of the memorized material than do younger adults (Poon, 1985).

When we are faced with such research, our first impulse is to say that during the aging process whatever mechanisms are involved in memory deteriorate. However, studies indicate that at least part of the deterioration is caused by something besides aging. In one study (Cavanaugh, 1983), adults in their early twenties or their late sixties came into the laboratory and watched television programs. Afterward they were asked about the content of the programs they had seen. But this experiment looked at the results in a different way. Before they saw the television programs, the adults took a vocabulary test. Older adults with high verbal ability, as measured by the test, did just as well at recalling programs as did young adults with high verbal ability. There was no apparent decline in memory with age. The customary decline appeared as expected among people with low verbal ability: 20 year olds recalled much more program content than did 65 year olds. But these 20 year olds did much worse than the 65 year olds with high verbal ability. The researcher suggested that people with high verbal ability use much more efficient methods when storing information in memory and that this difference explains the lack of decline in the first group of older adults.

Memory is only one form of cognition studied by psychologists. Cognitive psychologists also study age-related changes in sensation, perception, problem solving, learning, intelligence, and creativity. Other psychologists investigate personality, motivation, self-concept, and the effect of various social roles, such as marriage, parenthood, divorce, or retirement, on the individual. Another way psychologists may approach adult development is by examining the relation between a person's commitment and attitudes and his or her actual behavior (Lowenthal, 1977). Or they may explore the effect of various situations, such as stress or disease, on mental health. Much of the information gathered by psychologists can be seen in broader context by looking at the work of sociologists.

THE SOCIOLOGICAL PERSPECTIVE

Sociologists study age-related changes in social roles within the social institutions of a culture. Many of the topics studied by sociologists overlap with those studied by psychologists, but the sociological focus shifts from the individual to the group. Although sociologists are aware of the biological aspects of adult development and aging, these are more or less taken for granted. Both biological and psychological aspects of aging are considered, but only as they influence the social institutions in which people function.

No single sociological theory attempts to explain all the sociological aspects of aging (Passuth and Bengston, 1988), but many sociologists have adopted an **age stratification** model in which people are viewed as living through a sequence of age-related positions or

In the age-stratification model, people live through a sequence of age-related roles that prescribe their behavior. These roles show most clearly when people from different generations interact.

roles. Each position carries its own rules that prescribe a person's behavior (Riley, Johnson, and Foner, 1972). The influence of these roles shows most clearly in social interaction across generations. For example, when a 25 year old talks with a 70 year old, each will adjust his or her side of the interaction to take the other's age into account. This adjustment affects language, topic of conversation, whether one person defers to the other, and so on. Because age-related roles may change under the influence of history-normative events, society changes as new cohorts replace older ones (Featherman, 1981).

Another way that sociologists approach adult development and aging is through the concept of **socialization,** or the way in which people absorb the attitudes, values, and beliefs of their society. By studying transitions from one social role to another, sociologists hope to discover just how roles influence behavior and personality.

Sociologists also study adult development by looking at institutions as they respond to changing social conditions. For example, sociologists might consider the effects of retirement communities on family structure by studying family contacts, divorce and remarriage, and relationships between middle-aged adults and their aging parents. The influence of history-normative events may be explored by studying various cohorts in an attempt to discover how social or economic changes affect family size, mobility, or family roles (Featherman, 1981).

In a typical sociological study, Kenneth Ferraro (1983) examined the effect of moving on older adults. Approximately 3500 lower- and middle-class adults who lived in their own houses or apartments were asked about various physical disabilities, daily activities connected with self-care, illness, and hospitalization. Fourteen months later, the same adults again answered all these questions. During that period more than 200 had moved to another house or apartment in the same community.

Ferraro found that, although the health of adults who moved had been similar to that of other adults at the time of the first interview, both illness and hospitalization increased significantly more among the movers whether they had moved out of choice or necessity. What is more, neither the type of new housing nor a person's level of satisfaction with it had any effect on the level of illness or hospitalization.

Moving is apparently stressful, but whether the stress comes from the move itself, from the rupture of old social bonds, or from the unfamiliarity of the new environment is not clear. Results of other studies indicate that health may improve when older persons move into retirement communities or senior housing projects (Carp, 1976). Ferraro suggested two factors that could account for such improvement. First, needed services are clustered in or near such communities, making it easy to become acquainted with new surroundings. Second, social contacts with other older adults may provide support that is lacking in the wider community. If these factors are important, it may be possible to provide social support that would lessen the stress among older people.

THE ANTHROPOLOGICAL PERSPECTIVE

Anthropologists examine differences in developmental patterns across cultures. By studying patterns of development in various societies, they show us the potential range of human behavior and why development may proceed differently from one culture to the next (Spencer, 1957). Without this comparison, investigators might assume that the developmental patterns they have found in their own culture are universal and reflect human nature (LeVine, 1982).

Anthropologists have shown us that the way most older adults behave reflects in part the expectations of the culture and is not simply the result of the aging process (Fry, 1985). For example, some sociologists (Cumming and Henry, 1961) once believed that **disengagement,** or a gradual withdrawal from social roles and a decreased involvement with others, was typical of older adults. But anthropological research in other cultures has shown that in a number of societies older people do not withdraw; their level of psychological and social involvement remains relatively high.

Few aspects of life, from personality traits and social roles to attitudes, values, and beliefs, escape the influence of culture. Age-normative influences that are social in nature vary from culture to culture as do history-normative influences. As noted earlier, cultures even divide the life span in different ways.

Anthropologists also study many aspects of adult development and aging. They may investigate stages of the life cycle, the role and treatment of old people, individual differences in developmental patterns within a single culture, and the way a culture uses age as the basis of social organization.

This last issue was studied by Thomas Rohlen (1978), who found that Japanese society is ordered around differences in age. The form of the Japanese language reflects the age of the parties in a conversation as does the traditional dress of women. In business, seniority is the basis of rank, responsibility, status, and salary. Authority and career progress are age-graded, and the progress of a Japanese worker (traditionally male) is judged in comparison with that of his own cohort. Age is also linked with creativity and wisdom, and older people remain publicly active well into old age.

THE HISTORICAL PERSPECTIVE

Historians study differences in developmental patterns across time. In studying these patterns, they rely on birth, marriage, and death records; government population records, such as census documents; literature written during the period under study; and paintings and sculpture of the time.

A major focus of the historical approach has been the family and its changing role through the centuries. In their studies of the family, historians have discovered that, contrary to popular belief, the small nuclear family has characterized society in Europe and North America for centuries (Gies and Gies, 1987; Laslett, 1972). The large extended family that supposedly was common in an agriculturally based society turns out to have been a rarity. Other historians have looked at changes in the family in terms of the interaction among the social and psychological development of its members, the pace of the entire household's development, historical events, and changes in the culture (Featherman, 1981).

Historians may also study other aspects of adult development, such as changes in the marital relationship, in views of old age, in attitudes toward death, and in social policy relevant to the old. For example, historian Winthrop Jordan (1978) has traced the development of the concept of adulthood in the United States. He found that the word did not even exist in English until 1870. The concept of adulthood was late in developing because men and women were believed to have little in common. People talked instead of ''manhood'' and ''womanhood,'' as if men and women belonged to two completely different species. The concept of adulthood appears to have developed as society changed, with the current meaning of the term appearing as women began to vote and their entry into the labor market began to erode the linkage between masculinity and the idea of a career.

Historians, anthropologists, sociologists, psychologists, and biologists have increased our understanding of adult development and aging. But none of these approaches by itself adequately portrays the process because each describes development at a different level. Changes at any one level occurs in the context and under the influence of the other levels, so that development and aging involve an interaction among levels.

Aware of this interaction, many investigators have begun to use an interdisciplinary approach. In the study of some areas, such as the family, this approach draws on the resources of several disciplines to define research problems, choose the factors to be studied, and analyze the acccumulated data (Featherman, 1981).

DEVELOPMENTAL DESIGNS

Researchers investigating developmental questions are faced with the problem of distinguishing the effects of age-normative influences from history-normative influences. No matter what the topic, it is virtually impossible to separate the influences of age, cohort, and historical time. Yet the researcher's task is to determine how each contributes to the observed differences. Unless the influences of cohort and time of measurement can be ruled out, there is no way of being certain that a true age-related effect has been found. You may find it easier to absorb the following descriptions if you refer to the matrix in Table 2.3.

Four major types of research designs are used to study development: cross-sectional, longitudinal, time-lag, and sequential. Each looks at development in a different way, and Table 2.4 shows how the first three designs differ. Only a sequential design, which combines aspects of each of the other designs, is likely to shed light on all three influences.

CROSS-SECTIONAL DESIGN

In **cross-sectional designs,** two or more age groups, each from a different cohort, are studied at one time (Figure 2.1). A typical cross-sectional study is the study of memory for television programs, described earlier, in which the performance of 20 year olds and 65 year olds on the same task was compared during the same year. Researchers often choose this design because it is quick and relatively inexpensive to carry out.

The cross-sectional method reveals interindividual differences, but because each person is observed only once, it does not show intraindividual change. Even if we assume that the

Table 2.3 **COHORT × AGE MATRIX**

| | *Year* | | | | | |
Cohort[a]	*1900*	*1920*	*1940*	*1960*	*1980*	*2000*
I	0	20	40	60	80	100
II	×	0	20	40	60	80
III	×	×	0	20	40	60
IV	×	×	×	0	20	40
V	×	×	×	×	0	20

[a] In this matrix, Cohort I is the oldest, born in 1900.

Table 2.4   DEVELOPMENTAL RESEARCH DESIGNS

Design[a]	Ages	Cohorts	Times	Confounds
Cross-sectional	Multiple	Multiple	Single	Age/cohort
Longitudinal	Multiple	Single	Multiple	Age/time
Time-lag	Single	Multiple	Multiple	Time/cohort

[a] Sequential designs were devised in an attempt to get around the confounding factors in basic designs for developmental research.

differences we find are age-related, we are left with group averages instead of information about changes in individuals (Baltes, Reese, and Nesselroade, 1977).

Cross-sectional studies have a basic limitation: they confound age-related and cohort influences. In a typical cross-sectional study, there is no way to tell whether age differences are the result of developmental change or membership in different cohorts. Suppose we wonder whether young first-time mothers tend to use different child-rearing methods from mothers who have their first child at a relatively late age. We find a cross-sectional study in which researchers observed a group of 20-year-old mothers and another group of 40-year-old mothers in the same year. The differences in their styles of child-rearing were clearly not the result of an historical shift because both groups were observed in the same

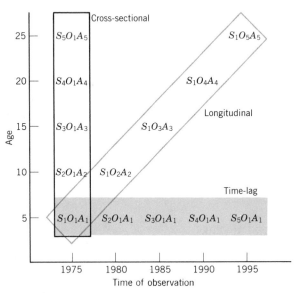

Figure 2.1   Experimental designs. In this comparison of developmental studies, the cross-sectional design uses five different samples (S_1–S_5), each a different age (A_1–A_5), observed on only one occasion (O_1). The longitudinal design uses one sample (S_1), observed on five different occasions (O_1–O_5) at five different ages (A_1–A_5). The time-lag design uses five different samples (S_1–S_5), each the same age (A_1), observed on only one occasion (O_1) but at different historical times. Each method looks at development in a different way. *Source:* Baltes, Reese, and Nesselroade, 1977, p. 122.

The mothering styles of these two women contrast sharply, but whether the effect is due to age or cohort differences is uncertain.

year and each was exposed to the same ''expert'' advice from pediatricians and popular books.

But we cannot be certain whether age or cohort differences are primarily responsible for the different styles of mothering. Women in the first group were born in the 1950s and those in the second group in the 1970s, and so they grew up under different circumstances. Women in the first group were likely to have grown up in intact families with mothers who did not work outside the home; women in the second group were much more likely to have grown up in single-parent families or reconstituted families, and to have had mothers who worked outside the home.

Despite the problem of distinguishing between age and cohort effects, cross-sectional studies, if interpreted cautiously, are often useful and the most practical. There are times when cross-sectional designs are the most appropriate (Nunnally, 1973). Cross-sectional studies can tell us how different age groups perform today on certain tasks or how they feel about certain issues. They will tell us only about age differences in 1990, however, and cannot be used to draw conclusions about developmental changes. If we are trying to find out about developmental change, cross-sectional designs can give us hints about possible age-related change. The differences that appear indicate what topics could be studied, using some other design, to discover whether the observed changes are actually age-determined.

One researcher feels so strongly about the influence of cohort effects on cross-sectional studies that he recommends they be tagged in a way that forces us to consider cohort effects. Warner Schaie (1973) once suggested that all such studies be relabeled, substituting the subjects' date of birth for their ages. In his view, many cross-sectional studies are primarily studies of intergenerational, not interindividual, differences.

It may not be necessary to go that far, but this sort of recommendation keeps us aware of the possible pitfalls of cross-sectional research. Consider the following situation. When 20, 30, 40, 50, and 60 year olds take the same intelligence test, the average score is progressively lower, beginning with that of the 40 year olds. It would seem that intelligence, at least as measured by IQ tests, begins to deteriorate during middle adulthood. But each of the age groups belongs to a different cohort. Is it possible that cohort differences, and not some inexorable developmental influences, cause the difference in scores? Perhaps a look at different developmental designs will help us answer that question.

LONGITUDINAL DESIGN

In **longitudinal designs,** a group from a single cohort is studied at several ages (Figure 2.1). Because all the subjects are from the same cohort, we know that any observed changes are not due to cohort effects. If, instead of giving an intelligence test to people from five different cohorts, we had tested a group of 20 year olds in 1940, and then again every decade until they were 60, we would have used a longitudinal design. The results from such a study might surprise us. Instead of beginning to decline at age 40, the average IQs of these subjects kept rising.

How can we reconcile the results of the cross-sectional and the longitudinal study? A good part of it is probably due to changes in society. Those 60 year olds tested in the cross-sectional study almost certainly had much less education than the 20 year olds. Because the 60 year olds in the longitudinal study were compared with themselves at age 20, the effects of education remained constant, and all their experiences over 40 years increased their scores on at least some aspects of intelligence.

Similar effects have been found for personality. In 1969 college students and 45-year-old adults took the same personality test (Woodruff and Birren, 1972). Scores indicated that the middle-aged adults felt themselves to be more competent and better adjusted than did the college students. It would appear that people's competence and adjustment tend to increase as they become older and settled in the community. But conclusions based on this cross-sectional comparison would be wrong. Twenty-five years earlier, the 45 year olds had taken the same test as college students—and obtained scores quite similar to their own middle-aged scores. Apparently, people who were in college during World War II had more confidence in themselves than people who were in college during the 1960s.

At first glance, longitudinal studies seem to be the ideal way to study adult development. They eliminate cohort differences, and they allow us to get at intraindividual change. But they can mislead us in another way. Longitudinal studies confound age-related change with historical change. People in the study are tested several times over a period of years, and any changes in society will affect their performance. For example, if we were studying political attitudes, societal shifts during the course of the study could lead us to conclude—inappropriately—that political attitudes change with age. If the study had been carried out from 1945 to 1965, we might have concluded that adults become more liberal with age; but if the study had been carried out from 1965 to 1985, we might have concluded that adults get more conservative as they get older.

Longitudinal studies have other problems as well. Testing the same people again and again makes them so familiar with the test that their scores may reflect a "practice" effect. In addition, as subjects age, some of the people in poorest health begin to die. Survivors in

◆ *Adulthood in Today's World*

THE BALTIMORE LONGITUDINAL STUDY

In 1958 researchers at the Gerontology Research Center began the Baltimore Longitudinal Study of Aging (BLSA), which they hope will go a long way toward uncovering the nature of the normal aging process. When the study began, all subjects, ranging in age from 25 to 84, were healthy men with better than average education and income. New subjects are added regularly, and in 1978 women were added to the study, most of them wives or daughters of the original group (Migdal, Abeles, and Sherrod, 1981).

Subjects younger than 60 are tested every two years, those in their sixties are tested every 18 months, and those older than seventy are tested every year. Each testing takes about 2 and 1/2 days to complete. During this testing session, subjects undergo physical examinations, an array of laboratory tests, aptitude, personality, and IQ tests, interviews, and behavioral observations. Major organ systems are evaluated, as well as the ability to adapt to stress.

Researchers have gathered data on medical, biochemical, physiological, nutritional, anthropological, psychological, and sociological aspects of the subjects' lives. By 1977, a total of 1088 men, ranging in age from 18 to 96, had been tested at least once. More than 200 had died (Shock, 1985). Not all the 600,000 records on these subjects have yet been analyzed, and more data are collected every year on both the original subjects and on subjects added since 1977.

In the early days of the study, most of the published information on physiological and psychological functioning was in the form of cross-sectional studies. But as longitudinal studies have been appearing, long-held assumptions about aging have been called into question. BLSA studies show that aging is highly individual, with few people following the pattern of age changes that appears in averages. Many of the accepted changes of aging are apparently the result of disease, and some of the expected physiological and intellectual declines have not appeared in very old individuals who retain their health (Shock, 1985).

lengthy longitudinal studies tend to be healthier, brighter, have more income, and higher ranking occupations than those who die or are not available for repeated testing (Schaie and Hertzog, 1982). As a result, a study that runs for 40 years will eventually be testing a group that lacks some of the people with the lowest scores, thereby raising the average score at older ages and causing the researcher to underestimate the effects of age.

As if these problems were not enough, the mechanics of a lengthy longitudinal study can be formidable, as the description of the Baltimore Longitudinal Study indicates (see accompanying box, ''The Baltimore Longitudinal Study''). Such studies are expensive; they are slow; and a researcher must remain committed to the project for years. In addition, people move or die, so that it is sometimes difficult to contact the same subjects for repeated testing. Finally, records must be stored for years.

Attacking the problem in another way might help us understand age, cohort, and time influences. By eliminating all age differences, a third type of design allows us to look at the influence of cohort and time.

TIME-LAG DESIGN

In **time-lag** designs, groups from several different cohorts are studied, but the studies are spaced so that each group is assessed at the same age (Figure 2.1). Using such a time-lag design, we might test IQ performance in 60 year olds. We would test individuals belonging to the 1900 cohort in 1960, those belonging to the 1910 cohort in 1970, those in the 1920 cohort in 1980, and those in the 1930 cohort in 1990.

The time-lag design does not show developmental differences, because we are studying each group only once, and all subjects are the same age. By eliminating age-related change, however, we are able to chart the effect of history-normative influences. Yet we cannot separate cohort effects from the effects of historical time. We have no way of knowing whether group differences are due to being born in a particular year (cohort) or to the general social climate at the time the test was given (historical time).

Time-lag designs are as time-consuming and expensive as longitudinal designs, and they require the same sort of commitment on the part of the investigator. However, other problems that are involved in longitudinal studies do not affect time-lag designs. Because each person is tested only once, there is no "practice" effect, and there is no worry that the subjects will move or die between tests.

SEQUENTIAL DESIGN

The best way to uncover developmental change and to find out how changes in society affect development would be to use all three designs to study a phenomenon. This procedure would enable us to estimate the effects of age, cohort, and historical time on the differences we find.

Such designs, known as **sequential designs,** were first suggested by Warner Schaie (1965). Schaie proposed three forms; the cohort-sequential, the cross-sequential, and the time-sequential. In the *cohort-sequential* method, two or more cohorts are tested at the same ages on two or more occasions. We might test members of the 1930 and the 1940 cohorts at ages 30 and 40, studying the 1930 cohort in 1960 and 1970, and the 1940 cohort in 1970 and 1980 (see Table 2.3). This method tries to separate age change from cohort difference and assumes that the fact that each cohort reached those ages at a different historical time will have no effect on the outcome.

In the *cross-sequential* method, two or more cohorts are tested at the same historical time on two or more occasions. We might test members of the 1930 and 1940 cohorts in 1960 and 1970, so that the 1930 cohort is studied at 30 and 40, and the 1940 cohort at 20 and 30. This method tries to separate cohort differences from historical time and assumes that age has no effect on the outcome.

In the *time-sequential* method, several cohorts are tested at the same ages on two or more occasions. We might test 30 and 40 year olds in 1960 and 1970, drawing on members of the 1920 and 1930 cohorts for the first test and members of the 1930 and 1940 cohorts for the second test. This method tries to separate age change from historical time and assumes that cohort has no effect on the outcome.

Sequential designs have been used in research with children and adults, but not all researchers are convinced that using these sequential designs would solve their problems. They have pointed out that, given the small groups used in most sequential studies, it often is not possible to determine whether observed differences between cohorts are actually true differences or due to changes in the nature of the group (Nesselroade and Labouvie, 1985). Some researchers have suggested that instead of using three different sequences, developmentalists use either cross-sectional or longitudinal sequences (Baltes, Reese, and Nesselroade, 1977).

In the cross-sectional sequence, a measure, such as an IQ test, may be given to five cohorts (20, 30, 40, 50, and 60 year olds). Ten years later, different groups from the same cohorts (now 30, 40, 50, 60, and 70 year olds) are given the same test. Using new groups for the second test avoids practice effects and makes it simpler to carry out the study. It also gives us an opportunity to compare age-related differences in different cohorts at different historical times.

In the longitudinal sequence, a group of 20 year olds may be tested every ten years until they are 60. When the 20 year olds are 30 and are given their first retest, a second group from another cohort (20 year olds) is selected. This second group is tested every 10 years until they are 50. This sequence allows us to assess the pattern of age change in two cohorts at two different times.

Another sequential approach, known as the most efficient design, combines elements of the cross-sectional and longitudinal sequences in a different, but systematic, manner (Schaie and Herzog, 1982). The first step in this sequential design is to conduct a cross-sectional study, using two or more cohorts. Several years later, these same groups are studied again, so that researchers now have longitudinal data on the subjects in the cross-sectional study. But they take one additional step: they conduct a new cross-sectional study, repeating the first study on new groups from the same cohorts they have been studying.

No matter how they are set up, sequential approaches are so time-consuming and expensive that they are rarely possible to carry out. By being sensitive to the particular factors that affect the results obtained with other types of design, however, investigators can avoid misinterpreting their findings.

Selecting an appropriate design is only the beginning of developmental studies. Other issues can also affect the results of research and the conclusions drawn from them, so that no matter how carefully the study is designed, its results may be misleading.

RESEARCH ISSUES

It is easy to assume that age is the source of the various changes that occur over time. Actually, age never *causes* developmental change, even though it provides a handy way of talking about changes that become more prevalent with age. A good way to think about age is as a *carrier variable;* age carries with it a variety of physiological, psychological, social, and environmental influences. For example, among children in our society, age is associated with schooling, and school may contribute to the development of verbal skills. Similarly, age is associated with income in adults, and financial resources may affect self-concept. Age-related changes in verbal ability may reflect age-specified school experiences, and age-related changes in self-concept may reflect age-specified increases in financial resources.

Such relationships mean that a good deal of developmental research is, by necessity, correlational, in which researchers uncover systematic relationships between two variables. In controlled experiments, every person in the study has an equal chance of receiving experimental or controlled treatments. But researchers cannot decide who will receive schooling or raises in salary. Since researchers cannot manipulate these conditions, they must study them as they occur naturally and note their effects. Instead of arranging conditions to test cause and effect, as they would in a controlled experiment, they look for systematic relations that occur at rates significantly higher than chance.

No matter what aspect of development they study, researchers want to be able to generalize their results from the individuals they have studied to other people and from the situations they have studied to other situations. Two issues that affect the applicability of research are the choice of samples and the measures of assessment.

SELECTING A SAMPLE

The nature of the **sample**—that is, the people selected to represent the population the researcher hopes to generalize results to—is important. In studies of adult development and aging, the nature of the sample differs, depending on the goal of the research. For example, if we want to study social interaction among older adults in general, a nursing home would not be a good place to do the study because only a very small percentage of older adults live in a nursing home and those who do are not typical older adults. But if we want to study the effects of life in a nursing home on social interaction, then the nursing home would be an ideal location. The nature of our sample also depends on whether we are trying to describe, predict, or explain age differences.

When the aim is *description,* a study is meant to describe differences that exist at the moment. In this case, the sample must be **random:** every member of each age group that the study will be generalized to must have an equal chance of being selected. Otherwise, the results are likely to be based on individuals who differ in important ways from the age groups of interest.

It is easy to see how the failure to use a random sample could affect the applicability of research results. Suppose you wanted to find out about the economic status of older adults. Are the elderly truly needy? To answer the question, you need a random sample of all older adults. A sample limited to residents of a retirement community would produce a rosy picture: it would seem that almost all older adults have above-average incomes. But a sample drawn from the inner city would produce a disturbing, dark view of age: you would find that few of these older adults have incomes above the poverty level.

When the aim of research is *prediction,* a study is meant to estimate differences that are likely to exist in the future. In this case, you would want a selective, nonrandom sample. Because the characteristics of the population are continually changing, the groups studied should reflect the probable makeup of the population at the future time predicted. Before the sample is drawn, a hypothesis about the characteristics of the population in the future is needed to guide selection of the sample.

Suppose you want to know what the economic status of older adults will be in 2020.

Studying a random sample of today's older adults would produce an erroneous picture of economic status in 2020. The United States is undergoing a shift from a predominantly industrial to a service-based economy. As the shift takes place, it is accompanied by cohort changes in occupation. This change means that few older adults in 2020 will have been factory workers; instead, the majority will be drawn from occupations that provide service. Pension policies and salaries as well as the tastes and needs of employees in service occupations may differ radically from those in manufacturing. In this case, the sample should be drawn selectively from today's older adults, so that their occupational backgrounds reflect the occupations of the cohort that will begin retiring in about 2010. In addition, because an increasing proportion of older women in 2020 will have had a history of employment, the sample should anticipate this situation and include an appropriate proportion of older women who are retired employees as opposed to older women whose work was confined to the home.

When the aim of research is *explanation*, the study is meant to enhance our understanding of the causes underlying observed age differences. Again, the sample should be selective, so that age-related factors, such as cohort differences, can be ruled out. For example, if education, health, or socioeconomic status were known to be related to the aspect of development under study, you would not want to use a random sample of adults. Because cohort differences are known to exist (on the average, 20 year olds have more education, better health, and higher socioeconomic status than 65 year olds), these differences alone could account for age differences. If you are trying to explain age-related differences in memory, for example, you would want to eliminate the possibility that they were simply the result of cohort differences in education. Therefore, you might want to compare 20 year olds in college with 60 year olds who had comparable educational background. Such older adults would not be typical of their cohort, but their performance would shed light on the basis of age differences that are not related to education.

Depending on the aim of the study and the phenomenon involved, sample characteristics that may be important include sex, education, socioeconomic level, ethnic group, and health. However, simply choosing an appropriate sample is not enough to produce results that can be generalized. The procedures used to assess the individuals studied must also be considered carefully.

SELECTING A MEASURE

Just as important as the nature of the sample is the choice of measures that are used to assess the characteristics or behavior of the individuals in the sample. Unless the measures are relevant to the task and appropriate to the age ranges being studied, little will be learned from the investigation. Two important factors that affect the adequacy of a measure are its reliability and its validity.

Reliability

Accurate measures have **reliability;** they can be applied with confidence that peoples' scores on the measure will be consistent, no matter where the measure is used, who administers it, or how many times it is repeated. If a measure is reliable, then individual differences in behavior will reflect actual differences among the people in the study. The consistency of an individual's scores on the same measure is known as **test–retest reliability.** Although illness, fatigue, worry, or distractions in the test situation can reduce the consistency of scores on reliable measures, those with high test–retest reliability are least affected. In some cases, test–retest reliability may be affected by time. The person who takes a test in 1995 has more experience and more knowledge than that person had in 1975, which helps to explain why scores on some tests of mental ability increase over the years. Even so, test–retest reliability is higher on tests of intelligence or ability than on measures of mood or attitudes, which are expected to fluctuate over time.

Validity

The **validity** of a research design refers to how well the study actually measures what it sets out to measure. Developmentalists are especially concerned with two kinds of validity: external and discriminant.

Unless a measure has **external validity,** which refers to how widely the information produced can be applied in other situations, it cannot tell us much about development. If measures have external validity, the results can be generalized outside the context of the study. Suppose you are studying memory and ask a cross-sectional sample of adults to come into the laboratory, memorize lists of unrelated words, and then later recall them. Younger adults are likely to do fairly well at the task, and older adults, poorly. But poor performance in this situation may have little relevance to the functioning of memory in daily life. Two thousand years ago, the Roman statesman Cicero wrote, ''I have never heard of any old man forgetting where he had hidden his money.''

Sometimes measures developed for use with children or younger adults may not test similar behavior in older adults. Digit span tests (which require subjects to repeat strings of digits they have seen or heard), for example, appear to measure attention span in young adults but memory in older adults (Schaie and Hertzog, 1985). Interpreting results on this test across adulthood could therefore lead to questionable conclusions. A study that uses intelligence tests to assess older adults' intellectual competence may also lack external validity. Intelligence tests were originally developed to predict success in school. Test developers made no pretense of measuring all kinds of intelligence—only those skills that are used in an academic setting. Because most older adults are unaccustomed to formal testing situations and few attend school, their scores on a typical IQ test may not be an adequate measure of their intelligence and may have little bearing on their ability to solve problems in daily life.

Cohort differences can also limit the external validity of tests for some age groups. For example, even though some IQ tests have special forms for adults, a test may become irrelevant, and therefore invalid, with the passage of time. In order to restore their validity, tests are revised to reflect cultural changes. It has been suggested, however, that earlier versions of adult intelligence tests, standardized on groups from the cohort now in old age, might be more appropriate for use with today's older adults (Nesselroade and Labouvie, 1985). If tests seem meaningless to older adults, who rarely use the abstract, context-free reasoning required, they may not be motivated to do well. In one study (Labouvie-Vief and Chandler, 1978), when researchers made the tasks attractive and meaningful to older adults, these individuals performed better than younger adults. Such age differences in performance highlight the importance of considering the appropriateness of a measure for all ages studied.

A second type of validity is also important. When a measure has **discriminant validity,** scores will have a very low relationship—or none at all—with scores on a different kind of measure. For example, if you are examining the effects of retirement on sociability, your confidence in your measure is strengthened if it correlates strongly with other measures of sociability but only weakly with measures of physical health.

With care, problems of validity can be minimized. Moreover, recognition of possible problems makes investigators wary of overconfidence in their results or of overgeneralizing them. As we explore the various aspects of adult development and aging, we will note from time to time when inadequate tests have produced research findings that may not accurately reflect people's functioning or abilities. Our exploration begins with an attempt to understand the biological bases of development and aging.

SUMMARY

ALTERNATIVE WORLD VIEWS

Developmentalists who use a **mechanistic model** to explain development tend to see the individual as relatively passive, to focus on observable changes in behavior, and to regard change as quantitative. In **social cognitive theory,** however, the individual is reasonably active and his or her goals, plans, and beliefs about the self are important. Developmentalists who adopt the **organismic model** see the individual as active, focus on internal changes in structure, and regard change as qualitative. Developmentalists who take a **dialectical approach** see the individual as interactive, focus on the relationship between the individual and society, and regard change as either quantitative or qualitative.

PERSPECTIVES ON DEVELOPMENT AND AGING

All biologists, psychologists, sociologists, anthropologists, and historians who study development and aging are interested in age-related changes in behavior, but the level of analysis varies from one discipline to the next. The levels interact, and development and aging cannot be explained by any one level alone.

Biologists focus on development at the cellular and anatomical level, studying biochemical and physiological changes across the life span of the organism. Psychologists study development as it affects individual function and social interaction.

Sociologists focus on groups, social institutions, and social conditions rather than on the individual. Many sociologists have adopted an **age-stratification** model, in which people are seen as living through a series of age-related positions or roles. Also heavily stressed is **socialization,** the process by which people absorb the attitudes, values, and beliefs of their cultures. Anthropologists study patterns of development in various cultures, thereby showing the potential range of human behavior. Historians study differences in developmental patterns across time, focusing on the way social institutions, social policy, and behavior change within a society over time.

DEVELOPMENTAL DESIGNS

In **cross-sectional designs,** two or more age groups, each from a different cohort, are studied on one occasion. This design reveals only interindividual differences and confounds age-related and cohort influences. In **longitudinal designs,** a group from a single cohort is studied at several ages. This design reveals intraindividual differences, but confounds age-related change with the effects of historical time. In **time-lag designs,** groups from several cohorts are studied, but the studies are spaced so that each group is assessed at the same age. This design confounds cohort effects with the effects of historical time. In **sequential designs,** researchers have tried to surmount some of the problems of other designs by combining aspects of more than one design into either a cross-sectional or longitudinal sequence.

RESEARCH ISSUES

Age does not cause developmental change, but carries with it a variety of physiological, psychological, social, and environmental influences. The nature of the **sample** determines whether research findings can be generalized across persons. When the aim of research is description, the sample must be drawn from the population of interest at **random.** When the aim of research is prediction, the sample should be selective and reflect the nature of the group for which the prediction is to be made. When the aim of research is explanation, the sample should be selective and controlled for relevant cohort differences and extraneous factors correlated with age.

Measures used in developmental research should have **reliability,** so that individual differences reflect actual differences among people in the study. **Test–retest reliability,** or the consistency of a person's scores on the same measure, is important. Measures used in developmental research should also have **validity** so that the investigator knows what observed differences reflect. Findings cannot be generalized past the measure used unless the measure has **external validity:** the items included must be relevant and the measures must be appropriate for all age groups studied. Studies will not be useful unless the measures used also have **discriminant validity:** the measures should correlate highly with the variable under study but only weakly—or not at all—with other variables.

KEY TERMS

age stratification	**organismic model**
cross-sectional design	**random sample**
dialectical approach	**reliability**
discriminant validity	**sample**
disengagement	**sequential design**
external validity	**social cognitive theory**
geriatrics	**socialization**
gerontology	**test–retest reliability**
longitudinal design	**time-lag design**
mechanistic model	**validity**

Part Two

♦

—— ♦ ——

Biological Aspects of Adult Development and Aging

Chapter 3

♦

Biological Explanations of Aging

♦

On January 11, 1988, Florence Knapp, then the world's oldest living person, died. Knapp, who was born on October 10, 1873 on a farm near Philadelphia, was 114 years and 94 days old. When she celebrated her 110th birthday, she was still alert and active. She took care of her garden, keeping it free from weeds, climbed stairs, and handled the details of daily life. Over the next few months she became increasingly frail and had trouble getting around. It was then that she moved to a nursing home, where she spent her last few years. Knapp's life spanned a major section of American history: when she was born, the Civil War had been over for eight years, Ulysses S. Grant was president, travel was by foot, horse, or railroad, and communication over long distances was by mail or telegraph. When she died, Ronald Reagan was president, transcontinental jets flew overhead, Americans had been to the moon, and television made us all eyewitnesses to history.

Florence Knapp was an unusual woman. She graduated from college in 1894, in a day when few men—and far fewer women—had advanced education. She chose a career as a teacher over marriage, for at the turn of the last century only a handful of women had both. She was a life-long feminist and actively supported the suffragist movement. In 1919, when she was 45, she demonstrated in Philadelphia, demanding the right to vote. She recalled marching down Broad Street, dressed in white and carrying a placard (Kotre and Hall, 1990). The next year the Nineteenth Amendment was ratified, and women could at last vote in every state.

Although almost no one lives as long as Florence Knapp did, the number of centenarians is increasing. In this chapter, we take up the topic of longevity, contrasting the maximum number of years scientists believe people are capable of living with the number of years most people reach. After reviewing research that has extended the life span in animals, we consider the possible effects of extending the human life span. Then we examine the process of normal biological aging and the factors that tend to accelerate deterioration. We close with an exploration of the various theories that have been advanced to explain biological aging.   ◆

LENGTH OF LIFE

As far back as records extend, human beings have fought against the brevity of life and tried to forestall the aging process—by determination, by prayer, or even by magic. Today the quest has moved into the laboratory. Researchers are trying to discover just *why* we age and what, if anything, can be done to slow the process.

Although we age in similar ways, we do not all age at the same rate. Appearances can be deceiving, and older adults may look 10 or 20 years older or younger than their chronological age. Function shows similar interindividual differences. Some people join the ranks of the old-old in their sixties, some are still young-old long past their eightieth birthdays, and a handful live for a century before their bodies begin to fail.

Longevity, which refers to the length or duration of life, can be considered in two ways. Average longevity, or the mean age of survival for members of any species, is known as the **average life span.** It is affected by nutrition, health care, and environmental hazards.

The oldest age to which any individuals survive is known as the **maximum life span.** It apparently reflects the unique biological characteristics of a species (Cutler, 1981), which somehow evolved in the course of evolution.

HOW DID OLD AGE EVOLVE?

A few species do not show an independent aging process. Like the salmon, they grow, become mature, reproduce once, and die abruptly—apparently as a direct consequence of a programmed hormonal flooding that is associated with the reproductive process (Walford, 1986). But virtually every animal that reproduces more than once ages, and many of these species show the same characteristics found in aging humans (Kirkwood, 1985). Skin, hair, posture, muscle strength and vigor, and the ability to react effectively to environmental stress change in similar ways. This similarity across so many species leads us to wonder how the process of aging evolved. Some theorists assume that aging is adaptive, a process that enhances survival of the species, while others see it as nonadaptive. No matter which version researchers accept, they assume that at least several thousand genes are involved in aging, and some speculate that most genes affect longevity (Johnson, 1988).

Adaptiveness of Aging

In the adaptive view, aging is good for any species. Because it leads to death, aging effectively eliminates old members of the species. This removal of the old clears the way for new generations, who can claim the space and food that would have gone to the departed generation. Aging is also beneficial because it provides a rapid turnover of the population. The quick succession of generations provides a wide array of genetic types. This turnover allows mutations to appear, improving the species' chances of adapting to environmental changes that might eliminate a nonaging group that had adapted to a narrow band of environmental conditions (Weizsacker, 1980).

Yet it is difficult to see how most species can reap these advantages. Few animals in the wild live long enough to reach old age, so death through aging is unlikely to benefit the group. In fact, so many individuals meet an early death that there is little opportunity for aging to evolve. Besides, for aging to evolve, its benefits to the group would have to outweigh the adaptive benefits to the individual of producing offspring that live to reproduce themselves (Kirkwood, 1985).

In the case of humans, these conditions may be met, and aging may have evolved through natural selection. We are one of the few species whose members live long enough to age, and in our case, the presence of nonreproducing old people seems to confer a distinct advantage on the group. Our long, slow period of childhood growth leaves our young dependent for many years. Having aged grandparents around to help with the care of infants and children increases the reproductive success of the family group. Older adults provide another adaptive function. By serving as the repository of information and wisdom, they assist the survival not only of their grandchildren but also of the entire group. In this view, older adults fill the role of group memory, transmitting a collection of roles, beliefs, and typical behavior (Birren, 1988; Gutmann, 1987).

Nonadaptiveness of Aging

Not all researchers agree that aging is adaptive. Instead, some see it as an inevitable by-product of evolution (Rose and Graves, 1989). They point out that evolution selects those traits that get offspring born and keep them alive until they can reproduce themselves. Since natural selection works through the survival of offspring, its force becomes progressively weaker as reproduction dwindles. Among those who take this view, three explanations are favored. The first says that aging evolved through the selection of many mutated genes whose function is beneficial during early life but harmful toward the end of the life span (Williams, 1957). The second explanation is that aging developed because natural selection has no way of weeding out mutations whose harmful effects appear only during later life (Rose and Charlesworth, 1980). A third view is that species have evolved by producing ''disposable bodies''; that is, they have devoted the metabolic energy that would be required for indefinite cell repair and prevention of aging to growth and reproduction (Kirkwood, 1981). Thus, aging is ''nonadaptive'' because it has no direct relation to the survival of species or individuals.

MAXIMUM LIFE SPAN

No matter how aging evolved, its result is a maximum life span that varies vastly from one species to the next and is determined by genes (Adelman, 1988) (see Table 3.1). In most cases, the factors that determine how long members of any species can live seem to remain the same.

Factors That Affect the Length of Life

Among animals with backbones, a species' longevity correlates with brain weight, body weight, metabolic rate, and deep body temperature (Kirkwood, 1985). Between two species of the same brain size, the species with the lower body weight generally lives longer, and between two species of the same body size, the species with the higher body temperature lives longer. Birds, which have a high body temperature, for example, tend to outlive mammals of the same size.

Within a single species, however, the relation is reversed. Among cold-blooded animals, whose metabolic rate is affected by the temperature of the environment, individuals with lower body temperatures live longer. Lizards that live in a warm climate have shorter life spans than animals that live in cold climates. Because human beings maintain a constant body temperature and a fairly steady rate of metabolism, changes in environmental temperature probably have no effect on human longevity.

Metabolism is extremely important: the more rapid the metabolic rate, the shorter lived a species. For more than three quarters of a century we have known that most animals consume a fairly constant number of calories per ounce of body weight over their entire life span (Rubner, 1908). Animals with a short life span, such as mice, tend to burn calories faster than longer lived animals, such as elephants. Animals that seem to break the rule by living long lives, even though they burn calories rapidly, generally have a very low metabolic rate while resting or sleeping. For example, because of its long rest periods, a bat burns no more calories per ounce during its 20-year life span than a mouse burns during its 4 years of life (Sacher, 1977). The notable exception to the rule of calorie consumption

Table 3.1 **MAXIMUM LIFE SPAN**

Species	Years
Tortoise	150.0
Human being	120.0
Whale	80.0
Indian elephant	70.0
Horse	62.0
Great apes	
Gorilla	50.0
Chimpanzee	50.0
Orangutan	50.0
Old World monkeys	
Baboon	40.0
Macaque	40.0
Gibbon	35.0
Brown bear	36.8
New World monkeys	
Spider monkey	35.0
Squirrel monkey	21.0
Dog	34.0
Cat	30.0
Cattle	30.0
Swine	27.0
Sheep	20.0
Goat	18.0
European rabbit	13.0
Guinea pig	7.5
Golden hamster	4.0
Mouse	3.5

Information from: Rockstein, Chesky, and Sussman, 1977; Walford, 1983; Washburn, 1981.

is the human being, who burns about four times more calories per pound than most other mammals.

The length of gestation and childhood also seems to be related to longevity. Length of gestation alone is a reasonably good predictor of longevity in many species, although human beings deviate from this rule. Our life span far exceeds the span expected for a nine-month gestation period. But we may not break the rule at all. For months after birth the human infant is like a fetus in brain development, physical development, and behavior. Human beings seem to be thrust from the womb ahead of schedule because further fetal brain development would make passage through the birth canal impossible. If we add our lengthy childhood, or immaturity, to our precocious birth, the comparatively long human life span no longer seems an exception to the typical pattern. Such a long period of immaturity may be extremely adaptive, for it permits the young to learn the adult skills that are necessary for survival (Bruner, 1964).

The maximum life span of a species appears to remain constant through historical time and across cultures. Although early humans of 100,000 years ago had the potential to live

85 or 100 or more years, almost none did because they succumbed to predators, accident, or disease. Excavations of the pre-Columbian grave site of a Native American tribe, for example, showed that few tribal members lived past the age of 45 and that the oldest person buried at the site was about 55 (Washburn, 1981). Yet the possibility was always there. At a burial site in the Aleutian Islands, anthropologists found that some Aleuts had lived past the age of 80. As we will see, it has taken more than 100,000 years for human survival to approach the maximum life span.

The Pseudocentenarians

Most researchers believe that humans have a maximum life span of between 110 and 120 years. From time to time, claims are made for individuals who live far past this apparent limit. In seventeenth-century England, Thomas Parr was said to have reached the age of 152; in eighteenth-century Philadelphia, Samuel Mecutcheon was said to have lived until 122; and in the early nineteenth century, Yarrow Mamout of Virginia supposedly lived past the age of 134 (Freeman, 1982). All these people lived at a time when it was virtually impossible to verify a person's age.

When researchers James Fries and Lawrence Crapo (1981) investigated the claims of 600 people who claimed to have been at least 120 years old, they found no one who had lived to be more than 114. That 114-year-old, Shigechijo Izumi of Japan, lived another six years, dying of pneumonia on February 21, 1986 at the age of 120 (*Newsweek,* 1986). The runner-up appears to be our own Florence Knapp, who reached 114. Izumi's and Knapp's life spans remain unchallenged. When Birdie May Vogt died in Florida on July 26, 1989, just eleven days short of her 113th birthday, she had been recognized by the *Guiness Book of World Records* as the world's oldest living person (*Reporter Dispatch,* 1989).

Typical of the inflated claims discovered by Fries and Crapo was that of Charlie Smith. According to the Social Security Administration, when Smith died in October 1979, he was 137 years old. His Social Security benefits had been based on work that began in 1955 when, at 113 years of age, he picked oranges. But his marriage certificate, discovered after much searching in Arcadia, Florida, showed that at the time of his marriage in January 1910, Smith was a lad of 35, not the venerable 66 of his claims (Freeman, 1982). When at last he died, Charlie Smith apparently was ''only'' 104 years old.

Occasionally we hear of remote communities where the average life span is extremely high and it is common to live past the century mark. Residents of these villages often say that they are 120, 134, or 150 years old. Three such settlements have received a good deal of publicity: the village of Vilcabamba in Ecuador, the Abkhasian region of the USSR, and the province of Hunza in Pakistan. Scientific investigations have discredited reports of extremely long life in each of these communities (Leaf, 1982).

In the case of Vilcabamba, the first studies seemed to indicate that many centenarians lived in the village. But further research made it clear that parents had been confused with children; that intermarriage was common, leading to the duplication of many names; and that when children died, parents often gave the same name to a new child. Vilcabambans who were younger than 60 or 70 generally gave their correct ages, but among those who had passed 70, ages became increasingly inaccurate. In 1944, when he was 61, one man claimed to be 70; in 1949 he claimed to be 80; in 1970, to be 121; and in 1974, to be 127. In 30 years, his claims had increased by 50 years, until he was overstating his age by 36 years. When records were carefully examined, none of the supposed centenarians had reached 100. The average 100 year old turned out to be 84, and the average 130 year old was only 95 (Mazess and Forman, 1979).

The extravagant ages reported for Abkhasia also have been discounted (Medvedev, 1974). Official birth registration is nonexistent for these old people, and baptismal records generally disappeared when churches were destroyed after the Russian Revolution. In the case of a man named Vakutia, who insisted that he was 130, extreme old age turned out to be a way of escaping service in the armed forces. Vakutia had deserted from the army after World War I simply by using his father's name and documents. He was actually only 78 years old. When a journalist later attempted to verify the asserted age of other Abkhasian residents, he was told by a Soviet gerontologist that no one in the area had ever reached the 120-year mark (Gerogakas, 1980).

All three areas of reputed centenarians are remote, located high in the mountains, and their residents live a rigorous rural life. In these areas, to be old is to gain authority and respect. It is easy for the local elders to claim an advanced age because literacy is low and records are sparse.

It would be a mistake, however, to dismiss these places completely. Even though few of the inhabitants reach or pass their hundredth birthdays, they do remain vigorous and active in community life to a very advanced age. Their low-calorie, low-fat diet, moderate alcohol and tobacco consumption, and active life-style are consistent with the recommendations of many researchers in the field of gerontology. They also parallel the life-style of Florence Knapp, who spent her 114 years in the country, living on the family farm, even though she taught school for 42 years. She neither smoked nor drank, and she adhered to a low-fat, low-calorie diet, centered around fresh fruits and vegetables (Woodruff-Pak, 1987).

AVERAGE LIFE SPAN

Until recently, the maximum and average human life spans have been widely separated. The average human life span varies from one culture to another and changes over historical time. Our ancestors were killed by wars, accidents, disease, predators, and malnutrition. Although accidents and warfare are still with us and other human beings have replaced bears and tigers as major predators, deaths from many other causes have plummeted.

For the past two centuries, average longevity has steadily increased. Expanded food supplies and better nutrition probably were responsible for any extensions before the middle of the nineteenth century, for they strengthened people's ability to resist infection. Then in the second half of the nineteenth century, advances in sanitation—hygiene, safer food and water—began to have an effect on longevity because they reduced contact with infectious microorganisms. Finally, medical measures, such as immunization, surgery, and antibiotics, began to reduce the death rate even further (McKoewn, 1978). It seems possible that another major advance may be on the horizon, created by a rapid deepening of our understanding that life-style has a major impact on health and longevity.

In 1900 the average person born in the United States could expect to live for 47 years; by 1985 expectations had increased to 75 years. Researchers predict that the average baby born in 2020 can expect to live for 78 years (U.S. Senate, Select Committee on Aging, 1987–1988). Most of the increase in **life expectancy,** or the number of years a person can expect to live, has come about because of reductions in premature death. Technically, life expectancy refers to the point at which 50 percent of the original cohort has died, which means that by 1947 only half of the babies born in 1900 were still alive. Life expectancy at later ages, say, 65, refers to the point at which 50 percent of the cohort members still living at age 65 have died. More people are reaching old age, but once they are 65, their life expectancy is only a few years longer than it was for 65 year olds in 1900. At that time, a person who was 65 could expect another 11.9 years of life; by 1985 it had grown to 16.8 years; and by 2000 it is expected to increase by yet another year (National Center for Health Statistics, 1986; Spencer, 1984).

The increase in average life expectancy is not the same for all groups. Women generally live longer than men. Fewer females die at birth, and at all ages they tend to survive infection and resist the effects of physical deprivation better than men. Women also appear less susceptible to the present number one killer in the United States—heart disease. This female advantage has not always existed. In 1900 women's life expectancy was only 2.0 years longer than men's at birth, and it had dropped to only 0.7 years longer once they reached the age of 65 (National Center for Health Statistics, 1986) (Figure 3.1). Several factors combined to change that picture. Smoking, accidents, and a higher degree of alcoholism increased male death rates while large reductions in childbirth deaths increased female life expectancy. In 1990 the life expectancy gap was 7.6 years at birth and 4.5 years at age 65; by 2050 it is expected to be 8.1 years at birth and 5.7 years at age 65 (Spencer, 1984).

Despite these external influences, many researchers believe that females may have a biological buffer that increases their chances of longevity. Some point to a more active female immune system (which responds more vigorously to disease and resists cancer cells better) and protection against heart disease by the female hormone estrogen (which keeps the levels of artery-clogging cholesterol low and increases the levels of artery-clearing "good" cholesterol) (Holden, 1987). Others suggest that metabolism may be a key: women burn calories at a rate that is 8 to 10 percent slower than that of men (Fischer, 1988). The finding of more long-lived females than males in most animal species supports the biological view.

Whites generally live longer than blacks, but the difference has declined sharply since 1900, when the life expectancy of a white baby was almost 16 years greater than that of a

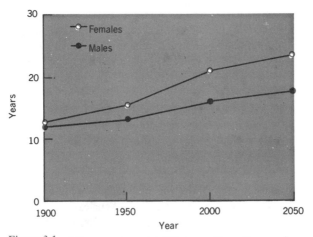

Figure 3.1   Life expectancy (at 65) across time. *Source:* Spencer, 1984.

black baby. The difference is still fairly large at birth (6 years in 1987) (*New York Times,* March 23, 1990), but by the age of 65, it has almost disappeared. In fact, among those who pass the 85-year mark, blacks of both sexes have a longer life expectancy than whites. The crossover occurs earlier for black men, whose life expectancy exceeds that of white men from the age of 73 (Wing et al., 1985). In both sexes, the crossover may occur because blacks are much less likely than whites to survive until their seventies. Thus, blacks who live into extreme old age may be especially robust. Because nutrition, sanitation, and medical care account for the increase in the average life span, it would be reasonable to assume that socioeconomic differences are responsible for most of this ethnic difference in life expectancy.

Variations in average life span across cultures are also related to a society's socioeconomic standards. In more developed nations, the average life span is much longer than that in less developed countries. This advantage is evident from the greater percentage of older adults in developed societies. In 1985, 11.5 percent of the population in the world's developed societies had passed their sixty-fifth birthdays; in less developed societies, only 4.2 percent were that old. The proportion of people in old age is growing rapidly in all societies, but developed countries will continue to have the edge. By 2025, 18.9 percent of their residents will be past 65 compared with 8.0 percent in less developed countries (Myers, 1990).

Extended longevity is moving the average life span closer to the maximum life span. Between 1980 and 1982, the number of Americans older than 85 increased more than 9 percent. Of the 2.4 million in this group, 32,000 were centenarians—75 percent of them women (U.S. Bureau of the Census, 1983). Another way to understand how average and maximum life spans are coming together is to look at survival rates. If no one succumbed to disease, those who did not die by accident would tend to succumb at about the same time. Plotted on a graph, the survival curve, which shows the percentage of population surviving at each age, would be rectangular (Figure 3.2). Today's survival curve is moving toward that shape. As the life span laid down in the general genetic program takes increasing control of the death rate and as society approaches the ideal curve, we can expect to see more and more centenarians. Just which of us reaches the 100 mark may be determined in good part by our own specific genetic program.

GENETICS OF AGE

The suspicion that genes may be at least partly responsible for the rate of aging has led to the adage that the best way to live to a ripe old age is to have long-lived parents and grandparents. That certainly seems to describe Florence Knapp's situation. A long life is not unusual among the Knapps. One of Florence's sisters lived to 107, and five other sisters and brothers lived well into their nineties. Three of her grandparents—all born before 1800—lived past the age of 80 (one until 95!). The fourth, born in 1800, died at the youthful age of 72 (Woodruff-Pak, 1987).

Research also gives some support to the adage. Identical twins (who have exactly the same genetic makeup because they develop when a single fertilized egg splits) tend to die within a few years of each other. Whether or not they live in a similar environment seems to have little effect on the time of their death. For example, one identical twin had a large family and lived on a farm; her sister never married and lived in the city. When they were

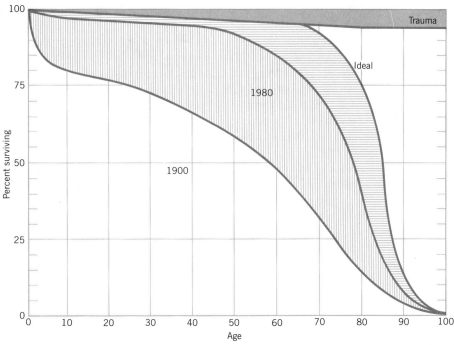

Figure 3.2   Survival curves. If premature death from disease were eliminated in the United States, the population would attain the ideal survival curve. By 1980 more than 80 percent of the discrepancy between the 1900 curve and the ideal curve had been eliminated. *Source:* Fries and Crapo, 1981, p. 73.

69, both twins had a cerebral hemorrhage on the same day, and they died within 26 days of each other (Rockstein and Sussman, 1979).

Although such coincidences are rare, the life span of identical twins is closer than that of fraternal twins (who have different genetic makeups because they develop from separate eggs). In a longitudinal study of all twins in New York State who had reached the age of 60 years, identical twins tended to die within 6 years and ten months of each other, whereas fraternal twins died about 8 years and five months apart (Falek et al., 1960) (Figure 3.3).

There is some indication that genetic influence on longevity is the result of differences in the susceptibility to disease. When a large group of men and women were followed for six years, differences in their susceptibility to disease seemed related to family differences in longevity (Hammond, Garfinkel, and Seidman, 1971). People from short-lived families tended to develop heart disease, diabetes, or other chronic diseases at an early age.

EXTENDING THE LIFE SPAN

Most of us would like to stay healthy and vigorous for as long as possible. Human attempts to stretch out the youthful years are carried out scientifically in the laboratory, where researchers are trying to extend the maximum life span. They have studied protozoa, rotifers, spiders, worms, flies, fish, hamsters, guinea pigs, mice, and rats, using chemicals, hormones, and various drugs that are reputed to extend life. They have removed the pituitary glands

Florence Knapp, who was the world's oldest living person when she died at the age of 114, celebrates her 113th birthday. Genetics probably contributed to her long life; life spans of 90 and 100 are not uncommon in her family.

of rats and manipulated the temperature of water in fish tanks. They have set some rats racing on exercise wheels and sharply restricted the food supply of others.

Many of these experiments have had tantalizing results, but only food restriction has provided clear evidence that the life span of mammals can be extended. Animals that get a highly nutritious diet with between 40 and 80 percent of the calories customarily eaten show increases in both life expectancy and life span. This restricted diet retards some, but not all,

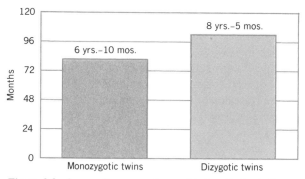

Figure 3.3 Longevity concordance of twins. Twin studies testify to a genetic influence on longevity; monozygotic twins, who share all their genes, have life spans that are closer in length than those of dizygotic twins, who share only half their genes. *Source:* Jarvik et al., 1960.

of the physiological changes associated with age, and it delays or prevents most of the diseases common to older mice. The important factor seems to be the reduction of calories, because reducing protein or fat sharply, but leaving calories at their normal level, has little or no effect on life span (Masoro, 1988; Weindruch and Walford, 1988).

Some researchers have found that when food restriction begins early in life, life span is lengthened but infant mortality increases, growth is stunted, childhood is prolonged, and behavioral development is impaired. But these drawbacks are eliminated and the diet is just as effective when researchers wait until the rats are six months old (and mature) to begin the restriction (Yu, Masoro, and McMahan, 1985).

Just why calorie restriction prolongs life is uncertain. It was once believed that it lowered the metabolic rate, so that the rat's allotted numbers of calories per ounce lasted several additional months. But studies have indicated that food-restricted rats burn energy as intensely as rats given free access to food (Masoro, 1988). As a result, their tissues use considerably more calories over the life span. Earlier research had shown that neither reduced body fat nor slowed growth and development was responsible for the extension. Recently, the focus has shifted to the effect of food restriction on the endocrine system, which influences biochemical processes in most tissues and organs. After reviewing the research, investigators Richard Weindruch and Roy Walford (1988) concluded that long-term dietary restriction prolonged life by affecting many physiological factors: it seems to upgrade repair and protective processes, increase metabolic efficiency, decrease the production of damaging agents, and change the signals received by the neuroendocrine network—especially the hypothalamus.

Weindruch and Walford have proposed a variation of undernutrition for human beings, although whether many people will be willing to trade the pleasures of the table for a strict dietary regimen is uncertain. (See accompanying box, ''A Researcher Becomes His Own Guinea Pig'') In the meantime, results from other research with rats provide a different prospect. Rats that exercise regularly but eat a normal diet do not live as long as food-restricted rats, but they live longer than sedentary rats and they seem to escape most of the diseases that cause many sedentary rats to die young (Holloszy, 1988).

QUALITY OF LIFE AMONG THE AGED

Suppose society were free of disease and most people lived at least 85 years. The situation would be very different from today, when the quality of the life span is linked with age and biological deterioration increases as we grow older, becoming prevalent in old age. If most of us reached 85 and the general health level of the population did not change, a society with a rectangular survival curve would be a society filled with nursing homes and populated by sick old people, unable to care for themselves.

But perhaps for most people, health does not begin to fail until a certain length of time before they die. If that is so, then the condition of extreme biological deterioration is better figured by the number of years until death than by the number of years since birth. Debilitating conditions, such as cancer, diabetes, mental deterioration, and heart, respiratory, and kidney disease, might be postponed. Heart attacks might strike at 80 instead of at 55; lung cancer might develop at 95 instead of at 60. People would generally be healthier longer.

The development of a large group of young-old individuals indicates that something of the sort may be happening. The proportion of vigorous old people is increasing, and some

◆ *Adulthood in Today's World*

A RESEARCHER BECOMES HIS OWN GUINEA PIG

A gerontological researcher who has successfully extended the lives of rats and fish has applied his methods to human beings. Roy Walford is his own guinea pig in an experiment to extend the human life span to 120, even 140 years. In mid-1989, after eight years on a food-restricted diet, Walford had lost 25 percent of his normal weight. He says his health is good, and he has no age-related diseases associated with secondary aging (Walford, personal communication).

Walford (1983; 1986) has reduced his food intake to between 1500 and 1800 calories a day, with a maximum of 15 percent fat and 25 percent protein. He distributes this calorie intake by fasting completely two days each week and adding the calories saved to his meals on the other five days. When a computer analysis showed that he could not provide a balanced diet with the specified calorie, fat, and protein restrictions, he added a lengthy list of vitamin and mineral supplements to his diet.

Many of the supplements are at the levels recommended by the National Research Council. But Walford parts company with their recommendations in several instances. He feels that it is unnecessary to take supplementary vitamins A and D, because they are already present in fortified milk and easily obtained in the diet. He also believes that longevity requires much more than the recommended amounts of some food elements. Convinced that he needed antioxidants to detoxify the free radicals he believes play a central role in aging, Walford added larger than recommended supplements of vitamins B_6, E, and C, selenium, beta-carotenes, and bioflavanoids, as well as pantothenic acid (a part of the B complex that has been implicated in extended life spans among mice and rats).

Although exercise is not a requirement in the calorie-restricted regimen, Walford runs and swims regularly. This exercise provides him with the equivalent of 15 miles of running per week. He also lifts weights. He believes that such exercise does not extend the life span but helps to maintain health and prevent secondary aging.

Because Walford was born in 1925, it will be 2065 before his experiment, if successful, is concluded. He contends that people who followed his life-style would have the appearance of today's 50 year olds at the age of 75 (Weinruch and Walford, 1988). Walford believes that it's never too late to begin food restriction, although the earlier in adult life a person begins, the more effective it is likely to be. "This may be too broad a statement," Walford recently told a journalist, "but caloric restriction will halve the rate of aging at whatever time you begin. If you start at 50, and you were genetically set to die at 80, then you might live another 60 years rather than 30" (Angier, 1990).

80 year olds are as healthy and vital as 60 year olds were only a decade or so ago. People are still aging, but many seem to be less vulnerable to stress, and their bodies are wearing out later than they once did. Thus, adding years to life will not necessarily add poor-quality years of dependency and lengthy hospitalizations.

The increasing group of older adults who exhibit "youth creep" is good news, but some older adults have survived what once would have been fatal illness only to be afflicted by

The presence of an increasingly larger group of vigorous, active, young-old individuals suggests that more people are retaining their health far into their later years.

disabling chronic conditions (Avorn, 1986). This prospect has led economists to warn that increased life expectancy could cause medical costs for older adults to reach staggering heights (Davis, 1986).

Some researchers disagree with this dismal picture. They suggest that, by the middle of the twenty-first century, medical costs may be less than they are today. Debilitating illnesses, such as cancer, heart disease, diabetes, arthritis, and stroke, generally develop when the aging process has led to a decline in resistance and adaptability (Walford, 1983). If the number of vital adult years is increased and the onset of these illnesses is delayed until an age near the end of the maximum life span, when the body has little physical reserve and the immune system has lost much of its protective power, then illnesses might be less likely to respond to treatment. In most cases, death would follow quickly (Fries and Crapo, 1981). If this analysis is correct, society will need fewer medical services, the terminally ill will require less intensive care, and people will spend fewer days in the hospital. A look at normal aging may clarify this issue.

TYPICAL AGING

When people talk about aging, they are usually referring to any age-related deterioration in body and behavior. As aging progresses, the body loses its ability to repair the damage wrought by living. When people enter the final biological stage of life, their ability to adapt to environmental challenge or insult decreases, diminishing their chances of survival (Rockstein and Sussman, 1979). When this process is considered, it is important to distinguish among primary, secondary, and tertiary aging.

PRIMARY AGING

Primary aging happens to all of us. It is lifelong, universal, and thought to be inevitable. It consists of gradual, age-related changes that can be observed in all members of all species. It may be the result of a genetic program.

Primary aging is also known as *normal aging*. It begins early in life, although the traces are not apparent for years. Some of the signs of primary aging are visible: graying or thinning hair, pigmented patches on the back of the hand, slowed movements, fading vision, or impaired hearing. The invisible aspects of aging diminish the body's adaptability in many ways. Response to temperature change slows. The effectiveness of the immune system to protect the body against infection declines. Recovery from physical exertion takes longer. Within the cells, the ability of DNA (deoxyribonucleic acid) to repair the continual damage it undergoes is gradually reduced. As we will see, this cellular change is important in the general aging process, for DNA is a complex chemical that guides development and functioning.

From cell to organ to system, primary aging goes on at all levels of the body. All body systems age, but not all systems or organs age at the same rate. A person could have a cardiovascular system that was young for his or her years and an excretory system that had aged far beyond his or her years. Because the farther aging advances in a system, the more vulnerable it is, such a person would be likely to develop kidney disease but unlikely to develop heart disease. The effects of aging are most apparent when activity requires the coordination of more than one organ system (deVries, 1983).

SECONDARY AGING

Secondary aging happens to most people, but it is neither universal nor inevitable. Secondary aging is the result of a life-long process involving disease, disuse, or abuse. But because the changes of secondary aging correlate with chronological age, they are often mistaken for the inevitable results of the primary aging process. The confusion of primary and secondary aging often makes it difficult for researchers to follow the course of normal aging. Most assessments of aging have relied on cross-sectional studies, in which age-related changes are obscured by cohort effects related to medical practice and life-style (Adelman, 1989). As more research is done and knowledge accumulates, an increasing number of changes that were once accepted as primary aging are being revealed as changes caused by secondary aging.

Three examples show the scope of reassessment. At one time wrinkles were thought to be a basic sign of primary aging; today we know that most wrinkles are the result of secondary aging, caused by accumulated radiation from the sun's rays. Only a few years ago, researchers agreed that the strength of the heart muscle at rest begins to decline by about 1 percent per year while people are still in their twenties (deVries, 1983). But studies have changed this view. When people with hidden heart disease (which is revealed only through stress tests) were eliminated from a sample, researchers found *no* change in the function of the resting heart over the years from 20 to 80 (Lakatta, 1985). An impaired ability to handle sugar released into the bloodstream has been portrayed as a "normal" aspect of aging. But researchers have discovered that physically trained older adults whose weight is normal handle sugar as well as young athletes do (Rowe and Kahn, 1987).

The relation between age and disease is so strong that more than 80 percent of people over 65 have at least one chronic disease, and 27 percent say that their normal activity is limited in some way by their physical condition (U.S. Senate, Select Committee on Aging, 1987–1988). Besides having some chronic disease that cannot be cured, only controlled, older adults tend to be troubled by acute illnesses. Most report being ill about once a year, and the disease is usually respiratory.

These various diseases are not caused by aging: 14 percent of older adults are disease free. Tom Hickey (1980) tells of a 103-year-old woman who complained that her left knee was causing her pain. When the physician said there was nothing he could do and suggested she accept the pain as a result of her advanced age, she retorted: "Well, the other knee doesn't hurt, and it's also 103 years old" (p. 4). Even though normal aging does not cause disease, the reduced resistance of aging bodies makes older adults more susceptible. And because disease becomes more prevalent with age, it contributes to the changes commonly associated with aging. Once a chronic disease develops, it can contribute to decay and deterioration in structure and function.

Disuse can also cause secondary aging in all body systems. Lack of exercise can cause muscles to atrophy and joints to stiffen. Many older people do not exercise because they believe they are incapable of it or because they think it is not good for them. Actually, by not using their bodies, they are hastening the effects of secondary aging.

Disease often limits people's activity and leads many to shun even those exercises they could safely undertake. For example, a woman with arthritis who avoids using her hands because of the pain and stiffness involved will soon find the hand unusable because of degenerative changes in the joints. Disease and disuse appear to interact, with disuse compounding the secondary aging effects of disease.

Abuse is the third cause of secondary aging. The obvious sorts of abuse that can lead to decay or deterioration are cigarette smoking, alcoholism, obesity, and malnutrition. Malnutrition is more likely to appear in older people living at or below poverty levels because they cannot afford to buy food for an adequate diet. Studies have found that about 6 percent of the men and 5 percent of the women between the ages of 70 and 80, and 12 percent of the men and 8 percent of the women older than 80 suffer from malnutrition (Guigoz and Munro, 1985). Specific deficiencies are more common. Among older adults living independently in New Jersey, for example, about one-fourth showed subnormal levels of thiamine and vitamin C, about one-fifth showed subnormal levels of vitamin B6, and about one-tenth iron deficiencies (Baker et al., 1979).

Some forms of abuse are not so obvious. For example, a degree of hearing loss generally accompanies primary aging. But exposure to loud noise—whether at work or in listening to rock music—can further limit a person's hearing. Studies have suggested that this environmentally induced damage to the auditory system already may be limiting the hearing of young adults.

Abuse, disuse, and disease contribute heavily to the changes associated with aging. At present nothing can be done about the effects of primary aging, but the effects of secondary aging can be delayed, slowed, and at times halted or even reversed. Among a group of men and women—all at least 70 years old—both health and work capacity improved after a 26-

day program that involved extensive dietary changes and regular exercise (Weber, Barnard, and Roy, 1983). A majority of these adults had cardiovascular disease, hypertension—or both—and some had mild diabetes. They ate a low-fat diet that was high in complex carbohydrates, and they walked twice each day for up to 40 minutes at a time. In several areas their functioning improved significantly. The fact that some of these people turned back the clock on some symptoms of secondary aging appears to indicate that not all the symptoms we attribute to aging are an inevitable, irreversible part of growing old.

TERTIARY AGING

Tertiary aging refers to a final, rapid deterioration that heralds the end of life. It is marked by pervasive changes in health, cognition, and social functioning, and the changes are different in quality and quantity from the changes of normal aging (Birren and Cunningham, 1985). The ability to ward off disease virtually disappears, and there is no physiological or cognitive reserve that can be drawn upon. Interest in other people and the world dwindles. Large portions of time are spent in sleep. Death usually comes within months but in some cases may be delayed for a few years.

The three types of aging seem to interact, producing what has been called the *cascade model* of aging (Birren and Cunningham, 1985). Aging, which begins as a slow trickling away of speed and strength, gathers strength and speed until it cascades over the brink.

SUCCESSFUL AGING

The cascade model describes the usual picture of aging. But what if we could avoid secondary aging? If we aged successfully, the end might come as it did to Birdie May Vogt, who died in her sleep at the age of 112. According to an employee at the nursing home where she lived, "She just kind of faded away" (*Reporter Dispatch,* 1989a). Successful aging would consist of decades of primary aging, followed by a brief period of tertiary aging that ended in a quiet slipping away sometime after the age of 85. Because individual genes probably control the rate of aging, some people would complete the cycle at 85, and others not until 90, 95, or 100.

Successful aging is a normal way to age, but it is not the way most people age or the usual picture given in geriatric textbooks. Among 80 year olds who aged successfully, thought would be clear, if somewhat slowed, and wisdom would grow. Heart function would remain normal unless the person were under stress. Blood pressure would not rise. Metabolism would remain normal. Kidneys would function normally. Immune function would not decline dramatically. Eyesight would remain clear, although reading glasses might be required. A game of tennis, a swim, or a hike through the countryside would be commonplace. Broken hips would be rare, because bones would not be brittle.

Successful aging sounds like an impossible dream, but we know this kind of aging is possible. In every study that shows impaired physiological or cognitive functioning with age, some of the older subjects perform at the same level as the average young person (Adelman, 1989). Current research suggests that the physical requirements for successful aging are a healthy diet and regular exercise, along with avoidance of cigarettes and heavy alcohol intake. The psychological requirements for successful aging are apparently social integration and a sense of autonomy and control over the environment. As we will see in

Chapter 5, when older people feel overprotected and unable to control their lives, they become passive, the functioning of their immune systems is depressed, and their health deteriorates (Rodin, 1986; Rowe and Kahn, 1987).

THEORIES OF AGING

If we set aside stories in which the gods bestow eternal youth or a pact with the devil keeps a person forever young, we are left with the fact that everyone ages. No matter how healthy our environment or our habits, organ systems gradually deteriorate. Even if we escape the ravages of secondary aging, our bodies become less and less able to adapt to stress and infection. Why should this be so? Just what processes cause us to age? Researchers believe that if they can solve this mystery, they might be able to protect us against the aging process or learn how to turn on the process of cell death in cancer cells, thereby destroying the cancer (Lockshin and Zakeri, 1990).

Over the years many theories have been developed to explain aging. Some have been discarded, and others move in and out of favor. None has yet been presented that can account for all the facts. Most theories of aging can be described as either programmed theories or wear-and-tear theories.

PROGRAMMED THEORIES OF AGING

Programmed theories of aging are based on the belief that aging is genetically controlled. The information that controls development is coded in genes, which are made up of molecules of DNA. Genetic information guides changes in the body just as a computer program controls the activities of a computer. As soon as the ovum is fertilized, the program is set and begins to run. At various points in development, the program causes particular genes to turn on or off. Evidence in favor of a programmed theory of aging includes the existence of a maximum life span in each species, the similarity in the life span of identical twins, and the tendency for the children of long-lived parents to outlive the children of short-lived parents. Several lines of research have provided other evidence of a genetic influence on aging.

Because identical twins tend to have similar life spans, some researchers believe that aging is governed by a genetic program.

Premature Aging

A clue to genetic influence on aging might be found by studying people who age in an abnormal fashion. Several conditions, including progeria, Werner syndrome, and Down syndrome, cause people to age prematurely.

Progeria (sometimes called the Hutchinson–Gilford syndrome) is an extremely rare disease that causes young children to resemble wizened old women and men. Its first signs may appear in infancy. As the disease progresses, children's hair becomes sparse and gray; their faces take on an ancient look; their joints become stiff and knobby; and the lack of subcutaneous fat makes their muscles, tendons, ligaments, and blood vessels stand out. Their skin becomes dry and mottled. Within their bodies, their cardiovascular system ages, so that the arteries of a nine-year-old resemble those of someone in the seventies. In the laboratory, cells taken from the skin of a child with progeria behave like those of an old person. Some time after the age of 7, but usually by about 13, most die from heart attack or a stroke. Researchers suspect that it is a genetic disorder (Tice and Setlow, 1985).

Until recently, no person with progeria had lived past 27. The world's longest lived progeriac was Meg Casey, who died in 1985 at the age of 29. Casey was only 4 feet tall and weighed less than 40 pounds. She wore a blond wig over her bald head, her spine was twisted, one arm was shorter than the other, and she walked with a stilted gait. She lived in her own home and headed her town's program for the disabled (Tracy, 1983).

Casey's longevity bolsters the evidence that progeria is not simply accelerated aging. If, as progeriacs are said to do, she aged at ten times the normal rate, she would have been more than 290 years old when she died. Despite their aged appearance, children with progeria escape some symptoms of normal aging (Walford, 1983). They do not develop cataracts, their bodies do not respond in the same way to the presence of sugar in the blood, and they show no evidence of mental slowness. Since some of these changes are probably the effect of secondary aging caused by environmental abuse, this difference in the aging pattern of progeriacs is not surprising. Only over many years, for example, would the environmental effect of dangerous light rays be likely to contribute to the formation of cataracts.

Werner syndrome is like progeria in many ways except that it develops between the ages of 15 and 20. As the disease progresses into the thirties, the individual shows many of the aging symptoms that appear in progeria. However, people with Werner syndrome develop cataracts and diabetes. Their life span is about 20 to 30 years less than normal. Werner syndrome is known to be a genetic disorder, inherited when both parents carry the same recessive gene (Tice and Setlow, 1985).

Down syndrome, also a genetic disorder, usually occurs when an error in cell division in a parent produces a sperm or an ovum with an extra chromosome (Number 21). People with Down syndrome are short and stocky and have characteristic facial features that led this disorder at one time to be called ''mongolism.'' They generally have some degree of mental retardation and often have congenital heart disease. They, too, age prematurely. Relatively early in life, their hair grays and their nervous system, glands, and immune system show some of the changes characteristic of aging. They often develop tumors. During their thirties and forties their brains undergo the same structural changes found in older individuals with Alzheimer's disease, which causes severe mental deterioration. Fewer than 3 out of 100 live past the age of 50 (Tice and Setlow, 1985).

Researchers believe that the genes that produce these extreme and rather rare types of premature aging may have other forms that contribute to the typical range of aging and to

The fact that most adults with Down syndrome age prematurely had led researchers to suspect that the same genes, in another form, are involved in the aging process.

individual differences in the rate of aging. Laboratory studies of cells from these patients may uncover the biochemical basis of abnormal aging and eventually lead to an understanding of normal aging (Omenn, 1977). Such study has shown that in most cases these prematurely aged cells display what is known as the Hayflick limit.

The Hayflick Limit

At one time it was believed that human cells, placed in a laboratory dish and given nourishment, would grow and divide indefinitely. Taken away from the control of the body, they were expected to be immortal. Then researcher Leonard Hayflick (1977) showed that human cells seemed to have a built-in life span. He took tissue from a human embryo, exposed it to an enzyme preparation that caused the cells to separate, and placed the separated cells in a laboratory container along with nutrient. The cells attached to the surface of the dish and began to divide. When the surface of the dish was covered with cells, he added enzymes to separate them, divided the total population in half, and cultured them. Again and again he grew the cells and divided the culture until at last, after about 50 doublings, the cells ceased to grow. There were, however, individual differences in the embryonic tissue. Some cells doubled only 40 times; others doubled 60 times.

This approximate boundary to the cell's ability to divide is known as the **Hayflick limit.** Hayflick also found that cells from adults would not divide nearly so often, but that individual differences in the number of cell divisions remained, ranging from 14 to 29 doublings. Age and cell doubling did not always correlate. For example, the cells from one 87 year old divided 29 times before they stopped, and the cells from one 26 year old divided only 20 times. Despite these wide individual differences, researchers have found a general age-related decline in the doubling of cells, once people younger than thirty are eliminated from the sample (Norwood and Smith, 1985).

When cells from other mammals were cultured, each species seemed to have its own reproductive limit. Mouse cells may double only 15 times, but cells from a long-lived Galapagos turtle may divide as many as 130 times. It appeared that the growth of body cells was linked with the life span of the species. Only cancer cells do not show the Hayflick limit; they reproduce indefinitely.

The Hayflick limit has been supported by many studies that have grown cells in the laboratory. As yet, however, the limit has not been demonstrated with cells in a natural environment. Some suggest that the various culture media used in the lab may lack an essential growth factor or that cells gradually accumulate a toxic factor from the medium (Norwood and Smith, 1985). Attempts to study the Hayflick limit in living animals have included the transplantation of various types of tissue, including the adrenal cortex, skin, pituitary glands, kidneys, and tissue from mammary glands. In all these cases, the tissue functions normally far longer than the Hayflick limit would permit but eventually becomes unable to reproduce itself (Harrison, 1985). Although it appears clear that the Hayflick limit may be surpassed in life, it also seems evident that there is a natural limit to the cell's ability to reproduce.

Programmed Destruction

But how does aging begin? According to **programmed senescence theory,** destruction itself is programmed. Within each cell are one or more genes that, when activated, begin the slow decline of the aging process and eventually lead to death. Another version of this theory suggests that aging begins when youthful genes are either turned off by the genetic program or overwhelmed by aging genes that turn on as middle age approaches (Lockshin and Zakeri, 1990). A third version proposes that the same genes have both youthful and aging effects, but that their function changes some time during the life span. The effect of the female hormone estrogen on women could be an example of this sort of program. Estrogen maintains the reproductive process in women and protects women from degenerative changes in the arteries that lead to high blood pressure. At menopause, estrogen production drops sharply, and women therefore face an increased risk of high blood pressure (Harman and Talbert, 1985).

The program for aging may be located in the hypothalamus, a gland about the size of a marble that is buried deep in the brain. The hypothalamus regulates many body functions, including temperature control, emotional and physiological reactions to stress, hunger, and sexual response. It carries out its job by signaling the pituitary gland to produce various hormones. According to one **endocrine theory,** a biological clock within the hypothalamus is set to reduce its signals to the pituitary. When the timer goes off, the amount of neurotransmitters to the hypothalamus decreases markedly. Because these transmitter chemicals carry signals from one neuron to another, communication between the hypothalamus and the pituitary is changed. The pituitary may respond with a hormonal imbalance that initiates the aging process.

Finally, the **immunological theory** of aging assumes that the program for aging is tied to the immune system and set for literal self-destruction. As people age, the immune system begins to attack its own body. The immune system is meant to protect the body by fighting microorganisms, foreign proteins, and cancer cells. It is the immune system that is responsible for the rejection of organ transplants or skin grafts. This theory draws on similarities between characteristic signs of aging and signs that accompany the process of rejecting a transplant: loss of hair, kidney disease, vascular disease, failure to thrive, and a shortened life span (Walford, 1983).

Programmed self-destruction is not the only problem with the aging immune system. It also begins losing its ability to recognize foreign substances and abnormal cells. This decline in function makes the immune system inefficient at protecting the aging body against diseases and cancer. As we will see, the immunological theory of aging is a combination of programmed theory and wear-and-tear theory.

WEAR-AND-TEAR THEORIES OF AGING

Wear-and-tear theories of aging are based on the belief that living damages biological systems. As people go through life, damage accumulates, but because biological systems can repair themselves, the damage does not show up as it would in a machine, where parts wear out and break down. Instead, the damage is functional; it limits the natural ability of biological systems to repair themselves. Various wear-and-tear theories focus on the importance of particular types of damage.

The **DNA-repair theory,** for example, is based on the fact that DNA undergoes continual damage, either in the process of metabolism or from contact with pollution or radiation. DNA can be damaged in a number of ways, and as soon as it is damaged, it sets about repairing itself. In a common type of damage, two adjacent organic molecules form a destructive bond, known as a dimer, on one strand of the double-helixed molecule. Within each cell are several endonuclei that serve as a repair crew. These endonuclei recognize the dimer, remove the damaged portion, and insert a new segment, using information contained on the complementary strand (Tice and Setlow, 1985). Another common kind of damage occurs when, instead of forming a dimer, one of the strands breaks. Less common is a break in both strands.

Cells work quickly and continually at repairing damage. A single cell can repair about 200,000 single-strand breaks or 500,000 dimers in an hour (Tice and Setlow, 1985). Yet, according to the DNA-repair theory, repair never quite keeps up with the rate of damage. As the cells' ability to repair themselves slows, DNA damage piles up. Because nerve cells and most muscle cells, including those in the heart, cannot divide and replace themselves, the accumulated damage gradually destroys their ability to function. Aging then is the result of the increasing store of unrepaired DNA. The DNA repair theory is falling out of favor, because no one has yet been able to produce clearcut evidence of a decline in repair abilities with age or an accumulation of unrepaired damage within cells (Tice and Setlow, 1985).

A second wear-and-tear theory is the **error catastrophe theory,** which also proposes cumulative errors but sees its source in the synthesis of protein within the cells. Proteins are involved in virtually every aspect of cell function. Since proteins are made by other proteins, errors tend to accumulate until they reach catastrophic proportions. At that point cells are unable to function. This theory was a favorite one until research demonstrated that old cells produce proteins as accurately as young cells. With no evidence to support the theory, it, too, has fallen out of favor with most investigators (Reff, 1985).

A third wear-and-tear theory of aging, known as the **cross-linkage theory,** assumes that aging is caused by a chemical reaction that permanently changes the nature of protein molecules. Cross-links are stable bonds between molecules or parts of molecules that cannot be repaired. The links change the molecules, making them rigid, so that they can no longer function in the same way. Cross-links are produced during metabolism and can be found in connective tissues and in DNA itself. As cross-links accumulate, tissues lose elasticity and become dry and leathery. In fact, the tanning of leather is an example of the cross-linkage process, for tanning involves the similar binding together of cells. The protein in our bodies is about 30 percent collagen, a supportive tissue that surrounds cells and blood vessels, and collagen is susceptible to cross-linking. Cross-linking seems responsible for some of the age-related changes that occur in the skin, such as its loss of elasticity, and may be implicated in stiffened joints and hardened arteries, but most researchers believe that it is not the major cause of aging.

A fourth wear-and-tear theory is the **free-radical theory,** which assumes that a different chemical reaction starts the aging process. Free radicals are chemical compounds that have a free electron, usually in an atom of oxygen. Some free radicals are produced during metabolism; others are simply present in the environment. These compounds are so unstable that they bond easily with other molecules. For example, they combine with molecules of unsaturated fats to form lipid peroxides, compounds that can decompose to form aldehydes (Walford, 1983). Because aldehydes are cross-linking agents, the free-radical and cross-linkage theories of aging are related.

Free radicals attack unsaturated fats in the membranes of body cells, damaging the membranes. They can also damage chromosomes. They are self-propagating, producing more free radicals each time they react with a molecule (Spence, 1989). Free radicals may contribute to the development of cancer, heart attacks, stroke, and emphysema (Marx, 1987), and many believe that they are a major source of aging. The body has a defense against free radicals in the form of scavenger enzymes (which can convert them to harmless water and oxygen) and vitamins C and E (which can inhibit their activity). Even so, some free radicals escape. Over the course of time, cell damage builds up and we age.

Another wear-and-tear theory, known as the **cellular garbage theory,** sees free radicals as only one factor in a massive accumulation of substances within the cell (Spence, 1989). Besides the reactive free radicals, many of our cells also accumulate a brown pigment known as lipofuscin. **Lipofuscin** contains lipid, protein, and carbohydrate. Although its origin is uncertain, some researchers believe that lipofuscin is a byproduct of metabolism. Lipofuscin is inert; it does not react with other body substances. But it tends to fill up cells, a fact that has led to the supposition that it may interfere with normal cell functioning and eventually lead to cell death. However, cells in the area of the brain where the largest accumulation of lipofuscin occurs are not lost during the aging process (Duara, London, and Rapoport, 1985). In addition, some older adults have little lipofuscin in their tissues, whereas some younger adults have a great deal of it (Sanadi, 1977).

Theories of primary aging will have to explain many aspects of the aging process (Walford, 1983). They must be able to answer the following questions: Why are cells subject to the Hayflick limit? Why do some people age prematurely? Why is the rate at which any species can repair damage to its own DNA related to its maximum life span? Why does the immune system become less efficient with age? Why do the fibers of connective tissue deteriorate with age? Why do biochemical changes take place in aging bodies? And why do almost all animals have a similar metabolic rate, using in a lifetime about the same amount of energy per pound of body weight?

None of the present theories accounts for all these aspects of aging, and it's unlikely that any single factor ever will (Eckholm, 1986). Since aging goes on at the level of cells, molecules, and organs, only a theory that draws on a combination of factors has prospects of explaining the complicated process. In the next chapter, we move our focus from aging at the cellular level to changes that appear in the various organ systems.

SUMMARY

LENGTH OF LIFE

Longevity, or the duration of life, can be considered in terms of **average life span** (the mean age of survival) or **maximum life span** (the oldest age to which any individuals survive). Theorists disagree as to whether the aging process is adaptive or has no relation at all to survival. Species longevity may be connected with the relationship among brain weight, body weight, metabolic rate, and deep body temperature. Although the maximum human life span probably has not changed in the past 100,000 years, only today have survival rates begun to approach that maximum span. Reports of remote communities filled with centenarians have been discredited, although people in these villages do remain vigorous and active to an advanced age.

The increase in average life span over the past two centuries seems largely due to better nutrition and sanitation, with medical measures adding to the increase during the past hundred years. Since 1900, **life expectancy** at birth has increased from 47 to 75 years among Americans, but for 65 year olds, life expectancy has increased only 4 years, from 78 to 82. Women generally live longer than men, and whites generally live longer than blacks, although once people pass the age of 85, blacks have a longer life expectancy. The population is moving toward a rectangular survival curve in which few people die from disease and most live until near the end of the maximum life span. Genetic influences on longevity have been established and appear to be the result of differences in the susceptibility to disease.

Researchers have extended the life span of laboratory animals by calorie restriction, which may delay aging through its effect on the endocrine system. Exercise does not delay normal aging among laboratory animals, but it seems to improve vitality and prevent age-related disease.

QUALITY OF LIFE AMONG THE AGED

The increasing health and vigor of people in young-old age may signal the postponement of age-related disease and the extension of health until a time closer to the end of the life span than has been the case. Some researchers have questioned this optimistic picture and believe that added years may be years of poor health and hospitalization.

TYPICAL AGING

Primary aging is universal and thought to be inevitable. It begins early in life and affects all body systems. As it progresses, the body's adaptability diminishes. **Secondary aging** happens to most people but is neither universal nor inevitable. Secondary aging is the result of disease, disuse, or abuse, but it can be modified by changes in life-style. The correlation of secondary aging with age causes it to be mistaken for primary aging. **Tertiary aging** is a final, rapid deterioration that heralds the end of life. Its changes are different in quality and quantity from the changes of primary aging. The three types of aging may interact in a cascade model of aging. In successful aging, people would move from decades of primary aging into a brief period of tertiary aging as their bodies wore out.

THEORIES OF AGING

Programmed theories of aging are based on the belief that aging is genetically controlled. It is believed that people who age in abnormal fashion from **progeria, Werner syndrome,** or **Down syndrome** could provide clues to the nature of the genetic program. Human cells seem to have a built-in life span, known as the **Hayflick limit.** According to the **programmed senescence theory,** aging is caused by the activation of destructive genes within each cell. According to the **endocrine theory,** aging is caused by signals from a biological clock within the hypothalamus. According to the **immunological theory,** aging is caused by self-destruction programmed into the immune system.

Wear-and-tear theories of aging are based on the belief that aging is the result of accumulated cell damage that is an inescapable effect of living. According to the **DNA-repair theory,** damage to DNA within the cells accumulates faster than it can be repaired. According to the **error-catastrophe theory,** damage accumulates as errors are made in protein synthesis within the cells. According to the **cross-linkage theory,** damage accumulates as permanent cross-links are formed between molecules or parts of molecules. According to the **free-radical theory,** damage accumulates when free radicals escape the body's methods for destroying them. According to the **cellular garbage theory,** damage accumulates as substances, including **lipofuscin,** build up within the cells.

KEY TERMS

average life span	life expectancy
cellular garbage theory	lipofuscin
cross-linkage theory	longevity
DNA-repair theory	maximum life span
Down syndrome	primary aging
endocrine theory	progeria
error-catastrophe theory	programmed senescence theory
free-radical theory	secondary aging
Hayflick limit	tertiary aging
immunological theory	Werner syndrome

Chapter 4

◆

Biological Changes Across Adulthood

◆

W alt Stack's days are full. Each morning he rides his bicycle seven miles across San Francisco to the Dolphin Swim Club at Fisherman's Wharf. From there he embarks on a 17-mile run that takes him across the Golden Gate Bridge to the town of Sausalito and back again. After his 3 1/2 hour run, he swims a quarter of a mile in the frigid waters of San Francisco Bay, pops into the sauna to warm up, has lunch, and rides his bicycle back home. This exhibition of physical endurance seems even more remarkable when Stack gives his age: 81. He has been following this routine almost 25 years. Before he retired, he got up at 2:40 A.M. in order to complete the schedule before he began work as a hod carrier.

Stack sees nothing strange in his daily feat. "Running's a habit, more than anything else," he says. "You get in the habit, and if you're motivated, you find you can do a lot of things. I think of motivation as a synonym for ego. Recognition is a thing that's important to a man. You do it because you have a strong feeling for it" (Brant, 1989, p. 32).

The feeling is so strong that it triumphs over physical damage. The day after Stack fell off his bicycle on one of San Francisco's notorious hills and fractured his collarbone, he made a few minor concessions to his injury. He took the bus to the Dolphin Club, ran only ten miles, and swam "underwater and backward" because the muscles in his neck tightened up.

Walt Stack's physical condition is unusual for an 81-year-old man. But his example shows clearly that growing old does not necessarily mean becoming weak and helpless. Stack's muscles still function as efficiently as those of much younger men. He is aging slowly but normally, and he seems relatively unaffected by the problems of secondary aging.

In this chapter our focus shifts from molecular and cellular aging to system aging. In considering the biological changes associated with normal human aging, we look at the various processes that are going on in the body of Walt Stack and every other person who has passed maturity. Biological changes are important because of their implications for other aspects of life. For example, secondary aging in the cardiovascular system can be responsible for poorer performance on intelligence tests. Secondary aging in the central nervous system can lead to drastic personality change. Visible signs of aging can affect self-image and self-esteem, and so changes in appearance are the first aspect of biological aging to be examined. Next we explore changes within the body, starting with the skeleton and teeth. From there we take up the various body systems in turn, looking at the cardiovascular, respiratory, gastrointestinal, excretory, endocrine, immune, and nervous systems. This tour of the aging body helps us separate the ravages of secondary aging from the inescapable, but less debilitating, decline connected with normal aging.   ◆

CHANGES IN APPEARANCE

The visible signs of age can be detected in a body we still consider young. A few gray hairs appear; wrinkles form at the corners of the eyes; our flesh is not as firm as it once was. The changes are gradual and accumulate so slowly that at first we are not aware of them. The day comes, however, when we can no longer ignore the evidence in the mirror.

The recognition is usually unsettling and may damage the ego and diminish self-confidence. A 30 year old, in good health, full of energy and functioning efficiently, suddenly realizes that he or she is no longer young. Because American society places a premium on youth, the recognition is difficult for most people in this country. Stereotypes about old age and the attitudes of others toward aging have combined to make growing old seem like a punishment (Weg, 1983).

Once the unsettling recognition of aging is passed, the 30 year old can brush aside the small signs in the mirror. Aging people rarely "feel" old; one man in his eighties said, "I don't feel like an old man, I feel like a young man who has something the matter with him" (Cowley, 1980, p. 41). The conviction that we are old generally comes from the reactions of others rather than from any inner sense of aging. Being treated like an old man or woman is probably more damaging to the self-confidence than the knowledge that the seventieth birthday has been passed. But few people accept old age without a struggle.

Billions of dollars are spent each year in attempts to reverse, slow down, or conceal the unmistakable signs of age. Moisturizing creams, facials, mudpacks, and hair dye are marketed to millions by cosmetic companies. Hair transplants, liposuction (in which fat deposits are suctioned off), tucks to raise sagging breasts, facelifts, and facial "peels" (in which layers of skin are lifted off by the application of a chemical), are offered by plastic surgeons. Cosmetic surgery was once primarily sought by women, but over the past 15 years the number of men having cosmetic surgery has increased dramatically. In most cases, cosmetic surgery does not make a person look younger. Instead, by removing or tightening excessive skin, it erases the tired appearance—but in most instances, the change is only temporary. The effects of most cosmetic surgery last 5 to 10 years, and deep chemical peels last up to 20 years.

As with all other aspects of aging, there are wide interindividual differences in appearance. A 35 year old may look 50; a 50 year old may look 35. How old a person looks on the outside seems to correlate with how old that person functions inside. When researchers compared biological assessments of older adults with judgments of their appearance, they discovered that those who *looked* oldest for their age were also biologically oldest on 24 different measures (Kligman, Grove, and Balin, 1985). Among the visible signs of aging, graying hair and loss of skin elasticity correlate most closely with chronological age.

HAIR

Hair begins to gray when the production of pigment in the follicles slows. No one is certain what initiates this process or why hair thins or changes its character with age. In fact, hairdressers know almost as much about age-related changes in hair as scientists do (Kligman, Grove, and Balin, 1985). Genes play a role in the rate at which gray or white hair replaces the natural color. Most people over 40 have some gray hair, but some get their first gray hairs while they are still teenagers. Others show only a few streaks at 60.

Each sex may undergo characteristic localized changes in the quality and quantity of hair. Once men are past 30, hair in the nostrils, eyebrows, and ears that once was fine, short, and colorless may gradually become dark, coarse, and long. Among women older than 65, the hair on their chins and above their lips may undergo a similar transformation (Kligman, Grove, and Balin, 1985).

On the scalp, hair changes in the opposite direction. Here, dark, coarse hair may be

In patterned baldness, a sex-linked form of hereditary baldness, the coarse hair on the scalp is gradually replaced by fine, downy, inconspicuous hair.

replaced by fine, short, colorless hair. Because this hair is inconspicuous, the scalp appears bald. The transition is called patterned baldness, and it is caused by sex-linked hereditary factors. While they are still young adults, men often find their hair receding at the temples. Gradually, the loss spreads over the crown of the head.

Only in the past few years has there been any way to deal with baldness except with wigs or toupees. Recently, the picture has changed. Among men in their twenties, minoxidil lotion—which contains a drug used to treat high blood pressure—may stimulate moderate regrowth of hair. Hair transplants are more often successful and can be used with men older than 30, but the lengthy process involved is expensive and uncomfortable.

Some scalp hair is actually lost in both men and women, and the process is well underway by middle age. By the time a person is 50, hair density has been reduced about 25 percent (Rockstein and Sussman, 1979). Some women discover that armpit and pubic hair diminishes after menopause and may even disappear. This loss is apparently related to hormone levels.

SKIN

Aging of the skin is more likely to disrupt self-image than aging of the hair. It is easy to color grayed hair, but no amount of moisturizers and wrinkle-resistant cream can permanently hide the marks of time. These tracings appear about ten years earlier in women than in men, because the oil-producing glands in women's skin begin to atrophy after menopause (Spence, 1989). Because men's oil-producing glands continue to function, their skin is thicker and oilier, postponing wrinkles. Shaving may also keep men's skin looking young, because the razor scrapes old cells from the top layer of skin, speeding the growth of new cells from lower skin layers.

Despite all the worry about wrinkles, many of us seem determined to hasten the aging process. Tanning is one way to induce secondary aging. The ultraviolet rays of the sun interfere with the cells' production of DNA and with protein synthesis in the skin, keeping the skin from regenerating. Tanning causes premature wrinkles, dryness, and leathery skin. It heightens the risk of skin cancer, which will not appear for decades, and may actually make it more difficult for the immune system to fight microorganisms and cancer cells (*New York Times,* 1989a). Some of the sun damage may be repaired by Retin-A, a treatment for acne that actually makes some wrinkles and age spots disappear (Hamilton, 1988). However, the cream—the only effective product yet discovered—has numerous side effects.

Sun, wind, and abrasion are responsible for so much of the damage we see that researchers find it difficult to separate normal aging from the cumulative effects of environmental damage (Kligman, Grove, and Balin, 1985). The extent of this damage becomes apparent when the furrowed, weathered facial and neck skin of an 80 year old is compared with the soft, youthful-looking skin on the buttocks. Although environmental damage is responsible for aging facial skin, in order to prevent this secondary aging, we would have to cover our faces as completely as we cover our buttocks.

A person's natural coloring is an important consideration in environmental damage. Fair-skinned blonds or redheads with blue or green eyes run the greatest risk, for their skin is most susceptible to sun damage. The darker the skin, the more resistant it is to solar radiation, so that blacks suffer the least damage from exposure to the sun. Surface skin cells replace themselves, but as we saw in Chapter 2, the rate of replacement slows markedly after a person is 50 (Grove and Kligman, 1983). As the ability to replace dead or damaged cells diminishes, aging becomes increasingly apparent.

The American quest for a bronzed skin hastens aging because the tanning process thins and wrinkles the skin and keeps skin cells from regenerating.

In the deep skin layers, cross-linkage stiffens elastic fibers and collagen, making the skin less pliable. As aging progresses, the skin becomes thinner and drier, fat deposits directly beneath the skin diminish, and muscles decrease in size. Eventually, the skin sags and wrinkles.

Many wrinkles are use-related; that is, they occur at an angle to the direction of muscle pull on the skin (Rossman, 1977). We recognize this connection when we call small wrinkles around the eyes ''laugh lines'' or forehead wrinkles ''frown lines'' or when we say that a person has the face he or she ''deserves'' at age 50. Habitual facial expressions accentuate wrinkles, but sunlight also accentuates them as it does other skin damage.

Although pigment-containing cells in the skin decrease with age, those that remain increase in size and sometimes cluster on the hands, forearms, or face. Variously called age spots, liver spots, pigment plaques, or lentigines, these brown freckles are common in whites with fair skin and are aggravated by exposure to the sun.

Keratoses, warty growths that may be dry and light-colored or greasy and dark-colored, may appear anywhere on the body. Although they become increasingly common with age, they are not necessarily a result of the aging process. Keratoses often appear on young adults, but because the growths are permanent and tend to enlarge and because new ones keep forming on susceptible individuals, they have been associated with aging (Selmanowitz, Rizer, and Orentreich, 1977). The use of sunscreens from an early age might prevent most—if not all—of these growths (Kligman, Grove, and Balin, 1985).

Skin tags, small pendulous skin growths, often appear on the chest, neck, eyelids, and armpits of older women (Spence, 1989). The growths are believed to be harmless and related to hormone levels.

Older people often complain that their skin itches or chaps easily. The dryness may be accentuated by vitamin A deficiency or excessive bathing, and the itching may be a reaction to the alkalizing effect of soap on dry skin. Other cases of itching may be due to drug reactions or be symptoms of various degenerative diseases.

A final mark of aging skin is decreased sweating. Fewer sweat glands are active, and those that are secrete less sweat. Aging sweat glands play a role in the older person's vulnerability to heat stroke, because they impair heat loss through the evaporation of sweat. On a somewhat brighter note, older people can save money on deodorants: the activity of apocrine sweat glands in the armpits and genital area, which are the source of body odor, also dwindles markedly (Kligman, Grove, and Balin, 1985).

PHYSIQUE

Unlike skin cells, muscle cells cannot replace themselves. In today's adults, the death and atrophy of muscle cells are age-related. Muscle density appears to increase progressively until about the age of 39 (Bulcke et al., 1979); then muscle mass begins to shrink as the muscle fibers decrease in number and diameter. Fat replaces some of the muscle. By using computerized tomography (CT scans), in which a narrow beam of x-rays is passed through the body from a number of angles, researchers have discovered how this change in the distribution of fat and muscle alters the male physique (Borkan et al., 1983). In men younger than 50, fat is deposited primarily *between* skin and muscle tissue, but among healthy men in their sixties and seventies, fat infiltrates in and between muscles. Even if weight is the same at age 60 as it was at 25, the bodies of most adults will contain more fat than they

◆ *Adulthood in Today's World*

WHEN YOUNG IS OLD

For professional athletes, old age may come at 30—or even sooner. Small declines in muscle strength or the efficiency of the circulatory or respiratory systems can write an ending to a dazzling career.

Some athletes continue to play professional sports into their forties, but they are few and their presence is confined to positions that require less speed, endurance, and strength. They may be place kickers in football or designated hitters in baseball.

Occasionally, athletes manage to stretch their careers. Tennis players rarely compete much past 30, yet Billie Jean King continued in professional competition much longer. At 39, this six-time Wimbledon champion tried to win the tournament one more time. When she reached the quarterfinals, King said, "I'm just surviving. . . . I'm playing just good enough to win. I'm so used to being on the edge of the ledge, maybe that will help me" (Vecsey, 1983). Apparently, it did help because King reached the semifinals, where she was beaten by 18-year-old Andrea Jaeger.

Does the fact that Billie Jean King reached the semifinals indicate longer professional lives for future athletes? Effective training techniques and better health levels in general may extend the careers of an increasing number of athletes, but there appears to be a limit to human plasticity.

When researchers examined athletic records gathered over 90 years, they found that better health has not budged the age at which athletes peak (Schulz and Curnow, 1988). No matter what sport they selected, the age of peak performance was stable. Each sport had its own peak age, and it seemed to depend on the type of physical proficiency required. Swimmers, sprinters, jumpers, and tennis players, who peak early, depend on reaction time, speed of limb movement, flexibility, explosive strength, and gross body coordination. Swimmers peak earliest—at 17 for women and 19 for men—and the others peak between the ages of 22 and 24. In these sports, women peak a year or two earlier than men. Long-distance runners and baseball players peak at 27 or 28, while golfers peak at 31. These sports require precise control, arm–hand steadiness, aiming, and stamina.

Yet older athletes continue to turn in spectacular performances in some fields. At distances greater than 40 kilometers, the fastest 40-year-old long-distance runner is nearly as fast as Olympic competitors. Speeds of older runners decline markedly, but the fastest 70-year-old long-distance runner can still run 70 percent as fast as male Olympic finalists. A researcher who studied speed and endurance in these athletes points out that the records of older men, who rarely run the hundreds of miles each week covered by Olympic athletes in training, should not be regarded as their best possible performance (Riegel, 1981). Instead, they represent minimum indicators of what the best older men can do.

once did. For most people, weight increases; men tend to gain weight until they reach their mid-fifties, and women until they reach their mid-sixties. At later ages, both sexes tend to lose weight.

With the loss in muscle mass goes loss of muscle strength, tone, flexibility, and speed of movement. Tests have shown that with the typical life-style of adults in the past generation, muscle strength begins to decline at about the age of 30, with losses in the strength of leg and trunk muscles progressing faster than those of arm muscles. Yet the decline is small— no more than 10 to 20 percent—until about the age of 70; then strength ebbs until the average adult has no more than 50 percent of earlier strength (Spence, 1989). At least half of this age-related decline may be the result of reduced physical activity (Smith and Gilligan, 1983).

The effects of aging, as opposed to inactivity, on performance may show clearest among athletes who continue to train into later adulthood (see accompanying box, ''When Young is Old''). Performance suffers least on brief events that require moderate amounts of energy, such as sprints or pole vault, and most on lengthy events that require a large expenditure of energy, such as the steeplechase or hurdles (Kozma and Stones, 1990). For example, the age difference on sprints between athletes in their early forties and those in their early sixties is less than 15 percent, but on hurdles the difference rises to about 35 percent.

CHANGES IN STRUCTURE

For many years it was believed that most people shrink several inches in height as they age, a belief that was consistently supported by cross-sectional studies. But Americans have been growing taller over the decades, and longitudinal studies show that the shrinkage, though real, is just over an inch in men and about two inches in women. This loss of height is due to altered posture, a thinning of the cartilage disks between the spinal vertebra, and a loss of water in the disks. Aging is also accompanied by changes in the composition of bone and the condition of teeth.

BONES

All through life, bone is resorbed and replaced; during young adulthood, 10 percent of the skeleton is remodeled each year (Exton–Smith, 1985). Until about the age of 30, bones get denser and heavier. New bone is formed throughout life, so that fractures heal—although more slowly—even among the oldest individuals. Yet, from about the age of 40, calcium is steadily lost from the bones, as more bone is resorbed than is replaced. Just why the balance alters with age is not known (Spence, 1989). In women, bone loss is slow until menopause, then it becomes rapid for five to ten years, after which the rate slows once more. In men, loss continues at a slow but steady rate. Even so, some people in extreme old age have denser bones that some 30 year olds (Exton–Smith, 1985).

Women's rapid bone loss after menopause, together with their lighter bones, puts them at greater risk than men for a condition known as **osteoporosis,** which literally means porous bones. In this state of pronounced degeneration, bones are brittle and break easily under stress. Among cohorts that have now reached later adulthood, some degree of osteoporosis exists in 65 percent of women and 21 percent of men older than 65 (Spence, 1989).

At one time physicians assumed that osteoporosis was an unavoidable consequence of aging, but today it is seen as a preventable condition (Marx, 1980). Its causes include a long-term dietary deficiency of calcium, probably dating from adolescence; lack of estrogen in postmenopausal women; cigarette smoking; heavy alcohol consumption; long-term treatment with corticosteroid drugs (such as prednisone) that suppress the immune system; and inactivity (which can induce osteoporosis even in healthy young people who are confined to bed) (Brody, 1987; Exton–Smith, 1985).

Physicians treat osteoporosis with estrogen, calcium, Vitamin D, injections of the hormone calcitonin (which inhibits bone resorption), anabolic steroids, parathyroid hormone, and fluorides—often in some combination. For example, a combination of fluoride, estrogen, and calcium seems to dramatically reduce the rate of fracture in patients with osteoporosis (Exton–Smith, 1985). Prevention is more effective than therapy, and researchers urge daily supplements of calcium, estrogen therapy during the postmenopausal years, and exercise that involves weight-bearing activities such as walking. In one study (Buskirk, 1985), women between the ages of 69 and 95 who exercised regularly for three years not only halted the loss of bone but also increased their bone density by 4.2 percent. In a control group of women who did not exercise, bone density dropped by 2.5 percent.

Joints also undergo degenerative change with age, and **osteoarthritis,** a chronic inflammation of the joints, sometimes develops. This disease appears to be related to mechanical stress. As the composition of collagen changes, the bone ends rub together, causing the joints to swell and become stiff and painful. Those joints that bear the greatest weight and receive the greatest shock, such as the legs and spinal column, appear to be particularly susceptible. The condition is unlikely to appear in young adulthood unless a joint has been injured or subjected to intense, prolonged stress (Spence, 1989). The incidence and severity of osteoarthritis increases from middle age until about the age of 80; after the age of 90, its initial appearance decreases sharply. Its development seems related to heredity, to hormonal influences, and to continual stress on the joints from poor posture, extreme overweight, and repetitive, job-related stress.

TEETH

Most people's teeth wear down so slowly that human teeth could last for 200 years if they were not lost through decay, root infections, or gum disease (Tonna, 1977). Within the tooth's central cavity, the fibers, blood vessels, and nerves form the tooth's pulp. With age, the pulp gradually loses cells until about half are gone by the age of 70. At the same time, the number of fibers increases while the number of blood vessels decreases. Almost one-half of today's 65 year olds and three-fourths of those older than 75 have or need dentures (Spence, 1989). Because of improvements in dental care, it is unlikely that so many of tomorrow's older adults will have lost their teeth.

A common cause of tooth loss is periodontal disease, an inflammation of the gums and surrounding tissue. It progresses as bacteria invade swollen, tender gums, increasing the inflammation and causing the gums to recede from the teeth. The process is accentuated by the presence of tartar on the teeth. If not treated, the spreading infection can cause bone loss, loosening the teeth so that they either fall out or must be removed.

The incidence of periodontal disease increases with age, but it is not part of normal aging and is often found among young people. There is, however, some connection between periodontal disease and osteoporosis, and where one condition is diagnosed, the other can often be found (Weg, 1983). Many factors are believed to be involved in the development of periodontal disease, including genetic influence, nutritional deficiencies, malocclusion, improper care of the teeth, and various diseases. Genes, nutrition, and disease are probably related to aging in most organ systems, including the invisible aging of the cardiovascular system.

CHANGES IN THE CARDIOVASCULAR SYSTEM

For centuries, scientists believed that aging of the cardiovascular system—the heart and blood vessels—was the basis of all physical aging. In the fifteenth century, Leonardo da Vinci, after dissecting corpses, wrote that the cause of aging was a slow constriction of blood vessels that cut off the body's nourishment (cited by Belt, 1952). In the seventeenth century, Thomas Syndenham wrote that a man was as old as his arteries. Although the search for the cause of aging is now conducted at the cellular and genetic levels, the health of the cardiovascular system is crucial, and its deterioration is associated with age. Once men pass 40 and women pass 65, cardiovascular disease becomes the leading cause of death in the United States.

Because the cells of the heart, arteries, veins, and capillaries cannot divide and reproduce, the cardiovascular system eventually wears out. Some of the changes in function and appearance are the inevitable result of normal aging, but many are connected with age-related disease (Lakatta, 1985). In fact, diseases of the heart and arteries are so prevalent that it is often difficult to decide just what age-related changes are the result of primary aging.

HEART

The heart never rests, pausing only a fraction of a second between beats (Figure 4.1). It is a muscular organ that pumps blood through the resting body at the rate of about 75 gallons per hour. During strenuous activity, the rate may increase to ten times that amount. In the course of a lifetime, the heart may beat 3 billion times (Rockstein and Sussman, 1979).

Age affects the appearance of this essential organ. Fat deposits collect on its surface, lipofuscin accumulates within the cells, the lining thickens, the valve between the left chambers of the heart thickens and becomes stiff, and the consistency of the collagen that surrounds the heart's fibers loses its elasticity. The normal aging heart either retains its youthful size or becomes slightly smaller when a sedentary life-style reduces the demands on it. But diseases of the heart and blood vessels are so prevalent that the typical heart becomes larger in later life (Spence, 1989).

There are few changes in the function of the normal heart at rest. This finding contradicts traditional reports of aging heart function, but most studies of "healthy" individuals include people with hidden cardiovascular disease. Such disease is undetected by resting electrocardiograms (EKGs) and reveals itself only under stress tests, such as walking on a treadmill. When a stress test is added, the proportion of people diagnosed as having cardiovascular disease *doubles* (Lakatta, 1990). Resting heart rate does not decline in older adults who are free of cardiovascular disease, nor does cardiac output (the volume of blood pumped by the heart in each minute) decrease. But among typical older adults, both measures decrease,

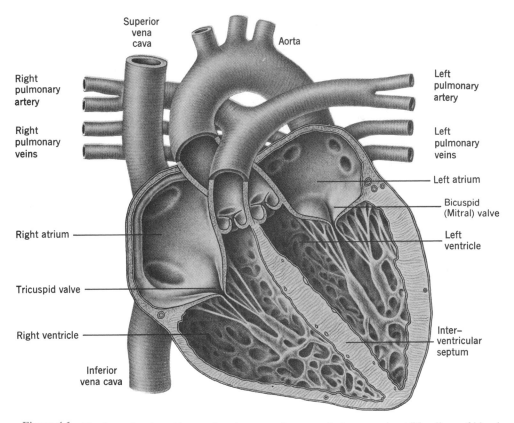

Figure 4.1   The four-chambered human heart, a muscular organ that pumps about 75 gallons of blood through the resting body each hour. *Source:* Nelson, 1984, p. 111.

indicating an apparent loss of strength in the heart muscle with age. Even the healthy heart works under a progressively increasing load, apparently caused by stiffening of the major artery (aorta) as it leaves the heart and a rise in blood pressure as the heart contracts.

Under conditions of stress, the healthy heart eventually becomes less effective than it once was. During exertion, the heart increases its rate in order to deliver oxygen through arterial blood (Figure 4.2). When younger men exercise vigorously, their hearts may begin to beat as rapidly as 200 times per minute. By contrast the hearts of men between 70 and 90 beat no faster than 125 times per minute under the same work load. No one is certain just why the maximum heart rate decreases with age and the older heart has trouble meeting the body's demands. But research indicates that decreased efficiency in the sympathetic nervous system, which regulates the heart, accounts for most of the changes in the older heart's response to stress, such as the longer time required for each contraction (Lakatta, 1990).

No matter how effectively the heart pumps, if the arteries are constricted, the oxygen-laden blood cannot pass through effectively. Indeed, most aspects of cardiovascular disease begin in the arteries.

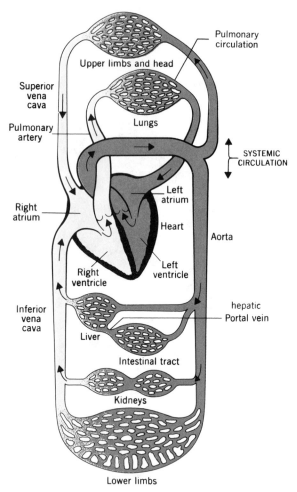

Figure 4.2 The circulatory system's distribution of blood throughout the body. Carbon-dioxide-laden blood flows through the veins into the right ventricle of the heart; from there it goes to the lungs, where carbon dioxide is removed and oxygen is taken up. From the lungs, the blood returns to the heart's left ventricle, where it is pumped to various portions of the body. *Source:* Nelson, 1984, p. 112.

ARTERIES

As arteries age, the structure of their walls gradually changes. The fibers of elastin, the protein that makes up about 30 percent of the arterial wall, are redistributed. They also become thin and fragmented, and some may be destroyed. While this process goes on, the elastin binds to calcium, making the arterial walls less flexible. As the elastin content of arteries decreases, their collagen content may increase. Finally, lipids, which are insoluble fat particles, begin to accumulate within the arteries, narrowing the passageway.

Just how much of this change is the result of normal aging is uncertain. Changes in the structure of connective tissue is probably part of the normal aging process, but the accumulation of collagen, calcium salts, and lipids resembles the condition of chronically in-flamed tissue, suggesting that the walls of the arteries have been injured (Kohn, 1977). Because arterial disease is fairly common among older adults, it is difficult to separate the deterioration that is the result of disease from the inevitable changes of aging.

These changes affect the functioning of arteries. Stiff arterial walls cannot expand as blood is pumped through them, so blood pressure gradually increases with age. This change is not a part of normal aging, but seems to be widespread in affluent societies. Even so, some people in affluent societies show no increase in blood pressure with age (Kannel, 1985).

Another characteristic sign of the aging cardiovascular system, the increased resistance to blood flow that often develops in the peripheral blood vessels, is not part of normal aging and does not appear among older people who have been screened for hidden heart disease (Lakatta, 1985). Resistance, combined with the lessened power of the heart, decreases the rate at which arterial blood flows through body tissues. This progressive decrease can explain much of the degeneration connected with secondary aging and supports the observation that we are as old as our arteries.

Some thickening and stiffening of arterial walls, known as **arteriosclerosis,** is normal and can be found in most older people. But the condition known as **atherosclerosis,** in which hard, yellow, fatty plaques are also deposited on the arterial wall, is not a normal part of aging and seems to result from a separate process (Bierman, 1985). The plaques contain lipids, collagen, and other substances. As the plaques grow, they gradually fill the artery, choking off the flow of blood. Although atherosclerosis is related to aging, plaques may begin to build up in childhood.

Atherosclerosis contributes to the development of **ischemic heart disease,** a condition in which plaques so obstruct the flow of blood to the heart that the heart muscle itself is starved for oxygen. Like other cardiovascular diseases, ischemic heart disease is age-related, found in 12 percent of women and 20 percent of men older than 65 (Spence, 1989). Ischemic heart disease can produce **angina pectoris:** periods of dull, pressing, constricting pain that appear during physical exertion or emotional stress. Angina often appears in middle or late adulthood and becomes less common in old age, perhaps in part because of a more sedentary life-style. Another consequence of ischemic heart disease is heart attack, or **myocardial infarction,** which occurs when plaques or blood clots suddenly block a major coronary artery, shutting off all blood to the heart. Diagnosing a myocardial infarction in older adults is sometimes difficult, because they may never feel any pain (Rowe and Minaker, 1985).

The amount of damage caused by a heart attack depends on how rapidly circulation can be restored, because as soon as the clot shuts off the blood, cells in the heart muscle begin to die. Today physicians inject clot-dissolving drugs into the veins of heart attack victims to clear the artery. When one of these drugs is given within an hour of the attack, the death rate is cut almost in half. Later administration cuts death rates by 20 to 30 percent. About one patient in four does not respond to the drugs. When this happens, cardiologists thread a catheter carrying a tiny balloon into the artery. When the balloon is inflated, the clot is compressed against the side of the artery, opening the vessel (Clark, 1988; Spence, 1989).

Most people with severe atherosclerosis also have high blood pressure, or **hypertension.** In people with hypertension, both the systolic pressure (the high reading when the heart contracts) and the diastolic pressure (the low reading when the heart relaxes) are elevated. The incidence of hypertension rises steadily with age and afflicts more women (66 percent) than men (59 percent) over the age of 65. Hypertension is not part of the normal aging process, and the causes of most cases are unknown. A number of factors have been connected to the condition, however, including genetic susceptibility, stress, obesity, alcohol, and high salt intake (Kannel, 1985). Arteriosclerosis sometimes produces high systolic pressure without affecting diastolic pressure. In the Framingham heart study, a continuing longitudinal study that since 1949 has followed more then 5,000 men and women of Framingham, Massachusetts, and their children, elevated systolic pressure without an increase in disastolic pressure became increasingly common with age, appearing in about 30 percent of women and men by the age of 80. More than half of these individuals previously had hypertension.

Both elevated systolic pressure and hypertension increase the risk of strokes, or cerebrovascular accidents, which result when a blood vessel in the brain ruptures or is obstructed by blood clots or fatty deposits. Massive strokes can be fatal; they kill more people than any other disorder except heart disease and cancer. When strokes are not fatal, they may be followed by partial paralysis, loss of memory, or aphasia, depending on the area of the brain that is affected. A piling up of small strokes can cause a degenerative brain disorder, as we will see in Chapter 6. Older adults appear to respond as well to hypertensive medication as younger adults, although they need careful monitoring because they may be more sensitive to the drugs' effects (Kannel, 1985).

CHANGES IN THE RESPIRATORY SYSTEM

Shortness of breath is one characteristic we associate with aging. It is a visible result of the respiratory system's reduced ability to gather oxygen and deliver it to the bloodstream. This decreasing efficiency can be traced to a series of structural changes in the body and in the lungs themselves.

As people age, the rib cage becomes increasingly rigid, and muscle fibers become smaller and fewer in number. This tendency is increased by the stooped posture of many older adults, in which the spine is curved. As a result of this change in the way people stand, the chest wall does not expand as far with each breath and less air is taken into the lungs.

Inside the lungs, cartilage in the trachea and bronchial tubes calcifies, making them increasingly rigid (see Figure 4.3). The walls of the tiny balloonlike air sacs, or alveoli, within the lungs deteriorate, gradually decreasing the functional respiratory surface of the lungs. Collagen in the walls of the alveoli develops cross-linkages, reducing the elasticity of these air sacs and thus the ability to expand with each breath. Chemical changes in the substance between the alveoli and the capillaries impede the exchange of gases, reducing the percentage of oxygen available to the bloodstream (Spence, 1989). The blood vessels that bring carbon-dioxide laden blood into the lung and take out oxygen-rich blood gradually thicken and become stiff.

Despite all these changes, the amount of air drawn in and expelled with each breath remains about the same in older adults, as does the rate of respiration. Other aspects of lung function are affected by aging. Vital capacity, or the maximum amount of air that can be drawn into the lungs with a single breath, declines each year, beginning when people are in their twenties. Between the ages of 25 and 85, vital capacity decreases by 40 percent. Because lung capacity remains steady and vital capacity drops, the residual volume of the

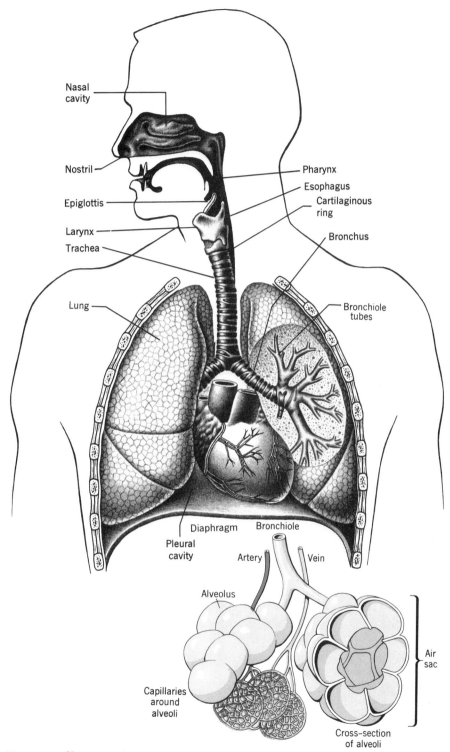

Figure 4.3 Human respiratory system, with enlargement of one of the alveoli. *Source:* Nelson, 1984, pp. 118–119.

lungs (which is the amount of air left in the lungs after exhalation) increases with age, rising from 20 percent of lung volume among 20 year olds to 35 percent among 60 year olds.

Older people have good reason to feel short of breath after exercise. Maximal oxygen uptake, which is the maximum amount of air a person can breathe in and expel during a 12-second period, begins to fall during the early twenties. By the age of 60, the average person has lost 30 percent of maximal oxygen uptake. There are wide individual differences, however, with fit older adults and former athletes having greater maximal uptake than others in later adulthood and beyond. Studies have shown that regular exercises increase maximal oxygen uptake, but it is unclear whether exercise improves the lungs' elasticity (Spence, 1989).

Discerning how much of the change in the aging lung is inevitable is difficult, because air pollution, smoking, and frequent respiratory infections can cause permanent damage that is easily mistaken for the effects of aging. It is clear, however, that various lung disorders that are common among older people are the result of secondary aging.

Emphysema, in which the walls separating the alveoli are destroyed, further reducing the already diminished respiratory lung surface, increases with age. People with the disease have large amounts of dead space in their lungs and take in so little air with each breath that they find any exertion difficult. The lung damage results in an ineffective exchange of oxygen and carbon dioxide, and the blood may carry so little oxygen that a person becomes confused, disoriented, or unconscious (Wantz and Gay, 1981). Emphysema is primarily the result of smoking, and when it appears among nonsmokers it is probably due to other types of environmental pollution. In fact, chronic bronchitis resulting from long-term exposure to environmental pollutants may lead to emphysema (Spence, 1989).

The increased incidence of pneumonia among older people may not be due to the aging of the lungs. The death rate from pneumonia climbs sharply among those past 65, but such infections are often the result of other disease or may develop when the aging immune system no longer responds to invading microorganisms. Some cases of pneumonia among older, bedridden individuals may be caused by inhaling food or other objects.

CHANGES IN THE GASTROINTESTINAL SYSTEM

Television would lead us to think that most Americans suffer from indigestion and constipation. These complaints do appear to increase with age, but the changes that accompany normal aging need not lead to these digestive difficulties (Weg, 1983). Although the esophagus, stomach, and intestinal tract alter in predictable ways (Figure 4.4), many of the digestive complaints of the elderly are the result of their life-style or the diseases of secondary aging.

Food moves through the esophagus by wavelike contractions that sweep food into the stomach. With age, these contractions may weaken, but in healthy older adults this weakening does not slow the passage of food into the stomach. Often, however, the muscle that closes the lower part of the esophagus fails to relax after a swallow, retaining food in the passage. Sometimes the muscle weakens and lets food from the stomach reenter the esophagus. Gas and stomach acid may pass into the esophagus along with the food, causing belching or heartburn (Spence, 1989).

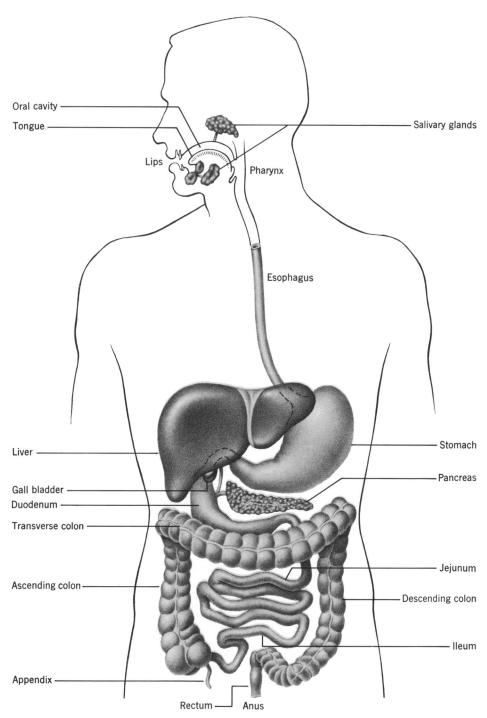

Figure 4.4 Major portions of the human digestive tract. *Source:* Nelson, 1984, p. 94.

Within the stomach, the secretion of hydrochloric acid, which is necessary for protein digestion, decreases steadily from the age of 50. When acid secretion falls too far, as it does in about 23 percent of men and 28 percent of women older than 70, atrophic gastritis develops. This chronic inflammation of the stomach lining destroys glands that produce mucous and the digestive enzyme pepsin. Atrophic gastritis is not the result of normal aging; it may be caused by repeated injury of the stomach lining by such things as aspirin, alcohol, bile salts and acids, and overproduction of gammaglobulin, a substance produced by the immune system (Bhanthumnavin and Schuster, 1977).

Our knowledge of age-related changes in the intestinal tract is meager because intestinal tissue deteriorates rapidly after removal from the body. Aging intestines secrete the same enzymes as youthful intestines, but in lesser amounts. The decrease appears to begin before the age of 30 (Rockstein and Sussman, 1979). Although age brings marked atrophy of muscle tissue, the mucous layer of the older intestine, and the layers beneath it, most older people absorb nutrients from their food as well as ever. There are, however, a few exceptions. Some older adults may absorb less calcium and vitamins B6 and B12 than they once did (Spence, 1989), and those past the age of 80 seem to absorb less of one of the simple sugars (Bhanthumnavin and Schuster, 1977). The lack of impairment in most nutrient absorption is probably due to the enormous reserve capacity of the small intestine.

With age, smooth muscle in the wall of the large intestine is reduced, and the remaining muscle loses some of its tone. These changes do not explain the prevalence of constipation among older people, which is probably due to decreased fluid intake, lack of fiber in the diet, and lack of exercise. These same factors, together with laxative abuse and drugs prescribed for other conditions, may lead to the development of **diverticulosis,** a condition in which irregular pouches develop along the walls of the large intestine. These small sacs can become obstructed, infected, and painfully inflamed. The condition is rarely seen in people younger than 30, but afflicts about 8 percent of those between the ages of 30 and 60, and about 40 percent of those older than 70. Diverticulosis might be considered a disease of modern society (Bhanthumnavin and Schuster, 1977).

Other gastrointestinal organs also show the effects of age. After people reach 50 or 60, the cells in their liver tend to change in structure, the liver may be more sluggish in responding to stimuli that provoke enzyme production, and the enzymes may be less concentrated. Because liver cells regenerate themselves and because we have about five times as much liver tissue as we need, the liver continues to function well (Spence, 1989). The primary effect of aging on the liver is to reduce its ability to metabolize certain drugs, so that drug dosages may have to be reduced for elderly patients.

The walls of the gallbladder tend to shrink and thicken with age, but in most people the organ continues to function efficiently. The primary function of the gallbladder is to store bile (which aids in the digestion of fat) after it is produced by the liver. When bile becomes supersaturated with cholesterol, gallstones may develop—a condition that becomes increasingly common with age.

Although gastrointestinal disorders become more prevalent among older adults, most of the disorders are also found in younger adults. Among older adults, however, the disorders are generally more serious. In about 56 percent of the cases, no organic reason can be found for the disorder (Rockstein and Sussman, 1979). Such functional disorders, whose symptoms include heartburn, belching, nausea, and diarrhea, are often the result of emotional or psychological problems, such as stress.

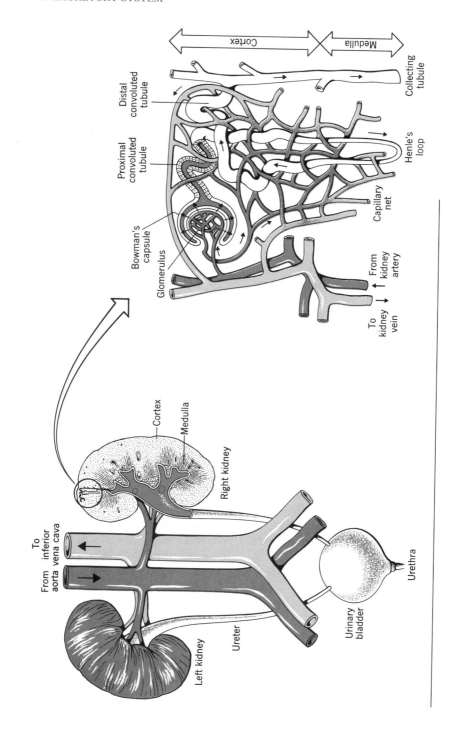

Figure 4.5 Excretory system, with enlargement of a nephron, or kidney tubule, which is the functional unit of the kidney. *Source:* Nelson, 1984, p. 183.

CHANGES IN THE EXCRETORY SYSTEM

Although there are major anatomical changes in the kidney with age, for most older people the organ continues to work in a reasonably efficient manner. The kidney's function is to cleanse the bloodstream of waste products; to regulate the salt, glucose, and alkaline (pH) levels of the blood; and to maintain the balance of fluids in the body (Figure 4.5). Aging of the kidney begins at about the age of 30, when the organ begins to shrink; by the age of 80, it may have lost 30 percent of its original weight (Spence, 1989). Within the kidney, glomeruli (which are tiny coils of arterial capillaries that supply blood to the working kidney units), gradually decrease until the 80 year old has only half the normal supply. Of the remaining glomeruli, more than 30 percent are abnormal.

Perhaps because of these changes in the glomeruli, the rate at which the kidney filters blood declines, falling steadily after the age of 21. By the age of 90, the filtration rate usually declines by about 35 percent, although in some people it has fallen as much as 50 percent (Vestal and Dawson, 1985). The speed with which blood passes through the kidneys and at which glucose is reabsorbed from the tubular fluid that eventually becomes urine also decreases. The urine produced by the older kidney is less concentrated than it once was.

Normal aging of the bladder can be a minor nuisance. Because its capacity gradually diminishes with age, the majority of people past 65 find themselves getting up in the middle of the night to urinate. This shrinkage in bladder capacity seems to be the result of muscle weakness and changes in connective tissue, which impair the bladder's capacity to expand and contract. Because of the shrinkage, the average older person's bladder holds less than half as much as that of a young person and after it is emptied, it may still be nearly half full (Spence, 1989).

Signals from the aging bladder also change. During young and middle adulthood, the sensation of bladder fullness, which causes the urge to urinate, is felt when the bladder is about half full. But among older adults, the urge is not felt until the bladder is nearly full, and some older people never receive the sensation. When the signal does come, it requires an immediate response. All these changes in the bladder explain the increased frequency of urination among older adults.

Muscle atrophy may be responsible for the involuntary passage of urine in either sex, a condition known as **incontinence.** However, older women who can control their bladders at other times often complain of stress incontinence, in which weakened muscles in the pelvic floor reduce the effectiveness of the muscle controlling the flow of urine. When stress incontinence develops, any sudden rise in pressure, such as a cough, sneeze, or laugh, leads to the leakage of urine (Spence, 1989).

CHANGES IN THE ENDOCRINE SYSTEM

Many aspects of development are affected by the endocrine system, including reproduction, metabolism, the body's internal environment, its responses to stress and disease, and even the process of aging itself. Although the effects of aging on the endocrine system are crucial, the system is so complex that our understanding of the process is meager. There are several ways in which aging could affect the endocrine system. It could reduce hormone secretion of the glands. It could produce a loss of responsiveness to hormones in the body's various receptor cells. It could lead to changes in the "second messengers" that transmit hormonal signals to the interior of cells. Or it could alter the level of enzymes that must carry out hormone-regulated activities (Marx, 1979).

Among the glands of the endocrine system are the pituitary, adrenals, thyroid, pancreas, thymus, and gonads (ovaries and testes) (Figure 4.6). Each of these glands affects body function by releasing hormones directly into the bloodstream. The endocrine system operates through an intricate system of feedback, which is supervised by the pituitary under the control of the hypothalamus. Any discussion of the thymus and gonads is omitted from this section because we will examine aging of the immune and reproductive systems separately.

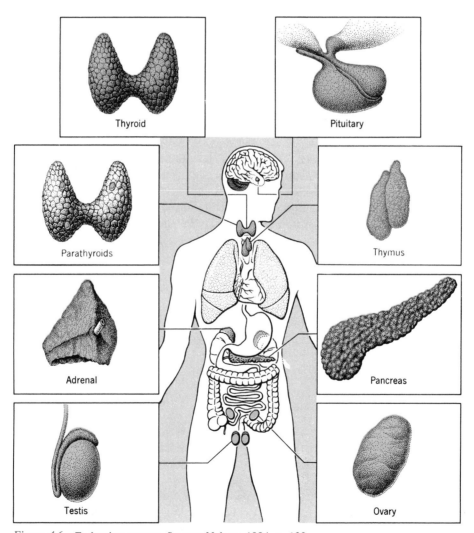

Figure 4.6 Endocrine system. *Source:* Nelson, 1984, p. 129.

PITUITARY FUNCTION

Age seems to cause no significant change in the size and weight of the pituitary, which is considered the master gland of the endocrine system. This gland is especially important because some researchers believe that it sets off the aging process when so instructed by the hypothalamus. In fact, when the pituitary gland is removed from the brain of young rats and three of its ten or more hormones are supplied by injection, the animals do not age. Cross-linkage within body cells slows, kidney damage decreases, the heart stays healthy, and the arteries seem to rejuvenate (Walford, 1983).

The structure of the pituitary shows characteristic signs of aging. Connective tissues increase, and there is a change in the way various cell types are distributed throughout the gland. Significantly less blood reaches the pituitary, but the gland's blood supply has been slowly decreasing since puberty.

One of the major hormones produced by the pituitary is growth hormone (GH), which affects metabolism and tissue growth and promotes tissue repair. The amount of GH in the bloodstream is affected by sex and obesity, and GH levels are extremely low in about one-third of the elderly. Women generally have higher levels than men, and the obese have higher levels than the nonobese. Although the fasting level of GH appears to decline with age, the pituitary never loses its ability to produce the hormone. In response to a sharp drop in blood sugar, the average increase of GH in the blood of people as old as 99 is similar to the response found in young adults (Andres and Tobin, 1977). The sensitivity to GH of receptors in body tissue seems connected to health; older men who are in excellent physical condition show greater responsiveness to GH (Spence, 1989).

A recent pilot study indicated that high levels of GH may slow the aging of skin, bone, and muscles (Rudman, Feller, and Nagra, 1990). Older men with abnormally low levels of GH received three injections of the hormone each week for a period of six months. Their bodies responded with a 9 percent gain in lean body mass, a 14 percent reduction in body fat, as well as slight gains in skin thickness and spinal density. In effect, these men's bodies had reversed the effects of nearly 20 years of aging.

After adolescence, the pituitary's production of thyroid-stimulating hormone (TSH) seems to show no change with age. Although TSH levels are highest in children and adolescents, there appear to be no age-related trends in blood levels among adults. Similarly, blood levels of adrenal-stimulating hormone (ACTH), the hormone that controls the adrenal glands, seem to remain constant, and the ability to secrete adrenal-stimulating hormones in response to stress is adequate.

ADRENAL FUNCTION

Several body systems are affected by the hormones produced by the adrenal glands, which perch just above each kidney. Epinephrine and norepinephrine, produced by the glands' inner region, initiate our physiological response to stress. The glands' outer region (cortex) produces a variety of steroids. Some are involved in the metabolism of fat and carbohydrates or influence kidney function. Some are sex hormones: the adrenal glands produce androgens (male hormones) and small amounts of estrogens (female hormones) in both sexes.

The adrenal glands show marked changes in structure with age. Lipofuscin accumulates within them, collagen proliferates, blood vessels enlarge, and some bleeding occurs. The adrenal cortex decreases in weight, and an increasing number of cells become abnormal.

With age, the production of adrenal hormones declines, yet the glands continue to function. Levels of steroids that regulate fat and carbohydrate metabolism remain constant in healthy adults. The decline in production of adrenal hormones is apparently due to the slower rate at which these hormones are metabolized with age. Hormones that affect the kidney's absorption of sodium and chloride also show little change in blood level, so that diminished production seems to have no effect on salt and water balance in older adults.

THYROID FUNCTION

Thyroid hormones play a role in the metabolism of fats and carbohydrates, and they also spur oxygen consumption and heat production by body cells. Another thyroid hormone causes the bones to absorb calcium and phosphate from the blood. With age, structural changes occur in the thyroid. In healthy adults, the gland itself increases slightly in volume (Minaker, Meneilly, and Rowe, 1985). Individual cells undergo characteristic changes, and fibers of collagen appear within the gland, yet the thyroid functions normally despite advanced age. Levels of thyroid hormones in the blood remain constant, even though hormone production declines with age. Apparently, production of thyroid hormones decreases because they take longer to degrade within body tissue as activity slows and oxygen consumption is reduced (Spence, 1989).

PANCREATIC FUNCTION

A primary job of the pancreas is to produce insulin, which is essential for the metabolism of carbohydrates. When carbohydrates have been changed to glucose within the body, insulin stimulates its transport into the cells. When this process breaks down, diabetes develops. Although insufficient production of insulin can cause diabetes, most people who develop the disease late in life produce normal or above-normal levels of insulin. "Maturity-onset" diabetes, which shows up during the forties or later, appears to be the result of a reduced sensitivity of body tissues to insulin (Spence, 1989). Recent research suggests that reduced insulin uptake is associated with the appearance of tangled polypeptide fibers within the pancreas, although it is not certain whether these fibers cause the decreased uptake or simply speed its progress (Hilts, 1989a).

No matter what the source of this insensitivity, tests show that the ability to dispose of glucose efficiently declines progressively during adulthood. In many older adults, the release of insulin in response to a rise in blood glucose is delayed in comparison with younger adults, and a smaller amount is released. Some researchers believe that this sluggish response among the elderly is the result not of an aging pancreas, but of changes in the insulin sensitivity of tissues (Minaker, Meneilly, and Rowe, 1985). In any case, glucose levels remain high in older adults, long after a load enters the bloodstream. Researchers are uncertain whether this widespread decline in the ability to handle glucose is part of normal aging or a disorder. Although more than half of adults past 65 show reduced glucose tolerance, fewer than 10 percent have any signs of diabetes (Rockstein and Sussman, 1979).

CHANGES IN THE IMMUNE SYSTEM

The immune system, which draws on components from various body systems, consists of the bone marrow, the thymus gland, the spleen, lymph nodes, and tonsils. Various types of white blood cells, which are the warriors of the immune system, are generated in the bone marrow. Those that are destined to become T-cells travel to the thymus, where they mature and are sent into the bloodstream. Some of these white blood cells become "killer" T-cells, which reject foreign tissue and destroy viruses, fungi, and parasites on contact. Others become "helper" T-cells and assist another group of white blood cells known as B-cells. B-cells have traveled from bone marrow to the spleen or lymph nodes; on maturity, they bear the primary responsibility for the production of antibodies that resist bacteria, toxins, and other foreign substances. However, most antigen responses of the B-cells seem to require the assistance of helper T-cells (Hausman and Weksler, 1985; Spence, 1989).

As the thymus shrinks, its production of hormones decreases, and it becomes less competent at fostering the maturation of T-cells. This change means that, although the number of T- and B-cells in the blood remains constant, the proportion of immature T-cells increases with age and the functioning of mature T-cells is less efficient. The B-cells also become less effective, producing fewer antibodies in response to various antigens. At the same time that response to foreign objects declines among older adults, the ability of antibodies to recognize their own cells is so impaired that they attack the body's own tissues. This autoimmune response is believed to contribute to the development of arthritis and perhaps other diseases among the elderly (Spence, 1989). The cells' diminished response to foreign objects may reduce the ability to resist infections or cancer.

It has been suggested that because of its responsibility for immune system function, the thymus is the principal pacemaker for aging (Walford, 1983). Although much of the decline in the immune system's efficiency has been related to shrinkage in the thymus gland, researchers still are not certain whether the system's decline is an effect of primary or secondary aging (Hausman and Weksler, 1985).

CHANGES IN THE REPRODUCTIVE SYSTEM

Some older adults have always quietly enjoyed their sexuality in a society that believed sex "didn't matter" in old age and that only abnormal old people were interested in it (Kay and Neelley, 1982). Changing attitudes, backed by research findings, appear to be making active sexuality more common in later years. In fact, sexual expression can continue throughout the life of reasonably healthy adults, and in Chapter 11 we will see how aging affects the expression of sexuality—which is also affected by historical and psychological factors.

Continued sexuality does not mean that the reproductive system remains youthful. Aging changes the structure and functioning of the reproductive system in predictable ways. Although we think of reproductive aging as beginning in middle age, some aspects of the process begin during youth.

MALE REPRODUCTIVE SYSTEM

Because reproductive function is closely tied to the endocrine system, we would expect changes in patterns of hormone release to be related to physiological changes with age. In

As long as adults remain reasonably healthy, they may continue sexual relations into their 80s or even their 90s.

the adult male, two hormones secreted by the pituitary gland, follicle-stimulating hormone (FSH) and luteinizing hormone (LH), control the production of hormones in the testes. FSH is necessary for the maturation of sperm cells, and LH stimulates the production of the male hormone testosterone within the testes (Figure 4.7). As testosterone levels rise in the bloodstream, they signal the pituitary to cut back on its secretion of LH.

After the age of 50, the blood levels of both these pituitary hormones rise, with FSH climbing more than LH. The rise apparently indicates increased production, because older men clear the hormones from their bloodstream as rapidly as younger men do (Harman and Talbert, 1985). Testosterone production was long thought to decrease after the age of 60, but the studies that established this belief were based on institutionalized men who were either sick or had been segregated from women (Adelman, 1989). When researchers studied healthy older men who lived in the community or in institutions that gave them opportunities to socialize with women, they found no decrease in testosterone levels with age (Harman and Talbert, 1985). The major difference between hormone production in younger and older men may be a smoothing out of daily rhythms of hormone release; young men show a morning peak in testosterone levels that does not appear among older men.

The relationship between hormonal levels and sexual activity is not clearly understood, but some minimum level of testosterone is probably necessary. As long as testosterone levels remain within the normal range, there is no correlation between hormonal levels and sexual activity in young men. But among older men, low testosterone levels are usually accompanied by low levels of sexual activity. This correlation does not mean that their low hormonal levels led to diminished sexual activity. Because some evidence indicates that sexual stimulation increases testosterone production, their low testosterone levels may be the *result* of diminished sexual activity (Harman and Talbert, 1985).

Sperm production continues throughout life, and among healthy older men of proven fertility, the number of sperm does not decrease. Although sperm tend to show reduced

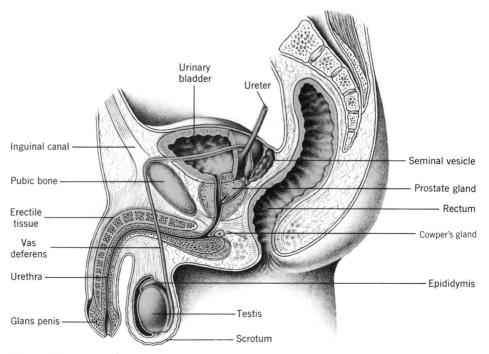

Figure 4.7   Male reproductive system and associated structures. *Source:* Nelson, 1984, p. 221.

motility with age, the less lively sperm are still capable of fertilizing an ovum. Some men in their nineties are still able to father children. Even so, with each passing decade of life, an increasing number of men stop producing sperm. Among men in their fifties, 68.5 percent have live sperm in their semen, but among men in their seventies the proportion has dropped to 48 percent (Harman and Talbert, 1985).

Cells in the prostate gland, which secrete the sperm-carrying semen, begin to age during the forties. At the same time, collagen replaces muscle tissue, and blood supply to the gland decreases. In most men, normal aging of the prostate is difficult to follow because abnormal, but harmless, cell growth enlarges the gland (Harman and Talbert, 1985). By the time men are in their fifties and sixties, the prostate may be 40 percent heavier than its earlier adult size, and among men who have reached their seventies, it may have doubled in size. Often the gland becomes so large that it interferes with bladder function and must be removed.

The penis may begin to show characteristic signs of aging as early as the thirties. Tissues and blood vessels undergo typical hardening and lose elasticity. Because erection depends on blood supply to the penis, these changes affect the speed and firmness of erection. Among men in their fifties, it takes about six times as long for an erection to develop as it does among men in their twenties (Solnick and Birren, 1977). By the age of 60, the angle of the erect penis generally has changed from 45 degrees to 90 degrees (Comfort, 1980). Unless some abnormal condition that interferes with penile blood or nerve supply develops, however, no further change will occur.

FEMALE REPRODUCTIVE SYSTEM

Aging in the female reproductive system is also linked to hormone production, and the consequences are clearer. Although men may be able to father children throughout the life span, few women past the age of 50 have given birth. The female pituitary gland produces FSH and LH, just as the male pituitary does. In women, FSH stimulates the growth of ovarian follicles, in which ova mature, whereas LH causes ovulation and the production of the female hormones, estrogen and progesterone. The ovaries also produce male hormones, as do the adrenal glands, and some of these androgens are converted into estrogen within the body (Figure 4.8).

Although men continue to produce new sperm throughout life, all the ova a woman will ever produce are present in immature form at birth. If loss of ova is considered a sign of aging, the ovaries begin to age as soon as a woman is born, for by the time she reaches puberty, at least half of the immature ova have been lost. After that time the loss slows, but as women approach the age of 50, only a few ova remain in each ovary (Finch, 1988).

A woman's reproductive aging begins during the forties. It is a collaborative effort of brain (hypothalamus) and ovary, and researchers have not been able to determine which makes the first move (Harman and Talbert, 1985). No matter which begins the intricate process, the net effect is a failure of the ovaries to respond promptly to FSH and LH sent by the pituitary. The ovaries' sluggishness leads to a drop in estrogen production and the

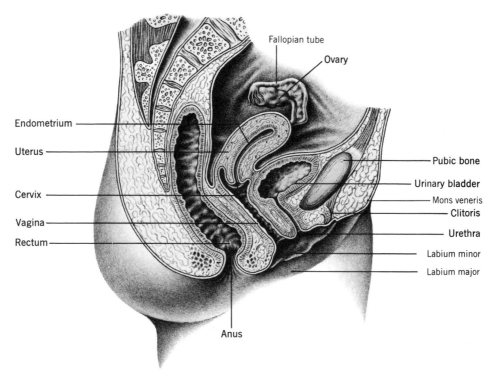

Figure 4.8   Female reproductive system and surrounding structures. *Source:* Nelson, 1984, p. 216.

maturation and release of fewer ova (Spence, 1989). Consequently, fertility gradually declines, menstrual periods become irregular, and cycles lengthen. The **climacteric,** or "change of life," has begun, and the ovaries gradually begin to shut down. When at last they stop functioning, menstruation ceases, signalling that a woman has reached **menopause.** With menopause, estrogen levels drop sharply, since the body's primary source of female hormones is now the conversion of androgens produced by the adrenal gland. But the pituitary continues to release FSH and LH, so that by two years after menopause, blood levels of FSH are 18 times higher than they were before the climacteric, and LH levels are three times higher (Harman and Talbert, 1985).

Although most people believe that all women suffer from headaches, backaches, nervousness, and hot flashes as they approach menopause, many women have none of these symptoms (Voda, Dinnerstein, and O'Donnell, 1982). Only 25 percent of the women in a large health-screening program reported any uncomfortable menopausal symptoms (Corby and Solnick, 1980). The expectation of various symptoms may lead women to attribute any physical symptom or change in mood to the climacteric. Among women who do experience symptoms, hot flashes are the most common. This sudden sensation of heat, often accompanied by sweating, coincides with pulses of LH released by the pituitary gland, which has led researchers to conclude that they are probably induced by activity in the hypothalamus (Harman and Talbert, 1985).

As estrogen levels decline, the vagina shortens and narrows as tissues in the vaginal walls become thinner and less expansive. This vaginal atrophy can be prevented by estrogen therapy, which also controls hot flashes and helps to prevent osteoporosis and heart disease. Although early estrogen therapy was connected with an increased risk of cancer and gallbladder disease, current therapy (which uses low doses of estrogen on a cyclic basis, supplemented with progestin) does not increase the risk (Harman and Talbert, 1985). Other research indicates that continued sexual activity, whether intercourse or masturbation, reduces vaginal atrophy and is accompanied by higher estrogen levels (Lieblum et al., 1983).

CHANGES IN THE NERVOUS SYSTEM

The myths and misconceptions that surround aging in the nervous system can create unnecessary concern about aging. We fear that growing old means becoming confused, disoriented, and unable to care for ourselves. But this vision of a nervous system in shambles is unwarranted. As we will see in Chapter 6, a relatively small proportion of old people develop any of the conditions commonly referred to as "senility," and they are never the result of normal aging.

Aging of the nervous system is critical because all other body systems are coordinated by this system. The central nervous system, made up of the brain and spinal cord, controls body functioning through nerve fibers in the voluntary muscles, through the autonomic nervous system, or through the brain's signals to the endocrine system. Although we have learned a great deal about the structure and functioning of the nervous system in the past decade or so, we still are not certain about the effect of normal aging on the system's anatomy.

Our uncertainty comes from the fact that until recently most of our knowledge of changes in the human brain was limited to evidence present after death. There are two problems with this kind of evidence. First, nutrition, cardiovascular status, respiratory function, cancer, organic brain disease, and the use of alcohol and drugs can have large effects on brain tissue, making it difficult to separate such changes from the effects of normal aging. Second, tissue deteriorates rapidly, so that the length of time between death and the preparation of tissue can affect findings, as can the methods used to prepare the tissue (Duara, London, and Rapoport, 1985).

Much of our basic knowledge is based on inferences from animal studies, but technological advances are beginning to produce new information about the aging human brain. CT scans, which were mentioned earlier, show cross-sections of living brain tissue. Positron emission tomography (PET) provides a picture of brain function. In this method, short-lived radioactive fluorine is attached to glucose, and the sugar is injected into the body. PET scans produce images of the active brain, allowing researchers to follow its function by tracing the uptake of radioactive glucose. Finally, nuclear magnetic resonance (NMR) scans are made by enclosing the body in a magnetic field and using radio waves to produce images of tissue, biochemical activity, and metabolism. As information from this new technological research accumulates, our understanding of the central nervous system—as well as all other body functions—may take a giant step forward.

CENTRAL NERVOUS SYSTEM

Studies of central nervous system aging have focused on the brain, which appears to shrink over the years (Figure 4.9). Most studies have reported decreased brain weight over the years, as well as increased space between the brain and the skull and expansion of the ventricles (the fluid-filled spaces deep within the brain). Using CT scans of hospital patients, researchers confirmed clear shrinkage beginning after age forty in men and age fifty in women (Takeda and Masuzawa, 1985). Although these researchers eliminated all patients with any sign of nervous system damage, their sample included patients with diabetes as well as those with cardiovascular, kidney, and respiratory disorders. Other studies using CT scans have found ventricular expansion accompanied by decreased brain volume with age, the rate accelerating after the age of 60 (Zatz, Jernigan, and Ahumada, 1982). Once again, however, typical and normal aging produce different results. When studies are limited to carefully screened, mentally normal adults, there seems to be no significant decrease in brain weight or ventricular expansion (Duara, London, and Rapaport, 1985).

Changes in Neurons

Like cells in the heart, brain cells cannot replace themselves. Neurons die, perhaps daily, but this loss has little effect on brain function. The typical loss appears to be limited to particular layers of neurons in certain regions of the brain, such as the cerebellum, a structure at the base of the brain involved in physical balance and motor coordination. Some studies have found progressive decline after age 60, with neurons disappearing from the cerebral cortex at the rate of 1 percent per year after the age of 70 (Bondareff, 1985). But such conclusions are based on postmortem studies and samples taken during brain surgery, which virtually eliminates the examination of the healthy brain. Among people who died from diseases unrelated to the brain, there was some brain shrinkage but no cell death (Terry et al., 1988). In this study, the weight loss apparently was due to the shrinkage of individual

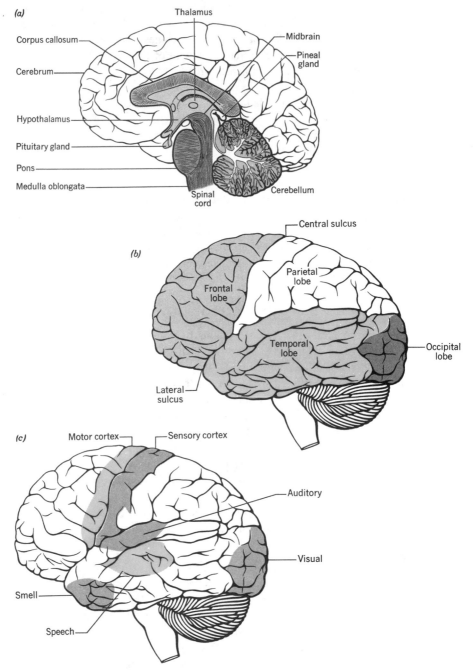

Figure 4.9   (a) Longitudinal section of the human brain, showing its major parts; (b) subdivisions of the cerebrum, showing its left hemisphere; (c) functional areas of the cortex, the 2 to 5 millimeter thick coating of gray matter that covers the cerebrum. *Source:* Nelson, 1984, pp. 170–171.

neurons, since people in their eighties and nineties had as many neurons as people in their twenties, but fewer of their neurons were large.

Over the years neurons may lose some of their dendrites (the fibers that bring nerve impulses into the cell body), and terminal branches of the axon (which conducts nerve impulses away from the cell) may disappear (Figure 4.10). However, such atrophy appears to go on throughout normal life, and it is accompanied by the growth of new fibers that may compensate for a good part of whatever loss occurs. Environmental stimulation also seems to foster the development of new connections between neurons in the older brain, just as it does in young brains (Cotman, 1990). Serious and permanent loss of neuronal connections is probably the result of organic brain disease, which will be discussed in Chapter 6.

Changes appear with age in the cell bodies of the brain. Dense granules surrounded by fluid-filled cavities, called vacuoles, may appear after the age of 60. **Senile plaques,** dark clumps of dead and dying neural fibers, may also appear in older brains, and at least a few seem inevitable once people are more than 90 years old. **Neurofibrillary tangles,** twisted bundles of paired helical filaments made up of various proteins, are also found in small

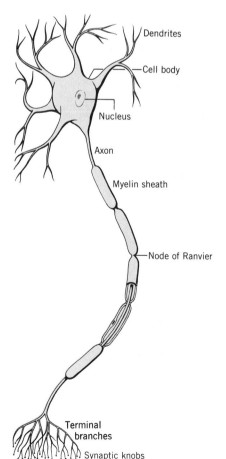

Figure 4.10 A brain cell, or neuron, and its major parts. *Source:* Nelson, 1984, p. 147.

numbers. All these changes (vacuoles, senile plaques, and neurofibrillary tangles), while sparse in the normal aging brain, are found in great numbers in diseased brains (Spence, 1989). In the normal aged brain, for example, neurofibrillary tangles are primarily confined to a portion of the temporal lobe, but in the diseased brain they often spread throughout the cerebral cortex (Duara, London, and Rapoport, 1985). Lipofuscin accumulates in the brain as it does in other parts of the body, but there is no indication that lipofuscin harms neurons or interferes with their functioning.

As the release of neurotransmitters into the space between neurons either causes a neuron to fire or keeps it from firing, any change in the concentration of these chemicals will affect brain function. Little is known about the effect of age on the production or uptake of neurotransmitters in normal aging (Rogers and Bloom, 1985), but significant changes are connected with abnormal states. For example, the destruction of pathways that carry one transmitter, dopamine, is connected with Parkinson's disease, a serious condition that becomes more common with age.

Brain Activity

Although nerve impulses are started and stopped by chemicals, the impulse itself is electrical. This electrical activity can be studied by attaching electrodes to the scalp and recording the impulses on an electroencephalogram (EEG). Several changes in brain activity are associated with aging, and characteristic differences appear between EEGs of healthy older people and those who are suffering from various degenerative diseases.

Brain waves differ in frequency and amplitude and are distinguished by frequency, or cycles per second (Hz). The more rapid the rhythm of the waves, the more alert and mentally active a person is. Delta waves, the slowest (1–3 Hz), predominate in deep sleep. Theta waves are slightly faster (4–7 Hz). Alpha waves, with a frequency of 8–13 Hz, appear when people are awake and relaxed or when they are meditating. Beta waves, the fastest (14–40 Hz), appear during aroused mental activity.

Slow wave activity, a combination of delta and theta waves, appears with increasing frequency as people age and may indicate a decrease of blood flow to the brain. Healthy adults who are less than 75 years old show no more slow wave activity than is found in the EEG of young adults. Once past the age of 75, however, about 20 percent of older people show an increase in slow wave activity. Cardiovascular disease has been proposed as the cause of this slowing. When slow wave activity is diffuse, that is, spread over the entire brain, it often is accompanied by impaired mental functioning as measured by IQ tests (Marsh and Thompson, 1977).

Some older people show bursts of high voltage, slow waves from small areas of the brain. This activity begins to appear at about the age of 50, and by the age of 65 the bursts are seen in the EEGs of from 30 to 50 percent of healthy older people. There seems to be no connection between such activity and any impairment (Marsh and Thompson, 1977).

Alpha waves seem to decline in amplitude with age. They may also become slower, falling at the low end of the frequency range. However, not all older adults show this alpha slowing. In fact, nearly a quarter of the 60 to 80 year olds in one study showed an increase in alpha frequency (Wang and Busse, 1969).

When the amount of alpha activity decreases, it is replaced by slow wave activity. Although slowed alpha generally is connected with decreased blood flow to the brain, especially during stress, it has been found in some healthy adults. In one longitudinal study, decline in alpha frequency over a 12-year period was correlated with drops in IQ scores, but only among adults in the highly educated, upper socioeconomic group (Wang, Obrist, and Busse, 1970).

Beta activity remains as fast as ever in healthy older adults, and some researchers have reported finding an increase in the amount of beta activity among 60 to 70 year olds. Among adults who are older than 80, beta activity seems to decrease in amount, and in severely deteriorated hospital patients beta activity is sharply reduced (Marsh and Thompson, 1977).

An important aspect of brain activity is metabolism within the cell. PET scans of carefully screened, healthy men between the ages of 21 and 83 show no change with age in the metabolism rate of glucose or oxygen. However, the rate of cerebral blood flow does diminish with age, perhaps as a result of arteriosclerosis (Duara, London, and Rapoport, 1985).

AUTONOMIC NERVOUS SYSTEM

The decline in the body's ability to respond to stress is primarily the result of aging in the autonomic nervous system (Figure 4.11). The autonomic nervous system regulates the body's internal environment. It controls such activities as heart rate, blood pressure, skin temperature, digestion, elimination, respiration, and reactions to emergencies or stress.

With age, many of the responses controlled by the autonomic nervous system slow or become weaker, so that it takes the body longer to adapt to changed conditions. This slowing may be the result of changes in the metabolism of neurotransmitters, to structural changes in neurons, or to the loss of neurons—although there appears to be no marked degeneration of the system's major branches with age (Everitt and Huang, 1980).

The autonomic nervous system exerts some control over many of the systems already discussed. For example, it regulates blood sugar levels and blood pressure. Age brings only slight changes in such measures, but some researchers believe that aging in the autonomic nervous system may be involved in the development of hypertension (Everitt and Huang, 1980).

The aging autonomic nervous system manages to maintain normal body temperature fairly well when no demands are placed on it, but falters when faced with extreme changes in environmental temperature. Impaired temperature regulation explains why older people are more likely to succumb to heat stroke in summer and hypothermia in winter. Similarly, it takes the pulse and breathing longer to return to normal after exercise. Sleep patterns also show the influence of aging in the nervous system.

SLEEP PATTERNS

Throughout the life cycle, the amount of time spent sleeping declines from the 16 hours each day of the newborn to the 7 or 8 hours of the adult. Older adults often complain that they sleep very little or that they frequently wake during the night. Their sleep patterns have changed, but most still sleep 7 to 8 hours out of every 24. When men and women between the ages of 65 and 95 were monitored in their homes, the average adult slept 8 hours and 15 minutes (Ancoli–Israel et al., 1985). Yet many of these same people complained about their inability to sleep at night.

The inconsistency becomes clear when we learn that, with age, sleep no longer comes in

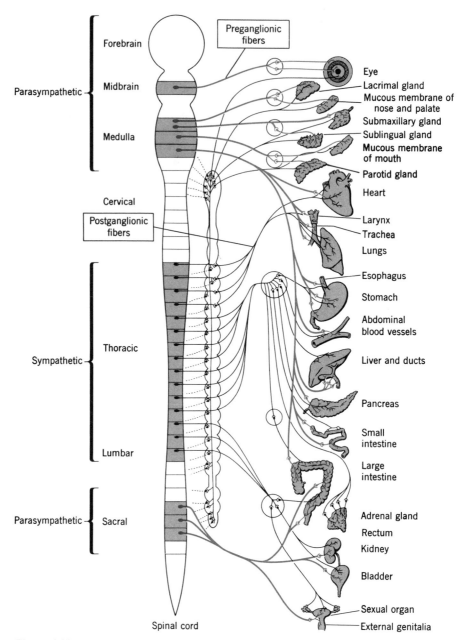

Figure 4.11 Autonomic nervous system, which controls the body's internal environment by innervating various organs. *Source:* Nelson, 1984, p. 144.

Older adults may sleep less at night, but they generally make up for the loss by taking a nap or two each day.

one chunk. The aging body rarely remains asleep all night without waking. Most older adults wake during the night, go back to sleep for a second stretch, then supplement their 5 or 6 hours of nightly sleep with a nap (or two) during the day. This pattern represents a change in one of the fundamental biological rhythms. The circadian (or daily) rhythm of sleep and waking does not disappear in older adults; instead its amplitude seems to be reduced, so that sleep becomes fragmented and waking hours are punctuated by periods of drowsiness (Richardson, 1990).

The changed sleep habits of older adults are accompanied by changes in nightly EEG patterns. Every 90 minutes or so during the night, sleep cycles through a series of stages that include a period called rapid-eye-movement (REM) sleep. REM sleep is characterized by rapid movements of the eyes beneath the closed lids and by a pattern of brain waves that resembles light sleep: a predominance of alpha rhythm, along with very slow theta waves and occasional bursts of beta activity. Heartbeat is irregular, breathing quickens, and blood pressure rises. Yet muscles become limp and virtually paralyzed. People are hard to waken from REM sleep, but, when roused, most say they have been dreaming. The proportion of REM to non-REM sleep generally remains steady across adulthood, although it declines among some adults in their eighties (Dement et al., 1985).

Sex differences in sleep exist from puberty. Men spend a larger part of the night in light, non-REM sleep than women do. The stage of deepest non-REM sleep is characterized by large, slow delta waves. Heart rate and respiration are slow and regular, and muscles are relaxed. Although most men older than 60 spend only a negligible amount of time in deepest sleep, sustained periods of slow wave sleep appears in a small but significant number of women. Through middle and late adulthood and young-old age, men wake more often at night, but once people reach their eighties, this sex difference disappears (Dement et al., 1985).

Frequent wakings during the night are sometimes due to the need to urinate, but respiratory impairment also contributes to the disturbance. Studies indicate that among supposedly healthy adults older than 60, one-third are roused at least five times each hour by **sleep apnea,** a condition in which breathing stops for at least 10 seconds (Ancoli–Israel et al., 1981). When this condition occurs, carbon dioxide levels rise, the person automatically wakes, and resumes breathing. Sleep apnea is rare among healthy adults in their fifties. Another disturber of sleep is **nocturnal myoclonus,** in which a sleeper's leg muscles twitch or jerk every 20 to 40 seconds over long stretches of time. Various studies indicate that about a third of adults older than 65 are troubled by this sleep disorder. Yet among healthy 85 to 94 year olds in Vilcabamba, Ecuador, researchers found a much lower incidence of both disorders (Okudaira et al., 1983). They suggest the difference could be due to the beneficial effects of the altitude, sleeping medication, strenuous physical exercise, or some other environmental difference. No matter what the cause, frequent disruption of sleep can reduce its quality and make a person feel that she or he is not getting an adequate amount.

Depression can affect sleep markedly, leading to frequent waking during the night, waking for good before daylight, and a feeling of tiredness on arising (Rodin, McAvay, and Timko, 1988). Depressed adults often complain of insomnia, which is not a normal accompaniment of aging. Insomnia can also be caused by excessive consumption of caffeine or alcohol or by the use of sleeping pills. Sleeping preparations, when used regularly, aggravate insomnia. The person builds up a tolerance for the drug, becomes dependent on it, and develops drug-dependency insomnia. Insomnia may be treated by eliminating sleeping medications and limiting time in bed, so that the bed is used only for sleeping and only during specific hours.

As with other aspects of biological aging, sleep patterns change little in some older people. In system after system, advanced aging and degenerative diseases come at early ages for some and are postponed or never appear in others. In the next chapter, we will investigate the health aspects of aging, discovering that the way we live can hasten or postpone the arrival of the frailty associated with old-old age.

SUMMARY

CHANGES IN APPEARANCE

There are wide interindividual differences in the rate of visible aging, and the level of visible aging correlates with the level of internal aging. With age, hair shows consistent, but different, localized changes for each sex, and by age 50, the density of scalp hair has been reduced by about 25 percent. Cross-linkage, changes in fat and muscle, and habitual muscle use play some role in wrinkles, but the major cause of skin aging is exposure to the sun. The shrinkage of muscles and the decline in their strength that accompany aging may be in part the result of reduced physical activity.

CHANGES IN STRUCTURE

A slight shrinkage in height may result from altered posture, thinning of spinal disks, and loss of water in the disks. Although calcium is steadily lost from the bones with age, osteoporosis can be prevented, and even some of the causes of **osteoarthritis,** which is related to mechanical stress, can be reduced. The major enemy of teeth is periodontal disease.

CHANGES IN THE CARDIOVASCULAR SYSTEM

As the cardiovascular system ages, lipofuscin accumulates, collagen stiffens, and additional collagen and fat are deposited in the heart. Cardiac output decreases in people with cardiovascular disease, but the decrease in maximum heart rate seems due to primary aging. Arterial walls become stiff, collagen, calcium, and lipids accumulate, and blood pressure often rises. Although changes in tissue structure are inevitable, much observed arterial change may be the result of secondary aging. Secondary aging produces **atherosclerosis,** which contributes to the development of **ischemic heart disease, angina pectoris, myocardial infarction, hypertension,** or stroke. Strokes may also result from pronounced **arteriosclerosis** (thickening and stiffening of arterial walls).

CHANGES IN THE RESPIRATORY SYSTEM

Stiffening of the rib cage, shrinkage of muscle fiber, and structural changes within the lung result in a marked decrease in efficiency. Vital capacity drops and residual lung volume increases. The decline in maximal oxygen uptake, which leaves people short of breath after exercise, is probably heightened by lack of exercise. Secondary aging may lead to **emphysema.**

CHANGES IN THE GASTROINTESTINAL SYSTEM

Although esophageal muscles contract more weakly in older adults and hydrochloric acid production drops, digestive problems such as atrophic gastritis and **diverticulosis** in the elderly are the result of secondary aging or life-style. As the liver ages, its ability to metabolize drugs is reduced.

CHANGES IN THE EXCRETORY SYSTEM

Changes in kidney structure and function do not prevent it from working efficiently, but bladder shrinkage often forces older adults to get up at night to urinate. Changes in signals from the aging bladder lead to increased frequency of urination, while weakened muscles may lead to stress **incontinence.**

CHANGES IN THE ENDOCRINE SYSTEM

The pituitary gland, which shows some structural change, may set off the aging process under instructions from the hypothalamus. The pituitary's ability to produce three essential hormones—growth hormone (GH), thyroid-stimulating hormone (TSH), and adrenal-stimulating hormone (ACTH)—is unimpaired by age. Although the production of adrenal hormones decreases with age, the glands continue to function, and the blood levels of each hormone tend to remain stable. Levels of thyroid hormones remain constant, even though production decreases, apparently in response to lessened activity. Changes in the pancreas make the body less effective in handling insulin, but it is uncertain whether this inefficiency is due to normal aging. Some adults older than 40 develop maturity-onset diabetes, a major disease of secondary aging.

CHANGES IN THE IMMUNE SYSTEM

The thymus, an endocrine gland that is a major component of the immune system, has been considered a primary pacemaker for aging. As the thymus shrinks, the proportion of immature T-cells in the bloodstream increases and the functioning of mature T-cells becomes less efficient, while B-cells produce fewer antibodies. But researchers are not certain whether the decline of the immune system with age is due to primary or secondary aging.

CHANGES IN THE REPRODUCTIVE SYSTEM

The structure and functioning of the reproductive system changes with age in both men and women. Many men continue to produce sperm into advanced old age; women cease producing mature ova by **menopause,** which usually arrives at about the age of 50, as the **climacteric** is completed.

CHANGES IN THE NERVOUS SYSTEM

With age the brain appears to shrink, and neurons are lost in some regions of the brain, especially the area that coordinates voluntary muscle activity. Research with carefully screened adults indicates that the shrinkage may not be part of primary aging, while some studies have found no neuronal loss with age but a shrinkage of neuron size. Major changes in the cell bodies of neurons include vacuoles, **senile plaques,** and **neurofibrillary tangles.** All these changes are found in small numbers in normal brains, but they are found in quantity only in diseased brains.

Studies of brain waves indicate that slow wave activity increases with age in some people and is found in healthy adults older than 75. Diffuse slow wave activity is often accompanied by impaired functioning on IQ tests. Alpha activity may slow or be partly replaced by slow wave activity, but beta activity decreases only among adults older than 80 or severely deteriorated hospital patients.

The autonomic nervous system regulates body systems effectively as long as no special environmental demands are placed on the body. But many responses controlled by the system slow or weaken with age, so that the body takes longer to adapt to changed conditions and may not respond effectively to stress.

Older adults tend to sleep about as much as they ever did, but not at one stretch. The proportion of REM sleep remains steady, although it may decline somewhat after the age of 80. Deep, slow wave sleep may disappear in older men, but some older women still spend significant amounts of time in this sleep stage. Sleep disturbances may be caused by **sleep apnea** or **nocturnal myoclonus.**

KEY TERMS

angina pectoris	menopause
arteriosclerosis	myocardial infarction
atherosclerosis	neurofibrillary tangle
climacteric	nocturnal myoclonus
diverticulosis	osteoarthritis
emphysema	osteoporosis
hypertension	senile plaque
incontinence	sleep apnea
ischemic heart disease	

Chapter 5

◆

Physical Health Across Adulthood

◆

On June 3, 1983, Harry Lieberman died at the age of 106. Lieberman, who had emigrated from Poland at the age of 29, manufactured candy for a supermarket chain until he retired in good health at the age of 74. Bored with his inactivity, he took up painting and established a successful second career. At 105, he told an interviewer that he felt his life was "paradise" because his painting would endure long past his own lifetime. "They can put you six feet down," he said, "but the spiritual work you leave lives forever. I don't ask for more" (Barasch, 1983). Lieberman's death was attributed to cardiac arrest: his heart simply stopped.

On November 7, 1980, actor Steve McQueen died in Juárez, Mexico, at the age of 50. McQueen, who projected the screen image of a tough, cool loner, refused a double for many of his dangerous stunt scenes and always drove his own racing car in such films as *Le Mans*. The cause of McQueen's death was mesothelioma, a tumor of the tissue that lines the chest and abdomen, a disease that is believed to be caused by exposure to asbestos dust. No one is certain just how the cancer came to develop, but McQueen may have come into contact with the dust when he worked as a merchant seaman in the early 1950s, or from the asbestos suit he wore when driving his racing car (Clark and Henkoff, 1980).

Why do some people live out a long, healthy life when others die prematurely or spend decades struggling with degenerative disease? Although we are not certain why some people remain healthy when others fail, we have discovered a number of factors that seem to have an important influence on health.

In this chapter, we begin by exploring the nature of physical health in adulthood. Next we consider the relationship between our health and the way we live, investigating aspects of life-style that promote good health and those that can speed deterioration. Pushing our exploration past the obvious connections of diet, alcohol, smoking, and exercise, we try to understand how stress and the manner in which we cope with it may also affect the quality of our later years.   ◆

PHYSICAL HEALTH

Our society has so thoroughly confused the concepts of aging and illness that we assume that to be old is to be ailing, and the absence of illness is often interpreted as the absence of aging (Hickey, 1980). A healthy old person may not feel, or be perceived as, "old." As an 86-year-old Iowan put it, "I just don't think I'm old. I got a lot of zip yet. You got to keep moving to keep young. Keep the old joints greased up" (Donosky, 1982). Although an increasing number of older people are keeping their health for a longer time, their bodies are usually less resilient after temporary illnesses, and many develop degenerative diseases. Such chronic illnesses alter the quality of life differently than do acute illnesses, whether we are 25 or 80.

ACUTE ILLNESS

All of us, from the youngest baby to the oldest centenarian, may develop **acute illness,** a physical disorder with a limited duration. Although the illness generally passes and we eventually feel as well as we ever did, some acute illnesses can kill. The once prevalent diphtheria, influenza, and cystitis (a bladder infection) are examples of acute illness.

Across adulthood, each individual tends to have fewer acute illnesses each year, although each separate illness is likely to be increasingly severe (Table 5.1). By the time people are in their thirties and forties, respiratory illnesses are the most common, accounting for 78 out of every 100 episodes of acute illness (Wantz and Gay, 1981).

Acute illness in older people is complicated by normal aging processes. For example, the symptoms of an older person suffering from pneumonia may be limited to confusion, unsteadiness, and a slight breathlessness (Rowe and Minaker, 1985). Temperature in older people may rise only slightly in response to a serious infection. The perception of pain may diminish, so that its source and location become difficult to determine. Because the immune system is aging, the response to treatment is slower and weaker than it once was. Because the older patient has less physical reserve (and about one-half the lung function of the average 30 year old), an illness such as influenza that may be merely a painful nuisance to a younger person can develop into pneumonia in an older person and may lead to death.

An additional factor that complicates acute illness in older adults is the probable presence of some chronic condition, such as cardiovascular disease or diabetes. More than four out of five people over 65 have at least one chronic health problem, and many have multiple problems (U.S. Senate, Special Committee on Aging, 1987–1988).

CHRONIC ILLNESS

Long-standing health problems are known as **chronic illnesses,** for they cannot be cured and they often get worse with time. The proportion of any cohort that has some chronic illness increases with age, as does the number of chronic illnesses a person is likely to have. In a longitudinal study of Californians, known as the Intergenerational Studies, the shift from acute to chronic complaints occurred when the subjects were in their forties. Instead of reporting sprains or strains, for example, they told of chronic pain, stiffness, and limited

Table 5.1 ACUTE ILLNESS, 1987 (RATE PER 100 POPULATION)[a]

Cohort	Infective and Parasitic	Respiratory		Digestive System	Injuries
		Upper	Other		
Men	20.3	31.2	41.3	6.0	30.5
Women	25.9	39.5	47.6	6.6	23.7
White	24.1	35.6	47.3	5.9	28.6
Black	19.2	33.8	24.6	9.2	18.5
By age					
18–24	22.5	29.8	58.3	7.9	33.3
25–44	18.2	28.2	46.0	5.0	28.5
45–64	7.8	21.4	28.3	3.3	18.2
>64	5.5	14.3	20.4	6.8	21.7

[a] The number of acute conditions that either require medical attention or restrict activity for at least one day declines with age, although each separate illness is generally more severe.

Source: U.S. Bureau of the Census, 1990.

movement. By the time these middle-class Americans were 50 years old, chronic bronchitis, emphysema, hypertension, and arthritis had appeared among them. Yet the great majority considered themselves in excellent health (Eichorn et al., 1981).

Their evaluations are not unusual. Most people in middle and late adulthood believe they are in good health. Among residents of three semirural counties in central Wisconsin, 88 percent of the adults between the ages of 45 and 64 said that their health was excellent or good (Levkoff, Cleary, and Wetle, 1987).

Disability

Chronic conditions often worsen as people get older, and the degree of disability increases with age. Disability is generally assessed in terms of a person's ability to function as measured by whether the person can handle the ordinary activities of daily living and the tasks involved in managing a home. Among women and men between the ages of 65 and 69, 85 percent have no trouble handling any of the activities of daily living and 82 percent have no trouble with any of the home tasks. Among those past the age of 85, however, the proportion of those who can manage all their personal activities has dropped to 51 percent, while about 45 percent can handle all the home tasks (U.S. Senate, Select Committee on Aging, 1987–1988). Even so, only 19 percent of the oldest adults are so severely disabled that they need assistance on at least four personal activities, while 24 percent are unable to manage four or more home tasks by themselves (Figure 5.1).

Studies traditionally find that older women are more likely to be disabled than older men (U.S. Senate, Select Committee on Aging, 1987–1988). When researchers traced disabilities in a national sample over a two-year period, they found that statistics can be highly misleading (Manton, 1988). The confusion arises because fewer women than men die at each given age and at each level of disability. Women tend to develop relatively less lethal conditions (arthritis, diabetes) than men (cancer, heart disease) and tend to use less intensive medical care—but for longer periods of time. In addition, men are more likely to be cared for at home, since they are likely to have wives, whereas women are more frequently cared for in nursing homes or hospitals, since they tend to be widows.

The degree of disability from any chronic illness is not determined solely by physiological measures. Attitudes and expectations—both of older people and of those around them—affect the level at which they can function. More than people of any other age, the degree of disability and functional loss in the elderly depends on behavioral and sociological factors (Rowe and Minaker, 1985).

Decline is not inevitable, and its failure to occur in many older adults points up the individuality of the aging process. In the Duke Longitudinal Studies, in which the health of 300 North Carolina women and men past the age of 60 was followed over a 15-year period, the health of 52 percent remained stable and that of 18 percent improved. Only 30 percent showed the expected decline (Maddox and Douglass, 1974).

Statistics usually lump illnesss and disabilities for all adults past 65 in a single group, leading to the myth that physical decline begins at 65. According to gerontologist James Birren, most Americans see older adults as "dying a little bit every day" (Langway 1982). When such statistics are analyzed, however, it becomes clear that the majority of people in their sixties are healthy and that significant health-related problems generally do not develop until people pass the age of 75.

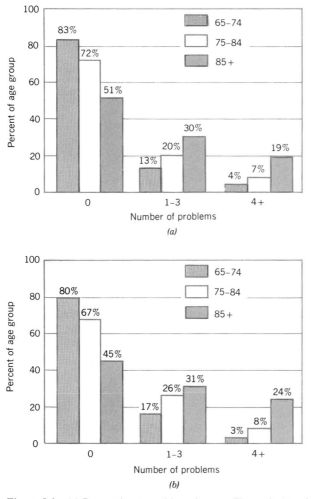

Figure 5.1 (a) Personal care problems by age. The majority of older adults—even those past the age of 85—have no problems with any of the actvities of daily living (bathing, dressing, eating, walking, using the toilet, getting in and out of bed, and going outside) that are used as a measure of disability. (b) Home management problems by age. A somewhat larger proportion of older adults need assistance with the tasks involved in managing a home (preparing meals, shopping, managing money, using the telephone, heavy housework, and light housework).

Among community-dwelling older adults surveyed by the National Center for Health Statistics, 70 percent regarded their health as excellent, very good, or good compared with that of other people their age (National Center for Health Statistics, 1987). Income was directly related to the way adults perceived their health. Only 11 percent of adults with an annual income of less than $10,000 said that their health was excellent, but 24 percent of those with incomes of more than $20,000 rated their health as excellent. Nearly 15 percent of low-income adults, but less than 6 percent of adults with high incomes, said their health was poor.

The majority of older adults enjoy an active social life and have no major health problems until they pass the age of 75.

Self-ratings of health have turned out to be relatively good predictors of mortality. When age, sex, and actual health were held constant, people who rated their health as poor were almost two and one half times as likely to die from ischemic heart disease as those who rated their health as excellent (Siegler and Costa, 1985). A similar connection between self-ratings and mortality held for death from any cause, even when researchers also controlled for such conditions as cardiovascular disease, chronic conditions, medication, and disabilities (Kaplan, Barell, and Lusky, 1988). Among more than 1200 older Israelis, those who rated themselves as being sick or very sick died at twice the rate of those who saw themselves as healthy or very healthy (Figure 5.2). Researchers who conducted this study are uncertain as to whether people are assessing their biological and physiological condition accurately or whether subjective ratings of health reflect emotional states, with stress, depression, or emotional problems promoting disease and optimistic feelings protecting health.

Health Problems of Older Adults

Determining the condition of an elderly person's health is often difficult. In order to assess health, one must know the person's actual physical condition, his or her level of functioning (which may be higher or lower than physical examinations and tests indicate), and what the older person expects of himself or herself, as well as what others expect the person to be able to do (Hickey, 1980). The stereotype of inevitable decline in the elderly can lead to preconceived expectations in old people, health professionals, and family members, and those expectations can interfere with improvements in health or function. For example, physicians may dismiss low levels of red blood cells as the "anemia of old age" and fail to treat it. Yet results from the Framingham study indicate that there is no decline in packed red cell volume with age and that a low red blood count signifies iron deficiency, pernicious anemia, or blood loss from intestinal malignancies (Rowe and Minaker, 1985). Too many older people assume that pain or loss of function is an inevitable part of aging and so fail to seek medical attention for serious, but treatable, illness.

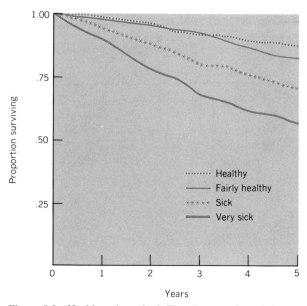

Figure 5.2 Health and survival. The chances of surviving over a five-year period are closely related to a person's subjective impression of his or her health. *Source:* Kaplan, Barell, and Lusky, 1988, p. 5115.

The most common health problems among older Americans are arthritis, hypertension, hearing impairment, and heart conditions, followed by osteoporosis and other orthopedic conditions (U.S. Senate, Special Committee on Aging, 1987–1988). Cancer and stroke together account for 30 percent of deaths among people older than 65, but heart disease is far and away the leading cause of death in the elderly (45 percent of all deaths) and the major reason for seeking medical care. The severity of cardiovascular disease is easy to demonstrate. If all cardiovascular disease could be eliminated, life expectancy would increase by 12 years from birth and 11 years from age 65; but if cancer were eliminated, life expectancy would increase by only 2 1/2 years from birth and 1 1/2 years from age 65 (Siegler and Costa, 1985).

The way in which a chronic disease can interact with normal aging to accelerate physical decline is clearest in the case of diabetes. Only 1 percent of people younger than 65 have developed diabetes, but among those between the ages of 65 and 74, 7 percent have the disease (Spence, 1989). That figure may grossly underestimate the incidence of diabetes, since it carries no warning symptoms, and some researchers have estimated that as many as half of adult diabetics are unaware that they have the disease (Kolata, 1987b). The implications for health are enormous. Diabetics have 17 times more kidney disease, 25 times more blindness, 5 times more gangrene, and twice as many heart attacks and strokes as other people (Wantz and Gay, 1981). Most of these disorders can be traced to the effect of diabetes on the circulatory system. The diabetic's blood vessels show accelerated aging, characterized by the formation of plaques and the calcification of arterial and venous walls. Plaques cut off circulation in the arms and legs. Changes in kidney blood vessels can decrease the kidney's efficiency in filtering the blood, and changes in small blood vessels of the eyes can lead to blindness. Through its effect on the nervous system, diabetes can cause complications in many body systems. Infections in feet or legs can cause gangrene, the bladder may become paralyzed, and impotency may develop in men, while women may find their sexual response impaired.

Diabetes may respond to medication, but weight loss seems to be the most effective treatment (Kolata, 1987b). Many people with maturity-onset diabetes are no longer diabetic after they lose weight. Exercise is a helpful adjunct to weight loss, since it promotes the entry of glucose into resistant tissue cells and enhances the cells' use of glucose. But the effect is short-lived. It lasts for only 72 hours, which means that diabetics must exercise regularly to get any benefit from their exertions (Kolata, 1987b; Spence, 1989).

THE PROCESS OF DYING

The probability that death will follow some degenerative disease means that many people will spend weeks, if not months, in the dying process. As death becomes certain, a person enters the **dying trajectory,** the emotional states through which an individual travels in the weeks, days, and hours preceding death (Glaser and Strauss, 1968). Depending on the patient's basic ailment and age and on decisions concerning medical technology, the trajectory may be rapid or slow, regular or spasmodic.

Chronic Illness and Medical Technology

Even after death has become certain, medical technology may prolong life, even though the person may be comatose or in continual pain. The patient is kept alive by a combination of five techniques: cardiopulmonary resuscitation (CPR) (which revives a person after cardiac or respiratory arrest); mechanical respirators (which take over for nonfunctional lungs); renal dialysis (which takes over for nonfunctional kidneys); artificial feeding (which provides nourishment for those who cannot eat or drink); and antibiotics (which control infection) (Hoopes, 1988). The result is a form of dying that has been called a "degradation ceremony," in which people meet their deaths in an ignominious manner (Shneidman, 1980).

Instead of trying to "heal" patients long after it is apparent that only heroic efforts are keeping them alive, says Avery Weisman (1972), we should be striving for an appropriate death. An **appropriate death** is the sort of death a person might choose—if the choice were available. This means that patients would be protected from needless medical procedures that only dehumanize and demean them. They would be allowed to die with dignity and with some control over the manner of their death.

Because such conditions are often difficult to meet in a hospital, hospices have been established in many communities. **Hospices** are institutions or wards within hospitals that use no technology to extend life but provide the dying with pain relief, attention, and affection. Most hospices coordinate a program of care that keeps the patient in the home as long as possible. Under the direction of physicians, pain is relieved in a way that keeps the patient alert. Hospice staff and volunteers help to fill the patient's need for love and affection, spending hours listening to the patient and providing physical contact. The family of the patient is seen as part of the treatment program.

Some patients want every possible technique used to prolong their lives; others do not.

The problem is that people with a terminal disease frequently do not make their wishes known while they are still capable of exercising judgment. And so when they are unconscious or mentally incapacitated, physicians and family must decide on how long to prolong life in the absence of any instructions. In a recent study (Uhlmann, Pearlman, and Cain, 1988), researchers tried to find out how accurate physicans and spouses were at predicting a patient's wishes. The patients were older than 65, had at least one degenerative disease, and all were expected by their physicians to live for at least six months. The physicians predicted their patients' preferences for cardiopulmonary resuscitation and resuscitation plus the use of a mechanical respirator at no better than chance. They also tended to *underestimate* their patients' wish to live with the aid of CPR and ventilators. The spouses were better at predicting the patients' wishes, but did only modestly better than chance. However, spouses tended to *overestimate* the patients' wish to live with the aid of medical technology.

Fears that medical technology will doom them to an unacceptable quality of life may be responsible for the recent increase in suicide among older adults, as we will see in Chapter 6. Some people have tried to prevent an unwanted extension of life in the event of terminal illness by setting forth their desires concerning the nature and extent of treatment. Such documents are known as **living wills,** and they are valid in some states (Figure 5.3). Other states do not recognize living wills but do accept health proxies, which are durable powers of attorney that allow a specified person to make health care decisions concerning the institution, withholding, or cessation of medical treatment of all kinds. The lack of such documents can lead hospitals to refuse to remove life support from people who are in a permanent vegetative state.

The Stages of Death

Whether patients' attitudes toward death go through a predictable series of stages in the death trajectory is uncertain. After interviewing more than 200 dying patients, Elisabeth Kübler–Ross (1969) proposed a five-stage theory of dying that has become widely known. The initial stage, which occurs when the patient first discovers that death is certain, is *denial and isolation,* in which the person simply refuses to believe that death is inevitable. Denial is soon followed by *anger and resentment,* when the patient envies healthy people and directs anger randomly—at the doctor, the nurse, the family. The third stage consists of *bargaining,* when the patient tries to postpone death by striking a bargain with God or the physician. Then the fourth stage, *depression,* takes over, when the patient prepares for the loss of everything he or she loves. If the patient has had enough time to work through the preceding stages, he or she enters the final stage of *acceptance.* Only now can the patient contemplate the end calmly and perhaps with quiet expectation.

Popular as this portrayal of dying has become, research has generally failed to support it. Investigators find that although the patients they study may exhibit any of the attitudes described by Kübler–Ross, they do not go through the stages in any particular order and may never enter some of the stages (Kastenbaum, 1985; Shneidman, 1980). Another problem with the theory is that it makes no allowance for individual differences that are likely to affect the dying trajectory (disease, gender, ethnicity, personality, developmental level, age, or immediate situation) (Kastenbaum, 1981). Finally, the theory is based on observations in industrialized society. It is unlikely that a dying person in the 13th century, for example, who was accustomed to seeing death almost daily and who had a deep religious faith, would feel the same denial and anger that may be common today.

LIVING WILL

I, _____, being of sound mind, make this statement as a directive to be followed if I become permanently unable to participate in decisions regarding my medical care. These instructions reflect my firm and settled commitment to decline medical treatment under the circumstances indicated below:

I direct my attending physician to withhold or withdraw treatment that serves only to prolong the process of my dying, if I should be in an *incurable or irreversible mental or physical condition with no reasonable expectation of recovery.*

These instructions apply if I am (a) *in a terminal condition;* (b) *permanently unconscious;* or (c) *if I am conscious but have irreversible brain damage and will never regain the ability to make decisions and express my wishes.*

I direct that treatment be limited to measures to keep me comfortable and to relieve pain, including any pain that might occur by withholding or withdrawing treatment.

While I understand that I am not legally required to be specific about future treatments, *if I am in the condition(s) described above I feel especially strongly about the following forms of treatment:*

I do not want cardiac resuscitation.
I do not want mechanical respiration.
I do not want tube feeding.
I do not want antibiotics.

I do want maximum pain relief.

Other directions (insert personal instructions): _____

_____

_____

These directions express my legal right to refuse treatment under the law of New York. I intend my instructions to be carried out, unless I have rescinded them in a new writing or by clearly indicating that I have changed my mind.

Signed: _____ Date: _____

Witness: _____

Witness: _____

Figure 5.3 Source: Society for the Right to Die, New York.

Chronic illness does not inevitably lead to an unwanted prolongation of life, but most of us still want to avoid the physical and mental degeneration that characterizes the diseases of secondary aging. Much of this degeneration depends on life-style, which means that for most of us the ability to reduce a good deal of secondary aging is within our grasp.

LIFE-STYLE AND HEALTH

The fewer chronic diseases we have in old age, the more rewarding the final phase of life will be. None of us wants to end our lives on medical support. Nor do we want to spend the last years confined to a bed or a wheelchair, depending on the care of relatives or paid attendants. Ideally, we would end like the famous ''one-horse shay'' in the poem by Oliver Wendell Holmes (1858), which ran smoothly for a hundred years, then simply collapsed when all its parts wore out at the same time.

If such a thing happened, there might be no apparent cause of death. At Case Western University, pathologist Robert Kohn conducted autopsies on 200 adults who died after the age of 85. In 26 percent of the cases, he could find no generally accepted cause of death (Bishop, 1983). There was no indication that atherosclerosis, heart disease, pneumonia, infection, accident, or any of the other customary killers had been responsible. Kohn concluded that the cause of death was ''aging itself.'' It has been suggested that such a ''natural'' death occurs when the body's ability to respond to any sort of stress has deteriorated so far that it cannot cope with even a slight disruption (Siegler and Costa, 1985).

The steady increase in life expectancy means that more and more of us will reach the hundred-year mark and that most of us will live longer than our parents and grandparents did. The evidence we have seen thus far shows that the disabilities of old age are not inevitable and not the result of normal aging.

The influence of life-long health habits on the quality and length of life has been amply demonstrated. As many as half of all premature deaths in the United States may be due to unhealthy life-styles (Carlson, 1986). Among the aspects of a person's life-style that have strong effects on health are nutrition, alcohol consumption, smoking, and exercise. The degree of stress in each person's life and the quality of the environment also affect health. Some of these relationships have appeared in longitudinal studies.

In the Intergenerational Studies (Eichorn et al., 1981), seven of the women and six of the men, all aged 34, were considered at high risk for cardiovascular disease because of such factors as parental deaths from the disease; overweight; and levels of cholesterol, triglycerides (fatty molecules associated with the development of atherosclerosis), and other lipids. By the time they were 50, five of the women and five of the men had developed hypertension, whereas none of the women and only one of the men in the low-risk category had either increased blood pressure or signs of arteriosclerosis. Personality was also important. Members of the study who were calm and not easily aroused or irritated as adolescents tended to have good health in middle age. Apparently, they were less susceptible to stress than other members of the study.

In the Duke Longitudinal Study of normal aging (Palmore, 1974), the healthiest members were nonsmokers of normal weight who exercised frequently. But the single best predictor of health was exercise. Compared with those who got little exercise, older adults who exercised a great deal were less likely to become ill or to die prematurely.

Functional health is linked with patterns of aging, and we know that secondary aging can be hastened—or perhaps initiated—by health habits. Habits established early in life provide the most benefit, but exchanging bad habits for good ones—even late in life—is likely to increase both the quantity and quality of our later years. If we take the responsibility for our own health and have the knowledge we need to maintain it, we are likely to have many additional disease-free years.

Most people have heard about the factors that have major effects on health, but many do not know that some of them are **synergistic.** When factors are synergistic, the effect of exposure to some combinations can damage health far more than the sum of each factor's probable harm. For example, a person who works with asbestos is 30 times more likely to develop lung cancer than a person who has no extraordinary exposure to the substance. A smoker is 10 times more likely to develop lung cancer than a nonsmoker. But a person who smokes *and* works with asbestos is 90 times more likely to develop the disease than people who neither smoke nor work with asbestos (U.S. Public Health Service, 1979).

THE EFFECT OF COHORT-RELATED FACTORS ON HEALTH

Social factors also affect the speed of secondary aging, with sanitation, nutrition, medical, and drug practices having strong influences on the quality of health. Since these aspects of life may change from one cohort to the next, health and disease is in good part the product of cohort-related factors.

When researchers began looking at the second generation in the Framingham Heart Study, they discovered significant cohort differences in risk factors for cardiovascular disease. As a group, children of the original subjects had lower blood pressure and lower levels of cholesterol in their blood and smoked fewer cigarettes than their parents had at approximately the same age (Riley and Bond, 1981). Because these three measures are major risk factors in the development of cardiovascular disease, it would seem likely that over their lifetimes, the children's cohort will show less heart disease than their parents.

Nowhere have health changes been more dramatic than in the drop in mortality from cardiovascular disease. Over the last few decades, deaths have declined by more than 30 percent—with the largest drop taking place during the 1970s (Levy and Moskowitz, 1982) (see Figure 5.4). Clearly, some environmental factor (or factors) has affected the development of cardiovascular disease or at least decreased its severity. The decline began before antihypertensive medications were introduced and before many people developed interest in healthy life-styles. Although improved medical services, introduction of coronary care units in the early 1960s, and improved control of high blood pressure have contributed to the decline, they cannot explain its magnitude. Many researchers have concluded that the combination of changes in life-style (decreased smoking, increased exercise, and changed eating habits) may be primarily responsible (Avorn, 1986). The decline is expected to continue well into the next century, as results from the Framingham study suggest.

Other statistics indicate a gray cloud behind the silver lining. Between 1966 and 1976, a pattern of increase in major diseases and disabilities from those diseases began to appear in all age groups. The trend was especially noticeable among 45 to 65 year olds. More people were unable to carry out their normal activities, activity was restricted for more days each year, and more chronic diseases were found (Colvez and Blanchet, 1981). Whether

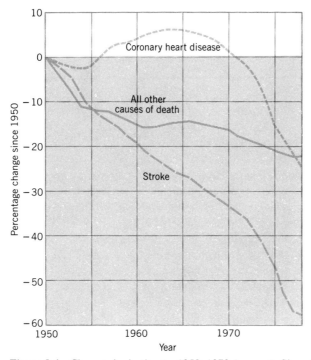

Figure 5.4 Changes in death rate, 1950–1978 (percent). Since 1950, the death rate from heart disease and stroke has dropped sharply among adults between the ages of 35 and 74. *Source:* Levy and Moskowitz, 1982, p. 123.

this pattern will continue for future cohorts is unknown, but the proportion of children with severe chronic impairments has more than doubled, apparently because improvements in medical care allows many to live who formerly would have died in infancy or early childhood (Brody, 1989).

NUTRITION AND HEALTH

Good nutrition contributes to health and resistance to disease. Just how much changing our diet would retard secondary aging is uncertain because we are only beginning to understand the subtleties of nutritional influence on health, behavior, and well-being. However, some studies have suggested that the rate of aging is affected by long-term food habits and that certain dietary patterns are associated with the diseases of secondary aging. As we saw in Chapter 3, research in a number of species indicates that restriction of calories without malnutrition—lowering calorie intake sharply while maintaining recommended levels of proteins, vitamins, and minerals—seems to retard the development of many diseases as well as to slow aging in various body systems (Weindruch and Walford, 1988).

Disease and the Typical Diet

The American diet of the 1980s, high in fat and low in fiber, has been linked with heart disease, hypertension, diabetes, and various forms of cancer. The typical diet contains between 450 to 600 milligrams of cholesterol per day, as compared with the recommended level of 300 milligrams (Cooper, 1988). That is why the surgeon general has called saturated fat, which is a major source of dietary cholesterol, our number one dietary problem (Byrne, 1988). Simple cholesterol levels tell only part of the story. Cholesterol, which is vital to cell function, comes in two major varieties: ''good'' cholesterol, or **high-density lipoproteins (HDL),** moves cholesterol along to the liver, where it is removed from the bloodstream and digested; and ''bad'' cholesterol, or **low-density lipoproteins (LDL),** collects in plaques and clogs the arteries. The key to avoiding cardiovascular disease is to maintain the balance of good and bad cholesterol within the body.

In an attempt to reduce the incidence of cardiovascular disease, the American Heart Association has recommended a ''prudent'' diet in which no more than 30 percent of the calories come from fat—a reduction from the 37 percent in today's typical diet (Byrne, 1988). Such a change could have widespread effects. Evidence from a longitudinal study of nearly 4000 middle-aged men with blood cholesterol levels in the upper 5 percent of the population indicates that reducing blood cholesterol levels lowers the incidence of heart attack and the risk of death from heart disease (Kolata, 1984). Among these men, for every point that cholesterol level fell, the overall risk of heart disease dropped by 2 percent (Monmaney, 1988). As yet no one has confirmed this connection for women or for older adults of either sex (who have 75 percent of all heart attacks). Nor do we know whether lowering cholesterol drastically has other effects on health, a fact that has led some researchers to be cautious about manipulating cholesterol levels with drugs among the elderly (Kolata, 1989). Cholesterol has also been implicated in the development of some cancers. Researchers have discovered that a gene responsible for the development of cancer in the pancreas, colon, and rectum cannot trigger the disease without the presence of a substance that plays a crucial role in the development of cholesterol (Schafer et al., 1989).

Diets low in fiber (especially the type found in dried beans and natural cereals) have been connected with disease in a number of ways (Burkitt, 1978). Several studies have shown that adding fiber to the diet can reduce overall cholesterol and triglyceride levels (e.g., Anderson et al., 1984; Brown and Karmally, 1985). In the Baltimore Longitudinal Study, men whose regular diets contained the most fiber had lower blood pressure (both systolic and diastolic), lower triglyceride levels, and lower fasting glucose levels than men whose diets were low in fiber (Hallfrisch et al., 1988). Such evidence has led the National Cancer Institute to recommend that Americans double their fiber intake—from 15 to 30 grams each day (Byrne, 1988).

The American taste for salty foods, such as potato chips and salted nuts, combined with the heavy use of salt in processed foods and the prevalent habit of salting food again at the table, worries many physicians. The body requires about 220 milligrams of sodium each day, but most Americans consume 10 to 24 grams of salt (which supplies 4000 to 9600 milligrams of sodium). It has been recommended that salt intake be reduced to less than 2 grams per day. Although there is undoubtedly a hereditary component to hypertension, excess salt consumption seems to be connected with its development. The disease is high in cultures where the customary consumption of salt is 4 grams or more per day (Kannel, 1985).

Obesity, another major dietary problem, has been associated with hypertension, heart disease, stroke, diabetes, and gallbladder disease. The link with cardiovascular disease comes about in part because obesity contributes to the causes of atherosclerosis: people whose body mass has a relatively greater proportion of fat tend to have high blood levels of LDLs and triglycerides (Cooper, 1988). Obesity is also associated with an increase in the body's own production of cholesterol (Bierman, 1985). Hypertension is common among obese people, and blood pressure tends to rise and fall as people gain and lose weight (Kannel, 1985). Obesity is also associated with resistance to insulin in muscle and fat tissue, believed to be a cause of maturity-onset diabetes. As we saw earlier, this kind of diabetes often disappears when people reach their normal weight. In fact, weight loss can improve all these conditions.

Among middle-aged adults, income is associated with obesity, but in a different way for men and women. Thirty-five percent of women and 5 percent of men with incomes below the poverty level are obese. As incomes rise, fewer women (29 percent) but more men (13 percent) are obese (U.S. Public Health Service, 1979). Although the change in body composition that accompanies aging alters the body's fat–muscle ratio, some researchers believe that the "inexorable" increase in obesity among the young-old can be prevented (Bierman, 1985).

Nutrition and Aging

Nutritional needs do not change radically with age, but the amount of various elements in the diet may need to be altered. On the average, the basal metabolic rate declines 5 percent every decade between the ages of 55 and 75 and 7 percent every decade after that time (Spence, 1989). Older Americans also tend to be less active than younger cohorts, and reduced activity may be at least partly responsible for resetting metabolism at a lower rate. When the physical activity of 76 older women was monitored, they ranged from sedentary to very sedentary in their life style. Their average activity level was one-third that of college students (LaPorte et al., 1983). As a result of lessened activity, older adults need fewer calories per pound of body weight than younger people. However, there are wide differences in individual activity, and older people use more energy than the young in performing the same physical task (Hickey, 1980). Many older people respond to slackening activity by eating less, so that calorie consumption generally declines with age. Among men in the Baltimore Longitudinal Study, the drop in calories was caused primarily by a drop in dietary fat (Elahi et al., 1983).

The actual need of older adults for specific nutrients has not been established, and in some cases, because of declines in digestive secretions, enzyme activity, or the absorption of nutrients from the intestine, older adults may need more—not less—of the same vitamin or mineral than they once did (Guigoz and Munro, 1985). For example, specialists in geriatric nutrition have recently recommended that the calcium intake for older adults be raised from 800 to 1500 mg per day. The most frequent dietary deficiencies found among older men and women are calcium, iron, magnesium, and vitamins A, C, and the B vitamins thiamine, niacin, and folic acid. Those whose diets are deficient in vitamins A, C, and niacin apparently run the greatest risk; studies in California have found excess deaths among such people over a three-year period (Guigoz and Munro, 1985). Dietary deficiencies may also lead to false diagnosis of permanent mental deterioration, because they can produce mental confusion, learning difficulties, and depression.

Dietary deficiencies in older adults are not usually the result of nutritional ignorance. Reduced income, lack of mobility, stress, attitudes, and loneliness can all affect the purchase, preparation, and consumption of food. Those with incomes below the poverty level cannot buy the right foods. Those who have the money but cannot get to the market have difficulty buying them. And those who are worried, depressed, lonely, anxious, or low in self-esteem have little appetite. Compared with those who live with other people, older people who live alone have a less adequate and less varied diet, eat fewer foods that require preparation, and are more likely to skip the evening meal (Davis and Randall, 1983). It would appear that older people who retain social ties, whether with spouse, family, or friends, are most likely to maintain an adequate diet throughout life.

SMOKING

The elimination of cigarette smoking would do more to improve American health than any other single step. Approximately 390,000 deaths each year are associated with tobacco, and another 10 million Americans have chronic diseases that were caused by smoking.

Cigarette smoking has been directly implicated in cancer. Besides having ten times as much lung cancer as nonsmokers, smokers have from three to five times as much cancer of the mouth and tongue, and more than twice as much bladder cancer (U.S. Public Health Service, 1979). Twenty percent of all cancer deaths are directly caused by smoking, and smoking plays a role in another 33 percent. Nine people out of every ten who develop lung cancer are dead within five years, and smoking is directly responsible for 75 percent of all lung cancer.

It generally takes about 20 years for lung cancer to develop, which means that deaths from lung cancer continue to rise even as the general rate of smoking has declined. Three times as many men as women die from lung cancer, but since the proportion of women who smoke has risen, so, too, has their rate of lung cancer. Lung cancer now causes more deaths among women than any other form of the disease. Between 1979 and 1986, cancer mortality rose 7 percent among men and 44 percent among women (*Reporter Dispatch,* 1989b).

The presence of tar, a proved carcinogen, in cigarettes is well known. Not as widely known is the fact that cigarettes contain another carcinogen—nitrosamines—as well as radioactive elements. Cigarette smoking can expose the smoker to 40 times the recommended maximum annual exposure to radiation (Brody, 1982).

Cigarette smoking is also directly implicated in heart disease. Twice as many smokers as nonsmokers die of heart disease. The more cigarettes smoked, the greater the risk; when

Smoking, which is responsible for nearly 400,000 deaths each year, is the major threat to health in the United States.

smoking exceeds a pack a day, the smoker is three, not two, times as likely to have a heart attack (U.S. Public Health Service, 1979). When tobacco smoke is drawn into the lungs, carbon monoxide enters the blood. The carbon monoxide replaces up to 12 percent of the oxygen in the red blood cells, cutting down the supply of oxygen to the heart and brain (Brody, 1982). The concentration of carbon monoxide in the blood may be responsible for the decrease in protective HDLs, heightened blood pressure, and increase of atherosclerosis among smokers. As nicotine in the blood also increases the heart's demand for oxygen, exercise may be followed by the crushing pain of angina, which develops when the heart muscle is starved for oxygen (Wantz and Gay, 1981).

The health toll does not stop there. Smokers are likely to have other problems with their lungs besides cancer. Their lung capacity is reduced, and their lungs are susceptible to various microorganisms and debris. About 70 percent of the cases of emphysema and chronic bronchitis are caused by smoking. Smokers are also likely to develop peptic ulcers, and when they do, they are more likely than nonsmokers to die from them. Smoking also doubles the incidence of **cataracts,** a condition in which the lens of the eye becomes opaque, or clouded, interfering with the passage of light through it. Researchers at Johns Hopkins University who discovered the link do not believe that cataracts are caused by contact with airborne smoke (*New York Times,* 1989b). They speculate that the damage develops when substances inhaled with the smoke are carried internally to the eyes.

Women smokers run additional risks. Those who take contraceptive pills for at least five years run an increased risk of heart attack until menopause—even if they stop taking the pill (Layde, Ory, and Schlesselman, 1982). Smoking also decreases their fertility by 25 percent, either by decreasing levels of certain hormones or by altering the timing of the ovum's passage down the Fallopian tubes to the uterus (Seligmann, 1985). As a result, women smokers take longer than nonsmokers to conceive. Pregnant women who continue to smoke are ten times as likely to miscarry as nonsmokers, have more stillbirths, and their babies who live generally have a low birth weight and run an increased risk of respiratory problems and death.

Given the lengthy list of gloomy statistics, long-time smokers may see little point in giving up cigarettes. But once a smoker stops, his or her health gradually returns to normal (Table 5.2). Within 7 years, the risk of bladder cancer has dropped to normal, and within 10 to 15 years, the added risk of other cancers has disappeared. Within 10 years, the added risk of coronary heart disease is also gone (Brody, 1982).

Table 5.2 **SMOKING AND CANCER**

Type of Cancer	Increased Risk	Period of Increased Risk After Quitting
Lung	10 times	10–15 years
Larynx	3–18 times	10 years
Mouth	3–10 times	10–15 years
Esophagus	2–9 times	Uncertain
Bladder	7–10 times	7 years
Pancreas	2–5 times	Uncertain

Source: Information from Brody, 1982.

THE TWO-EDGED EFFECTS OF ALCOHOL

Perhaps because of its legality and the fact that, in small amounts, it relieves anxiety and creates temporary euphoria, alcohol is our favorite drug. Alcohol works by depressing the central nervous system, slowing the rate at which neurons fire. Small amounts of the drug make people feel euphoric, but the euphoria is accompanied by slowed reaction time, decreased alertness, and impaired motor coordination. As levels of alcohol in the blood increase, people's speech begins to slur, they become unsteady, and they finally lapse into unconsciousness. As people age, their tolerance for alcohol is reduced. They metabolize the drug more slowly, and it may cause greater changes in brain chemistry and be more toxic than when they were younger (Zarit, 1980). Its effect on their behavior thus seems intensified, and it takes them longer to recover from a drinking spree. The long-term effects of alcohol vary, depending on the amount consumed.

Used in moderation, however, alcohol may be beneficial. It may protect against myocardial infarction, for example. At least 20 different studies have suggested that people who have one or two drinks a day are less likely to have heart attacks than nondrinkers (Bennett, 1988). It seems that small amounts of alcohol increase blood levels of HDL, the high-density cholesterol that helps rid the body of ''bad'' cholesterol. However, the form of HDL that is stimulated by small doses of alcohol is an early form of HDL and researchers have yet to confirm the transformation of this precursor into the late form that sweeps cholesterol from the blood. At least one study has also indicated that people who have no more than two drinks a day have lower blood pressure than nondrinkers or drinkers who exceed the two-drink limit (Darby, 1978). Researchers are unwilling to recommend that nondrinkers start drinking, but many have concluded that the evidence is strong enough to make it unnecessary to take away alcohol from the person who is striving for a healthy life-style but already has one drink each day (Liebman, 1984).

If the one- or two-drink a day person is a pregnant woman, however, researchers are virtually unanimous in urging her to give up alcohol. Four-year-old children of women who averaged two drinks a day during their pregnancy were found to have slow reaction times and difficulty paying attention (Streissguth et al., 1984). Even women who drink as sparingly as five drinks per week give birth to sluggish babies who have trouble adjusting to stimuli (Streissguth, Barr, and Martin, 1983).

The effects of heavy social drinking appear to be uniformly negative. Pregnant women who are heavy social drinkers have three times as many stillbirths as light drinkers, and their babies show clear effects of alcohol. They suck weakly, respond poorly, have abnormal heart rates, and their birthweights are below average. As for adults, heavy social drinking sends blood pressure up. In fact, researchers recommend that people with a family history of hypertension avoid excessive alcohol (Kannel, 1985). Heavy social drinkers also have higher rates of cancer than nondrinkers or light drinkers, and the synergy between alcohol and smoking quadruples the risk of cancer of the mouth and pharynx—even among those who smoke less than one pack of cigarettes per day (Liebman, 1984).

Americans seem to be getting the message of moderation. Alcohol consumption in the United States has been declining since 1980. By 1987 beer drinking had dropped 7 percent, wine drinking had fallen 14 percent, and hard liquor consumption was down 23 percent (Hall, 1989). The change seems related to new sensitivity to the dangers of alcohol and less tolerance of drunkenness and of alcohol in the workplace and on the highways. Cohort effects also seem to be at work in changing the pattern and levels of alcohol use. Older people, for example, consume the most whiskey, and as they die off, the baby-boomers who replace them prefer wine, beer, vodka, fruit juice, and soft drinks.

Despite the general decline in alcohol consumption, an increase in drinking among the elderly has been predicted. The present elderly have always been light drinkers, but cohorts now moving into late adulthood have always had a higher rate of alcohol consumption (Alexander and Duff, 1988).

EXERCISE

When the United States became a technological society, Americans gradually adopted a sedentary life-style. As technological advances decreased the amount of energy expended in physical labor, automobiles cut down opportunities and inclinations to walk. At the same time, the growing popularity of professional sports encouraged Americans to watch sporting events instead of participating in them.

Yet regular exercise appears to be a foe of the aging process. As we saw in Chapter 3, the cardiovascular and respiratory systems undergo characteristic changes with age. In addition, muscle strength and joint flexibility decline. We assume that these are the result of natural aging, but older Americans lead such sedentary lives that few older people who participate in studies have activity levels high enough to make a comparison of their performance with young adults meaningful (deVries, 1983).

Declining activity, not aging, may be responsible for a good deal of the "natural" deterioration of body systems. Inactivity causes muscles to shrink and reduces muscular en-

A lack of physical activity may be responsible for much of the "deterioration" that accompanies old age in many people.

durance. Researchers (Saltin et al., 1968) have found that putting young, well-conditioned men to bed for three weeks decreases their cardiac output by 26 percent, their maximum breathing capacity by 30 percent, and their oxygen consumption by 30 percent. Solely from disuse, their respiratory and circulatory systems in effect temporarily "age" nearly 30 years in three weeks.

Regardless of age, people who have become inactive generally find that exercise improves their mental health. Men and women who exercise regularly say they feel better, have more energy, and require less sleep. Many find their self-esteem improved, their anxiety decreased, and mild depression lifted. They feel more self-reliant (U.S. Public Health Service, 1979). An immediate psychological benefit of exercise appeared when researchers tested exercise against tranquilizers and a harmless sugar pill with ten elderly men who complained of high levels of anxiety. Walking for 15 minutes at a moderate rate was more effective than a dose of meprobamate (better known as Miltown or Equanil) in relieving anxiety, and the relief was apparent in electrical measures of muscle tension. The effect lasted about an hour.

The cardiovascular benefits of exercise showed clearly in a study that followed nearly 17,000 Harvard alumni for ten years (Paffenbarger et al., 1986). Those who regularly expended at least 3000 calories a week on nonvigorous activities reduced their risk of heart attack by 35 percent (compared with sedentary alumni), while those who spent the same number of calories on vigorous activities (exercise that raised the heart rate and worked up a sweat) reduced their risk of heart attack by 50 percent. The benefits were not limited to alumni who had been college athletes. In fact, cardiovascular disease was more prevalent among athletes who lived sedentary lives after graduation than among nonathletes who began exercising after college.

When researchers studied fitness directly, measuring performance on the treadmill instead of relying on people's reports of exercise, it became clear that exercise reduces death from cancer as well as cardiovascular disease. In an eight-year study of 13,000 adults, death rates were tied closely to heart and respiratory fitness, with mortality dropping as fitness rose (Blair et al., 1989) (Figure 5.5). Yet even modest exercise—the equivalent of a half hour's brisk walk five times a week—cut death rates in half compared with unfit, sedentary adults. The benefits of exercise remained after researchers corrected for such factors as age, smoking, cholesterol level, blood pressure, blood sugar levels, and family history of cardiovascular disease.

The protection provided by exercise appears to be the result of increased respiratory endurance, decreased triglyceride and LDL levels, increased levels of protective HDLs, increased red blood cells and blood volume, improvement in the condition of blood vessels in the heart, and better circulation (Cooper, 1988; Wantz and Gay, 1981). Regular exercise can even halt the course of disease. Six months of regular exercise reduced blood pressure significantly in adults with hypertension (Boyer and Kasch, 1970). In other cases, exercise reduced the pain of angina, allowing patients who were recovering from heart attacks to increase their activity (U.S. Public Health Service, 1979). Exercise for heart patients is probably most beneficial as part of a complete health program that includes nutrition and stress reduction, as described in the box, "Taking Care of Health."

The cardiovascular benefits of exercise may also prevent or postpone the cognitive slowing that has been associated with aging. The difference is already apparent toward the end of middle adulthood. Women in their late forties and fifties who regularly ran at least 30 minutes a day reacted faster to a warning stimulus (by taking their foot off the accelerator)

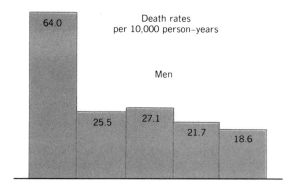

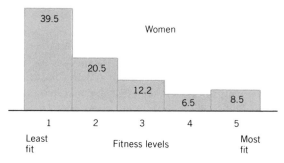

Figure 5.5   Physical fitness and survival. As heart and respiratory fitness increases, survival rises, but even moderate exercise (Level 2) has a dramatic effect on death rates. *Source:* Blair et al., 1989, pp. 2395–2401.

and moved more quickly to the brake pedal than working women who did not exercise (Baylor and Spirduso, 1988). The disparity continues throughout life. Women in their late sixties who had exercised regularly for at least ten years reacted as rapidly as college students (Rikli and Busch, 1986). Among adults between the ages of 55 and 88, those who exercised vigorously and regularly (more than five hours per week) had faster reaction times, better working memory, and reasoned more accurately than those who were sedentary (Clarkson-Smith and Hartley, 1989).

Exercise also slows—or prevents—the development of osteoporosis. As we saw in Chapter 4, women in old age who exercised regularly for several years had an increase in bone density at a time when sedentary women's bone density was declining (Buskirk, 1985). This increase in bone density may explain why regular exercise—walking at least one mile three times a week—seems to protect older adults from fractures (Sorock et al., 1988). The protective effect of exercise was strongest in men who exercised both before and after they retired, but women who exercised before retirement and then slacked off had no more fractures than women who continued their exercise program. The researchers suggest that, in the case of women, exercise before and/or during menopause may be extremely important in stimulating bone growth.

It has been estimated that exercise can add at least 15 years to the life of an inactive 70 year old (Burrus–Bammel and Bammel, 1985). There are no age limits on the beneficial

♦ *Adulthood in Today's World*

TAKING CHARGE OF HEALTH

Four years ago, Richard Szpak's life changed overnight. At 55, he was manager for a company that supplied pipe line used in the oil-drilling industry. He worked 12 hours a day, 6 days a week, and never let up. As he tells it, "I was a hard-charging guy. Always had to be first. It was blow the horn and get out of the way because I'm coming through" (Carlson, 1986, p. 36). His appetite was as fierce as his drive to work: he consumed rich foods in vast quantities. He weighed 185 pounds, about 25 pounds too much for his 5 foot, 8 inch frame. His blood pressure was high (165/103). Instead of hovering at the recommended level of 200 mg, his cholesterol had climbed to a dangerous level (330 mg) that increased his risk of myocardial infarction fivefold.

The day of reckoning came, and Richard Szpak had a severe myocardial infarction. While he was in the hospital, his nurse persuaded him to enroll at the Richardson Institute for Preventive Medicine, and that made all the difference. At the institute he learned about nutrition, stress management, and exercise. He took part in the exercise program: 45 minutes a day, three days a week. He changed his eating habits, reducing or eliminating foods highest in cholesterol (eggs, organ meats, most cheeses) and cutting back sharply on foods rich in saturated fat (butter, bacon, beef, and whole milk). He began eating more vegetables, switched to polyunsaturated fats (such as safflower, corn, soybean, and sesame oil). He made sure that his meals included plenty of fiber. Within a year, Szpak had dropped 20 pounds, controlled his blood pressure, and lowered his total cholesterol level while raising the proportion of HDLs.

At 59, Richard Szpak sees himself as a new man. He has been back at his old job for several years, but no longer feels the same pressures. "I now eat less and exercise more," he says. "I've even learned how to relax. Everything considered, I'm in better shape today than I was 10 or 12 years ago" (Carlson, 1986, p. 38).

Szpak's story is typical of that of an increasing number of Americans who are beginning to take responsibility for their health. A recent survey of more than one thousand chief executive officers disclosed that 64 percent of them exercise regularly, more than 90 percent are careful about their diet, 81 percent have had a complete physical examination within the past two years, and 65 percent know their blood pressure (Rippe, 1989). Perhaps the CEOs' new concern for health explains why so many corporations, from L. L. Bean and Bonne Bell to Safeway and AT&T, have inaugurated "wellness" programs. At Johnson & Johnson, for example, the Live for Life program has been underway since 1978 (Roberts and Harris, 1989). It begins with health screening, followed by eight-week courses aimed at any weak spots that are discovered. There are lunch-hour seminars on related topics, and fitness facilities are available. Overall, J&J employees have doubled their strenuous physical activity and lowered their blood pressure, weight, and stress levels. Nearly one-quarter of the smokers have given up the habit. The program has helped the corporation as well as the employees. During the first five years, absenteeism dropped 18 percent in the J&J companies where the program was available, and hospital costs at these companies increased only one-third as much as in J&J companies that had not instituted the program.

effects of exercise and few limits on the kind of exercise that is helpful. At 89, Lucille Thompson of Danville, Illinois, earned a black belt in Korean karate. At 75, Helen Zech-meister began lifting weights, and at the age of 78 she held the world records in her age group for the squat lift, dead lift, and bench press. She jogs two miles a day, swims several times a week, and does stretching exercises (*AARP News Bulletin,* 1983a). Researchers at Tufts University have discovered that weight-lifting by older people seems to alter the aging process (Stockton, 1988). After eight weeks of knee extensions on a Universal weight-training machine, young-old adults increased their strength by almost 200 percent and their muscle mass by 15 percent. Old-old adults, some as old as 96, increased their strength 180 percent and their muscle mass about 12 percent. Their mobility also improved; they found it easier to get up from a chair, for example, and they walked more rapidly and surely.

In order to produce such effects on an aging body, an older man or woman must engage in a regular exercise program that focuses on the rhythmic activities of large muscle masses, such as walking briskly, jogging, running, or swimming. The conditioning routine is similar to that used by younger people, but it must be initiated slowly and carefully (Buskirk, 1985). Whatever exercise is chosen must raise the heart rate to a predetermined level based on the person's age and present heart condition. In practical terms, this prescription means that 70-year-old men of average physical fitness need to raise their heart rate above 95 beats per minute and that well-conditioned men in the same age bracket need to raise their heart rate to above 103 (deVries, 1983). Exercises that focus on small muscle masses or isometric muscle exercises that use high levels of muscle contractions without any pauses for relaxation are undesirable and do not have the same beneficial effects.

The amount of exercise people engage in is linked to age, sex, and education. All groups become less active as they grow older. Women become inactive earlier than men, and people with lower levels of education become inactive earlier than college graduates (Ostrow, 1980). Only about one-third of older adults exercise regularly, and many of the rest believe that they have no need to exercise, or even that exercise is harmful. Their attitudes probably reflect stereotypes formed in childhood about appropriate behavior and levels of activity among the old. As more and more models of vigorously active old people appear, older men and women may change their attitudes. One source of active models is the National Senior Olympics, a biennial event intended to promote fitness and health among older adults. In 1989, 3500 women and men between the ages of 55 and 91 gathered in St. Louis to compete in 14 sports, from archery to volleyball. Each one, from 64-year-old Dominican nun Mary Martin Weaver to 82-year-old sprinter George Richards, had qualified in local competitions. One senior athlete, 64-year-old Tony Quinci, was so eager to participate that he pedaled his bicycle from Roswell, New Mexico, to St. Louis, a distance of 1403 miles, to compete (Mark, 1989). It took him 20 days to complete the trip and he failed to win the gold, but Quinci and his fellow competitors may have given us a glimpse of aging in the twenty-first century.

STRESS AND COPING

Being a nonsmoker who eats carefully and exercises vigorously lays a solid basis for a long and healthy life, but health—either physical or mental—is also affected by other aspects of living. Development takes place within a social context, and features of the environment continually affect us. The way we react to events and situations may increase or decrease our chances of avoiding the diseases of secondary aging.

STRESS

Stress can have a detrimental effect on physical and mental health. It can accelerate the aging process, it can lead to the development of physical disease or mental disorder, and it can impair a person's ability to respond to new challenges (Eisdorfer and Wilkie, 1977). **Stress** is an ambiguous term that covers any disruptive physiological and psychological responses to unpleasant or threatening stimuli. Such a stimulus, known as a **stressor,** can be located in the outside world or within the individual, and it can be either physical or psychological. Stressors can threaten our lives and our status, signal some loss, or attack our belief systems (Renner and Birren, 1980). Stressors can be as specific as the death of a parent or impending surgery, as chronic as an unhappy marriage or competition at work, or as elusive as the piling up of daily hassles—misplacing things, running out of money before payday, being unable to stick to a diet, not finding a taxi on a rainy night, or worrying about the future.

Stress and Health

Whether a potentially stressful situation affects health depends less on the nature of the situation itself than on how we perceive it and whether we feel we have the ability and resources to cope with it. If we perceive it as threatening, decide that nothing we can do will alleviate the situation, and react in nonadaptive ways, the effects can be major. Following a highly stressful event, people eat less and lose weight, their immune response wavers (levels of T and B cells drop), the adrenal glands pour steroids into the bloodstream, and they are pervaded by feelings of distress (Willis et al., 1987). Stressful events have been connected with triggering diabetes in individuals who were predisposed to the disease and with exacerbating existing cases of diabetes (Renner and Birren, 1980). Stress has been connected with heart attacks, hypertension, respiratory disease, ulcers, and other disorders of the gastrointestinal tract, anxiety, paranoia, mental deterioration, and depression.

Research with animals suggests that inescapable and uncontrollable stress may lead to a condition known as **learned helplessness,** in which a person simply stops trying to cope with a stressful situation. When animals develop learned helplessness, they quickly succumb to disease. In one study (Visintainer, Volpicelli, and Seligman, 1982), rats were injected with cancer cells and then given electric shock. Some of the rats could escape the shock by pressing a bar; others could neither stop the shock nor get away from it. Twice as many of the helpless rats developed tumors as did the rats who could turn off the shock or the rats in a control group who were injected with cancer cells but received no shock. Later research with animals indicates that inescapable stress weakens the immune system, paving the way for cancer and other diseases to develop (Laudenslager et al., 1983).

The Importance of Control

Not everyone who encounters intensive stress becomes helpless. Whether learned helplessness develops depends on how people perceive the stressful situation. An important factor is whether they see themselves as having control over their lives (Rodin, 1986). Control makes life seem more predictable, and to the extent that events can be predicted, their power to make us feel helpless is diminished. The sense of control apparently reduces the effects of stress by minimizing the autonomic nervous system's reactions to the event and the adrenal glands' production of steroids. The perception of control has other positive effects on health. People who feel a sense of control over their lives and who believe they possess the skills or ability to affect events may be more likely to take actions that improve their health—from seeking health-related information to taking appropriate care of themselves and following physicians' instructions.

Other important factors in the development of learned helplessness are a person's tendency to generalize the cause of the stressful situation and its stability. When people see their inability to control the situation as permanent, as the result of deficiencies within themselves, and as affecting many areas of life, the risk of developing learned helplessness is heightened (Abrahamson, Seligman, and Teasdale, 1978). In Chapter 14, we will investigate the importance of control in the lives of older adults who enter nursing homes and other institutions.

Control is not always positive. When the perception of control makes people feel that they are responsible for outcomes but that they lack the necessary skills to prevent an event, end it, or minimize its effects, control can be demoralizing (Bandura, 1986). The event becomes highly stressful, both physiologically and psychologically. And so when people feel guilty about the development of health-related problems, control itself can increase stress and produce adverse effects on health (Rodin, 1986).

The effects of control are so complicated that researchers have devoted many experiments to teasing out its effects. They have looked at how people with an internal **locus of control,** who feel they are in control of what happens to them, differ from people with an external locus of control, who believe their lives are governed by fate, luck, or chance. Those with an internal locus of control seem to take an active, problem-solving approach to life, while those with an external locus seem to see any attempt to overcome stressful experience as useless. In most cases, internals feel less stress than externals—but not always. *Extreme* internals, people who believe that almost everything that happens to them is under their control, are skillful at avoiding stressful events, but when avoidance is impossible they may blame themselves so severely that their attempts to cope are ineffective and they become highly vulnerable to stress (Krause, 1986). Perhaps that is why extreme internals report fewer stressful events in their lives, but a greater vulnerability to highly stressful, but unavoidable, events.

Stress in Context

The context of life events tends to reduce or increase their potential as stressors. Age, sex, marital status, ethnic background, socioeconomic level, and education all affect the way events are perceived and thus modify the level of stress that is likely to be experienced. Events that are expected, such as marriage or getting a first job for young adults, menopause or children leaving home for middle-aged adults, or retirement for older adults, may not be as stressful as nonnormative events (Brim and Ryff, 1980). When people can anticipate stress, they may be able to work it through beforehand, so that when the event finally arrives—elective surgery, retirement, the death of a spouse after a long illness—coping is far more effective. Unexpected events, such as the loss of a job, or events that happen at the "wrong" time of life, such as the death of a spouse in young adulthood, may be especially stressful.

Life's daily hassles may be more closely related to the state of health than major life

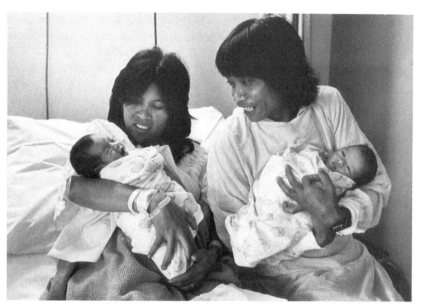

The birth of children is challenging as well as stressful. Because it can be worked through before the event, the stress from the experience itself is reduced.

events. Some hassles (losing the key to your apartment, having a flat tire) are temporary irritations, but others (poverty, marital conflict) may be repeated or chronic. Studies indicate that scores on a "Hassles Scale" are better predictors of morale, psychological symptoms, and illness than are major life events (Lazarus and DeLongis, 1983).

Stress Across Adulthood

The nature of hassles and stress-producing events tends to be related to age. The majority of hassles in younger people's lives are more likely to arise from finances and work, while hassles in the lives of older adults are more likely to be centered around their health and environmental and political issues (Folkman et al., 1987).

A person's age seems to have a powerful effect on the degree of perceived stress that accompanies any event. When asked to estimate the degree of disruption caused by major life events, older people produce consistently lower ratings (Chiriboga and Cutler, 1980). Older people also seem to worry less than younger people, report greater satisfaction with their jobs and less job stress, and are more likely to say that their lives are "free." Younger people tend to describe their lives as "hard" and "tied down" (Campbell, 1979). Studies of natural disasters, such as floods and tornadoes, have also shown that older people were less anxious than younger people and perceived less stress concerning their experiences (House and Robbins, 1983).

Do such findings indicate that older adults are under less strain than young and middle-aged adults? Probably not. Older adults are more worried about physical health than young and middle-aged adults. Under some conditions, they perceive community events such as social and economic change as particularly stressful, whereas middle-aged adults find the same situation generally reassuring (Miller, 1980). Political squabbles over funding of Social Security, Medicare, and long-term nursing care, for example, are likely to be much more stressful for older adults than for young or middle-aged adults.

The balance of stress is also likely to change in old age. Along with the negative stresses of earlier life go many positive stresses. The birth of a child, a promotion, buying a new house, and having children leave home, though potentially stressful events, are also challenging and full of promise. During later adulthood, the positive stresses decline sharply, leaving the balance skewed toward pain instead of pleasure (Chiriboga and Cutler, 1980).

Finally, older adults may be highly vulnerable to stress. The aging process affects the immune system, decreasing the ability to resist stress and making the person more vulnerable to the development of disease as a response to stress (Rodin, 1986). In addition, the prior presence of a degenerative disease, which is more likely in old age, may interact with the stressor, increasing the strain.

COPING WITH STRESS

The way we cope with stress plays a large part in determining whether life's hassles and events affect our health. **Coping** describes the thoughts and acts that are used to manage the demands of stressful situations. People can cope with stress by working on the troubling situation itself (a problem-solving approach) or by trying to change their reactions to it (an emotion-focused approach). Although people may use both techniques, researchers have found a clear and consistent age difference in the way people tend to cope with stress that accompanies life's hassles (Folkman et al., 1987). Adults in their late thirties and early forties tend to focus on the problem; they try to solve it, planning some constructive action and following it; seek social support, either concrete aid or sympathy; or confront the situation, fighting for whatever outcome they desire. Adults in their late sixties tend to focus on their emotions; they distance themselves, going on as if nothing had happened; accept responsibility, deciding they brought the situation on themselves; or reappraise the situation in a positive fashion, using it to find new faith. For the most part, men and women use similar strategies. Perhaps this age-related choice of coping strategies is adaptive, since the younger adults in this study could realistically hope to change situations, while older adults may have had less control over situations that bothered them. As the researchers point out, positive reappraisals and distancing may short-circuit the stress process and help explain why older people generally report fewer hassles than younger people do.

Some people seem to thrive on situations that would defeat others. In a longitudinal study that followed four cohorts of young and middle-aged men and women, about two fifths of people whose lives were filled with stressful situations seemed challenged by them (Fiske, 1980). They paid little attention to the stress, were open to new experience, and generally had close personal relationships. Among the young, women were more likely to feel challenged by stress, while men tended to feel overcome by it. Among those in their late fifties, the situation was reversed: men were more likely to be challenged, while women tended to feel overcome. At all ages, some people were overwhelmed by small amounts of stress. Although they had encountered little stress, they dwelt on it, talked about it constantly, and let it color all aspects of life.

Experience in coping with stress early in life may provide a source of strength that makes older people able to handle the stress and losses of age. Older people who have had little stress in earlier life seem unprepared to handle the stressors that accompany aging (Fiske, 1980).

Two extreme ways of coping with life have been found to affect the development of coronary disease. These behavior patterns, Type A and Type B, were first detected in a study of 3400 men between the ages of 39 and 59, none of whom had cardiovascular problems at the beginning of the study (Rosenman, 1974). Men with **Type A personalities** were highly competitive, impatient, and hostile when thwarted; they felt that life was a struggle against time. Such men seemed to have a strong need to be in control of stressful situations. Men with **Type B personalities** seemed relaxed, felt no pressure from time, and showed none of the hostility or competitive striving that characterized the Type As. Only about 10 percent of the men in the study were Type As; another 10 percent were Type Bs.

At first, it seemed that Type A was a prescription for cardiovascular disease: Type As were twice as likely as Type Bs to develop cardiovascular disease or myocardial infarctions and, among survivors of a first heart attack, five times as likely to have a second (Rosenman et al., 1975). Later research has shown that the connection between cardiovascular disease and personality is complex. It seems that the competitive striving against the clock that typifies Type As has no association with cardiovascular disease; the link with cardiovascular disease is forged by anger and hostility (Blakeslee, 1989a; Booth–Kewley and Friedman, 1987). Angry, hostile Type As react to stress in a characteristic manner: their sympathetic nervous system goes into overdrive, but their parasympathetic nervous system—which normally turns off the adrenal glands' production of steroids—seems too weak to calm them down. Since they are under prolonged stress, their hearts are subjected to extensive wear and tear (Blakeslee, 1989a). Cardiovascular disease is not the only threat that hostile Type As must face. As research with the immune system suggests, researchers have discovered that any condition that increases perceived stress increases a person's susceptibility to other disorders (Booth–Kewley and Friedman, 1987).

Stress is intimately connected with another factor that affects life-style: the environment.

ENVIRONMENT

People can never be separated from the environment, for it always surrounds them (Windley and Scheidt, 1980). The physical environment can affect physical and mental health, and it can affect them either directly or indirectly.

Noise, air pollution, and extreme temperatures can have direct effects on health. Prolonged exposure to high-intensity sounds can cause irreversible hearing loss. Noise can also act as a stressor; laboratory tests indicate that people respond to unpleasant or loud noises with the typical physiological reactions to stress, such as muscle tension, increased blood pressure, and the production of epinephrine (Holahan, 1982). It is not certain whether the stress from noise can damage physical or mental health. However, some studies (Crook and Langdon, 1974) have found a relationship between noise and headaches, nervousness, and insomnia, and others (Cameron, Robertson, and Zaks, 1972) have found a correlation between prolonged noise and the incidence of acute and chronic physical illness.

Polluted city air contains carbon monoxide, sulfur dioxide, nitrogen oxides, photooxidants from automobile engines, asbestos particles, and substances formed when automobile tires pass over the pavement. As the level of pollutants increases, the incidence of respiratory disease rises. In addition, when air contains high levels of carbon monoxide, heart patients develop symptoms of angina after much less exertion (Anderson et al., 1973). Older adults, especially those who have developed emphysema, are more sensitive than younger people to the effects of air pollutants. During temperature inversions, the heavy accumulation of pollutants near the ground surface can cause serious illness or death.

As we saw in Chapter 4, older adults' impaired ability to regulate body temperature makes them vulnerable to heat stroke. During a heat wave in July 1980, 148 heat-related deaths were reported in Kansas City; 72 percent of the deaths occurred in people past 65 (*Time,* 1980). The death rate was concentrated among older people in low-income areas; these residents tend to be in poorer health than other older adults and to lack air conditioners or other means of keeping cool. A similar heat wave in 1983 led St. Louis city officials to provide air-conditioned shelters for this group.

The effect of other environmental factors on health is generally less direct than the action of noise, air pollution, or heat. As people age, their senses are less effective, picking up less information from the environment, and they process the information they receive more slowly. When information is sharply reduced or distorted, people may become increasingly cautious, move more slowly, require more help, and interact less with other people and the environment. They may even become confused, disoriented, or extremely suspicious, and their level of adaptation to the environment changes (Howell, 1980).

In the view of Lucille Nahemow and Powell Lawton (1976), adaptation results from the interaction of individual **competence** (the ability of the person to respond) and **environmental press** (aspects of the environment that have some motivating force for the individual). Competence encompasses physical vigor and health, sensory functioning, and intellectual skills. People with a high level of competence can adapt to a wider range of press, including stressors. Moderate levels of environmental stress in relation to competence appear to lead to the most efficient adaptation and positive moods (Figure 5.6). When a person is functioning at adaptation level, he or she is minimally aware of the environment, and behavior and emotions are normal.

If environmental press is either extremely high or extremely low, an individual's health may suffer. For example, if older people's environment is oversimplified by reduced role demands, constraints on economic freedom, dwindling connections with friends and family, and reduced physical surroundings, they may adapt with very low levels of sensory and emotional experience (Nahemow and Lawton, 1976). Ultimately, their competence is reduced, and they lack the resources to adapt to any high environmental press.

Again and again, researchers have found that the environmental features of neighborhoods are more closely associated with the well-being of older people than are their personal characteristics (Scheidt and Windley, 1985). Much of the stress in their lives is created by various aspects of the environment, which can make some older adults virtual prisoners in their homes. High curbs, fast traffic, signals that do not give them time to cross the street, poorly labeled buildings, and windtunnel effects between some high-rise buildings may discourage city-dwelling adults from leaving their apartments (Holahan, 1982). How stressful any environment is depends in good part on how it is perceived. Older people generally live active and satisfying lives in quiet neighborhoods in small or middle-sized communities where the risk of crime is low, but activity and satisfaction seem to depend as much on the *perception* that there is little danger from crime as on the actual risk (Scheidt and Windley, 1985).

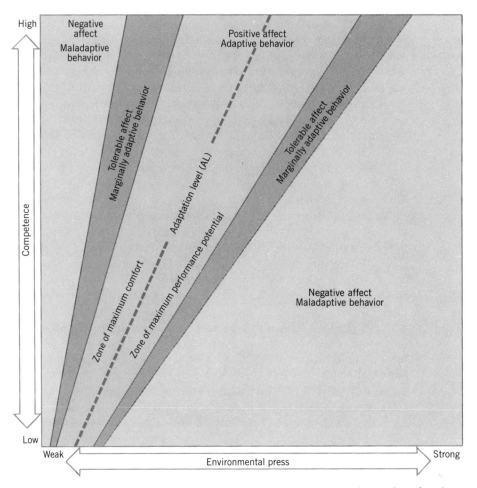

Figure 5.6 Adaptation to the environment. Adaptation results from the interaction of environmental press and competence. An individual's adaptation level is the point at which environmental press is average for his or her level of competence. *Source:* Lawton and Nahemour, 1973.

When older people fear being preyed on by muggers or purse snatchers, they adapt by cutting back on their exposure to stressors and thus reduce environmental press. If various services are available in their building, they may rarely leave the premises. In one study (Lawton, 1977), for example, tenants in housing with many services reported improved morale after a year, but were less likely to leave the property for any reason than were tenants in housing without services. The arrangement seems satisfying, but they may come to depend on it, so that they become bored, apathetic, and withdrawn. Ultimately, their mobility and competence are reduced (Parmelee and Lawton, 1990).

Reduced competence, together with a lack of independence and perceived control over their lives, may be responsible for the high levels of mortality among older individuals who are moved into institutions, especially those who already have physical or mental impairments (Lawton, 1977).

The crowds and noise of city life may produce a level of environmental stress that exceeds the older person's ability to adapt.

None of the factors that affect life-style acts in isolation. Nutrition, exercise levels, stress, and the environment work on all of us all the time. If we also smoke, we have added another factor that interacts with all the others. Together these factors play a major role in determining the speed with which we age.

SUMMARY

PHYSICAL HEALTH

Acute illness, a physical disorder with limited duration, becomes less common with age, although each incident of illness tends to be increasingly severe. Normal aging processes may complicate acute illness in older adults. The proportion of any cohort with a **chronic illness,** which cannot be cured and tends to get worse, increases with age. As death becomes certain, people enter the **dying trajectory,** but research indicates that their progression of emotional states may differ. **Hospices** have been created to make an **appropriate death** possible.

LIFE-STYLE AND HEALTH

Life-style has an important influence on health; as many as half the premature deaths in the United States may be due to unhealthy life-styles. Aspects of life-style may be **synergistic,** so that some combinations can damage health more than the sum of probable harm from each aspect. Such social factors as nutrition, sanitation, medical care, diet, and drug practices can lead to changes in general health from one cohort to the next.

The typical American diet (high in fat and cholesterol, low in fiber) has been linked with heart disease, hypertension, diabetes, and various forms of cancer. Lowering blood cholesterol levels (and increasing the proportion of **HDLs** to **LDLs**) reduces the incidence of myocardial infarction. Older adults need fewer calories per pound of body weight than younger adults, in good part because they are less active. However, older adults use more calories when performing the same physical task. Cigarette smoking is the most deleterious life-style factor; smoking has been implicated in various forms of cancer, heart disease, emphysema, chronic bronchitis, peptic ulcers, and **cataracts.** It also reduces fertility among women. Small amounts of alcohol may protect against myocardial infarction, but social drinking in excess of two drinks per day has been associated with hypertension and cancer.

Declining activity may be responsible for a good deal of the ''natural'' deterioration of body systems that is generally assumed to be the result of aging. Exercise, even when initiated late in life, sometimes can reverse physical declines that develop from inactivity.

STRESS AND COPING

Stress can accelerate the aging process, leading to the development of physical disease or mental disorder and impairing a person's ability to respond to new challenges. **Stressors** can be either physical or psychological, located in the world or within the person. Whether a potentially stressful event affects health depends on how it is perceived and how a person reacts to it. When people face uncontrollable stress and believe that their inability to control it is permanent and the result of inner deficiencies and that it affects many areas of their lives, they may develop **learned helplessness.** Control usually reduces stress, apparently through its affect on the autonomic nervous system, but control can also be harmful if it leads people to believe they are responsible but lack the skills needed to overcome it. People with an internal **locus of control** tend to react to stressors with a problem-solving approach, while those with an external locus of control may feel they are powerless to overcome stressors. Older people face fewer stress-producing events than do the young, but the balance of stress is likely to change in old age so that negative stresses outweigh positive stresses. Older people may also be more vulnerable to stress than the young.

A person's manner of **coping** with stress may determine whether it affects health. There are consistent interindividual differences in the way people cope with stress, as well as consistent age differences. Angry, hostile men with **Type A personalities** are at high risk for cardiovascular and other diseases, while those with **Type B personalities** run only a low risk.

ENVIRONMENT

Aspects of the environment (noise, air pollution, extreme temperatures) can have direct effects on health. Older adults are especially sensitive to air pollutants and temperature extremes. Adaptation to the environment results from the interaction of individual **competence** and **environmental press.** People function best at moderate levels of stress, and when environmental press becomes extremely high or extremely low, health may suffer. The stressfulness of any environment may depend on how it is perceived, and as people age, their level of adaptation to the environment may change. All factors that affect life-style interact, affecting the speed at which an individual ages.

KEY TERMS

acute illness

appropriate death

cataracts

chronic illness

competence

coping

dying trajectory

environmental press

high-density lipoproteins (HDLs)

hospice

learned helplessness

living will

locus of control

low-density lipoproteins (LDLs)

stress

stressor

synergistic

Type A personality

Type B personality

Chapter 6

◆

Mental Health
Across Adulthood

◆

T he first sign that something was wrong came when Allene Roach stopped taking phone messages. Then it became difficult to hold a conversation with her; seemingly deep in a coherent dialogue, this teacher at a bilingual Montessori school would simply turn her back in midsentence and walk off. Once she wandered away from home, and when she returned four days later, she had no idea where she had been. She became increasingly disoriented, never sure of the time or the date. Her memory was failing; she repeatedly asked the same questions and told the same stories again and again. Finally, about two years after the first indications of trouble, she was diagnosed as having Alzheimer's disease. Allene Roach was then 52 years old. Within another two years, she was unable to drive a car, her memory had deteriorated so severely that she could not be left alone, and unless she was given sedatives regularly, she hallucinated. There was no way to halt her mental deterioration, which would eventually end when her autonomic nervous system "forgot" how to function. Then she would die (Roach, 1983).

Alzheimer's disease is a form of mental deterioration and personality disintegration that is accompanied by physical changes within the brain. Although this disorder has a physiological basis, many mental disorders appear to develop from the individual's interactions with the environment, and others seem to have both physiological and environmental components.

Mental disorders are not limited to any phase of the life span. Children, adolescents, and young adults also have disorders that seem to come from the interaction of personality and experience, or in some cases from a physical cause. When all degrees of mental and emotional disorders are lumped together, no particular increase in prevalence appears with age, although the type of disorder may change. Among adults between the ages of 26 and 45, for example, up to 50 percent of admissions to mental hospitals are for schizophrenia or alcoholism; among adults older than 75, 85 percent of all admissions are for "brain syndromes" (La Rue, Dessonville, and Jarvik, 1985). The best guess is that from 15 to 25 percent of older persons have at least moderately severe symptoms due to mental disorders (U.S. Senate, Special Committee on Aging, 1987–1988)—not far off the 16 to 25 percent that has been found in various studies of adolescents and 20 percent for the population at large (Adelson, 1985).

In this chapter, we begin by exploring the organic brain disorders that were once thought to be an inevitable accompaniment of aging. Then we consider mental disorders with no identifiable physiological basis, first looking at psychotic disorders and then turning to the less severe but more common conditions, including depression, hypochondriasis, and alcoholism. The chapter ends with a brief overview of various mental health services. ◆

ORGANIC BRAIN DISORDERS

Organic brain disorders are related to physical changes within the brain; although they may have different causes, most are marked by similar symptoms. When behavioral and emotional changes have no identifiable organic basis and so are not related to known brain deterioration, they are called **functional brain disorders.** The signs of organic brain disorder may be slight or profound; they may appear slowly or develop with amazing speed. Five kinds of mental change generally accompany organic brain disorders:

1. *Impaired memory.* The person's inability to remember may be caused by a failure to register an event in the mind, to retain a memory that was registered, or to recall a memory voluntarily.

2. *Impaired intellect.* The person has trouble comprehending facts or ideas, handling arithmetical chores, or learning any new behavior.

3. *Impaired judgment.* The person finds it difficult to comprehend personal situations and make plans or decisions.

4. *Impaired orientation.* The person becomes confused about time, place, and people's identity, with confusion concerning time appearing first.

5. *Excessive or shallow emotions.* The person may react excessively to an event, perhaps throwing a temper tantrum, or be apathetic. Emotions may also shift rapidly, for no apparent reason (Butler and Lewis, 1982).

A person with organic brain syndrome may not show all five signs at once, and some signs may be more pronounced than others. For some, these symptoms may be reversed; they are suffering from **acute brain dysfunction.** For others, the symptoms are irreversible. They herald a steady decline that will become an inability to handle the simplest self-care and finally end with death; these people are suffering from **chronic brain dysfunction.**

ACUTE BRAIN DYSFUNCTION

From 10 to 20 percent of people with organic brain syndrome have acute brain dysfunction (La Rue, Dessonville, and Jarvik, 1985). Although the condition often develops swiftly, it may also come on slowly, depending on its cause. Whatever the specific cause, metabolism is disturbed throughout the brain. Acute brain dysfunction may result from medications, vitamin deficiencies, brain tumors, liver disease, thyroid disorders, anemia, multiple sclerosis, infectious diseases, cardiovascular disease, strokes, fever, infections, emphysema, mercury or lead poisoning, or acute alcoholic intoxication. The list is almost endless (Kolata, 1987). In most cases, the dysfunction has more then one cause.

Drug toxicity is frequently involved in acute brain dysfunction. Any drug that affects the central nervous system can produce the condition, especially if the patient has cardiovascular disease that reduces the brain's oxygen supply or if dehydration develops. An older person whose memory has been affected may forget that a prescribed medication has already been taken and take multiple doses without realizing it. As the body ages, the central nervous system becomes more sensitive to some drugs, and many drugs remain in the system longer because the liver and kidneys become slower at excreting them. Another problem is the tendency of older people to take a combination of drugs (often prescribed by more than one physician), along with self-prescribed over-the-counter medication. Among the drugs that can induce symptoms of brain dysfunction are antihypertensive medications, antiulcer medication, various narcotics given for pain, antihistamines, some antibiotics, cardiovascular medication (digitalis or lidocaine), and even laxatives (Kolata, 1987; La Rue, Dessonville, and Jarvik, 1985).

Nutritional imbalance is another often unsuspected cause of acute brain dysfunction. Lack of B vitamins is one source of dysfunction. Severe niacin deficiency, for example, can produce a series of psychological symptoms, beginning with depression and anxiety and ending in delirium, hallucinations, and even death. Thiamine deficiency can cause insomnia, irritability, extreme lassitude, and disturbed memory and the ability to concentrate. Deficiencies of Vitamin B_6 (pyridoxine HCl) can also lead to brain dysfunction.

Patients with acute brain dysfunction may be confused, stuporous, or actively delirious, and the level of awareness may fluctuate (Butler and Lewis, 1982). Some or all of the organic brain syndrome signs are present, and there may be hallucinations or delusions of persecution. Fever, muscular tremors, rapid heartbeat, sweating, flushed face, dilated pupils, and elevated blood pressure are also common. EEGs are always abnormal.

If properly identified, acute brain dysfunction generally lasts less than a week. It is treated by correcting the underlying condition. The patient may need oxygen, transfusions, blood glucose, fluids, massive doses of vitamins, treatment of infection, or control of body temperature. If the underlying condition is not diagnosed, however, the patient may develop a chronic brain dysfunction or even die. Approximately 40 percent of patients with acute brain dysfunction die—either from exhaustion or the underlying causes (Butler and Lewis, 1982). Often, however, complete recovery is possible. Chances seem best when social or environmental factors may have played a part in the development of the dysfunction, as when isolation leads to malnutrition or alcoholism.

CHRONIC BRAIN DYSFUNCTION

About 5 percent of the population who have passed the age of 65 have a chronic brain dysfunction, or **dementia,** that interferes with cognitive functioning either moderately or severely. In another 10 percent, there is mild cognitive impairment (La Rue, Dessonville, and Jarvik, 1985). However, the condition is most likely to develop during the seventies and eighties, so that the proportion of afflicted adults between the ages of 65 and 70 is actually much lower than statistics might suggest.

Some older men and women who seem to be suffering from one of the common forms of chronic brain dysfunction actually have a treatable, acute brain disorder. In one group of 60 patients, for example, 18 had a disease that could be relieved by treatment, such as chronic drug toxicity, liver failure, or hyperthyroidism (Freemon, 1976). In other cases, the apparent organic deterioration is a functional disorder—most often, depression. Because a misdiagnosis carries with it the assumption of irreversibility, it is important that physicians keep the less common, reversible brain disorders in mind when examining patients.

Alzheimer's Disease

The major cause of chronic brain dysfunction in older adults is **Alzheimer's disease,** a disorder that affects approximately half of those with severe intellectual impairment (Heston and White, 1983). The terminology for this disorder has shifted. Until recently, all cases that developed after age 65 were known as *senile dementia,* with the same condition in those younger than 65 called *presenile dementia,* or Alzheimer's disease, after the German neurologist who first identified the structural brain changes that characterize it. Most investigators believe that the two conditions are physiologically identical and prefer the term Alzheimer's disease, regardless of age. The age of onset is important, however, since among

Table 6.1   AGE AT ONSET RELATED TO SURVIVAL IN ALZHEIMER'S DISEASE

Age at Onset (yrs)	Percent with Onset	Cumulative Percent	Average Survival (yrs)	Longest Survival (yrs)
≥44	3	3	4.5	6.0
45–49	2	5	6.1	9.9
50–54	5	10	7.2	12.2
55–59	7	17	8.5	16.1
60–64	14	31	8.4	25.2
65–69	19	50	8.5	18.1
70–74	17	67	8.4	21.3
75–79	18	85	6.1	11.9
80–84	10	95	5.0	13.4
85–	5	100	4.1	8.3

Source: Heston and White, 1983.

younger patients, the disease tends to progress more rapidly and the chances of genetic involvement are higher (Heston and White, 1983) (Table 6.1). The condition is more common in women than in men.

Alzheimer's disease is the result of characteristic changes in the brain that at present can be identified with certainty only at autopsy. As noted in Chapter 4, the brains of people with Alzheimer's disease show gross dendritic atrophy, as well as many senile plaques and neurofibrillary tangles. The plaques, which have the consistency of a Brillo pad, are made up of a central core of the amyloid protein, surrounded by cells that normally support neurons as well as degenerating neural fibers. The twisted tubes of neurofibrillary tangles are composed of four different proteins. The picture is further complicated by the fact that a brain may have many senile plaques, but the person may never show Alzheimer-related behavioral symptoms unless the tangles are also present (Kosik, 1989). Yet among patients who develop the disease after the age of 75, there may be a multitude of senile plaques but no neurofibrillary tangles (Joachim and Selkoe, 1989). Apparently because of the death of neurons, brain shrinkage is more pronounced than in normal aging and the surface of the brain shows fewer folds.

Diagnosis of Alzheimer's disease is usually made by eliminating other causes of brain disorder. Thorough physical, neurological, and psychiatric examinations are necessary. CT and MRI scans, EEGs, taps of spinal fluid, and comprehensive blood analyses can rule out some possible causes. Psychological tests can rule out others, such as severe depression, which is a functional disorder. PET scans can help to confirm the diagnosis, for an Alzheimer's brain takes up glucose much more slowly than a normal brain (Roach, 1983).

Alzheimer's disease develops so slowly that family members do not realize for some time that the person is deteriorating. It may first show as an inability to write checks or make change. Sometimes it progresses even farther before the condition is apparent. For example, one morning at breakfast a 62-year-old salesman asked his wife what time it was. Before half an hour had passed, he asked her again. She stretched out her arm so he could see her watch, but he could not read the dial. She asked him a few simple questions about telling time from a book their children had used as preschoolers. From his answers, she became aware that he was having a real problem understanding time. Until that moment, she had no idea there was anything seriously wrong with him (Burnside, 1979).

The mystery of Alzheimer's disease is slowly being untangled. The hereditary component in Alzheimer's disease may be larger than was once believed. As longevity has increased, it has become apparent that nearly half of the first-degree relatives of Alzheimer patients (parents, children, siblings) develop the disease if they live to the age of 90 (Mohs et al., 1987). In addition, people with Down syndrome (an inherited chromosomal disorder that was discussed in Chapter 3) are likely to develop Alzheimer's disease if they live past 40, and the disease also appears among their relatives. A marker indicating a gene in a 500-gene stretch on Chromosome 21, located near the gene involved in Down syndrome, has been implicated in Alzheimer's disease that appears by the age of 52 (St. George-Hyslop et al., 1987). The gene ultimately responsible for amyloid protein production is also found on Chromosome 21, close to the family gene for Alzheimer's. Yet the three genes are not linked, and one may be inherited without the other (Joachim and Selkoe, 1989). Some cases of later onset Alzheimer's disease that runs in families but appears during the late fifties or early sixties may be due to a different genetic defect, since these patients lack the Chromosome 21 marker for Alzheimer's (Schellenberg et al., 1988).

Many cases, called sporadic Alzheimer's disease, seem to have an environmental cause. It has been suggested that a slow-acting virus is the culprit, or that environmental toxins are responsible—perhaps the high levels of aluminum that accompany acid rain. The neurofibrillary tangles in the brains of Alzheimer patients, for example, often contain high levels of aluminum—a substance that normally does not cross the blood–brain barrier (Turkington, 1987). For some reason, their systems apparently allow ions of aluminum to pass into the brain. Yet no one has been able to establish *why* their systems malfunction in this way. In fact, studies investigating the role of aluminum in the development of Alzheimer's disease have been inconclusive (Dieckmann et al., 1988).

Whatever the ultimate cause, Alzheimer's disease seems to affect behavior through its action on the brain's supply of the neurotransmitter, acetylcholine. Within the cortex of people who die of Alzheimer's disease, levels of an enzyme that synthesizes acetylcholine are from 60 to 90 percent less than are found in the brains of people without the disorder. Alzheimer's patients—whether young or old—have lost a significant proportion of the neurons that supply the critical enzyme (Coyle, Price, and DeLong, 1983). This loss leads to the death of neurons in other parts of the brain, especially in the hippocampus—a structure that is essential to memory—and adjacent areas. As a consequence, nerve impulses cannot get in or out of the hippocampus, and memory is gradually obliterated and cognitive functioning disrupted (Hyman et al., 1984).

The question is what instigates the process that destroys the enzyme-producing neurons. Many researchers believe that the key lies in the amyloid protein deposits that form the core of plaques (Marx, 1990b). Amyloid protein is produced by another protein that seems to be essential to the development and maintenance of the nervous system. But no one has been able to establish whether amyloid deposits cause the death of neurons, the development of neurofibrillary tangles, and the growth of plaques, or whether the protein simply accumulates as the result of some other unknown brain process (Joachim and Selkoe, 1989).

At present, Alzheimer's disease cannot be cured, but the inevitable decline of functioning may be slowed. Elizabeth Reno, a 46-year-old phone company supervisor, was able to handle her job for five months after receiving the diagnosis of Alzheimer's disease. She kept going by concentrated effort, writing notes to herself, conducting conversations with herself, trying to anticipate what others might say, rehearsing over and over what she wanted to do or say. "After work I would collapse," she said, "because I had to muster all the strength I could to make it through the day" (Clark, 1984). But the delay was only temporary. Within a few months after she stopped working, she had forgotten how to cook or drive a car, and she had trouble reading newspaper articles because the intent of the article slipped from her mind after a few paragraphs.

As memory fails, recall (the ability to remember voluntarily in the absence of the sought-for information) is destroyed before recognition (the ability to remember in the presence of the information). Substituting recognition for recall in daily situations may help patients manage their lives in early stages of the disease (Zarit, Zarit, and Reever, 1982). Labels on drawers and appliances ("turn off the burner"), an automatic-dial telephone, calendars, digital clocks, and notes left in conspicuous places can increase functioning and prolong independence. When family caregivers were trained to spend six hours each week stimulating and challenging patients' memory, problem-solving, and communication skills, the patients' cognitive skills showed no decline over an eight-month period, at a time when the cognitive skills of patients in a comparison group declined steadily (Quayhagen and Quayhagen, 1989).

Sometimes programs have been able to improve the functioning of Alzheimer's patients—at least temporarily. Many nursing homes use reality orientation in an attempt to delay the progress of Alzheimer's disease and other organic brain disorders. In **reality orientation,** repeated, continual attempts are made to keep patients in touch with reality. Staff members regularly remind patients of their own names, the name of the institution, and the day of

Labels on objects in their world, which substitute recognition for recall, enable Alzheimer patients to function for a considerable period after the disease first appears.

the week. Daily classes are held, in which a staff member repeats such basic information as the date, the weather, the names of other patients in the class, news events, and how to comply with nursing home routines. Clocks, bulletin boards, and name cards provide constant reminders. Research has not established the effectiveness of reality orientation, but some psychologists believe that it may slow the loss of memory (Smyer, Zarit, and Qualls, 1990). Attempts to alter behavior have been more successful. By using verbal instruction, modeling, and practice, researchers were able to reteach personal hygiene skills to Alzheimer's patients, so that they once again could take care of their own bathing, dressing, and toilet functions (McEvoy and Patterson, 1986). As the disease progresses, however, people become progressively less able to care for themselves. Finally, they cannot even feed themselves and require continual nursing attendance.

Perhaps one day a drug will be able to halt the progress of Alzheimer's disease. THA (tetrahydroaminoacridine), which inhibits the action of an enzyme that breaks down acetylcholine, has shown some promising results, although trials of the drug had to be stopped when a number of patients showed signs of liver damage (Marx, 1987a). Other researchers are working on a treatment that involves nerve growth factor (NGF), either injecting NGF directly into the brain or implanting within the brain genetically modified cells, which produce NGF. The hope is that such treatment might allow neurons that produce acetylcholine to survive and flourish, as it does in laboratory animals (Rosenberg et al., 1988). But some researchers have found that the amyloid protein itself causes neurons to sprout new, abnormal fibers, which themselves contribute to plaque formation. If this is the case, nerve growth factor might do more harm than good (Marx, 1990a).

The need for effective treatment is urgent, because Alzheimer's disease is the most prevalent form of organic brain dysfunction. Among older patients, 48 percent of all deaths attributed to organic brain dysfunction are due to Alzheimer's disease, and it plays a contributing role in another 12 percent, in which multi-infarct dementia is also present (Butler and Lewis, 1982).

Multi-infarct Dementia

Multi-infarct dementia is a second major form of chronic brain dysfunction. It is a disorder apparently caused when blood clots repeatedly cut off the supply of blood to the brain, often in the form of small strokes. The patient generally has hypertension, and atherosclerosis may be present. There are frequently signs of kidney failure, and the retina of the eye may be scarred. Multi-infarct dementia appears to cause about 20 percent of the deaths from chronic organic brain dysfunction, in adddition to its presence in the 12 percent who also have Alzheimer's disease (Butler and Lewis, 1982).

The first symptoms of multi-infarct dementia may appear at about the age of 50, although the average age of onset is 66. It is more common in men than in women, apparently because estrogen provides women with some protection against cardiovascular disease until menopause.

The brains of patients with multi-infarct dementia show cerebrovascular lesions, with areas of softened and deteriorated tissue. The first symptoms may be dizziness or headaches, or even a blackout, although about half the cases begin with a sudden, acute attack of confusion (Butler and Lewis, 1982). Sometimes the patient hallucinates or shows signs of delirium. Memory loss may be spotty, and the patient may retain a large measure of insight until relatively late in the course of the disease. Often a patient will have periods of seeming remission: memory suddenly clears and lucidity returns. The improvement is sometimes so impressive that only careful testing reveals the cognitive impairment (Sloane, 1980). In Alzheimer's disease, by contrast, the deterioration is smooth and gradual.

Treating the underlying hypertension and cardiovascular disease can slow the progress of multi-infarct dementia. Patients may live for 15 years or more, and death is usually the result of stroke, heart disease, or pneumonia.

Because patients with multi-infarct dementia hallucinate, a substantial minority of the people believed to be suffering from this organic condition may, in fact, be afflicted by a functional brain disorder. In one state hospital, investigators discovered that 30 percent of the patients referred to them as having multi-infarct dementia actually had paranoia, a functional mental disorder (Butler and Lewis, 1982).

Parkinson's Disease

A third chronic brain disorder, **Parkinson's disease,** may appear as early as the thirties, although it usually shows up when people are in their sixties. The disease develops slowly, beginning with a slowing of movement, a stooped posture with the head forward and elbows flexed, and a shuffling gait. The face lacks emotional expression, speech is slurred, and the voice becomes a monotone. A tremor appears about four to eight times per second, which is most noticeable in the fingers, forearm, eyelids, and tongue. Patients have good days and bad days. At times, they improve so much that they can control the tremors enough to do some task that requires fine muscular coordination, but the good days pass and the characteristic shaking soon returns.

Although some patients retain their cognitive powers, from 40 to 60 percent of individuals with Parkinson's disease show mental impairment and many also become apathetic and socially withdrawn (Bootzin and Acocella, 1988). The impairment may involve memory, learning, judgment, and the ability to concentrate. Some develop a deep depression. If left untreated, Parkinson's disease causes disability within five years. The disorder is twice as common in men as in women, although no one knows why.

Nor is anyone certain just what causes Parkinson's disease; it has been attributed to genetic influences, encephalitis, viruses, toxins, or disturbed metabolism in the brain. Some researchers lean to an environmental toxin theory, pointing out that (1) twin studies appear to rule out genetic causes, and (2) when multiple cases of Parkinson's disease appear in a single family, the onset of the disease clusters around a short span of time, as if some environmental exposure were involved. In one family, for example, mother, father, and child all developed the disease within a period of three years, yet their ages at onset (68, 58, and 37) were widely separated (Lewin, 1987).

Once the disease is underway, brain cells die in the substantia nigra, a small area on each side of the brain that produces dopamine. Giving these patients dopamine has no effect, because the neurotransmitter cannot cross the blood–brain barrier, but the drug L-dopa, a substance the body converts into dopamine, can pass the barrier and enter neurons, where it is converted to dopamine (Spence, 1989). Although L-dopa does not cure the disorder, it reduces or eliminates symptoms, allowing individuals to function in a relatively normal fashion.

Recently, researchers have discovered that deprenyl, a drug that combats depression by inhibiting the enzyme that breaks down dopamine and similar neurotransmitters, can mark-

♦ *Adulthood in Today's World*

DON NELSON, PARKINSON'S PATIENT

Eighteen months ago, Don Nelson, a 53-year-old Denver man, had cells from a six-week-old aborted fetus implanted deep within his brain. Nelson had had Parkinson's disease for 20 years, and the symptoms were most noticeable on the left side of his body. In a nine-hour operation, a neurosurgeon drilled a quarter-inch hole in the right side of Nelson's skull, then used ten long needles to implant the immature fetal cells.

Because the good days/bad days aspects of Parkinson's disease make it difficult to evaluate the results of such surgery, researchers monitored Nelson for four months before the operation. Again and again, they tested his hand movements and reaction times with a computer. They had him walk repeatedly down a 20-foot strip of plastic, while photo cells recorded his gait. They scanned his brain to estimate how many dopamine-producing cells were still functioning. This information made it possible for the medical team to evaluate any progress against an objective standard.

After six months, Nelson still had good days and bad days. On the bad days, he found it difficult to move, just as he always did, but encouraging results appeared. Despite a reduction in his drug dosage, his left side slowly but steadily improved. On good days he could walk 50 percent faster than he used to and work in his garden for as long as eight hours. Before his surgery his work limit was two hours (Blakeslee, 1989b).

Nelson continued to improve over the next year (Freed et al., 1990). By May, 1990, eighteen months after his surgery, when the fetal cells presumably had matured, Nelson had

edly slow the progress of Parkinson's disease. In a group of patients treated with deprenyl, the advance of Parkinson's disease was slowed from 40 to 83 percent per year compared with a control group (Tetrud and Langston, 1989). This slowing significantly postponed the need for L-dopa therapy.

Researchers have also been experimenting with transplants of dopamine-producing cells into the brain. Results from the more than 100 adrenal-to-brain transplants carried out in the United States have been discouraging, leading the American Academy of Neurology to urge a halt on surgical transplants until more animal studies have been done (Pool, 1988). Interest has since shifted to transplanting fetal cells directly into the brain, as described in the accompanying box, "Don Nelson, Parkinson's Patient." The goal is to have these cells, obtained from aborted fetuses no more than about eight weeks old, mature and produce dopamine. In Sweden, the process may have been successful in the case of a man who had developed Parkinson's more than ten years earlier (Lindvall et al., 1990). Researchers reported that five months after surgery, PET scans detected an increased uptake of energy in the area on one side of the brain where the cells had been implanted. The patient's muscles lost their rigidity, and his motor performance improved, particularly on the side of the body opposite from the implant. Since dopamine-producing fetal cells require a year of indepen-

regained normal function in both hands and had thrown away the cane he once needed (see photo). ''I'm walking better, my speech has improved, the volume of my voice is better,'' he told a journalist (*Reporter Dispatch,* 1990a). His tremors had disappeared, and he had even regained the ability to whistle.

dent life to mature, there may be further improvement. Yet the researchers warn that it is impossible to say whether the fetal cells will continue to develop. The jury is still out.

DEMENTIA AND THE FAMILY

When a family member develops dementia, family life changes. By the time the disorder has progressed far enough for a reasonably confident diagnosis, the patient requires a high level of attention and supervision. This care places such enormous physical, emotional, and financial burdens on primary caregivers that they are highly vulnerable to depression (Gallagher et al., 1989). In order to alleviate the overwhelming stress of caregivers, psychologists have developed a variety of programs, including support groups and respite service.

Support groups focus on sharing information and releasing pent-up emotions. Some are led by therapists, and others by members of the group. Participating in them tends to reduce the caregiver's isolation and makes them aware that others face similar problems and feel similarly about them. Respite service gives the caregiver ''time-off''—relief and rest away from the patient. An aide may come to the home, or the patient may be brought to a day-care setting or an institution.

Just how effective these programs are in enhancing the well-being of caregivers is un-certain. Caregivers consistently report satisfaction with both support groups and respite programs, and therapists who work with the caregivers generally see improvement. Yet studies have not been able to document improvements in caregivers' feelings about their burden, their levels of stress, or their sense of well-being (Toseland and Rossiter, 1989). Compared with caregivers on a waiting list, for example, caregivers in a support group program showed no change in life satisfaction, ability to cope, levels of depression, or social activity (Haley, 1989). Yet the caregivers said they were satisfied with the group, and two years later they still perceived the group as having been important in helping them to cope successfully over the succeeding months. In a longitudinal study of a Philadelphia respite program, researchers could find little impact on the physical or mental health of the care-givers or on their perceived burden (Lawton, Brody, and Saperstein, 1989). But there was one objective measure of success: the patients involved were able to live in the community an average of 22 days longer before being placed in an institution than were patients in a control group. And the caregivers were enthusiastic about the program, saying that it had provided them with the information and assistance they needed to cope with the burden of caregiving.

PSYCHOTIC DISORDERS

Normal mental activity is severely impaired in **psychosis,** and the patient's perception of reality is drastically distorted. Hallucinations and delusions are common; impulses are poorly controlled. Because they have lost the ability to deal adaptively with the world, people with psychoses often cannot handle the details of daily life. If the psychosis is in an acute stage, they are usually unable to hold a job or even to carry on a coherent conversation. The major psychotic disorders are schizophrenia and paranoid disorder.

SCHIZOPHRENIA

Schizophrenia is the most common psychosis. Between 1 and 2 percent of the population has either had a schizophrenic episode or will have one at some time in their lives (Robins et al., 1984). The disorder is characterized by disturbed thought, disturbed perception, and disturbed emotions. Delusions and hallucinations are common, and the patient's behavior is often bizarre. A schizophrenic might be highly active (running around and knocking things about), engage in moderately active but highly repetitive behavior (tearing paper, counting cornflakes, rubbing his or her head), or be completely immobile (not moving or speaking for days).

In most cases, schizophrenia first shows itself in adolescence or early adulthood. Men tend to develop the disorder early—usually before the age of 25—and to display negative symptoms: the virtual absence of speech or emotion, withdrawal, apathy, and impaired attention. Women tend to develop schizophrenia later—usually after the age of 25—and to display positive symptoms: hallucinations, delusions, bizarre behavior, and thought disorders (Lewine, 1981). About 1 percent of older adults have schizophrenia (Cohen, 1990), but it rarely appears for the first time in old age: 90 percent of older adults with schizophrenia developed the disorder before they were 40 (LaRue, Dessonville, and Jarvik, 1985).

When schizophrenia does make its initial appearance in adults past the age of 60, it is called **paraphrenia.** These patients seem to have a milder form of the disorder than patients with an early onset, and their symptoms virtually always include delusions, especially delusions of persecution. There is some question as to whether these patients suffer from schizophrenia or from a delusional disorder (LaRue, Dessonville, and Jarvik, 1985). Patients with paraphrenia generally have a good work history, but their intimate relationships are either unstable or nonexistent. They tend to be unmarried, to live in isolation, to have few surviving relatives, and to belong to lower socioeconomic classes (Post, 1980).

Schizophrenia appears to develop out of a complicated interaction of biology, personality, and society. Many researchers have adopted the view that the disorder develops when someone with a biological predisposition to schizophrenia encounters stressful events but lacks the coping skills to handle them.

Most cases of schizophrenia are treated with drugs, not therapy. Antipsychotic drugs make it possible for many schizophrenics to return to society, but they do not cure the disorder. Drugs simply relieve the symptoms, and most have serious side effects. But until more effective treatment is available, drugs will probably continue to be the treatment of choice.

DELUSIONAL DISORDERS

Although delusions are a frequent symptom of schizophrenia, they are the central symptom of **delusional disorders,** sometimes called **paranoia.** The basic abnormality is usually a grandiose delusion, as in the man who thinks he is God, or delusions of persecution, as in the woman who believes that someone is plotting to kill her. The person's intellectual processes are intact, but mood, behavior, and thought are all distorted by the basic delusion. If the basic delusion were true, the thoughts, attitudes, and behavior would seem logical.

Delusions in young people are generally fleeting and part of schizophrenia. Once people are past 35 or 40, chronic delusional disorders may develop, but they are extremely rare (Post, 1980). Delusions may develop in older people as part of an attempt to fill in the "blank spaces" in the environment that result when hearing, vision, or memory fail (Pfeiffer, 1977). In fact, deafness is often involved. Older people who develop delusional disorders (sometimes diagnosed as paraphrenia) usually have a long-standing hearing loss that interferes with their ability to follow normal conversations (LaRue, Dessonville, and Jarvik, 1985). An older man who is deaf may believe that people are deliberately speaking softly, so that he cannot hear what they are saying about him. One who cannot remember where he put his billfold, glasses, or keys may accuse others of stealing them. An older woman who has been having arguments with her daughter and whose taste perceptions have changed may accuse her daughter of trying to poison her.

Because such delusions explain bewildering events in the world, they are in a sense adaptive. Perhaps this adaptive function explains why delusions are sometimes seen in the early stages of an organic brain syndrome. In this view, the delusions can be an exaggeration of the understandable annoyance caused by the physical and environmental limitations that begin to curb some older people's activities and capabilities.

Some delusions that develop during old age may escape the notice of others. In one case, it was only after an older man died that his family discovered in his diary that he believed people followed him in the street whenever he went out. Many people who develop delusional disorders have been eccentric for years. The disorder does not affect their ability to care for themselves, and so others see no dramatic change in their conduct or appearance.

Trying to reason a person out of delusions of persecution is doomed to failure; it simply convinces the individual that the delusion is true. But simple delusions often can be dealt with, at least temporarily, by changing the social situation. A stable, friendly environment that is not connected with the delusions may end the fears—although not the person's belief in the delusion. Correcting any sensory loss that may be contributing to the delusion is helpful. Delusions often disappear when patients are given small doses of antipsychotic drugs. But older persons suffering from delusions of persecution are often suspicious of medication and reject any kind of therapy that marks them as being ill (LaRue, Dessonville, and Jarvik, 1985). Support, sympathy, and acceptance may also help those with delusional disorders to cope with daily life despite their fears.

OTHER FUNCTIONAL DISORDERS

Not all functional disorders interfere with daily life to the degree seen in psychotic disorders. Some people who find it difficult or even impossible to carry out their normal functions remain in touch with reality. In these people, thinking and judgment may be impaired, but personality does not disintegrate. The psychotic person believes that he or she is well; the person with milder functional disorders knows that something is wrong and wants relief.

Only a few functional disorders are included in this section, but those described are among the most common. Like the psychotic disorders, most develop before a person enters old age. Mental health may change in later years, perhaps because of changes in life situations, but the change is as likely to be for the better as for the worse. Bereavement or a disabling chronic illness may produce symptoms of distress in some individuals, whereas others, who no longer have to cope with adolescent children, the financial burden of college tuition, or the care of aging parents, may show improved mental health (Aldwin et al., 1989).

DEPRESSION

Depression, which is classified as a *mood disorder* by the American Psychiatric Association (1987), can occur at any time of life, including childhood. From 18 to 23 percent of women and from 8 to 11 percent of men have a major depressive episode at some time in their lives. About 50 percent of these people will have at least one recurrence of depression (Skodol and Spitzer, 1983). Depression is one of the most common—and most treatable—functional disorders of later adulthood. Whether depression becomes more common with age has not been established. Most studies are cross-sectional and include few adults older than 70 (Newmann, 1989). However, results from two longitudinal studies suggest that increased age itself is not associated with depression (Lieberman, 1983). When controlled for social class, increased age showed no association with depression, either among 360 ethnic men and women or 2300 Chicago adults from majority groups.

Depression is more than the fleeting sadness, despondency, or grief we all feel at some time or another. It cannot be chased away by a fine meal, a new suit, a vacation, or expressions of affection from a loved one. In a major depression, the despondent mood persists and may be accompanied by pessimism, low self-esteem, and feelings of foreboding. The depressed person's posture and facial expression often change to reflect mood. Although some patients are agitated and jittery, others show slowed speech and movement and stare into space. Most have trouble making decisions, perhaps because they find it difficult to concentrate on any activity or problem. They may begin to contemplate suicide. Among the physical symptoms of depression are insomnia, anxiety, loss of appetite, weight loss, fatigue, and bodily aches and pains (Klerman, 1983).

The causes of depression are often difficult to discover. There may be some clear-cut, precipitating event, or the disorder may seem to develop out of the blue, with no noticeable life event to explain it (Skodol and Spitzer, 1983). Often the loss of some important person, thing, or activity precedes the depression. Bitter disappointments, criticisms, and real or imagined threats may be in the background (Butler and Lewis, 1982). At times guilt appears to be implicated, a guilt produced by the conviction that the person has failed in carrying out life tasks (Stenback, 1980).

At one time it was thought that menopause could lead to a form of depression called involutional melancholia. The physiological adjustments to a new hormonal balance, together with the psychological adjustments to the loss of youth and the ability to bear children, were supposed to plunge middle-aged women into depression. The condition could be distinguished from other types of depression because these women had never had a previous depressive episode. Once researchers began to study the situation, it became apparent that there was no rise in depression at menopause. In fact, the rate of depression was about the same whether women were under 45 (premenopausal), between 45 and 55 (menopausal), or older than 55 (postmenopausal) (Weissman, 1979). And when depression did develop in middle-aged women, it was no different from depression in anybody else. As a result, involutional melancholia is no longer recognized as a separate mental disorder (American Psychiatric Association, 1987; Skodol and Spitzer, 1983).

Longitudinal studies have found that some life events can lead to depression, but only when they change the circumstances of a person's life (Lieberman, 1983). For example,

Although depression is the most common functional disorder of later adulthood, studies indicate that life events—not aging—are usually responsible.

demotion, losing a job, and poor health were found to be associated with depression, but the association appeared to come from the strain these events placed on marriage, parenthood, and economic and occupational situations. Such strains were most apparent among middle-aged men, who showed the highest rate of depression. Divorce was also associated with depression, but only when divorced people faced changes in their economic situation and when they had no supportive personal relationships to take the place of the marital partner.

Social support seems to provide some protection against depression among the elderly. The less social support older men and women have, the more likely they are to be depressed (Holahan and Holahan, 1987). Older people who are best able to maintain their social networks over the years tend to be those who feel some sense of control over their lives, in that they are confident that they can manage such social hassles as loneliness or separation from friends and relatives. In one study, this kind of confidence predicted the level of older people's social support the following year, while lack of it predicted depression (Holahan and Holahan, 1987).

A sense of control, which is so important for physical health, turns out to be equally important for mental health. Thus, it is not surprising that learned helplessness, which affects the way people react to events, also has been related to depression. When people attribute their failures to their own incompetence and see no way to change the situation, they may become severely depressed. In a study of older women (65 to 96 years), those who were depressed attributed their failures to their own lack of ability and their successes to good luck (Maiden, 1987). They felt personally helpless when comparing themselves to others in the same situation. Those who were not depressed attributed their failures to bad luck and their successes to their own ability. They felt helpless only in situations where they believed everyone would fail.

This focus on personal failure may be connected with an increase in the rates of depression that some researchers have attributed to age-cohort effects. In surveys of nearly 10,000 adults in three cities (St. Louis, Baltimore, and New Haven), the proportion of 25 to 44 year olds who had ever had an episode of major depression was about twice as large as among those between 45 and 64, and about eight times as large as among those older than 65 (Robins et al., 1984). The proportion of 18 to 24 year olds who had gone through a major depression was about as high as that of the middle-aged adults, indicating that the increased incidence was not likely to decline with younger cohorts. Psychologist Martin Seligman (1988) believes that the apparent rise in depression rates largely reflects the current emphasis on the self in contemporary society, which tends to make people blame their misfortunes, losses, and disappointments on themselves rather than on chance or the environment. Seligman points out that, despite this rise in depression among the general public, the rate among the Old Order Amish of Pennsylvania (who live in a traditional nineteenth-century farming culture) shows no change.

Among older adults, physical health is also related to depression. Some investigators have pointed out that other losses, such as the loss of work, status, prestige, financial security, friends, and relatives, can be handled fairly successfully as long as older people maintain their health (Jarvik, 1983). Disabling disease often means becoming dependent on children or caregivers, accepting their decisions as well as their help. This reversal of roles—which erodes the older person's sense of competence and control—may be harder to bear than other losses.

Not all people with disabling diseases become depressed. Life situations interact with personality, genetics, and biochemistry. Studies of twins and adopted people indicate that severe depression has a genetic component (Davis, Segal, and Spring, 1983). The rate of depression is eight times higher among biological relatives of adopted people who have had a bout of severe depression than among the biological relatives of adopted people who have never been depressed (Wender et al., 1986).

Several brain chemicals have been implicated in severe depression. Norepinephrine was the first, but later studies have added serotonin and perhaps acetylcholine to the list. Low levels of norepinephrine are associated with depression, whereas high levels of the transmitter are associated with manic episodes, which are the mirror image of depression. In a manic episode, there is elation, optimism, hyperactivity, and a feeling of power. Drugs that lift depression either block the reabsorption of norepinephrine, prevent its destruction, or increase its production. Low levels of serotonin also have been associated with depression, and the same drugs that increase the availability of norepinephrine also increase serotonin levels. Acetylcholine was added to the list when researchers discovered that blocking its destruction within the brain (thus raising its level) depressed a manic patient within minutes (Davis, Segal, and Spring, 1983). Perhaps it is the balance of neurotransmitters in the brain and not the deficiency or excess of a single transmitter that triggers depression.

Sometimes depression is caused by drugs, which can aggravate a depression that already exists, cause a depression to develop, or produce symptoms that resemble the disorder but are not a true depression (Klerman, 1983). Because symptoms may not appear until as long as 14 months after the person begins taking a drug, it is often difficult to discover the connection. Antihypertensive drugs are the most likely offenders, with true depression developing in 20 percent of older adults who take them. Other drugs that may be involved include female hormones, corticosteroids, and drugs used to treat Parkinson's disease, tuberculosis, and cancer. Sometimes a mixture of drugs, prescribed and over-the-counter, can lead to a depressed state.

When a depressed person talks about suicide, the message should be taken seriously; depressed individuals account for between 30 and 50 percent of all suicides (Murphy and Robins, 1968).

SUICIDE

The older the person, the more urgent any message of suicidal intent becomes. Suicide attempts by people younger than 35 fail more often than they succeed, but people older than 50 are likely to be successful in their attempts. Once they are past 65, the attempt rarely fails (Butler and Lewis, 1982). The high success rate among older adults may be traced to the fact that suicide attempts among the young are often meant to affect other people; attempts among the elderly are unlikely to be directed at others (Zarit, 1980).

The typical person who attempts suicide and survives is a native-born white woman in her twenties who does not work outside the home. She swallows sleeping pills, and the reason she gives for her attempt is either marital problems or depression. The typical person who succeeds in a suicide attempt is a native-born white man who is older than 40. He shoots or hangs himself or else uses carbon monoxide. The reason for his suicide appears to be poor health, marital problems, or depression (Shneidman and Farberow, 1970).

Throughout life, the suicide rate is higher in males than in females, and the difference

Table 6.2   CHANGING SUICIDE RATES; 1970, 1980, AND 1986 (PER 100,000)

	Men						Women					
	White			Black			White			Black		
Age	1970	1980	1986	1970	1980	1986	1970	1980	1986	1970	1980	1986
20–24	19.3	27.8	28.4	18.7	20.0	16.0	5.7	5.9	5.3	4.9	3.1	2.4
25–34	19.9	25.6	26.4	19.2	21.8	21.3	9.0	7.5	6.2	5.7	4.1	3.8
35–44	23.3	23.5	23.9	12.6	15.6	17.5	13.0	9.1	8.3	3.7	4.6	2.8
45–54	29.5	24.2	26.3	13.8	12.0	12.8	13.5	10.2	9.6	3.7	2.8	3.2
55–64	35.0	25.8	28.7	10.6	11.7	9.9	12.3	9.1	9.0	2.0	2.3	4.2
65–74	38.7	32.5	37.6	8.7	11.1	16.1	9.6	7.0	7.7	2.9	1.7	2.8
75–84	45.5	45.5	58.9	8.9	10.5	16.0	7.2	5.7	8.0	1.7	1.4	2.6
>84	45.8	52.8	66.3	8.7	18.9	17.9	5.8	5.8	5.0	2.8	—[a]	—[a]

[a] Represents or rounds to zero.

Source: U.S. Bureau of the Census, 1990.

widens across the life span (Table 6.2). Among women, the rate rises gradually, from 5.3 per 100,000 among white women in their early twenties and 2.4 among black women of the same age, to peak at 9.6 per 100,000 among white women between the ages of 45 and 54 and 4.2 among black women between the ages of 55 and 64. Women's suicide rate then falls to 5 per 100,000 among the oldest white women and virtually to 0 among the oldest black women. Among white men the rate in the youngest group is 28.4 per 100,000 (more than five times the female rate) and 16.0 among young black men (more than six times the female rate). Men's suicide rate rises continually throughout adulthood, reaching 66.3 per 100,000 among the oldest white men (more than 13 times the female rate) and 17.9 among the oldest black men (U.S. Bureau of the Census, 1990). Since 1981, the suicide rate among older adults, which had been declining for 40 years, has begun to rise again (Gottschalk, 1986). Cohort differences may be responsible for part of this rise, because different cohort groups have different suicide rates during every phase of the life cycle (Cohen, 1990).

These statistics encompass only those deaths officially ruled as suicides. Older adults often use methods that are not as direct as firearms, ropes, or pills. They may starve themselves, refuse to take prescribed medication, engage in hazardous activities, or delay medical or surgical treatment (Miller, 1978).

What leads an older adult to attempt suicide? In one completed suicide, Joseph Wiseman, a 72-year-old retired postal worker, shot and killed his 69-year-old wife, then turned the gun on himself. His wife had been confined to a wheelchair for 11 years, could neither talk, feed, nor bathe herself, and Wiseman, who was rapidly going blind, feared that he would soon be unable to care for her. In an averted suicide, a 72-year-old retired accountant downed a bottle of sleeping pills. He had Parkinson's disease and feared he was a burden to his children; he was also suffering from depression. The accountant had second thoughts and called police. Antidepressant drugs and group therapy lifted his depression and eliminated thoughts of suicide (Gottschalk, 1986).

Social isolation often seems to play a role in the suicide of older, depressed people. Among white males over 60 who committed suicide in Arizona over a five-year period, most had recently lost a confidant. They were also less likely to pay social visits than men who died from natural causes (Miller, 1978).

When a depressed person commits suicide, it is rarely during a deep depression. Instead, the step is usually taken as the depression lifts (Butler and Lewis, 1982). It is not clear whether a person appears to come out of a depression because the decision to commit suicide produces a temporary state of tranquility or whether it is only as the depression lifts that a person has enough energy to commit suicide.

HYPOCHONDRIASIS

Hypochondriasis, an exaggerated fear of disease, is another common functional disorder among older adults, ranking third, behind depression and delusional disorders. It appears to peak between the years of 60 and 64, and it is more prevalent among women than men (LaRue, Dessonville, and Jarvik, 1985). The American Psychiatric Association (1987) classifies hypochondriasis as a *somatoform disorder* because it involves symptoms of physical illness without an organic base. When it develops for the first time in old age, it may not be true hypochondriasis but an indication of depression or a signal that the patient has some underlying degenerative disease that he or she knows nothing about (Simon, 1980).

Hypochondriac patients are preoccupied with their bodily functioning, and this preoccupation interferes with family, friends, social organizations, or occupation. They may report a list of symptoms that include every organ and system in the body. Or they may shift from system to system. This week they have a slipped disk, next week emphysema, and the week after they are certain they have a malfunctioning kidney. Often they are in good physical

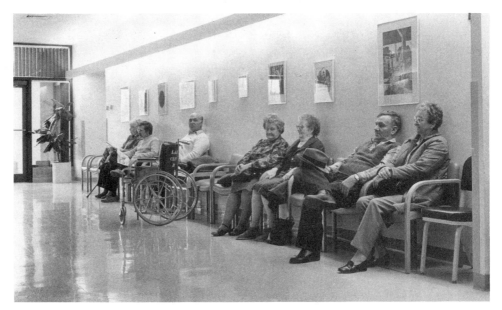

Hypochondriasis, or a fear of disease that is so exaggerated that it interferes with a person's family, social, and occupational life, appears to increase with age.

health, although they cannot be convinced of it. The worst news a physician can give a hypochondriac patient is, "There is nothing wrong with you" (Pfeiffer, 1977).

The disorder may be a response to accumulated stress, and seems most prevalent in situations where a person has suffered prolonged criticism, when the person is isolated because of economic problems, or when marital satisfaction has declined because of a spouse's disability (LaRue, Dessonville, and Jarvik, 1985).

Hypochondriasis serves an important function because it allows people to avoid their problems by escaping into the role of an invalid. It can make a person's sense of deterioration concrete; it gives such people a valid reason for interacting with medical personnel and other caregivers; it displaces anxiety from other problems; it allows them to identify with a deceased loved one who had a similar disease; it punishes them for whatever they feel guilty about; it allows them to escape unwanted duties or social interactions; it punishes those around them; it regulates intimacy with others (Butler and Lewis, 1982).

In addition to all these psychic functions, hypochondriasis allows a person to ask for help in an acceptable way. Often there is an underlying psychological stress that the individual cannot acknowledge. Because emotional disorders are unacceptable to the hypochondriac patient, he or she rejects any attempt to explain the emotional basis of physical symptoms (Pfeiffer, 1977).

ALCOHOLISM

The American Psychiatric Association (1987) considers **alcoholism** a *substance abuse disorder*. It results when a person becomes so dependent on alcohol that it interferes with health, personal relationships, occupation, and social functioning (Simon, 1980). Judging from admissions to psychiatric hospitals and outpatient clinics, the peak years for alcoholism are from 35 to 50. But in a New York City survey, there were two peaks of alcoholism, one between the ages of 45 and 54 and the other between the ages of 65 and 74 (Bailey, Haberman, and Alksne, 1965).

Although alcoholism appears to decline with age, and up to 55 percent of older adults do not drink at all, alcohol is clearly a problem for many men and women past the age of 60 (La Greca, Akers, and Dwyer, 1988). It was once believed that 10 to 15 percent of older adults were alcoholic, but more recent studies indicate that the proportion is closer to 2 percent (Alexander and Duff, 1988). Among older alcoholics, about two-thirds have lengthy histories of alcohol abuse, dating back to early or middle adulthood; the remaining third are late-onset alcoholics, who have turned to alcohol in old age because of grief, depression, loneliness, boredom, or pain. Women usually begin drinking later in life than men do, and there is some evidence that many late-onset alcoholics are women (La Rue, Dessonville, and Jarvik, 1985). A large majority of alcoholics are men, but sex differences may not be as great as is often assumed. Many alcoholics are also depressed, and male alcoholics may be diagnosed as "alcoholic," whereas a woman with the same symptoms may be diagnosed as "depressed" (Kaplan, 1983).

Some psychiatrists believe that the treatment for alcohol abuse should change with age (Zimberg, 1985). Young and middle-aged alcoholics need to become abstinent, and so are best treated in a detoxification program or with a drug that makes them violently ill when they take a drink. But older alcoholics seem to do best when treatment focuses on their social and emotional problems instead of on their abuse of alcohol.

As people age, their tolerance for alcohol decreases, which helps to explain why one-third of older adult alcoholics had no problem with alcohol during their younger years.

That approach worked with one 64-year-old man, whose alcoholism followed decades of social drinking without any alcohol-related problems. Not long after he retired from his job as a railway mechanic, his wife died. He had always been a social drinker, but the double loss of his job and his wife plunged him into a depression. He responded by drinking heavily and began behaving bizarrely in public. When he became unable to get along with his son, he sought help. Medication for his depression, combined with participation in a supervised discussion group composed of older patients with a variety of problems, lifted his depression and he was able to stop abusing alcohol (Brody, 1988).

Because alcohol affects the central nervous system, it temporarily impairs cognitive processes, and the abuse of alcohol may cause permanent damage. Cognitive impairments related to alcohol abuse tend to be much more pronounced among older alcoholics (La Rue, Dessonville, and Jarvik, 1985). This effect has led to the assumption that alcoholism accentuates cognitive aging, but research comparing young and old alcoholics with groups of nonalcoholics showed no interaction between alcoholism and age: the performance skills affected by alcohol tended to be different from those affected by age (Burger, Botwinick, and Storandt, 1987).

Chronic alcoholics may develop organic disorders. Extreme alcohol intoxication can cause acute organic brain disorder at any age. In some cases, the organic disorder is not directly caused by alcohol, but by dietary deficiencies. Alcoholics generally eat very little because alcohol provides energy (calories) without nutrients. Alcohol-related protein deficiency can lead to cirrhosis of the liver, a potentially fatal disease. Long-term deficiencies of vitamin B can lead to **Korsakoff's syndrome,** a chronic organic brain disorder.

A patient with Korsakoff's syndrome looks very much like a patient with Alzheimer's disease. However, differences between the two disorders exist. When researchers tested the memory of patients with the two disorders, they discovered that both groups had severely impaired episodic memory (Weingartner et al., 1983). They could not remember specific events. But unlike patients with Alzheimer's disease, those with Korsakoff's syndrome still had access to semantic memory. They could recall general knowledge (meanings, relationships, and rules for manipulating information). As a result, patients with Korsakoff's syndrome could assemble complex perceptual figures, identify words from fragments, and read inverted text. Patients with Alzheimer's disease simply could not handle these tasks.

Patients with Korsakoff's syndrome have both *anterograde amnesia,* the inability to form new memories, and *retrograde amnesia,* the inability to recall events that occurred before the disease developed (Sloane, 1980). However, some tend to fill in their memory gaps by inventing facts, a process known as *confabulation,* so that in conversation the amnesia may go undetected for a time.

Many cases of alcoholism seem related to some inherited physiological or biochemical abnormality. Sons and brothers of alcoholic men have an extremely high rate of alcoholism (from 25 to 50 percent), and identical twins are twice as likely to share the addiction as fraternal twins (55 percent compared with 28 percent) (Bootzin and Acocella, 1988). Studies have also uncovered differences between young-adult children of alcoholics and young adults whose parents did not abuse alcohol (Kolata, 1987a). Among sons and daughters of alcoholics, eye–hand coordination and muscle control improve *when they drink*—just the opposite of the normal response. They also show a smaller increase in blood levels of certain hormones that normally rise in response to alcohol. It may be that this inherited ability to tolerate alcohol makes it difficult for people to learn how to manage their drinking. They can drink quite a bit of alcohol without feeling or acting drunk, so that they lack the cues that help other people learn when to stop.

MENTAL HEALTH SERVICES

At one time little effort was made to treat functional mental disorders in older adults. Sigmund Freud (1924), the father of psychoanalysis, had felt there was little purpose in using individual psychotherapy with people who were more than 45 years old. They were, he thought, so inflexible that even when they gained insight into their problems, they could not make the necessary personality changes. In addition, if their memory was failing, essential childhood memories might no longer be recalled from the unconscious.

Although some therapists disagreed, many tended to believe that the disorders they saw in older adults were in large part organic, that organic brain disorders were an inevitable part of aging, and that "you can't cure normal aging" (Eisdorfer and Stotsky, 1977). As more has been learned about normal aging, as the biochemical involvement in some disorders has become apparent, and as new therapeutic techniques have been developed, therapy with older adults has become more prevalent.

It seems apparent that a good many older adults can benefit from present forms of therapy, with only minor modifications (Gatz et al., 1985). Many therapists believe that short-term, problem-centered therapy probably works best with older adults, who seem to improve more than younger adults in brief treatment. However, recent research indicates that once adults are older than 80, they require a longer course of therapy to reach the level of change seen in the young-old after brief therapy (Knight, 1988).

Older adults are not a uniform group, and their vast interindividual differences place generalizations about the effectiveness of therapy on shaky ground. It would appear, how-

Counselors at some senior citizen centers provide older adults with short-term therapy focused on problems in daily living.

ever, that individual psychotherapy, cognitive and behavioral therapies, group therapy, and family therapy are all effective (Gatz et al., 1985). These forms may be most suitable for older adults with problems of personal or family adjustment. In the case of depression, cognitive and behavioral therapies are generally effective when the depression seems primarily confined to emotional and cognitive symptoms, but are much less effective when weight loss, sleep disturbance, massive fatigue, and slowed movements are present (Gatz et al., 1985). The latter kind of depression often responds to drugs.

Some therapists have incorporated a form of ''life review'' into the therapeutic process, using reminiscence to reorganize and integrate the person's life. By reviewing their achievements, older adults enhance their self-esteem and can see that they may have overgeneralized their negative interpretations of past events.

Sometimes older adults are best helped by focusing on their real problems in daily living. Mental disorders may develop as a result of physical illness or social circumstance. When this pattern exists, the most helpful course may be to arrange for economic supports, coordinate various aspects of medical care, find home services for those with physical impairment, or develop an informal support network that ensures regular visitation by neighbors or friends. (Such social services will be explored in Chapter 14.) In a case described by Stephen Zarit (1980), for example, a 64-year-old woman who sought therapy for depression had recently been fired and had little income. Her counselor put her in touch with an employment agency that specialized in placing older adults, and she soon had a job. Within two months, her depression had lifted, she left therapy, and continued to function well on her own.

How does most therapy bring about positive changes? Five major processes may be involved: (1) therapy seems to increase hopes of change for the better and expand the sense of control, mastery, and competence; (2) the therapeutic relationship provides solace, bears witness to the importance of the person's life, and demonstrates the possibility of developing new relationships; (3) the recall of events stimulates emotional release; (4) insight gained through therapy helps integrate life experiences and provides meaning to life; and (5) learning helps change behavior, while cognitive processes help change self-defeating thoughts (Gatz et al., 1985). Although this analysis identifies relevant mechanisms of therapeutic change among older adults, much of it applies to therapy with any age group.

SUMMARY

ORGANIC BRAIN DISORDERS

Most **organic brain disorders,** which have a physiological basis, are accompanied by five kinds of mental change: impaired memory, impaired intellect, impaired judgment, impaired orientation, and excessive or shallow emotions. In **acute brain dysfunction** the symptoms are reversible. There are many causes of acute brain dysfunction, but in every case, brain metabolism is disturbed. When the causes are identified and treated, recovery occurs in about a week; when the causes are not identified, the patient may either develop a chronic brain dysfunction or die.

Chronic brain dysfunction, or **dementia,** is most likely to develop in late adulthood. The major cause is **Alzheimer's disease,** a slowly developing condition that is responsible for about half the cases. The disorder can develop in middle-aged adults and is more common in women than in men. Alzheimer's disease affects behavior through its action on the brain's supply of acetylcholine, a neurotransmitter. **Multi-infarct dementia,** a second major chronic brain dysfunction, is caused when blood clots repeatedly cut off the supply of blood to the brain. It may appear as early as 50 and is more common in men than in women. **Parkinson's disease,** a third chronic brain dysfunction, may appear as early as the thirties, although it is most common in the sixties. It apparently is related to a deficiency of dopamine, a neurotransmitter.

Nursing homes use **reality orientation** to keep patients with organic brain disorders in touch with the world about them. Before patients with dementia enter an institution, the attention, supervision, and continual care they require often place such stress on family caregivers that family members may develop depression. In an attempt to relieve this burden, therapists have developed support groups and respite services.

PSYCHOTIC DISORDERS

Mental disorders with no identifiable organic basis are known as **functional mental disorders.** In **psychosis,** a person's perception of reality is drastically distorted, and normal mental activity is severely impaired. **Schizophrenia,** the most common psychosis, is characterized by disturbances of thought, perception, and emotions. The disorder usually appears relatively early in life, and when it makes its initial appearance in older adults, it generally takes a milder form, known as **paraphrenia.** The causes of schizophrenia are not understood, although some genetic predisposition may be necessary for its development.

Delusions are central to **delusional disorders,** or **paranoia,** a condition in which behavior would be logical if the central delusion were true. The appearance of delusional disorders in older adults may be in part an attempt to compensate for sensory or memory loss. Changing the social situation is often an effective treatment.

Depression can appear at any time of life. Although it is the most common functional disorder of later adulthood, it is not caused by aging. Depression may be linked to learned helplessness and the perception that one has no control over life. Life events may lead to depression, but only when changes in the circumstances of a person's life place a strain on social roles. Several neurotransmitters have been implicated in severe depression, but it can also be caused by drugs. Between 30 and 50 percent of all suicides are among depressed individuals. Men are much more likely to commit suicide than women, with the suicide rate increasing steadily with age in white men but peaking between the ages of 45 and 54 in women. Social isolation has been implicated in suicide, which is most likely to occur as a depression lifts.

Hypochondriasis, an exaggerated fear of disease, is the third most common functional disorder among older adults. The condition allows people to avoid their problems by escaping into the role of an invalid and to ask for help in an acceptable way. **Alcoholism** apparently declines with age, with about two-thirds of older alcoholics having lengthy histories of alcoholic abuse. Through long-term vitamin B deficiency, chronic alcoholics may develop **Korsakoff's syndrome,** a chronic brain disorder that somewhat resembles Alzheimer's disease.

MENTAL HEALTH SERVICES

It was once believed that older adults with functional disorders would not respond to therapy, but most gerontologists reject this belief. Therapists are now optimistic about the benefits of therapy with the elderly and tend to favor short-term problem-centered approaches to treatment. Older adults with problems of personal or family adjustment often respond to individual psychotherapy, behavior therapy, group therapy, or family therapy. Older adults whose disorders have developed because of physical illness or social circumstances can probably be helped by providing social services.

KEY TERMS

acute brain dysfunction	Korsakoff's syndrome
alcoholism	multi-infarct dementia
Alzheimer's disease	organic brain disorder
chronic brain dysfunction	paranoia
delusional disorder	paraphrenia
dementia	Parkinson's disease
depression	psychosis
functional brain disorder	reality orientation
hypochondriasis	schizophrenia

Part Three

Psychological Aspects of Adult Development and Aging

Chapter 7

Sensation and Perception
Across Adulthood

A few years ago Harry Porter ran an aviation service out of the Chattanooga, Tennessee, airport. His favorite plane was a twin-engine Beechcraft, which he felt was considerably safer than a single-engine plane. Other than mechanical malfunctions, Porter believed that bad weather was the greatest danger he could face in the sky. Heavy fog or wind shear can bring down the best of pilots. Porter's occupation would not have seemed unusual except for the fact that he was 89 years old and still flying. By mid-1983, he had logged more than 17,000 hours of flying time since he learned to fly half a century earlier (*AARP News Bulletin,* 1983). Although he was still an active pilot, Porter no longer taught others to fly.

Harry Porter's achievement seems especially impressive when we consider that sensory ability generally declines with age and that most people's vision and hearing—two senses that are essential for pilots—undergo pronounced impairment long before their eighty-ninth birthday. Most of us accept the idea that glasses are inevitable and that we will begin to have trouble distinguishing some sounds as we get older. We are less aware that our sense of smell, taste, and touch, as well as our experience of pain, may also change.

The accomplishments of some individuals raise the question of whether our expected sensory impairment is entirely caused by the aging process. For example, at 101, John Henry Smart, a retired Utah farmer, had no serious visual problems. He told a photographer, "My eyesight's awfully good—I take the paper every day" (Barasch, 1983, p. 34). In fact, about 25 percent of 70 year olds and more than 10 percent of 80 year olds still have "perfect" 20–20 vision (Anderson and Palmore, 1974).

In this chapter, we investigate the sensory changes associated with normal aging. After considering some of the factors that may lead to sensory impairment, we take up the senses, one at a time, beginning with vision. After examining changes in the visual system and looking at specific visual disorders that become more common with age, we consider what implications these typical changes have for vision. From vision, we go on to hearing, smell, and taste, and close by considering the senses of touch and pain. In the process, we will discover how aging in the sensory systems affects the experiences of daily life and how changes in the environment can reduce its effects.   ◆

SENSORY AGING

Despite the existence of a few Harry Porters, virtually all of us will experience some loss of sensitivity to environmental stimulation as we age. When light and sound waves stimulate our eyes and ears, gaseous molecules stimulate our noses, soluble molecules stimulate our taste buds, and temperature or pressure stimulates our skin, the perceptual experiences that follow may become different in quality and quantity from our youthful perceptions.

As we get increasingly older, sensory problems generally become more intense, so that there is an age-related increase in the percentage of individuals with severe sensory limitations. For example, between the ages of 45 and 64, less than one person in 200 is legally blind; among centenarians, the ratio rises to five persons in 100 (Rockstein and Sussman, 1979).

Sensory information comes to us as energy changes in the environment. The changes are picked up by specialized receptors, converted into electrical nerve impulses, and processed by structures in the nervous system. The sensory loss that usually accompanies aging may be caused by deterioration of the receptors, degeneration in the peripheral nervous system (the nerve fibers that connect muscles, glands, and sense organs with the central nervous system), or changes in the central nervous system itself. Much of the decline may reflect normal developmental changes, but it may also be caused or speeded up by disease, environmental abuse, or disuse of the sensory system.

Without some kind of sensory information, we could not deal with the environment at all. The brain translates sensations into perceptions by organizing and interpreting the complex patterns of stimulation it receives in the form of nerve impulses. Any sensory loss that accompanies aging thus curtails access to knowledge of the world and may interfere with the ability to communicate effectively with others. A decided impairment in vision or hearing can isolate a person, producing serious psychological or social effects (Wantz and Gay, 1981). For example, a person with a severe hearing loss may find it so tiring to try to follow conversations that he or she simply stops listening, a habit that can lead to withdrawal from social interaction.

In an attempt to simulate some of the sensory loss encountered by many older adults, college students wore specially treated lenses over their eyes and put plugs into their ears (Pastalan, Mautz, and Merrill, 1973). Then the students went into everyday situations, such as supermarkets. The distorted visual and auditory information that came through the sensory

Sensory loss in some older adults may be severe enough to make an ordeal out of a trip to the supermarket, where glare, noise, and precariously stacked cans can create a disorienting situation.

barriers threw these young adults into a state of disorientation. They became cautious and moved very slowly, fumbling for items and faltering when they had to go up or down steps. Sudden perceptual changes are, of course, likely to create a more intense disorientation than gradual impairment, which enables an individual to make a series of small adjustments to sensory decline.

Yet the impairment that develops in many people has led psychologist Diana Woodruff (1983) to suggest that, compared to the young, many older adults are in a state of sensory deprivation. Severe sensory losses may reduce stimulation in the brain below the level required for efficient functioning. At this point, cognition could be affected, leading to disorientation and confusion that sometimes appears in older people without organic brain disorders. As yet, no research has demonstrated that age-related sensory restriction has such an effect.

VISION

The ability to see was important in human evolution, for sight enabled our early ancestors to locate prey and escape predators. Today vision remains central to a society that is heavily dependent on the automobile, the airplane, television, computers, and the printed word (Walsh, 1982). Severe visual impairment can sharply curtail an older person's independence. Many of the changes in vision that occur with age can be explained in terms of normal physiological aging in the structure of the eye, others are due to secondary aging; still others as yet cannot be explained and may be due to factors that are unrelated to the perceptual system itself (Whitbourne, 1985).

CHANGES IN THE VISUAL SYSTEM

Age can bring many changes in vision. Some of them are the result of changes in the eye's structure, and others the result of changes in visual processes.

Structural Changes That Affect Vision

Structural changes in the pupil and the lens have a decided effect on the ability to receive visual stimulation (Figure 7.1). With age, the pupil, the small opening in the center of the iris that allows light to enter the eye, gets smaller. This decrease in size, called **senile miosis,** begins in young adulthood, but its progress is slow. At the same time, the vitreous humor within the eye may become more opaque. By the age of 70, the amount of light that reaches the receptors at the back of the eye may be reduced by at least two-thirds, so that adults need a good deal more light in order to see as clearly as they once did (Spence, 1989).

Once adults are past 70, the pupil responds more slowly so that it takes older eyes longer to adjust to sudden changes in illumination, as when people enter or leave a dark movie theater. The impairment becomes pronounced when driving in the dark, a situation in which the headlights of oncoming cars and lighted intersections cause the level of illumination to change rapidly.

The pupil's responsiveness to changes in light is also modified. Although it continues to alter size in response to variations in light level (widening as light is reduced and constricting as light is increased), with age the difference in size between the light-adapted and the dark-adapted pupil diminishes, so that in the dark the diameter of the average 80 year old's pupil

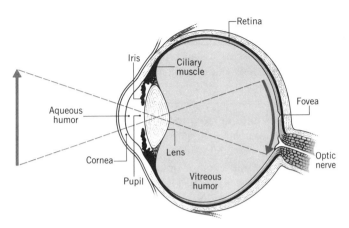

Figure 7.1 Structure of the eye. For clear perception, an image must be sharply focused on the fovea, a small indentation in the retina that is primarily responsible for color vision. The cones (color receptors), which respond in bright light, are densely packed within the fovea; and rods (black, white, and gray receptors), which respond in dim light, dominate the rest of the retina. *Source:* Kimble, Garmezy, and Zigler, 1984, p. 106.

is two-thirds of the average 20 year old's (Fozard, 1990). These changes are believed to be due to muscle weakness, along with the thickening of collagen fibers in the iris (Kline and Schieber, 1985). As a result, older people's vision at dusk or after dark may be comparable to the vision of young adults who are wearing very dark welder's goggles (Sekuler and Blake, 1987).

A second structural change with major effects on vision takes place in the lens of the eye. Cells in the lens grow throughout life, but none are shed, and so the lens gradually thickens, becoming densely packed with shrunken cells that have lost much of the water they once contained. This change reduces the transparency of the lens in 60 percent of the population past the age of 65, further diminishing the amount of entering light that reaches the retina and compounding the effects of senile miosis (Whitbourne, 1985).

Beginning at about the age of 35, the lens begins to turn yellow. Its color progressively deepens, reducing the ability to distinguish colors in the green–blue–violet range. Whether this distortion has serious implications is uncertain (Corso, 1990). Although early studies found a severe loss in color sensitivity beginning at about the age of 70, with 90 year olds unable to identify the color of about half the objects they were shown, later research found color vision remained highly accurate until the age of 90 (Dalderup and Fredericks, 1969; Fozard, 1990). Apparently, clear distance vision and color vision are so closely related that researchers must be careful to control for clarity of vision when assessing color vision (Kline and Schieber, 1985). Even so, older people are more successful at distinguishing colors in the longer wavelengths—yellows, oranges, and reds. Color appears to be one facet of environmental design in which prevailing practices pose fewer hazards for older people: stop and caution lights are still easy for them to interpret.

As the lens becomes increasingly dense and less transparent, the eye becomes more sensitive to glare, a factor that affects people at all ages when a photographer's flashbulb goes off or they suddenly encounter the headlights of an oncoming car on a dark night. Once people are older than 40, they become increasingly sensitive to such glare, with senile miosis aggravating their sensitivity (Whitbourne, 1985).

As the lens thickens, it becomes less flexible, so that it has difficulty changing its shape in order to focus properly at short distances. This ability of the eye to change its focal length is called **accommodation.** The lens's inability to accommodate to short focal lengths becomes noticeable around the age of 40 and keeps worsening until about the age of 60, when many older adults can no longer accommodate at all to near objects. Although no one knows why, women seem to develop the inability to focus at short range, called **presbyopia** ("old sight") approximately three to five years earlier than do men (Kline and Schieber, 1985). Most people first notice their presbyopia when they realize that they must hold a book or newspaper at arm's length in order to read it. The condition is easily corrected with reading glasses, and people who already require glasses for distant vision may need bifocals when they reach their forties. Not only is the ability to accommodate reduced, but the speed with which the process takes place also appears to slow with age. Perhaps as a result of the lens's greater rigidity, the muscles that control its accommodation tend to atrophy, with collagen replacing some of the muscle tissue (Whitbourne, 1985). Once again, the process begins as we approach our forties.

Other structural changes occur with age, but none has major consequences for vision (Whitbourne, 1985). The cornea, which covers and protects the iris and pupil, becomes thicker and less sensitive to mechanical stimulation, and it often loses its sparkle. This dimming of the eye's appearance may be due to changes in its ability to refract light and to a decrease in the amount of fluid that bathes its surface.

Changes in Visual Processes

Not all impairments in vision can be traced to structural change. The field of vision, which refers to the portion of the environment perceived effectively by the eye, remains constant until the age of 35. It then declines slowly until the age of 50, after which it progresses more rapidly, until by the age of 70 the visual field has shrunk to 140 degrees, compared with 170 degrees in young adults. Because depriving young adults of oxygen constricts their visual field, some researchers suspect that much of the shrinkage that occurs with age can be traced to changes in retinal metabolism (Kline and Schieber, 1985).

At present, no one is certain just why visual **acuity,** or the clarity of vision, declines so much with age. Acuity seems to increase until the thirties and then holds stable until the mid-forties. After the age of 50, it declines steadily until, by the age of 85, acuity has fallen to 20 percent of its earlier peak (Spence, 1989). Acuity for moving objects declines even more dramatically than for stationary objects, such as letters on eye charts that are commonly used as a measure of acuity (Kline and Schieber, 1985). For people of all ages, increasing contrast improves acuity, as does increasing the amount of illumination. But no matter how much the light level is raised, most 60 year olds do not see as clearly as 20 year olds. None of the factors that might contribute to reduced acuity—glare, yellowing of the lens, or senile miosis—can account for the dramatic loss in acuity that generally occurs.

The effects of age on depth perception are not clear, but if structural changes affect this aspect of vision, they do so indirectly. Our ability to see depth and locate objects in three-dimensional space is based on a combination of binocular cues (which require the cooperative use of both eyes) and monocular cues (which are available to one eye). Only perception using binocular cues has been studied systematically, and this research indicates that depth perception begins to deteriorate sometime between the ages of 40 and 50—just when other sorts of visual impairments seem to begin (Kline and Schieber, 1985). Any decrease in the amount of light that strikes the retina is likely to interfere with the cooperative use of the eyes; however, some researchers believe that deterioration in binocular depth perception may be caused in part by deterioration in cells within the visual cortex (Corso, 1981). Monocular cues include relative changes in the retinal image when a person moves, the way one object blocks the view of another, lineal perspective, and apparent differences in texture that depend on an object's distance from the eye. It seems reasonable that decreased acuity and increased susceptibility to glare would diminish the value of monocular cues, but the essential research is still lacking (Fozard, 1990).

VISUAL DISORDERS

The aging visual system has been associated with three disorders, but none is the result of normal aging. Because these disorders usually develop slowly and painlessly, they may be far advanced before their presence is discovered in older adults who do not have regular eye examinations.

Glaucoma, a steady increase in pressure within the eye, may develop when fluid is unable to leave the eye by its normal channel. As pressure constricts the blood vessels, nerve cells and fibers are starved for oxygen and die. Vision is gradually destroyed at the periphery of the visual field, so that untreated glaucoma leads first to tunnel vision and eventually to blindness. It first appears among people past the age of 40, but the greatest incidence is among older adults; 3 percent of the population past the age of 65 suffer from severe glaucoma, with another 6 percent having related problems (Verrillo and Verrillo, 1985). Some cases of glaucoma are the result of eye disease or injury; the cause of other cases is unknown, although genetic factors appear to be involved (Spence, 1989). Your chances of developing glaucoma are increased tenfold if a family member has had the disease and threefold if you are diabetic (AARP Pharmacy Service, 1989). Drugs or eye drops may either improve drainage or reduce the formation of fluid, thus halting further destruction of nerve cells. In some cases, however, laser surgery, which provides a way to drain the fluid, is required.

A second common visual disorder is **cataracts,** a condition in which a portion of the lens becomes opaque so that light cannot penetrate it. Cataracts also become increasingly common with age; 20 percent of people with cataracts are between the ages of 45 and 65, while 75 percent are older than 65 (Brody, 1982). No one has yet been able to discover a direct cause of cataracts, although people who develop them often have elevated levels of sugar in the blood. Extensive exposure to high levels of ultraviolet radiation is also suspected of being related to the growth of cataracts, which suggests that people who spend most of the time outdoors should wear dark glasses (Kline and Schieber, 1985). Most cataracts can be treated. When a cataract impairs vision, surgical removal of the lens and its replacement with a lens implant, contact lenses, or special glasses are usually helpful, although many patients are disappointed when only partial vision is restored. Patients who have been highly active before their surgery tend to regain the most vision (Corso, 1990).

The third visual disorder associated with aging is **macular degeneration,** in which the central portion of the retina deteriorates. This part of the retina is essential to tasks like reading, which require fine discrimination. Macular degeneration causes about 25 percent of severe visual damage among people younger than 80, and 40 percent of damage among people past 80 (Verrillo and Verrillo, 1985). The disorder may strike one eye or both, and it may be either hereditary or the secondary effect of other diseases. Neither medical nor surgical treatment can reverse the course of this disease, but the use of powerful magnifying glasses can restore some visual acuity. Because macular degeneration does not affect peripheral vision, most afflicted people can continue to function adequately in familiar surroundings.

IMPLICATIONS FOR VISUAL PROCESSING

As people age, they seem to process visual information more slowly than they once did. For example, even when their visual acuity is as sharp as a young adult's, people past 60 take longer to extract information from a display that is flashed briefly on a screen before them (Scialfa and Kline, 1988). Some older adults may learn to compensate for this slowing in daily life by using cues from their surroundings or taking advantage of advance information.

An aspect of vision that has been extensively investigated is the ability to detect when a light that flashes rapidly is not a steady source of illumination. The point at which a flickering light can be detected as such is called the **critical flicker frequency (CFF).** Most older adults find that the flickering light fuses into a steady beam at a level at which younger adults are still reporting a decided flicker. Some researchers have suggested that age differences in critical flicker frequency develop because the older nervous system takes longer to recover from stimulation, a condition known as **stimulus persistence** (Botwinick, 1978). For example, when researchers tested healthy, highly educated adults with alternate flashes of red and green light (which the eye fuses to produce yellow), those in their sixties reported seeing a yellow light significantly more often than did those in their twenties (Kline, Ikeda, and Schieber, 1982). The effect remained even when young adults were tested in dim light and older adults were tested with more illumination, indicating that changes in neural functioning, not a reduction in the amount of light reaching the retina, is responsible.

Another aspect of vision, known as contrast sensitivity, has also been found to change with age. **Contrast sensitivity function (CSF)** can be assessed by giving people brief glimpses of stationary patterns, made up of alternating light and dark bars of the same width, and asking them to detect the patterns. When the bars are wide and contrast is high, little age difference appears, but as the bars narrow and contrast decreases, older adults find the patterns more difficult to detect (Figure 7.2). Older adults also react more slowly to the appearance of the patterns, but the difference in reaction time cannot be fully explained by diminished contrast sensitivity, indicating that slowed processing in the nervous system may be involved. Contrast sensitivity function is a more important measure of vision than is acuity, because CSF provides a fairly accurate test of performance in everyday settings (Corso, 1990). CSF tests can predict how well visually impaired people will get around in the environment, the ability of experienced pilots to see objects on the ground at twilight or in fog, and how severely glare from various light sources will impair vision (Sekuler and Blake, 1985). Some studies suggest that disease, not the aging process, is responsible for changes in contrast sensitivity (Whitbourne, 1985).

Studies in contrast sensitivity underscore the wide range of interindividual differences in aging. In one study (Kline et al., 1983), one of the older subjects was a man in his late sixties who had 50 years of experience in shooting at targets. This marksman's response

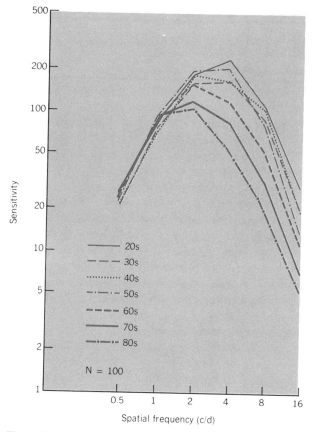

Figure 7.2 Age and contrast-sensitivity function. Age-related effects of the contrast sensitivity function for monocular vision, by decade of adulthood. Observers who normally used optical correction wore their glasses. *Source:* Sekuler, Owsley, and Hukman, 1982, pp. 689–700.

time and sensitivity to contrast was matched by only two of the college students, and no one surpassed his performance. Perhaps practice and experience can compensate even for aspects of aging that are considered inevitable.

IMPLICATIONS FOR DAILY LIFE

Significant eye impairments affect one in four older adults (Heinemann et al., 1988). As a result, many older adults find it increasingly difficult to read, to recognize faces and facial expressions, to perform physical tasks that rely on visual guidance, to recognize important features of their environment, and to see at night (National Advisory Eye Council, 1983). Among a group of visually impaired adults between the ages of 62 and 97, poor vision, not age, was associated with a decline in leisure activities (Heinemann et al., 1988). Sixty percent of these women and men reported giving up such activities as gardening, cooking, sewing, knitting, auto maintenance, and writing after their vision had worsened.

◆ *Adulthood in Today's World*

THE AGING DRIVER

How serious is the problem of the aging driver on American highways? Senile miosis, slowed response to changes in illumination, reduced transparency of the lens, increased sensitivity to glare, lessened acuity for moving objects, a shrunken visual field, and diminished depth perception all would seem to affect driving skills. Because less light reaches the older driver's retina, he or she may have to make critical decisions on the basis of incomplete, or even erroneous, information (Whitbourne, 1985).

Yet a two-year study of older drivers indicates that, between the ages of 25 and 75, age alone is a poor predictor of the ability to drive (*AARP News Bulletin,* 1989). Drivers between the ages of 65 and 74 have a safety record that is nearly as good and sometimes better than that of drivers between the ages of 25 and 54. Once drivers pass the age of 75, they are twice as likely to be in an accident as drivers in the younger group. However, the most dangerous drivers are not those older than 75 but drivers under the age of 25.

Studies indicate that the older driver's ability is not seriously impaired during daylight hours. Adults in their sixties were as efficient as those in their twenties when tested on daytime driving with eyes open (Sterns, Barrett, and Alexander, 1985). However, on basic skills related to driving, such as visual search and quick reactions, drivers in their sixties were much slower than drivers in their twenties—although there were vast interindividual differences, with some older drivers scoring as well as most younger drivers. The excellent driving record of some older drivers can be explained by the fact that they show few, if any, of the typical visual changes associated with aging. Others maintain good records by driving more cautiously, reducing their speed, staying off busy expressways and out of rush-hour traffic, and no longer driving at night.

There is no doubt that older drivers are at a disadvantage after dark. When drivers in their sixties were matched for visual acuity with drivers in their twenties, the older drivers still needed between 65 and 77 percent more driving distance to read road signs at night (Sivak, Olson, and Pastalan, 1981). This drop in legibility means that older drivers have less time to make driving decisions when driving at night, a factor for which they can partially compensate by reducing their speed. Older drivers' susceptibility to glare means that it takes them longer than the young to recover from the effect of oncoming headlights and to adjust when moving rapidly from lighted intersections to shadowy roads. Once again, however, some older drivers can see in dim light as well as younger drivers and are no more bothered by glare than the young (Sterns, Barrett, and Alexander, 1985).

Since 1979, the American Association of Retired Persons has offered a refresher course for older drivers, which helps them cope with traffic problems on today's highways and informs them about the effects of aging on their driving skills (*AARP News Bulletin,* 1989). Such courses not only make safer drivers out of older adults, but also earn them discounts on their car insurance. By keeping drivers on the road, the courses postpone the jolt to self-esteem and independence that comes when people in an automobile-based society discover they can no longer drive.

Even adults who have escaped serious visual disorders may find their worlds contracting (Whitbourne, 1985). Changes in depth perception may cause them to collide with furniture, trip over curbs, or fall down stairs. Senile miosis and sensitivity to glare may make a trip to the supermarket an unpleasant, threatening experience. In response, they may feel insecure and avoid unfamiliar settings. The resultant self-isolation may lead to curtailed physical activity and eventually to poorer health.

By now we know enough about typical changes in vision to make life easier and simpler for people whose impaired sight has begun to interfere with their life but does not yet threaten their ability to see. Glasses are obvious ways to increase the amount and quality of visual information, but changing the environment can also be effective. Increasing light levels, reducing glare, and heightening contrasts are ways to compensate for decreased retinal illumination (Whitbourne, 1985). Halls, staircases, entrances, and landings are primary candidates for increased lighting. Because of the effect of glare on the aging eye, the use of diffused light in public places would make navigation easier and safer for older adults. If the lights are yellowish instead of blue, the problem of glare will be further minimized. Older people frequently fall on stairs, and the accident tends to occur at the top of the landing. Windows often make a corridor much brighter than the staircase, so that when people turn away from the light to go down stairs they must adapt to lower levels of illumination. Slowed adaptation to light levels can lead them to misjudge the first step. Simply placing a light above the top stair can sharply reduce these accidents.

Other simple, but effective, changes include painting wall switches to contrast with walls and covering the horizontal treads of stairs with different materials from those used on the vertical risers. In places like restaurants or theaters, where dim lights cannot be avoided, carrying a penlight to read a menu or find a seat can turn a trial into a pleasure (Sekuler and Blake, 1987). Adjustments that can assist older adults to drive with safety are discussed in the box, ''The Aging Driver.'' Impaired vision is not the only environmental constraint on older adults. Some of the changes in the aging visual system are paralleled by changes in the auditory system.

HEARING

Much of the information from the environment comes to us through our ears. Sound waves, caused by pressure changes in the atmosphere, travel through the air and strike the ear drum, causing it to vibrate and transmit an amplified sound wave through the bones of the middle ear and then deep into the inner ear, where the sound receptors are located in the cochlea (Figure 7.3). These sound receptors, called hair cells, produce a signal that passes along the auditory nerve to the brain. A sound has both intensity, which determines its loudness, and frequency, which determines its pitch. The higher a sound's frequency, measured in hertz (Hz), the higher the pitch.

CHANGES IN THE AUDITORY SYSTEM

As we grow older, the ability to receive and interpret sounds declines, with a gradual loss of hearing that begins during the thirties for many people and accelerates after the age of fifty (Whitbourne, 1985) (Figure 7.4). By the time men are older than 32 and women are

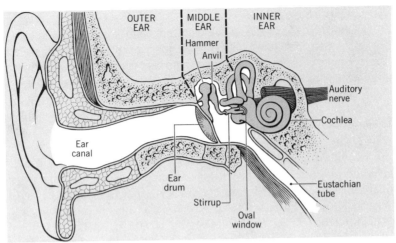

Figure 7.3   Major structures of the ear. *Source:* Nelson, 1984, p. 163.

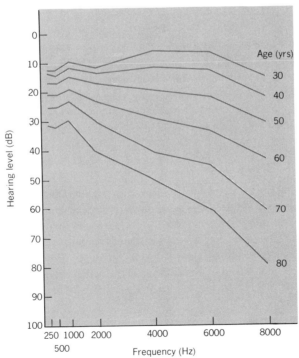

Figure 7.4   Hearing and age. Hearing level frequency by age decade in adulthood. *Source:* Lebo and Reddell, 1972, pp. 1402–1403. Copyright © 1972 by the Laryngoscope Company. As adapted by Whitbourne, 1985.

older than 37, nearly all show some degree of impairment, however slight; men are especially vulnerable to the loss of hearing. Younger cohorts may begin to lose some hearing at an earlier age, however, because of their exposure to loud environmental noise and music. Such losses can be detected by the capacity to detect pure tones. In these tests, interindividual differences are greatest in the perception of high-frequency sounds and increase with age, so that the spread of ability at 8000 Hz is 3 1/2 times as great among 65 year olds as it is among 25 year olds (Corso, 1981). (The human voice has a customary range of about 120 to 600 Hz, although a soprano can soar well above 1000 Hz. The highest note on a piano is 4100 Hz, and the highest frequency that can be detected by human beings is about 20,000 Hz.)

Although not everyone suffers a large loss of hearing, a sizable minority have so great an impairment that it interferes with daily activities. Estimates of hearing impairment among older adults range from 12 percent to more than 50 percent, and some researchers believe that about 33 percent of people past the age of 65 have a loss that is large enough to have unfavorable social consequences (Whitbourne, 1985). Part of this hearing loss is caused by a buildup of wax in the outer ear, which may impair the ability to hear sounds in the low-frequency range, but most hearing loss is due to changes in the inner ear (Spence, 1989).

AUDITORY DISORDERS

The progressive, age-related loss of the ability to hear high-frequency sounds is known as **presbycusis,** which means ''old hearing.'' It first affects sounds that are above the range of human speech, so that its onset usually goes unnoticed until it progresses into those frequencies (Spence, 1989). The disorder originates in the cochlea, the fluid-filled chamber in the inner ear, and it may be the result of damage or of aging. There are four kinds of presbycusis, each the result of different structural changes and each affecting hearing in a different way. *Sensory presbycusis* is caused by atrophy and degeneration of the hair cells. It produces a loss of high-frequency sounds but does not interfere with the discrimination of speech. *Neural presbycusis* is caused by the loss of auditory nerve fibers. It affects the ability to distinguish the sounds of speech, especially in the higher frequencies, but it does not affect the ability to hear pure tones. *Strial presbycusis* is caused by vascular changes within the cochlea and affects hearing at all frequencies. Speech discrimination remains good until the loss progresses past a certain level. *Mechanical presbycusis* is caused by atrophy of the vibrating membrane within the cochlea. It causes a gradual loss of hearing in all frequencies, but becomes progressively worse as frequencies increase (Whitbourne, 1985). In most cases, a person with presbycusis has more than one type (Verrillo and Verrillo, 1985).

As people begin to develop presbycusis, they find themselves missing certain high-frequency sounds: the song of birds, the ring of a telephone, the ticking of a clock. High-frequency consonants, such as *s, z, t, f,* and *g,* become inaudible, and a person must strain to follow a conversation. It becomes difficult to distinguish one-syllable words, so that ''sit'' sounds just like ''fit.'' Older individuals may also find some women's speech harder to distinguish than the speech of men, for men's voices tend to be louder and lower in pitch. By the age of 80, a person may miss 25 percent of the words in a conversation (Feldman and Reger, 1967).

It is difficult to distinguish age-related presbycusis from that caused by damage to the

Steady exposure to loud noise can so damage hearing that many industries must provide noise protectors for their employees.

inner ear. People who live in environments with low noise levels show less hearing loss than those who live in noisy environments, but there is some loss at high frequencies in all cross-cultural studies (Olsho, Harkins, and Lenhardt, 1985). Despite improved general health, the rate of damage-related presbycusis in the United States may be increasing at all ages. Most Americans live in a noisy environment, and excessive exposure to noise can permanently impair hearing by destroying hair cells or damaging other cochlear structures. For example, the vibration of extremely loud sounds can literally tear apart the hair cells, eliminating the ability to hear sounds in that frequency range. If exposure is infrequent, the muscles around the stirrup (the delicate, stirrup-shaped bone in the middle ear that transmits amplified sound to the cochlea) restrain its movements, but they cannot protect the hair cells from excessive noise that continues for long periods. Permanent damage caused by noise exposure is so similar to age-related damage that some researchers call it premature presbycusis (Corso, 1990).

The loudness of a noise is measured in decibels (dB). As the intensity of a sound increases by 20 decibels, it is experienced as being ten times louder. Among familiar sounds, a whisper is about 30 decibels; normal conversation, about 60 decibels; traffic noise at a city intersection, 75 decibels; a vacuum cleaner, 80 decibels; a power lawn mower, 96 decibels; a subway train, 100 decibels; a rock band, 115 decibels; a jet at takeoff, 140 decibels. Sounds louder than 80 decibels are usually annoying; at 130 decibels sound becomes painful.

Gunfire can cause sudden, permanent deafness, but steady exposure to loud noises at lower levels damages hair cells more slowly, with destruction at all levels more pronounced for men than for women (Corso, 1990). Unprotected workers in assembly plants, airports, and construction jobs often suffer permanent damage, with the magnitude of hearing loss related to the length of time on the job (Sekuler and Blake, 1985).

Sometimes presbycusis is reversible. These cases are often caused by massive doses of aspirin, which can reduce the ability to hear by 10 to 40 decibels, particularly for high-frequency sounds. The daily amount of aspirin required to cause hearing loss is 4 to 8 grams (16 to 24 tablets), which is about the dosage prescribed for arthritis patients. When the aspirin is discontinued, hearing returns in a day or so (Sekuler and Blake, 1985). Aspirin-induced presbycusis is often accompanied by another age-related hearing difficulty known as tinnitus.

Tinnitus is a persistent ringing, roaring, or buzzing in the ears. Its incidence rises from 3 percent among young adults and 9 percent among the middle-aged to 11 percent among those between 65 and 74 (Rockstein and Sussman, 1979). Tinnitus also frequently accompanies presbycusis that has been caused by exposure to excessive noise, leading some researchers to speculate that it comes from spontaneous activity among neural receptors bordering on regions of hearing loss (Corso, 1990). Others have suggested that wax, tumors, middle-ear infections, bone growth in the middle ear, drugs (including aspirin), or allergies are responsible, but in most cases the cause is not known. When the noise can be traced to some physical problem within the ear, surgery is often effective; when no physical cause can be found, psychotherapy, biofeedback, a hearing aid, or a device producing a mild sound that masks the internal noise may be effective.

IMPLICATIONS FOR AUDITORY PROCESSING

Whether or not people have presbycusis, the processing of sounds is affected by age. Older adults process pure tones more slowly than do the young. Among men, reaction time almost doubles (from 0.2 to 0.37 second) between the ages of 20 and 60; among 70 year olds, reaction time increases further, to 0.53 second (Corso, 1981). However, this difference may not be simply a matter of slowed processing. When asked to make a decision about sounds, such as indicating when they detect a sound in the presence of noise, older adults take much longer than younger adults to make their decision, even though both groups have the same ability to detect tones. Older adults seem more cautious in making "certain" that they hear a tone before they indicate its presence (Kline and Schieber, 1985). For this reason, an apparent impairment in hearing may have little to do with whether sounds have actually been detected.

Under ideal conditions, age differences in the comprehension of speech match the ability to detect pure tones. When older and younger adults are matched for hearing loss, both groups hear isolated words equally well. These findings indicate that when sounds are not distorted, impairment is limited to changes in structures within the ear, whether caused by damage or aging (Whitbourne, 1985).

Under adverse conditions, however, age differences widen substantially, suggesting that auditory processing within the brain is the dominant influence on performance. Sentences that can be comprehended under test conditions become unintelligible when words overlap or are interrupted. This effect begins to appear as early as the thirties and becomes pronounced by the sixties (Corso, 1981). Because of this effect, older adults who can follow a conversation under ideal circumstances may have trouble when several people are talking together or in such situations as a cocktail party.

The rate of speech is also important. At normal speaking rates (140 words per minute), increasing the intensity of speech brings the older individual's comprehension to almost 100 percent. But when speech is speeded up to 350 words per minute, older adults cannot understand more than 45 percent of the words, no matter how loudly they are spoken. Yet younger adults can understand the rapid, but louder talk (Calearo and Lazzaroni, 1957). Although the comprehension of older adults deteriorates drastically when speech is extremely rapid, speaking more slowly than normal does not improve comprehension—at least not when speech is heard in the laboratory, where the use of earphones eliminates the visual cues provided by a speaker's slowed lip movements (Corso, 1990).

In fact, older adults may understand a good deal more of what is said by people around them than these studies indicate. When researchers had younger and older adults listen to various sentences, most adults between the ages of 60 and 75 were as adept as college students at using the linguistic context of a sentence as an aid to comprehension (Hutchinson, 1989). All the subjects had relatively normal hearing for their age. Although the sentences were heard against background noise, the older adults did about as well as the young in understanding such sentences as "The bird of peace is the dove" or "The cigarette smoke filled his lungs." But when context was of no help, as in "I will now say the word cards" or "Mr. Smith knew about the bay," wide age differences appeared.

IMPLICATIONS FOR DAILY LIFE

Having to guess at conversation they have just heard may have adverse psychological consequences for older people with hearing impairments. As Blasa Aparicio, a 101-year-old woman, explained, "It's difficult when you can't hear well, because they ask you one thing and you answer another. You have no control of your hearing. It's embarrassing" (Barasch, 1983, p. 20). Such embarrassment can make an older person feel inferior and helpless in a social situation. If older people with presbycusis withdraw and stop trying to distinguish what people are saying or if continued difficulty in making themselves understood causes others to reduce their conversation, social isolation can follow.

Older men and women can take certain steps to reduce their isolation. Hard surfaces exaggerate background noise and may cause echoes, so when in a crowded room, the older person can move away from large windows and plaster walls and stand near soft materials that absorb sound, such as draperies, bookshelves, or upholstered furniture. A high-backed upholstered chair can also shield its occupant from much of the background noise (Sekuler and Blake, 1987). And, of course, focusing on a speaker's lips increases an older person's comprehension dramatically, as does a conversational partner who lowers his or her voice, speaks slowly and distinctly, and remembers not to turn away while talking.

Remarkable advances have been made in hearing aids, but none returns perception to pre-impairment levels. Until recently, hearing aids magnified all sounds equally. If hearing loss is primarily in the higher frequencies, increasing sound intensity enough to make higher frequencies audible may make lower frequencies far too loud. Simple amplification also increases the level of background sounds such as the hum of an air conditioner or conversations among people in another part of the room. In early presbycusis these hearing aids may be more or less satisfactory. Among adults who have tried them, 90 percent of 60 year olds and 70 percent of 70 year olds seem satisfied; but among 80 year olds, less than 40 percent find them useful (Olsho, Harkins, and Lenhardt, 1985). Many older adults buy hearing aids without an adequate medical evaluation of their impairment. For them, bitter disappointment often follows, and some may react as did the sharp-eyed centenarian, John Henry Smart, who said: "Hearing aids are a joke. I bought two of 'em and throwed both of 'em against the wall. They're no good!" (Barasch, 1983, p. 34).

Newer, more expensive, hearing aids amplify sounds selectively. These digital hearing aids use computer circuitry to analyze sounds in terms of frequency, rhythm, and loudness. Using this information, the aid enhances speech and tunes out distracting background noise (Kirsch, 1989). These aids may cost as much as $2000, compared with $550 to $1000 for conventional hearing aids, and they are bulky because the earpiece is connected to a pocket-size computer. To a 73-year-old Memphis man, the extra expense was worth it. He wore a conventional aid for about eighteen months, and then gave it up because it was useless unless he took it to an audiologist for adjustment every other week. Now he wears a digital aid, which has required adjustment only three times in the last year and which, he says, has helped ''tremendously'' (Marklein, November 1989).

At any age, adults with neural presbycusis are not helped by increases in sound intensity. For them, a **cochlear implant** may be the answer. In this device, an exterior microphone transmits sounds to an implanted receiver-processor that in turn sends vibrations to electrodes that have been inserted into the cochlea. The implant takes over the function of the destroyed hair cells, picking up sounds, converting them to electrical impulses, and sending them directly to the auditory nerve. Implants require a lengthy adjustment period, because they produce a distorted sound like that from a poorly tuned radio full of humming, crackle, and static. Implants seem to work best when they are combined with lip-reading; they make loud warning sounds, such as automobile horns, slamming doors, approaching trucks, or the signal emitted by a smoke detector, audible.

As a consequence of uncorrected impairment, some older people may become withdrawn, insecure, depressed, confused, or isolated. As we saw in Chapter 5, deafness has been connected with delusional disorders. Among older adults in mental hospitals, the rate of deafness is especially high among those who have been diagnosed as having delusional disorders (Post, 1980). It has been suggested that deafness may develop so slowly that older people at first attribute their inability to follow conversations to the fact that people are whispering. Yet others deny that they are speaking too softly. Continued denials of what seems an obvious fact to older persons leads them to assume that others are lying and trying to hide information. Older persons' suspicion and hostility may make friends and acquaintances avoid them, and a simple search to explain why speech cannot be heard develops into an adaptive delusion.

An experiment with college students indicates that, at least in a few cases, the explanation may be valid (Zimbardo, Andersen, and Kabat, 1981). Three groups of men who had been screened to eliminate anyone with psychological problems were told that they were participating in a study of the effects of hypnotism on creative problem solving. When they were hypnotized, men in two of the groups were told that when they came out of their hypnotic state they would have difficulty hearing. Men in one ''deaf'' group were told that they would not remember the instructions to become deaf; men in the other ''deaf'' group were told that they would remember the instructions. Men in the control group were told that they would feel a compulsion to scratch their ears but would not remember the suggestion.

During the preliminary phase of the experiment, two confederates of the experimenter kept up a running conversation (which the men could not hear). Finally they asked each student who had been hypnotized if he would like to work with them on the creative problem-solving task, which required them to create stories about pairs of people shown in ambiguous relationships. Students who did not know why they were deaf generally refused to work with the confederates, and on a personality test they filled out, they were more irritated, agitated, hostile, tense and unfriendly than men in the other groups. Although the students with unexplained deafness said they were not suspicious, the stories they wrote about the pictures showed the judgmental attitude toward others that is a hallmark of paranoia. Afterward, the men received full explanations of the study, and none showed any lingering effects. Even so, this experiment has been criticized for its use of deception. From the results, researchers concluded that the search for a rational explanation for their inability to hear might lead some middle-aged and older adults who are already predisposed to be suspicious into developing paranoid reactions.

Yet most hearing-impaired older people are not actually isolated, even though some say they are. In other research, older adults' reports of loneliness and isolation correlated with their degree of hearing loss, but their actual isolation—when measured by social activity—was unrelated to their impairment (Corso, 1990). Perhaps the effort involved in conversing with hearing-impaired adults places a strain on relationships, making the adult with presbycusis feel isolated even in social situations.

When hearing loss is their only problem, however, older adults seem to adjust to it. In a group of healthy, middle-class individuals between the ages of 60 and 89, those with presbycusis were no more anxious, depressed, hostile, or worried about their health than those who had no hearing impairment (Thomas et al., 1983). Nor did the hearing loss affect these adults' intelligence test performance exactly as expected. In some studies (e.g., Ohta, Carlin, and Harmon, 1981), hearing loss has been closely related to losses in intellectual functioning. Among the adults in this study (Thomas et al., 1983), those with impaired hearing had lower scores on a verbal test of cognition but did just as well as those without impairment on a nonverbal test. Perhaps, as Susan Whitbourne (1985) suggests, hearing loss isolates older adults from the cognitive stimulation involved in conversation, listening to television and radio, and general exposure to cultural influences—all of which affect verbal intelligence scores. If so, adults with presbycusis who regularly watch closed-captioned television programs, as well as those who read widely, should show less decline than adults who lack these forms of cognitive stimulation.

SMELL AND TASTE

Although we get much less information through the nose and mouth than we do through our eyes and ears, smell and taste are important human senses. Both can save our lives—our olfactory sense can detect dangerous odors in the air, and our gustatory sense can detect the bitter taste that often signals the presence of poison. The final flavor we assign to food is a combination of smell and taste, and when smell is temporarily impaired, as occurs with a cold, food may taste flat.

CHANGES IN THE SENSE OF SMELL

The proficiency of smell generally declines with age. Olfactory receptor cells live for only about five to eight weeks, and then die and are replaced by new cells. This process goes on throughout life, but it appears that as people age, more receptor cells may be lost than are replaced. Layers of cells in the olfactory bulbs, which receive input from the receptor cells, also show some thinning. As yet, no one is certain how this change relates to declines in olfaction (Bartoshuk and Weiffenbach, 1990).

The loss of olfactory ability is by no means universal and is often related to disease. Early in Parkinson's disease, the ability to detect and identify odors declines (Doty, Deems, and Stellar, 1988), and in early Alzheimer's disease, there is a loss of the ability to identify odors but not the ability to detect them (Koss et al., 1988). Identifying an odor that has been isolated from any cues presents a cognitive challenge even to young adults, and so the nature of the loss in Alzheimer's disease suggests that after odors are detected, the information is not processed properly within the brain. Other health-related factors that damage the sense of smell include viral and bacterial infections. These conditions may change nasal tissues in such a way that less air reaches them, thus curtailing the amount of stimuli that contacts receptors (Doty and Snow, 1986). As with other age-related declines, healthy people often fail to conform to the statistical norm. In a test of retired university staff members, those between the ages of 60 and 90 were *more* sensitive to some odors than adults between the ages of 20 and 50 (Rovee, Cohen, and Shlapack, 1975).

Age-related losses in the ability to detect odors also depend on the structure of molecules in the vapor that stimulates the sensory receptors. At about the age of 50, the ability to detect the odor of mercaptans (the chemicals added to odorless natural gas and propane to enable their detection) begins to decline, but the ability to detect the odor of roses shows no change until the age of 70. Other studies have shown that the odor of natural gas must be approximately twice as intense for adults in their seventies to detect as for young adults. In fact, only a few adults older than 60 could detect the odor of propane at intensity levels commonly used as a warning (Bartoshuk and Weiffenbach, 1990). Because many homes use gas for heating or cooking, this finding is cause for concern and may indicate that the use of mercaptans to warn consumers leaves many older adults vulnerable to accidents from leaking gas. Illness may be responsible for a good deal of this failure, because healthy adults past the age of 65 can recognize natural gas when only 10 parts per million are in the air.

Unless an odor is dangerous, as when it comes from leaking gasoline or gas from an unlighted stove, the pleasantness or unpleasantness of the scent may be more important than simple detection (Engen, 1977). People's preference for odor seems related to age. Children prefer fruity odors, such as strawberry, but adults prefer the smell of flowers, such as lavender, and their preferences do not change after the age of 30. Familiarity appears to have a good deal to do with odor preference. When people are asked to rate odors, they generally dislike any that are unfamiliar (Engen, 1974). Thus, our past experiences play a large role in determining whether a particular odor will evoke appreciation or disgust.

It might be expected that the intensity of an odor would affect a person's reaction to it. Age appears to reduce sensitivity to concentrated smells. In a study that compared adults' reaction to menthol (a common ingredient of sweets, cigarettes, and toiletries), older adults required a much larger change in the concentration of the scent before indicating that its intensity had increased (Murphy, 1983). As menthol concentration rose, younger adults said that the smell became more pleasant, but older adults tended to rate most concentrations about the same. Yet, as with other studies, the two groups overlapped. In fact, one 70-year-old man had the same threshold for the odor as the average young adult, and he reacted just as the younger group did to changes in intensity.

Some odors not only seem less intense and harder to identify with age, but also become less unpleasant (Bartoshuk and Weiffenbach, 1990). When asked to rate their reactions to diesel exhaust fumes and to the mercaptans in natural gas, people past 65 found them much less objectionable than did younger people. This diminishing unpleasantness of foul odors could affect older people's social relationships (Whitbourne, 1985). An insensitivity to pet or body odors might drive away younger people who find the smells offensive.

As with other body systems, the sense of smell may deteriorate through misuse, and exercising the ability to detect odors may help preserve it. If that is so, then odors that people enjoy or value and so seek out may be less vulnerable to age-related loss (Whitbourne, 1985). Yet except when disease is responsible, declines in sensory ability are usually minor. In most cases, the concentration of naturally occurring odors is so intense that losses rated as ''significant'' in the laboratory have little effect on daily life.

CHANGES IN THE SENSE OF TASTE

Like the receptor cells for smell, the receptors for taste are continually replaced, but there may be no age-related decline in the overall numbers of taste buds. Researchers have discovered wide interindividual differences in the density of taste buds across the tongue, but the density has no relation either to age or to sex (Miller, 1988). Ninety year olds are as likely to have a dense clustering of taste buds as 22 year olds.

Although taste-bud density does not decline with age, taste sensitivity weakens. Early studies indicated that for people who have reached 60, tastes must be more concentrated for them to be detected, but others showed no change after the age of 40. Much of the earlier discrepancy was due to differences in the methods used to assess the threshold; with the adoption of more accurate technology, results are in general agreement (Bartoshuk and Weiffenbach, 1990).

We perceive a multitude of flavors, but there are only four basic tastes: sweet, salty, sour, and bitter. Thresholds for salt clearly rise with age, so that older adults require a more concentrated solution before they can detect it. Rises also appear in the thresholds for sour and bitter tastes. Research with older men indicates that medication is responsible for at least part of the difference in age-related responses to salt and sour (Spitzer, 1988). Men on hypertensive medication have significantly higher salt thresholds than men with normal blood pressure, and older men who take other prescribed drugs cannot detect sour until the solution reaches three times the intensity detected by men who take no medication. Even among unmedicated men, however, there was some decline in sensitivity to these flavors.

The ability to detect sweet shows virtually no change with age. If anything, older adults are *more,* not less, sensitive to weak sugar solutions than younger adults. As the intensity of a sweet solution increases, the reactions of young and old are identical (Bartoshuk et al., 1986).

Sensitivity to weak solutions in the laboratory bears little relationship to taste responses in the higher concentrations that we encounter in food. Researchers have concluded that, compared with sensitivity to odors, taste remains remarkably intact in older adults (Bartoshuk and Weiffenbach, 1990).

IMPLICATIONS FOR NUTRITION

What does all this mean for older adults? It is widely believed that as people grow older, food no longer tastes as good and that this decline in enjoyment of food is responsible for loss of appetite and consequent malnutrition in some elderly. Research on the appeal of food indicates that whatever loss of appetite develops is not due primarily to the loss of receptors for taste and smell.

The enjoyment of food comes not from taste alone, but from a combination of smell, taste, color, temperature, and texture. Research using blended food shows that older adults are as adept as the young in identifying mixtures of salt or sugar with cornstarch and water, but that the ability to detect blended foods declines with age (Bartoshuk and Weiffenbach, 1990; Verrillo and Verrillo, 1985). For example, 78 percent of college students, but only 33 percent of older adults, could identify blended strawberries on the basis of taste and odor; 63 percent of college students, but only 7 percent of older adults, could identify blended carrots. The major reason for this decline has little to do with taste, but a great deal to do with odor and memory (Corso, 1990).

As we saw, some odors seem much less intense to older people than to younger adults; this diminished sensitivity may be responsible for much of the decline in the enjoyment of food (Moore, Nielsen, and Mistretta, 1982). The case of a woman whose taste threshold rose sharply after radiation therapy for cancer of the neck also supports this proposal. Even after the woman's taste threshold returned to pre-radiation levels, she complained that various tastes remained ''weak'' (Marks and Stevens, 1980).

Perhaps because of their diminished sensitivity to odors, most older adults tend to prefer strongly flavored food. This tendency has led some psychologists to suggest placing various seasonings on the table, enabling older diners to add flavors that might seem too strong to other family members (Sekuler and Blake, 1987). Another means of increasing the intensity of flavors is to chew carefully, swishing the food around in the mouth. Swishing heightens taste by increasing the food's contact with the tongue and heightens aroma by increasing the food's exposure to odor receptors.

Trygg Engen (1977) has suggested that sensitivity to tastes and smells is more affected by smoking than by any aging process. Although there is little research to support the suggestion, anecdotal evidence is plentiful. One healthy 75-year-old man who abruptly quit

Older adults who have a diminished sensitivity to the intensity of aromas and tastes may not be motivated to vary their diet, a situation that could lead to malnutrition.

his two-pack-a-day habit reported with some surprise that the flavor of food suddenly became intense and his meals tasted better than they had in years.

Finally, Claire Murphy (1983) has suggested that older people's failure to find an odor less pleasant after extended exposure to it may go a long way toward explaining some cases of malnutrition. The sense of smell is often crucial in the identification of flavor. With the nose blocked, it is almost impossible to tell the difference between raw apple and raw potato. It is also possible that the pleasantness of taste follows the same pattern after exposure. Murphy proposes that because the same food continues to taste good, the older adult is not motivated to seek a varied diet. If a few foods are cheap and taste reasonably good, they make up the entire diet, eventually leading to malnutrition.

TOUCH AND PAIN

Touch and pain are considered **somesthetic senses** because their receptors are located throughout the body (soma), primarily in the skin but also in the viscera. Receptors within the skin or nerve endings in the cornea and deep within the body send signals through neurons to the brain, carrying the message that some object has come into contact with the body or that real or possible injury threatens. Other somesthetic senses inform us of temperature, the position of body parts, or body posture and movement.

CHANGES IN THE SOMESTHETIC SYSTEM

Although we know much less about the effects of aging in the somesthetic system than about any other kind of sensory aging (Verrillo and Verrillo, 1985), most researchers have assumed that sensitivity to touch begins to decline when people are in their fifties and that the loss of sensitivity is due to a decrease in the number of receptors and their individual sensitivity. It has been proposed that this loss of sensitivity then reverses itself during the sixties and seventies as the skin thins with age (Rockstein and Sussman, 1979).

Yet this picture is clouded by conflicting evidence. It is by no means clear that all aspects of somesthetic sensitivity decline, that sensitivity declines in everyone, or even that the skin thins with age.

The effect of aging on skin receptors has been confirmed. Beginning in childhood, the **Meissner corpuscles,** a type of sensory receptor believed to respond to light touch and perhaps to vibration, grow in size, change in shape, and decrease in number. These receptors are concentrated on the soles of the feet, the palms of the hand, and the hairless side of fingers and toes. Free nerve endings, found in the skin, in the cornea, and deep within the body, show no changes with age (Whitbourne, 1985). **Pacinian corpuscles,** sensory receptors in the skin that may respond to deep pressure and to vibration, appear to grow in size with age, which may indicate a decreased sensitivity, but to decrease in number (Verrillo and Verrillo, 1985).

Sensitivity to touch in body regions that are thickly covered by hair shows no change in later life, but sensitivity to touch on the palms and fingers declines (Whitbourne, 1985). The loss of sensitivity to vibration shows clear changes. There is a progressive loss of the hand's sensitivity to vibration between the ages of 10 and 65 years—but only to vibration at higher frequencies (Corso, 1990). The decline of sensitivity to vibration in the feet is

Although sensitivity on the palms and fingers declines with age, a loving touch is as important as it ever was.

much larger, with some studies showing impaired sensitivity in the feet of 40 percent of older adults but in the hands of only 5 percent (Skre, 1972).

Age-related losses in sensitivity to touch and vibration may be connected to changes in body temperature. As skin temperature drops, Pacinian receptors lose sensitivity. Studies indicate a significant lowering of skin and body core temperature in people past the age of 65 (Verrillo and Verrillo, 1985). Although some people with reduced vibratory sensitivity seem to be healthy, degenerative diseases such as diabetes and anemia, as well as thiamin deficiency, are known to impair sensitivity (Kenshalo, 1977).

CHANGES IN THE PERCEPTION OF PAIN

Pain can be caused by pressure, heat, cold, twists, scratches, and punctures—any sort of stimuli that warn the body of possible danger. If we were unable to feel pain, we would not realize when we had been injured. Cuts, burns, sprains, broken bones, and appendicitis would go unnoticed. But evoking the perception of pain is not a mechanical matter like flipping a light switch. Although pain is apparently a separate somesthetic sense, with its own receptors, neural pathways, and centers within the nervous system, a multitude of factors determine whether a stimulus will be perceived as painful, the degree of pain involved, and whether it can be borne (Verrillo and Verrillo, 1985). Among the factors that affect the perception of pain are ethnic background, socioeconomic status, motivation, attitudes, emotions, beliefs, suggestion, prior experience, attention to the painful stimulus, and personality. People who are highly anxious or neurotic, for example, show increased sensitivity to pain and find it difficult to tolerate, whereas stoic people generally have a high tolerance for pain (Whitbourne, 1985). The picture is further complicated by the fact that reports of pain in a laboratory situation may not be related to reports of pain in daily life. In the laboratory, subjects feel less anxiety; they know that the pain is temporary and that they can stop it at any time (Verrillo and Verrillo, 1985).

Pain is usually studied in two ways: the threshold level, which is the amount of stimulation required to create a perception of pain; and the tolerance level, which is the amount of pain a person can stand. In laboratory experiments, the tolerance level is especially sensitive to the relationship between the subject and the experimenter, the actions of the experimenter, and the instructions received by the subject (Gelfand, 1964).

Perhaps because of all the factors that influence the perception of pain, researchers have been unable to demonstrate conclusively whether sensitivity to painful stimuli decreases, increases, or remains the same as people age (Corso, 1990). Research with animals, where many of the confounding factors do not appear, indicates that the pain threshold rises with age, so that it takes more stimulation to evoke a reaction (Nicak, 1971). Physicians are inclined to endorse this notion, since they have discovered that some generally painful procedures cause virtually no pain in older adults, and some have suggested that a diminished perception of pain helps to explain why burns are often more serious and widespread among the old (Kligman, Grove, and Balin, 1985).

A number of studies have attempted to control for the confounding factors that determine the perception of pain. In one study (Clark and Mehl, 1971), investigators used the signal detection method to assess sensitivity to painful heat. People were asked to rate the intensity of pain from radiant heat, but the light was hot on only half the trials, forcing them to decide whether they could detect the stimulus (the activation of sensory receptors) as well as determining the degree of pain (affected by cognition and emotion). Under these circumstances, there was no difference in the pain experienced by men, no matter what their age, and by young women. But from the age of 60, women seemed to experience less pain at the same levels of stimulation. As we saw in the discussion of visual processing, older adults seem to be more cautious in making judgments. Such was the case in this experiment. Older men and women reported pain only when they were certain the pain was present, but younger men and women tended to report the stimulus as painful before they were sure it actually hurt.

Some theories of pain attempt to explain why the perception of pain and its intensity is so unpredictable. According to the gate-control theory, sensations travel from receptors and free nerve endings up the spinal cord to the brain. A gatelike mechanism in the system may be open, closed, or partially open. Unless signals can get through the gate, the person will feel no pain (Melzack and Wall, 1982). The gate is affected by several factors, including signals from the brain. During anxiety or fear, for example, the brain opens the gate, allowing messages from pain receptors to flood through to the brain and increase the perception of pain.

Deeply involved in the perception of pain are the body's own painkillers. Endorphins, a type of neurotransmitter manufactured by the brain, act like opiates. Beta endorphins provide long-lasting pain relief, such as would come from an injection of morphine, whereas enkephalins provide brief, but powerful, relief. Both kinds of endorphins send messages to the spinal cord that close the gate, blocking the transmission of pain signals to the brain. The diminished pain that some older people report from normally painful conditions such as appendicitis, peritonitis, or heart attack may be not so much the result of diminished sensitivity to pain as to endorphin production.

As we will see in the next chapter, reduced sensory functioning is apparently involved in age-related changes in the processing of information, because the ability to learn and remember depends in good measure on what we perceive.

SUMMARY

SENSORY AGING

Despite the existence of people whose sensory apparatus seems to show little evidence of failure, a substantial number of older people develop sensory impairment. Indeed, reduced sensory functioning is probably the most nearly universal loss of ability associated with aging.

With age, sensory systems slowly become less sensitive to stimulation from the environment, curtailing access to knowledge of the world and sometimes interfering with the ability to communicate with others. Compared with the young, many older adults may be in a state of sensory deprivation that could be responsible for some cases of disorientation and confusion. Reduced sensory function is probably the most universal loss of ability connected with aging. However, some people show little sensory impairment even at advanced ages.

VISION

With age, the pupil decreases in size (a condition known as **senile miosis**), the difference in size between the light-adapted and dark-adapted pupil diminishes, and it responds more slowly to changes in illumination. The lens thickens, yellows, and becomes less transparent and more sensitive to glare. The eye becomes less sensitive to color. As the lens loses flexibility, **accommodation** becomes less efficient and **presbyopia** may develop. Visual **acuity** declines, especially for moving objects, as depth perception is generally impaired. The major eye disorders of later adulthood, **glaucoma, cataracts,** and **macular degeneration,** are not the result of normal aging.

The processing of visual information also slows with age. This slowing may be the result of **stimulus persistence,** an explanation that has been supported by changes in **critical flicker frequency.** Changes in **contrast sensitivity function** can predict performance in everyday settings.

HEARING

During young adulthood, a small, but gradual, hearing loss develops that increases with age. The progressive loss of ability to hear high-frequency sounds can take four forms: sensory **presbycusis,** neural presbycusis, strial presbycusis, and mechanical presbycusis. Presbycusis can be the result of aging or exposure to noise, and damage-related presbycusis is often accompanied by **tinnitus.**

The processing of sounds is affected by age, although the slowness may be heightened by older adults' caution in responding. Under ideal conditions, speech comprehension mirrors hearing ability, but under adverse conditions speech may become unintelligible. Outside the laboratory, however, older adults are as skilled as the young in their use of linguistic context as an aid to comprehension.

Hearing aids may help some older adults, especially the new digital aids that amplify sounds selectively. Those with neural presbycusis may be helped by **cochlear implants.** Some researchers have linked deafness to delusional disorders. Although it has been suggested that uncorrected impairment may lead to social isolation in older adults, those who are in good health seem to adjust to their hearing loss.

SMELL AND TASTE

Sensitivity to odors may decline with age, as more receptor cells are lost than are replaced. The decline may be related to disease, especially Parkinson's or Alzheimer's disease. Older adults may need an increased concentration of an odor before they can detect it, and they seem less sensitive to concentrated smells. Although taste-bud density does not decline with age, taste sensitivity to salty, sour, and bitter weakens somewhat, but the sensitivity to sweet shows no change with age. Medication may affect sensitivity to sour tastes. Changes in taste are probably not responsible for lessened enjoyment of food, and older adults' declining ability to identify flavors is probably the result of changes in olfactory sensitivity and memory. Smoking may be another factor in declining enjoyment since it seems to affect sensitivity to tastes and smells. Some cases of malnutrition may develop because older adults may not tire of a single food and so fail to eat a varied diet.

TOUCH AND PAIN

Touch and pain are **somesthetic senses,** and not much is known about the effects of aging on these senses. In hairless areas of the body, where **Meissner corpuscles** transmit touch, sensitivity declines with age. Sensitivity to high-frequency vibration, transmitted primarily by **Pacinian corpuscles,** declines from the age of ten, but sensitivity to low-frequency vibration shows no age-related change. Any age-related changes that appear may also be related to changes in body temperature.

Many factors affect the perception of pain, including ethnic background, socioeconomic status, motivation, attitudes, emotions, belief, suggestion, prior experience, attention to the painful stimulus, and personality. The effect of aging on sensitivity to pain has not been demonstrated, although the pain threshold appears to rise in aging animals. Reports that some older people have little pain from normally painful conditions may be explained by diminished sensitivity to pain or by the body's manufacture of endorphins.

KEY TERMS

accommodation	contrast sensitivity function (CSF)
acuity	critical flicker frequency (CFF)
cataracts	glaucoma
cochlear implant	macular degeneration

Meissner corpuscles

pacinian corpuscles

presbycusis

presbyopia

senile miosis

somesthetic sense

stimulus persistence

tinnitus

Chapter 8

♦

Learning and Memory Across Adulthood

♦

A s she progressed through her seventies, Alice Phillips noticed that she had begun to forget things. She had trouble recalling where she had placed her keys, her glasses, and a letter she intended to answer. She found it difficult to remember appointments or to carry out tasks she had planned to do. At first she passed it off as a natural accompaniment of aging. She decided that her mind was simply getting rusty. But then Phillips enrolled in a major research project near Seattle, Washington, where researchers were studying the course of cognition in older adults. Her participation in that program helped her to recapture confidence in her mental ability, regain cognitive skills she thought she had lost, and discover a talent for writing she did not know she possessed. At 76, she wrote her first book, *A Practical Guide to Independent Living for Older People,* based on what she had learned by observing herself during the project (*New York Times,* 1986). Alice Phillips is not the only older American who enjoys exercising mental skills and learning new things.

Age does not destroy the ability to learn, a fact that is underscored by the return of older adults to formal education. Researchers used to wonder about the ability of older adults to profit from formal education—about their ability to learn much of anything. But during the last decade, the presence of older adults in the classroom has become commonplace. One of their number, Frederick F. Bloch, received a Ph.D. in history from New York University at the age of 81, culminating a course of study he began 15 years earlier when he retired from business (Johnston and Anderson, 1983). His plans were to spend his remaining years writing books and perhaps teaching a few classes.

As we will see in this chapter, cognitive processes do not become radically different in older adults. Some of the observed changes in learning, attention, and memory may be smaller and less important than was once believed. After a brief discussion of information processing, we explore the way learning skills change with age. Because learning usually requires attention, we will investigate changes in the ability of older people to attend to more than one thing at a time and to switch their attention from one task to another. Remembering is how we demonstrate learning, and so we will look at the aspects of memory that seem to change with age as well as those that appear to remain the same. The chapter closes with a consideration of the factors that influence learning and memory.   ◆

INFORMATION PROCESSING

Whether we are looking at a sunset, chatting with a friend, balancing a checkbook, reading a book, fantasizing about our next vacation, or trying to fix a squeaking floorboard, we are processing information. All aspects of cognitive function, from recalling whether the front door is locked to writing a poem, may be considered in terms of the way information is processed.

The terminology used in the **information processing** view of cognition comes from an analogy between the human mind and the computer. As the computer accepts information that is fed into it, human beings take information from the environment. The information is manipulated, stored, classified, and retrieved; its patterns are recognized. The basic mechanisms of cognition, which are processes like recognition, scanning the environment, learning, or the integration of information from various senses, correspond to the computer's hardware. The knowledge that has been accumulated over the years corresponds to the computer's data base, and the strategies used to process information correspond to the computer's library of software (Perlmutter, 1988). As we saw in Chapter 2, this view of human thought processes takes a mechanistic approach that assumes we can understand complex cognition by analyzing it into simple processes and isolating them in the laboratory.

Learning and memory depend on time-based processes that transfer information within the cognitive system. Memory has to do with the retention and retrieval of information or skills that have been learned. But it is very difficult to separate the two processes because people cannot demonstrate learning without using memory and memory cannot be demonstrated unless something has been learned.

Whether we look at learning or memory, the cognitive system can be seen as using several kinds of operations or several levels of processes to handle information. Whether the topic is learning or memory, the information must be acquired, stored, and retrieved. This sequence assumes that people are not simply passive recipients of information. They participate actively in the processing, and the way they deploy their attention and other cognitive resources affects what and how much they learn or remember, as do their expectations, emotions, and attitudes.

Most researchers accept the fact that, *on the average,* aging is accompanied by a decline in the ability to process new information. The decline consistently appears in experimental tasks related to learning, reasoning, and memory skills. Yet the decline is less severe, later in onset, and true for a smaller proportion of the population than was once believed. In almost every case, some adults in the older group perform better than some adults in the younger group.

EXPLAINING THE DECLINE

The average age-related decline in information processing could be produced by changes at any one of the levels of cognition: the basic mechanisms, the knowledge base, or the strategies used to manipulate information. Researchers have advanced several explanations for the decline, but none accounts for all age differences.

One set of explanations focuses on basic mechanisms. A version of this explanation is the **speed hypothesis.** In this view, decline in performance is due to age-related reductions in the speed of sensory or motor processes (Salthouse, 1989). As we saw in Chapter 7, a hallmark of aging is slowed processing of visual and auditory information, and reaction time also slows. Thus, it takes older adults longer to perceive and register in consciousness the various test items and also longer to speak or write the answers. Since most tests are timed, the scores of older adults suffer, leading to underestimations of their ability. Researchers have indeed found that age gaps are greatest on tests that depend on perceptual speed and that scores continue to decline across later adulthood (Cunningham, 1989). Although this explanation accounts for some of the decline, the scores of older adults still lag behind those of the young, even in tests that allow extra time.

A variation of the speed hypothesis may account for a much larger proportion of the decline. According to the **generalized slowing hypothesis,** processing slows throughout the brain as well as in perceptual and motor processes (Cerella, 1990). In this view, cognition is seen as computation across networks of neurons. With age, basic mechanisms slow at each step in the thought process, either because of breaks in the network that require detours through other neurons or because at each step some of the original information is lost. In a study that required adults to rotate letters mentally, researchers discovered an apparent slowing with age, but only among adults in their late sixties (Jacewicz and Hartley, 1987). Those who were in their late fifties seemed to process the letters as rapidly as did young adults. Other researchers have found that when speed is accounted for, some—but not all—age differences disappear (Schaie, 1989).

Another explanation that focuses on basic mechanisms is the **component efficiency hypothesis.** In this view, most tasks require several distinct processing operations, and with age, one or more of the processes becomes less efficient or less effective (Salthouse, 1988). This explanation, though popular, is very difficult to research, since it is extremely difficult to isolate the various processing operations involved.

A fourth explanation involving basic mechanisms is the **resource-reduction hypothesis.** In this view, aging leads to a reduction in the quantity of one or more essential cognitive resources, such as attentional capacity, the capacity of consciousness (working memory), mental energy, or the speed of processing (Salthouse, 1988). Many researchers assume that a reduction of resources is probably a major force in age-related cognitive decline, but the exact nature of the resources involved is rarely specified. Research by Timothy Salthouse and his associates (Salthouse, Kausler, and Saults, 1988) indicates that age seems to affect processing resources, which in turn affect cognitive performance, but that a portion of the typical age-related decline remains unexplained.

Some explanations assume that cognitive decline is the result of software problems. In the **inefficient strategies hypothesis,** observed age-related decline results from a tendency among older adults to use less effective strategies in manipulating information than they once did (Salthouse, 1988). In other words, poorer performance is the result of the way in which older adults go about carrying out cognitive tasks.

Another explanation is the **disuse hypothesis,** which assumes that at least part of the cognitive decline is due to the fact that older adults are rarely required to exercise the abilities tested in the laboratory, and so they have lost part of their efficiency (Salthouse, 1989).

A final explanation is the **changing-environment hypothesis.** In this view, age differences are more likely to be the result of cohort differences in the physical or social environment (Salthouse, 1989). As succeeding generations become healthier and better educated, they perform better on tests than older cohorts, so that age-related declines actually reflect improvements in succeeding cohorts.

It seems likely that most age-related declines can be attributed to some combination of these explanations. For example, disuse is usually accompanied by a failure to draw on cognitive reserves, which are a kind of resource capacity. Some researchers believe that although older people rarely perform up to their capacities when tested in the laboratory, performance eventually is affected when poor health leads to eventual declines in basic cognitive mechanisms (Kliegl and Baltes, 1987). An examination of age-related changes in learning, attention, and memory may help to clarify some of these explanations.

LEARNING ACROSS ADULTHOOD

Our knowledge of learning across adulthood is complicated by the fact that learning is an invisible process. We cannot observe it; we can only infer its presence by observing some change in a person's behavior. If a person learns something and no occasion rises for its use, we have no way of knowing that learning has taken place. When behavior does change, unless we can eliminate other factors that can affect performance, such as drugs, fatigue, or motivation, we cannot be certain that the change is the result of learning. Similarly, if a person appears to forget something, it is possible that he or she has not really forgotten, but is simply tired or lacks the motivation to do whatever has been learned.

Researchers have used various methods to get around these problems, including the study of other species such as rabbits, rats, and monkeys (Woodruff–Pak, 1990). Most studies of learning use techniques that come from the mechanistic approach to development. Investigators attempt to discover what characteristics of a task affect learning, whether these influences change with age, and how they may affect learning in daily life. Age differences have been found in conditioning, verbal learning, and the learning of various skills, such as word processing.

CONDITIONING ACROSS ADULTHOOD

Conditioning is considered the simplest form of learning, and the pattern of age changes depends on whether classical or operant conditioning is examined. In **classical conditioning,** some normally involuntary response, such as the blink of an eye, is conditioned to a new stimulus. For example, researchers studied the eyeblink response in men and women, ranging in age from 18 to 85, by having each person sit in a comfortable chair, while speakers mounted about a foot from each ear sounded a tone just before a puff of air was blown into the eyes (Solomon et al., 1989). When adults blinked at the sound of the tone, even though no blast of air followed, they were conditioned. Young adults conditioned rapidly, as did those in their forties, but after the age of 50 the speed of conditioning slowed dramatically and the proportion of adults who eventually developed the conditioned response dropped (Figure 8.1). Among adults in their eighties, only about 35 percent developed the response and the conditioning required more than twice as many trials as it did in those younger than 50. It is important to note, however, that some of the oldest adults conditioned as rapidly as did most of the younger adults.

In this study, the researchers screened their subjects for hearing deficits, gross cognitive impairment, sensitivity to the puff of air, and the rate of spontaneous blinking. There were no significant age differences on any of these measures. If the older adults could hear the tone, showed no obvious mental deficits, blinked spontaneously as often as the young, and were as sensitive to the blast of air, how can we account for their slowed learning and frequent failure to condition? One explanation is that the length of time allowed for the appearance of the response masked many cases of conditioning. As we saw in Chapter 7, there is some sensory decline with age. The puff of air was released just 400 milliseconds after the tone began, which may not have given some older people enough time to register the sound and respond to it. (People condition fastest at times ranging from 400 to 1200 milliseconds; see Woodruff–Pak, 1990).

Because conditioning differences that appear with age follow similar patterns in rabbits

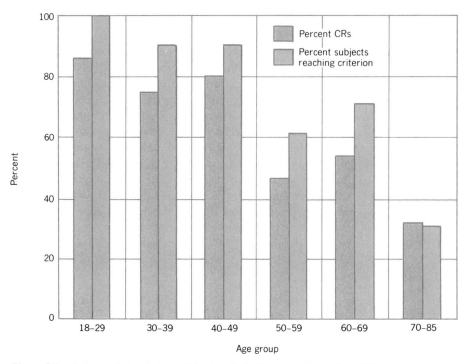

Figure 8.1   Aging and classical conditioning. Both the percentage of conditioned responses acquired and the percentage of people who acquire a conditioned response decline steadily across adulthood. *Source:* Solomon et al., 1989, p. 36.

and humans, Diana Woodruff–Pak (1990) has suggested that the cause may also be similar. In aging rabbits, cell loss within the cerebellum, a portion of the brain that is primarily involved in the coordination of movement, is highly correlated with slowed conditioning. If the cerebellum is indeed the site of memory for simple conditioning, the decline that is characteristic of many older adults may be affected by changes in the central nervous system.

In classical conditioning, people are generally unaware of the response that is being conditioned. A person may transfer an emotion or some involuntary muscular response to a new stimulus, but he or she is not trying to do anything. There is no voluntary action the person can take toward a goal.

In **operant conditioning,** what the person chooses to do either brings some reward or removes some unpleasant situation. The consequences of the action produce reinforcement, and as a result of reinforcement, behavior changes. When action brings a reward, there seem to be no differences in conditioning across the life span. Even psychotic older patients and patients with organic brain syndromes have been successfully conditioned. For example, through the use of prompts and reinforcement, patients up to 90 years of age who had been bathed by an attendant at a nursing home began bathing themselves (Rinke et al., 1978).

The effectiveness of operant conditioning in modifying behavior can be seen in its application to the case of an 82-year-old heart patient who regularly stayed in bed all morning, rarely exercised, did not take his medication, and failed to drink his orange juice. Each time he walked around the block without being reminded, drank a small glass of orange juice, or took his medication, he earned tokens, which could be exchanged for such privileges as a weekend dinner at a restaurant of his choice. Within a few weeks, his walks had increased from once every seven days to three times a day, he was drinking three glasses of orange juice a day, instead of one—or none—and he was taking each of his three medications regularly. During the same period, his angina pain disappeared (Dapcich–Miura and Hovell, 1979).

Yet when operant conditioning requires some action that prevents an unpleasant situation, age differences often appear—at least among nonhuman species. Numerous experiments have found that aging rats have difficulty learning to avoid painful situations (Woodruff–Pak, 1990). A typical test involves learning to stay on one side of a small chamber in order to avoid an electric shock. Older rats learn the required response and retain it for short periods as well as do younger rats, but by the next day many older rats have forgotten it. Researchers are uncertain whether this ability is similarly impaired in older adults. Conditioning has received less attention from researchers than more complicated forms of learning, such as verbal learning.

VERBAL LEARNING

When investigators study verbal learning, they are looking at the processes involved in rote learning. The goal is to have the subject repeat specific information presented by the researcher. The experiment generally takes the form of either a serial-learning task or a paired-associate task. The serial-learning task is the simplest. As the person watches a screen, a list of words appears, one at a time, and the person tries to memorize them. Learning is demonstrated by repeating the list. In a paired-associate task, a person learns pairs of words, such as ''moon-zebra.'' Then, when given one member of the pair, the person produces the other.

The performance of older adults on cross-sectional studies of verbal learning invariably declines with age. In one paired-associate study, older adults who had twice seen each pair in a lengthy list recalled about 40 percent of the pairs, but young adults recalled more than 60 percent (Balota, Duchek, and Paullin, 1989). When they are required to learn an entire list, older adults need more time than either the young or the middle-aged. Once older adults have learned the pairs, however, they remember about as many of them over subsequent months as do younger people (Poon, 1985). In almost every study, the performance of young and old groups overlaps, with some older adults performing as well as the young.

There is no way to be certain whether observed differences in verbal learning are due to aging or to cohort effects. Because the results of cross-sectional studies are probably magnified by cohort effects, a look at a longitudinal study may be helpful. In the Baltimore Longitudinal Study, well-educated men of high socioeconomic status were retested after eight years (Arenberg and Robertson–Tchabo, 1977). The men, born between 1885 and 1932, ranged from 32 to 75 years of age at the time of the first testing and represented six cohorts. At that time, there was little difference in learning among those who were less than 60 years old, but large age differences among the older men.

In both tests, the men were given a paired-associate and a serial-learning task. Results on the two tasks were similar. In the paired-associate task, the youngest cohort, who had been in their thirties at the time of the first testing, showed a small improvement over the eight years. Middle-aged men, who had been in their forties and early fifties at the time of the first testing, showed a small decline. But older men, beginning with those who had been 55 at the first testing, showed a large decline, which became quite steep among those who had been between 69 and 76 eight years before. Interindividual differences were smallest within the youngest cohort and increased with age. At least in the area of verbal learning, there seems to be a decline after the age of 60.

SKILLS LEARNING

Many jobs in today's marketplace demand skills that were not taught when today's middle-aged and older adults were in school. Yet if older persons wish to stay in the workforce, they may have to update their skills. Given the results of learning experiments, the question arises as to whether declines in learning abilities will severely handicap older men and women in the acquisition of new skills.

Older people can learn new cognitive skills. For more than a decade, laboratory studies have shown that with instruction older people markedly improve their performance in problem-solving, reasoning, and other advanced cognitive skills (Willis, in press). For example, older adults who were given a six-week training program in discussion and role-playing of problems showed improved functioning in social cognition (Zaks and Labouvie–Vief, 1980). When compared with a control group and a group that had participated only in discussions, they were better at taking the perspective of another person. They did a better job at understanding the way a scene would look to a person standing from another vantage point. They also showed superior skills in referential communication, in which they had to describe an object (usually a geometric figure) clearly enough so that an unseen listener could pick the object out of an array of similar figures.

A group of researchers at the University of Maine addressed the question of skill-learning directly by studying the acquisition of word-processing skills in young, middle-aged, and older women (Elias et al., 1987). All the women were high school graduates with about a year of college or business school, all were in good health, and none had serious hearing or uncorrected visual problems. All were proficient typists, and all were at the same level of computer literacy. Instruction in the use of a commercial word-processing program was spread over seven 3 1/2 hour sessions. The older women, who were in their early sixties, took longer to learn various aspects of the program than did the middle-aged women (in their early forties) or the younger women (in their early twenties). In an exam given after the first three lessons, the older women were having more trouble mastering cursor movement, moving blocks of text, and setting margins than women in the other groups. By the completion of training, however, the only difference in word-processing skills seemed to be in speed of execution. It took the older women longer to complete the final document (input, edit, print, enter corrections from hard copy, and print a corrected version), but the finished document was as accurate and error-free as that produced by the younger groups.

It would seem that even if cognitive skills have deteriorated somewhat from disuse, the overlearning of some competing but obsolete skill, or lack of motivation, it is possible to regain at least some of the former skill. One factor that influences learning is the ability to pay attention.

If this woman took laboratory tests of learning, she might show impaired performance relative to young adults. Yet in daily life she has learned new skills and works comfortably with computers.

ATTENTION

If older people cannot keep their attention focused on a learning task, they are unlikely to learn much. Keeping attention focused on the task at hand is known as *sustained attention,* and it is an important aspect of learning. Attention also functions in other ways, as when we select important signals from the array of stimuli (*selective attention*), perform two tasks at once (*divided attention*), and monitor first one, then another task (*switching attention*) (McDowd and Birren, 1990).

Typically, sustained attention is measured with vigilance tasks, in which a person must monitor a single source of information in order to detect objects or events that occur at unpredictable, infrequent intervals. Although older people appear to be less accurate than young people overall, the process of allocating attention does not seem to change with age. At any age, people make more mistakes over time on a vigilance task, and accuracy declines no faster in older adults than it does in young people. In fact, when a vigilance task was part of a longitudinal study, the passage of years brought no increase in the decline of accuracy over time (Giambra and Quilter, 1985).

Selective attention, which refers to the ability to focus on relevant information while screening out irrelevant aspects of a situation is, of course, basic to learning. Whether age differences appear in selective attention appears to depend on the situation. If the task of searching for information is simple and the irrelevant information need not be processed, then age seems to have no effect on selective attention. But as soon as the irrelevant information must also be processed and the search for relevant information becomes demanding, age differences are apparent (McDowd and Birren, 1990). In one study, researchers asked young adults in their twenties and older adults in their seventies to select a target from displays of X's and O's (Plude and Doussard–Roosevelt, 1989). Older adults were slower than young people, but more accurate. As more features had to be considered and the task's difficulty increased, the gap in speed between age groups became wider. By manipulating the task, researchers concluded that the increased slowness of older adults did not come from any difference in search strategies or sensory slowing, but from a generalized slowing in the central nervous system that affects attentional processes.

Divided attention, in which attention must be distributed between two or more tasks, also suffers with age. But again, the complexity of the task is important. When the task is extremely simple, such as indicating whether or not a specific target is present or absent in a pair of displays, there are no age differences (McDowd and Birren, 1990). When the task becomes more complicated, however, the performance of older adults falls behind that of the young. This age difference in divided attention became apparent when researchers tested the ability of experienced drivers to allocate their attention to two tasks on a second-by-second basis (Ponds, Brouwer, and Wolffelaar, 1988). The first task involved simulated driving and used a computer display similar to that in video games; it required the ''driver'' to turn a steering wheel to keep a car in the correct lane. The second task required noting the dots in a visual display and pressing a button when at least nine dots were present. All the drivers were able to handle the two separate tasks, but when both tasks were presented at the same time (the dot display was superimposed in the center of the computer screen ''highway''), the performance of older drivers on the driving task deteriorated significantly more than that of young and middle-aged drivers. The researchers were unable to determine whether the decline with age was due to generalized slowing, in which slowed processing interferes with the ability to merge two subtasks into one integrated activity, or to slowed motor responses, which make it difficult to combine steering and pushing buttons in a rapid series of responses.

Unlike divided attention, in which both sources must be monitored continually, attention switching involves shifting the focus of attention back and forth between two sources. Until recently, few studies had been done on this form of attention. Researchers had assumed that older adults would not only be slower than the young, but less accurate as well (McDowd and Birren, 1990). Yet a study that required adults to switch from a narrow to a broad focus of attention brings that assumption into question (Hartley, Kieley, and McKenzie, 1987). No age differences appeared in the rate at which older and younger adults reallocated their attention.

Attention is a complicated procedure that involves a variety of functions, including alertness and arousal, whether attention is automatic or requires effort, attention span, the selection of signals for processing, whether we have advance knowledge of the target, and how prepared we are for its appearance. These factors determine what information will be processed and the degree of processing it will receive (Hoyer, 1987). For example, if we have enough time to prepare for an event, we will be faster and more accurate at detecting its appearance. Although older adults require more time to process advance information (500 milliseconds, compared with 250 milliseconds for younger adults), age differences in many attentional tasks disappear when there is adequate preparation time. By examining the efficiency of memory, we may discover whether age differences reflect the failure to learn or the inability to remember what has been learned.

MEMORY ACROSS ADULTHOOD

Many older people report that they forget things, but that does not indicate that forgetfulness is an inevitable consequence of aging. Older men and women in Cambridge, England, told researchers that their most frequent lapses came in not being able to recall a word that was on the "tip of the tongue," forgetting where they had placed an object or whether they had done some task, forgetting something someone had told them, and forgetting to take an object with them (Sunderland et al., 1986). Yet not all older people complain about memory lapses. When the National Center for Health Statistics conducted a survey of nearly 15,000 people older than 55, only 15 percent said that they frequently had trouble remembering and more than 25 percent said that they never had problems with their memory (Cutler and Grams, 1988). In fact, 20 percent of the adults past 85 said that they never had trouble with their memory.

Many older people retain their ability to remember details far into old age, but there is no doubt that aging is usually accompanied by changes in the memory system. Not all parts of the system change in the same manner, and the changes may be easier to understand if we divide the system into capacities and contents. **Memory capacities,** which consist of the basic mechanisms and strategies, may decline, but **memory contents,** which refer to the knowledge stored in the data base, may increase (Perlmutter, 1986).

At the shallowest level of the memory system is **sensory memory,** a basic mechanism that holds environmental information (sights, sounds, touches, smells, or tastes) for a second or so. The information then decays, so if it is to be used, it must be processed at a deeper level. Once past the sensory store, memory may be seen as divided into two basic systems: short-term memory and long-term memory. Aging appears to affect each system differently. Although it has proved extremely difficult to separate sensory memory from selective attention, most researchers agree that aging has only small, unimportant effects on sensory memory (Poon, 1985).

Older adults' skill at Scrabble™ may improve with age because they continue to add information to their store of knowledge.

SHORT-TERM MEMORY

Short-term memory is a limited capacity system that keeps information in consciousness. It can hold a telephone number long enough for it to be dialed, but because short-term memory is not permanent storage, unless the material is maintained—as when you repeat a phone number over and over to yourself as you walk to the phone—it is generally lost within about 15 seconds. If you have ever been interrupted as you picked up the telephone and found that you had to look up the number again, you have experienced the unintentional loss of information from short-term memory. In terms of the computer analogy, short-term memory might be compared to the CRT tube of a computer system (Perlmutter, 1986). If the displayed information is not saved (transferred to long-term memory), it will be lost when the power is switched off (attention is withdrawn).

Because short-term memory holds information that is being consciously processed, it includes a control system that is capable of attention, selection, and manipulation (Baddeley, 1986). It is here that we apply whatever strategies we have developed, organizing material to make certain that it is permanently recorded, or encoded, so that we can retrieve it later.

The capacity of short-term memory is usually studied by the digit-span test. A person hears or sees a string of digits or letters and repeats as many of them as he or she remembers. Short-term memory apparently holds about seven (±2) items, and anything over that amount must be retrieved from long-term memory (Miller, 1956). Simple span tests indicate that the passive capacity of working memory is relatively unaffected by age (Dobbs and Rule, 1989).

If the holding function of short-term memory (its storage aspect) does not decline, then age changes in short-term memory must be related to the workings of the control system (the processing aspect). This is just what researchers have found. As soon as material in short-term memory must be manipulated or additional information must be processed, substantial age differences appear (Hultsch and Dixon, 1990). This effect showed clearly when adults were asked to solve three addition problems (Foos, 1989). As they solved each problem, they held the answer in mind until they had worked all of them and then gave the answers from memory. Older adults did significantly worse at retaining the answers than young and middle-aged adults, whose performance did not differ.

Short-term memory also seems to slow with age. Although older people can retrieve as many items from short-term memory as younger people, it takes them longer to do so. In one study (Anders, Fozard, and Lillyquist, 1972), adults looked at a list of digits and then told researchers whether a test digit was part of the original list. Older adults needed more time than the young to make up their minds, even when the original list contained only one digit. As the number of digits on the list approached the limits of short-term memory, people in their thirties needed more time than those in their twenties. Time in such experiments is measured in milliseconds, so that it may take a 35 year old 100 milliseconds longer than a 20 year old to run through five digits and a 75 year old, an extra 300 milliseconds. Whether such a difference reduced the effectiveness of memory would depend on the task.

The reason for the reduced efficiency of working memory has not been established. Some researchers believe that declines are signs of diminished processing resources. Others have suggested that they are the result of a decreased flexibility in processing, which makes it more difficult to shift from one process to another (Dobbs and Rule, 1989). Still others have suggested that the problem may arise from the intrusion of irrelevant information into working memory, where it either displaces desired material or makes it difficult to retrieve specific information from long-term storage (Hasher and Zacks, 1988).

LONG-TERM MEMORY

Long-term memory is assumed to be a system with unlimited capacity. It is the storehouse of our past experience, holding the contents of memory: memories of childhood, our knowledge about the world and about how to do things, and even information about the way our thought processes work. As information is encoded, it is transferred to long-term store, where it is held until needed. At retrieval, the information is transferred back into short-term memory, where it can be consciously manipulated (Figure 8.2).

Age does not seem to affect the retention of information; once material has been placed in long-term storage it is kept as efficiently by 80 year olds as by 20 year olds (Poon, 1985). Even if a person is unable to retrieve the information, once it is stored, it is believed to be in long-term memory but inaccessible. Presumably, given the right cue in the right situation, the information could be retrieved.

Memory for various skills that we have learned is relatively unaffected by age. This kind of memory, known as **procedural memory,** refers to skills that are practiced and automatic, and that may be primarily cognitive (such as reading) or involve a motor component (such as driving, playing the piano, or typing). A large proportion of procedural memory cannot be expressed in words, but we can demonstrate it. Older adults exhibit procedural memory every day, and as we have seen, older typists are as efficient as younger typists, and older musicians do not lose their skills. Procedural memory is so different from other memory that it is often unaffected by brain damage that destroys memory about the world, which is known as **declarative memory.**

The contents of declarative memory seem to be organized similarly in young and old adults (Salthouse, 1982). Regardless of age, adults have stored two major kinds of world knowledge: episodic and semantic memories. **Episodic memories** include everything that happens to us, so that each memory is linked with a time and a place. Recalling a childhood birthday party, last week's football game, or the name of a person you met at a dance

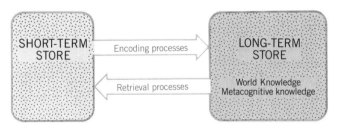

Figure 8.2 Memory system. This model of the memory system represents two aspects of memory: capacities and contents. The basic memory capacities include short-term memory, a limited-capacity store that keeps information in consciousness; long-term memory, a store that is assumed to have unlimited capacity; and the encoding and retrieval processes that transfer information back and forth between the two stores. The contents of memory consist of our knowledge about the world (semantic and episodic) and metacognitive knowledge (our understanding of the way the memory system works).

Age does not affect the retention of information; with the proper cues, long-forgotten memories can be recalled.

retrieves an episodic memory. **Semantic memories** are organized factual knowledge such as the fact that basenjis are dogs and dogs are mammals, that the United States is made up of 50 states, and that the past tense of ''break'' is ''broke.'' It is generally believed that episodic memories are vulnerable to the effects of aging, but that semantic memories are generally unimpaired (Craik and Simon, 1980).

Episodic and semantic memories accumulate throughout life, and since the memory system retains old information as it adds new, most older people have larger knowledge bases than they once did. In many situations, older adults may be able to compensate for declines in the memory system's efficiency by relying on their stored knowledge. Researchers have found that in situations where world knowledge is involved, older adults may do as well as the young. This pattern became apparent when researchers asked adults to memorize lists of names: well-known politicians, big-band musicians who were well known before 1945, top male singers of the 1980s, and common surnames (Hanley–Dunn and McIntosh, 1984). On lists of names that were supported by their own store of knowledge (current politicians and big-band musicians), adults in their seventies outperformed college students. (Older adults are generally more interested in politics and have a larger store of political knowledge than young adults.) On the list of male singers, which had been compiled from *Billboard* magazine, college students outperformed the 70 year olds. On the list of common surnames, there was no age difference at all.

Most studies of memory do not assess the contents of long-term storage, but reflect the efficiency of the processes used to enter and retrieve material (Perlmutter et al., 1987). Encoding processes are usually tested with recognition experiments, because recognition involves little retrieval effort. In a typical recognition experiment, two groups of pictures or words are shown in succession, and people say whether the pictures or words in the second group are new or were included in the first group. In most cases, researchers have found only small age differences in recognition.

Recall experiments, in which stored material must be remembered spontaneously or in response to some cue, presumably test the retrieval process. When people are asked to learn a word list and recall it spontaneously, the number of words recalled begins to decline as people enter their thirties and becomes smaller with each passing decade. As we have seen, when the words are related to their world knowledge, the decline in older adults' performance may fail to appear. Reliance on world knowledge helps explain why, when given a retrieval cue (the name of a category, such as ''animals''), people can remember more words from the list and age differences generally diminish (Poon, 1985). Because the cue improves performance, it appears that older people often learn more than tests indicate but have trouble retrieving the information from storage.

Once they leave school, about the only occasion people have to memorize word lists is when planning a trip to the supermarket. The question is whether the sort of memory that is used in the course of daily life shows any decline with age. One important use of daily memory is in reading and recalling meaningful information. In most cases, it is the gist of what we have read, not its literal wording, that we want to remember: Did our congressman come out in support of a bill that affects us? Did the review in yesterday's newspaper indicate that a new film was worth going to see? Older adults tend to do about as well as young adults when asked to sum up the content of a passage in a sentence. When they read well-organized material and are allowed to proceed at their own pace, they do best. But age differences appear when the text is presented rapidly, primarily because older adults tend to read more slowly than the young (about 121 words per minute compared with 144) (Myer and Rice, 1989). Age differences also tend to appear when the information is disorganized or scrambled (Light, 1990).

The picture becomes more complicated when we look at individual differences. Among adults with high verbal ability, older adults do just as well as younger adults in extracting the important ideas from a prose passage, but consistent age differences appear among adults with low verbal ability (Hultsch, Hertzog, and Dixon, 1984). Further research indicates that differences in verbal ability reflect individual differences in the same processes that affect the recall of word lists: working memory and the speed of various processes related to language comprehension (Hultsch, Hertzog, and Dixon, 1990).

Studies that examine another facet of daily memory, the ability to recall everyday activities, have produced mixed results. People rarely make a conscious effort to remember their various activities, but they generally can tell you whether they have taken a suit to the cleaners, had their lunch, or watched a specific television program. Researchers have simulated this situation in the laboratory by asking adults to perform simple actions, such as ''smell the flower,'' ''lift the spoon,'' and ''look in the mirror.'' When the list of actions is short, older adults recall them about as well as the young, but when the list stretches out, the same age differences emerge that appear in other retrieval tasks (Knopf and Neidhardt, 1989).

Some of these age differences may be related to another aspect of memory contents: the strategies people use to help them learn and remember.

MEMORY STRATEGIES

Retrieval and encoding failure often seem to be the result of **production deficiencies.** That is, older adults often fail to use memory strategies spontaneously, even though they can use them if reminded to do so (Perlmutter, 1983). Memory strategies are believed to elaborate on information or to process it at a deeper level, making it more likely that material will be encoded in the first place and increasing the ease of later retrieval.

Material that is handled at the sensory level receives only shallow processing; when material is handled at the semantic level, so that meaning is attached to it, it receives deeper processing. Thus, noting that a green hillside is covered with black dots is an example of shallow processing. Realizing that the black objects are animals processes the information at a slightly deeper level. Noting that the animals are black cattle processes the material at an even deeper level, but noting that they are Angus cattle and, therefore, destined to become beef elaborates on the memory as well as deepens the processing. As processing deepens, the duration and retrievability of the memory is likely to increase.

Material can also be processed without moving to a deeper level. Repeating the words in a list again and again maintains the memory as long as the repetition lasts. However, the memory trace then begins to decay at the same rate as any other material that has been processed at this shallow level.

Any encoding strategy that increases the depth of processing is believed to increase learning. Several strategies can be used to move information to a deeper level. One is to organize it by category, for example, grouping together all the animals on a list to be remembered. A second strategy is to use some sort of verbal aid to memory, such as making a word out of the first letter of each item to be remembered. A third is to construct a vivid image of items to be remembered, such as visualizing a dog at the helm of a sailboat to remember the paired-associate words dog/boat. A fourth strategy, known as the *method of loci* (or places), is also based on imagery. The person visualizes a familiar setting, such as a childhood home or a neighborhood street, and imagines each item (perhaps a shopping list of milk, macaroni, oranges, and yogurt) in a particular location. The milk might be in the birdcage, the macaroni on top of the television set, the oranges on the sofa, and so on. Once at the supermarket, the person takes an imaginary stroll through the setting and visualizes each item placed along the route. A fifth strategy is to devise a systematic plan for rehearsing the material. No matter which of these five strategies is used, the amount of material remembered should increase. Researchers frequently find that college students use such strategies spontaneously in memory tests but that older adults do not. It has been suggested that the failure to apply deep processing to information is responsible for inferior recall and recognition found in older adults.

In one experiment (Zacks, 1982), researchers asked college students and adults in their seventies to memorize a list of common words drawn from several categories. As expected, the students were much better at the task than the older adults. But when the researcher kept students from using strategies by requiring them to repeat each word in the list out loud until the next one disappeared, their performance plummeted and they did only slightly better than the older adults. Other studies have indicated that when older adults are forced to use a strategy (for example, by instructing them to indicate whether each word in a list belongs to the category of clothing, insects, countries, birds, or fruits), older adults recall about as many words as do the young (Mitchell and Perlmutter, 1986).

Another way to find out whether older adults use memory strategies is to warn them that they will be tested on their retention of the material they are learning. Presumably, when people know they are going to be tested, they will make an extra effort to learn the material, using whatever strategies they find work best for them. In such situations, age differences widen, suggesting that older adults are not using the kind of strategies best suited for rote memory (Perlmutter, 1986).

But experimental tasks resemble school tests, which require rote memory for material taken out of context. Perhaps, suggests Marion Perlmutter (1986), strategies that are most effective on experimental tasks are no longer relevant to the lives of mature adults. She points to a study in which adults kept a diary about their use of strategies in their daily lives (Cavanaugh, Grady, and Perlmutter, 1981). Younger and older adults used similar strategies, although older adults tended to use them somewhat more consistently. These findings are supported by later research in which older adults were better at remembering to complete assigned chores than college or high school students. Adults between the ages of 60 and 80 were more likely to remember to call a friend, make an appointment, or mail a letter—and also more likely to complete the task on time—than were the young (West, 1984).

A study that compared recall of word lists in young, middle-aged, and older women also indicated the importance of matching strategy to situation (Zivian and Darjes, 1983). The major difference in this experiment was the fact that half the middle-aged women were also university students. The students, whether young or middle-aged, performed similarly, with the middle-aged students recalling as many words as the 20 year olds. But the middle-aged women who were not in school performed much worse than the two student groups, although better than the older women, who were between 60 and 86 years old. Apparently, when our everyday situation requires us to process material so that it can be produced on demand, we maintain memory strategies that we might otherwise cease to use.

Few people use all their potential powers of memory. When researchers set out to test the powers of memory, they discovered that mentally fit adults in their sixties and seventies could learn to perform feats of recall that resembled those of professional memory experts (Kliegl and Baltes, 1987). These adults learned some of the same strategies that experts rely on when they memorize lengthy lists of words and digits. In one strategy, they recoded digits into a list of historical dates they had learned; in another, they used the method of loci, attaching words to be remembered to a series of locations within the city. The best subject, a woman of 69, could correctly recall a string of 120 digits presented at the rate of one digit every 8 seconds. This woman outperformed young adults of average intelligence who had learned the same memory strategies. When tested under speeded conditions, however, all old people performed worse than the young. This pattern shows the existence of a large reserve capacity at all ages, but a smaller reserve capacity in the old.

METAMEMORY

Several reasons have been suggested for the failure of older adults to use spontaneous encoding or retrieval strategies. At one time researchers believed that older adults were simply unaware of possible memory strategies. They did not use them because they did not know as much as younger adults about **metamemory,** which refers to an understanding of the way the memory system works.

Since psychologists have explored older adults' knowledge about the memory system, this explanation has fallen out of favor. When researchers compared adults' knowledge of metamemory with their recall of a word list and a prose passage, they discovered that knowledge of memory strategies predicted how well young adults would do on the recall

◆ *Adulthood in Today's World*

B.F. SKINNER OUTWITS AN AGING MEMORY

When psychologist B. F. Skinner (1983) reached the age of 79, he shared some of the means he had discovered for getting around the problems of an aging memory. Skinner contended that shortcomings in the environment are responsible for many of the intellectual lapses encountered by older adults. An environment that produces an abundance of cues and reinforcements for a younger person will lack the appropriate stimuli for a person whose senses have dulled and whose processing of information has slowed.

Most of the difficulties Skinner encountered with memory were problems of retrieval, and he developed the systematic use of cues to ease recall. At one time he found himself responding to reports predicting rain in the Boston area by resolving to take an umbrella. Too often, however, he found himself forgetting his resolution and leaving the house without the umbrella, only to be caught in a shower. He solved his problem by learning to hang an umbrella on the doorknob or put it through the handle of his briefcase as soon as he heard predictions of rain. As he left the house, the sight of the umbrella reminded him to carry it along—and perhaps to take his raincoat.

When he forgot names, Skinner used such cues as going through the alphabet and testing each letter to see if it began the person's name. Given half an hour, he usually recalled the name. Because forgetting a person's name when trying to make an introduction is embarrassing, the situation is aversive and one that most people try to avoid. In addition, having forgotten names in similar situations in the past may set up enough anxiety to increase the likelihood that the name will be forgotten in the new situation. Skinner's solution was to

test but bore no relation to the recall of older adults (Cavanaugh and Poon, 1989). Apparently, what older adults have learned about the workings of the memory system no longer seems important to them. In the box, ''B.F. Skinner Outwits an Aging Memory,'' we can see how the use of such knowledge helps older adults evade memory problems.

Older adults seem just as proficient as the young in their ability to predict what knowledge they have in permanent storage. This ''feeling of knowing'' is a metamemory process that is part of daily life. Asked a series of general knowledge question, such as ''What was the former name of Muhammad Ali?'', older adults were as accurate as the young in assessing whether they definitely knew the answers, definitely did not know, or ''could recognize if told'' (Lachman and Lachman, 1980). (A multiple-choice test later confirmed the ability to recognize the correct answers.)

If ignorance about the memory system is no greater among older adults, why do they fail to use memory strategies? Most tasks presented in the laboratory require focused attention and a conscious effort to process the material. If the resource-reduction hypothesis is true, older adults have less energy available for information processing and so are either unable

eliminate the aversive aspects of the situation by appealing to his age, by flattering his listener, or by recalling instances in which he had forgotten his own name.

Lapses of memory in the midst of a conversation are also unpleasant. Skinner found that when he digressed, he sometimes forgot why he began the digression and what he was talking about when he began it. His solution was to rearrange the situation. He stopped "interrupting himself," and he tried to use only simple sentence constructions to keep him on track. When someone else was talking and he was trying to keep in mind a point that he wished to make, he either pulled out a pad and made a note or rehearsed the point to himself, keeping it in short-term memory.

Notes, whether written or taped, were other cues that Skinner found valuable. After repeatedly forgetting to make important changes in articles that occurred to him in the middle of the night or while he was doing other things, Skinner began carrying a notepad and pencil or keeping a tape recorder beside his bed. As he put it: "The problem in old age is not so much how to have ideas as how to have them when you can use them" (Skinner, 1983, p. 240). By recording his thoughts, he made them available when he sat down at his desk to write.

Because Skinner's work was intellectual, he found that providing an abundance of cues helped compensate for retrieval problems. Reference books, rereading relevant material, and the use of a thesaurus increased his responses to any problem he was writing or thinking about. Good files; a tape recorder; a word processor; an abundant supply of pens, pencils, and paper; and an increasing reliance on detailed outlines enabled him to continue the production of scholarly and popular papers until his death at the age of 86. His last book was published when he was 85, and less than two weeks before his death he was working on a paper he described as "my summing up of what psychology is all about" (*New York Times,* August 8, 1990; Sobel, 1990).

or reluctant to carry out the demanding strategies involved in effortful processing. Reduced resources thus result in the use of inefficient strategies.

Another explanation may be that even when older adults use encoding strategies, retrieval problems interfere with their ability to recall what they have learned. In a study that "forced" adults to use deep processing on a text passage, it was the young and not the old who profited from the technique (Simon et al., 1982). Adults read a 500-word text about a family with financial problems. When they were asked to supply advice to the family after reading the text, young adults (18 to 32) recalled far more of the main ideas in the story than did the middle-aged (39 to 51) or older (59 to 76) adults. But when they were simply asked to read and remember the story, middle-aged and older adults recalled at least as many of the main ideas as did the young. The researchers suggested that, although the two older groups may have processed the material as thoroughly as the younger group under the first condition, their recall suffered because at the time of retrieval, they were unable to reinstate the mental operations they used at encoding. Faced with the additional demands of the task, older adults may have encoded the material in a less specific and distinctive manner than that used by younger adults. If so, they would require different or more general retrieval cues for successful recall (Craik and Simon, 1980). Neither of these explanations may describe a consequence of normal aging, but instead may reflect factors that are specific to the task, the individual, or the situation.

INFLUENCES ON PERFORMANCE

By itself, age is not a good predictor of performance on learning and memory function. Although there is a tendency to attribute every lapse of memory to aging, young people forget, too. Most 70 year olds attribute their inability to remember where they placed their car keys to "old age," but 20 year olds also forget where they have placed their keys. Even so, as they pass through their middle and late adulthood years, many people find that learning new skills does not seem to come as easily as it once did and some do tend to forget things. In relatively healthy adults, however, such changes are minor and unlikely to affect daily functioning (Perlmutter et al., 1987).

It has been extremely difficult to discover just how much of this decline is due to the effects of aging and even whether aging itself actually affects the ability to learn. No matter what aspect of processing researchers examine, their findings often conflict with those of other studies (Hultsch and Dixon, 1990). The conflict may arise in part from the wide span of scores among older adults. This diversity may be the result of factors related to the task itself, of factors within the person, of psychosocial factors, or perhaps it arises because the tests used to assess learning and memory lack validity outside the psychological laboratory.

TASK FACTORS

Although older groups do worse than younger groups in laboratory experiments, changing the conditions of the experiment can increase or narrow differences, depending on the technique used. Among the factors that may contribute to age differences are pacing and interference.

Pacing

Slowness exerts a major influence on older people's ability to learn and remember in the laboratory. Whether slowing is peripheral or generalized, the pace at which experiments are conducted has a major effect on the performance of older adults (Poon, 1985).

In paired-associate tasks, the experiment is paced in two ways: by the length of time the pair of words appears together (the study period) and by the length of time between the presentation of the first word in each pair and the presentation of the two words together (the testing period). Lengthening either period improves the performance of older adults. They seem to take more time to learn and more time to recall an answer. Younger adults also do better with more time, but older adults narrow the performance gap noticeably when the testing period for both is lengthened. When trying to recall an answer, a person must first register the word, then search long-term memory for its partner, and finally come up with it before the pair appears on the screen together. When the testing interval is only 1.5 seconds long, older adults do much worse than younger adults; when the interval is increased to 3 seconds, older adults improve much more than the young (Canestrari, 1963). When both periods are lengthened, older adults do their best.

An operant conditioning experiment that required men to learn complicated light patterns showed that older men can adapt to all but the very fastest pace. In this study (Perone and Baron, 1982), men earned money by duplicating a ten-light sequence produced by pressing four keys in the proper order. When a light sequence was thoroughly learned, 67- to 75-year-old men did as well as 18 to 20 year olds as long as they had at least a second to produce the response. But when they were given only half a second, the performance of older, but not younger, men suffered. In the learning of new light sequences, the gap between the performance of younger and older men widened considerably. By the fifth presentation of the sequence, however, the older men did as well as the younger men except at the half-second interval.

Pacing problems are not confined to the elderly. Once people reach the age of 40, rapid pacing begins to cause poorer performance on paired-associate tasks (Monge and Hultsch, 1971). This slowing may explain why many adults in their late thirties leave fast-paced industrial jobs where work is done under a constant, externally imposed time pressure (Davies and Sparrow, 1985).

Interference

Another possible aspect of the task that can affect the result of learning and memory studies is interference. In the disruption known as **proactive interference,** old material interferes with new material to be learned. If the task requires paired-associate learning, for example, old associations interfere with the new ones. Given a list of common associations (blossom/flower; hot/cold), older adults have more trouble than young adults in forming new associations to the words (blossom/cold; hot/flower) (Lair, Moon, and Kausler, 1969). That is, previously established habits are believed to become so strong in older people that they have difficulty forming new ones. Others have agreed that interference affects learning, but not interference from old information. They point to retroactive interference as the culprit. In **retroactive interference,** learning new material interferes with previously learned material. For example, if a person learns a list of words and then a second list, the information from the second list will make it more difficult to recall the first.

Although retroactive interference may be strong in older adults, young adults are known to be subject to it, as well as to proactive interference. Whether interference is stronger in older adults seems impossible to discover because so many other factors are also at work in these experiments (Arenberg and Robertson–Tchabo, 1977). Before the presence of interference can be compared, equal learning of the original material must be established, but when individuals learn at different rates, there seems no way to equate the two groups. However, in one study (Schonfield, Davidson, and Jones, 1983) that began with almost perfect performance in both young (18 to 30) and older (63 to 77) adults, proactive interference seemed stronger in the elderly. Among young adults, proactive interference disrupted only recall, but both recognition and recall suffered among older adults.

PERSON FACTORS

Factors within the person may affect the ability to learn and remember at any age, but some of them seem increasingly likely to be related to memory problems among older people.

They may explain why, given an identical task, older adults show a much wider range of performance than do the young. Physiological factors, such as physical or mental health, nutrition, and the use of alcohol, may impair performance among older adults, and researchers often are unaware whether such problems are affecting the people in their study. Psychological factors are equally important; hopes, fears, expectations, moods, and self-esteem may also be implicated in the older adult's ability to learn and remember.

Physical Health

As physical health deteriorates, it may become more difficult to learn and to recall what was previously learned. People with early, undiagnosed Alzheimer's disease or other organic brain disorders do poorly in learning and memory studies, and their scores can affect the average scores of the older group (Chapter 6). The link between learning and health goes far beyond brain disorders, and a mounting number of studies suggest important relationships between health and cognitive functioning at any age (Perlmutter and Nyquist, 1990). In one study of adults ranging in age from 20 to 89, there was little correlation between age and digit-span memory, but there was a clear connection between health and memory span among the older adults (Perlmutter and Nyquist, 1990) (Figure 8.3).

It may be that cardiovascular and respiratory fitness, which affect the brain's supply of blood and oxygen, are involved. If that is the case, physical fitness may have an important

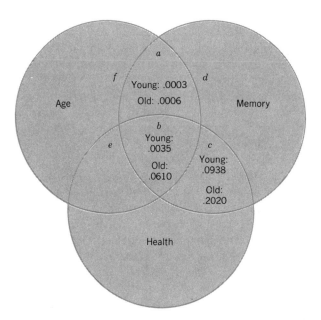

Figure 8.3 Effects of age and health of memory. The section marked *a* shows the direct effect of age on memory span using simple correlations; the section marked *b* shows the joint effect of age and health; and the section marked *c* shows the direct effect of health. The total effect of age and health on memory span ($a + b + c$) is much larger among older adults (60 to 90 years: +.2636) than among younger adults (20 to 50 years: +.0976). *Source:* Perlmutter and Nyquist, "Health and Cognitive Performance across Adulthood." Unpublished paper, University of Michigan, 1989.

As these adults learn the skills of modern dance, they may also be improving various cognitive skills, including attention, memory, and the ability to grasp complex relations.

effect on memory. As we saw in Chapter 5, middle-aged and older adults who are on a regular, vigorous exercise program react faster, have more efficient short-term memories, and reason more accurately than sedentary adults of the same age (Clarkson–Smith and Hartley, 1989). Although these adults, whose activity levels exceed those of most younger adults, may differ from their peers in other ways as well, researchers have found that exercise programs can improve cognitive functioning. Studies have shown that exercise improves memory in middle-aged and older mice and that aerobic exercise improves performance on digit-span tests (Perlmutter et al., 1987). Physical conditioning increases the attention span of the elderly and improves their performance on simple cognitive tasks (Ohlsson, 1976). The ability to grasp complex relationships in nonverbal material also increases after physical training (Elsayed, Ismail, and Young, 1980).

Mental Health

Mental health may have an equally powerful effect on learning and memory. Adults who are anxious or depressed are unable to do their best in laboratory experiments. Although general levels of anxiety appear to remain fairly stable across adulthood, the proportion of adults who suffer from anxiety when faced with a learning or memory test may be higher among older adults. Some studies have found older adults to be considerably more anxious than the young during tests, while others have found them less anxious (Kausler, 1990). Because anxiety leads people to worry and to focus on themselves instead of on the task, it can pull their attention away from the task at hand, lowering their scores. Indeed, after steps are taken to reduce anxiety in older adults, age differences on memory tasks narrow (Perlmutter et al., 1987).

Although anxiety and depression are correlated among college students, as we saw in Chapter 6, there seems to be no age-related increase in the incidence of depression. Among older adults who suffer from depression, researchers have found improvements in memory following treatment (Perlmutter et al., 1987). The connection between depression and memory may operate indirectly. Among older adults, those who are depressed are more concerned about memory lapses and complain more bitterly about them than do those who show no signs of depression (O'Hara et al., 1986). Yet when given a free recall test, both groups remember the same number of words. Perhaps depression leads people to focus on memory lapses that are ignored by the optimistic, and perhaps this dismal focus among the depressed eventually leads to actual declines in memory.

Nutrition

The role of nutrition in memory functioning is not clear, except for the marked memory disorders—and even delirium—that accompany severe vitamin deficiencies. Memory failure is a major symptom of beriberi, produced by thiamine deficiency; pellagra, produced by niacin deficiency; and pernicious anemia, produced by deficiency of vitamin B_{12}. Among healthy elderly adults, those with low blood levels of vitamins C and B_{12} do poorly on memory tests, even when researchers correct for age, gender, income, and education (Goodwin, Goodwin, and Garry, 1983).

Alzheimer's disease appears to affect behavior by depleting the brain's supply of the neurotransmitter, acetylcholine, whose known precursor in the body is choline (Chapter 6). Although no connection has been made between dietary choline and lecithin (another source of choline) and memory performance, some researchers have suspected that deficiencies of choline may be connected with memory failure in adults without Alzheimer's (Perlmutter et al., 1987).

Alcohol

Alcohol in the bloodstream affects the central nervous system and impairs memory processes. The blackouts that may accompany heavy drinking are the result of alcohol's effect on short-term memory, which interferes with the encoding of new memories (Loftus, 1980). But developmentalists are concerned about alcohol's possible long-term effects on learning and memory. Research with a group of California men indicates that over the years regular consumption of high doses of alcohol takes a toll (Parker and Noble, 1977). Among men who customarily drank heavily at a single sitting, cognitive processes and memory were impaired, but among those who had regularly consumed the same amount of alcohol but spread it out so that they were having only a drink or two at a time, there was no sign of impairment. Apparently, getting smashed every Saturday night takes a greater toll of memory processes over the years than having a drink or two each evening. These cognitive defects may be reversible. Several studies indicate that performance among middle-aged drinkers improves once they abstain from alcohol (Perlmutter et al., 1987).

Drugs

Because so many older adults take prescription or over-the-counter drugs, some of the age-related differences in memory may be due to drug effects. It is known, for example, that diazepam, a tranquilizer marketed as Valium and widely prescribed for tension or anxiety, impairs memory performance (Block et al., 1985). The standard dosage for adults is 2 to 10 milligrams three or four times a day—a level that produces symptoms similar to the kind of memory loss associated with Alzheimer's disease. Just how many other medications commonly prescribed for anxiety, pain relief, or sleep may have similar effects is unknown, but changes with age in the way the liver metabolizes drugs, as well as the tendency of older adults to take several medications, may lead to unsuspected effects on cognitive functioning.

Motivation

Motivation invariably affects performance. A person who has no interest in the outcome of an experiment is unlikely to strive for peak performance. Some researchers have assumed that older adults see laboratory experiments as meaningless and have no motive to learn a list of words or word pairs. If they are not motivated to do their best, older adults will not do as well as the young on learning and memory tests. However, other investigators believe that older adults who participate in research tend to be especially interested, involved, and motivated.

Some cross-sectional studies indicate that the need to achieve declines with age, especially among women, although one longitudinal study suggests that cohort effects may be responsible for much of this decline (Kausler, 1990). The need to achieve provides intrinsic motivation. Often, however, we act because of extrinsic motivation—the promise of reward or the avoidance of punishment. Researchers have found that offering money for high performance increases motivation (measured by increased arousal) and performance. However, the young improve as much as do older adults, and so age differences do not change (Warren et al., 1985).

Older adults' motivation may also be influenced by their beliefs in their own memory abilities, strengths, and weaknesses. Research by Albert Bandura (1989) indicates that our judgment of our own competence in a particular situation, which he calls **self-efficacy,** has a powerful effect on how well we learn and remember in various situations. Older adults anticipate the outcomes of their actions and set goals for themselves based on the way they appraise their capabilities. The stronger their self-efficacy, the higher the goals they set, and the more firmly they are committed to them. Even though older adults may have extensive knowledge about the workings of memory, their belief that their own ability to remember in a particular situation is poor may lead them to perform below their capacity (Hertzog, Hultsch, and Dixon, 1989). For example, after training in the use of a new memory strategy, older adults' performance improved, but their confidence in their ability to remember did not (Rebok and Balcerak, 1989). Later, when asked to memorize another list for later recall, only a minority of the older adults adopted the new, more effective strategy. Among younger adults, however, confidence in their ability to remember increased along with their scores, and a majority switched to the new technique on the next recall task.

Yet when older adults are convinced of the usefulness of a new strategy, they do adopt it. Offered a method of learning to connect names and faces, a group of retired middle managers used the strategy effectively, doubling the number of names they could recall (Yesavage, Rose, and Bower, 1983). In this study, the retired adults were told to identify a prominent facial feature (a large mouth), produce a concrete image from the person's name (''Whalen'' became ''whale''), and then produce a second image associating the feature with the transformed name (a whale in a person's mouth). The retired adults remembered the most names when they were also told to judge the pleasantness or unpleasantness of the associative image they had formed. Presumably, this judgment forced them to process the image at a deeper level. Because this memory technique has obvious practical applications, the older adults may have had more incentive to focus their available energy on the encoding strategy.

Cautiousness

If people do not respond, there is no way to discover whether they have learned anything. When the errors of older adults are analyzed, they turn out to be primarily errors of omission (Arenberg and Robertson–Tchabo, 1977). Instead of giving wrong answers on paired-associate or serial-learning tasks, older adults tend to stop answering. As we saw in Chapter 7, older adults take longer to decide whether they have heard a sound in auditory tests. This caution not only makes older adults slower to respond, but it also makes them seem to have learned less than they have—especially in experiments that give them only a second or so to answer and exact no penalty for incorrect answers. In one experiment, researchers were able to reduce errors of omission by paying older adults for their answers, even when they were wrong (Leech and Witte, 1971). When this technique was used, the adults were less cautious. They responded more quickly, and they needed fewer trials to learn the material than did adults who were paid only for correct answers.

PSYCHOSOCIAL FACTORS

Factors within the typical environment, whether the immediate situation or that of the larger society, may also affect the older adult's ability to learn and remember. Among these factors are individual expertise, the stimulation and cognitive demands of the immediate environment, and the structure of society.

Expertise

When they encounter unfamiliar tasks, people of any age find it difficult to perform well. Each step demands active, conscious control by the learner, a kind of attention that is known as *effortful processing*. But once the task is mastered, it is carried out rapidly, accurately, and with little conscious effort, drawing on a kind of attention that is known as *automatic processing*. This progression from effortful to automatic processing occurs for intellectual tasks like solving mathematical problems or playing chess, as well as for motor tasks like ice-skating or riding a bicycle. Perhaps the reason most older adults do poorly on laboratory tests of learning lies in their unfamiliarity with the task. In paired-associate tests, researchers may be pitting older adults who are near-novices with college students who are experts at such tasks (Salthouse, 1987). If older adults were tested on tasks on which they, too, were experts, age-related differences might narrow sharply. Indeed, several studies have indicated that when adults are tested on well-mastered skills, age differences shrink or disappear (Hoyer, 1987). As we saw in Chapter 1, older typists are as fast as younger typists, because their experience has enabled them to compensate for peripheral slowing by looking farther ahead in their copy than do younger typists (Salthouse, 1987). In this case, older typists used different strategies to reach the same level of competence.

Personal Environments

The life situations of older individuals may also affect their ability to learn and remember. As we saw in Chapter 1, older adults who live in undemanding, unchallenging environments may become hyperhabituated and virtually stop learning new things or exercising their imagination. Adults of the same age who live in complex, demanding environments may continue to exercise their cognitive abilities far into old age.

This tendency seems to be present at all stages of life. Workers whose jobs are intellectually demanding have more flexible minds than workers with routine, closely supervised jobs. In a ten-year longitudinal study, researchers found that workers of all ages whose jobs required thought and independent judgment, tended to rely more on logical reasoning, be more independent in their judgment, and were better able to see both sides of an issue than workers in dull, routine jobs (Miller, Slomczynski, and Kohn, 1987). This effect was as strong among workers between the ages of 46 and 65 as it was among younger workers. Apparently, people exercise more of their cognitive potential when their life situation makes its use rewarding.

When older adults regularly seek out intellectually stimulating situations, they are much less likely to show the declines in learning and memory that appear in most studies. This view is supported by a study of adults between the ages of 20 and 90, in which they reported the number of hours they engaged in various activities during the preceding month (Perlmutter, Nyquist, and Adams–Price, 1989). As expected, older adults spent far fewer hours each week in mental activities, but the effects of regular mental activity were clear. There was a positive correlation between older adults' performance on cognitive tests and their levels of everyday mental activity—especially creative activities. Perhaps creative activities provide retired people with the same sort of mental challenge and opportunity for self-expression that intellectually demanding jobs provide for workers.

Social Structure

The structure of society may also account in part for observed age differences in learning and memory. Such a relationship may not be obvious, but it is the result of cultural expectations. Each culture defines appropriate levels of power and activity for various age groups, and these definitions give rise to stereotypes concerning the way mental processing changes across the life span. The stereotypes operate on aging individuals in two ways—from within the person, as he or she tries to conform to social expectations, and from without, as others exert social pressure on the person to conform to appropriate age roles. Studies have confirmed that these expectations vary across cultures and that the American stereotype of aging involves dramatic declines in power and activity (Heise, 1987). David Heise (1987) describes the expectations of American society for men: "A child's mind should be immature, full of shallow, lively thoughts. A male adult's mind should be the ideal problem-solver—a quick powerful computer. As the adult male moves into middle age, he should think slower while retaining his depth, becoming the conservative theoretician. Elderly mental

processes should return to the shallowness of childhood, but now in a plodding fashion''
(pp. 251–252).

ECOLOGICAL VALIDITY

The list of factors that inflate age-related differences found in learning experiments is a
lengthy one, but there is an even more fundamental source of older adults' performance.
Warner Schaie (1987) contends that the way we set about testing learning and memory lacks
ecological validity. In other words, the ability of older adults to memorize word lists rapidly
bears almost no relation to their intellectual competence.

When researchers assess the abilities of children, they are looking for the emergence of
various intellectual structures or for predictions about the children's ability to perform in
the school system. But when we assess the abilities of adults, we are concerned with the
maintenance or decline of intellectual structures and with predictions about older adults'
ability to function in their everyday lives. Because everyday competence may require such
different abilities from success in school, tests that predict well for children may not be
valid for adults.

The validity of these tests is questionable because the requirements of memory change
with age. Children come into the world with little, if any, memory contents, and they must
continually soak up new knowledge if they are to become efficient adults. For the young,
rapid and efficient memory capacities are essential. With maturity, however, the contents of
memory are vast, and the need to acquire new information, though never ending, declines.
Memory always works best in familiar situations, and we remember best the things that are
relevant to our past experience. Thus, when people live in relatively stable environments,
memory becomes more efficient and increasingly adaptive over the years. With this in mind,

This teacher of the Talmud is unlikely to show memory declines because of his continual use of
memory and his life in a relatively stable environment.

Marion Perlmutter (1986) has suggested that typical changes in the memory capacities of healthy adults may actually increase their environmental fitness. Cognitive systems would be highly inefficient if they retained everything. Consider the waste if waiters recalled every order they had taken over a 30-year career. With age, the increase in memory contents may compensate for much of the decline in capacities. As we will see in the next chapter, the same factors that affect memory in adults also affect attempts to assess intelligence.

SUMMARY

INFORMATION PROCESSING

All cognitive functioning can be considered in terms of **information processing,** in which people take in information from the environment, then manipulate, store, classify, and retrieve it. Learning and memory are two time-based processes by which information is transferred within the system, and it is difficult to separate them. On the average, aging is accompanied by a decline in the ability to process new information. Some explanations for the decline focus on basic mechanisms: the **speed hypothesis,** the **generalized slowing hypothesis,** the **component efficiency hypothesis,** and the **resource-reduction hypothesis.** Other explanations include the **inefficient strategies hypothesis,** the **disuse hypothesis,** and the **changing-environment hypothesis.**

LEARNING ACROSS ADULTHOOD

The rate of decline in simple learning skills and the age at which it begins has not been established. With age, **classical conditioning** appears to take longer to establish, and some researchers believe that age differences are due to cell loss within the cerebellum. When a person's actions result in positive consequences, **operant conditioning** appears to be equally effective at all ages. But age differences may exist when the required action prevents an unpleasant consequence. Average scores on tests of verbal learning decline with age, although there are wide interindividual differences. Older adults can learn cognitive skills, even if their skills have deteriorated from disuse or lack of motivation.

ATTENTION

The process of sustained attention, in which people must focus on a single task over time, does not appear to change with age, although older adults generally make more mistakes than do the young. Selective attention does not change when the search for information is simple, but when the search becomes demanding, age differences are apparent. Age differences in divided attention are apparent in complex, but not in simple, tasks. There appear to be no age differences in the ability to switch attention from one task to another.

MEMORY ACROSS ADULTHOOD

Memory capacities (basic mechanisms and strategies) may decline with age, but **memory contents** (stored knowledge) generally increase. The memory system includes **sensory**

memory, where environmental information is fleetingly registered, **short-term memory,** where information is kept in consciousness, and **long-term memory,** where memory, knowledge, and past experience are stored. In short-term memory, where information is organized for permanent encoding, speed and flexibility appear to decline with age. Long-term memory consists of **procedural memory,** which is relatively unaffected by aging, and **declarative memory.** In declarative memory, information is stored in the form of **episodic** or **semantic** memories, and this storage is not affected by aging. With age, retrieval may decline for episodic memories, but recall of semantic memories shows little change. Encoding failure may present a problem because of **production deficiencies,** with the elderly failing to use memory strategies spontaneously even though they have as good a grasp of **metamemory** as the young. Older adults may fail to use strategies because their everyday situations do not require them to produce material on demand. In addition, older adults may encode information in a less specific and distinctive manner than the young, making retrieval more difficult.

INFLUENCES ON PERFORMANCE

The extremely wide span of scores among older adults may arise from a variety of factors. Among the factors that impede older adults' learning in the laboratory are pacing, in which time limitations lead to decreases in performance, **proactive interference,** and **retroactive interference.** Physiological and psychological factors within the person such as physical health, mental health, nutrition, alcohol use, drug use, motivation, and cautiousness may affect the performance of many older adults. **Self-efficacy** seems to have a powerful effect on motivation. Psychosocial factors such as expertise, personal environments, and social structure may also affect performance. Finally, the tests used to assess learning and memory may not have ecological validity, because the requirements of memory change with age.

KEY TERMS

changing-environment hypothesis	**metamemory**
classical conditioning	**operant conditioning**
component efficiency hypothesis	**proactive interference**
declarative memory	**procedural memory**
disuse hypothesis	**production deficiencies**
episodic memories	**resource-reduction hypothesis**
generalized slowing hypothesis	**retroactive interference**
inefficient strategies hypothesis	**self-efficacy**
information processing	**semantic memories**
long-term memory	**sensory memory**
memory capacities	**short-term memory**
memory contents	**speed hypothesis**

Chapter 9

◆

Intelligence, Creativity, and Wisdom Across Adulthood

◆

One day in 1960, a trio of mathematicians paid a visit to philosopher Bertrand Russell, then nearly 90 years old. The visit was expected to be primarily an act of homage, allowing the mathematicians to say they had met the legendary figure. But it became an animated discussion when the men discovered, to their astonishment, that Russell's wit and acute understanding were unimpaired. Russell had not considered mathematical logic for 30 years, but his handling of technical mathematics awed these experts. "It was not merely that his brain was beautifully clear for somebody of 87," reported one of the mathematicians, "it was beautifully clear for anybody of any age" (Clark, 1976, p. 549). Russell's retention of cognitive competence is not as rare as most people believe. At the age of 97, pianist Mieczyslaw Horszowski performed in concert at Carnegie Hall (Rockwell, 1990). At the age of 86, Helen Hooven Santmyer, a resident of an Ohio nursing home, published a 1344-page novel, . . . *And the Ladies of the Club,* which she had written in longhand in a bookkeeper's ledger. Two years later her novel was picked up by a major publishing house, became a Book-of-the-Month Club selection, and rose high on the best-seller list (McDowell, 1984). In the fall of 1989, the 80-year-old operatic singer Hans Hotter, "his towering presence barely stooped, his cavernous voice still surprisingly potent," received rave reviews when he sang the role of Schigoich in Berg's *Lulu* (Rockwell, 1990). The next year actress Jessica Tandy garnered universal praise for her performance in the film *Driving Miss Daisy,* winning the Academy Award for best actress, as well as best actress award at the Berlin Film Festival (Fabrikant, 1990). At 80, Tandy was a mere slip of a girl compared with playwright-director George Abbot, who a few years earlier had directed a revival of a Broadway musical at the age of 100.

The fact that a good many very old people show little, if any, decline in their cognitive ability and creativity does not seem as surprising today as it did only a few decades ago. Although cognition changes with age, those changes vary widely from person to person and are hastened or slowed by the same factors that affect learning and memory. As the health and vigor of older adults improve, we can expect a growing group of women and men whose lives remain exciting and productive into their eighties, nineties, and even beyond.

We have already looked at the cognitive processes of perception, attention, learning, and memory. In this chapter, we examine changes in intelligence, creativity, and wisdom across adulthood. After exploring the nature of intelligence, we look at the ways in which researchers measure intelligence and how current tests were developed. Building on this background, we see how test performance changes with age and what that change means. Widening our view of intelligence, we examine creativity in adulthood and the possibility that age alters the style of artists and musicians in predictable ways. The chapter concludes with a look at wisdom, an aspect of cognition that may not develop until middle or even late adulthood.   ◆

NATURE OF INTELLIGENCE

Everybody seems to know what intelligence is, but no psychologist has been able to produce a formal, useful definition that satisfies everyone. Like learning, intelligence is invisible and

The man paying his taxes and the town tax collector both display intelligence by functioning competently in the environment

must be inferred from behavior. That is exactly how we assess the intelligence of others in daily life—in terms of how closely their behavior corresponds to our idea of an exceptionally intelligent person. Does that mean that our implicit views of intelligence change when we assess people of different ages? A series of studies with adults in Connecticut suggests that this is true. Researchers asked adults about the characteristic behavior of exceptionally intelligent 30, 50, and 70 year olds, and discovered that being curious about the world and reasoning with new concepts was judged less important as people aged, while competence in everyday situations took on increasing importance (Sternberg and Berg, 1987). Apparently, our views of intelligent behavior shift to correspond with the sort of developmental tasks that we see as appropriate for adults at various ages. The situation is comparable to the way we view intelligence in children; we do not expect two year olds and ten year olds to display intelligence in the same manner.

Yet for decades, researchers assumed that intelligence in 70 year olds consisted of the same cognitive abilities displayed in the same tasks as in 20 year olds. This assumption led to the conclusion that, because the average scores on standard intelligence tests declined with age, intelligence declined as well. In the past few years, some researchers have begun to question this assumption and have been looking at adult intelligence in a new way. But no matter what position they take on this question, most researchers can agree with a broad, general definition, that **intelligence** involves mental operations that enhance the ability to function effectively in the environment. The problem arises when we attempt to become specific. When we talk about intelligence, are we referring to a single general attribute or to a group of processes, and, if so, what are they and how many are there? Throughout this century, researchers have been wrestling with these questions.

HISTORICAL VIEWS OF INTELLIGENCE

Over the years, most attempts to pin down intelligence in this way have relied on **factor analysis,** a statistical technique by which researchers examine people's performance on a variety of tasks, looking for relationships among them. Factor analysis is based on the belief that highly correlated tasks measure some common ability and that perhaps the ability reflects an aspect of a characteristic like intelligence.

Factor-analytic research on intelligence convinced some investigators that intelligence is a general ability. For example, Charles Spearman (1927) noted that performance on all sorts of intellectual tasks showed a moderately high positive correlation. This correlation led him to argue that a general factor of intelligence, which he called g, pervaded all cognitive function. He saw g as the ability to grasp relationships quickly and to use them effectively. Spearman admitted that specific abilities existed. In fact, he regarded each task as requiring a different ability, but he maintained that g was common to all intellectual tasks and affected the level of performance on them. A person with a low level of g would be poor at any intellectual task, and individual patterns of ability would be determined by the levels of the various specific abilities a person possessed.

Using similar techniques, others found it difficult to conceive of intelligence as a "common central factor" and denied that g existed. For example, Lewis Thurstone (1935) proposed that intelligence was based on seven factors, which he called **primary mental abilities:** verbal comprehension (the ability to understand the meaning of words), number (the ability to work with numbers), space (the ability to visualize relationships of space and form), perceptual speed (the ability to grasp visual details rapidly, noting similarities and differences in objects), memory (the ability to recall words or sentences), reasoning (the ability to induce a general rule from various instances), and word fluency (the ability to think of words rapidly). Because these factors are specific to different areas of functioning, each person would develop a unique pattern of abilities.

This approach was not specific enough for J. P. Guilford (1973), who maintained that intelligence could not be confined to seven abilities. Instead, he believed that the kind of mental operation used on a particular task was as important as whether the task had to do with numbers, symbols, words, or behavior (which he called the four "contents" of intellect). He saw human intellect as structured by the action of five different mental processes on these four contents, to produce six forms of information. Guilford's five mental operations were evaluation (judging the accuracy or appropriateness of information); convergent thinking (the production of logically necessary solutions); divergent thinking (the production of alternative solutions); cognition; and memory. The six forms of information were units, classes, relations, systems, transformations, and implications.

When all the possible interactions are considered (5 x 4 x 6), 120 factors emerge. Guilford's concept of intelligence was broader than that proposed by other theorists because he included divergent thinking, a cognitive process generally related to creativity because it involves the ability to provide alternative solutions for problems that do not have a single answer.

No matter how many individual factors are involved, many researchers assume that the quality we refer to as "intelligence" is the product of two fundamental types of skills: fluid intelligence and crystallized intelligence. In this view of intelligence, which was proposed by Raymond Cattell (1971), **fluid intelligence** corresponds to the basic cognitive processes and is similar to Spearman's *g*. Fluid intelligence is required to identify and understand relationships and to draw inferences on the basis of that understanding (Horn, 1982). Figuring out the rules governing a number series, for example, draws on fluid intelligence. **Crystallized intelligence** corresponds to acquired knowledge and developed intellectual skills; it may be regarded as reflecting the application of fluid intelligence to cultural content. Solving an arithmetic problem or defining a word draws on crystallized intelligence. Crystallized intelligence is also shown in a person's breadth of knowledge and experience, quantitative thinking, judgment, and wisdom (Horn, 1982). This way of looking at intelligence is useful in the study of adult development because the two types follow different developmental paths, which diverge widely during the last few decades of life.

RECENT MODELS OF INTELLIGENCE

More recently, Howard Gardner (1983) has proposed a theory of **multiple intelligences,** in which each different intelligence can be identified by its susceptibility to destruction without affecting other kinds of intelligence, the existence of prodigies within that domain, specific and unique mental operations, a distinct developmental history that displays levels of competence, a plausible evolutionary history, a symbol system that encodes it, and support from laboratory experiments and standard tests. Gardner believes he has identified seven broad forms of intelligence: linguistic, musical, logical-mathematical, spatial, bodily-kinesthetic, intrapersonal (knowledge of self), and interpersonal (knowledge of others). These forms of intelligence are believed to interact with and build on one another. What is generally known as common sense is, he suggests, a highly developed skill in either spatial and bodily-kinesthetic intelligence or the two forms of personal intelligence. Although Gardner contends that each different form of intelligence is located in specific portions of the brain, except for language there is little evidence for a direct connection between specific brain functions and the structure of intelligence (Rybash, Hoyer, and Roodin, 1986). (The *structure* of intelligence refers to the way in which various cognitive processes and abilities are interrelated in their functioning.)

According to Robert Sternberg (1985), intelligence is best viewed as composed of three parts: components, context, and experience. In his **triarchic model** of intelligence, the *componential* part of the model refers to the basic cognitive processes involved in learning and in executing plans and decisions, as well as the higher processes of planning, monitoring, and judging performance. The *contextual* part of the model refers to the way we apply those processes in the range of situations we encounter—adjusting to the environment, changing it, or moving to a more compatible environment. The *experiential* part of the model consists of how effectively we apply those processes to novel tasks and how rapidly we can become expert at them so that processing becomes automatic. Across adulthood, many of the basic components of intelligence may show decline, but most of the higher processes may remain stable. Research has not established whether older adults are generally as successful as younger adults in maintaining the best possible fit between themselves and their environment. With age, adults seem to become less efficient at handling novel tasks but the ability to attain automatic processing may remain stable (Berg and Sternberg, 1985).

Another way to describe intelligence is in terms of the **dual-process model,** in which intelligence consists of mechanics and pragmatics. In this view, proposed by Paul Baltes and his associates (Baltes, Dittmann–Kohli, and Dixon, 1984), the first process, which they call *mechanics,* refers to basic cognitive processes and whatever cognitive structures are involved in perceiving relationships, classifying the world, and reasoning logically. *Pragmatics* refers to world knowledge, expertise, and **metacognition,** which is the ability to think about our own cognitive activity. This second process involves the application of the mechanics in various contexts. When the development of intelligence across adulthood is seen in terms of the dual-process model, any declines in mechanics of intelligence may be compensated for by improvements in the pragmatics of intelligence—improvements that may appear as wisdom or increased social intelligence.

THE ORGANISMIC VIEW OF INTELLIGENCE: PIAGET

The organismic theory of cognitive development developed by Swiss psychologist Jean Piaget (1983) was intended to describe the way intelligence developed at the species level. Piaget amassed evidence to show that widespread, consistent changes in the way children thought emerged with predictable regularity. He concluded that intelligence develops through four invariant stages, and in each stage the structure of thought is qualitatively different. In the sensorimotor stage (birth to about 2 years), perceptions and actions are intertwined, and there is no symbolic thought. In the preoperational period (2 years to about 7 years), thought is symbolic but intuitive. In the concrete operational period (7 years to about 11 years), thought is logical but limited to concrete situations. Cognitive development is believed to culminate at about adolescence, with the attainment of **formal operational thought.** In this formal operational period, thought is logical and abstract and can be applied to hypothetical situations.

Piaget did not extend his theory across the life span except to say that the development of formal thought continued ''throughout adolescence and all of later life'' (Piaget and Inhelder, 1969, pp. 152–153). As research has continued, it has become apparent that, although there are important age changes in the predisposition to think in certain ways, the changes may not be entirely the result of a reorganization in the structure of thought as Piaget proposed. Formal thought may not be as prevalent as Piaget once supposed, and its presence may be closely related to formal education (Perlmutter, 1988).

Research with older adults indicates that in most cases performance on Piagetian tasks of cognitive development declines with age. As a result, some investigators supposed that cognitive development eventually reverses itself, with the more advanced cognitive skills disappearing first (Storck, Looft, and Hooper, 1972). In one of the few experiments involving formal thought (Overton and Clayton, 1976), college women performed significantly better than older women, and women in their sixties and seventies were progressively less able to solve tasks involving formal reasoning, such as discovering the factors that determine the speed of a pendulum as it travels through its arc. But Piagetian tasks probe abstract reasoning in the field of science, logic, and mathematics—areas that are not part of the average adult's daily experience. When formal thought is not relative to daily problems, adults may cease to use it. In one study, although formal thought had declined among older nonscientists, older scientists were better than young scientists at formal thought (Sabatini and Labouvie–Vief, 1979).

A number of researchers have investigated the performance of older adults on tasks of concrete operational thought, especially on conservation (the understanding that irrelevant

Teaching pre-calculus demands the exercise of logico-mathematical thought, making it unlikely that this man's performance on tests of formal reasoning will decline.

changes in the appearance of objects do not affect their quantity, mass, weight, or volume). The results have been mixed. Some researchers (Chance, Overcast, and Dollinger, 1978) have reported no difference in conservation abilities, and others (Papalia, 1972) have found that older adults are less able to solve more difficult conservation tasks but have no problem with simpler tasks, such as the conservation of number. The proposal of cognitive regression in old age has not been clearly supported, and the nature of the tasks themselves may go a long way toward explaining the poorer performance of some older adults. Designed to be used with children, the tasks involve repetitive questioning that may seem tiresome or ludicrous to adults and thus lead older people to give childlike responses.

AN INTEGRATED VIEW OF INTELLIGENCE: THE THREE-TIER SYSTEM

Each of the various approaches, whether it tries to reduce cognition to basic processes or retains a holistic view, has identified major aspects of intelligence. In an attempt to integrate the diverse findings into an integrated model of cognition, Marion Perlmutter (1988; 1989) has proposed a **three-tier model** in which intelligence is composed of separate levels that can be characterized as (1) processing, (2) knowing, and (3) thinking (Figure 9.1). Approaches using factor analysis generally focus on the first two tiers, while the organismic approach focuses on the third tier. The first tier begins functioning at birth; the second emerges during childhood; and the third emerges later and may continue to develop throughout adulthood. As each new tier is added, the system becomes more powerful, effective, and efficient.

The three-tier model is helpful in understanding changes in intelligence across adulthood. With age, the processes in Tier 1, a biological tier, may deteriorate, either because of poor health or biological aging during the final years of life. Tiers 2 and 3, which are psycho-

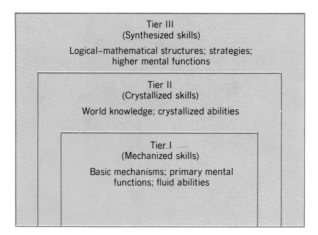

Figure 9.1   Three-tier model of cognition. *Source:* Perlmutter, 1989, p. 257.

logical tiers, are relatively immune from aging. Because they have made the cognitive system so powerful, their functioning can be maintained even in the presence of minor declines in the speed or quality of Tier 1 abilities. This strength means that the basic mechanisms of cognition, which are the abilities that underlie fluid intelligence, are much less important in later adulthood than they were in childhood, adolescence, or young adulthood.

Processing

Tier 1 consists of the basic cognitive processes, such as attention, perceptual speed, memory, and reasoning, as shown in Figure 9.1. It incorporates what Sternberg calls the componential aspect of intelligence and Baltes calls the mechanics; these are the abilities that produce fluid intelligence. During infancy and very early childhood, some growth in this system may take place, but after that point cognitive processes remain stable and functional unless they are damaged by disease or poor health. We draw on this processing tier when we are faced with seemingly meaningless tasks—as all tasks first appear to the infant or young child. As we saw in Chapter 8, the processes of Tier 1 tend to slow as people age, but age differences in the efficiency of processing may often reflect the conditions of the research task, which lacks context and relevance to daily life, rather than any change in the biological system (Rybash, Hoyer, and Roodin, 1986).

Knowing

Tier 2 consists of our store of world knowledge. Knowing develops with external experience and provides the data base that allows us to act in an adaptive manner. It incorporates what Baltes called pragmatics and is related to the experiential aspect of Sternberg's theory; these are the abilities that produce crystallized intelligence (Figure 9.1). This system grows throughout life, recording our external experiences. Through the action of this tier, we habituate to unimportant events and come to anticipate important events. Although growth of the knowing tier slows during middle and late adulthood as we encounter fewer novel

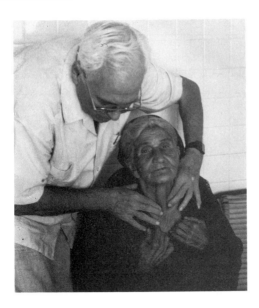

Diagnosing a patient's ills draws on the pragmatics of intelligence, an aspect of the Knowing Tier of intelligence, which does not decline with age.

events, some researchers see development in this tier as the dominant feature of adult intelligence (Rybash, Hoyer, and Roodin, 1986). As various skills or domains are mastered, we switch from effortful to automatic processing in specific areas of knowledge (Chapter 8). Once expertise develops, problem solving becomes intuitive in that particular domain. Some researchers contend that age-related declines in basic processes may reflect a reassignment of these processes from fluid intelligence to domains of expertise, making it impossible to assess adult intelligence accurately (Rybash, Hoyer, and Roodin, 1986).

Thinking

Tier 3 can develop only after the emergence of metacognition. Metacognition includes metamemory (see Chapter 8), and it gives the mental system the power to construct additional tiers of thought. The thinking tier consists of our strategies for dealing with information and the higher mental functions that allow us a greater degree of adaptive function (Figure 9.1). It incorporates the logical-mathematical thought that is characteristic of Piaget's formal operations; it may also incorporate what has been called postformal thought.

Piaget's theory assumes that biological maturity and cognitive maturity go hand in hand, with intelligence reaching its peak as formal reasoning develops. Once the peak is reached, there is a period of stability and then an inevitable decline. If we take a broader view of intelligence, what appear to be declines in adult cognition may actually indicate the emergence of a new organization of thought. In the model of thought that characterizes formal operations, mature thought is seen as conscious, logical, and abstract; emotion, intuition, imagination, and interpersonal identification are kept subordinate and are even viewed with suspicion. But this vertical model of thought, says Gisela Labouvie–Vief (in preparation), may not be the most mature model of thought, for it leads to rigidity and a closure of thought to change and novelty. She sees an additional stage, called **postformal thought,** which emerges from experiences during adulthood that lead to questions, doubts, and contraditions. As experience deepens and the social environment becomes increasingly complex, the thinker reevaluates the nature of reality and subjectivity. With the reevaluation, thought follows a lateral model, in which conscious, logical thought and intuitive, emotional thought participate in a dialogue, with neither dominant. Thought moves from the highly literal to the interpretive, and the thinker gains increasing autonomy.

The dialogue that characterizes postformal thought has led some researchers to call it **dialectical thinking** (Basseches, 1984). In a dialectic, opposing ideas or versions of reality interact to form a synthesis on a new level. The synthesis then interacts with its opposing version to form a new synthesis, and so on. In the postformal dialectic, adults understand that only change is constant; they know that aspects of reality continuously change and evolve, and they maintain their equilibrium by repeatedly integrating these changing systems in the changing world.

How do postformal thinkers see the world? They realize that it is impossible to discover absolute truth; that their own ways of thinking influence whatever information they take in. This leads to the understanding that *all knowledge is relative and nonabsolute* (relativistic thinking). They realize that thoughts, emotions, experiences, people, and objects embody contradictory aspects. For example, people can be kind and cruel, generous and greedy, loving and cold, at the same time. This leads to the understanding that *contradiction is a basic aspect of reality*. Instead of having to discard one alternative in a contradictory situation, they learn to combine them in a larger framework. This leads to an *integration of contradiction into an overriding whole* (dialectical thinking) (Kramer, 1983).

There is some experimental evidence for this development. Researchers have found that when given logically inconsistent statements, younger adults took the information presented and concentrated on analyzing it in order to reach a conclusion, but older adults directed their attention toward the inconsistent premises, using their personal experience and knowledge to introduce supplementary premises that might resolve the inconsistencies (Labouvie–Vief, 1985). In the interpersonal field, middle-aged adults have proved to be better than the young at interpreting contradictions between people's statements and their facial expressions or gestures. Young adults relied on verbal statements, but middle-aged adults used all the available information (Labouvie–Vief, 1985).

Middle-aged adults are also more adept than the young at reasoning about social dilemmas. This tendency became apparent when Fredda Blanchard–Fields (1986) asked adolescents, young adults, and middle-aged adults to resolve a series of dilemmas, such as an adolescent boy's conflict with his parents over a visit to grandparents and a conflict between a couple over whether to abort an unplanned pregnancy. In these dilemmas, most adolescents took one side or the other and rarely tried to deal with the opposing view. The young adults were aware of the discrepancies in viewpoints but tended to say that a neutral party could reach the "truth." By contrast, middle-aged adults tried to separate the facts from the interpretations of the involved parties, and then reconcile the differences. They tended to see each party's perspective as valid and unique. When researchers looked at differences in the way younger and older adults function in the world, they found that younger members of the Vermont legislature produced twice as many bills as older members, but that the older members were twice as likely to have a bill passed (Labouvie–Vief, 1985). The younger legislators operated on a trial-and-error method, but the older legislators proceeded in a cautious and deliberative fashion, which seemed to make them more effective at reconciling differences among legislators' views.

The view that postformal thought is a cognitive stage that requires a complete reorganization of thought has not been universally accepted. Relativistic and dialectical thinking did become more common with age in a study that matched young, middle-aged, and older adults on educational level (Kramer and Woodruff, in press). In line with theory, only adults who had developed formal operations were able to reason dialectically, indicating that dialectical thinking is a stage beyond formal thought. But relativistic thought, which was present in all adults who had developed formal operations, was also present in many who had *not* developed formal thought, indicating that relativistic thought may develop first. Some researchers believe that postformal thought is not an additional stage of thought but a *style* of thinking that emerges during adulthood and requires no reorganization of thought (Rybash, Hoyer, and Roodin, 1986).

PSYCHOMETRIC INTELLIGENCE

Intelligence cannot be measured without some kind of a yardstick, and the traditional measuring tool has been the standardized test, in which test norms are developed by giving the test to large groups of people. Once the distribution of normal scores is established, the score of any individual can easily be compared and evaluated in terms of its relationship to the performance of the standardized group. If the test is a valid measure of intelligence, a person's score can be used to predict his or her performance in other situations assumed to require intelligence. As we saw in Chapter 2, the problem of external validity is central to intelligence testing.

THE ROLE OF INTELLIGENCE TESTS

The field of mental testing is known as **psychometry.** Psychometric tests of intelligence were first developed to predict the academic success of school children. Alfred Binet, a French psychologist, believed that children who were failing in school should not be dismissed without being examined to see if they could learn in special classes. But no efficient way existed to pick out students who could profit from special instruction. With psychiatrist Theodor Simon (Binet and Simon, 1905), Binet developed a set of 30 problems that emphasized judgment, comprehension, and reasoning. The problems, which were arranged by difficulty, were given to normal children, mentally retarded children, and mentally retarded adults. Behind the construction of the scale was the belief that the test performance of a less intelligent child would resemble the performance of a younger child with average intelligence.

The scale went through several revisions and was soon used on normal children as well as on those believed to be mentally slow. It produced a measure of a child's mental level, and in 1911 the scale was extended to cover adults (Anastasi, 1976). Binet's test drew the attention of psychologists in other countries, who adapted it to their own societies. In the United States, a revision of the Binet scale known as the Stanford-Binet was the first to use the concept of IQ, or intelligence quotient, which refers to the ratio between a person's mental and chronological ages. Although psychometrists no longer use the intelligence quotient, the term ''IQ'' has become firmly attached to the intelligence test and now refers to an individual's score on a scale that has been normalized so that the average score made by people in his or her age group is 100. All versions of the Binet test are individual intelligence tests that require a highly trained examiner; thus, they are time-consuming and expensive.

The first group intelligence tests were developed for the United States Army, where they were used to screen a million and a half recruits in World War I. This screening marked the first widespread use of intelligence tests with adults. Two timed tests on various aspects of cognitive function were developed: the Army Alpha test, used routinely with the majority of recruits, and the Army Beta test, designed to be used by illiterates or immigrants who did not know English. Each test produced a single score based on a group of subtests. These army tests became the model for later group IQ tests (Anastasi, 1976).

Intelligence tests are now widely used in research with adults and have been the basis of many studies of the effect of aging on cognition. Two of the major tests are the Wechsler Adult Intelligence Scale (WAIS), which is influenced by Spearman's view of intelligence, and the Primary Mental Abilities test (PMA), which is based on Thurstone's concept of intelligence (Morrow and Morrow, 1973). The WAIS consists of two scales: a verbal scale with six subtests and a performance (nonverbal) scale with five subtests. Subtests on the verbal scale measure information (the range of general information), comprehension (the ability to evaluate past experience), arithmetic, similarities, digit span, and vocabulary. Subtests on the performance scale include digit symbol (a timed coding task that tests speed of learning), picture completion (a test of visual alertness and visual memory), block design (a test of ability to perceive and analyze patterns), picture arrangement (a test of understanding of social situations through the arrangement of pictures in sequence to tell a story), and object assembly (a test of ability to deal with part–whole relationships). The PMA uses five separate scales, which test number, word fluency, verbal comprehension, reasoning, and spatial ability, for these five abilities seem more or less independent. The PMA does not evaluate perceptual speed and memory, Thurstone's other primary mental abilities.

Despite the widespread use of these tests, it is still unclear how performance on them relates to an individual's everyday functioning in the world. The tests grew out of the school situation, where their purpose was to predict the future academic performance of children. Thus, they compare the performance of older and younger people on youth-oriented tasks. The tests were constructed as a measure of ''academic intelligence.'' Ulric Neisser (1976) has pointed out that they require the rapid solution of uninteresting arbitrary problems that have been stripped of any connection with ordinary experience. As Neisser has noted, many academically intelligent people seem no better than unintelligent people at managing their own lives. Although researchers have become interested in developing measures that assess the application of intelligence to problems in daily life, no such test has yet been produced. And so adult intelligence is still measured with the sort of test developed to assess children (Schaie, 1990).

Whether test scores reflect the competence of older adults is unknown. Think about the activities of most retired people you know. Are they more likely to be interested in computer programming or gardening? Reading *Scientific American* or *Reader's Digest?* Few older adults encounter any environmental press (see Chapter 5) that would lead them to engage in abstract academic tasks. If the majority of older adults live in an environment that de-emphasizes academic and cognitive achievement, then traditional IQ tests are unlikely to measure their competence, because any aspect of intelligence that does not help predict performance in the schools has been omitted from consideration. The inadequacy of IQ tests

◆ *Adulthood in Today's World*

HOW MUCH DOES IQ HELP AT THE RACETRACK?

The inadequacy of IQ tests as a measure of practical intelligence became clear when psychologists studied the ability of ardent harness-racing fans to handicap horses. Handicapping horses consists of determining a horse's chance of winning a particular race and expressing those chances in the form of odds. Stephen Ceci and Jeffrey Liker (1987) went to an East Coast race track and studied middle-aged and older men who customarily attended the track at least twice a week during racing season. On the basis of the men's performance at handicapping ten races, Ceci and Liker separated them into "expert" and "nonexpert" handicappers. Those who were labeled experts did as well as the paid track handicappers who produce the post-time odds at the track. All the men took the WAIS intelligence test.

There was *no* correlation between the men's IQ scores and their ability to handicap horses. The experts' IQs ranged from a low of 81 to a high of 128; the nonexperts' ranged from 83 to 130. One of the most proficient handicappers, a construction worker with an IQ of 85 who had been coming to the track for 16 years, picked the winner in all ten races and picked the top three horses in five of the races. One of the worst performances was turned in by a lawyer with an IQ of 118 who had been coming to the track for 15 years. He picked the winning horse in only three races and the top three horses in only one race.

In an effort to discover the cognitive nature of handicapping, Ceci and Liker asked each man to handicap 50 pairs of horses and then explain the reasoning he used when assigning odds. They discovered that handicapping was a complex cognitive task that involved determining how six aspects of the horse's and jockey's past performances interacted with the condition and nature of the track to affect the horse's chances of winning. The experts assigned weights to each variable and systematically combined the variables in complex ways in order to compute the odds. The nonexperts considered each variable independently.

In accounting for the lack of any relation between IQ scores and track expertise, Ceci and Liker pointed to the almost total lack of context for problems on IQ tests. They believe that the cognitive abilities that a person acquires depend on contextual variables (such as environmental opportunities and challenges) as well as on the person's underlying mental capacities (intelligence). And so people develop specific styles and modes of thought that are often unrelated to successful performance on academic tasks.

at measuring other cognitive skills is shown clearly in the box, "How Much Does IQ Help at the Racetrack?"

Intelligence tests can measure only the sort of cognitive skills that are assessed by the various subtests. If intelligence is reflected in the ability to function effectively in the environment, the mental operations involved are displayed in the solution of problems that require us to combine our general and specific knowledge to surmount obstacles, reach goals, or render life's complexities a little more manageable. Yet most intelligence tests probably do not tap such problem-solving skills. When tests are constructed around topics that have relevance to an adult's life, older adults often do better than younger adults (Cornelius and Caspi, 1987). Asked about problems involving landlords, relationships with friends and family, work, and financial matters, older adults perform competently, with those in their sixties and seventies providing more effective solutions than either young or middle-aged adults. Although scores on this everyday problem-solving test showed some correlation with scores on standard cognitive tests, the correlation was relatively modest and limited to crystallized intelligence skills (Figure 9.2). Other global qualities of intelligence like creativity, flexibility, and wisdom also escape the measuring net thrown out by standard intelligence tests. The narrow focus of current tests may have some bearing on the pattern of age changes in test scores that appears in many studies.

When researchers apply the psychometric approach to the measure of intelligence, they look at scores on various subtests. Taking a single figure as a measure of IQ follows Spearman's view of intelligence, but it does not give us an accurate picture of cognitive function. If scores on some subtests rise and scores on others fall, both increases and declines in various mental abilities could be masked. In other words, the same IQ score may have different meanings at different ages (Schaie, 1990). In addition, the picture of intelligence across adulthood may show a different pattern, depending on whether researchers use a cross-sectional or a longitudinal study, as we saw in Chapter 2.

CROSS-SECTIONAL AND LONGITUDINAL STUDIES

Early cross-sectional studies produced a pessimistic picture. The earliest studies were the most depressing. When soldiers took the first Army Alpha and Beta tests, their performance was inversely related to age, with each cohort scoring lower than the cohort born after it.

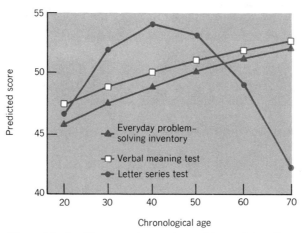

Figure 9.2 Intelligence and everyday problem solving. Scores on the everyday problem-solving test and the verbal-meaning test increase with age, perhaps because both tests tap the breadth of one's cultural knowledge. But scores on the letter series test, which taps fluid intelligence, decline with age. *Source:* Cornelius and Caspi, 1987, p. 150.

This systematic pattern was evident from about the age of 25 (Yerkes, 1921). Community studies a few years later confirmed the army findings, although they indicated substantially lower scores with age on some subtests and little difference on others. As new intelligence tests were standardized, the difference did not appear until about the age of 40, but the disparity was still present (Schaie, 1979).

The classic picture of aging that developed from cross-sectional studies was one in which most abilities peaked in early midlife, remained on a plateau until the late fifties or early sixties, and then began a gradual decline that accelerated after the late seventies (Schaie, 1989). Fluid intelligence (measured by performance tests) appeared to remain stable through middle adulthood and to decline in later adulthood, but crystallized intelligence (measured by verbal tests) continued to increase until the mid-sixties. This pattern was seen in both sexes, in whites and blacks, in various socioeconomic levels, and in institutionalized adults as well as in community residents.

In cross-sectional studies with all-male samples, John Horn (1982) attempted to discover precisely what changes in cognitive functioning are responsible for declines in fluid intelligence. It has been suggested that perceptual slowing accounts for many of the changes in test performance that appear with age, but Horn believes that declines in perceptual speed are a consequence of another decline: a lessening of the ability or inclination to concentrate on simple intellectual tasks. He points out that giving older people extra time decreases but does not eliminate age differences and that older people who can solve fluid intelligence problems solve them just as rapidly as the young do.

A second factor that leads to lowered performance on tests of fluid intelligence appears to be an increasing obliviousness to incidental environmental features. That is, older adults seem to pay little attention to things about them that are not obviously relevant to the task at hand, whereas younger adults note these features and remember them a few minutes or hours later when their relevancy becomes apparent. It may be that older adults have limited cognitive capacity that can be concentrated on a task, as well as less extra capacity to pick up possibly useful extraneous information surrounding it (the resource-reduction hypothesis discussed in Chapter 8).

Horn has linked these factors to specific cognitive processes, suggesting that older adults have trouble organizing information at the encoding stage, keeping their attention focused, and forming expectations about a task. These three processes, he says, account for about half the age decline that appears in performance tests of fluid intelligence.

But until the age of 65, this loss of fluid intelligence is balanced by a rise in crystallized intelligence of about the same amount. Older adults do better than the young on vocabulary tests, on tests that require them to understand analogies, and on tests of divergent thinking, in which they must come up with multiple uses for some common object, such as a brick or a paper clip. Horn believes that older people have more knowledge available than the young and that older adults have organized their store of knowledge so that it is more cohesive, more correct, and more accessible (Figure 9.3).

Indeed, some older adults continue to perform as well as the average young person on IQ tests. Interindividual differences in intelligence are wide, as we have seen, and even where IQ declines are ''significant,'' they are often only a few points. The average age difference for fluid intelligence, for example, increases by about 3.75 points each decade in old age (Horn, 1982).

When longitudinal studies were examined in terms of the entire group, a somewhat similar

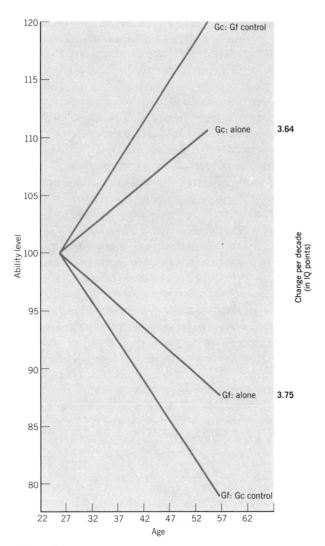

Figure 9.3   Aging of fluid and crystallized intelligence. This comparison of age differences in IQ scores shows a steady decline in fluid intelligence (Gf) that is matched by an increase in crystallized intelligence (Gc). When Gf is controlled, the rise in Gc becomes sharper, and when Gc is controlled, the drop in Gf becomes sharper. *Source:* Horn, 1982, p. 267.

picture emerged. In the California Intergenerational Studies, middle-aged adults (36 to 48) tended to show a modest increase in IQ levels over their scores at the age of 17 or 18 on every subtest of the Wechsler Adult Intelligence Scale. When these same adults were tested 12 years later, the picture was mixed (Sands, Terry, and Meredith, 1989). On verbal tests, improvement still outweighed decline, a result the researchers attributed to increased knowledge and experience, but on speeded performance tests, such as Object Assembly and Block Design, scores generally declined. When individual items on the tests were analyzed, it became apparent that cultural and social influence were responsible for some of the changes. For example, knowledge of the test item ''Koran'' improved over a span of years when events in the Middle East were widely publicized. Scores also improved on items that were frequently encountered by these California adults, while declining on items that were not part of their lives, such as those dealing with heating methods in cold climates. Intelligence does not always decline with age. Lissy Jarvik (1973) describes an 82-year-old woman in a New York State Longitudinal Study, whose scores on nonspeeded intellectual tasks were higher than they had been 20 years earlier. On speeded psychomotor tests, her scores had declined less than 1 percent per decade.

One of the most extensive studies of intelligence across adulthood was carried out by Warner Schaie (in press, 1990, 1989). Its sequential design combined cross-sectional and longitudinal elements as described in Chapter 2, and used the Primary Mental Abilities (PMA) test. Schaie followed two groups of adults over a 14-year period and compared their scores on the PMA with those of four cross-sectional groups. His data cover ages from 22 to 81 and allow him to compare successive cohorts with birthdates from 1889 to 1959. When Schaie looked at individual scores on the various subtests, he discovered that at the age of 60, 75 percent of his subjects showed no decline on at least four of the five subtests, as did just over 50 percent at the age of 81. Almost no one, including those in their eighties, declined on every subtest (Figure 9.4). From this analysis, Schaie concluded that during old age people selectively maintain some abilities, while others deteriorate. Because tasks differ from one person to the next, patterns of scores on the subtests will also differ.

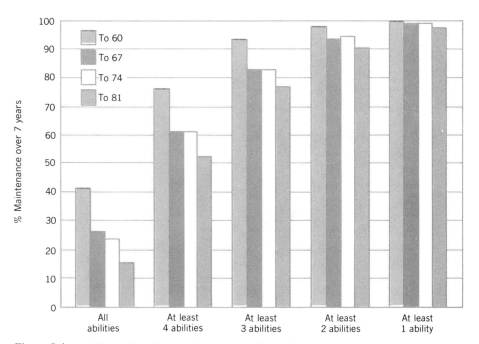

Figure 9.4 Stability of intelligence. Proportion of individuals who maintained stable level of performance on PMA subtests over seven years. *Source:* Schaie, 1990, p. 297.

Cohort Differences

The notion that intelligence inevitably declines with age is also challenged by Schaie's analysis of his data by cohorts. When examining scores on subtests, Schaie found that, at the same age, different generations perform at different levels of ability. In Figure 9.5, the performance of various cohorts are compared with the performance of the oldest cohort, whose members were born in 1889. On most of the PMA subtests, such as inductive reasoning, verbal comprehension, and spatial ability, younger cohorts did best. On word fluency, however, the advantage was with the oldest cohort, and the number skill subtest indicated a dramatic decline in the youngest groups.

Cohort differences have generally been explained as the result of increases in the general health and educational levels of the population. As the educational level rose, as sophisticated technology increasingly pervaded society, and as radio and then television brought the world into the home, succeeding generations grew up in quite different worlds and consequently performed better on intelligence tests. Improvements in nutrition and the conquest of childhood diseases had similar effects (Schaie, 1990). This view receives some support from the fact that over the years, as IQ tests have been standardized, each new test finds IQ peaking at a slightly later chronological age (Schaie, 1983). In 1916 the Stanford-Binet test assumed a peak in adult intelligence at age 16. By 1930 the peak had moved to age 20; by 1939 it was 20 to 24 years; by 1939 peak age had moved to between 25 and 30; and by the mid-1950s the peak came between the ages of 25 and 35.

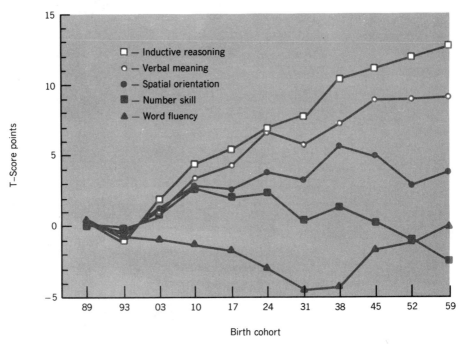

Figure 9.5 Cohort differences in cognitive abilities. Cumulative differences on primary mental abilities for cohorts born from 1889 to 1959. The dip in some abilities shown by younger cohorts may indicate that age differences in test scores are narrowing. *Source:* Schaie (in press).

This explanation seems to account for subtests whose content is most closely related to increased schooling, such as Verbal Meaning (which reflects world knowledge) and Inductive Reasoning (which reflects skill in problem-solving strategies). Other explanations must be sought for the pattern of scores for word fluency (in which scores bottom out among the 1931–1938 cohorts, members of the baby-bust generation) and number skill (in which scores drop steadily among the 1945–1959 cohorts, members of the baby boom generation).

When Schaie carried out a time-lag analysis, comparing the scores of five different cohorts at the same ages, he found evidence that over the next decade, age differences in test scores between young adults and the young-old will be sharply reduced and that scores will overlap so much that older people in their early sixties will be able to compete on equal terms with the young. That is because the noticeable declines that customarily appear after the age of 60 have been magnified by cohort effects. However, once people reach their eighties, earlier cohort increases seem to fade away as poor health and age-related changes exact their toll. Schaie also suggests that as education levels become similar across all age levels, the trend of scores among the young-old to increase will disappear.

Yet it is important to remember that the declines described may have little effect on daily life. If at the age of 30, a person could produce 40 words beginning with ''s'' in three minutes, but at the age of 70 he or she can produce only 36 words (a test of word fluency), the practical difference may well be nonexistent (Schaie, 1983).

Sex Differences

Most studies of American children indicate that girls have an advantage over boys in verbal abilities whether we look at complex written material, logical relations, or remote associations. Boys appear to be better at mathematical reasoning and problem solving and at spatial ability (Hall, Lamb, and Perlmutter, 1986). The differences are not large, and there is a wide overlap between the scores of boys and girls, but some researchers believe that biology is implicated in this development (McGuinness, 1985).

When IQ test performance across adulthood is analyzed, traditional differences in performance generally appear. In the California Intergenerational Studies, women tended to show greater increases in verbal IQ than in performance IQ, whereas men showed just the opposite pattern (Eichorn, Hunt, and Honzik, 1981). In Schaie's sequential study, women in older cohorts consistently performed better on tests of inductive reasoning and word fluency and men on tests of space and number, but in the most recent cohort (born in 1959), there was no difference in inductive reasoning and women outscored men on the number subtest. In addition, recent cohorts of men have outscored women on the word fluency subtest. Apparently, changes in sex roles, and thus in life experience, are narrowing the differences between the sexes in some aspects of intelligence.

The possible cultural roots of sex differences in IQ were reaffirmed by researchers in Israel, who found that age, education, and cultural origins explained sex differences in scores among middle-aged Israelis (Shanan and Sagiv, 1982). Educational level had a powerful effect, with men doing better on all subtests among those with less than ten years of education, but outscoring women on only one subtest among those with more education. In the educated group, age was also important. There were no sex differences on any test among highly educated adults between the ages of 46 and 55. Among older adults in the group (aged 56 to 65), there were no significant sex differences between men and women with

European backgrounds, but significant differences between men and women with Middle Eastern backgrounds. Less education, lower socioeconomic levels, and a subordinate position in the culture combined to produce the sex differences, leading the researchers to conclude that social position is a major determinant of intellectual functioning. But social position does not explain age-related declines in intelligence, which some researchers have connected with failing health.

DOES TERMINAL DROP ACCOUNT FOR AGE-RELATED DECLINES?

A number of studies have found a connection between physical health and intelligence test scores. In Schaie's study, for example, the average scores of individuals with cardiovascular disease tended to decline earlier on tests of *all* mental abilities than did the scores of other subjects (Schaie, 1990). The connection between health and intelligence is so strong that researchers have identified a phenomenon called **terminal drop,** in which people who are only a few years from death show a distinct drop in performance, no matter what their age. This tendency was discovered in a longitudinal study of older men. Those who died during the 12-year study had shown much steeper declines at their last testing than did those who had survived (Kleemeier, 1962). Research since then has indicated that people generally show a decline in cognitive functioning sometime during the five years preceding their death. What has not been resolved is whether the decline is pervasive or whether it affects only some abilities (White and Cunningham, 1988).

Recent research indicates that declines in verbal skills are the most strongly related to terminal drop. In the Duke Longitudinal Study, for example, the verbal portions of the WAIS and the Wechsler Memory Scale (which is a combined measure of logical memory and paired-associate learning) predicted both survival and distance from death (Siegler, McCarty, and Logue, 1982). Among a cross-sectional group of more than 1000 older adults in Florida, only vocabulary skills were related to distance from death—and only in adults who were 70 or younger (White and Cunningham, 1988). Adults in this category tended to die within two years of testing. Other researchers, who had earlier confirmed the terminal drop in verbal ability, reasoning, and long-term memory, have also found that short-term memory, as measured by the digit-span test, declined a few years before death in members of a longitudinal Swedish study who were followed throughout their seventies (Johansson and Berg, 1989). In Schaie's study, terminal drop was apparent in four PMA tests: verbal meaning, word fluency, number, and spatial orientation (Cooney, Schaie, and Willis, 1988).

Perhaps, as Schaie (Cooney, Schaie, and Willis, 1988) suggests, fluid abilities generally deteriorate with age, and so ''normal'' declines may obscure the effect of terminal drop, whereas deterioration in crystallized abilities, which are relatively unaffected by normal aging, are fairly easy to detect. Even though terminal drop affects scores on measures of intelligence, it cannot, by itself, account for all the measured decline. Intelligence is probably affected by the same wide range of causes that, as we saw in Chapter 8, affect performance on tests of learning, attention, and memory.

REVERSING THE DECLINE

Convinced that changing the environment of many older people would reveal unsuspected intellectual potential, researchers have been probing intellectual competence in old age.

Despite the decline in inductive reasoning shown by the average older adult in laboratory studies, many elderly men and women continue to serve efficiently in professions that require clear thought and the solution of intricate problems.

Because fluid intelligence consistently declines with age, most investigators have focused on providing older adults with training and practice in fluid intelligence skills. At Pennsylvania State University, Sherry Willis (in press) and Warner Schaie (Schaie and Willis, 1986) have been training adults between the ages of 64 and 95 in inductive reasoning and spatial orientation (the ability to rotate objects mentally). The program consists of five one-hour sessions of instruction and practice in a single skill.

The program has been effective in improving abilities in both skills, and the results for inductive reasoning resemble those for spatial orientation. Inductive reasoning requires that a person identify the rules governing a pattern of relationships and then apply those rules to predict how the pattern will continue. A typical inductive reasoning task involves figuring out the rule governing a sequence of letters or numbers. During the course session, older adults learned to figure out the rule governing patterns of musical notes and travel schedules as well as letters. After completing the course, among those adults whose IQ tests had shown a decline in inductive reasoning, 45 percent managed to wipe out the decline entirely, returning to the levels at which they had tested 14 years earlier. Another 15 percent showed significant improvement, although they still reasoned somewhat less effectively than they had 14 years earlier. Decline in inductive reasoning was not universal. Scores among the majority of adults had either remained stable (54 percent) or actually improved (8 percent). The training program was even more effective with these adults: 53.6 percent showed significant improvement in reasoning ability (Willis, in press).

Age differences did not disappear among the adults who took this training course (Figure 9.6). Although some of the age differences were the result of cohort differences, biological aging seemed to bear part of the responsibility. The two youngest cohorts improved so greatly that their post-training ability was *higher* than it had been 14 years earlier, but members of the oldest cohort, which was 81 at the time of the training program, still tested below their initial scores—although they did show significant gains (Willis, in press).

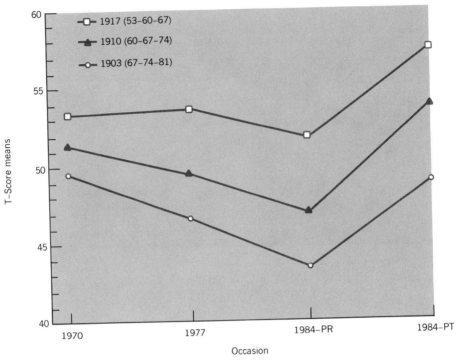

Figure 9.6 Training effects for three cohorts. Training improved the scores of all birth cohorts (1903, 1910, 1917) on tests of inductive reasoning, but age-related differences remained. (Training occurred between the 1984 pre- and post-tests.) The two younger cohorts performed above their original scores on the final test, when they were 74 and 67 years old, respectively, but the oldest cohort (81 at the final test) did not completely eliminate age-related decline. *Source:* Willis, in press.

Other researchers have shown that having a teacher provide instruction in fluid intelligence skills is not necessary. In two separate studies involving figural relations, self-instruction was as effective as instruction with a tutor. Figural relations describes the ability to see how objects change as they move in space and to detect the perspective of objects in relation to each other. Tests of this ability may require a person to identify rotated figures, show how parts of objects fit together in a whole, or discover a figure that is imbedded in another figure. In the first study, healthy older adults (62 to 92 years) who practiced solving problems in small groups where they discussed their progress, improved about as much on figural relations as did similar adults who received specific instruction and training (Blackburn et al., 1988). Although the training group showed greater transfer of their new ability to related tasks, their advantage did not last. On a later test, the scores of adults in the training group had slipped somewhat, while those who learned through a self-discovery program scored as high as they had at the conclusion of the program. In the second study, healthy older adults (63 to 90 years) who worked individually on a practice booklet without any assistance from an instructor showed as large a gain on figural relations as did those who received specific instruction and training (Baltes, Sowarka, and Kliegl, 1989). In this case, both groups showed a similar transfer of skills to closely related tasks. Older adults apparently have a substantial reserve capacity that they can activate on their own.

Younger groups also have a sizable reserve capacity, and they improve as much or more than older groups with such instruction. A popular measure of fluid intelligence is Raven's Progressive Matrices, a test that requires a person to examine 60 designs (matrices) from which a section has been removed and then choose which of six or eight alternatives would complete the design. After only a single brief individual session, in which an instructor solved three sample matrices and encouraged adults to solve three others, similar improvement appeared among young, middle-aged, and older adults (Denney and Heidrich, 1990). Although age differences did not disappear, the plasticity that exists, even in older adults, means that cognitive functioning is more open to modification than was once assumed.

CREATIVITY

Valuable as creativity is, little agreement exists about what it is or how to measure it. **Creativity** involves novel responses; in a creative act, previously unconnected elements are brought together in a new, unusual, and adaptive way. For this reason, creativity has been connected with divergent thinking, a cognitive operation that is not measured by intelligence tests even though it is related to intelligence in Guilford's structure of intellect.

Creativity is usually discussed in terms of the four "p's": personality, process, products, and persuasion. In the *personality-centered approach,* creativity is assumed to be a characteristic of the person, of a special combination of thought, motivation, and personality, and so researchers examine these aspects of notable creative individuals who are now working. In the *process-centered approach,* creativity is assumed to be the product of particular ways of processing information, and so researchers use tests to explore the way originality, fluency, spontaneous flexibility, and divergent thinking change over the life span. In the *product-centered approach,* the creative process produces some product that others judge to be creative, and so researchers focus on the output of creative individuals of the past who have made enduring contributions to the arts, humanities, and the sciences. In the *persuasion-centered approach,* creativity is a social phenomenon in which creativity depends on a person's ability to exert an impact on others, convincing them of his or her creativity. Unless others admire or appreciate the work, the person is not creative (Simonton, in press).

ASPECTS OF CREATIVITY

At first, researchers looked for a connection between creativity and intelligence. It soon became clear that many highly intelligent people show few signs of creativity, but that a certain level of intelligence (probably about 120 IQ) appears necessary for creativity to flourish. In studies of successful writers, artists, and architects, performance on intelligence tests is consistently above the norm, but outstanding creators score no higher than the moderately successful (Barron, 1969). Divergent thinking is generally conceded to be one aspect of creativity, but it is not the only requirement. According to Teresa Amabile, the personal characteristics that underlie creative work are (1) expertise in the field; (2) concentration, persistence, and divergent thinking; and (3) intrinsic motivation—enjoyment in doing the work (Kohn, 1987). The role of expertise means that creativity is domain specific. Thus, general tests that have been developed to tap divergent thinking and other aspects of creativity are unlikely to give us an accurate assessment of creativity (Simonton, in press).

Process-centered studies generally reveal a decline in divergent thinking with age and a lessened preference for complexity—even when the adults studied have similar educational and IQ levels (McCrae, Arenberg, and Costa, 1987). Yet most of these studies have not focused on people with demonstrated creative ability. When researchers compared highly educated, active women (ages 25 to 74) who had never shown evidence of high creativity with women (ages 22 to 87) who were professional artists and writers, two divergent patterns appeared (Crosson and Robertson–Tchabo, 1983). The noncreative women showed customary age differences in their preference for complexity, with younger women preferring more complex designs than the older women. Among creative women, however, no significant difference appeared at any age. In an attempt to understand this discrepancy, the researchers propose two possible explanations: (1) traits, preferences, and abilities that are important to an individual tend to be retained into old age; and (2) when experts continuously exercise highly established skills, they are unlikely to decline with age.

THE COURSE OF CREATIVITY

Product-centered research shows a fairly rapid rise in productivity, peaking in midcareer, followed by a decline. The timing of the peak, along with the size of the subsequent decline, differs from one area of specialization to the next. Lyric poets, pure mathematicians, and theoretical physicists tend to peak early, whereas novelists, historians, philosophers, medical researchers, and other scholars tend to peak as much as two decades later (Simonton, in press). The decline in productivity is not steep, and creative individuals in the last decade of their careers generally produce at about half the rate of their peak years—and at a greater rate than during the first decade of their career (Simonton, 1990).

Dean Simonton (in press) has concluded that there is no indication that age-related declines in creativity are the result of declines in cognitive function. For one thing, sometimes a second peak of creative productivity takes place during later adulthood—in the sixties, seventies, or even later. For another, the timing of the major peak is not necessarily predicted by chronological age, but by *career* age. In other words, the average age of peak productivity comes 22 years after a person enters his or her career. For those who embark on a creative career earlier or later than the prototypical age 20, the peak age will shift accordingly and the probability of making a major contribution remains high (Simonton, 1988).

Declining productivity neither halts the production of creative works nor ends the possibility of producing a masterpiece. Although the odds are in favor of producing masterworks during the middle of one's career, the seeming advantage is based on sheer output. Creators produce more masterworks during their years of peak productivity because they are also producing more pot-boilers. The proportion of major works to minor works remains the same at all ages (Simonton, in press). At 89, Sophocles wrote his tragedy of old age, *Oedipus at Colonus.* Francisco de Goya produced his famous lithographs and ''black paintings'' while he was in his seventies. Pablo Picasso and Georgia O'Keeffe were painting magnificently at 90. Tolstoy wrote *Resurrection* at 71, and P. G. Wodehouse was writing comic novels during his nineties. At the age of 61, Scott O'Dell, a successful author of novels for adults, switched to the field of children's literature and wrote *Island of the Blue*

Dolphins, a book that won national and international literary honors. His productivity remained high over the next three decades; O'Dell had completed his twenty-sixth book for young people and was well along on his twenty-seventh when he died at the age of 91.

CREATIVE STYLE: IS THERE A LATE STYLE?

Along with the brief upswing in productivity that may appear during the later years, many creative people also show predictable changes in their style. Researchers have speculated that the emergence of this late style may be prompted by psychological changes within the creator, perhaps spurred by an awareness of death's approach. Rudolf Arnheim (in press) describes the late style as reflecting detached contemplation. This detachment indicates a shift in motivation, as older adults become less interested in interacting with the world. Their diminished interest in the differences they see in the world around them is accompanied by a focus on the world's essential underlying similarities. This changed motivation produces an increased depth and comprehensiveness of view. Among painters, for example, the earlier works tend to show dynamic action, with the characters acting as causal agents, but in the later works the characters all seem to be subjected to a common fate. The changed world view leads to differences in composition and in the use of light. The change is especially apparent when artists return to a subject they have painted earlier in their careers, as in Rembrandt's two versions of "The Return of the Prodigal Son" or Titian's two

Figure 9.7 In *Christ crowned with Thorns* (1570), an example of the late style in painting, similarities are more important than differences. Instead of arranging the figures in a structural hierarchy, Titian has knit them together in a structure that intertwines torturers and victim without focusing on the principal theme (Arnheim, in press).

versions of ''The Rape of Europa''. One critic describes the change in Titian's style as the departure of any sense that the world is ''ideal, controllable, perfectly finished'' (Brenson, 1990). Titian's earlier belief in destiny now appears to be tempered by a sense of fatality (Figure 9.7).

Simonton (1989), who describes this late style as the ''swan-song phenomenon,'' has studied its effects in the works of 172 classical composers who lived over a period of five centuries. He found that swan songs tended to be shorter than earlier compositions, marked by less complex and less original melodies, less emotionally intense, but profound. The swan songs are generally superior works, as judged by critics, and they tend to be so concise and so direct that they are also more popular. Simonton interprets the swan song as an expression of resignation, or even contentment, rather than a cry of despair or tragedy. Arnheim interprets the late style as an expression of wisdom and notes that its appearance is not inevitable, perhaps because not all creative people become wise.

WISDOM

Wisdom is an aspect of cognition that is traditionally supposed to ripen with age, yet until recently, most developmental psychologists have neglected its investigation. The neglect has been due in part to psychology's aversion to explanations of human activity that could not be tied to observable behavior, in part to the twentieth-century tendency to equate all knowledge with technical-analytical expertise, and in part to an accompanying tendency to denigrate the value of older adults (Holliday and Chandler, 1986). As psychology began to retreat from the strictly mechanistic view of human beings, the view that technology could solve all human problems waned, and the appreciation of older adults increased, the stage was set for a new consideration of wisdom.

Each society seems to regard wisdom as a positive characteristic and to link it with maturity, but the qualities that make up wisdom and the path that leads to it differ from one culture to the next. In Eastern societies, rational intellect has traditionally been seen as a possible impediment to wisdom, which consisted of the direct experience of life's meaning. Such an experiential understanding required intuition and compassion. Wisdom could be reached by meditation and through observing and interacting with a wise teacher.

Western societies have tended to see wisdom as composed of cognition, emotion, and intuition. In the Judeo-Christian tradition, as in the East, it requires time to become wise, but the old do not necessarily possess wisdom. The path to wisdom is seen as threefold: through formal education, the teaching of one's parents, or a divine gift. The Greek tradition embodied two types of wisdom: an understanding of the ultimate nature of things and an understanding of the good. For the Greeks, wisdom went beyond formal knowledge and included moral behavior. The Greeks also included another aspect of wisdom—knowing what one did not know (Clayton and Birren, 1980).

The Greek notion that a mark of wisdom is knowing what one does not know has become central to a modern view of wisdom. John Meacham (1983) contends that wisdom does not consist of a body of knowledge but of the realization of personal ignorance; wise people continually consider what they know within the context of what they do not know. Meacham believes that the wise and the unwise may not differ in the particular facts they have stored but in the way they apply those facts in their lives. He also predicts that wise people are likely to deny being wise, because they appreciate how much they do not yet know.

Most people believe that wisdom becomes stronger with age and is most likely to be found in older adults. When adults of all ages were asked to rate various psychological attributes and to state which they expected to change across adulthood, young, middle-aged, and older adults agreed that wisdom was one of the few desirable characteristics that increase with age (Baltes et al., in press). Most believed that wisdom begins to develop at about the age of 55. Even so, studies indicate that older adults appear to be more aware than the young or middle-aged that age does not necessarily bring wisdom and to perceive understanding and empathy as more important than experience or age in its development (Clayton and Birren, 1980). This view was also expressed by an 84-year-old retired British schoolmaster, who was interviewed by Ronald Blythe (1979): "I don't think you grow in wisdom when you're old, but I do think that, in some respects, you grow in understanding. The very old are often as tolerant as the young. The young haven't yet adopted certain formal codes, and the very old have seen through them or no longer need them" (p. 186).

With their return to the study of wisdom, researchers have explored the popular meaning of the concept, attempting to develop formal theories of wisdom and to study its development.

IMPLICIT THEORIES OF WISDOM

When people say that someone is wise, what do they mean? Before researchers can study wisdom, they have to define it in such a way that it can be studied. When Stephen Holliday and Michael Chandler (1986) asked people of various ages to describe wise people, they discovered that a general agreement as to the meaning of wisdom and its characteristics did not change with age. Whether people were young, middle-aged, or older adults, they agreed that wisdom was determined by five major factors. The first, and most important, was *exceptional understanding* as based on ordinary experience, which included such characteristics as "sees things in a larger context," "understands self," "has learned from experience," "uses common sense," and the like. The second factor, also highly important, was *judgment and communication skills,* which pertained to understanding and correct judgment in the management of everyday matters. It encompassed such characteristics as "understands life," "is worth listening to," "weighs consequences," and "is a source of good advice." The third, moderately important factor was *generally competent,* which included such characteristics as "curious," "alert," "intelligent," "creative," and "educated." The fourth factor, *interpersonal skills,* included such descriptions as "fair," "sensitive," "sociable," "even-tempered," and "kind," and it indicates that wise people express their skills in social situations. The last factor, *social unobtrusiveness,* was marked by such characteristics as "discreet," "nonjudgmental," and "quiet."

Clearly, "wise" is not simply another word for "intelligent"; if it were, competence would have been the most important factor in people's views of wisdom. In order to see how wisdom related to other personal qualities, Holliday and Chandler compared people's descriptions of a wise person with their descriptions of people who were intelligent, shrewd, perceptive, and spiritual. In each case, there was some overlap, but the concepts were clearly separate. "Wise" seemed to be a broader and richer concept, overlapping most strongly with ''perceptive,'' but also carrying marked elements of ''intelligent'' and, to a lesser degree, ''spiritual.'' There was very little overlap with the concept ''shrewd.''

As they examined their findings, the researchers concluded that one reason wisdom is so difficult to study is that it does not fit comfortably into any psychological theory of competencies. Traditional intelligence tests are obviously of little help, since intelligence appears to be related to wisdom as it is to creativity: a certain level is necessary for wisdom to develop, but intelligence is no guarantee of wisdom. Some researchers have tried to develop cognitive theories of wisdom by expanding their view of intelligence.

COGNITIVE THEORIES OF WISDOM

The proponents of a cognitive theory of wisdom are convinced that wisdom is most likely to be found among the old, but that whether it actually appears depends on a person's life experience, motivation, and personal resources (Baltes et al., in press). The average older adult may not be wiser than the average younger adult, but when deep wisdom develops, it will be among the old.

Starting from an informal definition of wisdom as good judgment and advice about difficult but uncertain matters of life, Paul Baltes and his colleagues (Baltes et al., in press) propose that wisdom is actually expertise in the fundamental pragmatics of life. In the earlier discussion of the dual-process model of intelligence, we saw that pragmatics encompassed world knowledge, expertise, and metacognition. When applied to wisdom, the pragmatics of life refers to knowledge about the variation and conditions of life at all ages, human nature and conduct, life tasks and goals, social relationships, and the uncertainties of life. Baltes has developed five criteria that he believes describe the expert knowledge of wise people: (1) a rich store of factual knowledge about life; (2) a rich store of procedural knowledge (knowing ''how'' to do things); (3) an understanding that life is embedded in a series of interrelated contexts that can involve tension and conflict; (4) an awareness that all judgments are relative to a given cultural and personal value system; and (5) an awareness that no analysis of a life problem can be complete or definitive, since the future is not predictable and the past cannot be wholly known.

When wisdom is defined in this way, it seems very close to the application of postformal thought by an expert in knowledge about life. In fact, Baltes and his colleagues have been studying wisdom by asking adults to solve life dilemmas—the same method that has been used to study postformal thought. Some researchers believe that wisdom is more than an expanded intelligence and have begun to look at the part personality may play in its emergence.

INTEGRATIVE THEORIES OF WISDOM

One reason wisdom has proved so elusive to researchers is their failure to consider the role of personality in its development. Lucinda Orwoll and Marion Perlmutter (in press) believe that wisdom is as dependent on personality as it is on cognition and that is why great wisdom is so rare. Extreme wisdom entails exceptional growth in both personality and cognition.

Many personality theories have incorporated links between wisdom and personality, describing wise people as having exceptionally mature, well-integrated personalities. For example, Erik Erikson (1982), whose view of personality development will be explored in Chapter 10, saw wisdom as the peak of *self-development* and described it as an "informed and detached concern with life itself in the face of death itself" (p. 61). He proposed that wisdom develops in the old when they find meaning in life and accept the imminence of their own death, successfully resolving the struggle between integrity and despair. They are able to relinquish leadership while maintaining continuity to the past. Another aspect of wisdom that Erikson describes is *self-transcendence,* in which a person's sense of self expands beyond personal identity and its immediate context to embrace all of humanity, producing an "all-human and existential" identity. Wisdom, which depends on both these facets of the self, does not flower until old age. Yet Erikson's theory allows for earlier forms of wisdom at other stages of life, as people grow in response to life's challenges at various ages.

Extraordinary self-development and the transcendence of the self, when combined with cognitive growth, say Orwoll and Perlmutter, structure the way in which wise people view themselves, others, and the world. Their advanced personality development allows them to experience their emotions in a way that fosters self-awareness, while their advanced cognitive development leads to complex self-appraisals. Wisdom emerges from a developmental spiral, in which self-transcendence promotes the processing of new information and leads to a clearer perception of existing information. The resulting growth in wisdom-related cognition impels a more mature level of insight into motives and emotions, which in turn leads to further cognitive growth. The process eventually produces penetrating insights and fosters the emergence of wisdom.

Given the powerful effect of personality on wisdom and the focus on productivity and problem-solving abilities in a technological society, formal education may not be an effective method of transmitting the sort of knowledge that is required for wisdom. Wisdom may instead depend on the type of experiences a person has, their number, their timing, and the way in which they are processed. If we could learn more about the acquisition of wisdom, we might develop an increasing pool of wise adults who could play a valuable role in society. Orwoll and Perlmutter (in press) believe the best way to learn more about the way wisdom is acquired is to study wise people in the hope of discovering how particular cognitive and personality processes interact. The possible link between personality and wisdom sends us to the next chapter, where we will trace the development of personality across adulthood.

SUMMARY

NATURE OF INTELLIGENCE

Intelligence involves mental operations that enhance the ability to function effectively in the environment. Attempts to discover whether intelligence is a single general attribute or a group of processes have relied on **factor analysis,** and no consensus has been reached. Some researchers propose that intelligence can be divided into **fluid intelligence,** which corresponds to basic cognitive processes, and **crystallized intelligence,** which corresponds to acquired knowledge and developed intellectual skills. The **multiple intelligences** model proposes seven broad forms of intelligence that interact with and build on one another. The **triarchic model** of intelligence proposes that intelligence consists of a componential part (basic processes), a contextual part (application to the environment), and an experiential part (application to novel tasks and development of expertise). The **dual-process model** proposes that intelligence consists of mechanics (basic processes) and pragmatics (world knowledge, expertise, and **metacognition**).

In Piaget's organismic view of intelligence, development peaks at adolescence where the logical, abstract thought known as **formal operational thought** develops. The performance of older adults on Piagetian tasks of cognitive development is generally worse than that of younger adults, but that may be explained by the environment of older adults or the nature of the tasks themselves.

The **three-tier model,** which proposes that intelligence is composed of a processing, knowing, and thinking level, integrates diverse findings from various approaches to intelligence. Tier 1, which consists of basic cognitive processes, may deteriorate toward the end of life, but Tier 2, which consists of world knowledge, and Tier 3, which consists of strategies and higher mental functions, may show continued growth. Those who attain **postformal thought,** which is a Tier 3 process, display relativistic thinking, understand that contradiction is a basic aspect of reality, and combine the contradictions into **dialectical thinking.**

PSYCHOMETRIC INTELLIGENCE

The effect of aging on cognition has been studied using intelligence tests, a measuring technique from the field of **psychometry** that was developed to predict future academic performance. Thus, these tests measure the ability to solve arbitrary, context-free problems and do not consider any aspect of intelligence that is not part of the academic situation. Two major tests in use are the Wechsler Adult Intelligence Scale (WAIS), and the Primary Mental Abilities test (PMA).

Cross-sectional studies of intelligence show an apparent decline in IQ, with slight age differences appearing in middle adulthood and a sharply increased gap after about age 70. On subtests, crystallized intelligence shows little change, but fluid intelligence generally declines. Much of the age-related decline in fluid intelligence scores may develop because older adults seem to have trouble organizing information, keeping their attention focused, and forming expectations about a task. Until about the age of 65, however, the decline is usually matched by a rise in crystallized intelligence. Longitudinal studies, when examined in terms of the group, show a somewhat similar pattern, with rising test scores during middle adulthood, followed by small, but significant, decline after the age of 60. But when individual longitudinal scores are examined, it becomes apparent that declines are selective, affecting some subtests and not others, and that interindividual differences are wide, with many people showing stability, or even rising scores. Cohort differences indicate that subtests related to formal education show increased performance in each subsequent cohort, while other subtests show the effect of historical change, with older adults scoring higher than young adults on one subtest.

Sex differences in test scores generally show traditional differences, with women scoring higher on verbal tests and men scoring higher on mathematical reasoning, problem solving, and spatial ability. However, cohort differences indicate that sex differences are narrowing sharply as sex roles have changed. The average test scores of older adults may be pulled down by **terminal drop.** Declines in fluid intelligence scores can be lessened, and often completely reversed, by training and practice in the relevant skills.

CREATIVITY

Creativity involves the bringing together of previously unconnected elements in a new, unusual, and adaptive way. The personal characteristics that have been connected with creativity include expertise; concentration, persistence, and divergent thinking; and intrinsic motivation. Although there are many exceptions, the production of creative works seems to decline after a midcareer peak, with the timing of the peak varying depending on the field of specialization. The peak is related to career age, not chronological age, and a second peak often appears in late adulthood. The proportion of major works to minor works remains constant across adulthood. During their later years, many creators show evidence of a late style, reflecting detached contemplation.

WISDOM

Wisdom has been linked with age in most traditions. Implicit theories of wisdom indicate that it is marked by exceptional understanding, judgment and communication skills, general competence, interpersonal skills, and social unobtrusiveness. In some cognitive theories of wisdom, wisdom is seen as expertise in the fundamental pragmatics of life. In integrative theories, wisdom develops when a mature, integrated personality (characterized by extraordinary self-development and self-transcendence) interacts with cognitive growth.

KEY TERMS

creativity

crystallized intelligence

dialectical thinking

dual-process model

factor analysis

fluid intelligence

formal operational thought

intelligence

metacognition

multiple intelligences

postformal thought

primary mental abilities

psychometry

terminal drop

three-tier model

triarchic model

Chapter 10

◆

Personality
Across Adulthood

◆

Ada Cutting Perry died on September 27, 1983, at the age of 103. She spent most of her married life on a ranch in California, where her husband raised alfalfa and worked as a carpenter. She was the mother of five children, the last born when she was 47 years old. Three years before her death, she reflected on her ability to adapt, which had enabled her to handle crop failures and floods, financial reverses, and widowhood:

I realize I am always adapting to the next lesson in life.... After we had moved here to Berkeley, my husband died; and while I was overcoming my grief, I began to watch the birds outside my window and in the garden quite closely. I learned such a lot about them; it was another world.

Then after 70, I couldn't see the birds very well, so I turned to plants. Taking care of indoor plants, close work like that I could still do. And haiku—I even took a turn at writing poetry once my eyes weakened and I couldn't read as well as before.... I've kept changing my activities to fit my physical limitations. In my eighties I adapted to not going out so much as before....

I don't feel too different about being a hundred. After all, it's just a matter of good health and circumstances. I'm glad that I still have the use of my legs, my arms, my hands, my brain. I'm so thankful for common everyday health. I'm hungry. I enjoy food, and I love to eat something that's not good for me.

I have one more adaptation I must make in life, then I'll be through. It's something I don't talk to a lot of people about because most of them would be bored with it. But I want to adapt to the idea of death.... I hope I can adapt to it as well as I have to everything else. It might be around the corner. (Painter, 1985, pp. 124–125)

Ada Perry saw herself as a person who could adapt to change and exert some control over her surroundings, and so she found life meaningful and satisfying—as many older adults do. In this chapter, we will explore personality in the adult years, trying to impose some order on the mountain of often conflicting research that has been carried out over the past few decades. After discussing the concept of personality, we investigate what happens to personality across adulthood, first looking at ways in which it seems to remain stable. Then we turn to change, exploring the effect of context and cohort on personality and the various theories that have been put forth to describe personality development in adults. We close the chapter by considering similarities and differences in the personality of women and men and a theory that ties gender differences in personality to the experience of parenthood.

◆

THE NATURE OF PERSONALITY

Each of us is unique. Our ways of thinking, feeling, and reacting to the environment are not exactly like anyone else's. But we do not respond at random. Within each individual is a thread of consistency that accounts for similarities in his or her behavior in various situations and explains why, placed in the same situation, two people respond differently. That consistency is called **personality,** and without it, we would have no individuality. From infancy, socialization tends to push people into prescribed paths, making them more and more alike. But personality ensures that we will react differently to society's push, which distinguishes us from our relatives, our friends, and the rest of our fellow citizens.

Personality is reflected in behavior, attitudes, values, feelings, moods, and motivations. It is central to the way we perceive ourselves. It affects the way we meet people and solve the problems of living. Clearly, personality is a basic part of being human. Yet psychologists are still trying to explain just what personality is, how it develops, and why—or whether—it changes. The major approaches to adult personality are either mechanistic, in which personality is broken down into particular characteristics, such as shyness or hostility; or organismic, in which personality is often seen as developing through structured stages. But we can also look at personality in other ways: we can study personality states—enduring moods, such as happiness or satisfaction; or we can take a cognitive view of personality and focus on a person's *perception* of herself or himself instead of on the person's behavior. More recently, some researchers have tried to relate personality to its context, looking for the consequences of cohort and history on various life tasks (Kogan, 1990).

When measuring personality, researchers have used various methods. Most assessments of personality rely on standardized tests that are considered objective, for each person is scored on exactly the same questions, administered in the same way, and the results can be quantified. The resulting scores make it possible to compare the dimensions of a person's personality with norms established for the test. Most standardized tests take the form of the self-report inventory, in which a person responds to statements (such as "When I get bored, I like to stir up some excitement"). The 16 Personality Factor Questionnaire (16PF), a self-report inventory developed through factor analysis, is frequently used in studies of aging and personality.

A second way of assessing personality is to have a trained investigator interview people, observing them closely, and then rating them on a standard scale. This method has been used in some longitudinal studies of development. A popular rating scale, the Q sort, involves sorting 100 personality statements (such as "gets anxious easily") into a nine-point distribution that describes the person. The results of observer ratings often correspond closely with a person's self-report, and both types of rating tend to be consistent over time (Mischel, 1981).

Sometimes personality is rated subjectively by asking a person to reflect on his or her own personality and then to rate it directly. Instead of answering questions or responding to statements, the person looks at pairs of opposing adjectives (such as hostile/friendly or impulsive/controlled) and indicates which position on a ten-point scale between the adjectives best describes his or her own personality.

Other studies of personality use projective tests, which require a person to respond to ink blots with whatever comes to mind or to respond to ambiguous pictures by describing what is going on in them. Projective tests are subjective because the situation is ambiguous, the answers are not standard, and their meaning must be interpreted. A projective test that is frequently used in studies of personality is the Thematic Apperception Test (TAT), which consists of 19 ambiguous black-and-white pictures and one blank white card. The task is to describe what happened before the pictured scene, what is going on in the picture, and what will happen next. For the blank card, the person imagines a scene and responds to it as to the other cards (Anastasi, 1976). The TAT measures thoughts and fantasies, so any connection with dimensions of personality is indirect.

PERSONALITY TRAITS

Personality characteristics such as loyalty, shyness, or honesty are known as **traits,** which are enduring dispositions toward thoughts, feelings, and behavior. Traits tend to be stable over time and indicate a certain predictability of behavior. A person who is generally sociable and outgoing is unlikely to be withdrawn and shy at a party.

The assumption behind trait theory is that many traits exist, at least to some degree, in all people. Everyone is more or less dependent, more or less affectionate, more or less aggressive. Since there are literally thousands of possible traits (Allport and Odbert, 1936), psychologists have sought to organize important traits into a model of personality that can be effectively studied. The same five major factors (neuroticism, extraversion, openness, agreeableness, and conscientiousness) have emerged from studies using somewhat different approaches (McCrae, Costa, and Busch, 1986). In Paul Costa and Robert McCrae's (1989) **five-factor model,** each of these factors describes a broad dimension of personality, and together they seem to underlie most of the traits studied by psychologists or used by people in daily life to describe the people they know (Table 10.1). Costa and McCrae believe that these dimensions of personality can predict and explain attitudes, behavior, and feelings.

A look at the first three factors (neuroticism, extraversion, and openness), which have been studied most intensively, shows how they relate to personality (McCrae and Costa, 1984). People who are high on the *neuroticism* dimension tend to be high in all traits for that dimension: worrying, temperamental, self-pitying, self-conscious, emotional, and vulnerable. They tend to complain about their health, smoke heavily, may have drinking problems, report sexual and financial problems, and may be unhappy and dissatisfied with life. People who are high in *extraversion* seem to value power and humanitarian concerns highly, tend to be happy, and show high levels of well-being. This personality dimension influences occupation, with introverts tending to seek out jobs that are task-oriented, such as architec-

Table 10.1 **THE FIVE-FACTOR MODEL OF PERSONALITY**

Factor	*Adjective Definer*
Neuroticism	Worrying versus calm
	Insecure versus secure
	Self-pitying versus self-satisfied
Extraversion	Sociable versus retiring
	Fun-loving versus sober
	Affectionate versus reserved
Openness	Imaginative versus down to earth
	Preference for variety versus preference for routine
	Independent versus conforming
Agreeableness	Soft-hearted versus ruthless
	Trusting versus suspicious
	Helpful versus uncooperative
Conscientiousness	Well-organized versus disorganized
	Careful versus careless
	Self-disciplined versus weak willed

Source: McCrae and Costa, 1986.

ture or accounting, and extraverts seeking out jobs that involve dealing with people, such as social worker or sales representative. People who are high on the dimension of *openness* also tend to score high on theoretical and aesthetic values and low on religious and economic values. Openness is connected with above-average IQ scores; highly open individuals are more likely to change jobs, quit, or be demoted. They are also often involved in lawsuits. Their lives tend to be eventful, and their experience of both good and bad events is generally intense. This dimension also affects occupation, with open individuals tending to become psychologists, psychiatrists, or ministers and shunning the occupations of banker, veterinarian, and mortician.

Another way of looking at personality is through the **six-factor model** developed by Norma Haan and her colleagues (Haan, Millsap, and Hartka, 1986). The factors in this model of personality are self-confident/victimized, assertive/submissive, cognitively committed, outgoing/aloof, dependable, and warm/hostile. People who are high in *self-confidence* are calm, comfortable with themselves, and certain that they will be accepted by others, while people who are low on this dimension tend to be neurotic, self-defeated, victimized, and expect others to be harmful. Those who are high on the *assertive* dimension tend to take a direct, vigorously aggressive approach to living, while those who are low on the dimension tend to take a withdrawing, controlled, rule-dependent approach. People who are high on *cognitive commitment* tend to be innovative, introspective, have wide interests, and do not worry about conventions; those who are low on the dimension display an emotionally driven passivity and lack of certainty. Those who are highly *outgoing* are cheerful, warm, and gregarious, while those who are low on the measure tend to be reserved and cautious in their reactions to others. Those who are high on the *dependable* dimension tend to show dependable, controlled productivity, while those who are low on this dimension are undependable, rebellious, and self-defeating. Finally, people high on the *warm* dimension are sympathetic, giving, and protective of others, while those who are low tend to be cool, withdrawn, and cautious.

Not all psychologists are comfortable with trait approaches to personality, for they believe that using traits to study personality is misleading. They point out that calling someone ''shy'' does not explain the behavior but merely labels it; that using traits to describe behavior may obscure intraindividual differences, and that, from one situation to another, a person's behavior is much less consistent than we suppose.

Behavior is not entirely predictable, and traits are unlikely, by themselves, to determine specific behavior in specific situations. A sociable, outgoing person is more likely to run for political office than a person who is habitually withdrawn and shy. Yet some sociable people run for office, and others do not. Knowing a person's traits tells us about the range of responses he or she is likely to make, but it does not allow us to predict what that person will do in a given situation, such as receiving an extra $10 in change at the supermarket, being fired from a job, or being tempted to have an extramarital affair. Yet if behavior over a long period of time is considered, the effect of traits can be seen (Epstein, 1979).

Traits interact with situations. Some people may be outgoing at parties, but restrained and aloof in a new situation. Anxious people may be no more anxious than others when a situation is calm and unthreatening, but when some threatening event occurs, their apprehension may develop more rapidly and be more intense. When we keep this interaction in mind, traits can be helpful in understanding many aspects of personality.

PERSONALITY STATES

Another way to look at personality is through its effect on a person's predominant emotional state, mood, or motives. A number of researchers have studied feelings of well-being, happiness, and satisfaction among adults. Some believe that environmental conditions are the major influence on well-being, some believe that personality is the major influence, and others point to age as a powerful force.

Interested in the effect of age on satisfaction, Paul Cameron (1975) studied this state in more than 6000 people of all ages. After assessing children, adolescents, and adults at home, school, work, and play, he concluded that satisfaction was the same among the young, the middle-aged, and the old. Mood seemed to be determined primarily by social class, sex, and the immediate situation—not by age.

In studies of life satisfaction and well-being, mood often plays an important role in the ratings. Adults are asked to respond to such statements as ''I am just as happy now as when I was younger'' or ''This is the dreariest time of my life'' or ''Taking all things together, how would you say things are these days—are you happy, somewhat happy, neither happy nor unhappy, somewhat unhappy, or unhappy?'' Although most studies focus on older adults, some have questioned the young and middle-aged as well. In all groups, health is related to feelings of well-being, with the strength of the relationship increasing as people age. By the time people reach their fifties, health is the best predictor of overall satisfaction with life and with one's job, and second only to friendships as a predictor of satisfaction with one's community (Willits and Crider, 1988). Health remains the strongest predictor of life satisfaction among older adults, trailed by money, social class, social interaction, and marital status. Yet when women are asked what gives them their greatest satisfaction in life, middle-aged women say that their families are the greatest sources of satisfaction *and* dissatisfaction, while older women say that their material well-being, including their living arrangements, is their greatest source of satisfaction, with family and health being equally potent sources of dissatisfaction (Bearon, 1989).

The determinants of happiness, an essential part of satisfaction with life, do not appear to change with age.

Among gifted men and women in their sixties, who had been followed since childhood by Lewis Terman, the deepest life satisfaction came from their families (Figure 10.1). A simple joy in living was also a major source of life satisfaction for both sexes. Friends and culture weighed heavily on life satisfaction for women whereas men derived much of their satisfaction from their occupations (R. Sears, 1977; P. Sears and Barbee, 1978). When these gifted adults reached their seventies, their personal goals and commitments were strongly associated with their feelings of well-being (Holahan, 1988). Adults who were happiest, calmest, and most optimistic had goals that kept them involved in personal growth, other people, and personal activities, and they retained a desire to achieve, to work, and to contribute to society.

When disengagement theory (see Chapter 2) was prominent, it was assumed that the disengaged elderly would be more satisfied with life than older adults who remained active and engaged. Yet it was the most intensely engaged and active adults in the Terman study who were the most satisfied. Some studies with average adults have produced similar findings, but other research has found that activity levels have only a small effect on well-being (Okun et al., 1984). The discrepancy may be explained by the finding that high levels of activity can have negative as well as positive effects on happiness and general well-being (Reich, Zautra, and Hill, 1987). The researchers suggest that the interaction of competence and environmental press, which was discussed in Chapter 5, may be responsible. As long as activity levels are within the range of competence, they increase the happiness and well-being of older adults, but when the demands exceed their competence, the resulting stress produces dissatisfaction and unease.

The effect of personality on well-being and happiness cannot be discounted. In a study of 35- to 85-year-old men, the personality dimensions of neuroticism and extraversion were

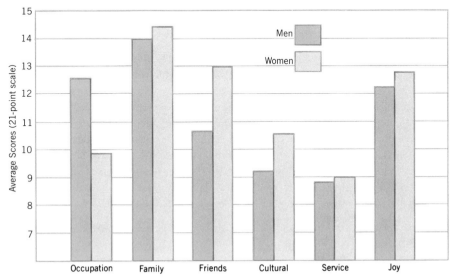

Figure 10.1 Life satisfaction of the gifted. In 1972 older men and women in the Terman study of the gifted reported on the relative importance of six sources of life satisfaction. ''Joy'' refers to overall pleasure in living. *Source:* Goleman, 1980, p. 40.

related to happiness (McCrae and Costa, 1983). Men who were high in neuroticism were more likely than others to feel dissatisfied or unhappy, and men who were high in extraversion were more likely to feel happy or satisfied. The relationship held regardless of the psychological maturity of the men. Personality may affect well-being in another way—our feelings about the aging process. It has been suggested that people who are afraid of growing old will be unhappy, dissatisfied older adults, but among a group of adults between the ages of 55 and 89, the direction of the relationship was just the opposite (Kercher, Kosloski, and Normoyle, 1988): People who were unhappy and dissatisfied with life tended to fear getting old.

Most studies find that contentment and satisfaction increase with age. In a survey of adults in 13 nations, young adults expressed the most dissatisfaction with their lives, and adults older than fifty were the most satisfied—although their satisfaction centered on different areas of life (Butt and Beiser, 1987). Among adults in their mid-twenties, life's major satisfaction came from their occupations, while satisfaction for those in early middle age had expanded to include human relationships. In late middle age and later adulthood, human relationships were still a major source of satisfaction, but material surroundings had replaced occupation as a major source of well-being.

When a 75 year old says she or he is ''happy,'' does it mean the same thing as the 25 year old's report of happiness? In other words, does the nature of life satisfaction change with age? After reviewing the evidence, Richard Schulz (1982) summed up the apparent effects of aging on these attitudes. He believes that older people's feelings about life are just as intense as those of the young, although their quality may change. A person's attitude toward life may not be as ''pure'' as it once was because years of living have tinged positive emotions with negative overtones and negative emotions with positive overtones. As Schulz puts it, love may be less euphoric and more bittersweet the fourth time round. Because the body's regulatory systems change with age, as we saw in Chapter 4, once an older person becomes aroused, it takes longer for the feeling to subside than it does in the young. For the same reason, within any one day, an older person is likely to show fewer changes in mood than a young adult.

Schulz believes that negative feelings and attitudes are not necessarily more prominent among the old. Although age often brings such negative events as loss of spouse, poor health, or decreasing income, these may not evoke the expected negative mood. As people age, their expectations may change, and these changing expectations may well offset negative life experiences. In one group of middle-aged and older women, aspirations changed with age, as predicted (Bearon, 1989). Women in their forties looked forward to positive developments in the coming years, whereas women in their late sixties and early seventies simply hoped to maintain their lives on their present course. Similar findings appeared in a study of both sexes (Ryff, 1989), with middle-aged adults wanting to improve themselves and accomplish more, but many older adults saying they were uninterested in changing anything in their lives.

SELF-CONCEPT

In the cognitive view of personality, a person's self-perceptions are central to personality. The organized, coherent, and integrated pattern of perceptions related to the self is known as **self-concept** (Thomae, 1980). Self-concept includes self-esteem, self-image, and beliefs about one's values, abilities, and personality traits. We construct our self-concepts from the meanings we attach to our interactions and our interpretations of them. All of us are motivated to search for some kind of personal meaning in life, and as our lives progress, our belief systems evolve and our values change (Reker and Wong, 1988). Thus, we continually reconstruct ''reality,'' and in the process we may change our self-concepts.

Self-esteem arises from the sense of personal competence, power, or capabilities, as well as the sense of personal virtue or moral worth. Many studies show no change in self-esteem across adulthood, but about half show higher levels of self-esteem among older adults (Bengston, Reedy, and Gordon, 1985). Because this research is cross-sectional, there is no way to know whether self-esteem tends to increase with age or whether today's older adults simply had higher levels of self-esteem when they entered adulthood.

At least among older adults, high self-esteem seems to be accompanied by a concern for others. When women in a low-income senior housing project were asked to contribute to the building's entertainment fund, those who were high in self-esteem contributed more money than those whose self-esteem was low (Trimikas and Nicholay, 1974). Their findings led the investigators to speculate that self-esteem contributes to group cohesiveness in older adults and may reduce social isolation.

Self-image, an important part of self-concept, appears to have four dimensions: well-being, interpersonal qualities, activity, and unconventionality. These dimensions emerged from a longitudinal study of college men, among whom well-being was made up of self-perceptions concerning happiness, lack of tension, and confidence (Mortimer, Finch, and Kumka, 1982). The interpersonal dimension consisted of self-perceptions concerning sociability, interest in others, openness, and warmth. The dimension of activity included self-perceptions of activity, strength, competence, and success. The unconventional dimension

This city councilwoman's self-concept depends upon her self-esteem, her self-image, and her perceptions of her values, her abilities, and her personality traits.

was made up of perceptions of the self as impulsive, unconventional, and a dreamer. The closeness of these aspects of self-image to dimensions of personality suggests that self-concept and personality are closely related (McCrae and Costa, 1988). Because these findings emerged from a study limited to men, caution should be used in applying the findings to women.

Another way of examining self-concept is through the structure of a person's identity. Identity refers to only a part of the personality, but it reflects a person's social, occupational, and community roles, and it can be seen as various answers to the question, "Who am I?" Daniel Ogilvie (1987) studied identity structure by asking late middle-aged and older adults to rank their various identities in terms of their relative importance and how much time they spent in each one. For example, one man listed his most important identity as retired salesman; somewhat less important were his identities as investor and grandfather. Trailing those identities were his identities as golfer, handyman, son-in-law, and husband. Less important still were his identities as maintainer of his yard and garden, brother, son, and reader. Least important were his identities as church usher and stamp collector. Ogilvie discovered that among his 32 subjects, self-concept affected life satisfaction in a straightforward way: the more time people spent in their major identities, the more satisfied they were with their lives. The retired salesman was somewhat less satisfied with his life than many of the older adults studied, since he spent most of his time as reader, husband, son-in-law, and handyman; more time working as home gardener than as investor, golfer, or grandfather; and no time as a salesman. Among these adults, time spent in various identities was three times as powerful as health in predicting satisfaction. The adults in this study also rated themselves on personality traits, and the self-perceived traits were often identity specific. One of the men, for example, rated himself as autonomous, active, and in control—but only in relation to his identity as committee member. The same man also rated himself as dependent, passive, and controlled—but only in relation to his identity as a patient. Ogilvie believes that seeing self-concept in terms of identities explains why people often seem inconsistent.

Self-concepts do not necessarily reflect reality; they reflect only our construction of it. If aspects of self-concept help to protect a person's psychological well-being, any change—such as a perception of the self as "old"—will be resisted. An older person may completely exclude the notion of old age from his or her self-concept, and many do, seeing themselves as "middle-aged" long past their seventieth birthdays. On his eighty-fifth birthday, financier and adviser to presidents Barnard Baruch summed it up: "To me, old age is always 15 years older than I am" (Simpson, 1988). According to one researcher (Turner, 1979), older adults who have a middle-aged self-concept tend to be better adjusted and have higher morale than those who see themselves as old. Along with a middle-aged self-concept go better health, employment, high levels of activity, and the absence of major illness or the loss of a spouse. Life events apparently play as large a role in self-concept as they do in satisfaction.

STABILITY IN PERSONALITY

Many people, whether professionals or average citizens, are certain that aging affects personality in predictable ways, and they have developed stereotypical ideas about the nature of these changes. Hans Thomae (1980) has collected the stereotypes and reports that American graduate students see old people as stubborn, touchy, bossy, and apt to complain excessively. Germans see the elderly as inactive and withdrawn, and textbooks in German elementary schools portray them as incompetent, dependent, and passive. These stereotypes, explains Thomae, are overgeneralizations from specific, isolated cases. The lack of social role that isolates older adults from society may affect the average person's picture of aging, which is heavily influenced by stereotypes in the media.

The stereotype itself, however, creates a role for the aged, who may feel forced into playing the "old role" by society. Florida Scott–Maxwell, a Jungian analyst, made this point forcefully when, well into her eighties, she wrote: "My kitchen linoleum is so black and shiny that I waltz while I wait for the kettle to boil. This pleasure is for the old who live alone. The others must vanish into their expected role" (1979, p. 28).

Only a minority of older individuals fit the stereotypical picture of the aged person. At every age, adults show similar, wide differences in personality, and studies indicate that personality characteristics rarely change from young adulthood to old age among healthy adults who live in the community (Costa and McCrae, 1989). An imaginative young person becomes an imaginative old person, a sociable young person becomes a sociable old person, and so forth. In the few instances of age-related change that seem to occur, the changes are slight, and the differences among individuals of the same age are greater than the differences between age groups.

When they reflect on their past, individuals may believe they have changed more with age than they actually have. A middle-aged person's recollection of his or her adolescent personality tends to be faulty. Middle-aged individuals generally believed that they had changed greatly in 15 years, but their self-report scales in 1969 showed little change since they had taken the same test in 1944 as adolescents. When asked to retake the test, answering it as they believed they had done as adolescents, there was a great disparity in scores, with the retrospective test portraying a much more negative image than shown in their actual adolescent self-reports (Woodruff and Birren, 1972). In another study (Costa and McCrae, 1988), adults in a longitudinal study were asked how much they believed their personality had changed over the past eight years. When their 1988 test scores were compared with their 1980 scores, the personalities of those who believed they had changed "a good deal" in their personality were as stable as the scores of those who believed they had "stayed pretty much the same."

Early cross-sectional studies attempted to discover whether various personality characteristics increased or decreased with age. Among the traits investigated were egocentrism, dependency, introversion, dogmatism, cautiousness, conformity, imaginativeness, risk-taking, sociability, happiness, activity, need for achievement, life satisfaction, social responsibility, creativity, and hope. In most cases, for every study that found an age-related change, another found stability in that characteristic. In only one trait—introversion—were consistent changes found with age. Most of the studies found that as people grow older, they shift from outer to inner concerns. This inward shift tended to be accompanied by increased cautiousness and conformity (Reedy, 1983).

Some researchers concluded that the evidence for increased interiority reflected older adults' disengagement from society. According to disengagement theory, the disengagement was mutual (Cumming and Henry, 1961). Limited physical and psychic energy supposedly led older adults to withdraw from active participation in a society that was simultaneously withdrawing from the old, taking from them active social roles. Disengagement was re-

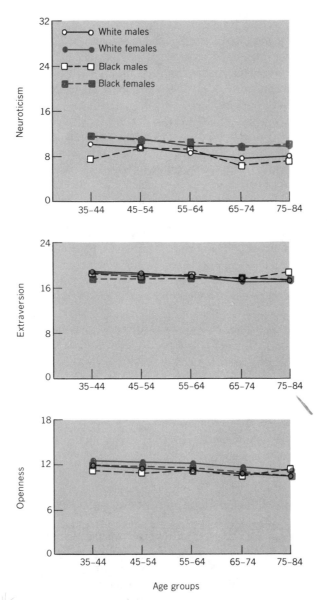

Figure 10.2 Stability of personality. Personality tests given to a national sample of almost 10,000 adults showed that age has little effect on personality. *Source:* Costa et al., 1986.

garded as ''natural'' and as the most satisfactory way to adjust to aging. But for most adults, interiority did not seem to translate into disengagement, and among adults in the Duke Longitudinal Studies, disengagement appeared to be a pattern found primarily among people who had always been relatively uninvolved in society (Maddox, 1970). Today most researchers regard disengagement as merely one pattern of adult personality development.

Striking levels of constancy appeared in a recent cross-sectional study when Costa and McCrae (1989) tested a national sample of almost 10,000 adults whose ages ranged from

35 to 84. Age had little effect on mean levels of neuroticism, extraversion, and openness to experience, although there were slight declines in all three factors (Figure 10.2). Many longitudinal studies have also found stability in mean levels of various personality variables across time (e.g., Costa and McCrae, 1988; Siegler, George, and Okun, 1979). That is, the average level of investigated traits or dimensions shows no change with age when people rate their own personality.

In a cross-sequential study that covered a seven-year period, investigators found that most personality traits remained stable over the years (Schaie and Parham, 1976). The only age-related changes they could identify were increases in excitability and humanitarian concerns. This sort of change appeared in Scott-Maxwell, who wrote:

"Age puzzles me. I thought it was a quiet time. My seventies were interesting, and fairly serene, but my eighties are passionate. I grow more intense as I age. To my own surprise I burst out with hot conviction. Only a few years ago I enjoyed my tranquility; now I am so disturbed by the outer world and by human quality in general that I want to put things right, as though I still owed a debt to life. I must calm down. I am far too frail to indulge in moral fervour (1979, pp. 13–14).

If some people show large increases in a particular trait and others show large declines, the mean level of that trait within the group will not change. Thus, studies reporting stability in mean levels of various personality traits tell us nothing about **normative stability,** which refers to constancy in personality in regard to an individual's rank among other members of his or her cohort. In normative stability, the cohort average and personality characteristics may or may not change in relation to the population as a whole, but the individual's scores remain at the same level in relation to those of other members of his or her own cohort. For example, a 30-year-old woman who scores higher in extraversion than most of her peers will continue to score higher than most peers at the age of 75, although in relation to a 25 year old, she may have an average score. Normative stability is revealed by longitudinal studies that report correlations; high levels of correlation indicate little change in rank ordering of personality traits within the cohort. In major longitudinal studies, correlations on personality stability range from +0.34 to +0.75, with most correlations above +0.50, the level that indicates substantial stability of personality (Costa and McCrae, 1989).

Perhaps part of this stability comes from temperament—the biological basis for personality that each of us brings into the world. Researchers who have studied identical and fraternal Swedish twins aged 27 to 81, some of whom grew up in the same family and others who were separated during infancy, found a moderate genetic influence on personality that lingers throughout adulthood (Plomin et al., 1988). They found a genetic influence on emotionality, activity, and sociability, the three traits they studied. In addition, the researchers found stability in such traits as neuroticism and extraversion. The only significant personality change that occurred with age was a weak tendency for older adults to become less active (Pederson et al., 1988).

CHANGE IN PERSONALITY

Although correlations across age are impressive, they are far from perfect. It is clear that individual personality can—and often does—change. The clearest evidence for change appears when others rate personality. At the University of California, where men and women in the California Intergenerational Studies (now aged 55 to 62) have been studied since birth, Q-sort measures of personality have produced evidence of "substantial and meaningful" shifts in personality (Haan, Millsap, and Hartka, 1986). When personality was analyzed in terms of the six-factor model, normative stability was evident between most adjacent periods of life, but across the life span—from early childhood to late adulthood—correlations on all factors were below +0.40. Apparently, most personality change is too gradual to be captured by studies that follow people for no more than 10 or 15 years. Pronounced shifts in personality appeared as people left adolescence and entered early adulthood, apparently related to the profound shifts demanded by roles connected with marriage and occupation. The least stable dimension of personality was self-confident/victimized, with assertive/submissive and warm/hostile also showing instability in some periods of life. The dimensions of cognitive commitment, dependability, and outgoing/aloofness showed normative stability—except for reshuffling during the transition from adolescence into early adulthood.

When the researchers turned from normative stability to mean levels of personality factors, another sort of change was evident. From adolescence, all the factors except dependable and assertive/submissive showed a steady, accelerating trend across adulthood, indicating that some aspects of personality tended to intensify across adulthood as initial deficiencies were resolved. Other aspects of personality seemed to change in response to historical events and individual experiences. For example, assertiveness seems to reflect a person's reaction to circumstances, which may allow or require either assertive or submissive reactions. Other researchers have found longitudinal trends in motives. Among adults between the ages of 20 and 40, there were clear increases in the need for achievement, autonomy, and dominance, along with decreases in the need for affiliation and abasement (Stevens and Truss, 1985).

How can we reconcile studies that show strong stability with those that show meaningful change? Those who claim to find only trivial changes across adulthood and those who claim to find sizable and psychologically significant change have focused on different aspects of personality, which they have measured in different ways (Kogan, 1990). The possibility and probability of personality change in adulthood may become clearer if we examine contextual views of personality development.

CONTEXTUAL THEORIES OF CHANGE

It may be possible to explain some personality change in terms of life experiences within the context of historical events. In this contextual approach to personality, the various roles that we assume during the course of life (worker, spouse, parent, grandparent, retiree) interact with general historical influences, such as depression or war. And so, marriage during World War II may have had different consequences for the personality and motives of women than did marriage during the 1980s. Instead of looking at the course of extraversion or assertiveness over the life span, contextual theorists may look at the way life events (such as getting a divorce, or becoming a parent) affect such qualities (Kogan, 1990).

In an attempt to relate historical events to the course of human lives, researchers found that the Great Depression of the 1930s had profound effects on boys whose family incomes were reduced by more than one-third (Elder, 1986). By adolescence, most were socially inept, inadequate individuals without initiative or purpose in life. Yet another historical event, military service during World War II, enabled many of these men to construct new identities. As middle-aged adults, they were more assertive and showed greater social competence than did men in their cohort who had never seen military service. Their military experience apparently had broad effects on their lives. The veterans achieved higher socio-economic status than nonveterans, and their marriages were more stable.

Some contextual theorists have been tracing the effects of personality on the life course by examining the interaction of temperament and social roles. In one study (Caspi, Elder, and Bem, 1987), researchers followed the lives of men and women who had been explosive children given to temper tantrums in late childhood. As eight to ten year olds, these adults—part of the California Intergenerational Studies—were known for fits of temper characterized by biting, kicking, striking others, swearing, screaming, and throwing things. Men with histories of violent tantrums became ill-tempered, irritable, moody men who had lower occupational status, more erratic worklives, and less stable marriages at age 40 than men who were not given to childhood tantrums. Women with histories of violent tantrums tended to marry men of lower occupational status, had less stable marriages, and were more ill-tempered as mothers than other women. The researchers believe that an explosive, irritable style of interacting with others not only kept leading these people into situations that perpetuated their bad tempers, but also evoked the sort of responses from others that maintained their explosive tendencies.

Other contextual theorists have investigated the effect of social clocks on personality, trying to discover whether adhering to or departing from the clock's schedule led to major changes in personality. In one study (Helson and Moane, 1987), researchers asked women who were seniors in college about their future plans for marriage, parenthood, and occupations. Some had established a traditional feminine social clock, which called for starting their families by age 28; others had established a masculine occupational clock, which called for advancing in their careers by age 28; the rest had not committed themselves to any schedule. At the age of 43, those women who had set a goal for themselves—whether feminine or masculine—showed increased dominance, independence, self-control, tolerance, and psychological mindedness. This was true whether or not they had managed to adhere to the schedule of their social clock. But those women who had failed to set up a social-clock goal for themselves by the time they were 21 failed to show these changes. Setting long-term goals in the early adult years—or the failure to do so—may moderate or intensify the effects that basic roles have on personality.

Research with ill-tempered individuals turned up stability in personality, while research on women's social clocks found change. Perhaps instead of seeing contextual theories as committed either to stability or change, we should regard them as exploring the social and historical contexts that contribute to stability or change—or both (Kogan, 1990).

STRUCTURAL THEORIES OF CHANGE

For some personality theorists, adults progress through a series of stages in which the structure of their personalities changes as their emotional energies are focused on different issues. The timing of this progression is not specific, but seems related to the life circumstances of the individual. For example, establishing a career or becoming a parent leads to similar personality changes in people regardless of their age. In a society with rigid, age-related roles, nearly all people of the same age would be occupied with the same issues, but in an age-irrelevant society, which the United States may be moving closer to, the stages of personality development would be less closely related to age. Somewhat different, but related, theories of adult development have been put forward by Erik Erikson, Daniel Levinson, and Roger Gould.

Erikson's Psychosocial Theory

One of the most comprehensive theories of personality development was set forth by Erik Erikson (1980, 1982). It is the only theory that covers the entire life span and the only one that considers late adulthood in any depth. Erikson's theory grew out of Freudian psychoanalysis, but shifts the spotlight from the child within the family to the individual within a changing, evolving society. Erikson's theory is organismic, but his focus on the interaction of individual, society, and history has led some developmentalists to regard it as also being dialectical (Buss, 1979; Riegel, 1977). The importance of social and historical factors shows clearly in Erikson's biographies of Gandhi (1969) and Martin Luther (1962), in which their accomplishments are seen to depend not only on their talents but also on the fact that their

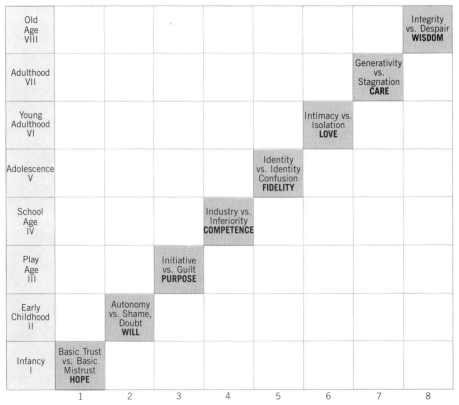

Figure 10.3   Erikson's stages of development. From the major conflict in each life stage, a different strength may develop. Erikson places the stages in a steplike arrangement in order to stress the fact that each step grows out of the previous one and that the strengths and weaknesses of each period are present in some form all during life.

personal conflicts were exactly what were needed for them to be able to solve the problems of a particular historical situation (Erikson and Hall, 1987).

Erikson refers to his theory as a theory of ego development, meaning that he is tracing the development of the conscious self throughout life. His theory might also be regarded as describing the development of changing values and personal meanings over the life course (Reker and Wong, 1988). In devising his theory, Erikson drew on his clinical experience as a psychoanalyst and on his studies of healthy adolescents and of the Sioux and Yurok Native American tribes. The theory is meant to apply to both sexes and, because of its cross-cultural background, to people in all societies. Whether personality develops similarly in men and women will be discussed in a later section.

Erikson divides the life span into eight stages, from infancy to old age, and in each developmental stage there is a characteristic emotional crisis that arises out of the conflict between two opposing trends (Figure 10.3). The life task of each period is to resolve its conflict so that the self is strengthened, "laying another cornerstone" for the mature personality (Erikson, 1962). Erikson's use of the word "crisis" is not meant to indicate impending disaster, but to stress the fact that the resolution of the conflict can send development in either direction, either fostering or impairing it. In each stage of development, the social world widens, so that the infant, whose society began with a dim image of the first caregiver—generally the mother—at last becomes an elder whose view of the world encompasses humanity.

Because the way each crisis is resolved affects the nature of the developmental conflict in all subsequent stages, the theory is not clear unless the early stages are covered. In addition, the strengths (or weaknesses) of each period are present in some form throughout life. For example, hope, the strength that grows out of the infant's struggle between trust and mistrust, in old age becomes faith; and autonomy affects adults' independence in matters relating to occupation and politics.

The Stages of Childhood   In infancy, the first stage of development, the individual faces the conflict between *trust* and *distrust*. The task of this first year of life is to develop a basic trust, which grows out of the baby's certainty that caregivers will be present when needed. Out of basic trust develops hope, which is the ego strength of infancy.

After the successful resolution of this—or any—developmental crisis, the defeated quality (in this case, mistrust) does not disappear from a person's personality. Instead, the balance between the opposing trends shifts, so that trust dominates mistrust, but a certain degree of mistrust continues (and is needed) throughout life. A person without a trace of mistrust would be gullible and constantly taken advantage of. A person without any trust would be suspicious of others and withdraw from society.

In the second stage, which lasts until about the age of three, children first feel the impact of socialization. At the same time they are demanding to determine their own behavior. Thus, the developmental crisis is the struggle of **autonomy,** the feeling of self-control or self-determination, against *doubt* and *shame.* If autonomy predominates over shame, the basic strength of early childhood, a rudimentary will, develops. Erikson sees several consequences of the failure to develop autonomy. If doubt and shame prevail, the child may develop into a compulsive adult who is overcontrolled in matters of time, money, and affection. Or the result may be an adult whose abiding wish to "get away with things" is accompanied by an apologetic, ashamed manner. Yet successful development does not eliminate shame or doubt from life, and a certain amount is present in healthy personalities.

During the later preschool years, children are in the third developmental stage, which Erikson calls the "play age," when the developmental crisis is the struggle between *initiative* and *guilt*. When initiative predominates, a sense of direction or purpose, which is the basic strength of the play age, flourishes. When guilt dominates initiative, the child becomes convinced that he or she is basically "bad." The adult filled with guilt may become excessively inhibited or develop a self-righteous moralism. Instead of seeing the possibilities of life, he or she is concerned with what cannot or should not be done.

As children begin school, they enter the next developmental stage, and their social world widens beyond the family. Children learn to gain recognition by producing things, and discover that completing a task brings pleasure. The crisis of the school age is the struggle between this new sense of *industry* and *inferiority*. If industry predominates, the child will develop the basic strength of the school age, a sense of competence. If instead the child feels inadequate and becomes convinced that his or her skills are not up to the requirements of the new world of school, a sense of inferiority develops.

Adolescence and Identity   Adolescence, the fifth of Erikson's stages, is important because identity is a central concept in Erikson's theory, and it is during adolescence that a sense of identity becomes the focus of personality development. By **identity,** Erikson means that an individual possesses a stable sense of self that is confirmed by experience, so that the individual's self-perception matches the perceptions others have of him or her. This new identity is not simply an extension of the self-concept of childhood. As adolescents go through a period of rapid physical growth and attain genital maturity, develop new cognitive abilities, and face choices that will determine adult roles, they begin to question the resolution of the crises of previous developmental stages. Each aspect of the self-concept is reevaluated, and the adolescent begins to form a new ego identity that will enable him or her to fit within the wider social world.

Occupational identity is one obvious concern of adolescence, but not the only one. There is the matter of gender identity, of just how the adolescent will incorporate masculinity or femininity into the self-concept. Ideals suddenly become important. The adolescent can think about religion, ethics, morality, and politics in a new way; and choices made in these areas will affect choices of other kinds. Both boys and girls face the task of forming an identity at this age, but the content of the task may differ, for it is heavily influenced by culture (Erikson and Hall, 1987).

The developmental struggle of adolescence is between *identity* and *identity confusion*. Once ego identity is established, fidelity, which is the basic strength of this stage, can emerge. The individual is able to commit his or her loyalty to some cause or goal. When a young person makes no occupational or ideological commitment, identity confusion predominates. As Erikson (1980) describes identity confusion, deep inside, you do not know whether you are a man (or woman), whether you will ever be attractive, whether you will be able to master your drives, who you really are, who you want to be, what you look like to others, or how to make the right decisions without committing yourself to the wrong friend, sexual partner, leader, or career.

Stages of Adult Development   Once past adolescence, we are into the realm of adult development. Adulthood encompasses three stages of personality development that roughly correspond to young adulthood, middle adulthood, and later adulthood. In young adulthood, Erikson's sixth stage, the task is to develop **intimacy,** a development that requires the previous establishment of some sense of identity. In intimacy, young adults are able to fuse their identities and commit themselves to relationships that demand sacrifice and compromise. In the developmental crisis of young adulthood, *intimacy* struggles with *isolation.* Out of the successful resolution of the struggle emerges the basic strength of young adulthood: love. When the struggle is not resolved successfully, isolation predominates, and a person's relationships with others lack spontaneity, warmth, or any deep emotional exchange. There may be a fear of intimacy, in which fusion with another is seen as a loss of personal identity. The establishment of sexual relationships does not necessarily signify the development of intimacy. In fact, a person whose sexual activity is purely recreational may feel extremely isolated because he or she never perceives the partner as a person (Erikson and Hall, 1987).

In middle adulthood, Erikson's seventh stage, the struggle is between **generativity** and the forces of *self-absorption* and *stagnation.* Generativity concerns the establishment of the next generation. It can be expressed in the bearing and rearing of children, in guiding other people's children or younger adults, and in contributing to society through productivity or creativity. Generative acts are infused with the strength of middle adulthood, which is care. Some people express generativity through their occupations: the teacher, the artist, the writer, the nurse, the physician. Some express generativity by working to maintain or improve society. In fact, Erikson sees generativity as the driving power in human organization.

Generativity may be reflected in the striking rise in altruism that researchers have found emerging during middle adulthood. In one study, when a pregnant woman asked shoppers in a large metropolitan mall to donate to fight birth defects, generosity generally increased with age (Midlarsky and Hannah, 1989). Among those who were entering middle age (35

The major task of middle adulthood is to develop generativity, a quality this high school teacher expresses through his work.

to 44), the proportion of people who gave jumped sharply—85 percent of them donated, compared with 67 percent among the 25 to 34 year olds.

When generativity fails to predominate, stagnation pervades a person's life. Such people may develop a need for "pseudo-intimacy." They are generally bored and tend to treat themselves as if they were their own spoiled only children, indulging their every whim. Erikson believes that generativity is an expression of a human drive to procreate and that people who decide not to have children need to direct their generativity into a socially fruitful channel in order to avoid an eventual sense of frustration and loss (Erikson and Hall, 1987).

The eighth and final stage of the life cycle is later adulthood, when the task is to develop **ego integrity,** a sense of coherence and wholeness in one's life. A person accepts that life, sees meaning in it, and believes that he or she did the best that could be done under the circumstances. The struggle in late adulthood is between *integrity* and *despair*. When despair predominates, a person fears death and wishes desperately for another chance. When integrity predominates, wisdom, which is the strength of old age, can emerge. Along with wisdom goes a shift in identity. Out of the psychosocial identity that first came together in adolescence emerges an existential identity, which comes from facing the border of life and realizing the utter relativity of your own psychosocial identity (Erikson and Erikson, 1981).

In the struggle to find meaning in their lives, older adults may go through a process known as **life review,** in which they survey, observe, and reflect on their past. According to Robert Butler (1975), anticipation of death starts the process, which can resolve old conflicts and fears, provide insight into past experiences, and make one's life seem significant. During the review, they may feel sadness and undergo some psychological discomfort, caused by the resurgence of unresolved conflicts.

Life review is different from reminiscence, in which people simply muse on their past experiences—often counting only the happy hours. Instead, life review is a structured process that requires people to contemplate the kind of life they have led, what they would change if they relived their lives, and the hardest things they had to face in their lives (Haight, 1988).

Among a group of homebound older adults, those who completed a structured life review under the guidance of an attentive researcher were more satisfied with their lives and scored higher on measures of psychological well-being than did adults who either received a friendly visit from a researcher or had no visit at all (Haight, 1988). Such studies have led to the conclusion that life review facilitates the development of integrity.

Yet some researchers contend that instead of leading to maturity, the life review may be primarily defensive. In a study of older adults who resided in homes for the aged, those who had completed a life review were more serene and more satisfied with life than those who had not (Lieberman and Tobin, 1983). However, instead of developing integrity, some of these individuals appeared to have been reworking the past in order to create a mythic image of the self that protected their present self-concept.

Other researchers have pointed out that life review may be a relatively new development in human history (Marshall, 1980). When life expectancy was short, death came most often to the young, and its arrival was unpredictable, there may have been little time or reason to reflect on one's past. And in the centuries before individualism developed, when each death was seen in relation to the community, a life review may have been inconceivable.

Whether integrity is reached through life review or some other means, Erikson has indicated that later adulthood may be changing in this society. He has suggested that because of recent increases in life expectancy, the stage of generativity may stretch farther into the life span, lasting much longer than it generally has in the past (Erikson and Hall, 1987). This lengthening of generativity may extend the period of middle adulthood. Productivity and creativity are still open to people for decades after they can no longer bear and care for young children. Older adults have traditionally expressed generativity as grandparents, but Erikson foresees longer working careers and a larger proportion of older artists, writers, and musicians in society.

Testing the Theory   The intricate meshing of individual, society, and history that is the core of Erikson's theory harmonizes with the developmental view of the human life span, but its complexity makes the theory difficult to test. Clear definitions of terms are not given, nor are the concepts clearly defined. This vagueness means that different researchers may use different objective standards when setting up a study. Nevertheless, an increasing number of investigators are applying Erikson's theory in research on adult development.

Many tests of the theory have focused on the development of identity among college students. The bulk of such studies support the theory. Young people—both men and women—appear to consider alternative identities during this period and form personally meaningful commitments (Waterman, 1982). In one study (LaVoie, 1976), adolescents of both sexes who had established identities apparently had successfully dealt with the earlier Eriksonian stages: they were confident of their sexual identity, they had good self-concepts and a sense of basic trust and industry, and they seemed generally well adjusted. Adolescents who had not yet established firm identities seemed generally maladjusted and lacked personality integration.

Some longitudinal studies also seem to support Erikson's theory. The life patterns of a group of Harvard men generally followed the theory's stages through middle adulthood, as did those of a group of nearly 400 men from high-crime, inner-city neighborhoods (Vaillant and Milofsky, 1980). The failure of these men to master one of the earlier stages usually meant that they did not go on to master subsequent stages. The stage that men from either group had attained by the age of 47 bore no relation to social class during high school or to education, but progression through the stages was correlated with whether basic trust, autonomy, and initiative had developed during childhood. However, the researchers found that an adequate description of adult personality required the insertion of another stage between the young adult stage of intimacy and the middle adulthood stage of generativity. This stage, which they called *career consolidation versus self-absorption,* was a time when men made a clear career identification, as measured by satisfaction, commitment, and skill. Even though a man had pulled free from dependence on his parents and developed a long-lasting, interdependent, intimate relationship, he was unable to develop generativity unless he first consolidated his own career identity. One of the men in the study summed up the progression by describing his own life: "At 20 to 30, I think I learned how to get along with my wife; and at 30 to 40 I learned how to be a success in my job. At 40 to 50 I worried less about myself and more about the children" (Vaillant and Milofsky, 1980, p. 1349).

Yet these researchers believe that healthy personality development will progress up the Eriksonian staircase only in cultures that hold individualism in high esteem and where caste and culturally dictated roles do not govern individual development. It works best, they propose, in individualistic, economically favored societies. They also believe that the model applies to women only in societies that give them the same options that are open to men. Other structural theories of personality change are related to Erikson's model.

Levinson's Seasons of Life

Psychologist Daniel J. Levinson (Levinson et al., 1978) speaks of his theory of adult development as portraying the "seasons of a man's life." It is an accurate description, for Levinson's theory begins with the close of adolescence, and his primary source of data was a series of in-depth interviews with 40 men. The theory may also describe the course of women's personality development, but only preliminary reports have as yet come from Levinson's study of women (see Brown, 1987).

The men (ten executives, ten biologists, ten factory workers, and ten novelists) whose lives provided the framework for this theory were born between 1923 and 1934, and they were from 35 to 45 years old when first interviewed. Their socioeconomic backgrounds ranged from working- to upper-class, their religions were diverse (Catholic, Jewish, Protestant), their educational levels extended from high school dropout to doctoral degrees, and five of the sample were black. In addition to the extensive interviews (from 10 to 20 hours with each man), Levinson's information included a shortened version of the TAT, an interview with most of the wives, and a followup interview with the men two years after the first series of interviews. Added to these descriptive studies was information on the lives of other men—both real and fictional—made by analyzing biographies, fiction, poetry, and drama. The interviews took place during the latter part of young adulthood and early middle age. Because each man's interviews were concentrated into a three-month span, much of the early material is retrospective and necessarily colored by the men's status at the time of the interview, but the material for the middle life period is abundant.

Information on a similar group of women born between 1935 and 1947 is still being analyzed. These women form three groups: businesswomen at major corporations in the New York City area, college and university professors, and a random sample of women, predominately homemakers (see Brown, 1987). Studies with women by other researchers indicate that most women progress through the same developmental stages as Levinson's men and at roughly the same time (Roberts and Newton, 1987). However, some distinctive differences have appeared, as we will see.

Like Erikson's theory, Levinson's conception of the life cycle grows out of psychoanalytic ground. Freud, Jung, and Erikson are the primary influences on Levinson's theory, which is both organismic and dialectical. Levinson acknowledges a kinship between his periods and Erikson's developmental stages, but sees a difference in emphasis. Erikson's focus is within the person, whereas Levinson's focus is on the boundary between self and society. He finds no conflict between the two theories and regards his own as building on and expanding the base established by Erikson.

Levinson focuses on **life structure**—the underlying pattern of each man's life. In developing this idea, he tried to consider the nature of the person and the nature of society, regarding each as equal in importance. When external events seemed to affect the pattern, he tried to see how each man's personality might have helped to cause the event and how it buffered the event's effects. When some inner conflict erupted to change the pattern, he tried to see what external events might have touched off the conflict or affected the way it was resolved.

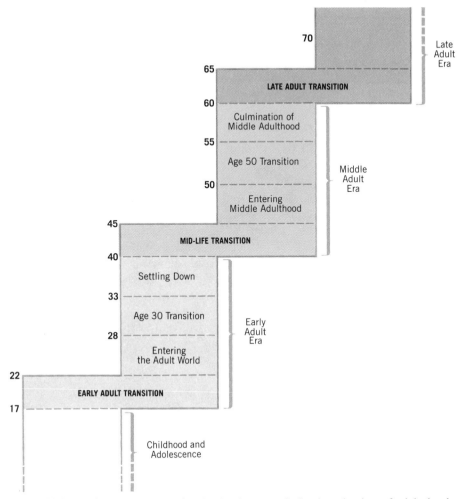

Figure 10.4 Levinson's seasons of male development. In Levinson's view of adult development, each adult era is bridged by a transitional period when the life structure is questioned, new possibilities are explored, and crucial choices are made. *Source:* Levinson et al., 1978.

When analyzed, nearly all the men's lives fell into a similar pattern (Figure 10.4). The men progressed through a relatively orderly sequence of periods that alternated between stable phases (when developmental tasks are solved and goals are pursued within the existing life structure) and transitional phases (when the structure is questioned, new possibilities are explored, and crucial choices are made). These choices could change the life structure, perhaps drastically.

Beginning with a transition out of adolescence (17 to 22 years), there are three major periods in Levinson's theory: early adulthood (ages 17 to 45), middle adulthood (ages 40 to 65), and late adulthood (past age 60). Also projected is a possible new period, late-late adulthood (after 80), which may develop to accommodate the increase in life expectancy. The periods overlap because each is bridged by a five-year transition that is part of both periods. These transitions between major developmental periods are generally crucial turning points in a man's life. The timing and length of each period and the development that takes place within it vary from man to man depending on the biological, psychological, and social conditions of his life. However, individual differences are usually no greater than two or three years.

Early Adulthood (Ages 17 to 45)   Early adulthood begins during the transition from adolescence when the developmental task is to move out of the adolescent world. Autonomy, which first occupied a man in early childhood, again becomes a concern. Now he needs to become psychologically independent from his parents. By about the age of 22, the move is complete, and a stable phase of approximately six years begins. During this "entering the adult world" phase, a man works to establish himself in the adult world, where he is considered a novice. He attempts to create a stable life structure, while keeping open as many options as possible. His life aspirations take shape, and he establishes a "dream." He forms an occupational identity and learns to relate to women as friends, collaborators, and intimate companions. These tasks are quite similar to Erikson's developmental tasks of establishing identity and intimacy. During this period of early adulthood most of Levinson's men married and established a home and family. Despite this stress on intimacy, few of his subjects had an intimate male friend, and most never had a close, nonsexual relationship with a woman.

The age of 28 marks the age 30 transition, a five-year span that is often a time of crisis, when flaws in the life structure become apparent and new choices must be made. By 33 the transitional phase has ended, and the second stable phase of early adulthood, the "settling down" period begins. No longer a novice, a man now works at furthering his career and gaining prestige. He tries to establish a place in society and build a good life. Toward the end of this period, he is busy at "becoming one's own man," when he once again is engaged in the process of establishing his autonomy, this time trying to reduce his dependence on individuals and institutions. If he has had a mentor, an older adult whose advice and counsel has helped him get on with his career, the relationship may be broken off or at least may become more distant.

During their novice phase, many women form a dream, but only a few of them report the masculine sort of individualistic dream, in which occupation is the central component (Roberts and Newton, 1987). The same proportion of women either fail to form a dream of any kind or else report a dream that centers around a self defined in terms of relationships to others (as wife, mother, or colleague). About half the women form a "split dream," in which relationships and occupation get equal attention. The age 30 transition is also important for women but in a different way. During this transitional period, many women are reappraising their lives in terms of family and career, with women who earlier stressed the relational aspect of their lives now developing more individualistic goals, and those who have focused on their occupations suddenly becoming concerned with marriage and family. For most women, there is little evidence of "settling down" during their thirties. Indeed, this last decade of young adulthood seems unsettled and full of attempts to integrate their new commitments into their life structures. Despite this instability, as her thirties come to a close, a woman tends to go through a period of "becoming one's own woman."

Midlife Transition (Ages 40 to 45)   At 40, a man's midlife transition begins, and he starts to cross the bridge into middle adulthood. During this period, which usually lasts about five years, a man appraises his life thus far, usually discovering that he has failed to match his early aspirations and that his dream is out of reach. He loses many of his illusions, reevaluates his job, his marriage, his assumptions and beliefs. He works at making a better balance between self and society. His life structure changes as he makes new choices. Sometimes the choices are drastic: He may divorce, remarry, change jobs, move to another city.

For 80 percent of the men in this study, the midlife transition was a time of major crisis. The process of reappraisal awakened old conflicts, and the men were in emotional turmoil. Slight declines in strength and energy, coupled with the first visible traces of age, became apparent. Men were forced to deal with this evidence and with the recognition that they would one day die. As a man resolved the problems of this transition, he sometimes began to act as a mentor to younger adults, providing them with guidance and counsel. This process is similar to Erikson's idea of attaining a generativity that extends beyond the family by taking responsibility for the next generation.

Middle Adulthood (Ages 40 to 65)   Like early adulthood, middle adulthood consists of two stable phases divided by a transitional phase. During the years from about 45 to 50, a man is "entering middle adulthood." With the conflicts of the midlife transition resolved, life may be more satisfying and productive than at any other time. Active questioning seems to be over. The task of building a new life structure based on the choices made during the transition occupies a man for the next five years. During this period, qualities like wisdom, judiciousness, and compassion may flourish. Although for many men these years are filled with growth and continued generativity, for others they are a period of stagnation and decline.

As men enter their fifties, they must deal with the age 50 transition. The period is similar to the age 30 transition, when modifications may be made in the life structure. The period may be a time of crisis, especially if a man went through the midlife transition with little change. Levinson believes that it is impossible to get through middle adulthood without at least one crisis. Once past the transition, another stable phase, the culmination of middle adulthood, begins. This part of the life span may be one of great fulfillment and is much like the settling down phase of early adulthood. It lasts until the late adult transition, which starts at about the age of 60 and forms the basis for later adulthood.

As none of the men studied by Levinson was older than 47 at the last contact, the theory necessarily becomes sketchy after the midlife transition. Although Levinson believes that the general sequence of development he depicts is universal, he points out that his findings may apply only to men in this culture at this historical period. Since all men in the study came from the northeastern section of the United States, the applicability of its findings to men in other areas of the United States or to other countries has not been tested. We do not know, for example, whether a midwestern farmer or a West Virginia coal miner experiences these sequences in the same way as men in the industrialized Northeast. Perhaps a look at another structural theory of adult personality development would be helpful.

Gould's Transformations

Psychiatrist Roger Gould (1975, 1978) sees adult personality as progressing through a series of transformations in which self-concepts are reformulated as childhood illusions are faced and conflicts are resolved. His view of development grew out of a cross-sectional study he designed after noting that outpatients who came to the university psychiatric clinic tended to have similar problems at similar ages. After observing men and women from adolescence through middle adulthood in group therapy sessions, he studied 524 white, middle-class American men and women between the ages of 16 and 60. From their responses to a questionnaire, in which they responded to such statements as "My personality is pretty well set" and "Life doesn't change much from year to year," he discerned a pattern to life made up of predictable transitions, in which concerns were similar to those expressed by the patients he had observed. Like Levinson, Gould found adulthood to be a time of change, not a time of stable emotions and motivations.

Late adolescence, the years from 16 to 22, was a time of ambivalence. The major concern was forming an identity and leaving the parental world. This change required challenging a false assumption: "I'll always belong to my parents and believe in their world." Among young adults, aged 22 to 28, autonomy seemed established, and their energies were devoted to attaining their goals. At the same time they were challenging the false assumptions that there was only one right way to do things, and that whenever they felt unable to cope with their problems, their parents would step in and show them "the right way."

The next group of adults, between the ages of 28 and 34, seemed to be going through something that resembled Levinson's age 30 transition. They were questioning some of the goals they had set in their early twenties, and many were reevaluating their marriages. Fewer agreed that "For me, marriage has been a good thing," and many more indicated that they wished "my mate would accept me for what I am as a person." Economic problems became sharper, and there was an increase in the number agreeing that they did not have enough money to do what they wished. Their major tasks were to challenge the beliefs that life was simple and controllable and to open themselves to the desires, tendencies, and talents they had shut out of their lives during their twenties.

Adults approaching the midlife decade, between the ages of 35 and 45, were still questioning values, but a new element had entered the picture. Time had begun to press sharply, and with it came the realization that any major life changes that were to be made must be made soon. Their major task was to come to terms with the possibility of death—for both themselves and their loved ones. Their motivations for work changed, and for many, there was a period when their occupations seemed boring and devoid of meaning. This phase of life, like Levinson's midlife transition, was an unstable period, full of turmoil and personal discomfort.

Once people were into middle age, the years from 45 to 50 became stable. Marital satisfaction rose, friends became more important, and money seemed less important. There was a positive acceptance of life. This acceptance increased during the fifties among the oldest age group in the study. An awareness of time running out sharpened, and more people said that there was not enough time left to do all the things they wanted to do. Concerns about health also rose, but personal relationships became even more important, and marital satisfaction was even higher than it was during the forties. Many indicated a flowering of generativity—a desire to contribute in some way to society.

The results of Gould's study agree in good part with Levinson's findings. At the approximate time Gould's cross-sectional data were collected in Southern California, about 1970 or 1971, the northeastern men in Levinson's study were being interviewed, and many were in the midlife transition. It is possible that the widespread midlife crisis that appeared in both studies is in part a reflection of cohort effects. One of the questions that faces developmentalists is whether the midlife crisis exists (see accompanying box, "Is There a Midlife Crisis?").

Jung's Quest for an Integrated Personality

Carl Jung (1969), like Erikson and Levinson, devised a theory of personality development that had its origins in psychoanalysis. The key to Jung's theory is his belief that healthy development requires people to draw on all parts of their personality, then unite them into a balanced, integrated self. Within each person, he believed, were conflicting forces and tendencies that had to be recognized and reconciled. Because few people ever managed to complete the quest for an integrated personality, attempts to realize the self continued throughout adulthood.

Youth, the first stage in Jung's theory, begins at puberty and lasts until the approach of middle adulthood. During youth, people give up their childhood dreams, come to terms with their sexuality, and focus largely on their relations with the world. Youth is thus a time of extraversion, an orientation toward the external world. This orientation is necessary because young adults are concerned with establishing themselves in careers, finding mates, and having children. Because women are engaged in mothering children and men are absorbed in making their mark on the world, women tend to suppress the masculine aspects of their personality and men to suppress their feminine aspects.

As people enter middle adulthood, physical and social changes demand corresponding changes in people's personalities, goals, and interests. In Jung's words, "We cannot live the afternoon according to the programme of life's morning, for what was great in the morning will be little in the evening, and what in the morning was true will at evening have become a lie" (Jung, 1969, p. 399). Some people develop new interests and some show gradual changes in personality, but those who feel threatened by impending change become rigid and intolerant. During this period, aspects of the personality that have been suppressed begin to assert themselves. As the pressure of their culturally prescribed sex roles wane, men become more nurturant and less assertive, and women more active and tough-minded. In the next section, we will see that similar views have been put forth by other theorists.

In old age, the balance between another pair of conflicting forces shifts. With the family grown and careers coming to a close, women and men show a shift toward introversion, which is an orientation toward the inner, subjective world. They begin to cultivate their own interests and explore their inner selves. Jung saw the resulting steady increase in interiority as part of the search for an integrated personality. In his words, "For a young person, it is almost a sin, or at least a danger, to be too preoccupied with himself; but for the aging person it is a duty and a necessity to devote serious attention to himself" (Jung, 1969, p. 399). As we saw earlier, an increase in introversion with age has appeared in many personality studies.

GENDER DIFFERENCES IN PERSONALITY

Considering the personality of men and women together can be misleading. If men score low on a dimension and women score high, lumping their scores together results in a score

◆ *Adulthood in Today's World*

IS THERE A MIDLIFE CRISIS?

Both Levinson and Gould discovered the presence of a midlife crisis in the adults they studied. The concept has become widely popular, in part owing to journalist Gail Sheehy's *Passages* (1976). This book, which relied on Levinson's and Gould's theories, used interviews with men and women to locate a "predictable crisis" at about the age of 35 in women and at 40 in men. *Passages* became a national best-seller, and portions of the book appeared in eight different national magazines and in newspapers throughout the country. As a result, the midlife crisis entered the American vocabulary and the American conception of the life course. We became convinced that a midlife crisis awaited each one of us. Yet our fears may be groundless.

When developmentalists talk about a **midlife crisis,** they are generally referring to a state of physical and psychological distress that arises when developmental tasks threaten to overwhelm a person's internal resources and systems of social support (Cytrynbaum et al., 1980). Many researchers believe that such a crisis is neither widespread nor inevitable, and some object to the term. George Vaillant (1977), who reported the results of a 40-year longitudinal study of 95 Harvard men, complains that the midlife crisis brings to mind "the renegade minister who leaves behind four children and the congregation that loved him in order to drive off in a magenta Porsche with a twenty-five-year-old striptease artist" (p. 222). Vaillant agrees that some inner exploration and reevaluation takes place during the forties, but he fails to see high drama or major crisis in the process.

Many of the men in his study divorced, changed jobs, or became depressed between 35 and 50, but Vaillant notes that divorce, job disenchantment, and depression occur at about the same frequency throughout adult life and that crisis is the exception, not the rule, at midlife. Some of the men in his study said that the years between 35 and 49 were the happiest in their lives. Of course, these men were not typical: they were white, upper-socioeconomic level, well-educated Harvard men, and the intent of the study was to show development under the most favorable circumstances. Perhaps cohort influence spared these men. They were born between 1920 and 1922, so that they passed through the midlife transition 6 to 12 years before the men in Levinson's study did. Their experiences in the Great Depression of the 1930s and World War II would have been very different from those of Levinson's men and could have affected their subsequent development.

But the midlife crisis also failed to show up in the lives of men and women who took part in the California Intergenerational Studies. These adults, though mostly middle-class, are less privileged than the men in the Harvard Growth Study. Some were born between 1920 and 1922, and the rest in 1928 and 1929, so that they span the age range in Levinson's and Vaillant's studies. At midlife, most of the men found their jobs satisfying and their careers rewarding (Clausen, 1981). Both men and women appeared to have become more self-confident, insightful, introspective, and more open to others. They seemed better equipped to handle stress, deliberately processing new information, integrating it with their knowledge, and then using their understanding to reach their goals (Haan, 1981).

A direct attempt to locate the male midlife crisis found that it occurred in only a few men and that it could come at any time from 30 to 60 (McCrae and Costa, 1982). The midlife crisis also failed to appear in a national sample of more than 10,000 Americans (Costa et al., 1986). Between the ages of 34 and 54, the mean levels of neuroticism remained remarkably stable for both sexes; if the midlife crisis were common, there should be a peak in neuroticism around the age of 40. These researchers feel that most people never have a midlife crisis, that a crisis can occur at any age, and that when it does erupt, it is usually due to a long-standing emotional instability.

Investigators who conducted a three-year study of American women tend to agree (Baruch, Barnett, and Rivers, 1982). They suggest that if the study of middle age had begun with women, the midlife crisis might never have become part of our vocabulary. They focused on women between the ages of 35 and 55 and found that it was during their twenties and not at midlife that uncertainties and dissatisfactions tended to surface. These women rarely mentioned anticipated developmental events (such as marriage, childbirth, or menopause) as marking major turning points in their lives. Instead, they reported that unexpected events (such as divorce, automobile accidents, or job transfers) or normative events that occurred off-schedule (such as the early death of a parent) were likely to cause life crises.

Finally, among the men and women studied over the years at the University of Chicago, no evidence could be found for the midlife crisis (Neugarten, 1973). As adults made the transition to middle age, new developmental issues arose, having to do with family roles, generativity, and occupational life. Men and women seemed to have less energy and power and became more introspective and reflective, but the drama of a major life crisis was missing.

Some researchers have suggested that the midlife crisis is a white, middle-class phenomenon that has developed because of increased leisure, high technology, and the acceptance of self-fulfillment as a goal. Liberated from the toil of past centuries, a large segment of the population is now free to engage in introspection and self-expression (Cytrynbaum et al., 1980). Other researchers (Haan, 1981) believe that the midlife crisis may have been exaggerated by taking the self-descriptions of participants at face value or by using the concerns of people in therapy as a framework for studying the average person. A man or woman in therapy is more likely to dwell on personal problems than on personal strengths.

Bernice Neugarten (1979) has suggested that the normal turning points in life, such as marriage, parenthood, occupational achievement, or retirement, lead to changes in self-concept and identity. But when they are expected and occur ''on time,'' a crisis is unlikely to develop. When we anticipate an event, whether it be graduation or widowhood, we tend to rehearse it mentally beforehand. When the event finally arrives, much of the anguish has been worked through. Our strategies for handling it are adequate, and our sense of the life cycle's continuity remains whole.

midway between the two that reflects neither group. Should there be a great disparity between the sexes on any trait or dimension, the result would be as illuminating as learning that a person with one foot in a bucket of hot water and the other in a bucket of ice water was standing in water that was, on the average, tepid.

Most of the longitudinal studies we have encountered reflect the effect of aging on the male personality. Yet it is generally assumed that men and women differ in self-concept, aggression, dependence, emotional expressiveness, and social orientation (Frieze et al., 1978). These differences are believed to be strengthened or created by traditional patterns of socialization. From childhood, girls are taught to be passive, dependent, warm, and emotionally expressive, and boys are taught to be assertive and independent. By adulthood, the differences are believed to be firmly established.

Gender differences in personality do exist, but variations among each sex are generally wider than the average differences between the sexes. The size, consistency, and meaning of these gender differences are still controversial, with many personality measures showing no consistent differences between women and men. Even when reported differences are "statistically significant," they are so small as to be meaningless in terms of daily life (Huyck, 1990). It also appears that sociohistorical context has a powerful influence on the degree of difference, so that gender differences vary across societies and across time in the same society.

SEX-RELATED TRAITS

Men are believed to have higher self-concepts, including self-esteem and self-confidence, than women. This personality difference is supposed to develop because society values stereotypical masculine traits more highly than it does stereotypical feminine traits. Studies indicate that such beliefs are not entirely accurate. During young adulthood, men and women have similar levels of self-esteem and both sexes value themselves more highly than they did as adolescents (Frieze et al., 1978). However, women tend to have less self-confidence than men, seeing themselves as not nearly as competent. When young adults are asked to predict their performance on a task or to evaluate their own abilities, women consistently rate themselves lower than men do (Bandura, 1986; Tavris and Offir, 1977).

Aggressiveness is another aspect of personality that is considered to be stronger among men. This is one stereotype that research has supported again and again. No matter what type of measure is used—behavior, self-report, observation—men score higher on aggression than women. The difference between the sexes is much higher when aggression is expressed physically than when it is expressed verbally. Some researchers have suggested that because the culture defines aggression as unfeminine, women feel guilty and anxious about being aggressive and tend to inhibit such impulses (Frieze et al., 1978).

Women see themselves as more sensitive, submissive, helpful, gentle, and kind than men see themselves, and other people rate women as higher on these traits (Hoyenga and Hoyenga, 1979). Men see themselves as more ambitious, assertive, competitive, and independent than women see themselves, and other people view them in the same manner. However, the difference is a matter of degree and often depends on the situation. A traditional woman may be independent and assertive when she makes decisions at work or manages her household, and a traditional man may be gentle and sensitive with his family.

Because of their socialization, women and men may experience the world in different ways. Their basic experiences may be so different that, even when they give similar responses on personality scales, their reports may not be equivalent (Huyck, 1990). Carol Gilligan (1982), who was drawn to the study of personality development from her work on moral development, charges that most theories of personality development omit women and so present a lopsided picture. Throughout childhood, separation and autonomy are seen as basic to masculinity, whereas attachment and empathy are seen as basic to femininity. By adolescence, each sex has a different interpersonal orientation and a different range of social experiences.

Erikson has indicated that the various developmental tasks do not differ for men and women, but that the content of the tasks may vary from one society to another and at different times in the same society (Erikson and Hall, 1987). However, Gilligan sees the disparity between the sexes as so great as to place them on opposite sides of a great gulf.

Gilligan (1982) has studied identity and moral development in college students, pregnant women who were considering abortion, and the relation between moral judgment and views of the self among males and females who were from 6 to 60 years old. In her analysis of personality development, Gilligan concluded that relationships are at the center of women's experience of life. The key to female development is women's recognition of the continuing importance of attachment throughout the life span. As a result, they place autonomy and identity in the context of relationships and view morality as a problem of care and responsibility. Underlying the ethic of care is a psycho-logic of relationships. Because relationships are central, moral problems can be considered only in a context that takes into account the consequences of a decision.

In male development, autonomy is ripped from the web of relationships. Separation defines the self, and this self-definition affects later intimacy and generativity. For example, in Levinson's theory, which stresses autonomy, relationships with others are subordinate to the male dream—but not to the female dream. All his men seem distant from others, and few of them have close friends. Morality is seen as a problem of rights and justice. Underlying the ethic of justice is the formal logic of fairness. Because relationships do not enter into rights, moral problems can be abstracted from context and considered in isolation.

Although Erikson attempts to integrate the female ethic of care into his tasks of intimacy and generativity, the path that leads to them makes the integration difficult. Between trust and intimacy, he places only autonomous tasks: autonomy, initiative, industry, and identity. When men confront the task of intimacy, their primary experience has been one of separation, for society endorses these values as masculine. For men, intimacy changes their adolescent identity and prepares them for the struggle between generativity and stagnation that can lead to the ethic of care.

As women have worked on these tasks, society has pulled them the other way, teaching them to be dependent, gentle, and compassionate. Indeed, adolescent women may be working on identity and intimacy simultaneously, for they tend to define themselves in terms of relationships. From childhood, they are pointed toward generativity and its ethic of care, and for many the postponement of its development until middle adulthood, when their children may be grown, seems strange.

Gilligan sees the consequences of this socialization as being responsible for much of the misunderstanding between women and men in all areas of life. Both use the same moral vocabulary, but for men and women the words describe radically differing experiences of self and social relationships. Communication becomes garbled, and cooperation and care become the casualties.

Among the men and women in the California Intergenerational Studies, the relationship between adolescent personality and the culture's sex roles seemed to have an important influence on the course of adult personality development. Looking only at men and women who were above the mean in psychological health at the age of 50, Florine Livson (1981) found that those who adhered to traditional sex roles had a relatively smooth course, being above the mean throughout adulthood. Those who adopted nontraditional sex roles traveled a bumpier road. They tended to be in relatively poor psychological health at age 40 and then improved dramatically during the decade, becoming just as successful at age 50 as the traditional men and women. By adolescence, each group had developed a central personality style that evolved and became more complex over the years. In all groups, intelligence scores and socioeconomic level were similar.

The development of these men and women gave some support to Erikson's theory. The traditional men and women tended to pass through the stages at the appropriate times, but the nontraditionals seemed unable to adhere to the timetable. At 40, they seemed in a midlife crisis. According to Livson (1981), the developmental paths of nontraditional women and men were parallel because both had personalities that did not fit conventional sex roles. During young adulthood, both groups accepted traditional sex roles, leading them to suppress their cross-sex traits. The suppression caused them to pause, if not regress, on the path of personality development. As they moved toward middle age, their social roles changed, and they felt free to express this "hidden" side of their personalities. Their psychological health improved, and they were ready to resume their developmental tasks. These men and women, who were born between 1920 and 1922, when sex roles were more rigid than they are today, may have found that in middle age their basic personalities were in tune with what some researchers believe to be a universal trend—for gender differences in personality to narrow sharply during the last half of the life span.

TOWARD ANDROGYNY

As men and women age, gender differences in personality appear to diminish, proposes David Gutmann (1987), and both sexes may move toward **androgyny**. Androgyny comes from the Greek words for male (*andro*) and female (*gyne*), and it refers to a self-concept that incorporates a high level of both masculine and feminine characteristics. A move toward androgyny is central to Gutmann's theory of personality development, as it was in Jung's theory. Gutmann sees basic gender differences in personality as having evolved with the requirements of young children in mind. He has proposed that, in the course of evolution, parenthood came to play a pivotal and controlling role over the entire life span, driving personality development across adulthood—even after children grew and left home. He calls this development the **parental imperative**.

In Gutmann's view, parenthood is a state of chronic emergency, in which the sort of maternal and paternal behavior that is encouraged by traditional female and male traits supplies the infant's need for physical and emotional security. The usefulness of these traits, he says, becomes apparent when we look at subsistence societies, which may be closer to the conditions of scarcity and danger in which the species evolved. In such societies, traditional male characteristics (such as aggression, autonomy, competence, and control) provide the child with physical security, for they send the father out to hunt large game and to guard the child against predators. Traditional female characteristics (such as nurturance, sympathy, gentleness, and understanding) provide the child with emotional security, for they keep the mother near the child and home.

According to Gutmann, evolution provides only the *potentials* for gender roles. Society channels these potentials through socialization, so that men and women come to enjoy exercising the traits that characterize their own gender. A cultural consensus gives meaning to traditional gender roles and surrounds them with moral incentives.

When a child is born, the young father's behavior changes; he directs his masculine potentials toward creating and controlling security for his family, ignoring any longing for pleasure, passivity, or dependence that might interfere with the child's safety. (A passive, dependent, sympathetic father might not be tough enough to provide adequate economic or physical security.) The young mother directs her feminine potentials toward the child, muffling any aggressive or assertive qualities. (An aggressive, insensitive mother might harm her child or drive off her husband, leaving her child unprotected.)

Gutmann claims not that each sex lacks the qualities of the other, but that each suppresses those qualities in carrying out parental roles. Once the child has grown and left home, both parents are free to reclaim the qualities that they have suppressed throughout the child-rearing period. As men's aggressiveness cools and they no longer draw their main pleasure from providing for others and serving as a source of security, they enter what Gutmann calls the "season of the senses." They become more interested in love than in power, taking pleasure in diffuse sensuality, enjoying food, aesthetic pleasures, and human associations. They also tend to become dependent and to defer to their wives. At the same time, women take over the power that men have relinquished. They tend to become more aggressive, assertive, and dominant, and they now prefer autonomy to nurturance and understanding. As each gender takes on some of the qualities of the other, men and women become androgynous.

Is Gutmann's theory supported by research? Socialization does not have the same effects on everyone. Differences in these traits among women and men are as large as, if not larger than, the differences between the average woman and the average man. Studies have found that many contextual factors, such as family background, occupation, educational level, and satisfaction with job and family contribute to individual differences in androgyny.

There is, however, some indication that people tend to move toward androgyny in later adulthood. A number of studies have found that men and women are least alike during late adolescence and young adulthood, and become more similar toward the end of middle adulthood (Huyck, 1990; Sinnott, 1986). Gutmann's (1987) own research in the United States and several other cultures is based primarily on the result of TATs, and it has been largely cross-sectional, although a five-year longitudinal study among Navajo and Druse men indicated age shifts toward dependency and diffuse sensuality. Looking at the other end of the scale, researchers have found that young fathers rate themselves higher on masculine traits and young mothers rate themselves higher on feminine traits than do men and women among cohabiting couples, childless married couples, and married couples expecting their first child (Abrahams, Feldman, and Nash, 1978). In another cross-sectional study (Feldman, Biringen, and Nash, 1981), expectant mothers were least autonomous, and grandmothers were most autonomous. Among men in this study, compassion increased steadily from single adulthood to grandfatherhood. However, middle-aged parents continued to show traditional sex differences, even though their children were no longer at home. It was not until men and women became grandparents that the androgynous trend appeared.

There seems little chance of untangling the influences of genetics and society on these shifts in personality, and Gutmann stresses the role of socialization in developing them. However, rigid parental roles that were adaptive for our early ancestors are not necessarily the most adaptive roles in a highly technological society of relative abundance. Mothers no longer must spin yarn, weave cloth, make all the clothing, grind grain to obtain flour, bake bread, tend the vegetable garden, and scrub clothes in the nearby stream. Fathers no longer must guard against predators, go after big game, or assume total financial support of the family. When child care is no longer so labor intensive, the parental imperative becomes less important and perhaps less adaptive.

Changes in personality required by parenthood may be much briefer and less intense among future cohorts (Self, 1975). It is even possible that the changes may differ from those proposed by Gutmann. Among a group of well-educated, middle-class parents, parenthood had an unexpected effect on the personality of fathers (Feldman and Aschenbrenner, 1983). Longitudinal measures, taken a month or so before the baby's birth and again when the child was six months old, indicated that fathers showed increased nurturance, responsiveness to babies, warmth, sensitivity, emotional expressiveness, and tolerance for others' shortcomings. These men had become more *feminine,* and 77 percent of them shared in the house-cleaning, shopping, and cooking. But there was no decline in their masculine identity or in their dominance scores, and their scores on autonomy increased. The care of a small infant made *both* parents more feminine, indicating the influence of life situations on personality.

Working as a volunteer with AIDS babies, this man demonstrates the androgynous trend toward compassion and nurturance that often appears in later life.

As more parents share the responsibility for their children's physical and emotional security, and as more young women see their occupations as more than just a way to mark time until they have children, the development of androgyny may not wait for the postparental years.

That may not be a bad thing. More than a decade ago, researchers reported that androgynous college students had higher self-esteem than any other group (Spence, 1979). At that time, only about one out of three men and women fitted the stereotype for his or her gender, in which men see themselves as high only in masculine traits (self-reliance, independence, assertiveness) and women see themselves as high only in feminine traits (affectionate nature, sympathy, understanding). Apparently, we feel better about ourselves when our self-image combines the best of both genders. College students with undifferentiated personalities, who were low in both masculine and feminine traits, had the lowest self-esteem of all, indicating our need for strength in these gender-related characteristics.

SUMMARY

THE NATURE OF PERSONALITY

Personality assures individuality, and the presence of **traits** indicates a degree of predictability in behavior. Personality may be assessed by standardized, objective tests (self-report inventories or rating scales), by subjective self-assessment, or by projective tests. In Costa and McCrae's **five-factor model** of personality, traits are organized into five broad dimensions: neuroticism, extraversion, openness, agreeableness, and conscientiousness. In Haan's **six-factor model,** the dimensions are self-confident/victimized, assertive/submissive, cognitively committed, outgoing/aloof, dependable, and warm/hostile. Although behavior in specific situations cannot be predicted on the basis of traits, their effect can be seen over long-term behavior.

Health appears to be a major predictor of life satisfaction, and its strength increases across adulthood. **Self-concept** is a subjective construction that may not reflect reality. Self-esteem either remains stable or increases across adulthood.

STABILITY IN PERSONALITY

Only a minority of old people fit the sterotypical picture of aging; the range of personality is as wide among older adults as it is among the young. Studies of single traits have found that only one trait—introversion—increases with age; however, disengagement appears to characterize only a minority of older adults. Cross-sectional studies have found little change in the mean level of personality dimensions with age, and longitudinal studies indicate that **normative stability** is also the rule for the majority of traits on self-rating scales.

CHANGE IN PERSONALITY

When personality was rated by others, substantial shifts in personality appeared in a major longitudinal study, with steady, but slow, increases in the mean level of some factors. Contextual theories of personality assume that various social roles interact with general historical influences to produce personality change. Structural theories of personality assume that personality develops in stages that are structured by the normative life tasks of each period of life.

Erik Erikson has proposed a comprehensive theory of personality development, in which each person passes through eight stages from infancy to old age. At each stage, there is an emotional crisis that arises out of the conflict between two opposing trends, and in each stage the individual's social world widens. **Autonomy** first develops in early childhood. **Identity,** which is central to the theory, develops during adolescence, when society allows a **psychosocial moratorium** that permits the individual to work on the development of ego identity. In young adulthood, the task is to develop **intimacy;** in middle adulthood, to develop **generativity;** and in old age, to develop **ego integrity.**

In Daniel Levinson's theory of personality development, each man's **life structure** goes through an orderly sequence of periods that alternate between stable phases and transitional phases, which are crucial turning points. In Roger Gould's view of personality development, each person progresses through a series of transformations, in which self-concept is reformulated. Both Levinson and Gould found the **midlife crisis** to be prevalent, although other research has not found an increase in the frequency of crises at midlife. Jung saw adult personality development as a quest for an integrated personality in which such opposing forces as introversion/extraversion and masculinity/femininity were balanced.

GENDER DIFFERENCES IN PERSONALITY

Men and women differ in personality, but variations among each gender are generally wider than the average differences between the sexes. Socialization appears to widen personality differences between men and women. Men are usually more self-confident and aggressive than women, and women are generally more sensitive, submissive, gentle, helpful, and kind. Women are socialized to place autonomy and identity in the context of relationships and to view morality as a problem of care and responsibility. Men are socialized to remove autonomy from any relational context, to subordinate relationships to personal goals, and to view morality as a problem of rights and justice. As adults age, gender differences seem to diminish and both sexes may move toward **androgyny.** David Gutmann explains the development as the result of the **parental imperative,** an evolved tendency for parenthood to drive personality development across adulthood.

KEY TERMS

androgyny	life structure
autonomy	midlife crisis
ego integrity	normative stability
five-factor model	parental imperative
generativity	personality
identity	self-concept
intimacy	six-factor model
life review	trait

Part Four

Sociological Aspects of Adult Development and Aging

Chapter 11

♦

Relationships Within Generations

———— ♦ ————

In 1982, 16 adults, whose ages ranged from 23 to 84, were living together as a "family." Members of the Shared Living House, a commune that was established in 1978 by the Back Bay Aging Concerns Committee, resided in a former boarding house. Each contributed to the rent, and each shared in household tasks. Nathan Saperstein, the oldest member of the commune, was responsible for polishing the furniture and for seeing that the premises were secure—he checked all the doors at eleven o'clock each night and put out the lights. Saperstein, a bachelor who used to live in an apartment by himself, explained, "Other places you don't even know your neighbor. Here, you're part of a family" (Zabarsky, 1982).

A commune of unrelated adults does not fit the traditional picture of important adult relationships in which a woman and man marry and establish a family. Indeed, the nuclear family is alive and well, although its structure is often complicated by the pattern of divorce and remarriage. But the rising tide of single adults, made up of the never-married, divorced, and widowed men and women in our society, has not eliminated the need for relationships. Not all unattached people want to live by themselves, and some have formed unconventional units to avoid social isolation. Arrangements like the Shared Living House provide social contacts without restricting privacy or independence.

"No man is an island, entire of itself," wrote poet John Donne in the seventeenth century. Donne was referring to all of us when he wrote those words, and they evoke general agreement. The importance of social relationships and the serious consequences of social isolation are usually taken for granted. Individual development occurs in a human context, and the person who grows up without social interaction or affection has little chance of being normal. Even in adulthood, the absence of other people can be devastating. It is no accident that prisoners are punished by being thrust into "solitary."

Relationships that one person finds fulfilling may be stifling and uncomfortable for another. As we look at the variety of bonds that form within a single generation, it becomes clear that interindividual differences need to be recognized no matter what aspect of adulthood we consider. In this chapter, we investigate the nature of adult relationships that are usually, but not always, between members of the same generation. In exploring specific types of relationships, we begin with mates, considering the way we select a marital partner, roles within marriage, and the progression of the relationship across adulthood. This takes us into an examination of the effects of divorce, remarriage, and widowhood, as well as ways of handling intimate relationships outside the traditional marriage. Whether or not a person marries, relationships with siblings continue and can have powerful effects on life. After exploring bonds between adult siblings, we close with a consideration of the course of friendship across adulthood. Among members of the same generation, the closest relationships are generally with sexual partners.   ◆

MATES AND MARRIAGE

There appears to be a universal human need for emotional relationships with other people, and the relative strength of this need is linked to sex and age (Huyck, 1982). It seems stronger in women than in men, in younger women than in older women, and in older men than in younger men. As we have seen, women traditionally have been socialized to define themselves in terms of relationships, whereas men have been socialized to subordinate relationships to other goals. In American society, a primary means of satisfying the need for human connection is through an intimate relationship with a mate. Studies indicate that married adults are healthier than those who remain single and that they have a lower rate of mental illness (Traupmann, Eckels, and Hatfield, 1982). Whether being married is good for physical and mental health or whether people who are healthy are more likely to marry is uncertain, but the relationship consistently turns up.

CHOOSING A MATE

The connection between love and marriage seems natural to us, but this link is not considered necessary in all cultures or in all historical times. To complicate the picture, we are not always certain just what we mean by "love." Researchers have as much trouble agreeing, in good part because love is a uniquely personal experience that resists analysis. Finding it impossible to reduce love to either feelings or behavior, Bernard Murstein (1985) proposed that love is a *decision*—"a decision to regard another person as a love object, the conditions for defining love varying from individual to individual" (p. 103). Other researchers have concluded that love is so elusive because it comes in a variety of forms.

In Robert Sternberg's (1986) **triangular theory of love,** love involves three components: intimacy, passion, and decision/commitment. *Intimacy* represents the emotional aspects of love: feelings of closeness, connectedness, and bondedness. *Passion* represents love's motivational aspects: the drives that lead to romance, physical attraction, and sexual consummation. *Decision/commitment* represents love's cognitive aspects: the decision that one loves another person and the commitment to maintain that love. From these three components, Sternberg lists eight different kinds of relationships, the nature of each depending on the relative contribution of each component (Table 11.1). For example, liking, characterized by

Table 11.1   **TRIANGULAR THEORY OF LOVE**[a]

	Component		
Kind of Love	Intimacy	Passion	Decision/ Commitment
Nonlove	−	−	−
Liking	+	−	−
Infatuated love	−	+	−
Empty love	−	−	+
Romantic love	+	+	−
Companionate love	+	−	+
Fatuous love	−	+	+
Consummate love	+	+	+

[a] + = component present; − = component absent. Most loving relationships will fit between categories, because each component of love is expressed along a continuum, not discretely.

Source: Sternberg, 1986, p. 123.

intimacy but lacking either passion or commitment, produces friendship, while infatuated love is passion without either emotional intimacy or any commitment. In Sternberg's theory, consummate love is the sort we all strive for.

Other researchers divide love into two major kinds: passionate love and companionate love (Hatfield and Walster, 1978; Rubin, 1973). **Passionate love** is made up of emotional intensity, deep absorption in the partner, and ardent sexual passion. In Sternberg's terminology, it is probably closer to romantic love than to infatuated love. **Companionate love** is a tranquil, stable love, in which the partners trust and depend on each other and enjoy each other's company. In Sternberg's theory, companionate love is formed from intimacy and commitment, but lacks passion. Some relationships are predominately passionate, and others predominately companionate. Passionate love appears to have a natural life span of about two years, but it often settles down into companionate love, marked by moments of passion.

Passionate love may, however, continue to remain a vital part of some relationships. Among a group of middle-aged women, most of whom had been married 30 years, passionate love played a significant role in their marital relationship and was strongly correlated with marital and sexual satisfaction (Traupmann, Eckels, and Hatfield, 1982). Continued romance also characterized some of the happy couples in the California Intergenerational Studies. One man, who had been married 30 years, said, "I still have stars in my eyes" (Skolnick, 1981). Some research indicates that companionate love deepens after marriage and that romantic love diminishes during the first 15 or 20 years of a marriage, only to reawaken after the children have departed and the couple once again have time for themselves (Murstein, 1985).

In the United States, the ideal marriage is based on an intense romantic relationship. This association has not always existed, and in many societies romance is not expected to precede marriage. Cultures often regard marriage primarily as a means of preserving the ancestral line, of transmitting property, and of cementing alliances between families. As countries become industrialized, however, old patterns slowly give way, and freedom of choice in marital partners tends to develop (Murstein, 1980). The decline of arranged marriages has probably been accelerated by employment among women, which enables them to postpone marriage and to choose a partner based on romance rather than on economics.

According to John Money (1977), the American mating system developed from a combination of the Scandinavian and Mediterranean systems, a mixture of incompatible elements. The tradition of romantic mating is believed to have come from Scandinavia, where young people selected their own mates in an atmosphere of sexual equality. Betrothal and pregnancy were expected to precede marriage, and—because the family was the foundation of the fishing and farming culture—unless the woman became pregnant, marriage was unlikely to take place. In the Mediterranean tradition, family approval was required (although a young man might select his own bride). The marriage transaction, which involved a dowry from the bride's family, took place in an atmosphere of sexual inequality. The bride was required to be a virgin, and the groom was expected to be sexually experienced. American society combined romantic mate selection with virgin brides and the double sexual standard, a practice that prevailed until the development of cheap, effective contraceptives led to a relaxation of the double standard.

Despite the ideal of romantic mate selection, various social factors influence the choice. Most mates tend to be similar in many ways. They are generally of the same religion, race,

When choosing a mate, people generally select someone of the same religion, race, ethnic background, economic status, intelligence level, and social class.

and ethnic group and have a similar economic status and educational background. This is not accidental. Some sort of contact is required in order to select a mate, and neighborhoods tend to be populated by people of similar backgrounds who send their children to the same schools. Such neighborhood and school segregation limits the chances for young people to meet members of other groups. Although marital choice rests primarily with the individual, many parents (either implicitly or explicitly) still retain a veto power over their children's choice of mate—especially during adolescence and early adulthood. As society has become more fluid, marriage across racial, ethnic, and religious groups occurs more often, but the tendency to stay within one's own group remains strong (Murstein, 1985).

The similarity between mates goes further than social background. Marital partners are generally similar in physical attractiveness, although the reason for this similarity is not so clear. Perhaps we tend to seek out someone who is as attractive as possible, but not so attractive that he or she is likely to reject us. Or perhaps we look for physical attractiveness but are rejected by people who have similar goals and believe they can find better looking partners.

There is hardly an area of life in which mates are not likely to be similar. Married couples generally have similar attitudes, similar values, similar intelligence, similar sex drives, and similar levels of interest in sex. They also tend to have similar personalities, but this trend is much weaker than any of the others (Murstein, 1985). Similarity between mates is lower among couples who marry during pregnancy. In such cases, for example, the likelihood of both partners having the same socioeconomic background drops sharply (Coomb et al., 1970)

In an attempt to account for the choice of a marriage partner, Murstein (1980) has proposed an equity theory of mate selection, in which each person brings certain assets and liabilities to the relationship, and the choice to marry depends on their exchange value. After a stage of initial attraction, people assess the compatibility of their values and attitudes, and, if a prospective partner passes this hurdle, they decide whether the pair can function in complementary roles. Because lovers are generally on their best behavior before marriage, neither partner may have enough evidence to make a wise decision. Murstein's research indicates that people with many assets and few liabilities *choose* each other and that people with fewer assets and more liabilities *settle* for each other. He also found that, despite some changes in male and female roles, men continue to have higher status than women, which gives them more power during courtship.

The decision to marry is influenced by social and economic context, which may vary according to social class and ethnic group. The timing is often a compromise between society's standards (the "proper" age for marriage), economic demands (economic resources, career stage, income), and the urges of the partners (Ankarloo, 1978). Indeed, these external influences may either keep people from thinking about marriage so that no one seems "right" or lead them to perceive members of the other sex as possible marital partners, making a choice imminent.

MARRIAGE

More than nine out of every ten Americans marry at some time (Table 11.2), but age at first marriage has varied over the years. In 1890 half of all women were married by the age of 22.0 years, and half of all men were married by the age of 25.5. During the first half of the twentieth century, the median age at marriage dropped until in 1956 half of all women had married by the age of 20.1 years. For the past several decades, marital age has been rising, and by 1988, it was not until the age of 23.6 that half of all women were married (U.S. Bureau of the Census, 1989). The longest delay occurs among young women who postpone marriage in order to establish careers. Men's age at first marriage also has been increasing over the past quarter-century, but to a lesser degree, with the median age at marriage rising from 22.5 in 1956 to 25.9 in 1988.

Marriage may serve as protection against **loneliness,** which is characterized by an unpleasant deficiency in the quality of social relationships. Loneliness is a subjective personal experience that depends on the way a person perceives his or her isolation and lack of communication with others, not on the actual situation. In a group of more than 500 adults between the ages of 25 and 74, the loneliest people were the widowed or divorced who were either living alone or as single parents (de Jong–Gierveld, 1987). They were lonelier than single adults, perhaps because the loss of a marital partner contributed to their perception of loneliness.

Marital Roles

Once married, mates have to learn to live together. During the first year of marriage the partners generally fall into complementary roles that affect the way decisions are made and

Table 11.2 **WHO IS MARRIED?**

Sex	Age (yrs)									
	18–19	*20–24*	*25–29*	*30–34*	*35–39*	*40–44*	*45–54*	*55–64*	*65–74*	*>74*
Men	3.1%	20.7%	52.3%	68.8%	76.6%	81.8%	84.1%	84.1%	81.5%	68.8%
Women	9.9%	36.0%	63.3%	73.4%	76.7%	76.7%	76.6%	76.1%	53.0%	23.8%

Source: U.S. Bureau of the Census, 1989.

tasks divided. For example, one partner may become dominant and the other submissive; or one partner may become nurturant and the other receptive. In any marriage, the division of power between the partners is central to marital roles, with one partner (usually the man) having the upper hand. This is, of course, the traditional marital arrangement, but it does not describe all marriages. When researchers followed a thousand young couples for several years, they discovered nine different types of marriages (Table 11.3). In three of these types, representing about a quarter of the marriages, the wife was clearly in charge (Miller and Olson, 1978). Money is a strong determinant of power in a marriage, and women with high incomes tend to be equal or dominant partners.

When asked, most young couples say that the marriage of equal partners is their ideal, yet few actually have that sort of marriage. In the study of a thousand couples (Miller and Olson, 1978), 80 percent said that they had a cooperative marriage in which leadership was shared, yet the researchers rated only 12 percent as being equal partners. Marriage seems to be organized around inequalities, and attempts to change it run up against a lifetime of socialization. In a study of 300 American couples, those who had consciously tried to rearrange their marriage along less traditional lines said they found it difficult to do so (Blumstein and Schwartz, 1983). Yet among all these couples, a majority felt that their relationship was one of equal partners, with men most likely to be the dominant partner in marriages where both husband and wife accepted the validity of the male-provider role.

As they learn to deal with issues of power, authority, and control, most childless couples find that the early years of their marriages pass through similar, predictable phases (Kurdek

Table 11.3 **VARIETIES OF MARRIAGE[a]**

Wife led, disengaged	Low conflict; low affect
Wife led, congenial	Low conflict; average affect
Wife led, confrontive	High conflict, moderate affect
Husband led, disengaged	Low conflict; low affect
Shared leadership, cooperative	Moderate conflict; moderate affect
Husband led, engaging	Moderate conflict; high affect
Husband led, confrontive	High conflict; moderate affect
Husband led, conflicted	High conflict; high affect
Husband led, cooperative	Moderate conflict; moderate affect

[a] Using factor analysis of couples' responses to tests of marital conflict and tapes of their marital interaction, researchers found that most marriages could be characterized by three factors: (1) dominance, (2) conflict, and (3) affect. The dimension of *affect* consists of humor or laughter, spouses' disapproval of each other, and the husband's level of self-doubt.

Source: Miller and Olson, 1978.

and Schmitt, 1986). During the **blending phase** of the first year, they learn to live together and to think of themselves as part of an interdependent pair. The second and third years, known as the **nesting phase,** are often a time of stress and disillusionment, as the partners explore the limits of their compatibility and come to terms with the amount of time that should be spent on shared activities. By the time the marriage enters the **maintaining phase** that begins in the fourth year, family traditions are established and stress declines. Each partner's individuality reappears and the marriage is on an even keel. When couples cohabit before marriage, they are likely to have already passed through some or all of these stages. Nevertheless, the commitment implied by marriage can demand new adjustments.

Sexuality in Marriage

During the first year of marriage, passionate love is intense, and levels of sexual activity are usually high. Although the frequency of sexual activity tends to decline with age, American couples are having sex more effectively and use a greater variety of techniques than did couples at midcentury (Rosen and Hall, 1984). For many of today's couples, sex appears to be more pleasurable than it was for their parents. When Alfred Kinsey (Kinsey et al., 1953) interviewed American women at midcentury, 45 percent of the wives who had been married for 15 years almost always experienced orgasm and another 27 percent experienced orgasm at least one-third of the time. Twenty years later, when Morton Hunt (1974) interviewed American women, the rate of consistent orgasm had risen to 53 percent among wives who had been married for 15 years, and another 32 percent experienced orgasm at least one-half of the time.

The marriage of most middle-aged women studied by Lillian Rubin (1979) also followed this trend. Describing her marriage of 33 years to an electrician, a 52-year-old homemaker said: "Sex? It's gotten better and better. For the first years of our marriage—maybe nine or ten—it was a very big problem. But it's changed and improved in a lot of ways. Right now, I'm enjoying sex more than I ever did in my life before—maybe more than I ever thought I could" (p. 75). More than half the women in this study had sexual intercourse once or twice a week, and another fifth did so three or four times each week.

The degree of sexual satisfaction men and women derive from marriage seems to depend on whether they feel they are being treated unfairly by the marital arrangement. Among a group of Wisconsin couples, those who felt that their partners were getting a better deal out of the marriage were generally dissatisfied with their sexual relationships and felt angry and distant after sex (Hatfield et al., 1982). In contrast, men and women who felt either that marriage was a better deal for them than for their partner, or that both husband and wife had an equally good (or bad) deal, tended to be more satisfied with their relationships and to feel loving and close after sex.

Among older couples, the physiological aging described in Chapter 4 need not rob marriage of sexual pleasure. Although orgasmic contractions are fewer and less intense in late adulthood, they are just as pleasurable as they were in earlier years. Research with older adults indicates that many older people give up sexual activity altogether, with health and marital status strongly affecting responses. In one study of older adults, only 25 percent of those who had passed their seventy-fifth birthday were still sexually active. In another study, 47 percent of those between the ages of 60 and 71 still had regular, frequent intercourse, as did 15 percent of those past the age of 78 (Comfort, 1980). Among the elderly couples in the Duke Longitudinal Study, happily married couples reported engaging in sexual activity more than once a week (Busse and Eisdorfer, 1970)

The major reasons for ending sexual activity are health and the absence of a partner. For some older adults, sexual activity is ended by chronic disease, whether alcoholism, drug abuse, diabetes, hypertension, cardiovascular disease, or thyroid or neurologic disorders. For many more, sexual activity is curtailed by lack of a partner. Because women generally live longer than men and also tend to marry men older than themselves, they are likely to outlive their mates. Thus, the rate of sexual activity tends to be higher in older men than in older women. But a major reason for diminishing sexual activity among many older adults may be lack of interest over the years. Sex researchers have discovered that the best insurance for continued sexual activity into old age is frequent sexual activity between the ages of 20 and 40 (Walters, 1987).

Sexuality in old age should be regarded as a potential to be enjoyed, not an obligation. Erik Erikson refers to sex in later adulthood as a source of closeness that may or may not culminate in intercourse and as ''generalized sensuality, which has something to do with play and the importance of the moment'' (Erikson and Hall, 1987). As a 70-year-old woman described sexuality, ''It's not so much how powerful the orgasm is or how many orgasms you have. It's just touching and being together and loving'' (Kotre and Hall, 1990).

As we have seen, historical factors can affect the experience of aging, and changed sexual attitudes may affect sexuality among older adults. The change may already have begun. In one study, 70 and 80 year olds reported rates of intercourse much like those Kinsey found among 40 year olds in the 1940s and 1950s (Starr and Weiner, 1981). As today's younger adults age, the level of sexual activity among older men and women may rise.

Marital Satisfaction

In general, marital satisfaction is high in the early years and then drops after the first child is born. Satisfaction seems lowest when children are adolescents and living at home; then it rises when the children leave and the couple are again alone. Most older adults rate their marriages as ''happy'' or ''very happy'' (Bengston, Rosenthal, and Burton, 1990). The problem with these findings, which are relatively consistent from one study to the next, is that they are all cross-sectional. It is possible that satisfaction rises in the later years because the unhappiest marriages have been ended by divorce or that people who remain married for 30 or 40 years cannot bring themselves to say that they invested all that time and energy in an unhappy, unsatisfying enterprise (Huyck, 1982). It is also possible that cohort effects or age-related factors outside the marriage influence reports of satisfaction.

In a study of married couples that combined a lengthy questionnaire with in-depth interviews, the happiest couples—no matter what their ages—were those with the most egalitarian relationships (Blumstein and Schwartz, 1983). In these relationships, each partner felt equally powerful, an equal participant in decisions, and free to initiate sex. The unhappiest marriages were those in which traditional gender roles were reversed, leading the husband to feel that their wives did less than their fair amount of housework, were too ambitious, too career-oriented, or made too much money. Wives were also unhappy when they perceived themselves as the more powerful partner.

Among a group of middle-aged Michigan couples, marital satisfaction bore no relation to the couple's division of power, their levels of sexual activity, communication skills, or problem-solving ability (Laurence, 1982). Instead, the happiest marriages were those in which there was a solid balance: each partner had a strong personal identity and an equally strong identity as part of a couple. Partners who felt this way realized that a good marriage required hard work and were deeply committed to the relationship. This finding is supplemented by other research indicating that the major influence on marital stability over the years is commitment to the spouse and to marriage as an institution. Less vital but still important is the spouse's possession of valued personal characteristics. Other factors that characterize long-term, happy marriages are economic stability, viewing one's mate as one's best friend, liking one's mate as a person, agreement on life goals, and a humorous, playful attitude (Bengston, Rosenthal, and Burton, 1990).

Marital satisfaction appears to be made up of two unrelated factors. One dimension consists of positive interactions, such as working cooperatively, having stimulating discussions, and laughing together. The other consists of negative sentiments, including sarcasm, disagreements, criticisms, and anger. In a cross-sectional study of three married generations, negative sentiments declined steadily with age, while positive interactions began at a high level among the young married adults, dropped sharply among the middle-aged, and rose somewhat among the oldest adults (Gilford and Bengston, 1979). Apparently, the rise in satisfaction among older couples is due as much to the decline of negative feelings as it is to the joy of doing things together.

Not all longitudinal studies find the expected dip in marital satisfaction at midlife. Among members of the California Intergenerational Study, marital satisfaction was as high after 16 to 18 years of marriage (when many had adolescent children living at home) as it had been ten years previously (Skolnick, 1981). Among these couples, neither length of marriage nor stage of the family cycle was associated with marital satisfaction. The happily married couples in this group were alike in several ways. Wives and husbands liked, admired, and respected each other, and they enjoyed each other's company. Their marriage had improved over time, and, given a second chance, they would marry the same person again. Their relationship was close, and their personalities were very much alike. It has been estimated that such **companionate marriages** are found among only about 20 percent of American couples in young and middle adulthood. Such marriages resemble the ideal that most young couples hold as they begin married life.

The other 80 percent of American marriages are believed to be **institutional marriages,** in which material concerns, not emotional bonds, hold the marriage together. The marriages of unhappy couples in the California Intergenerational Studies were most likely to be of this type. They were utilitarian living arrangements, but that by itself was not enough to make a marriage unhappy. Unhappy husbands and wives also tended to have personalities that clashed.

The individual personality traits that predicted marital satisfaction among these California couples were linked with traditional sex roles: self-confidence in the men and nurturance in the women. It would seem that aspects of their personalities harmonized with the marital roles they grew up expecting to assume. In addition, both husbands and wives scored high on social maturity and achievement.

The results of this study are in line with other research on personality and marital satisfaction. Such characteristics as emotional maturity, the ability to demonstrate affection, consideration, self-esteem, and adaptability have been found to predict marital satisfaction

◆ *Adulthood in Today's World*

MARRIAGE AND MEMORY

"The fact that we think so much alike is one of the strongest ties that has held us together. We have always done everything together. Always helped one another. For sixty-one years." The woman in her eighties who described the course of her marriage in this way was clearly high in marital satisfaction (Erikson, Erikson, and Kivnick, 1986, p. 112). After interviewing this couple and observing them together, the researchers agreed that the marriage was indeed a happy one. She and her husband seemed to do everything together. They had a gentle, playful, teasing relationship. Each figured in almost every sentence uttered by the other. Their lives were inextricably intertwined.

Yet 40 years earlier, this woman had spoken of her marriage with bitterness. She told interviewers for the California Intergenerational Studies that she had nothing in common with her husband, that they quarreled incessantly, that he offered little to her or to their three sons, that he required as much attention as another child, and that her marriage was oppressive and unrewarding. She wanted very much to leave her husband.

What happened to make this woman forget the unhappy years? Erik Erikson and his associates found that her experience followed a common pattern among the parents of subjects in the California Intergenerational Studies. In accounting for this transformation of memory, the researchers admit that it may simply be a matter of loyalty. People who have become close to their partners during their later years might feel disloyal if they mentioned the shortcomings the partners had exhibited in earlier years. But Erikson and his associates think it is much more likely that the present satisfaction derived from marriage has colored these people's memories so that they remember only the good aspects of marriage. Instead of remembering her marriage as a time of strife and argument, this woman recalled it as a time of mutual struggle against the outside world.

in various cross-sectional studies. It would appear that well-adjusted people are more likely to find satisfaction in marriage than are poorly adjusted people

A longitudinal look at marriage in old age came when researchers reported on the *parents* of California Intergenerational Study subjects who had been interviewed and tested repeatedly for more than half a century, along with their children. These adults, now between the ages of 75 and 95, were interviewed in 1981 by Erikson and his associates (Erikson, Erikson, and Kivnick, 1986). Only a few reported unsatisfactory marriages. Most of them described their marriage as a *life-long* relationship of mutual affection, supportiveness, understanding, and companionship. They spoke as if their married lives had been one long period of bliss. These husbands and wives were obviously devoted to each other, but their memories had rewritten the history of their relationship. Forty years earlier, many of these people had gone through painful marital problems, yet the very memory of their unhappiness now seemed wiped away (see the accompanying box, "Marriage and Memory").

Three years later, the 17 surviving couples were reinterviewed by other researchers, who found that marital satisfaction in this cohort had followed four different paths (Weishaus and Field, 1988). Most of the marriages fell into two types, *stable-positive,* in which satisfaction had been moderate to high (as measured by ratings taken at various times during the marriage) across the entire 50 to 69 years of marriage; or *curvilinear,* in which satisfaction dropped during midlife and then rose again in later adulthood. A few of the marriages were either *stable-neutral,* having always lacked intimacy and emotional highs, or *stable-negative,* in which dissatisfaction had been a feature of the relationship almost from its beginning. All of the couples—even those who were dissatisfied—had shared as well as separate interests, were committed to the marriage, and accepted each other. But those who had stable-positive or curvilinear marriages also expressed deep affection and love for their partners, seemed to understand them, and were uncritical of either their mates or their marriage.

DIVORCE

If Americans never truly believed that all marriages were made in heaven, they once did believe that marriages were "forever." In cases of desertion or adultery, divorce was possible, but even the injured party was stained with the brush of public disapproval. Divorce simply did not happen to "nice" people. Most people in a bad marriage struggled along, often "for the sake of the children." Today, people are much less likely to cling to an unsatisfactory marriage, and the rate of divorce has skyrocketed. After rising steadily through the 1960s and 1970s, the divorce rate seemed to level off in the 1980s. Yet researchers at the University of Wisconsin predict that 56 percent of recent first marriages will end in divorce (Bumpass and Castro–Martin, 1989). This figure does not include an additional 6 percent in which the couple will permanently separate but never get a legal divorce₁

At the time of the Civil War, about 4 marriages out of every 100 ended in divorce; by 1970, divorce ended 44 out of every 100 marriages. Yet approximately the same proportion of marriages remained intact during the 1970s as during the 1870s. In the last quarter of the nineteenth century, about as many marriages were prematurely dissolved by the death of the husband or wife as are now dissolved by divorce. Over those years the rise in divorce rate and the decline in death rate nearly balanced each other. It was not until 1974 that the number of divorces (977,000) was greater than the number of deaths among married people (947,000) (Glick, 1980). The difference is that in the past many happy marriages were ended by death, and today the unhappy marriages wind up in the divorce court.

Although people are marrying later, they are quicker to divorce (Table 11.4). A decade or so ago, the typical divorce occurred after six or seven years of marriage; today, it comes three or four years into the marriage. Today, nearly 40 percent of all divorces occur among couples younger than 30 (Yarrow, 1987). But age is no insurance against divorce; 21 percent of all divorces involve middle-aged women, and another 2 percent involve women older than 60 (Uhlenberg, Cooney, and Boyd, 1990). Since there were 1,187,000 divorces in 1985, it appears that nearly 24,000 older women divorce each year.

We would expect that the level of marital satisfaction predicts the stability of a marriage,

Table 11.4 **WHO IS DIVORCED?**

Sex	Age (yrs)									
	18–19	*20–24*	*25–29*	*30–34*	*35–39*	*40–44*	*45–54*	*55–64*	*65–74*	*>74*
Men	0	1.5%	5.4%	8.0%	10.9%	10.8%	8.8%	7.3%	4.8%	3.2%
Women	0.3%	3.2%	7.6%	11.2%	13.6%	14.5%	13.1%	9.0%	5.5%	2.7%

Source: U.S. Bureau of the Census, 1989.

but that is not always the case. Some marriages that seem to be of high quality end in separation or divorce, whereas other marriages that seem dismal survive. According to Graham Spanier and Robert Lewis (1980), the quality of a marriage is determined by a balance of its rewards and tensions, including each partner's social and personal resources, satisfaction with established life-styles, and reward from interacting with the spouse. But the stability of that marriage is strongly affected by forces outside the marriage—alternative attractions (another possible mate, a crucial career decision) and external pressures. Costs and rewards combine with pushes and pulls to determine whether the marriage breaks up.

A number of factors appear to predict the likelihood of divorce. If the woman is pregnant at the time of marriage or if the partners are younger than 20, the marriage's chances of survival are reduced. If the couple is black, divorce is more likely; if the couple is Hispanic, divorce is less likely. Low income is associated with a high probability of divorce, as is infrequent attendance at religious services (Glenn and Supanic, 1984).

But divorce has become more prevalent than in previous times among all groups, not just among the young, the pregnant, black, poor, and religiously indifferent. Wider changes in society have contributed their share to the increased divorce rate. Women are more deeply involved in the labor force, preparing them to be self-supporting, and child rearing has declined in significance as woman's central role. The availability of welfare also reduces women's dependence on continuation of a marriage. There has been a reduction of legal barriers to divorce and of social disapproval afterward. Finally, society emphasizes personal fulfillment, while demanding that marriage supply a level of happiness that earlier generations never expected it to provide. Add to these changes a greater freedom to have sexual relations before marriage, to cohabit, to establish single households, and to remain childless, and marriage seems slated to become a more voluntary and less permanent arrangement (Furstenberg, 1982).

Demographic factors tell us who is most likely to divorce, but how do divorced people see their situation? People are unlikely to say that their marriage failed because they never went near church or synagogue, but a large minority blame money as one factor in divorce. When researchers asked divorced people why their marriages had broken up, women were most likely to blame communication problems (70 percent), basic unhappiness (60 percent), incompatibility (56 percent), emotional abuse (56 percent), and financial problems (33 percent) (Cleek and Pearson, 1985). Men also placed communication problems at the top of the list (59 percent), followed by basic unhappiness (47 percent), incompatibility (45 percent), sexual problems (30 percent), and financial problems (29 percent). Most expected reasons for divorce trailed behind. Among women, 30 percent attributed their divorce to their husband's alcoholism, 25 percent to his infidelity, and 22 percent to physical abuse.

Among the men, 11 percent blamed their wives' infidelity and 9 percent said it was the result of their own alcohol abuse.

Although no-fault divorce laws have made it easier to end a marriage, divorce is still a painful process that moves through three inevitable stages (Wallerstein and Blakeslee, 1989). The *acute stage* begins when the failure of the marriage becomes apparent. It crests with the decision to divorce and then lasts for several more months—sometimes as long as two years. The divorced partners find that they have lost one of their social roles (wife or husband) and that they have taken on a role for which society has not yet established any expected standards. Friends may disappear as they "choose" husband or wife as friend or as they find that the presence of an unattached person does not fit into their social scheme. During the acute stage, people act in uncharacteristic ways, acting out their feelings and perhaps going through a series of short-lived sexual affairs. Unhappiness is prevalent in all age groups. When adults past the age of 50 who had been divorced within the past nine months were interviewed, 60 percent of the men and 50 percent of the women said that they were unhappy. The older the person, the more psychological distress he or she displayed (Burrus-Bammel and Bammel, 1985).

As they enter the *transitional stage,* people become involved in their new roles, try to solve their problems, and may experiment with new life-styles. One adult may go back to school, another may move to a new home, a third may seek out old friends. This phase is often made up of repeated progress and regression. The final, *stable period* begins as relationships settle down and people feel comfortable in their new lives (Wallerstein and Blakeslee, 1989).

Divorce's economic consequences fall heavily on women. A woman's income and standard of living usually drop, and the decrease is especially pronounced when small children are involved. The average woman with minor children finds that her standard of living declines 73 percent during the first year after divorce, while her husband's standard of living increases 42 percent (Weitzman, 1985). Divorced women of any age are at a disadvantage. Among middle-aged and older women, divorce has stronger economic consequences than does widowhood. Divorced women past the age of 40 have fewer resources, are less likely to own their own home, and are more likely to be in the labor force than are widows (Uhlenberg, Cooney, and Boyd, 1990).

The physical and psychological consequences of divorce are also high. During the acute stage, divorced people are often filled with anger, guilt, and depression, and time does not necessarily heal the wounds. Compared with all other groups in society (married, single, widowed, remarried), divorced people have the highest rate of emotional disturbance, accidental death, and death from heart disease, cancer, pneumonia, high blood pressure, and cirrhosis of the liver (Brody, 1983b). Older adults seem especially vulnerable to the long-term toll of divorce, perhaps because older adults—especially older women—have a more limited range of options than do younger adults (Bengston, Rosenthal, and Burton, 1990)

Some people never bounce back after a divorce. When researchers reinterviewed a group of adults ten years after their divorce (now aged 32 to 75), a third of the women and a quarter of the men complained bitterly of loneliness and felt that life was unfair and disappointing (Wallerstein and Blakeslee, 1989). Their divorce still occupied their emotions. Among those who had divorced late in life, many still leaned on their children for support and companionship. Yet for some people, the ultimate consequences of divorce are good.

About half the men and women in this study had no regrets. For them, divorce was a closed book, and they were happy with their present lives.

REMARRIAGE

About 40 percent of all marriages are remarriages, and the average remarriage follows divorce by about three years (Glick and Lin, 1986). The majority of divorced people remarry, and the younger the person is at the time of divorce, the more likely she or he is to find another mate. In a study of more than 200 recently divorced adults in Pennsylvania, 66 percent said that they were reluctant to consider another marriage, but in less than three years 28 percent of the disenchanted had remarried (Furstenberg, 1982). At any age, men are more likely to remarry than women, and once women enter middle age, remarriage is closely related to educational level, with highly educated women being the least likely to remarry (Figure 11.1). According to the Census Bureau, 76.3 percent of all women who divorce before they are 30 eventually remarry; among women who divorce during their thirties, 56.2 percent remarry; but among women who divorce during their forties, only 32.4 percent remarry, and among those older than 50, only 11.5 percent ever remarry (Yarrow, 1987). Marriages among older adults are virtually always remarriages, but in most cases

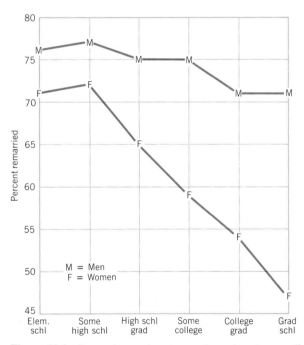

Figure 11.1 Remarriage, education, and gender. Among divorced women between the ages of 35 and 44, remarriage is closely related to educational level, perhaps because more education makes a woman more employable and self-reliant and because women tend to look for men with higher incomes than their own. *Source:* U.S. Bureau of the Census, 1970.

both partners have been widowed, not divorced. About 20 percent of older widowers, but only 2 percent of older widows, remarry (Bengston, Rosenthal, and Burton, 1990). These older adults usually marry someone they knew before their spouse died or someone they met through a mutual friend or relative.

Second (or third or subsequent) marriages seem different in several ways from first marriages. The factors that complicate remarriages have been spelled out by Frank Furstenberg (1982). First, the expectations and habits formed during the first marriage influence a partner's behavior in a subsequent marriage. Most remarried couples use the first marriage as a baseline by which they judge the new marriage and generally take care to develop a different style for the new union. Second, contact with the previous spouse is often unavoidable. Partners at remarriage are likely to be parents, and the children are usually young. Their presence often makes contact with the previous spouse necessary, and, whether the new spouse likes it or not, present and former mates become linked. When both partners in the remarriage have children from a former marriage, relationships can become complicated.

Third, people remarry under changed personal circumstances. They are older, and their social status, level of maturity, and wealth of experience are different. In addition, the difference in age between husband and wife is likely to be larger than that in most first marriages. The average age gap increases from two years to just over five years. Two factors are believed to be responsible for the increase: Men who remarry tend to look for younger women, and women who remarry are usually reluctant to marry anyone with less power, money, education, or status than they have. These tendencies have combined with the longer female life span to produce an increasingly larger pool of unmarried middle-aged and older women. Women seem to be responding to the problem by marrying younger men; in 22.5 percent of remarriages, the bride is now older than the groom (U.S. Bureau of the Census, 1989).

A final factor that makes remarriages different from first marriages is that a second marriage puts a person into a different marriage cohort (Furstenberg, 1982). Thus, the marital relationship is played out under the influence of different cultural standards and historical events.

Marriage is often just as good the second time around. When people remarry, they are likely to do so with fewer romantic illusions and lowered expectations. Among older adults, for example, most marry for companionship (Bengston, Rosenthal, and Burton, 1990). Among the remarried adults in the Pennsylvania study, most said that, compared with their first marriage, they had better communication with their mate, felt more trust and goodwill even during disagreements, were more likely to make decisions jointly, and shared domestic chores in a fairer manner (Furstenberg, 1982). Remarried adults who were contacted ten years after their divorce expressed similar feelings (Wallerstein and Blakeslee, 1989). In most second marriages, the level of marital satisfaction, personal happiness, and worry seems to be about the same as that in first marriages. Women in second marriages often say they are very happy, and men are unlikely to find a middle ground; either they are very happy or very unhappy (Huyck, 1982)

Despite similar levels of satisfaction, second marriages seem less stable than the first. Researchers have estimated that among all marriages since 1975, 50 percent will end in divorce, but among those that are second marriages, 60 percent will end in divorce (Kan-

Second marriages tend to be as happy as first marriages, perhaps because the partners have fewer romantic illusions.

trowitz and Wingert, 1990). The risk is heightened if one of the partners has custody of children from the previous marriage. Among adults recontacted ten years after their divorce, a consistent pattern appeared (Wallerstein and Blakeslee, 1989). One of the partners was in a lasting second marriage, while the other partner was either still single or had gone through a second or even a third divorce.

WIDOWHOOD

When couples do not divorce, sooner or later either the wife or husband is widowed. The death ends the cycle of a family and casts the surviving spouse into a different role, one

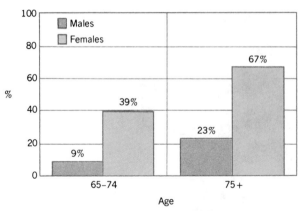

Figure 11.2   Widowhood by gender and age.

that requires painful readjustments. In most marriages, it is the wife who is left to make a new life for herself, and as people grow older, the disparity widens. Among the comparatively youthful 65 to 69 year olds, for example, 34 percent of women are widowed, but only 7 percent of men. A decade later, among the 75 to 79 year olds, 60 percent of the women but only 18 percent of the men are widowed. Among the oldest Americans, those over 85, 82 percent of the women but only 43 percent of the men are widowed (Sweet and Bumpass, 1987) (Figure 11.2).

The Bereavement Process

The desolation that follows the loss of a loved one is known as **bereavement,** and it has been called the ''most severe psychological trauma most people will encounter in the course of their lives'' (Parkes and Weiss, 1983). The person who grieves experiences physiological and psychological symptoms. During acute grief, a person may feel tightness in the throat, shortness of breath, a choking sensation, the need to sigh, an empty feeling in the pit of the stomach, weakness, and pangs of intense distress (Lindemann, 1944). A 30-year-old widow tried to describe her feelings, saying, ''I had heard the expression, 'heartache,' and I had read it, but this is the only time I really knew what it feels like. It is pain inside me, physical pain, all the way up. It's very tight and I get very hurt. It's inside the heart that I hurt'' (Parkes and Weiss, 1983, p. 1). The grieving person may be unable to sleep, eat, or carry out daily activities.

Colin Parkes (1972) has proposed that normal grief moves through four predictable stages that blend into one another. Immediately after the death, a person is shocked and may feel little emotion other than emptiness or *numbness.* After a few hours or days, this protective numbness gives way to *yearning,* the second stage of grief, in which the acute reactions described earlier flood through the person. During this stage, the desire to recover the person who has died is paramount and the bereaved seems to engage in a continual search for the lost one. There is a continual reworking of memories, in which the survivor goes over and over the death, trying to decide what might have happened had different actions been taken. For example, a widower whose wife died of cancer might think, ''If only I had insisted that she see a doctor sooner.'' Feelings of guilt alternate with feelings of anger, in which survivors angrily blame someone else—the doctor, the hospital, God, or the deceased person—for the death and, thus, their grief.

Once the intense yearning is over, the survivor accepts the permanence of the loss but enters the *disorganization* stage of grief. He or she often becomes depressed. Anger has not completely disappeared, but its strongest expression is over. Finally, the *reorganization* stage begins. In order to recover from bereavement, a person must accept the loss intellectually and emotionally, and reorganize her or his self-concept. This reorganization requires the establishment of an identity and world view that reflect the new reality (Parkes and Weiss, 1983). The recovery process is generally underway within a year, for in that time most survivors have developed some intellectual and emotional acceptance of the loss. The process of normal grieving can be lengthy, however, and up to 25 percent of widows and widowers are still depressed one year after the death of a spouse (Norris and Murrell, 1990). The new identity may not be firmly established for another two or three years. For some people, recovery may never come.

Whether survivors actually move through identifiable stages of grief remains a matter of controversy. There is, however, general agreement that normal grief includes feelings of guilt, anger, depression, anxiety, and restlessness, as well as a preoccupation with the image of the dead person (Kalish, 1985).

Several factors determine how disruptive the death is for the widowed partners (Lopata, 1975). They include the survivor's degree of dependence on the deceased partner; the way in which the couple had been immersed as a team in the family, community, and occupation; the social and economic resources and limitations of the surviving partner; and the steps taken by the survivor either to assume the role of a widowed person or to move into another social unit or life-style.

How rapidly a widow is able to come to terms with her husband's death depends in part on whether his age or ill health made the death seem ''on time.''

Another factor that affects immediate adjustment is whether the death is seen as being "on time." The accidental death of a young husband presents a much more difficult adaptation than the death of an older husband, especially if the older spouse has been suffering from a chronic disease. In the case of the young widow, the unanticipated nature of the death plunges her into an existence for which she has no economic or social plans. The older widow usually has made plans and has also gone through a period of psychological preparation for widowhood. Faced by the deaths of her friends' husbands, her own husband's declining health, or his terminal illness, she is likely to have gone through mental rehearsals and even begun the grieving and reconstruction of family life that prepare her to meet the event when it actually happens (Marshall and Levy, 1990).

A prospective study has thrown some light on the factors that impede the recovery of older widows (Goldberg, Comstock, and Harlow, 1988). More than a thousand older women had been interviewed as to their socioeconomic status, physical health, social support, and psychological status. Several years later, each woman who had recently been widowed was reinterviewed about six months after her husband's death. Among these women, aged 65 to 78, the only factors from the earlier interviews that strongly predicted the development of emotional problems were a scarcity of friends and a lack of closeness to their children.

The Experience of Widowhood

The status of widowhood varies from one society to another. Some cultures have a specific role for the widow; she may be responsible for organizing social rituals, act as arbitrator, or serve as matchmaker (Lopata, 1980). Among high-caste Hindus, who forbade remarriage, a widow was expected to throw herself on her husband's funeral pyre. Although this regulation was more honored in the breach than the observance, it acted as an ideal and helped enforce other behavior on widows who did not join their husbands in death (Lopata, 1975).

The special role of widow seems linked to the subordinate status of women in most societies. Only for women does the death of a spouse require social roles and rituals. Searches of anthropological studies have found no society that supports a special role for widowers; the only references are to remarriages by the surviving husband (Lopata, 1980).

American behavioral scientists have also largely ignored the widower. Most studies have focused on widows, in part because there are so many of them. The apparent lack of interest in widowers may also have come about because a man's primary identity comes from his occupation, and society expects the death of a wife to have little or no effect on that part of his life. Some research indicates that men find the adjustment to the death of a spouse much harder than do women. Compared to widows, widowers have poorer health, greater social isolation, weaker emotional ties to the family, and are less likely to find a confidant. Yet other studies have found no gender differences in adjustment (Bengston, Rosenthal, and Burton, 1990). Since differences in social support, mental health, and general well-being narrow sharply as widowed men and women become older and their health begins to fail (Feinson, 1986; Wister and Strain, 1986), some of the differences that have been found may reflect the fact that women tend to be widowed at a younger age than men.

Among the middle-aged and young-old, however, the widower seems to be more isolated and lonely than the widow. Women tend to be the "kin-tenders," who maintain social and family ties, and they also are more likely to have a close friend other than their spouse. Practical problems come from the structure of the traditional marriage. The widower suddenly faces a struggle for survival—he must cook, clean, and take care of the domestic chores most men in present older cohorts have never tackled. Yet most widowers are much better off financially than widows and may be more accustomed to managing money. It is no wonder that widowers tend to remarry rapidly.

Although society believes that most widows would remarry if they had the opportunity, a large proportion have no interest in reentering the married state. Among more than 500 widows in St. Louis who had not remarried, 36 percent said they had no interest in finding another husband because they liked being single and the independence that went with it (Gentry and Shulman, 1988). Few of these widows said that it was the shortage of potential partners that kept them from remarrying, but a large proportion said they simply had not found anyone as nice as their late husbands (Table 11.5). This last reason may reflect the tendency of many widows to sanctify the memories of their husbands, idealizing them to the point where the widows cannot find any man who could possibly live up to the image they have created. Among older widows in Chicago, more than 75 percent said they had no interest in remarrying (Lopata, 1973). Some, like many of the widows in the St. Louis group, liked their independence; other said they had no wish to play the wife role or did not want to have to care for another sick man. Some viewed another marriage as impossible, either because they had sanctified their late husbands or because they perceived a scarcity of possible partners.

The failure to remarry does not mean that widows give up sexual activity. Among widows between the ages of 26 and 30, 55 percent are sexually active (Gebhard, 1970). The frequency of sexual activity declines once widows pass the age of 30, but throughout life their rate of sexual activity exceeds their rate of remarriage. Among older widows, 20 percent agree that men continually make them sexual propositions and that some of the offers come from friends of their husbands. As we have begun to understand the importance of sexuality across the life span, some researchers have proposed that society seek alternative solutions to the sexual needs of older widows (Corby and Zarit, 1983). Among their suggestions are cohabitation with younger men, polygamous marriage, and homosexual relationships.

The desire for independence may help explain why so many widows choose to live alone. Younger widows who live with others generally are the heads of households composed of themselves and their children. Among women past the age of 40, recent widows are 25 to

Table 11.5 **WHY WIDOWS STAY SINGLE**

	Age Category					
Reason	≤35	*36–45*	*46–55*	*56–65*	*66 +*	*Total Sample*
Not enough men	0	0	6%	1%	3%	3%
Not found anyone as nice	54%	32%	36%	40%	43%	40%
Too old	0	0	1%	3%	15%	8%
Children disapprove	0	11%	0	0	1%	2%
Like being single	31%	32%	42%	48%	30%	37%
Still mourning	15%	21%	13%	5%	6%	8%
Economic	0	4%	3%	2%	3%	3%

Source: Gentry and Shulman, 1988, p. 195.

50 percent more likely than recently divorced women to be living alone, perhaps because so many of them own their own homes (Uhlenberg, Cooney, and Boyd, 1990). Although widows have more financial problems than widowers, the majority are not in dire circumstances. It is the widow younger than 60 who is most likely to find her standard of living declining (Morgan, 1986). Among more than 300 older widows who lived in a midwestern metropolitan area, less than half said that their economic circumstances had declined since the death of their husbands, and only one-fifth said that they had problems getting along on their current income (O'Bryant and Morgan, 1989). The overwhelming majority (68 percent) said they were "comfortably" fixed, and 12 percent said they were "fairly well off." Far from being the financially inexperienced widows of earlier studies, these women tended to have considerable financial knowledge. A large majority of them had handled the couple's household bills, and about one-third reported having had credit in their own names, a personal checking or savings account, or their own investments at some time during their marriage. Women who seem to be at greatest financial risk are those who have had neither experience in managing money nor any discussions with their late husbands regarding economic plans for their widowhood

This optimistic picture of widowhood, taken about 18 months after the death of the women's husbands, may present only a temporary picture. A more sobering study, which analyzed financial situations five years after a spouse's death, indicates that *both* widows and widowers who maintain their own households suffer a sharp decline in economic well-being compared to married couples and that about half can expect to live at least one year below the poverty line (Zick and Smith, 1986). Clearly, many widows continue to have economic problems.

Even so, in the two decades since the first comprehensive studies of widowhood, widows seem to have become better equipped to handle life without their husbands. Those with extensive experience in the labor market, good education, and relatively high scores on nontraditional gender tasks tend to be better equipped to handle their own financial affairs (O'Bryant and Morgan, 1989). An ever larger proportion of American women fit that description, suggesting that an increasingly large number of widows will resemble the small group found among those whose husbands died in the late 1940s and 1950s (Lopata, 1975). Once past the period of mourning, these women became independent, taking on roles and developing life-styles that they never would have considered as girls or wives.

ALTERNATIVE LIFE-STYLES

Marriage is not the only way to form close relationships. Although younger adults are more likely than members of older cohorts to take another path, some people have always found alternative ways to fulfill the need for intimacy. The most common alternative solutions are heterosexual cohabitation, homosexuality, and singlehood.

Cohabitation

The path to intimacy closest to marriage is heterosexual **cohabitation,** in which two unmarried, heterosexual people live together. Cohabitation differs from common-law marriage, which is recognized in some, but not all, states. In **common-law marriage,** a cohabiting couple declare themselves to be married and are so regarded by the state. Their assets are mingled, and they file joint tax returns. Like traditional marriages, common-law marriages can be dissolved only by death or divorce (Hirsch, 1976).

Cohabitation first came to public attention when it became popular with college students toward the close of the 1960s. By the mid-1980s almost half of all Americans between the ages of 25 and 35 had lived together before marriage (*Wall Street Journal*, 1988). Among those marrying between 1980 and 1984, 44 percent had cohabited, a rate that climbed to 58 percent among those who had remarried during the same period. In 1987, 2,334,000 couples were reported to be cohabiting; in 143,000 of these couples, either the man or the woman was older than 65 (U.S. Bureau of the Census, 1989).

According to Philip Blumstein and Pepper Schwartz (1983), who conducted a major study of American couples, cohabitation is so unstable and takes so many different forms that it is simpler to regard it as a "situation that may change at any moment" rather than an institution. Among the cohabiting couples they studied, the two partners often had very different concepts of what cohabitation meant. Partners often had trouble making certain that they both wanted the same thing out of the relationship, and many of the cohabiting couples had developed no basis for trust, no mutual cooperation, and no ability to plan for the future. As a 25-year-old woman who had been cohabiting for two years explained, "I think he has some questions in his mind if he really belongs in this kind of relationship. We discussed this recently, that in his mind he kind of lives with his suitcase packed" (Blumstein and Schwartz, 1983, p. 423).

Perhaps for this reason, a number of researchers do not regard cohabitation as a separate institution, but as an additional step in the courtship process—at least among young adults. In such cases, living with a member of the other sex is not seen as putting young people on a path that leads away from marriage. Indeed, some researchers believe that cohabitation will soon become the norm (Lewis, 1989).

Even some long-term cohabitations seem tentative. One of the older cohabitating couples studied by Blumstein and Schwartz (1983) had been together for nearly eight years, but they still looked no farther ahead than six months. Said the 60-year-old male partner, "We started out and decided to try it for six months and see how it went together. Then we could always renew our agreement at the end of six months—which we've done fourteen times now." (p. 409)

Despite the temporary nature of many cohabiting relationships, married and cohabiting couples seem to derive about the same amount of satisfaction from their relationships, and when the data are controlled for age and length of relationship, the two types of couples are very similar (Macklin, 1978). Cohabiting couples go through the same blending, nesting, and maintaining phases as do married couples—and on the same timetable (Kurdek and Schmitt, 1986). They seem to divide tasks in a similar manner, make decisions similarly, and communicate in the same manner. Those who have no intention of marrying tend to keep their finances separate, hold less traditional views concerning gender roles, and tend to see each other in flattering ways (Blumstein and Schwartz, 1983)

Cohabitants who go on to marry tend to hold traditional views of gender roles, and most combine their finances at the start of their relationship. After their marriage, they seem little different from married couples who had never cohabited: They are similar in emotional closeness, satisfaction, conflict, and egalitarianism in the marital relationship. However, those who cohabit before marriage are more likely to divorce than those who do not (Lewis, 1989). Their higher divorce rate may be explained by the fact that people who cohabit are less likely to hold traditional views of marriage.

Homosexual Relationships

Some individuals reserve their intimate relationships for members of their own sex. In a detailed study of homosexual life styles conducted over a decade ago in San Francisco, only about 10 percent of gay men were in *close-coupled* relationships, in which the partners lived together, shared a close emotional bond, and were monogamous (Bell and Weinberg, 1978). Another 18 percent lived in an *open-coupled* relationship, which was more like an open marriage. Each partner was free to seek outside sexual relationships. *Functional* relationships, which resembled the life-style of swinging singles, accounted for 10 percent of the gay men. They lived alone, had sexually active lives, and seemed self-reliant and comfortable with their homosexuality. The 12 percent of gay men who were *dysfunctional* lived alone and sometimes had active sex lives, but they were unhappy and troubled about their situation. Finally, *asexual* gays lived alone and had little sexual activity. The 16 percent in this category led quiet, withdrawn lives and had little contact with others. They were not, however, troubled about their sexual orientation.

The lives of lesbians followed similar patterns, although the most prevalent relationship among homosexual women was the close-coupled variety; 28 percent were in monogamous relationships. Open-coupled and functional relationships among lesbians were about the same as among gays, but lesbians were less likely than gays to be dysfunctional (5 percent) or asexual (11 percent) (Bell and Weinberg, 1978).

This study may not reflect the actual life of most homosexuals, for it was conducted before the threat of AIDS affected homosexual life-styles and increased the proportion of coupled relationships. In addition, all the subjects volunteered to take part, and all were drawn from a single area of the country. Even among this group, the categories were unlikely to be permanent (Gagnon, 1979). Although only 28 percent of the men studied were living with a partner, most of them had had at least one long-term relationship in the past.

Later researchers have found that when gays or lesbians form close-coupled or open-coupled relationships, they go through the same blending, nesting, and maintaining phases that distinguish marital relationships (Kurdek and Schmitt, 1986). Although the prevalence of marriagelike arrangements appears to be growing within the homosexual community, legal marriage is not yet possible. In San Francisco, however, the Board of Supervisors has endorsed a referendum to allow public registration of "domestic partnerships" between homosexuals (extending marital status to their union), and the referendum has been placed on the ballot (Bishop, 1989). Several cities (West Hollywood, California; Ithaca, New York; Madison, Wisconsin) already provide for such registration (Lewin, 1990). The New York State Court of Appeals has ruled that homosexual couples who have lived together for ten years can be considered a "family" under New York City's rent-control regulations (*Newsweek,* 1989). Each of these changes has come in response to lobbying by homosexual individuals, who want access to the economic advantages our society extends to married couples.

Considering the difference in male and female socialization, as well as the importance women learn to place on relationships, the greater prevalence of close-coupled relationships

Many gay men form close, stable relationships, and some gay couples are rearing children.

among lesbians is not surprising. When researchers compared gay men, lesbians, and heterosexual men and women, they found that whether a person was male or female had more to do with their attitudes toward intimacy than whether they were heterosexual or homosexual (Peplau, 1981). Other researchers have found that lesbian relationships, formed with *two* people who have been socialized in ways that stress long-term emotional commitments, are generally warm, tender, and caring and that the partners often become overinvolved emotionally (Nichols and Lieblum, 1983). As a lesbian in her forties who had been in a relationship for 14 years saw it: ''Two women are going to be more sensitive than a man and a woman. Now I don't think it's the men's fault—don't get me wrong. It is just that men are of a different nature. I used to think that men were no good, but as I have gotten older and matured, I think society has laid a lot of trips on them, and I don't think many men know their own identity and so they can't be very sensitive'' (Blumstein and Schwartz, 1983, p. 480).

Homosexual couples may find unanticipated problems in their relationship because they cannot use gender as a guideline for decisions and interactions between partners. This conclusion came through clearly in Blumstein and Schwartz's (1983) study of American couples. Gay couples found that easing the demands of the male role was less of a problem than assuming roles that traditionally had been held by women. Lesbians found themselves in a double bind: they wanted an intense home life, but they also wanted a strong, ambitious, and independent partner. The balance of power was so important to lesbians that they resented being placed in a more powerful role. This double bind may explain why, although lesbians' relationships were more likely to be intense, intimate, and monogamous than those of gays, lesbian couples were more likely to break up than gay, cohabiting, or married couples.

Little research has been done on aging homosexuals, so we are left primarily with speculation about the course of their relationships over the life span. Research on aging lesbians is virtually nonexistent. What research has been done with men indicates that the stereotype of the lonely, frustrated, depressed, aging gay male does not fit those who have been studied (Kimmel, 1978). The life course of middle-class gay males between the ages of 55 and 81 roughly corresponded to that set forth by Daniel Levinson (1978) for adult male development. For example, all long-term relationships among men in the study either flourished or began during what Levinson calls the Settling Down period.

Perhaps, as some researchers have suggested, the homosexual community functions almost like an extended family for most gay men (Francher and Henkin, 1973). If so, gay friendship networks may be as supportive in time of need as children or other relatives would be. Given the large changes in society's attitude toward homosexuality over the past 25 years, different cohorts of homosexuals are likely to experience various aspects of development in radically different ways.

Singlehood

Thirty-five years ago, anyone who remained single was regarded with suspicion by most people. Judgments rendered on single women were extremely harsh; in 1957, 80 percent of Americans believed that they were either "sick," "neurotic," or "immoral." By the 1980s, that judgment had been reversed: 75 percent said that single women were simply women who had chosen a different way of living (Yankelovich, 1981).

The change in public attitudes reflects a change in society. Today, only about 5 percent of adults past the age of 65 have never married (U.S. Bureau of the Census, 1989). The proportion of single older adults will shrink as the marriage-minded baby-boom generation moves into later adulthood, but when today's young adults are ready to enter retirement, more of them may still be single (Bengston, Rosenthal, and Burton, 1990) (Table 11.6). Because an increasing proportion of people are marrying at a later age, demographers cannot agree on the ultimate size of the increase (Rich, 1987).

The rising popularity of the single life may seem like a new development, but a large single population is not a new factor in American life. If we assume that most people who marry will do so by the age of 40, the figures from Essex County, Massachusetts, for the years 1875–1885 may prove startling. During those years, the proportion of unmarried men between the ages of 35 and 39 ranged from 14 to 29 percent in various areas of the county. The proportion of unmarried women of that age ranged from 23 to 31 percent (Ankarloo, 1978). In 1987, 12.4 percent of American men and 8.4 percent of American women were unwed at that age (U.S. Bureau of the Census, 1989).

Why were so many Massachusetts women unmarried? There is no way to be certain, but historical events apparently played some part in the development. Industrial areas of Mas-

Table 11.6 **WHO IS SINGLE?**

Sex	Age (yrs)									
	18–19	20–24	25–29	30–34	35–39	40–44	45–54	55–64	65–74	>74
Men	96.8%	77.7%	42.2%	23.1%	12.4%	6.9%	5.9%	5.8%	4.7%	4.3%
Women	89.8%	60.8%	28.8%	14.6%	8.4%	6.4%	4.5%	4.2%	4.8%	6.4%

Source: U.S. Bureau of the Census, 1989.

sachusetts were attracting immigrants—both from the Massachusetts countryside and from other nations. The highest rate of unmarried women (and the lowest rate of unmarried men) appeared in industrial areas, where women worked in the labor force. The lowest rate of unmarried women (and the highest rate of unmarried men) appeared in rural areas, where women's work was confined to home and farm. The family's need for the earnings of adult children may have prevented some from marrying. Finally, possible husbands for some of the women may have been killed during the Civil War.

When today's single adults are asked why they have not married, most say that the personal freedom, career opportunities, and availability of sexual partners outweigh the economic, emotional, and sexual security of marriage—at least for the present. Interviews with single men turned up eventual intentions to marry, accompanied by the fear that they might remain single forever (Gabriel, 1987). Thirty year olds hoped to ''make a commitment'' before they were 40; 40 year olds said that men were not confirmed bachelors until they were in their fifties. An increasing number of women may feel like the 39-year-old president of a public relations firm who enjoys having ''total control over her environment'' and sees no reason to bother with marriage: ''The difference between being unhappily single and unhappily married,'' she said, ''is that, in the first case, one phone call can turn it around. The other takes a lot more work'' (Salholz, 1986). There are, however, two kinds of single adults: self-selected, who prefer the single life; and socially selected, whose real or imagined handicaps have left them unable to attract a mate (Corby and Zarit, 1983).

Whether people are single by choice or by chance, social conditions play some role in their fate. The increased tolerance of alternative life-styles and the active social and sexual

Less restrictive social attitudes, together with a technology that has made the single life easier, have contributed to the growing number of adults who choose not to marry.

life now available to singles make the unmarried life more attractive to self-selected men and women. Technology has made their lot comfortable: frozen foods, microwave ovens, laundromats, permanent press clothing, improved transportation, and other services that cater to single adults have simplified life. Among self-selected women, more education and expanded opportunities have made them financially independent. They no longer *have* to marry. The relative shortage of marriageable middle-aged and older men has increased the pool of socially selected women.

How does the single life affect intimate relationships? Among single adults who live alone, some ''swing,'' and others have long-term sexual relationships. The fear of AIDs and other sexually transmitted diseases has apparently reduced the proportion of swingers— or at least changed their sexual practices. Some single adults are celibate. Although the majority of singles say they are satisfied with their sex lives, they seem less satisfied than the married. Among several hundred Dayton, Ohio, adults, 80 percent of the married reported sexual satisfaction as compared with 51 percent of the singles. Although single adults had a greater variety of partners, married adults had sex more often (Cargan and Melko, 1982).

Nonsexual relationships do not appear to be a problem for single adults. They have friends and family, and some studies have found that their physical and mental health is no different from that of people who live with others (Rubenstein, Shaver, and Peplau, 1979). Young singles in the Dayton, Ohio, sample were just as physically healthy as married adults, but they seemed under more stress. Single women were more likely than married women to be lonely, have nightmares, crying spells, and irrational fears. Single men were more likely than married men to be lonely and despondent and to feel guilty and worthless (Cargan and Melko, 1982).

Yet loneliness affected only some young singles. There is actually no one ''single type'' of unmarried adult. Among a group of older single men (Rubinstein, 1987), three distinct types appeared. Some of these men were sophisticated and outgoing, interested in people and events, and had many friends and high levels of social interaction. Another type included ''socialized isolates.'' They spent much of their time alone, but whenever they felt the need of company, they reached out for it. They had friends, but not many. Over the years their social lives had focused on their families, and they had few remaining relatives. Only the third type, ''the outsiders,'' seemed truly isolated. Their social relationships tended to be cursory, unemotional transactions, and none had any friends.

Only a minority of older singles are lonely. Older women tend to have very close family relations with their own parents, aunts and uncles, siblings, nieces and nephews (Bengston, Rosenthal, and Burton, 1990). Their stronger family relationships may explain why only a quarter of older single women but a third of older single men say that they are lonely at least ''some of the time'' (Rubinstein, 1987). Older single adults are lonelier than married people, but they are not as lonely as the widowed. Half of older single adults say that they are ''rarely lonely,'' compared with less than a third of the widowed. In general, however, older single adults' satisfaction with life is much like that of older married adults, and they seem better off than the widowed and divorced (Corby and Zarit, 1983). They escape the pain of divorce and the grief of being widowed. Most adults who have chosen the single life are independent people who prefer solitary pursuits and do not appear to miss the family involvement they might have had as spouses or parents.

SIBLINGS

Most of us have at least one sibling. In the population as a whole, only about 10 percent are only children (Cicirelli, 1982), and 82 percent of older adults have at least one surviving sibling (Shanas and Heinemann, 1982).

The sibling relationship is unique in several ways (Cicirelli, 1982). It is the most enduring of all relationships, beginning with birth (or in early life) and ending with the death of the sibling, generally outlasting the parental relationship by several decades. Siblings have more in common with each other than with anyone else. They share a genetic heritage, cultural surroundings, and early experiences. The relationship is one of approximately equal power and freedom. Finally, no sibling has to ''earn'' the relationship; it is awarded by circumstances of birth. Our brothers and sisters certainly affect our development during childhood, and if they are older, they were present in the family from the day we were born.

As children grow up and leave home, sibling relationships generally diminish in importance. Yet most people remain in contact with brothers and sisters, and in some cases the bonds are intense. For example, a group of four brothers were as close as the three musketeers, whose motto, ''All for one, and one for all,'' reflected their relationship (Bank and Kahn, 1982). These college-educated brothers, whose ages ranged from 36 to 45, lived within a 100-mile radius; their contacts were frequent; and they shared common values, resolved their conflicts openly and rapidly, relied on one another, and defended one another against outsiders.

Especially intense sibling loyalty appears to develop when children either lose a parent (by death, desertion, or divorce) or else perceive their parents as weak or hostile. Their social support system is either missing or unpredictable, and they cling together for support (Bank and Kahn, 1982). Sibling loyalty rarely runs so deep.

Researchers have discerned three more typical patterns of relationships among adults (Cicirelli, 1982). Some siblings feel a mutual apathy, getting together only at ritual family events. In such cases they are likely to see little of each other after the death of their parents, although it is extremely unusual for them to lose touch completely. Some siblings are close, and others maintain an enduring rivalry. Sisters seem more likely than brothers to develop extremely close relationships, and cross-sex relationships are generally closer than the relationships between brothers.

Throughout life most people express feelings of closeness to their siblings whether or not they often see or hear from them. A large majority of middle-aged adults say they get along well with their siblings, find their relationships satisfying, and feel that their brothers or sisters are interested in them. Yet less than half say they discuss intimate topics with siblings, and only a handful talk over important life decisions with them (Cicirelli, 1982).

As people get older, their relationships with their brothers and sisters seem to deepen. Feelings of closeness intensify with age, even though visits, telephone calls, and letters may decrease in frequency. Siblings may provide important connections to the past, giving older adults an opportunity to share reminiscences and shore up their identity. The link to the past is reflected in the tendency to reevaluate sibling relationships in the wake of marriage, the illness or death of parents, or the death of another brother or sister (Rosenthal, 1985). The existence of brothers or sisters may also provide a sense of security, because siblings are generally ready to help one another if main sources of support, such as spouse or children, break down (Bengston, Rosenthal, and Burton, 1990). There seems to be a clear pattern of mutual aid in sibling relationships, with assistance infrequent among young adults, extended in times of crisis among middle-aged adults, and often expanding to encompass the role of substitute parent or spouse during old age (Cicirelli, 1982).

Siblings do not usually provide the closest relationship in later life: only about 14 percent of older men and 27 percent of older women rely on a sibling as a confidant—typically a sister. Among the widowed elderly, however, siblings are often close friends and sources of emotional support (Bengston, Rosenthal, and Burton, 1990). After the death of a spouse, widows and widowers often renew contacts with brothers and sisters and reestablish associations with them. Although closeness to brothers has no effect on an older person's well-being, depression tends to be more prevalent among older adults without a close bond to a sister (Cicirelli, 1989).

Whether the pattern of sibling relationships that have been detected in cross-sectional studies will reflect relationships in future generations is unknown. Various changes in society could alter the present pattern. Perhaps sisters will no longer be seen as the confidant of choice or a defense against depression among younger cohorts who grow up with less traditional gender roles (Cicirelli, 1989). In addition, the encouragement of emotional openness, the loosening of strong family ties as ethnic groups move from first and second to third generation, increased geographical mobility, and the increased frequency of divorce and reconstituted families could change the course of this family bond. For many people, the role that might be played by siblings is filled by friends.

FRIENDS

Friendship differs from other close relationships because its ties do not depend on kinship or the law; it is a purely volitional relationship. Because neither custom nor law forces us to maintain a friendship, the bond is fragile and can be broken by a single defection of either party. However, we judge our friends less harshly than we do our families. We expect help from families in time of need and judge them harshly if they fail to come through. Because friends are not obligated to help, we do not condemn them if they fail us and are highly appreciative when they provide aid (Antonucci, 1990).

THE NATURE OF ADULT FRIENDSHIP

Like lovers, friends tend to be similar in many ways: age, sex, race, ethnic or religious group, social background, proximity, interests, and attitudes. This similarity is important in maintaining friendship because of the function served by these relationships. Friendships appear to provide self-affirmation and ego support, with the friend validating our identity, and our acceptance by friends contributing to our self-acceptance. Friends also provide intellectual stimulation and interesting activities.

Friendship often proves difficult to study because it is such a subjective classification. For example, older adults who lived in Manhattan hotels listed their friends and indicated their daily contacts with others (Cohen, Cook, and Rajkowski, 1980). But the people labeled as ''friends'' were often seen infrequently and considered neither intimate nor important, whereas "nonfriends" were often a source of regular interaction and a significant minority were considered both intimate and important.

Friendships are often linked to people's other life roles. Being married makes other married people available as friends, for many adult friendships are between couples, not individuals. Becoming parents makes other parents available; friendships may develop out of children's social lives, with such activities as scouting, music lessons, Little League, or car pools bringing parents with shared interests together. When their children's interests are the only basis for friendship, the bonds tend to dissolve as the children drift into differing paths. Friendships often develop between coworkers, and when a person changes jobs or retires, occupational friendships may dwindle. As is true of friendships between parents, some other basis for shared experiences is required to maintain the bond.

Friendship patterns are strongly related to social class, marital status, and gender. People with extensive formal schooling and prestigious occupations generally have more friends than working-class adults with little schooling. Married couples usually have more friends than single or widowed adults and see them more often (Aizenberg and Treas, 1985), but among retired adults, the unmarried spend twice as much time with friends as do married couples (Larson, Mannell, and Zuzanek, 1986), and among adults older than 75, widows and widowers see their friends more often than do the married (Field and Minkler, 1988). Childless older people have more contact with friends and acquaintances than older people with children.

Older adults frequently say that their friends provide more important and satisfying companionship than their children do. Studies support their statements, indicating that friends have a stronger relation to well-being than do families (Adams and Blieszner, 1989; Antonucci, 1990). A recent study in which retired adults (ages 55 to 88) wore electronic pagers helps explain why friends are so closely associated with well-being (Larson, Mannell, and Zuzanek, 1986). Each time the pager beeped, these adults wrote down what they were doing, whom they were with, what they were thinking about, and how they felt. When with their families, they were carrying out humdrum activities—housework, eating, watching TV, riding in the car. Their thoughts were on TV, food preparation and eating, the weather, personal care, home maintenance, financial matters—or nothing. When they were with their friends, they were engaged in active socializing—hobbies, sports, religious and cultural activities. Their thoughts were on other people, food preparation and eating, games, their current activity, religious activities, volunteer work, exercising, and historical and social ideas. Clearly, being with friends is much more stimulating than being with family. Older adults may count on their families, but they enjoy their friends

For those who live on into old-old age, the death of friends may mean social isolation. A 92-year-old widow noted this tendency with some distaste:

Friendship is one's own responsibility. Old age shouldn't make one less friendly or interested in making new friends. All my old friends are in the graveyard, and if I hadn't made some new ones, where would I be? I think a lot of old people just aren't very sensible. They only have old friends, and then they live to be ninety or something, like me, and then they start moaning because their friends have gone before, as they say. My advice to the aged woman is find some young people. Don't go to these dreadful old folks' clubs, but find some young people (Blythe, 1979, p. 266).

GENDER DIFFERENCES IN FRIENDSHIP

Friendships are very different among men and women. Bonds between male friends seem to be based on shared activities and shared experiences, in contrast to the mutual assistance, emotional support, and intimacy that seem to characterize bonds between female friends (Fox, Gibbs, and Auerbach, 1985). As a result, men's friendships tend to be limited to certain segments of life, whereas women's friendships involve all aspects (Wright, 1982).

These differences, as well as sex-role socialization, have led to the assumption that men are likely to hide their feelings and private thoughts from friends, but that women are likely to express them. Among college students, for example, men are much less interested in intimate communication with friends than are women (Caldwell and Peplau, 1982). Yet in a study of young, single, Catholic, middle-class adults, men seemed to confide in their male friends about as much as women confided in their female friends (Hacker, 1981). Married women were more likely than single women to disclose themselves to friends—a trend that was also present, but weaker, among men. In the case of cross-sex friends, men were likely to hide their weaknesses from female friends and women to conceal their strengths from male friends, indicating a tendency to fulfill sex-role expectations (Table 11.7).

Some researchers have suggested that friendships become more important to men in later life. The loss of work and family roles that occurs with retirement and the emptying of the nest supposedly lead men to find increased value in friendship (Blau, 1973). Autobiographical sketches written by Harvard graduates during middle and later adulthood provided an indirect look at the course of men's friendships (Reisman, 1988). At middle age (25 years after graduation), only 15 percent of married men, 12 percent of divorced men, and 6 percent of single men spontaneously mentioned their friends in these sketches, although virtually all mentioned careers and family. In older adulthood (50 years after graduation), 21 percent mentioned friends, and, even though most were retired, almost every man again mentioned careers. The increase is not impressive. Among parents in the California Intergenerational Studies, a pronounced change in male friendships appeared to occur as these men moved from young-old to old-old age (Field and Minkler, 1988). Now between the ages of 75 and 93, the men not only tended to see their friends less often than they had 14 years earlier, but also valued their friendships significantly less. They also tended to shift from the more intimate, one-to-one activities of middle age to group activities.

Table 11.7   **GENDER DIFFERENCES IN SELF-DISCLOSURE[a]**

	Same-sex Pairs		*Cross-sex Pairs*	
	Women	*Men*	*Women*	*Men*
Reveal strengths and weaknesses	77%	86%	50%	62%
Reveal only weaknesses	18%	0	33%	0%
Reveal only strengths	0	9%	0	31%
Reveal neither	5%	5%	17%	7%

[a] When it was a matter of revealing both strengths and weaknesses, men and women reported high rates of self-disclosure to a friend of the same sex. But in this young, educated, mostly single group, men concealed their weaknesses from female friends, and women concealed their strengths from male friends. The pattern follows the culture's gender-role standards.

Source: Hacker, 1981, p. 393.

Women's friendships seem to run a different course in later adulthood. When researchers followed the friendships of single, widowed, and divorced older women for three years, they discovered that a woman's status in the community was the best predictor of her friendship patterns (Adams, 1987). Women labeled ''high society,'' who had been active in cultural groups, had relatively high incomes, wore more expensive clothes, and tended to look young for their age, had contracted their friendship networks. They had dropped their casual friends to cherish a few close relationships. One said that since her husband had died, ''I'm footloose and fancy free. I have time for real friendship.'' ''Pillars of the community'' had been active in church and fraternal organizations, had less money and less expensive clothes than the high-society women, and looked their age. These women had expanded their friendship circles, making new friends outside their neighborhood and community as they dropped old friends connected to earlier responsibilities. ''I'm no longer tied up in couple things,'' said one of these women. ''I can travel without worrying about the children.'' The third group of women, labeled ''marginal,'' belonged to fewer organizations, had lower incomes, were more likely to use social services, dressed in poorer quality clothes, and looked older than their age. Marginal women had expanded their friendship networks, adding to their few close friends a number of new casual friendships, made through senior centers. ''I've made more friends since my divorce than I ever had before,'' said one. Instead of finding aging a time of physical decline and social loss, many of these women discovered that the elimination of social role obligations had liberated them. Among the mothers in the California Intergenerational Studies, contacts with friends and commitments to them remained unchanged as they moved from young-old into old-old age (Field and Minkler, 1988). Friendships were just as important for them as they had been 14 years earlier.

Relationships with mates, siblings, and friends are important influences on the shape and quality of our lives. In the next chapter, we will investigate the nature of the family and relationships across the generations.

SUMMARY

THE IMPORTANCE OF RELATIONSHIPS

Individual development occurs in a human context, and the person who grows up without social interaction or affection has little chance of being normal. The need for human relationships is also central in adulthood, but the degree of human contact that seems to be required varies from one person to the next.

MATES

In U.S. society, a primary means of satisfying the need for human connection is through an intimate relationship with a mate. In the **triangular theory of love,** love is viewed in terms of intimacy, passion, and decision/commitment, whereas in other research, love can be distinguished as **passionate love** or **companionate love.** Mates tend to be similar in many ways. Marriage may protect people against **loneliness.** The division of power between marriage partners is central to marital roles, and in the traditional marriage the man has the upper hand. Whether marriages are equal partnerships or one partner is dominant, they go through **blending, nesting,** and **maintaining phases.** Levels of sexuality are highest during the first year of marriage. Sexual satisfaction appears to depend on whether people feel they benefit as much from the relationship as does their partner. Cross-sectional studies indicate that marital satisfaction is curvilinear, with the low point occurring during the children's adolescence. Most satisfactory marriages are either **companionate marriages** or **institutional marriages.** In later adulthood, when most marriages improve, couples may forget the dissatisfactions and marital problems of the past.

Divorce now tends to occur after three or four years of marriage, with social changes playing a major role in the increase in divorce rates. The painful process of divorce moves through three stages: the acute stage, the transitional stage, and the stable period. Divorced people lose one of their social roles, and women usually find that their income drops. The divorced have higher rates of serious illness, emotional disturbance, and accidental death than any other group in society. A high percentage of divorced people remarry, and the remarriage may be quite different, as it is influenced by efforts to avoid the style of the previous marriage, contact with the previous spouse, changed personal circumstances, and different cohort effects. Second marriages seem less stable than the first.

The death of the marital partner forces the survivor, usually the wife, into a new social role. During **bereavement,** the survivor may move through four stages of grief: numbness, yearning, disorganization, and reorganization. Reorganization is generally underway within a year of the spouse's death. Among the factors that determine the disruption caused by widowhood are how much the survivor depended on the deceased partner, the survivor's social and economic resources, and whether the death is seen as being "on time." Some studies find that men have a more difficult adjustment than women, but the difference may be due to the fact that men are widowed later in life. Most widowers remarry rapidly, but many widows have no interest in remarriage.

Heterosexual **cohabitation** precedes almost half of all marriages, although some people see it as an alternative to marriage. It differs from **common-law marriage** in that cohabiting partners can dissolve their arrangement without going through the courts. The degree of commitment felt by the partners determines the form that cohabitation takes. Satisfaction among cohabiting and married couples is very similar.

Homosexual relationships seem to fall into types that are similar to various heterosexual relationships, but they are less likely to be permanent. Lesbian relationships are more likely to be intense, intimate, and monogamous than gay relationships, but lesbian couples tend to break up more quickly. The inability to use gender as a guideline for decisions and interactions complicates homosexual relationships.

The proportion of adults who choose to remain single appears to be growing, although the postponement of marriage has made it difficult to predict the eventual size of the single group. The desire for personal freedom, the prevalence of career opportunities, economic independence, and the availability of sexual partners seem to be primary reasons for staying single.

SIBLINGS

Siblings have much in common: their genetic heritage, their cultural surroundings, and their early experience. Although sibling relationships generally diminish in importance during adulthood, most siblings maintain contact. Siblings tend to be apathetic about their relationships, to be extremely close, or to be rivals. Bonds between siblings tend to deepen during later adulthood, and mutual aid is common.

FRIENDSHIPS

Friendships are voluntary associations and can be broken by either party. Friends tend to be similar in many ways, and friendships are often linked to other life roles, with shifts in the other roles affecting the friendship bond. Male friendships are typically based on shared activities and shared experiences, whereas female friendships are characterized by mutual assistance, intimacy, and emotional support.

KEY TERMS

bereavement	institutional marriage
blending phase	loneliness
cohabitation	maintaining phase
common-law marriage	nesting phase
companionate love	passionate love
companionate marriage	triangular theory of love

Chapter 12

Relationships Between Generations
──── ◆ ────

A t the age of one year, Katherine Anne Pruzan is growing up in a nontraditional household. Since she was born, her 34-year-old father, Mark, has been at home with her on unpaid paternity leave as her primary caregiver. Katherine's mother, Jo Ann, also spent time at home on maternity leave but only for the first three months after Katherine's birth. Thirty-two-year-old Jo Ann's job as field director for a marketing and research company pays substantially more than Mark's job as county welfare frauds investigator, so it seemed sensible for her to return to work instead of Mark.

"Someone has to watch the baby," explained Mark. "I don't want a surrogate parent from eight to six. Why have a child in the first place?" (Melvin, 1983, p. WC6) Once Mark returns to his job, Jo Ann plans to work part time, meshing her hours with Mark's so that Katherine's care will be managed smoothly.

Few families have adopted the sort of arrangement that seems to be working well for this couple, and paternity leave would have been unthinkable a decade ago. But when employment among mothers of infants passed the 50 percent mark, the workplace was bound to change. In 1990 Congress passed a bill requiring businesses with more than 50 employees to offer parents up to 12 weeks' unpaid leave for the care of newborn infants or ill family members. Although President Bush vetoed the legislation, an increasing proportion of the country's businesses offer some form of family leave. Choices for today's families are wider than they once were, and alternative family forms have become more popular.

In this chapter, which investigates relationships between generations, we begin with a look at the family, where we learn the rules of relationships and what to expect from them. After exploring the family as a system, we move to the parent-child relationship, considering traditional as well as nontraditional ways of relating to children. Next, we examine another bond that crosses generations, the relationship between grandparents and grandchildren, as well as relationships with great-grandparents—a role that longevity has made increasingly common. Returning to the parent–child relationship, we investigate its changing nature across adulthood as child becomes parent and parent enters old age. The chapter closes with a look at the problems of caring for aging parents.   ◆

THE FAMILY AS A SYSTEM

Our most important relationships occur within the context of the family. Our first relationships are with our parents, and—unless we are abandoned or orphaned—we grow up and are socialized within the family unit. Siblings, grandparents, and perhaps stepparents become important; in some families, aunts, uncles, and cousins also play important roles. Our relationships with our first family endure as we find mates, establish new families of our own, and continue the cycle of generations. Even those who remain single maintain a role in their family of birth.

One way to look at the family is to see it as a social system whose structure is affected by the addition, development, and departure of individual members and sometimes by the demands of the culture and changes in the environment (Hill and Mattessich, 1979). The system is established with the marriage of mates and lasts until that bond is dissolved by

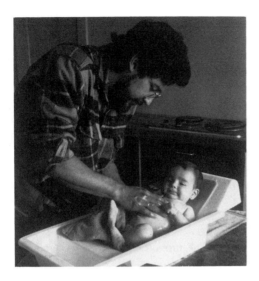

Some businesses have begun to offer paternity leave, a development that could lead to major changes in the lives of many young couples.

divorce or death. Within the system, each member has a series of roles that at any time are determined by age and gender and by relatedness. Each family goes through stages of development that occur whenever new members are added by birth or adoption, present members leave to take jobs or establish their own families, or any family member moves into a new role, as when a child becomes an adolescent.

Because the family is a system, a change in any of its parts changes all the other parts. When the first child is born, wife and husband acquire the new roles of mother and father. The addition of a second child shifts the relationships of mother, father, and firstborn to one another and creates new relationships with the infant. Although many of the changes in family roles, such as school entry, puberty, and retirement, are age-related, others, such as divorce, are not. Family roles and structure are also affected by changes in type of residence (as from renter to homeowner), changes in status (parenthood, grandparenthood, widowhood), changes in job (through promotion or switching occupations), and historical events (depressions, wars, sweeping technological change) (Hill and Mattessich, 1979).

All families respond to the needs of their members and actively manipulate the environment so as to fill those needs, but the location of the family in historical time affects the particular way in which the family views needs and the range of possible responses. As Glenn Elder (1978) has pointed out, the basic facts of birth, sexual maturity, and death differ in their social meaning across cultures and at various times in the same culture. Social expectations tell us when ''the time is right'' for school entry, completion of education, economic independence, leaving home, marriage, childbirth, and retirement. The timetable in rural areas may differ from the timetable in small towns or in cities in the same society, just as the timetable may vary from one ethnic or socioeconomic group to the next. If society changes its expectations or the roles it assigns people at various ages, the structure and function of the family may change (Hill and Mattessich, 1979).

Another factor that affects the family system is the age of husband and wife at each step of family life (Elder, 1978). A marriage begun at the age of 23 is a different experience from a marriage begun at the age of 35. Age also affects the experience of parenthood.

When children come early in life, neither husband nor wife is likely to be established in a career, the couple has few assets, and economic constraints on the young family are likely to be sharp. When child-bearing is postponed, the family's situation is likely to be comparatively secure, lessening economic pressures.

Cohort differences affect family life just as they affect cognition and emotional development. A historical event affects each cohort at a different stage in the members' careers. The experience of World War II, for example, had very different effects on the lives of the cohort that was in high school during the early 1940s, the cohort whose members fought in the war or worked in the factories, and the cohort whose sons were on the battlefields. Historical events can make it easier or more difficult to attain life goals, so that even if social expectations remain the same, the opportunities for reaching those goals change (Hill and Mattessich, 1979). Today, for example, it is very difficult for a young couple to buy a first house. With fewer people able to own a home and those who do buy homes making the purchase later in life, family structure is having to adjust to a new social reality. Marriage and childbirth might be postponed, or the proportion of three-generation families may increase.

Over the past 50 years, family structures have changed in other ways. In North America, increases in life expectancy and decreases in fertility have led to the emergence of the **beanpole family,** in which there are more living generations but fewer members in each generation (Bengston, Rosenthal, and Burton, 1990). As the proportion of four- and five-generation families grows, relationships with parents, grandparents, and great-grandparents increase in duration. They may also increase in intensity, because so many years of common experiences accumulate and because there are fewer siblings, aunts, uncles, nieces, nephews, and cousins to absorb emotional investment.

Families have also become more diverse (Bengston, Rosenthal, and Burton, 1990). The growing number of teenage pregnancies has condensed some family structures so that generations are separated by only about 15 years, producing mothers and daughters who relate more like sisters and grandmothers who are thrust into a new role when "the time is wrong." Other family structures are characterized by large age gaps, in which the chronological distance between generations may dilute the strength of relationships. Childlessness has truncated some family systems, matrilineal systems have developed among unmarried women who give birth, and the cycle of divorce and remarriage has produced highly complicated family structures that have incorporated stepparents and stepgrandparents into the system.

Despite alterations in the cycle, the family continues to fulfill its primary functions. In addition to meeting its members' needs, the family serves a social purpose. It socializes children, preparing them to take on adult roles and transferring the culture from one generation to the next. Anthropologist Margaret Mead (1978) saw the transmission of culture as occurring in one of three styles: postfigurative, cofigurative, and prefigurative. In the **postfigurative culture,** at least three generations take the culture for granted. As no one questions the culture, the child also takes it for granted. Most aspects of the culture are not put into words; they are simply *there* and remain below the level of consciousness. Authority comes from the past. Tribal societies and small religious and ideological groups within larger societies are primarily postfigurative. Such cultures are stable, and the course of family life remains the same from one generation to the next.

In the **cofigurative culture,** not the past but the present is the standard. The parental generation assumes that each generation's behavior will differ from that of the previous generation, and children accept the behavior of their peers as a model. Elder peers establish standards for the young and set boundaries to their behavior. This describes the experience of immigrant groups within a postfigurative culture, whose children are socialized into the new society. Most complex societies, which have had to develop a way to incorporate change, combine cofigurative with postfigurative styles.

In the **prefigurative culture**, neither the past nor the present serves as a trustworthy guide. Society is changing so rapidly that the lessons of parents and elder peers are unreliable, and the future is unknown. Mead believed that atomic energy had thrust the world into a prefigurative state and that generations who grew up after World War II could not rely on the culture of the past. As a result, society would remain unstable until members of the post–World War II generation became grandparents, for their tradition could be passed on as a reliable guide. Members of that generation are now in middle adulthood, and some have already become grandparents.

Whether or not Mead's analysis is correct and we are now about to move out of the prefigurative style, American society has been changing rapidly since World War II. Under the influence of such factors as extended education, divorce and remarriage, early retirement, and second careers, the American life cycle has become fluid, with many role transitions (Neugarten and Neugarten, 1986). Expectations are not as rigid, and timetables are not as strict, making chronological age a less reliable guide to family events. Changes are especially apparent in our expectations concerning parenthood.

PARENTHOOD

The majority of couples eventually have children, but the course of parenthood in this country has been changing in several ways. From 1870 to 1976 the overall birth rate declined steadily, interrupted only during the decade between 1947 and 1957, when the post–World War II flurry known as the baby boom yielded a fertility rate of 3.7 births per woman. Two more decades of declining birth rates bottomed out in 1976, when the national fertility rate dropped to 1.74. For the next decade, the birth rate remained relatively stable, but in 1988 it began to rise again, and by 1989 the national fertility rate reached 2.0009 (*Reporter Dispatch*, 1990b).

Thanks to cheap, reliable contraceptives, births are more likely to be planned than those in previous generations. Births are also coming somewhat later than once was customary as an increasing number of women are establishing themselves in careers before they pause to have a child. In 1988, 42 percent of married women between the ages of 20 and 24 and 29 percent of married women between the ages of 25 and 29 were childless. Twenty-eight years earlier, only 24 percent of the 20- to 24-year-old married woman and 13 percent of the 25- to 29-year-olds had never given birth (U.S. Bureau of the Census, 1990). As a result of this trend, the major increase in births has come among women in their thirties—a shift that is likely to continue. In 1975 only 34 percent of women between the ages of 30 and 34 said that they were planning to have a child someday, but in 1988, 54 percent said they were still planning to have a child (Berke, 1989).

One consequence of reduced family size is a decrease in the proportion of the life span that parents devote to child rearing. Most of the increase in child-free years comes during middle age, when children have become independent. When a woman has only two children, her child-bearing period is usually compressed, so that she is younger when her last child leaves home. Those who postpone childbirth until their thirties rarely have more than one child (Kotre and Hall, 1990).

The proportion of mothers employed outside the home has increased, especially among women with preschool children. In 1988, 57 percent of all married mothers with children younger than six years were in the labor force, compared with only 19 percent in 1960 (U.S. Bureau of Labor Statistics, 1989). The rate of outside employment was slightly lower among separated (53 percent) mothers of young children but considerably higher among divorced mothers (70 percent).

The high divorce rate has increased the number of one-parent families. As the 1980s came to a close, more than 15 million children (25 percent of those younger than 18 years) lived with one parent—usually the mother. The Census Bureau predicts that 60 percent of today's children will spend at least some time in a one-parent family (Kotre and Hall, 1990). Some of those children will eventually have a stepparent. Almost 7 million children were living in stepfamilies in 1985, and demographers predict that one-third of all children born during the 1980s will spend part of their childhood with a stepparent in the home (Kantrowitz and Wingert, 1990).

Because of these trends, talking about the traditional nuclear household, in which the mother stays at home and the father is the sole breadwinner, means talking about a minority of American families. Life in today's family cannot be understood without considering employed mothers, stepparents, and single-parent households.

PREGNANCY AND CHILDBIRTH

The experience of parenthood begins before the birth of a child. From the first awareness of conception, relationships within the family begin to shift, as the couple makes psycho-

The marital relationship begins to change during pregnancy, as couples make psychological and practical provisions for their expected child.

logical and practical provisions to accommodate a new member within the family system. Because pregnancy requires the pair to make a transition from romantic to committed love, it may be a stressful period for some, but for others it is a time of personal growth. Couples who know what to expect during pregnancy, childbirth, and a baby's first year generally cope best with all aspects of the process (Entwisle and Doering, 1981).

Even when the partners eagerly anticipate the birth, they may harbor negative emotions. The woman often worries whether the baby will be normal, about the physical changes her body is undergoing, how she will be able to give birth, and how the process will change her. She worries about changes in her work and home roles and how motherhood will affect her relationship with her husband and other important adults in her life. The man frequently worries about how the birth will change his life and his relationship with his wife. He may be envious of his wife's ability to reproduce and feel excluded from the intimate and mysterious process of birth, while at the same time feel burdened with an overwhelming sense of responsibility. Couples handle such feelings most successfully when they can share their concerns with each other or with some confidant (Osofsky and Osofsky, 1984).

The marital relationship has clear effects on the course of pregnancy. Among 100 middle-class couples who participated in a longitudinal study (Grossman, Eichler, and Winickoff, 1980), women with high marital satisfaction or egalitarian marriages had fewer physical and emotional symptoms—as did those who had wanted the baby at the time of conception. Other studies indicate that emotional symptoms during pregnancy are related to a woman's earlier relationship with her own mother, the effects of pregnancy on her life and work patterns, her ability to adjust to them, and the amount of support provided by her husband, family, and community (Osofsky and Osofsky, 1984).

Discrepancies in sexual desires and curtailment of sexual activity may add to marital tension. Some men say there is no change in their sexual desire during their wives' pregnancies, some say their desire increases, and others say their desire wanes or disappears entirely. According to Susan White and Kenneth Reamy (1982), in large studies of pregnancy, most—but not all—women report a progressive decline in sexual interest, sexual activity, and orgasm during pregnancy. However, most women also say that they want to be cuddled and held more by their husbands. When the wife's and husband's sexual reaction to pregnancy is greatly discrepant, the result may be sexual frustration and a strained marital relationship. Wives in the longitudinal study who seemed to adapt best to labor and delivery had husbands who were satisfied with their marriages as a whole and who were content with a low level of sexual contact (Grossman, Eichler, and Winickoff, 1980).

A working woman's feelings about her job may also affect the course of her pregnancy. Among 120 pregnant employed women, those who enjoyed their work adapted well to being pregnant and were less anxious, depressed, tired, and guilty during their pregnancies than women who disliked their jobs (Newton and Modahl, 1978). Rather than finding it difficult to adapt to the idea of motherhood, women who enjoy their occupations may also enjoy their pregnancies—perhaps because they have a generally positive attitude toward life.

In a traditional hospital birth, the father is generally ignored during labor and shut out of the delivery room. When natural childbirth methods are used, the father becomes an active participant and coach. This involvement in the birth process may make it easier for a man to adjust to his new role as parent. Fathers who have such a part in childbirth afterward say that they felt their role was important (Romalis, 1981).

Once their infant is born and the joy and exhilaration that often accompany the birth are past, couples must adjust to the physical presence of the new family member. These adjustments generally require the expenditure of much time, emotion, and energy. During this period, some women develop **postpartum depression,** which includes crying jags, nightmares, and fears or worries about the baby. Although it usually lasts only a short time, some women find themselves depressed for several months.

Shifting hormone levels may play a role in this emotional reaction, but researchers have found that answers given by pregnant women to two questions were the best predictor of postpartum depression. Those who were most likely to become depressed had replied yes to the questions, ''Do you often feel that your husband (or boyfriend) does not love you?'' and ''Can you honestly say at this time that you really do not want to have a child?'' (Brody, 1983a). Women who feel this way may be especially vulnerable to the strain of adapting to the role of mother. If a woman has sole responsibility for child care, she may feel isolated, if not trapped. If she is deeply committed to her career, she may be especially vulnerable to a bout of depression. However, some researchers believe that postpartum depression may be triggered by a simple cause: lack of sleep (Laws and Schwartz, 1977). Few new mothers escape a period of weeks or months in which their sleep is interrupted several times a night.

In a longitudinal study that followed women from the last month of pregnancy until their babies were 16 months old, most women had a much more positive outlook at the close of the study than during the first few months after the birth (Fleming et al., 1990). Even so, moods early in the study correlated strongly with women's later moods; those who were the most anxious, depressed, elated, or content during pregnancy were usually the most anxious, depressed, elated, or content more than a year later. Women's positive feelings toward their babies increased steadily throughout the study, but their feelings toward their husbands followed a U-shaped curve: highest during pregnancy and 16 months after the birth, and lowest when the baby was 3 months old (Figure 12.1).

A father's adjustment to his new role has received little notice. Available studies indicate that fathers are under many of the same stresses that mothers encounter, that they feel they have lost a good share of their wives' attention, and that they tend to have trouble developing their changed role in regard to their wife and infant (Alpert and Richardson, 1980).

CHILDREN AND MARRIAGE

Parenthood is generally a stressful, but rewarding, experience. When parents were asked whether, if they could live their lives over, they would have children, 90 percent said they would (Yankelovich, 1981). Among the rewards they found in parenthood, they mentioned joy, fun, self-fulfillment, maturity, and pride. Among the stresses were restrictions on personal and economic freedom and disruption of the marital relationship. Life in a household with children is very different from life in a childless home. There is usually less conversation between the parents, and some of the spontaneity that characterizes a couple's emotional and sexual life may disappear. Depending on the situation, the care of children can either raise or lower the parents' perception of well-being.

The nature of the couple's relationship before the child's birth has a strong influence on the way both parents approach parenthood. Couples who have a close, intimate relationship are most likely to find parenthood a rewarding experience. Women in such relationships generally feel great warmth toward their babies and are sensitive to their infant's needs,

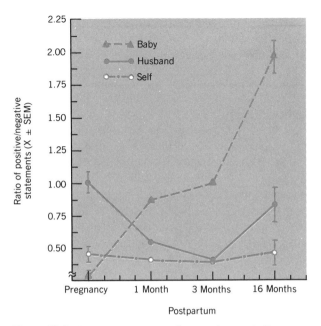

Figure 12.1 Postpartum course of women's mood. Changes across time in the proportion of positive to negative statements made in reference to the baby, husband, or self. *Source:* Fleming et al., 1990, p. 140.

perhaps because the relationship with their spouse fills their own emotional needs (Cox et al., 1989). Their husbands generally have positive attitudes toward their babies and toward their own role as parent. Other research indicates that unhappily married men may withdraw from their infants as well as from their wives (Dickstein and Parke, 1988).

Differences in parental responsibility for infant care and household responsibilities may account for a good deal of the dissatisfaction among mothers with young children. With the birth of the first child, chores tend to be divided along more traditional lines, no matter what arrangement the couple had previously established (Cowan, Coie, and Coie, 1978). If a couple has been sharing household tasks and the new mother suddenly finds herself with more work as well as the burden of child care, conflict may develop, and marital satisfaction may plummet.

A second aspect of motherhood that can reduce satisfaction arises from the mother's responsibility for organizing family life and seeing that necessary tasks are carried out. As mothers work to make the system run smoothly, they are likely to run into resistance from their children and to receive little support from their husbands for their efforts. Researchers have suggested that the situation reduces self-esteem and contributes to the depression found among mothers of young children (Maccoby, 1980).

At 44, one mother recalled her situation when the children were young:

They want what they want when they want it! There is no sense of fairness—no sense that you have to have a little peace and quiet. You're there to dispense what they want and sometimes you feel like a nothing because you're just there for everyone. I think in these darker periods you start wondering if there's any point to it. But fortunately, these feelings are more prevalent when the children are small, and looking back, I think other mothers took steps to prevent that overburdened feeling—which I didn't do (Baruch, Barnett, and Rivers, 1983, p. 89).

A third factor that affects satisfaction with motherhood is the woman's age (Figure 12.2). Among first-time mothers between the ages of 16 and 38 who were not employed outside the home, younger mothers were the least satisfied, although they generally had fewer caregiving responsibilities and more social time away from the baby than older mothers (Ragozin et al., 1982). Satisfaction increased steadily with age, and the effect was especially pronounced among mothers of babies born prematurely, perhaps because older mothers may be better equipped to handle the additional stress.

The birth of a second child requires further adjustments in family relationships. A new balance must be struck between parental and marital roles, and there is added stress involved in fitting the demands of a fourth family member to various housekeeping and child-care tasks. In a study that followed 16 families for two years after the birth of their second child (Kreppner, Paulsen, and Schuetze, 1982), researchers found that parents handled these problems in several ways. Some parents played interchangeable roles, passing the same respon-

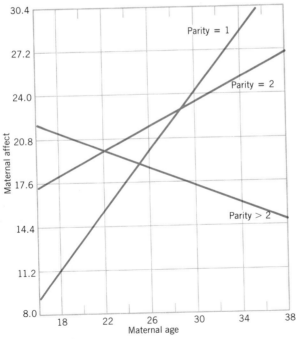

Figure 12.2 Maternal feelings and age. Among first-time mothers of young babies, the older the woman, the more pleasure she derived from the maternal role. Only among women with three or more children did younger mothers find motherhood more satisfying. In this study, maternal affect was a combination of the mother's gratification from interactions with her baby, the general emotional tone of their relationship, and her sensitivity to the baby's needs. *Source:* Ragozin et al., 1982, p. 631.

sibility back and forth, depending on the situation. Other couples divided responsibilities, with the father taking greater control of the older child and the mother devoting herself to the new baby. In other families, fathers focused on household tasks while mothers took most of the responsibility for child care. A year or so later, as the new baby emerged from babyhood, the situation changed again. Instead of seeing themselves as parents of a child and a baby, mother and father tended to see themselves as parents of "children," and they reacted on the basis of each child's personality as opposed to his or her developmental stage. Family priorities changed, and the parents' own needs and wishes began to receive attention.

Among a group of midlife women, two kinds of relationships with children, "autonomous" and "coupled" mothering, were found (Baruch, Barnett, and Rivers, 1983). In **autonomous mothering,** rewards came from seeing children as individuals instead of as extensions of the mother. Mothers felt proud of their children, enjoyed doing things with them and watching them mature, and liked the kind of people they were. An autonomous mother, a 37-year-old college administrator, described some of the rewards she got from her maternal role: "Children teach you a tremendous amount. The older they get, the more important are the questions that arise, and you have to think and rethink the issues you've grappled with before in childhood or adolescence. I look on it as a tremendous opportunity because it means I'm always growing. They're really just lovely people, each very different, and it's kind of neat for me to see how different three people can be who came out of the same gene pool" (Baruch, Barnett, and Rivers, 1983, p. 84).

In **coupled mothering,** rewards came from children's importance to the mother's sense of identity. These mothers felt that children gave meaning to their own lives and provided them with a sense of being needed; as mothers, they felt special and irreplaceable. A coupled mother described her relationship with her children: "It's the kids that keep me going, really. This is how I feel. I don't see how people can be married and not have kids. The kids are my life, that's it in a nutshell, and I live for my kids and I do things for my kids. I'm in the car running here and there. I'm always running for everybody. I can't say no" (Baruch, Barnett, and Rivers, 1983, p. 84).

Both kinds of mothers tended to derive much pleasure from their offspring, but compared with coupled mothers, autonomous mothers were higher in self-esteem, felt that they had more control over their lives, and were less likely to complain of anxiety or depression.

Youngsters have such a powerful influence on family life that researchers have suggested marital satisfaction is determined by the presence, number, and age of a couple's children (Rollins and Galligan, 1978). These factors are believed to affect the way each parent perceives the quality of the spouse's performance as husband or wife, the sacrifices each makes in carrying out family roles, and the quality of each parent's own performance as wife or husband. In today's world, when two out of every three mothers are employed outside the home, occupation may be as important a factor as the number and ages of children.

WORKING PARENTS

Families in which both parents have outside employment have become the norm in the United States. The proportion in which the mother has no outside employment has shrunk steadily, dropping from just under 43 percent among mothers with babies and preschoolers

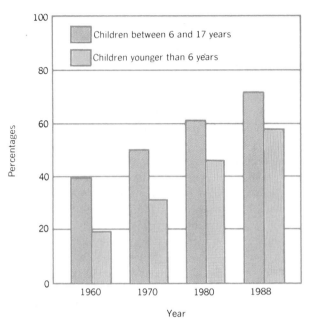

Figure 12.3 Employed married mothers. *Source:* U.S. Bureau of the Census, 1989.

to 28 percent among married mothers of schoolaged children (U.S. Bureau of the Census, 1989) (Figure 12.3).

Objections to maternal employment come from those who believe a small child requires the presence of a full-time mother. Most of the evidence, however, indicates that maternal employment is not detrimental to young children (Clarke-Stewart, 1989; Hoffman, 1989). Yet lingering doubts about day care have led some parents to work different shifts. More than a million American families have adopted the split-shift approach to day care, and in most cases the husband works nights and the wife works days (Dullea, 1983). For example, Patricia Craemer, who works as a reservation agent for Delta Air Lines, arrives home each day 20 minutes before her husband Richard leaves for his shift as a mechanic for the same airline. Richard says, "We don't want anybody else taking care of Erika. Nobody can do that better than her parents" (p. B12). Shift work may affect the marital relationship. Some couples find that their relationship improves because they value their fleeting time together, but others find that their sex life suffers (Dullea, 1983). Shift workers encompass a minority of families with employed mothers.

Among nonshift-working parents of three to six year olds, the mother's employment did not affect the nature of the relationship between children and their parents (Stuckey, McGhee, and Bell, 1982). Each parent tended to adhere to a gender-typical parental role, with the mother spending more time on caregiving and quiet play and the father spending more time on active play. When the mother's employment did not match parental attitudes toward working mothers, however, both parents tended to be dissatisfied. Other studies have produced similar patterns and indicate that satisfied mothers have more positive interaction with their children than dissatisfied mothers (Houser and Beckman, 1980).

When both parents work, the question of who handles "the second shift" inevitably arises. Sociologist Arlie Hochschild (1989) describes the second shift as consisting of the additional jobs of child-rearing and household tasks that have traditionally fallen to women. In the course of a year, it amounts to an extra month of 24-hour days. As women's outside employment has become the rule rather than the exception, men have begun to assume some of the household tasks and responsibility for children, but rarely is the work shared equally. Among the families Hochschild studied, only 18 percent of the men shared the work equally; another 21 percent did a substantial amount—more than a third but less than half; and 61 percent did even less. Men with egalitarian views of gender roles in marriage were most likely to assume an equal share of second-shift duties (Table 12.1). Traditional men, who identified with their jobs, expected their wives to identify with home and family, and believed men should exert the most power in the marriage, helped a moderate amount. The largest group, men with transitional views, supported their wives' working but expected them to take the major responsibility at home; these men did the least work on the second shift. Couples who shared the second shift generally had the happiest marriages.

When women receive little assistance on the second shift, they often find themselves suffering from role overload. Some women cope by cutting back at work, as did Nancy Weston, a bank vice-president and mother, who dropped back to 25 hours a week when her daughter was two years old (Kantrowitz, 1988). Weston took a 40 percent cut in pay but believes that the move was a good idea: "I like to feel that I'm really a fast-tracker," she says, but "I'm much happier. I feel like my life is balanced" (p. 64). Like Weston, one-third of mothers who work have chosen part-time work. Among the other two-thirds, many cope with overload by cutting back at home, discovering that a number of "necessary" tasks are not as necessary as they once thought (Pleck, 1985). They may cook less elaborate meals, clean less often, or withdraw from community responsibilities. Most women also cut back on personal needs: they give up reading, hobbies, television, visiting friends, exercise, and time alone (Hochschild, 1989).

The drudgery of the second shift does not seem to make women as unhappy as staying home does. In general, employed mothers are happier, higher in self-esteem, have less depression and fewer psychosomatic symptoms, and show fewer signs of stress than mothers who stay at home (Hochschild, 1989; Hoffman, 1986). The least happy women are those who stay home but would rather be in the workplace. Among mothers of eight- and twelve-month-old infants, most of these women showed symptoms of mild depression (Hock and DeMeis, 1990). During middle adulthood, women who scored highest on all measures of well-being had high-prestige jobs, were married, and had children (Baruch, Bennett, and

Table 12.1 **MEN AND THE SECOND SHIFT**[a]

	Shared	*Moderate Amount*	*Little*
Egalitarian men	70%	30%	0
Transitional men	3%	10%	87%
Traditional men	22%	44%	33%

Source for data: Hochschild, 1989.

[a]When both parents work, the man's participation in child-rearing and household tasks is strongly affected by his gender ideology.

Rivers, 1983). Juggling three roles, they were happier than women who faced the strains of fewer roles (either nonemployed wives or single employed women).

Maternal employment is part of modern family life. Because it diminishes rigid sex-role stereotypes, it may equip children to meet their adult roles more effectively. And because employment gives women added sources of identity and self-esteem, it may make it easier for them to allow their growing children to develop autonomy.

SINGLE PARENTS

The number of parents without partners continues to rise, so that an increasing number of adults can expect to spend some time rearing their children by themselves. Although in most cases the single parent is a divorced mother with custody, sometimes the mother has never married, the divorced father has custody, the absent partner has died, or the single parent (mother or father) has adopted a child. In 1989 more than 6 million women and about 955,000 men were heads of households composed of their own children younger than 18 years (U.S. Bureau of the Census, 1989).

An increasing number of single women in their thirties are having children by choice—either arranging for artificial insemination, applying for adoption, or asking a friend to father a child. Most of these women are middle-class professionals in their thirties or early forties. When she reached 40, Marilyn Levin, a psychotherapist whose biological clock was ticking loudly, looked for a way to start a family. "I tried therapy. I did the singles scene. I gave finding a relationship top priority. It was unproductive. Finally I said, 'That's it,' and went ahead on my own" (Seligmann, 1990, p. 44). She opted for artificial insemination and at the age of 45 has a 2 1/2-year-old daughter. Marilyn Levin belongs to a minority of single mothers, however. The majority of mothers who bear children without a partner are younger women, many of them adolescents, and they have fewer financial resources and less education than Levin. Their children are less likely to be the result of a deliberate choice.

Most of what we know about relationships in the one-parent home comes from studies of divorced, middle-class mothers and their children. But no matter what the structure of the one-parent family, many of its problems have nothing to do with gender or the marital status of the parent.

In all one-parent families, a single person is responsible for dealing with all tasks and demands that are ordinarily shared by two parents. Having to take full responsibility for meal preparation, cleaning, home and car maintenance, financial management, child care, and meeting children's emotional needs produces more problems for the lone mother or father than any other aspect of the single-parent role. After interviewing more than 200 separated, divorced, widowed, and married parents, Robert Weiss (1979) found that children are more likely to help out in single-parent families. They take care of some household tasks, shoulder extra responsibilities, and often participate in major household decisions.

Some of the problems that beset single parents cannot be handled by turning to the children. The single parent may be lonely, lack a sexual partner, have no source of emotional support, have nowhere to turn in emergencies, and find his or her social life sharply curtailed. Many single parents work at building up support networks to help with social and emotional problems. They turn to their own parents and relatives, the other parent, friends, lovers, counselors, and such groups as Parents Without Partners.

The responsibilities of single parenthood even affect performance on the job. Child care limits job mobility, cuts into the parent's working hours and earnings, changes work priorities, and hampers job transfers. It also restricts the kind of work the parent does, the possibility of promotion, and relations with coworkers and supervisors (Keshet and Rosenthal, 1978). An employer's request that they work overtime can be highly stressful, and parents who refuse to work extra hours often feel they have jeopardized their standing with the company and made their coworkers resentful. The 47-year-old director of social work at a New York hospital who is the mother of a 12-year-old daughter explained, ''The worst thing is the fear of what will happen if I can't find anybody. It's a desperate feeling. If I can't reach someone, a friend or a neighborhood teenager, I'd have to either leave work or decide it's OK for Katie to be alone until I get there. But I don't like for her to be home alone'' (Elder, 1989).

Despite the problems that accompany the single-parent role, it has many rewards. Single parents are often closer to their children than are parents in intact homes, and child–parent interactions are more open and cover a broader range of situations. Single parents may have additional responsibilities, but they also tend to feel proud and happy about their accomplishments. Often they develop new aspects of their personality, as women are forced to become more self-reliant and men are forced to become more nurturant.

STEPPARENTS

When divorced women and men remarry, the ceremony often creates stepparents. In 1988 about 11 percent of this country's children were living in a home with a stepparent, and it has been predicted that about 35 percent of today's children will spend part of their childhood with a stepparent (Child Trends, 1989; Glick, 1984). Because society has not developed expectations for the role of stepparent, men and women who suddenly find themselves cast in this role have few guidelines.

In most cases, children live with their mothers, so that the role of the stepfather has received the greater share of attention. According to Judith Wallerstein and Sandra Blakeslee (1989), a stepfather is like a main character in a play who arrives in the middle of the second act. ''He may be welcomed as rescuer, rejected as alien, loved as potential provider and source of love and affection, resented as an object of envy, or hated as a potential rival'' (pp. 245–246). Among the 113 children followed by Wallerstein and Blakeslee for ten years after their parents' divorce, the age and sex of the children had an enormous influence on relationships with stepfathers. Few stepfathers ever developed close relationships with children who were older than nine years of age at the time of the parents' divorce, and stepfathers tended to find it easier to develop close relationships with stepdaughters than with stepsons. Stepfathers who waited to impose discipline until they had developed an affectionate, trusting relationship with the children generally fared best. Cross-sectional studies of younger children show a different pattern. Stepfathers often develop warm relationships with very young boys, but generally find their young stepdaughters hanging back (Clingempeel and Segal, 1986).

Stepmothers seem to develop warmer relationships with stepchildren when they have had a lengthy prior acquaintance with them. In one study (Clingempeel and Segal, 1986), the longer the stepmother and the biological father had lived together (both before and after marriage), the warmer the relationship between the children and their stepmother.

Relationships between stepparents and stepchildren are sometimes complicated by the fact that each parent has children from a former marriage. In such cases adjustment calls for multiple shifts in roles and relationships. Family structure becomes most intricate when the children can be divided into "his, hers, and ours." When both parents have children from a former marriage, marital quality (as measured by both self-report and observations of interaction between the spouses) is lower than when only the wife has children from her former marriage (Clingempeel, 1981). Conflicting loyalties on the part of the stepfather, who has to divide his time and attention between his biological children (who live with his former wife) and his stepchildren, may be responsible for the lowered marital quality found in this study.

In all stepparent families, marriages in which former spouses were seen a few times each month were happiest (Clingempeel, 1981). When former spouses were seen too often (at least once a week), the frequent contact, together with the lack of any social guidelines for such roles as stepfather, noncustodial parent, and former spouse, may have placed the new marriage under so much strain that it never became solid. When former spouses were seen infrequently (less than once a month), marital quality also suffered. The reason for this effect is uncertain, but the researcher suggests that when there is very little contact with a former spouse, children may become resentful that they are being denied membership in their other biological family. That resentment may erode their relations with their stepfathers, ultimately affecting the relationship between husband and wife.

THE EMPTY NEST

Eventually, children grow up and leave home, taking at least partial responsibility for their own support. When the last child has departed, parents are left with an "empty nest," a situation that once was believed to be especially difficult for parents. Textbooks sometimes discussed the **empty nest syndrome** as if it were an expected part of adult development and as if all parents grieved when their children left home. Men were supposed to find the situation less traumatic because their occupations provided a major source of meaning in their lives. After two decades of a life centered around children, women who lost this focus were thought to be ripe for a bout with depression. And when menopause and the empty nest coincided, as they often do, a crisis was seen as virtually inevitable.

Then Bernice Neugarten (1970) and her coworkers studied midlife women, comparing those with all their children home, those who were in the transitional stage (having launched some of their offspring) and those with empty nests. The study indicated that, instead of causing a stressful period, the empty nest was a time of life when satisfaction was greater than in earlier stages of parenthood. Coping with the problems of children at home appeared to be more taxing than the emptiness that followed the children's departure. The notion that women who were not employed outside the home would be especially vulnerable to the empty nest syndrome also failed to hold up. Home- and community-oriented women displayed even greater satisfaction than work-oriented women. The absence of the empty nest syndrome in this study is not an isolated finding. Studies consistently find that morale tends to be higher among women whose children have left home than among those who still have a full nest (Cooper and Gutmann, 1987). Most empty nest women say that they looked forward to their children's departure. The minority of women who are unhappy when the children leave generally have a history of emotional problems (Lowenthal and Chiriboga, 1972).

Most parents find that the departure of their grown children brings them new freedom and an increased satisfaction with marriage.

It is not difficult to discover why parents fail to be devastated by the departure of their offspring. Unless they are footing the bill for one or more college educations, disposable income suddenly rises. Time expands as parents no longer have to supervise children, and as laundry, cleaning, marketing, and cooking chores shrink. Wife and husband once again have the privacy they enjoyed as newlyweds, so that intimacy can flourish and sexuality can be spontaneous. Travel no longer must be scheduled around school vacations. Among a group of midlife women, almost every one described the departure of her children with a sense of relief. A nonemployed, middle-class, 50-year-old mother of three said, ''When the youngest one was ready to move out of the house, I was right there helping him pack. We love having the children live in the area, and we love seeing them and the grandchildren, but I don't need for any of them to live in this house ever again. I've had as much as I ever need or want of being tied down with children'' (Rubin, 1979, p. 16). In recent years, the freedom of the empty nest has been constricted by the return of adult children. As we will see in Chapter 15, a changing economic climate has driven an increasing number of adult children back to the shelter of the nest.

The effect of children's departure does not, of course, depend solely on the relationship between parent and child. The marital relationship is likely to have a powerful effect on satisfaction in the empty nest. When husband and wife have stayed together only for the ''sake of the children,'' the empty nest may be torn apart by divorce. When husband and wife care deeply for each other, their new privacy may lead to a second honeymoon. Some couples may develop separate lives, living together amicably but without great affection while each follows his or her own interests. The diversity of marital style during the empty nest period may be greater than at any other time (Troll, Miller, and Atchley, 1979).

As with other life transitions, timing is important in determining the effects of the empty nest. When children leave home at what parents perceive as the ''right time,'' the transition is likely to be smooth. But the empty nest can lead to emotional turmoil when a child leaves too early, as when a 15 year old runs away. When children fail to leave, the level of family stress may mount. One angry, bewildered father tried to explain his situation, saying, ''Last night we had a confrontation. . . . A disgust on my part for a twenty-year-old not in school, not working, not putting anything into the house. . . . It's all taking . . . food, car, clothing'' (Hagestad, 1984). Parents in this man's situation often have a sense of personal failure.

Perhaps our view of the devastating impact of the empty home has grown from our perception of the typical family as one in which the mother is a homemaker with no outside employment, a person whose identity depends on the roles of wife and mother. But even among married women who were between 45 and 64 in 1960, 36 percent had a job outside the home; and among women of the same age in 1988, 52.7 percent were employed outside the home (U.S. Bureau of the Census, 1990). As the identity and interests of more and more women have a broader base than home, children, and spouse, it would seem increasingly unlikely that the departure of children would lead to an emotional crisis.

The final launching of children is no surprise to parents. The empty nest is an expected state of family life, and parents begin to prepare for it long before the day their last child departs. Parent–child relationships continue, and bonds of affection and support are maintained. According to one woman, the empty nest is surrounded by telephone wires (Troll, Miller, and Atchley, 1979).

GRANDPARENTHOOD AND GREAT-GRANDPARENTHOOD

Once the nest is empty and grown children have become parents themselves, family relationships change yet again. Parents become grandparents, a role that usually comes when people are in their forties and fifties. The stereotypical view of white-haired grandparents, with grandmother dispensing comfort and cookies and grandfather rocking on the front porch as he whittles toys for grandchildren, bears little resemblance to reality. Today's grandparents are likely to be in the prime of their careers; the chances are good that both grandparents go off to work each morning.

Becoming a grandparent in middle adulthood is nothing new; in 1900 people became grandparents at about the same time they do now. But when people in 1900 became grandparents, they were still absorbed in the business of rearing their own children. In 1900 about half of all women in their early fifties had children under eighteen; by 1980 only one-fourth still had fledglings in the nest (Cherlin and Furstenberg, 1986). Smaller families, born at an earlier age, mean that today's grandparents are unlikely to be dividing their identity and attention between two generations of young children, so that among today's adults with an increased life expectancy, grandparenthood has emerged as a lengthy period of life that is distinct from parenthood (Bengston, Rosenthal, and Burton, 1990). In today's beanpole family, a grandparent may know her or his grandchildren as infants, adolescents, young adults, and parents. Thus, the once rare role of great-grandparent is becoming increasingly common.

Because increased life expectancy has created four—or even five—living generations, grandparents may not be the family elders but an intermediate generation. About 50 percent of adults past the age of 65 have great-grandchildren, and 20 percent of the women who die after the age of 80 are great-great-grandmothers—matriarchs in five-generation families (Hagestad, 1986; 1988). In families where teenage pregnancy is the rule, a woman may be a grandchild and a grandparent at the same time. While researching such families, sociologists found one seven-generation family in which the oldest member, the great-great-great-

great grandmother was 91, and the youngest grandmother was only 34 (Burton and Bengston, 1985). Among the growing group of women who delay child-bearing until their late thirties and early forties, grandmotherhood will arrive later—when they are in their sixties, or even older. That will make them grandparents at about the time most of today's older adults become great-grandparents—during their late sixties and early seventies (Doka and Mertz, 1988).

Increased life expectancy has affected grandparenthood in another way. Today more children have living grandparents, because there are more older people, creating a larger pool of prospective grandparents. It is no longer uncommon for children to have all four grandparents alive throughout their childhood.

The prevalence of divorce may also affect the experience of grandparenthood. The parent of the adult child who loses custody of the children may find contact with these grandchildren so restricted that opportunity to be actively involved in their lives is lost (Bengston, Rosenthal, and Burton, 1990). The pattern of divorce and remarriage has complicated relations with grandchildren in another way. When young divorced parents remarry, as they are likely to do within three years of the divorce, children often find themselves with four sets of grandparents. For example, one-third of all grandparents interviewed by researchers had at least one stepgrandchild (Cherlin and Furstenberg, 1986). Stepgrandparents enter children's lives in some way, and no one knows just how this abundance of grandparents will affect relations between grandparents and grandchildren.

PATTERNS OF GRANDPARENTHOOD

The age span of grandparents—and grandchildren—is so large, the grandparent–grandchild relationship so varied, and the research so scanty that sweeping generalizations about these relationships are impossible. Ethnic group, religion, socioeconomic level, personality, and child custody also affect the relationship. Grandparents have no prescribed function, and so they can relate to a grandchild in any way they please. The same grandparent may develop a different kind of relationship with each grandchild.

In one of the first studies of grandparents, Bernice Neugarten and Karol Weinstein (1964) discerned five different styles among middle-class grandparents. Grandparents who adopted the *formal style* carefully separated themselves from the child-rearing role and offered no advice. They were interested in their grandchildren, providing special treats and indulging them, but never played surrogate parent. Grandparents who adopted the *fun-seeking style* played with their grandchildren, enjoying them as a source of leisure activity, and cultivated an informal relationship. *Distant* grandparents were benevolent but remote. They had only fleeting contact with their grandchildren, emerging at such occasions as Christmas and birthdays and then disappearing. An occasional grandmother became a *surrogate parent*, a style that developed when the mother worked and the grandmother became primary caregiver. Finally, a few authoritarian grandfathers acted as a *reservoir of family wisdom*, with the grandfather dispensing skills or resources and the parents playing a subordinate role.

More recently, Andrew Cherlin and Frank Furstenberg (1986) concluded that grandparenthood could be described with only three styles: companionate, which characterized 55 percent of the grandparents they interviewed; remote, which characterized 29 percent; and involved, which characterized the remaining 16 percent. **Companionate grandparents** saw the grandchild at least once every two or three months, and their relationship had an affectionate, informal quality. (They seem to resemble fun-loving grandparents.) **Remote grand-parents** tended to see their grandchild infrequently, and their interactions were formal and reserved. (They seem to resemble both formal and distant grandparents.) **Involved grand-parents** also saw the grandchild at least once every two or three months, and the relationship was characterized by frequent exchanges of service (helping each other with errands, chores, and so forth) and by parentlike behavior, in which the grandchild consulted the grandparent concerning important decisions, exchanged ideas, talked over problems, received advice, and was sometimes disciplined. (Involved grandparents seem to resemble surrogate parents, but Cherlin and Furstenberg found some grandfathers in this category.)

Age and geographic distance are powerful determinants of a grandparent's style. Older grandparents—those in their late sixties and seventies—tend to adopt formal or remote styles of grandparenthood, whereas younger grandparents are more likely to be fun-loving, companate, or involved grandparents. However, this relationship may not be due as much to the age of the grandparent as to the age of the grandchild (Cherlin and Furstenberg, 1986). By the time grandparents near the end of their sixties, most of their grandchildren are adolescents or young adults, and the companionate, fun-seeking relationship may no longer be possible. No matter what the age of the grandchild, without frequent contact the involved grandparent style is unlikely to emerge. Most of the involved grandparents saw their grandchildren nearly every day, and most of the remote grandparents tended to be separated from their grandchildren by geographical distance.

Great-grandparents most often adopt a remote style with their great-grandchildren, in good part because of diminished strength and energy. One great-grandmother explained that she had passed the responsibility of grandparenthood on to her own children. ''When you're a grandparent, you love 'em, you're glad to have them come, you fix 'em food, do things for 'em, because they're precious to you,'' she said. ''When you're a great-grandparent, you're older and you can't do as much. It's different'' (Wentowski, 1985, p. 594). Among one group of great-grandparents, only a third had a close relationship with one or more great-grandchildren (Doka and Mertz, 1988). In every case, the great-grandparent lived within 25 miles of the great-grandchild.

SATISFACTION WITH GRANDPARENTHOOD

The majority of adults adjust easily to grandparenthood and find a great deal of pleasure in the relationship. Those who are less positive about the relationship tend to be younger than 50 or older than 80. Perhaps this is another instance of people's perceptions of the ''right time'' for life events. When women become grandparents ''too soon,'' an event that occurs when both they and their daughters give birth during adolescence, they may resent the role. Among ''early grandmothers'' (ages 25 to 38) in one study, 83 percent rejected the role (Burton and Bengston, 1985). These women had been forced into adult status as teenagers, before they had a clear sense of who they were or what they might do with their lives. Then, still feeling like young women and often trying to develop intimate relationships with men, they suddenly found an ''old-age'' role (in their perception) thrust on them. As one 31-year-old grandmother expressed it, ''I'm really a grandmother in name only. . . . You may think I'm a terrible person for feeling this way but I can't help it. I am just too young to be a grandmother. That's something for old folks, not for me'' (Burton and Bengston,

1985, p. 68). At the other end of the chronological scale, an 80-year-old grandparent may feel too old to have to bother with the noise and disorder that are a feature of child's play.

Few grandmothers are eager to babysit, and many resent being asked. But among those who live nearby, except for grandparents who are still active in their careers, most babysit for younger grandchildren. Their vocal complaints indicate ambivalent feelings. One grandmother, who acted as babysitter so that her daughter could work in a shop owned by the grandmother, said, "Sometimes they get under my skin, but it's like an abscess, you'll miss it once it's gone, or a toothache [turns to granddaughter], huh, Janice?... Hey, I'm a prisoner, you know, I'm the dumping ground [laughs]. You know, you always think, boy, when my children are grown I can have a decent rug and decent furniture. Oh no, you start all over again with grandchildren" (Cherlin and Furstenberg, 1986, pp. 85–86).

Some grandmothers find themselves taking full responsibility for grandchildren; they become "skip-generation" parents. When a daughter cannot manage the parental role, whether because of extreme youth, drugs, alcohol, or abuse from a cohabitor, grandmothers often assume the maternal role. At 62, Ruth Rench gained custody of her five-year-old granddaughter, who had been sexually abused by one of her mother's male friends. Rench and her granddaughter, now eight, are not an unusual family; 95 skip-generation families make up the Fort Worth, Texas, chapter of Grandparents Raising Grandchildren (Seligmann, 1990). In families where adolescent pregnancy is the custom, "early" grandmothers may refuse to step in, and so the maternal role falls to the great-grandmother. One "skip-two generations" parent, a woman of 56, complained bitterly, "My daughter and granddaughter keep making these babies and expect me to take care of them. I ain't no nursemaid; I ain't old; and I ain't dead yet" (Burton and Bengston, 1985, p. 61).

For the majority of adults, grandparenthood seems to follow a three-stage career (Cherlin and Furstenberg, 1986). The first stage, which one grandmother called "the fat part" of grandparenthood, covers the years from the grandchild's birth until adolescence, which most grandparents prefer and remember most fondly. The second stage covers the grandchild's adolescence, when the relationship becomes less fun-seeking and more formal, even though grandparent and grandchild may share such leisure activities as watching television, reminiscing, and joking. Some grandparents feel that the second stage is a "cold spell in an otherwise warm climate." The final stage begins as grandchildren reach adulthood, when most marry and eventually have their own children. Among a group of young adult grandchildren, most expressed strong affection, respect, and closeness for at least one grandparent (Kennedy, 1990). They also expected their grandparents to be liaisons between them and parents, to provide personal advice, to understand them when no one else did, to act as a role model, or to be somebody whose occupation they might choose to imitate.

The gender of parent and grandparent also makes a difference, perhaps because of women's role as kin-keeper. Grown grandchildren usually feel closer to grandmothers than to grandfathers, and closer to their maternal grandmother than to their paternal grandmother (Kennedy, 1990; Matthews and Sprey, 1985).

Being a grandparent provides a variety of satisfactions, and after studying nearly 300 grandparents, Helen Kivnick (1982) found that the rewards and meanings inherent in the role could be grouped into five categories. *Spoil* included the lenient attitudes grandparents display toward their grandchildren and the opportunity to indulge them. *Centrality* included the central importance of activities with grandchildren, the sense that being a grandparent gave meaning to life, and the incorporation of the role in the person's identity. *Valued elder* described the role of resource person for grandchildren and the concern that children would remember them when grown. *Reinvolvement with personal past* included the pleasure of reliving earlier experiences through relationships with grandchildren and reminiscences about the grandparent's own grandparents. And *immortality through clan* described the grandparent's sense of personal immortality through descendants.

Great-grandparents find their situation similarly rewarding and emotionally fulfilling, with most of the great-grandparents in one study emphasizing the sense of personal and family renewal they derived from the role (Doka and Mertz, 1988). One great-grandparent said, "Seeing them grow keeps me young" (p. 193). Many found happiness in the diversion the great-grandchildren brought into their lives ("I enjoy the contact and attention"), and a few found the major satisfaction of great-grandparenthood was its function as a mark of longevity ("I never thought I'd live to see it") (p. 194).

Young grandchildren have added benefits for grandparents and great-grandparents (Hagestad, 1981). Interactions with grandchildren give older adults opportunities to break norms regarding age-appropriate behavior. They can be "foolish," giggling and playing games that their age and dignity would normally forbid. The hugs and cuddles that children expect (or endure) from their grandparents also give older adults opportunities for touching in a culture that restricts most expressions of physical intimacy.

Most grandchildren seem to enjoy their grandparents. A special bond may develop in which positive relations can develop without any of the friction that is often present between parents and children. Grandparents can enjoy and indulge their grandchildren without feeling the degree of responsibility that may burden the parent. The added perspective on life that grandparents have, now that they have survived the parental role, may also contribute to the special quality of the relationship.

A special bond often develops between grandparent and grandchild, a bond that lacks the friction characteristic of many parent–child relationships.

The relationship a grandchild develops with a grandparent stretches far into the future, for it appears that the way the child experiences this relationship affects the way he or she relates to grandchildren half a century later (Kivnick, 1982). Yet the grandparent–grandchild relationship is largely controlled by the intermediate parent generation. After a divorce, relationships are often strengthened when grandparents provide emotional and material aid to the custodial parent—usually their daughter (Cherlin and Furstenberg, 1986). In other cases, however, the bonds are ruptured, when the custodial parent (usually a daughter-in-law) moves away or refuses to allow access to the grandchild. According to Helen Kivnick (1982), this deprivation could affect children two generations later when the deprived grandchild has difficulty establishing a rewarding relationship with his or her own grandchild.

RELATIONS WITH AGING PARENTS

Contrary to popular belief, the elderly are not isolated from their adult children. Most old people have frequent contact with their grown children, and the family provides them with consistent emotional and social support as well as with aid in times of crisis. Yet even old people who have close relationships with their children tend to accept the myth that the family has become alienated from its older members. After describing their own deep involvement with their children and grandchildren, many older adults say, ''But, of course, my family is different'' (Shanas, 1979). As we will see, the relationship between adult children and their parents may be closer than it has ever been.

TODAY'S FAMILY IN PERSPECTIVE

Myth has it that our forebears lived in three-generation families, that grandparents were venerated, and that, by comparison, today's family is a cold, isolated place—no longer a haven in a heartless world. A review of historical research indicates that the three-generation family has always been rare, primarily because few adults lived long enough to see their grandchildren born, and many of those who did lived only a few years. Older adults did seem to be venerated, but there were few of them, and those who survived usually held the family pursestrings. In Colonial America, fathers held onto the land so tightly that many sons had to postpone their own marriage for years. Parental control even extended to the choice of children's marital partners. Before the American Revolution, for example, daughters nearly always married in the order of their birth—a practice that declined in the nineteenth century—and sons whose fathers died before they were 60 years old married at an earlier age than sons whose fathers lived to be 60. According to Andrew Cherlin (1983), relationships between parent and child in Colonial America seem to have been relatively cold and distant, with the authoritarian position of fathers creating considerable tension between generations.

The tension appears to have lasted into the nineteenth century, when fathers who relinquished control of the land or family business generally retained the title or else set up elaborate legal provisions for the support of themselves and their wives. Three-generation families were indeed more common in the nineteenth century than they are today, but they usually involved grandparents who could contribute to the household economy. In nineteenth-century England, for example, grandmothers who could act as primary caregivers or

♦ *Adulthood in Today's World*

ARE CHILDREN ABUSING THEIR PARENTS?

One night Betty's 23-year-old son held a knife to her throat and threatened to kill her. That incident started a pattern of physical abuse that went on for years. Betty says of her son, now 52, "All he wants to do is beat me up" (Martin, 1989). Over a five-year period, workers in the Bronx (New York) Elder Abuse Project have uncovered a number of such cases: vicious battering, extortion of money, sexual assault. In one case, a son killed his father's guide dog in order to make the older man completely dependent. Such reports of aging adults who have been beaten or shamefully mistreated by their children lead the public to assume that the problem is widespread and that the family has deteriorated past the point of no return. Yet research presents a much different picture of **elder abuse,** which refers to physical violence, chronic verbal aggression, and the neglect of aging parents or grandparents (Callahan, 1988; Pillemer and Finkelhor, 1988).

When researchers interviewed a random sample of 2000 older adults in the Boston area, they discovered that 3.2 percent had been physically abused—pushed, grabbed, shoved, hit, kicked, choked, assaulted with a gun or knife (Pillemer and Finkelhor, 1988). But when the investigators conducted in-depth interviews with these abused elders, they discovered that only 24 percent of them had been mistreated by a child—cutting the rate of parents abused

handle housework were generally welcome, and farming families might take in grandparents during the spring and summer when crops had to be planted, tended, and harvested, only to return them to the poorhouse when winter arrived (Bengston and Treas, 1980). In today's families, members are held together by emotional bonds instead of by economic needs (Hagestad, 1986). This change in the nature of the "glue" that binds families means that family ties between adults are now voluntary and thus closer, warmer, and more affectionate than the bonds between earlier generations. As the box, "Are Children Abusing Their Parents?" demonstrates, the impression created by media accounts of elder abuse is exaggerated.

The increased intensity of intergenerational ties has led some experts to predict that more than one-third of older Americans will, at some point in their lives, live with an adult child (Gatz, Bengston, and Blum, 1990). Although fewer than 5 percent of older adults now live in three-generation families, another 16 percent live in two-generation families, usually with an unmarried or childless offspring (Coward, Cutler, and Schmidt, 1989). The older the adult, the larger the proportion who reside with members of another generation of kin; just under 10 percent of adults older than 90 live in three-generation families, while 37 percent live in families of two generations.

The elderly move into a child's home only when they are poor, so sick that they cannot care for themselves, or—in a few cases—where a spouse has died. The parent who moves in is usually a mother (80 percent), and the child who provides the home is more likely to

by children to less than 1 percent. The majority of victims (58 percent) had been assaulted by a spouse, and about half (52 percent) of all victims were men, not women. In fact, men were at higher risk than women; 5.1 percent of the older men in the Boston area, compared with 2.3 of the older women, had been abused. Whether abuse came from spouse or child, its intensity was about the same, but women were generally more severely injured than men.

When a child assaults an older parent, it often turns out that the child is a mentally handicapped adult who has become caretaker of the older person by default (Callahan, 1988). In many other cases, the "caretaking" child is financially dependent on the older parent. Either way, the older person has become vulnerable, not through his or her own dependency, but through the dependency of the young or middle-aged child. Sometimes the dependency is the result of drug abuse, as in the case of Gerald, a 27-year-old man who had extorted $39,000 over a three-year period from his parents. Gerald kept the flow of money coming by slamming his father's face into a plate of food or throwing furniture at him whenever he refused a demand for cash (Martin, 1989).

Elder abuse exists and requires attention, yet only a minority of cases fit the stereotypical picture provided by the media. Although most providers of services to the elderly know about abuse dealt out by children, few seem to be aware of the incidence of spousal abuse among older adults (Pillemer and Finkelhor, 1988). Elder abuse does not reflect a disintegration of the family but instead seems to be related to other problems in society.

be a daughter (66 percent) (Hagestad, 1986). In most cases, the grandchildren already have left the nest. The majority of parent–adult child households, however, are established in the home of the aging parent, when an unmarried adult child moves back into the parent's home.

INTERGENERATIONAL SUPPORT

Despite each generation's fondness for independence and the establishment of their own homes, the contact between parents and adult children is generally frequent and relatively close. American society is concentrated in nuclear households, but bonds with the elder generation are so strong that the American family is considered a **modified extended family,** in which the generations live apart but are linked by mutual aid and affection (Litwack, 1960).

Intergenerational support can be demonstrated by interaction, by affection, or by assistance in the form of money or services. Elderly parents see or hear from their adult children frequently (Moss, Moss, and Moles, 1985). Whether the older generation lives in the country or the city seems to have no effect on the amount of contact (Krout, 1988), but gender, marital status, social class, and geographic distance do. Daughters are more likely to be in contact with their elderly parents than are sons, and they contact their mothers more frequently than their fathers (Hoffman, McManus, and Brackbill, 1987). Widows are generally in closer contact than married parents; unmarried children see their parents more often than do married children. Working-class men, especially those who are upwardly mobile, are more likely to be in contact with their parents than are middle-class men.

Geographic distance seems to determine the amount of contact (Moss, Moss, and Moles, 1985). Three out of four older parents live within half an hour's drive from at least one child, and they see that child often. Those who live in the same neighborhood generally see their children daily, those within 10 miles see them at least once a week, and those tho live more than 500 miles away see them at least once a year.

Most parents and children report a feeling of closeness, but when there is any discrepancy, parents tend to see the relationship as closer than does the child. This discrepancy is believed to reflect the **developmental stake** of parent and child (Bengston et al., 1985). Each person's stake in the relationship reflects the way in which the bond enables the person to attain personal goals. Parents, who often see their children as perpetuating parental ideals and valued institutions, have a stake in a close relationship, and so they tend to deny differences. Children, who need to see themselves as distinct from their parents, have a stake in autonomy, and so they tend to magnify existing differences.

The relative closeness of relationships in today's family may explain why influence travels up and down the generations. Studies have found consistent attempts of parents (whether aging or middle-aged) and children (whether middle-aged or young adult) to influence one another in almost every sphere of life (Hagestad, 1984). About one-third of older parents' attempts to influence their middle-aged children in the areas of health, work, and finances were successful, and the children were especially grateful for advice on child-rearing. The older parents said that they followed their children's advice concerning health, living arrangements, money, dress, and household management about two-thirds of the time. Young adults were the most influential concerning health matters, current social issues, and the way their parents used their free time; middle-aged parents said that they followed their children's advice about three-quarters of the time.

In the areas of politics, religion, and gender roles, researchers have found that children's influence on their parents' views increases as the parents age (Bengston, Rosenthal, and Burton, 1990). Middle-aged parents interviewed in the early 1970s said that events in the turbulent 1960s would have been incomprehensible and frightening without the interpretations they received from their children (Hagestad, 1981). Young-adult children had influenced these parents on matters of work, life-style, and social issues. In another study, 60 percent of middle-aged mothers said that they had been influenced toward a more liberal sexual attitude by their daughters' behavior (Angres, 1975).

INTERGENERATIONAL ASSISTANCE

In the modified extended family, gifts, services, and financial assistance also flow up and down the generational tree. Housecleaning, babysitting, meal preparation, and transportation are the sort of services that generations often exchange. Aid is especially likely to flow from parent to child during the early years of the child's marriage, and, especially among the middle class, aid may continue for many years. The proportion of older parents who provide financial assistance to their children exceeds the proportion of children who get financial aid from their parents (Table 12.2). Even older adults who need considerable help themselves continue to give financial aid, gifts, and other services to their grown children and

Table 12.2 FINANCIAL AID BETWEEN GENERATIONS

Older Adults	All Older Adults	Sex		Age	
		Women	Men	<75	>75
Receiving aid from children	11.3%	11.9%	10.2%	8.9%	14.3%
Need aid from children	18.6%	22.1%	13.0%	21.3%	15.0%
Those needing help who get it	34.6%	31.6%	42.9%	29.4%	44.4%
Giving aid to children	47.2%	42.6%	53.3%	54.8%	36.4%

Source: Hoffman, McManus, and Brackbill, 1987.

grandchildren (Gatz, Bengston, and Blum, 1990). In fact, when all three generations are considered, grandparents are the primary providers of money and emotional support (Bengston, Rosenthal, and Burton, 1990).

Social class affects assistance patterns, with working and lower class families generally assisting their older parents by providing services within the home, whereas middle-class families tend to provide emotional support and money (Chappell, 1990). Gender also influences the form of assistance; daughters generally provide hands-on care and emotional support, and sons generally provide supervision and financial aid. When no daughter is available, however, sons give direct care. Despite any need by older adults, assistance continues to flow in both directions until older parents are severely impaired.

Eventually, as health deteriorates and income becomes inadequate, older family members may need extensive care. Because of gender differences in longevity, the dependent adult is likely to be a widow—an older mother (or grandmother) who had herself served as caregiver for an ailing spouse. When an aging parent's health problem requires considerable

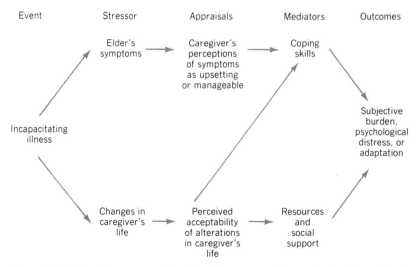

Figure 12.4 Caregiver stress and coping. The amount of stress involved in caring for an ailing parent depends on the actual stressors, the caregiver's perception of the situation, available resources, and the caregiver's coping skills. *Source:* Gatz et al., 1990, p. 412.

care, two kinds of stress are involved: the health problem itself and changes in the caregiver's life caused by the health problem (Gatz, Bengston, and Blum, 1990). Family, work, finances, and friendships compete for the caregiver's time and energy. How heavy the burden becomes depends on the demands involved, the caregiver's perception of the situation, and the resources and coping skills of the caregiver (Figure 12.4). The degree of psychological stress felt by the caregiver is likely to be especially heavy when the older parent suffers from an organic brain syndrome, as we saw in Chapter 6. Most research has focused on such situations, but many aging parents who require care suffer not from some form of dementia, but have a fractured hip, severe emphysema, or are incapacitated by a stroke.

For some caregivers, their job creates added stress; for others, it becomes an escape, as it was for one 52-year-old woman in the University of Southern California's Three Generational Study. "I never would have believed that anyone would use Aircraft Engineering and Manufacturing Corporation for therapy," she told interviewers, "but I do ... I would never think of not going to work. . . . I go in there, I feel great" (Gatz, Bengston, and Blum, 1990, pp. 412–413). Outside employment means that some paid caregiving is available and that other family members are likely to help with household chores. Yet 12 percent of women who cared for an ailing mother had quit their jobs to take care of her and another 13 percent had either cut back on their working hours or were considering quitting (Brody et al., 1987). Mothers of these women tended to be older and to require more extensive care.

Because its members are linked in an intricate web of relations, changes in the life of a dependent older member radiate throughout the family system, affecting the lives of all. Virtually every family member in the Three Generations Study spoke of at least one relationship with another family member that had been changed by an aging parent's health-related dependency (Mellins, Boyd, and Gatz, 1988). An adult child who becomes caregiver for an ailing mother has less time for her adolescent children or her husband. Family pressure mounts markedly if the web is also disturbed by tensions in the caregiver's marriage or if young adult children are having financial problems, marital discord, or problems with drugs. At this time middle-aged children, especially women, find themselves part of the "sandwich generation." They are caught in a **life-cycle squeeze,** trapped between responsibilities for an ailing parent (or grandparent) and for adolescent or young adult children.

The life-cycle squeeze becomes especially constrictive when middle-aged adults must care for frail parents who live in another city. Among the middle class, the phenomenon of long-distance care has appeared, apparently the result of today's mobility combined with increased longevity. No one knows how many people are involved, but it seems clear that many who are responsible for making long-distance arrangements and who spend their weekends traveling hundreds of miles are under extreme stress. A 42-year-old management consultant in Manhattan, who traveled to Chicago each week to care for her 91-year-old father and 87-year-old mother, said, "To take on parenting of your parents is the true mark of being an adult, but sometimes I feel that my whole life is on hold" (Collins, 1983, p. C10). Some of the consequences of long-distance care have been broken marriages, financial crisis, and lost jobs (Collins, 1983). A network of "case-management" services has developed to aid people caught in this squeeze.

Although the care of ailing parents may be demanding, some caregivers seem to take it in stride. In one study, the majority of middle-aged daughters who had cared for their

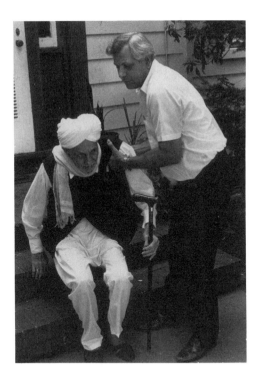

Grown children and parents continue to aid one another, with services, money, and emotional support flowing up and down the generational ladder.

mothers said that they were glad they had provided the care and felt satisfied about having done it (Lewis and Meredith, 1988). Other studies have found that, despite the increased stress felt by all caregivers, one quarter of them said that their satisfaction with life had also increased (Chappell, 1990). Apparently, feelings of accomplishment and self-satisfaction may counterbalance the stresses and strains that go with caregiving.

SUMMARY

THE FAMILY AS A SYSTEM

The family can be regarded as a social system whose structure is affected by the addition, development, and departure of its members; by the demands of the culture; and by changes in the environment. The family system is established with the marriage of mates and lasts until the marriage is dissolved by divorce or death. Each member of the system has a series of roles that are determined by age, gender, and relatedness. As life expectancy has increased and fertility has declined, the **beanpole family** has developed, in which there are more generations but fewer members in each generation. The purposes of the family are to meet its members' needs and to socialize children. Cultures may be **postfigurative,** in which authority comes from the past; **cofigurative,** in which the present is the standard; or **prefigurative,** in which neither the past nor the present is regarded as reliable.

PARENTHOOD

Although most people have children, reduced family size has decreased the proportion of the life span that is devoted to child-rearing. The increase in maternal employment outside the home, together with the rising divorce rate, has reduced the traditional nuclear household to a minority of American families. Family roles begin to shift early in pregnancy, and both partners worry about how the change will affect their lives and their relationship. Pregnancy is affected by psychological and environmental variables, including the marital relationship, a woman's feelings about her job, and attitudes toward the pregnancy. Afterward, both partners may face stresses as they adjust to their new roles, and some women undergo **postpartum depression.**

Among the stresses of parenthood are restrictions on personal and economic freedom and the disruption of the relationship between the spouses. The major responsibility for infant care, the return to a traditional division of household tasks, and the responsibility for keeping the family system functioning may be at the base of a young mother's dissatisfaction. By midlife, many women have developed either an **autonomous mothering** relationship, in which they see their children as individuals; or a **coupled mothering** relationship, in which the children are important parts of the mother's identity. Marital satisfaction may be determined by the presence, number, and age of a couple's children.

Maternal employment does not appear to be detrimental to young children, and its effects on the mother are often positive. The least happy women are those who stay at home but would rather be in the workplace. Egalitarian husbands are most likely to share the "second shift" with their wives, and transitional men help even less than traditional men do.

Being a single parent affects social life and job performance. Despite the heavy financial and psychological burden of filling both parental roles, the single parent may develop new aspects of personality.

Although young boys at first take readily to a stepfather, over time girls seem to develop closer relationships with him, but close relationships seem limited to stepchildren who are younger than nine when the stepfather enters the family. Warm relationships with stepmothers seem to require time to develop.

Parents generally react to the empty nest with relief, and the marital relationship often improves. The **empty nest syndrome,** a negative reaction to children's departure that was once considered inevitable, rarely develops. Both the marital relationship and the timing of the children's departure help determine the effects of the empty nest.

GRANDPARENTHOOD

The relationship between grandparent and grandchild is affected by ethnic group, religion, socioeconomic level, personality, and child custody. Age and distance have powerful effects on a grandparent's style. The majority of grandparents develop a **companionate** style, although some older or distant grandparents develop a **remote** style, and grandparents who live close by may develop an **involved** style. Grandparenthood seems to follow a three-stage career: (1) from the grandchild's birth to his or her adolescence; (2) adolescence; (3) adulthood.

RELATIONS WITH AGING PARENTS

Most older adults have frequent contact with their grown children. The generational bonds are so strong that the American family is considered a **modified extended family.** Fewer than 5 percent of American households contain three generations, but another 16 percent of older adults live in two-generation households. Discrepancies in parents' and adult children's views of their relationship have been attributed to the **developmental stake** each has in the relationship. Influence between generations runs up and down generational lines, and, no matter what their age, parents and children consistently attempt to influence one another. **Elder abuse** is rare and is more likely to come from a spouse than from a child. The generations exchange money, gifts, and services, but older parents give more to their children and grandchildren than they receive. When parents enter the old-old group, adult children may be caught in a **life-cycle squeeze,** in which they are responsible for two generations besides themselves. How heavy the burden of care becomes depends on the demands involved, the caregiver's perception of the situation, and the resources and coping skills of the caregiver.

KEY TERMS

autonomous mothering

beanpole family

cofigurative culture

companionate grandparent

coupled mothering

developmental stake

elder abuse

empty nest syndrome

involved grandparent

life-cycle squeeze

modified extended family

postfigurative culture

postpartum depression

prefigurative culture

remote grandparent

Chapter 13

◆

Occupational Patterns
Across Adulthood

◆

What makes an occupation rewarding? What turns off an employee? The first impulse is to say that salary and social status determine the way people feel about their work. These factors are important, but the answer is not so simple. Asked to talk about her job, Babe Secoli, who has been a checker in a supermarket for 30 years, says: "I love my job. I've got very nice bosses. I got a black manager and he's just beautiful. They don't bother you as long as you do your work. And the pay is terrific. . . . I'm a couple of days away, I'm very lonesome for this place. When I'm on a vacation, I can't wait to go, but two or three days away, I start to get fidgety. I can't stand around and do nothin'. I have to be busy at all times. I look forward to comin' to work. It's a great feelin'. I enjoy it somethin' terrible" (Terkel, 1974, pp. 377, 380).

Secoli stands eight hours a day at her register, and her feet hurt. By middle-class standards, her pay is low. She has no authority. Yet she is not alienated, and she likes her job.

At the other extreme is Ray Wax, an upper-middle-class stockbroker about the same age as Secoli, a man whose commissions put him in a privileged economic group. Wax commutes each day from an affluent New York suburb to Wall Street. Asked about his work, he says: "People like me start out with a feeling that there's a place for them in society, that they really have a useful function. They see it destroyed by the cynicism of the market. . . . I can't say what I'm doing has any value. This doesn't make me too happy. . . . I'll continue with my personal disillusionment. (Laughs.) Oh, I'd like one morning to wake up and go to some work that gave me joy" (Terkel, 1974, pp. 446–447).

Despite high financial returns and social status, the stockbroker is clearly alienated. He says he feels that he is no more important than a ribbon clerk, who takes orders but makes few decisions.

Neither Secoli nor Wax may reflect the views of the majority of people who hold similar jobs. It would be fairly easy to find alienated supermarket checkers and dedicated stockbrokers. A variety of factors help determine whether a person's occupation is disillusioning or fulfilling, and in this chapter we investigate some of them. We begin with an exploration of the role of work in our lives and how we come to be in one job rather than another. Next, we look at the way careers tend to develop, looking at the stage of the prototypical career, as well as at the influence of occupations on personality and on the factors that determine work satisfaction. Gender affects the course of occupation, and so we turn to the working lives of men and women—and the differences between them. As fewer people die in midcareer, retirement becomes more important to all of us, and so we explore influences on the decision to retire and the ways in which people adjust to retirement. We close by considering the ways in which retirement may change as we reach the twenty-first century.

CHOOSING AN OCCUPATION

Most of us would work even if we did not have to take a job in order to support ourselves. Having a job indicates that we have grown up, and it serves as a measure of maturity and responsibility. A young man who could not find work put this feeling into words: "Who wants to have that kind of time on his hands? I hate myself; then I hate everyone else. . . . It's a rotten deal when you can't find a job and don't earn your own money. Who wants to draw unemployment money, then borrow from the parents? I feel myself getting younger by the day—becoming a kid, feeling sorry for myself, and getting lazier by the minute. No good. After a while you're ready to return to elementary school!" (Coles, 1978, p. 226).

Occupation is also entwined with the sense of identity, so that it is rare to hear people talk about themselves without including some reference to their work. The link is so close that sudden unemployment can threaten identity and self-esteem.

PURPOSES OF WORK

Work can give meaning to our lives, for it defines our position in society and provides us with satisfying activity, an outlet for creativity, and a source of social stimulation. If work does not do these things, we feel that something is wrong, and we may become alienated like Ray Wax, the stockbroker. Several years ago, Studs Terkel spent months traveling across the country and listening to Americans talk about their jobs. He sees work as a "search . . . for daily meaning as well as daily bread, for recognition as well as cash, for astonishment rather than torpor; in short, for a sort of life rather than a Monday through Friday sort of dying. Perhaps immortality, too, is part of the quest" (Terkel, 1974, p. xiii). Work is so vital to our sense of self that when asked what a healthy person should be able to do, Freud replied with three short words: *Lieben und arbeiten* (to love and work). According to Erik Erikson (1968), this simple rule means that people need to become productive without becoming so immersed in their work that they lose the ability to be sexual, loving persons. In his view of the life span, the sense of industry, on which work is based, develops during middle childhood.

Most of us who are able to work are part of the labor force: 75 percent of men and 62 percent of women past the age of 16 are either employed or looking for work (U.S. Bureau of the Census, 1989) (Table 13.1). Not counted in the labor force are women whose occupation is homemaker; people who are retired, in school, in prison, ill, or disabled; and those who do not wish to work. About 75 percent of the labor force work at jobs. **Jobs** are occupations in which upward advancement is limited and movement is primarily horizontal.

Table 13.1   **CIVILIAN LABOR FORCE, 1968 TO 1988, BY RACE AND SEX[a]**

	1960	*1970*	*1980*	*1988*	*2000*
White men	83.4%	80.0%	78.2%	76.9%	76.6%
White women	36.5%	42.6%	51.2%	56.4%	62.9%
Black men	83.0%	76.5%	70.6%	71.0%	71.4%
Black women	48.2%	49.5%	53.2%	58.0%	62.5%
Hispanic men	NA	NA	81.4%	81.9%	80.3%
Hispanic women	NA	NA	47.4%	53.2%	59.4%

Source: U.S. Bureau of the Census, 1990.

[a] Over a period of nearly three decades, the proportion of men in the labor force dropped, in part because of the trend toward earlier retirement. At the same time, the proportion of women in the labor force increased.

A carpenter may move from one employer to another, accumulating experience and developing skills, but the job responsibilities remain more or less the same.

The rest of the labor force work at careers. **Careers** are occupations that are characterized by interrelated training and work experiences, in which a person moves upward through a series of positions that require greater mastery and responsibility and that provide increasing financial return. An executive, a banker, a college professor, or an officer in the armed forces has a career. If the carpenter should develop the knowledge and experience to become a contractor, he or she would move onto the career ladder, advancing in position with advances in age. This distinction between jobs and careers has been challenged by researchers who believe that the career trajectory describes only a handful of professions and that most job sequences are idiosyncratic and follow no predictable pattern (Treiman, 1985).

PROCESS OF SELECTION

Ideally, each person would work at the job or career that best suits his or her interests, abilities, and personality. However, life does not seem to work in that way, and occupational choice is often accidental and guided by what may seem to be irrelevant factors. Sex, social class, proximity, apparently unrelated decisions, and luck can play at least as great a role in career choice as factors that match individuals with the best-suited occupations.

Gender restricts job access—even though discrimination based on gender is illegal. Women are now hired as fire fighters, but few apply and those who do face an uphill battle to win consideration for the job. Because many women are too small or have paid too little attention to developing muscle power to be able to handle the physical demands of fire fighting, all women are seen as incapable of its demands, no matter how strong they are. Until recently, a girl was encouraged to consider a job as no more than a way station until she entered her "true" occupational roles—wife and mother. As we will see, such socialization practices may also affect women who do not choose to marry or have children, as well as those who wish to embark on a dual-occupational identity, combining the roles of home and workplace. Gender can also restrict job access for men. Few men decide to become kindergarten teachers, although they may be nurturant and enjoy working with young children.

Social class affects occupational choice, with adolescents in the upper socioeconomic brackets directed toward careers and those in the lower brackets directed toward jobs. Some of this influence comes from parental attitudes toward the value of education or the possibility of attaining it. The cost of lengthy professional training may effectively put careers out of the reach of some young people who have both the aptitude and inclination for law, medicine, or science.

Proximity can be a powerful force in occupational choice. A young person who grows up in the Pacific Northwest is more likely to go into some kind of work connected with forestry than one who grows up in Manhattan. Similarly, someone who lives near Detroit is more likely to work in auto production than someone who grows up on a midwestern farm. Childhood experiences are important because the availability of role models is likely to increase the chances that children will aim their sights on a particular occupation.

Luck is also important. Classified ads, job listings with employment agencies, and campus interviews fill some jobs, but informal connections are more likely to lead to employment. Knowing someone in an organization—or knowing someone who knows someone—is a common path to jobs and careers. Between 50 and 90 percent of blue-collar workers are believed to have found their jobs through informal channels (Reid, 1972) Openings in business and academic occupations are often filled by contact with the "old-boy network," in which a member (male or female) of the network, comprised of friends, acquaintances, and former coworkers in a particular field, relies on other members to fill openings or to provide new career slots.

A person must be aware that a job exists before he or she can begin training for it—or even consider it. Few children have any idea of the variety of occupations that are available, nor do they understand the barriers that may stand between them and what they think they would like to do. A 12-year-old boy might, for example, dream of becoming an astronaut without realizing that a congenital eye defect, one that does not interfere at all with his school or play activities, has put his dream forever out of reach.

Although children do not have to choose an occupation, the educational choices they make as young adolescents may—without their awareness—shut off some careers, narrowing their future selection. The decision not to take third and fourth year math courses in high school, for example, puts a student so far behind others of the same initial ability that by the twelfth grade a wide range of math-related careers has been eliminated (Abeles, Steel, and Wise, 1980). When adolescent pregnancy leads to marriage or the adoption of the parental role, or both, college education—and with it, most careers—is shut out for many youngsters. In a study that matched young people for aptitudes, aspirations, and socioeconomic background, fewer than 2 percent of adolescent mothers and 10 percent of adolescent fathers had completed college by the age of 29, compared with 22 percent of women and 27 percent of men who postponed parenthood until they were at least 24 years old (Card and Wise, 1978).

Individuals are most likely to find occupations that match their interests and abilities if they know what those interests and abilities are and what occupations require those talents. At a time when young people are making occupational decisions, however, most may not know themselves very well, nor realize what day-to-day work in a particular field entails. They are likely to go by stereotypes they have picked up from the media and casual contacts and may either pass over fields that would be rewarding or else embark on lengthy preparation in a field that has no resemblance to their stereotypical ideas of it (Anastasi, 1976).

Vocational tests have been developed to assist people in making wise occupational choices. The Strong–Campbell Interest Inventory, for example, uses the answers to several hundred specific items (Do you "like" or "dislike," or are you "indifferent" to, e.g., making a speech?) about activities, amusements, categories of people, school subjects, and various occupations to determine a person's interests and the sort of work environment he or she would find congenial (Campbell, 1974). The pattern of scores is compared with the pattern of choices made by people who have been successful in various occupations.

The Strong–Campbell Interest Inventory groups answers in several ways. It provides typical scores for 162 specific occupations; it provides 23 basic interest scales that relate to general occupational interests; and it interprets answers in terms of personality themes that are derived from the research of J. L. Holland (1985). Holland proposed that people in a particular occupation tend to show certain correlations in the strength of six personality themes: realistic, investigative, artistic, social, enterprising, and conventional. A farmer, for example, is likely to score high on realistic and conventional themes and low on their opposites, social and artistic themes. Holland believes that these themes reflect a person's

Table 13.2   **PERSONALITY THEMES AND OCCUPATIONAL CHOICE**[a]

Investigative	*Social*	*Realistic*
aeronautical engineer	clinical psychologist	airplane mechanic
anthropologist	foreign missionary	electrician
astronomer	high school teacher	filling station attendant
biologist	marriage counselor	fish & wildlife specialist
botanist	physical education teacher	photoengraver
chemist	playground director	plumber
geologist	psychiatric case worker	railroad engineer
meteorologist	speech therapist	surveyor
physicist	vocational counselor	tool designer
research scientist		tree surgeon
science writer		
zoologist		

Artistic	*Conventional*	*Enterprising*
art dealer	bank examiner	business executive
author	bank teller	buyer
cartoonist	bookkeeper	hotel manager
commercial artist	computer operator	industrial relations consultant
composer	court stenographer	political campaign manager
musician	financial analyst	realtor
playwright	quality control expert	restaurant worker
poet	statistician	sports promoter
stage director	tax expert	stockbroker
symphony conductor	traffic manager	television producer
		traveling sales representative

Source: Holland, 1985.

[a] Occupations frequently chosen by individuals who display Holland's personality themes.

major personality characteristics and that when the themes of a chosen occupation match a person's personality, his or her job satisfaction, job stability, and occupational achievement are likely to be high (Table 13.2). In this view, choosing a particular occupation is choosing a way of life.

Holland's analysis fits comfortably with the five-factor model of personality (Chapter 10). The five-factor category of extraversion, for example, encompasses Holland's social and enterprising themes, and the five-factor category of openness to experience encompasses Holland's investigative and artistic themes. Occupational choices predicted by the five-factor theory generally correspond to the predictions made by Holland (Costa, McCrae, and Holland, 1984). Consistent gender differences appear in Holland's personality themes, and the differences mirror gender differences in occupation. Women, no matter what their age, are more likely than men to display artistic, social, and conventional themes. Of course, people do not choose their occupations solely on the basis of their personality. As we have seen, other factors also have powerful effects on vocational choice.

OCCUPATIONAL DEVELOPMENT

The developmental course of most occupations was once related primarily to age. In the nineteenth century, most people worked on jobs related to physical strength, which meant that the kind of job a person held was determined by age. According to Tamara Hareven (1978), workers younger than 20 or older than 45 were employed in agriculture or at unskilled labor. A permanent job was rare, and most careers were ''disorderly.'' Progression was not necessarily upward, and no principle of seniority protected the older worker. After working hard for 20 or 30 years, skilled employees in their forties or fifties were suddenly moved to semiskilled or unskilled positions, there to work until they died. A factory worker might move up from sweeper to skilled textile operator to supervisor, only to be made sweeper again after the age of 50.

The great change that has taken place in the world of work becomes clear when we contrast the ''average'' male worker in 1870 with his counterpart a century later (Miernyk, 1975). In 1870 the average man entered the workforce when he was 14 years old and worked an average of 3120 hours per year (a 60-hour work week) with no vacations until he died, still at work, at the age of 61. In 1970 the average man entered the workforce at the age of 20 and worked an average of 2000 hours per year (a 40-hour work week with a two-week vacation) until he retired at the age of 65. Over his lifetime, the average 1870 worker would have earned $90,000 (in 1970 dollars) for 146,640 hours of toil. The average 1970 worker would have earned $360,000 for 90,000 hours of labor—four times the real income for two-thirds as much work. (The average 1970 college graduate would have entered the workforce several years later but would have earned much more than $500,000 by retirement.)

THE STAGES OF AN ORDERLY CAREER

Today's workers not only work less and get paid more, but their work careers have changed as well. In the twentieth century, seniority, tenure, health insurance, pensions, and other forms of occupational protection have made orderly job histories and careers possible. According to Donald Super (1957, 1980, 1985), the orderly course of vocational development goes through seven phases (Table 13.3). It begins in adolescence, when a person's ideas about work crystallize and tentative occupational decisions are made. In this **crystallization stage,** the adolescent explores various fields, and he matches—as closely as possible—personal needs, interests, capacities, and values with the opportunities that present themselves. The selection may be vague or unrealistic, but the usually irrevocable choice between broad areas, such as humanities or science, is made, and a vocational self-concept is developed. The adolescent may see himself or herself as an engineer, a restaurant owner, or an architect, although usually without much knowledge of what the occupation entails. This selection is, of course, an essential part of what Erikson saw as the formation of identity (Chapter 10).

From the crystallization stage, a person moves into the **specification stage,** when more is discovered about specific careers and reality shapes occupational decisions. This period is a transitional phase and is occupied by job training. The specification stage roughly

Table 13.3 **LIFE STRUCTURE AND CAREERS**

Levinson's Stages of Life Structure	*Super's Career Stages*
Late adult transition (60–65)	Deceleration (60–65)
Culmination of middle adulthood (55–60)	
Age 50 transition (50–55)	
Entering middle adulthood (45–50)	Maintenence (45–60)
Midlife transition (40–45)	
Settling down (33–40)	Consolidation (35–45)
Age 30 transition (28–33)	Establishment (25–35)
Entering the adult world (22–28)	Implementation (21–24)
Early adult transition (17–22)	Specification (18–21)
	Crystallization (14–18)

Sources: Levinson et al., 1978; Super, 1957, 1980, 1985.

corresponds to the undergraduate years at college. In these years, young people who do not go to college may, without much forethought, take a dead-end job, since they are usually not ready to marry or set up their own households.

During the **implementation stage,** which begins at about 21 or 22, a person makes an initial commitment to a vocation and takes an entry-level position. Additional training, either on-the-job or graduate work, may occupy a good part of this period. There is often some job shifting as the person searches for the "right" position with prospects for advancement. During this period many college graduates enter their first full-time positions, and many working-class adults settle into jobs with reasonable pay, the possibility of promotion, and long-term security.

In trades, business, and most professions, the new employee may find a **mentor,** an established, often powerful, sponsor who takes a personal interest in the young man or woman. The mentor generally provides guidance, advice, and additional contacts and smooths the way for promotion and advancement within the field. The relationship between mentor and protégé seems to pass through four phases (Kram, 1985). During the *initiation phase,* which lasts about six to twelve months, the relationship first develops. The heart of the relationship is the *cultivation phase,* which lasts two to five years. During this phase the mentor fulfills the roles of confidant and sponsor. When the protégé rises in the company or occupation and must demonstrate his or her own competence, the *separation phase* begins. At this time, both parties may feel the pang of separation. Finally, they move into the *redefinition phase,* when the relationship is reestablished but as a friendship of equals.

Compared with successful men in George Vaillant's (1977) Harvard Study (see Chapter 10), those with relatively unsuccessful careers rarely had mentors during their twenties or thirties. Women corporate executives who make it into the top ranks usually emphasize the influence of a mentor on their success (Hennig and Jardim, 1977). The scarcity of women in executive positions makes female mentors difficult to find, however, and women with male mentors sometimes discover that unfounded rumors of sexual involvement damage their careers (Hurley, 1988). Not all young workers find a mentor; among the men in Daniel Levinson's (1978) study (see Chapter 10), the mentor was more the exception than the rule.

By about the age of 25, the **establishment stage** of the orderly career begins. For the next decade a person settles down and becomes established in a chosen field. Then, at about 35, the **consolidation stage** begins, when a person, now regarded as experienced and knowledgeable, advances as far as possible and consolidates his or her gains. At about the age of 45, careers move into the **maintenance stage,** a transitional period when goals have either been met or seen to be out of reach. At this time, the drive to achieve diminishes, and workers tend to cut back on the time they devote to work. The maintenence phase lasts until a person sees retirement looming ahead and begins to shift priorities. This shift in priorities ushers in the final career period: the **deceleration stage.** This cycle of crystallization, specification, implementation, establishment, consolidation, maintenence, and deceleration describes the careers of workers with ''orderly'' work patterns. Many people, however, establish themselves late, some drift, and others find their established careers destabilized by nonnormative events (accidents, illness), history-normative events (war, politics, recessions), or shifts in their interests and values (Super, 1985).

HOW OCCUPATIONS AFFECT DEVELOPMENT

During our working lives, we spend about one-third of our time in the occupational environment. It should come as no surprise, therefore, to find that work affects the course of human development. Prolonged occupational exposure has a cumulative effect on cognition and personality, and it affects women and men similarly (Kohn, 1980; Kohn and Schooler, 1983; Miller et al., 1979).

The complexity of a job, how closely it is supervised, and the sort of pressure it places on the worker—not the status of a job—influence a worker's intellectual flexibility. A job's complexity refers to the degree to which it requires thought and independent judgment. Meeting the challenge of a complex job generally leads to increased intellectual flexibility. In a ten-year longitudinal study, researchers found that the complexity of work continues to affect intellectual flexibility even when social background and original levels of flexibility are taken into account (Kohn and Schooler, 1983). That is, if two workers with equivalent levels of intellectual flexibility were to start their careers in jobs that differed in complexity, the person in the more complex job would eventually outstrip the other in intellectual growth. Because intellectual flexibility is related to values, self-concept, and social orientation, job complexity may alter a person's self-esteem, anxiety, receptiveness to change, standards of morality, authoritarian conservatism, and degree of alienation. The influence of work is even seen in the way people spend their leisure: workers in jobs that demand intellectual flexibility tend to spend their free time in such intellectual activities as reading or attending plays (Miller and Kohn, 1983). The autonomy and challenge inherent in complex jobs apparently lead workers to value self-direction and encourage feelings of creativity.

When workers in an assembly plant began participating in management decisions, the workers themselves could see how the increased complexity of their jobs soon began to affect the way they approached various aspects of their lives. Attitudes toward authority at work, for example, carried over to the home. One worker at this plant told a researcher, ''I say things to my (eight-year-old) daughter that I know are a result of the way we do things at work. I ask her, 'What do you think about that?' or 'How would you handle this problem?''' (Crouter, 1984). Researchers found improvement in listening and communication skills within the family, a greater toleration for give-and-take in family life, and increased democracy in conflict resolution.

At the other end of the scale, studies indicate that fast-paced, repetitive, sedentary, and mindless work can be deadening and alienating, and lead to health disorders (Geyer, 1972). Such jobs, which have had all complexity stripped away, tend to produce workers who prize conformity over autonomy and believe that they have little control over their lives.

SATISFACTION WITH WORK

Given the enormous changes in the character of working conditions since 1870, we would expect to find today's workers happy and contented. Yet job alienation is just as visible as it was a century ago (Miernyk, 1975). Workers may not have been satisfied in the nineteenth century, but they were probably too busy and too exhausted to contemplate their situation. Greater freedom, the democratization of the workplace, as well as a newfound affluence, appear to have developed hand in hand with anxiety, discontent, and alienation.

What makes a job or career satisfying? According to Mark Twain, the satisfaction is not in the job itself but in the worker's view of the job. When Tom Sawyer was faced with the drudgery of whitewashing a fence, he pretended the job was a rare privilege that required great skill. His act was so convincing that the neighborhood boys paid him for the privilege of doing his work. As Twain pointed out, Tom had discovered ''that Work consists of whatever a body is *obliged* to do, and that Play consists of whatever a body is not obliged to do. And this would help him to understand why constructing artificial flowers or performing on a treadmill is work, while rolling tenpins or climbing Mont Blanc is only amusement'' (1876, p. 29).

Following Twain's line of reasoning, Renee Garfinkel (1982) decided that, unless work includes the element of creating, producing, or achieving, it can destroy a person's self-concept and sense of well-being. The contented supermarket checker who began this chapter took pride in her knowledge of thousands of item prices, her speed and accuracy, and her ability to detect shoplifters. Her job included the element of achievement, and she liked it so much that she came to work 45 minutes early every morning. The alienated stockbroker felt that his job was superfluous, that his middle-income customers had no hope of making much money in the market, and that he had no opportunity to make decisions. For him there was no sense of personal achievement in his career.

Drawing on a national survey of working conditions, researchers discovered that job satisfaction was related to the challenge presented by a job, by its financial and security rewards, by the availability of resources that allow workers to do the job well, and by the comfort or convenience of the job (Seashore and Barnowe, 1972). Salary turned out to be an important factor among low-income workers, but not among blue-collar or white-collar workers with high incomes. This finding fits with other research indicating that satisfaction among workers who have jobs is more affected by salary, whereas, among those with careers, it is most affected by opportunities to advance (Kanter, 1976).

Job satisfaction usually increases with age, and researchers have proposed three explanations for this development (White and Spector, 1987). The **grinding down hypothesis** assumes that older workers have declining expectations. There are no substantial changes in workers' needs or desires, but ground down by the realities of the work situation, they are satisfied with less (Davies and Sparrow, 1985). The **Lordstown hypothesis** assumes that cross-sectional studies have picked up a cohort effect, in which each cohort is more dissatisfied with typical working conditions than the cohort that preceded it. Each successive cohort is better educated and has grown up with more comfortable living standards and higher expectations. The Lordstown hypothesis takes its name from the General Motors plant in Lordstown that opened in the 1960s, almost entirely staffed by young workers and beset by high levels of worker unrest for a decade. Its workers, unlike earlier cohorts, were more willing to question authority, less materialistic, and more optimistic about the fulfillment that jobs should provide. The **job-change hypothesis** assumes that older workers have better, more fulfilling jobs than do novices in the job market. Not only are their jobs higher on the occupational ladder, but also over the years they either change jobs until they find a position that is compatible with their needs and interest or else their values and needs change to become compatible with their work.

Whether these workers are satisfied depends on how well their positions match their needs, the extent of their perceived control, salary, job level, and length of time on the job.

Repeated national surveys on job satisfaction failed to support the Lordstown hypothesis, and studies of white- and blue-collar men provided no indication that workers' expectations and aspirations decline with age (Davies and Sparrow, 1985). However, a study of several hundred city managers of both sexes between the ages of 23 and 73 supported the job-change hypothesis (White and Spector, 1987). Increased job satisfaction with age was the result of the extent to which the characteristics of the position matched the worker's needs, the extent to which the worker felt he or she had control over the work situation, salary, job level, and length of time on the job. When these aspects of work were removed, there was no relation between age and job satisfaction. Some studies have found that older workers are less satisfied with their salaries than with other aspects of their jobs (Morrow and McElroy, 1987). Other studies suggest that the sources of satisfaction derived from work change over time, so that salary or specific working conditions become less important than, say, control over the work situation and the intrinsic pleasure of accomplishment (Bray and Howard, 1983). Whether they find their work satisfying or meaningless, each sex tends to approach occupations differently.

MALE OCCUPATIONAL PATTERNS

Men have been socialized toward the role of worker. They grow up expecting to work for the rest of their lives, to find meaning in that work, and to take the responsibility of providing for others. Although the majority of married men have financial assistance from employed wives or other family members (U.S. Bureau of the Census, 1989), until very recently socialization has proceeded as if men were the sole breadwinners. During childhood, boys learn the social skills that enable them to get along in the world of work. As they participate in organized sports, they get lessons in competitiveness, confidence, teamwork, persistence in the face of heavy odds, and leadership (Eccles and Hoffman, 1984). They learn to follow as well as to lead, to lose as well as to win, and to see a team victory as more important than individual success.

When men set out on their careers, they are prepared to be autonomous, competitive, and task-oriented. In Valliant's (1977) study of Harvard graduates, men seemed to devote their thirties to their occupations, focusing so intently on mastering their work and climbing the career ladder that they paid little attention to other aspects of life. As noted in Chapter 10, their focus is so intent that it has led to the proposed stage of *career consolidation* in adult development, to be inserted between Erikson's periods of intimacy (the twenties) and generativity (the forties). Indeed, in most major studies of adult development, a pattern of concentration on intimacy, then on career consolidation, and only afterward on generativity has been detected.

HOW ORDERLY IS THE MALE CAREER?

As we saw in Chapter 10, Levinson (1978) views the male life structure as evolving through a relatively orderly sequence, in which the stages of early adulthood roughly parallel the developmental course of careers (Table 13.3). In Levinson's theory, career development plays an important part in the formation of a life structure. During the early adult transition, the first serious career choice is made, but the work of forming an occupation does not end there. Whether a man makes an early, intense commitment to an occupation (as did some of the biologists in his study), remains undecided, or makes a major occupational shift during his twenties, the formative process extends throughout the novice period, which lasts through the age thirty transition. Among the men Levinson studied, even orderly careers were marked by this lengthy procedure, which was as true of working-class men as it was of executives.

Throughout the settling down period, in which career consolidation takes place, the men in Levinson's study were working at advancing their careers, and most had set rough time-tables for reaching various occupational levels. Their sense of well-being seemed to depend on how fast they reached these goals. Five different career patterns developed during this period. For some men, life went according to their timetables, and they advanced within a stable life structure. A second group of men stayed with the life structure they had established, but failed to advance as they had hoped—or even slipped back. For a third group of men, the life structure they had formed early in the settling down period became intolerable, and toward the end of the period, they broke out and tried to establish a different life structure. A fourth group of men advanced so swiftly and did so well that their old life structure could no longer accommodate their new status and income. They, too, had to establish a new life structure. Finally, a fifth group of men did not conform to the orderly sequence. Their life structure remained unstable throughout the settling down period, and no clear occupational direction appeared. One man, for example, led a nomadic existence, moving around the country and working variously at careers in radio, art, sales, and counseling. As men entered the midlife transition, they faced the task of making a place for themselves in the world of middle adulthood and, depending on how they had met their timetables, the task of modifying and consolidating their occupational goals.

Job consolidation and the settling down process seem to indicate a tendency to stay with a job once the implementation period is over. Although men tend to show a pattern of substantial upward mobility in job level and salary, researchers have discovered that men change their jobs and occupations often. Many workers change jobs in a random way, moving from one job to another with no visible upward progression. Such sideways shifts may sometimes be a sign of drift, but many are the result of layoffs, plant closings, or involuntary transfers (Treiman, 1985). Men change occupations far more often than the pattern of orderly career development would predict. In one longitudinal survey, nearly 90 percent of men had changed occupations at least once by the time they were 54 to 68 years old (Jacobs, 1983). A search of 23 professional and technical occupations revealed that in only 5 of those occupations were more than half of the men who started their careers in the field still practicing it at age 55 (Evans and Laumann, 1983). Men in the California Intergenerational Studies reported a number of job changes during their thirties and forties, with top executives and professionals and those who were moving up in the middle class being especially likely to have changed jobs (Clausen, 1981). Such men in their early forties reported an average of two job changes within the past decade, and those in their late forties and early fifties reported an average of 1.4 job changes. Blue-collar workers in the study reported no job changes in the previous decade, but they were interviewed before the plant closings and consolidations of the 1980s occurred.

As men in the California study passed 45 and entered the stage of career maintenance, all but the most successful cut back on their working time, by about four hours each week. Top executives and professionals showed the opposite trend. They increased their investment of time, working a 51-hour week at the age of 50, as compared with a 48-hour week among top executives and professionals in their early forties.

PREDICTING CAREER SUCCESS

A man's success in his chosen occupation seems to be affected by his personality and intellectual abilities. Among men in the California Intergenerational Studies, those who made it to the top could be distinguished from other men in early adolescence by their intellectual capacities and interests and their adherence to the "work ethic"—they were ambitious, productive, dependable, and not self-indulgent. During the middle years, work-ethic attributes tended to narrow among men, but their cognitive skills and intellectual interests could be ranked by occupational level, with blue-collar workers scoring lowest. Scores progressed steadily through the professional and top executive levels, and upwardly mobile middle-class men scored especially high.

Similar relationships appeared in a longitudinal study of managers at AT&T (Bray and Howard, 1983; Howard, 1984). At the beginning of their careers, men who climbed the corporate ladder differed from those who stayed on lower rungs in intellectual capacities, interpersonal skills, and ambition. They also showed a strong desire to be a leader and to direct operations. At midlife, the successful managers were now more highly involved in their work—a quality that diminished in those who did not rise in the corporation. Successful men also showed increased behavioral flexibility and somewhat less authoritarianism, while those who were less successful became more rigid and authoritarian.

Other personality attributes that tend to impair personal effectiveness were unlikely to be strong among successful men. In the California Generational Studies, men in the top levels scored lowest on anxiety, fearfulness, punitiveness, and the tendency to withdraw when frustrated, to feel victimized, and to complicate simple situations (Clausen, 1981). Working-class adolescents who moved up to the middle class tended to be more dependable, considerate, likable, sympathetic, and warmer than middle-class adolescents. As middle-aged men, these upwardly mobile men remained warm and sympathetic, developed intellectual skills and interests, tended to be conventional, and were unlikely to push limits.

FEMALE OCCUPATIONAL PATTERNS

Women have always worked, whether within the home or in the labor force. A major change in the occupation of women is the movement of mothers into the labor force, so that women now make up 45 percent of all workers, compared with 38 percent in 1970 (Cowan, August 21, 1989). Mothers of young children, who were once least likely to be employed, now are more likely to be working outside the home (57.1 percent) than are married women who have no children (48.9 percent) (U.S. Bureau of the Census, 1989).

This shift has attracted so much attention that little notice has been paid to a change in the character of women's work. Since 1961, for example, women have moved from a minority share of jobs in seven large categories to a majority of positions as insurance adjusters (up from 9 percent); examiners and investigators, bill collectors (up from 22 percent); real estate agents and brokers; photographic process workers; checkers, examiners, and inspectors; production-line assemblers; and typesetters. In three other categories, they hold almost half the jobs: accountants, bartenders, and busdrivers. Such changes often reflect a change in the nature of the job rather than a dropping of barriers (Hacker, 1988). In 1970, when only 17 percent of typesetters were women, the job was done with hot lead; today, when women have 70 percent of the positions, type is set electronically. Women took over the field of insurance adjusting when the position changed from going out into the field and inspecting smashed fenders to sitting at a computer console and entering claims information. Although women still hold only a handful of positions in some of the more prestigious fields, their numbers are growing. In 1971, 4 percent of judges and lawyers were women; in 1989, women accounted for about 20 percent of the positions. During the same period, women physicians increased from 9 percent to 20 percent, and the proportion of women engineers swelled from an almost invisible 1 percent to 7 percent (Cowan, August 21, 1989; U.S. Bureau of the Census, 1989).

THE FEMALE CAREER

For the most part, women's childhood preparation aims them at motherhood. As we have seen, women are socialized to be nurturant, dependent, gentle, and compassionate. Until recently, women who chose to work outside the home were expected to go into nursing, teaching, librarianship, or office work, all occupations in which they could use their nurturant skills or act as ''office wives,'' helping executives wield power but never thinking of such achievement for themselves. Women who choose nontraditional occupations are forging new ground; they have few role models to use as patterns and must go against a lifetime of socialization.

What leads a woman to choose a nontraditional occupation? Interviews with women working in skilled trades (such as carpentry, construction work, mechanics, tool and die making) indicate some common factors (Schroedel, 1986). Most of the women either had fathers who treated them like boys or grew up with a lot of brothers around the house. They liked the outdoors and were in peak physical condition. Some got their jobs because of industry's response to the women's movement and federal regulations regarding sex discrimination. Others had working-class husbands who urged them to stick it out in the face of their coworkers' harassment.

When women try to climb the corporate ladder, even their childhood activities serve them poorly (Hennig and Jardim, 1977). Taught tennis, swimming, and gymnastics, girls have tended to excel at individual performance but often have had no chance to learn the lessons that can be derived from team sports. And as we have seen, team play has been critical to job performance in management situations, where workers must operate in a network that depends on friendship, persuasion, favors, promises, and connections.

Although some management consultants (Hennig and Jardim, 1977) believe that women's climb up the corporate ladder is slowed by excessive caution in corporate strategy, other consultants say the major problem lies in the narrow band of acceptable characteristics and actions that women must embrace if they are to be promoted (Morrison, White, and Van Velsor, 1987). Women must be tough and independent, while depending on others. They must contradict female stereotypes without forfeiting all traces of femininity. They must put their job first, sacrificing their family when a conflict arises. They must work harder and longer than men to get the same opportunities.

Although an increasing number of women are succeeding in traditionally male occupa-

Socialized to be nurturant, dependent, and helpful, and mostly confined to individual sports that give no lessons in team play, women are at a disadvantage in the corporate business world.

tions, the average woman experiences slight downward career mobility over her working life (Treiman, 1985). One reason is that women tend to begin their careers in higher status occupations than men do, often beginning as clerical workers whereas many men begin as semiskilled or unskilled workers. Another reason has to do with women's marital and maternal status. Women with children, especially those who have three or more, tend to show downward mobility; those without children, especially those who remain single, show upward mobility.

Women who remain single tend to have orderly careers, and their working lives may resemble those of men in many ways. However, many married women do not follow the "typical" career plan, either delaying entry into the labor force until their children begin school—or even until they leave home—or else starting their careers "on time" but interrupting them to bear and rear children. In a study that traced the working careers of retired women, Norah Keating and Barbara Jeffrey (1983) discovered five different occupational patterns among women who had recently retired. Only one of these resembled the "orderly" career pattern. No married women, but 55 percent of the single women, had had the continuous, orderly career pattern found among men, and 30 percent of the married women had unstable careers, interrupted as many as five times. No single women had so many interruptions; 23 percent of the single women had dropped out of the labor force once, and another 22 percent had dropped out twice during their careers. These women had been born between 1910 and 1920 and were subject to a particular set of social influences and historical events.

Interruptions in women's occupational lives have been connected with lower income and lower job prestige. Women's failure to progress as far and as fast as men on the climb up the management ladder has also been attributed to their practice of taking time out for child-rearing. Time out for children usually comes between the ages of 25 and 35, the very years when people with orderly careers are in the establishment stage, laying the foundation for occupational success. Perhaps that helps explain why women who delay child-bearing until they are at least 27 earn about 10 percent more than women who have their first child before they are 22—even when their education and experience are comparable (*New York Times,* August 21, 1986).

Women who refuse to place their jobs before their families are shunted to the **"mommy track,"** whose occupants are seen by management as "not really serious" about their work. Although the mommy track describes women's desires to work *and* to have children as well as recognition by employers that both desires can be accommodated, it can also result in the restoration of discrimination against women—albeit in a sophisticated guise (Dionne, 1989). Yet when employers recognize the existence of the mommy track, usually by providing variations in working schedules and/or child care, many women's working lives become easier. By 1987, 11 percent of employers provided some sort of child-care benefits, but only 2 percent sponsored day-care centers (U.S. Bureau of the Census, 1989). More popular were varied working schedules, which had been adopted by 61 percent of businesses (U.S. Bureau of the Census, 1989) (Table 13.4).

Some companies have instituted job-sharing, which allows mothers of young children to find time for their families while continuing to hold responsible jobs. At Time, Inc., Susan Oestreich and Mary Jane Berrien share the position of advertising sales manager. Berrien, the mother of two children younger than four, works Mondays, Tuesdays, and Wednesdays. Oestreich works Wednesdays, Thursdays, and Fridays. Each woman retains complete benefits and earns 60 percent of her full-time salary (Lawson, 1989).

Table 13.4 **WORK SCHEDULE VARIATIONS FOR THE MOMMY TRACK**[a]

Flextime	43.2%
Voluntary part-time	34.8%
Job sharing	15.5%
Work at home	8.3%
Flexible leave	42.9%
Other leave or scheduling policies	2.1%

Source: U.S. Bureau of the Census, 1989.

[a] Many employers have responded to the need to balance work and family by arranging flexible working schedules. More than 60 percent of employers provide at least one schedule variation and some provide several.

Other companies provide flexible hours, a practice called flextime. **Flextime** allows employees to choose their own hours, as long as they work the prescribed number of hours and are on the job during the "core period," which usually runs from about 10 A.M. to noon and from 2 to 4 P.M. Flextime was initiated as a way of reducing traffic congestion during working hours, but it has become a primary tool in allowing women to meet the needs of their families without taking time from work. Denise Francis, a payroll administrator at Steelcase, Inc., an office-furniture company in Grand Rapids, Michigan, has the freedom to set her own schedule as long as she puts in 40 hours each week. Francis, who is divorced and has two daughters, told a journalist, "It makes my life easier. If one of my kids is sick and the doctor says, 'Bring her in,' I can just go" (Cohn, 1988).

THE PROBLEM OF PAY

No matter what their occupation, women generally earn less than men. In 1988, the average woman earned only about 70 cents for every dollar earned by the average man—up from 62 cents about 20 years ago (Cowan, August 21, 1989). Economist Victor Fuchs (1983) believes that career interruptions are only one of the factors responsible. He sees male and female gender roles as the strongest factor and points out that early socialization practices affect women's choice of subjects in school, occupation, location of employment, and hours of work. Because traditional socialization emphasizes the maternal role, it weakens women's commitment to work outside the home, making them likely to refuse job transfers or to drop out of the labor force at any time. Fuchs believes that women who are committed to continuous, full-time employment are often discriminated against because employers form expectations based on the "average" behavior of women. Most employers, for example, believe that women's attention to their families keeps them from putting in as much time on the job as men. Yet researchers have found that up to 70 percent of women workers spend more time on their jobs than do men in similar occupations who have equivalent responsibilities (Bielby and Bielby, 1988).

Another factor that lowers the average woman's wage is the existence of "female ghettos" within various fields, in which virtually every worker is a woman (Cowan, August 21,

1989). In the field of real estate, for example, women handle most of the residential sales, whereas men handle most commercial sales—the lucrative side of the real estate business. Among bakers, women run supermarket bakeries, often at minimum wages, and men work in higher paying commercial bakeries. Although women now hold 39 percent of all executive, administrative, and managerial jobs, they tend to be concentrated at the low end, working as apartment managers, retail store managers, and the like. As the 1980s closed, women filled only 3 percent of the top management positions in the country's largest corporations (Cowan, August 21, 1989). The problem is compounded by the fact that when women enter a field in large numbers, wages tend to drop—not only for the women, but also for the men who remain. One study indicated that each time the proportion of women in a specific occupation rose by 1 percent, the median earnings for that occupation dropped by $42 per year (Hacker, 1988).

A final problem faced by many women is the disparity in pay between typically male and typically female jobs of **comparable worth.** That is, when an occupation that is filled primarily by men (painter, carpenter, automobile mechanic, janitor) requires approximately the same level of skills and responsibility as an occupation that is filled primarily by women (typing-pool supervisor, senior legal secretary, mental health technician, maid), the male job consistently pays more money. The Supreme Court has halted some specific discriminations, holding that the Corning Glass Works, for example, had violated the law by paying male night inspectors higher wages than female day inspectors (Pear, 1985). Yet the discrepancy in pay still exists in most comparable jobs. An attempt by the state of Washington to introduce a comparable-worth pay scale among government workers has shown that solving the problem of pay disparity is not easy (Kilborn, 1990). Washington State has reduced the gender pay disparity from 20 to 5 percent, but budget limitations led to reduced cost-of-living increases for jobs commonly held by men coupled with pay boosts for jobs commonly held by women. The salary of proficient secretaries with shorthand skills has increased 28 percent in the past four years, but the salary of transportation engineers has increased by just over 11 percent. The result has been a departure of male workers to the private sector, where wages are about 30 percent higher, as well as a shortage among workers of either sex for jobs requiring special skills. In addition, men have been reluctant to apply for jobs commonly held by women, despite the increase in wages. Since the comparable-worth program was initiated, the proportion of male government employees has dropped from 50 to 47 percent.

Because researchers have generally focused on male workers, we know little about gender differences in attitudes toward retirement. But when people of either sex are dissatisfied and have no sense of achievement or control over their work, they may spend the last decade or so on the job marking time, counting off the years and months until retirement. Highly satisfied workers may have mixed feelings about the approach of retirement.

RETIREMENT

The concept of retirement, of withdrawing from the labor force yet continuing to be paid, is a relatively new development, one that appears to be connected with industrialization. As we discovered earlier, during the nineteenth century only a minority of the population lived long enough to reach today's retirement age, and the average worker was still employed at the time of death. Those who survived continued to work as long as they were physically able, and in predominantly agricultural areas there was always work for them to do.

Several forces associated with industrialization made the practice of retirement possible (McConnell, 1983). First, beginning in about 1870, as productivity mounted and fewer people were needed to provide the country's goods and services, the demand for labor declined. The change was most striking in the field of agriculture, where jobs shrank from 50 percent of the workforce in 1870 to 38 percent in 1900 and 4 percent in 1975 (Foner and Schwab, 1981). Second, as technology transformed many occupations, the skills and knowledge of older workers quickly became obsolete. Third, as large business and governmental bureaucracies developed, careers began to be governed by impersonal rules and regulations that made organizations run smoothly but made no allowance for interindividual differences. Finally, private pensions and the establishment of the Social Security system in 1935 provided an economic base that made the retirement of older workers possible and established the arbitrary age of 65 as the normative time of departure from the labor force. If the age of retirement bore the same relationship to life expectancy today as it did in 1935, because of increased longevity, people would be expected to work until they reached the age of 80 (Swensen, 1983).

By institutionalizing retirement, the Social Security system reduced unemployment, sweeping workers out of the labor market. The sweep accelerated after World War II when the program expanded to cover nearly all workers (including the self-employed), permissible retirement age was lowered to 62, and private pension plans began to spread (Morrison, 1986). As people retired early and lived long, the pool of retired workers grew rapidly. In 1900, 68.3 percent of men older than 65 and 9.1 percent of older women were still in the workforce (Riley and Foner, 1968); by 1987, only 16.3 percent of older men and 7.4 percent of older women were still employed (U.S. Bureau of the Census, 1989) (Figure 13.1).

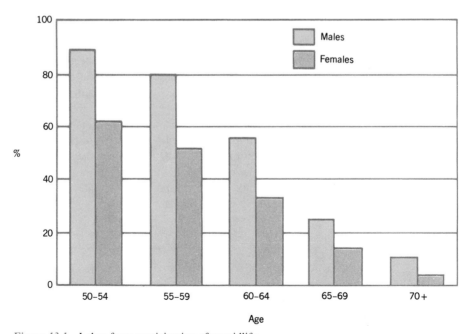

Figure 13.1   Labor force participation after midlife.

Among those who continue to work, many have their own businesses. As we will see, changes in society, in the Social Security system, and in employment practices may produce a new concept of retirement in the twenty-first century.

Investigators have been especially interested in whether the aging process diminishes the value of workers, what factors contribute to retirement decisions, and how retirement affects people psychologically and physiologically.

THE PROBLEMS OF THE AGING WORKER

One factor that may push an older worker into retirement is job discrimination. Most people believe that the aging worker is less efficient, less adaptable, slower, and weaker on the job than younger adults. Such stereotypical beliefs about older workers can translate into discriminatory employment practices. Studies have shown that interviewers who screen job applicants assume that older adults are more difficult to train and place in jobs, more resistant to change, likely to be less productive, and to be less suitable for promotion (Waldman and Avolio, 1986). As a result, when older and younger people have the same job qualifications, the younger candidate usually gets the position. Other research indicates that older workers are laid off first and rehired last; that when they do find another job, it generally carries less prestige and less pay than their old position; that they are passed over for promotion; and that they are less likely than a younger worker to get education and retraining that would upgrade their skills (Wanner and McDonald, 1983).

Perhaps this discrimination explains why workers older than 65 are three times as likely as the general population to be self-employed (Quinn and Burkhauser, 1990). Steven August, a 61-year-old former advertising executive who freelances his advertising skills, would probably agree. His self-employment is a matter of necessity, not choice. At the age of 58, August, who says, ''I love what I used to do and I hate being tossed on the scrapheap,'' lost his long-time job as associate creative director at a New York advertising agency (Lewin, April 22, 1990). When he looked for a new position, he got subtle messages of discouragement that made him realize his former career was over. Once he was told that a firm's creative director was only 40 and might feel uncomfortable talking to him. On other occasions he was told that ''it must have been great to be in advertising back when it was fun.''

The Age Discrimination in Employment Act, passed in 1967, attempted to protect workers younger than 65 from being retired, fired, or passed over for hiring simply because of their age. In 1978 the law was amended to cover workers up to the age of 70. No one knows how much age discrimination still goes on, but most specialists in the field of employment agree that it is still a serious problem (Robinson, Coberly, and Paul, 1985). For example, workers between the ages of 55 and 64 showed a decline in real earnings over the preceding ten years—at a time when the average full-time worker showed a 12.4 percent gain (Wanner and McDonald, 1983). Yet nearly a third of these men had had some sort of recent occupational training.

Is there any basis for age discrimination in the workplace? If older workers are less productive than younger workers, then their employment at similar salary levels could be costly. No one has yet demonstrated that there is much difference between the job performance of the old and the young (Robinson, Coberly, and Paul, 1985). Although productivity declines occur in a few occupations, in most there are no significant age differences, and in others older workers are *more* productive than younger workers. Declines in reaction time and speed are usually compensated by older workers' superior flexibility, creativity, and experience. Some studies have found that when older workers are more productive than younger workers, the difference disappears when output is corrected for job experience (Davies and Sparrow, 1985). Older workers are also steadier than younger workers. They are less likely to be absent from work, and they are less likely to be injured on the job (Martocchio, 1989). Finally, among workers who are at least 65, health insurance costs tend to diminish because of Medicare coverages. Employers have found that health insurance costs are less for workers on Medicare than for young workers with children (Marklein, 1990).

Among professional workers, training is important to the maintenance of performance. Age-related declines in performance in such professions as aerospace engineering is the result of an obsolescent knowledge base rather than from any loss of physical or mental skills (Davies and Sparrow, 1985). Among service engineers in the office equipment industry, the quality of work declined with age, but only among engineers who had received no training within the past five years (Sparrow and Davies, 1988). As for managerial positions, age seems to have no effect on performance, although it leads to the use of different strategies in formulating similar decisions (Taylor, 1975).

The widespread belief that young employees are innovative and that older employees are inflexible and conservative is probably wrong. Young employees are intent on learning company politics, advancing their careers, and avoiding risks. Older employees, being near retirement, risk little by proposing radical innovations. It has been suggested that instead of a roster of young Turks and old fogies, most companies are staffed by young fogies and old Turks (Schrank and Waring, 1983).

Studies of skilled and semiskilled jobs indicate that workers in their twenties turn in the poorest job performance and that peak performance comes from the mid-thirties to the early forties (Sparrow and Davies, 1988). Among workers in their fifties, performance declines but is still higher than among workers in their twenties.

Although older workers may be slower than younger workers, they are as productive because of their superior flexibility, creativity, and experience.

Because older skilled and semiskilled workers tend to be concentrated in dying industries, their skills often become obsolete. When this happens to a younger worker, employees frequently provide retraining. But when they consider the number of productive years remaining to the older worker against the cost of retraining, it may be more economical to train a new worker. In addition, the older worker's experience often has pushed his or her wages to the high end of the salary scale, further increasing the annual cost. Skill obsolescence and higher salaries, together with beliefs that aging is associated with rigidity and low productivity, tilt the scales against the older worker. However, because age is a rough index of knowledge and experience, this practice deprives companies of the experience and wisdom of employees with long employment histories (Schrank and Waring, 1983).

When industrial plants shut down, blue-collar workers may find themselves suddenly thrust out of the middle class. Employees who fare the worst are those in their forties and fifties whose training is limited and who feel unable to relocate in another community. At 39, Frank Burton, a "rubber rat" in an Akron tire factory, found his $30,000 a year job gone when Firestone stopped making tires (Manning and McCormick, 1984). Nearly 1000 hours of training in computer science was of little help, because no one in Akron needed his new skills. At 42, Burton was earning $7000 a year working the graveyard shift behind the counter of a convenience store. The switch from manufacturing to service not only lowers a worker's standard of living, but also undermines self-esteem and identity. Older workers may do even worse. After a plant closes or moves, workers older than 54 are without work for 27 weeks, whereas workers younger than 45 generally find work within 13 weeks (Love and Torrence, 1989). Even when workers are matched on education, job tenure, marital status, and willingness to relocate, older workers still face an additional four weeks on unemployment, and when they finally find a job their new wages are 16.5 percent less than those earned by younger workers.

Many older unemployed workers cannot find jobs. Unemployment figures for older workers seem low compared to rates among younger workers. In 1988, when the rate for workers between the ages of 25 and 54 was 4.5 percent, the official rate for workers aged 55 to 64 was 3.2 percent and 2.7 percent for those 65 and older (Quinn and Burkhauser, 1990). But because many older workers have become discouraged and dropped out of the job market in the belief that no one will hire them, their inclusion would send unemployment rates for those older than 60 climbing. Unemployment may be the first step to early retirement for as many as 20 percent of working men (Robinson, Coberly, and Paul, 1985). If they are eligible for retirement benefits, older workers may decide to take them as soon as their unemployment checks run out, making them "reluctant retirees."

THE RETIREMENT DECISION

Reluctant retirees are only part of the increasing number of people who are choosing early retirement, in which they leave work any time after their sixty-second birthday and accept reduced Social Security benefits. Nearly two-thirds of large companies allow full pensions at 62 for employees who meet service requirements and reduced pensions as early as age 55 (Quinn and Burkhauser, 1990). The factors behind the decision to retire differ, depending on whether a person chooses early or "on time" retirement.

In some occupations, where physical condition and reaction time are critical, full retirement comes especially early. For example, police officers tend to retire before they are 50.

For the most part, however, workers who retire ''very early,'' that is before the age of 62, tend to be either wealthy and in good health or strapped financially and in poor health.

Since 1968 early retirement—which refers to retirement beween the ages of 62 and 64—has become increasingly popular. Some workers retire because they have been unable to find new employment after being laid off, but other factors influence the majority of early retirement decisions. Finances appear to be the most important influence, and workers who can expect an income that permits them to live comfortably are the most likely to retire early. Researchers have found that the proportion of workers who retire in their late fifties and early sixties rises sharply in companies that provide attractive benefits for those who retire early (Rhine, 1984).

Among workers in several national longitudinal studies, poor health and positive attitudes toward retirement were associated with early retirement (Palmore, George, and Fillenbaum, 1982). Health is apparently the major factor in the decision. Job dissatisfaction appears to lead to early retirement only when a worker's occupation is central to his or her life (McConnell, 1983), but 90 percent of health-related retirements occur among workers younger than 65 (Ward, 1984).

Among men in the longitudinal studies who retired ''on time'' or later, education, occupation, and financial considerations were of major importance (Palmore, George, and Fillenbaum, 1982). Those with high levels of education and high-status occupations tended to work longer and often worked past retirement age. People in high socioeconomic brackets appeared to have more opportunities to work and more incentive to continue working. Similarly, self-employment also predicted continued work, whereas working for others, pension plan coverage, and mandatory retirement rules predicted retirement at age 65. These considerations appeared to have little effect on women's decision to retire. Only age predicted retirement among women in these longitudinal studies (George, Fillenbaum, and Palmore, 1984). (Most retired workers in these surveys stopped working before mandatory retirement was pushed to age 70.)

Attitudes toward work and retirement appeared to be of little importance, but they may have influenced retirement decisions indirectly (Palmore, George, and Fillenbaum, 1982). Work attitudes influenced the likelihood of continued full-time employment or part-time employment after retirement. Workers who had said earlier that they preferred work to leisure or that they would work if they did not have to generally stuck by their words. By the end of the studies, they were working more hours each year than other workers.

The condition of a worker's health had little connection with the decision to retire at 65 or later. This finding contradicts the conclusions of many cross-sectional studies, but the researchers suggest that poor health is a socially acceptable reason for retirement and that, in retrospect, it may take on exaggerated importance to the retired worker.

ADJUSTING TO RETIREMENT

The transition from work to leisure is sometimes seen as a negative process involving a series of losses: the loss of income, occupational identity, social status, associates, and the daily structure of time and activities (Robinson, Coberly, and Paul, 1985). Yet studies consistently indicate that most retired people are satisfied, continue to feel useful, and maintain their sense of identity. Retirement is unlikely to be followed by depression, decline, or death.

When we examine studies of retirees closely, it becomes apparent that retirement is good for many people, has no influence on others, and is bad for the rest (McConnell, 1983). Prior attitudes, personality characteristics, economics, and health all affect the way a person adjusts to a life of retirement. For some people, the abrupt loss of the work role, with its associated sense of power and the belief that their work contributes to society, can lead to a troubled transition. Such people are likely to have made work a central part of their lives and to be members of high-status professions. High occupational status does not foretell an unhappy retirement, however. Among high-status retired employees from seven large corporations, 55 percent said that retirement had given them "the best years of my life" (Kimmel, Price, and Walker, 1978).

It has been suggested that retirement is likely to be pleasant for people who have a comfortable income, are relatively healthy, retire voluntarily, are not wedded to their work, and have made some sort of plans for their new lives (McConnell, 1983). Economics seems particularly important. Between 1974 and 1978, as inflation increased, the proportion of retired people who said they would prefer to be working rose from 31 to 46 percent (Foner and Schwab, 1981).

Until recently, only a minority of women spent their lives in the labor force, and so most of the information on adjustment to retirement has come from studies of retired men. When researchers studied 6000 retired union members, for example, 75 percent of the sample were men, yet in the retired population at large 75 percent are women (Tolchin, 1989). Among the retired union workers, 23 percent said they had retired too early, but in a longitudinal study of 5000 men, 80 percent of those who had retired said that retirement fulfilled or exceeded their expectations (Parnes, 1981). Once those who retired because of poor health were eliminated, the remaining retirees were just as satisfied with life as the workers (Table 13.5). Loss of the work role appeared to have no negative impact on happiness, but marital status did (Beck, 1982). Divorced, widowed, or separated men were more likely than married men to say they were unhappy. In addition, reluctant retirees, who had retired five or more

Table 13.5 **RETIREMENT AND LIFE SATISFACTION[a]**

"Very Happy with"	Nonretired (N = 503)	All Retired (N = 299)	Healthy Retired (N = 185)
Housing	70%	67%	72%
Local area	68%	64%	66%
Health condition	59%	47%	62%
Standard of living	62%	54%	59%
Leisure activities	54%	57%	65%
Things overall	59%	51%	60%

Source: Parnes, 1981, p. 188.

[a] When adults with 12 years of education were compared, there was no difference between healthy retired people (those who did not retire for health reasons) and workers in their satisfaction with most areas of life.

♦ *Adulthood in Today's World*

JOBS FOR OLDER WORKERS

There may be more job opportunities for older workers than the average reluctant retiree believes. As the baby-bust generation enters the labor market and the pool of available workers shrinks, some companies have begun to look for employees among the over-65 group. For about ten years, The Travelers, a Connecticut insurance firm, has filled its temporary jobs from a job bank made up of men and women who have retired from various insurance companies. On any given day, about 180 retirees are usually working in its offices (Lewin, 1990). The Home Depot, a chain of home-improvement centers, has found that customers prefer to do business with retired people from construction-related fields, whose age and experience convince shoppers that they are getting reliable advice (Marklein, 1990). Texas Refinery Corporation, which produces building products, has found that older workers make better sales representatives than young adults in their twenties (Marklein, 1990). Each year, nine of their top ten sales reps are older than 50.

Days Inn, a motel chain, turned to older adults when the absentee rate among reservation

years before they expected to leave the labor force, tended to be less happy than men who had retired at the expected age.

When adjusting to retirement is traumatic, the stress may be due to the abrupt change connected with the shift from worker to retiree. The sudden removal of a useful social role may make a worker feel bereft, useless, and unhappy. In fact, studies have consistently shown that workers prefer part-time work to complete retirement and that many would prefer a phased retirement, in which they gradually reduced their working hours during several transitional years. The feeling is so strong that 25 percent of the older men and women in the Social Security Administration's massive Retirement History started work on a new job (either full or part-time) after they left their major employer (Quinn, Burkhauser, and Myers, 1990). Workers at both ends of the economic spectrum—the wealthy and the poor—were most likely to take another job. Two years later, more than 75 percent of those who moved to new employment were still working.

A new trend may make adjusting to retirement easier. Polaroid Corporation has initiated a program that provides several routes to retirement, perhaps cushioning its shock (Clendinen, 1983; Lewin, 1990). In one option, employees may take a "rehearsal retirement"— up to three months' leave of absence with all their benefits intact. If they find that retirement does not agree with them, they may come back to work. About half do return to the job, with one man back at work after only three days of leisure. Another route consists of tapering off working hours. A worker may cut back to a four-day work week, taking a 20 percent salary cut. A third program pays a year's college tuition for workers who have been

agents climbed to 30 percent and the turnover rate to 180 percent each year. But newspaper ads urging older adults to apply for work went unheeded, primarily because most older men and women who saw the ads did not believe them. Not until the company posted notices at senior centers across the country did older men and women begin to apply for work (Lewin, 1990).

Today, the program is successful, and Days Inn's productivity has improved. With more than 20 percent of its 600 reservation agents older than 60, the motel's absentee rate has dropped to 3 percent, and turnover has virtually come to a halt. Since the program began in 1987, almost none of the reservation agents has left. Older workers have also increased Days Inn profits to the tune of $1.8 million per year—simply because older workers get off the phone more quickly. When younger workers manned the reservation lines, the average phone call lasted 235 seconds; with older workers on the phones, the average call now lasts 175 seconds (Marklein, 1990). Even so, some older adults find the idea that companies are actively seeking their services hard to believe. After seeing a posted notice, one skeptical woman called the toll-free reservation number and demanded to speak to an "older worker." Her doubts were put to rest when she discovered that the woman who answered the call was 78 and her supervisor was 73 (Lewin, 1990).

with the company at least ten years and want to leave Polaroid for second careers as elementary or high school teachers.

Xerox Corporation allows people who are at least 55 years old and have been with the company for at least 15 years to move to less demanding jobs that do not involve arduous shift work. The people in this program take a small cut in pay but still get more money than other workers in these less strenuous jobs (Lewin, 1990). Only a few employers allow people who would otherwise retire to move into part-time work, but such programs are popular with retired workers. After eight years of retirement, when she discovered that hobbies, crafts, and travel did not fill her life, Anna Martino went back to the Travelers. The former accounting supervisor, now 74, has been working in the personnel department for two years.

IBM pays for educational programs that help train employees who are near retirement age for alternative careers or postretirement hobbies. It also provides two years of full company benefits and partial salary for retiring employees who want to teach (Fanning, 1990). The accompanying box, "Jobs for Older Workers," describes other job opportunities for retired people.

As the labor force shrinks and the proportion of healthy, young-old people grows, programs like those of Polaroid, Xerox, and The Travelers may be more the rule than the exception. Retirement expert Malcolm Morrison (1986) suggests that before too many decades have passed, society will expect older adults either to postpone retirement, move to a different postretirement job, or engage in some other productive activity that brings minimal economic rewards but provides broad benefits to society. Similar suggestions have come from psychiatrist Carl Eisdorfer, who suggests that older men and women could be trained as teachers' aides or paid to serve as foster grandparents to retarded or disabled children in institutions (Kotre and Hall, 1990). If social expectations for the young-old years change, the concept of retirement may be altered in significant ways.

SUMMARY

CHOOSING AN OCCUPATION

Work serves many purposes. It is a measure of maturity and responsibility, a reflection of identity, a source of meaning, a definition of social position, a satisfying activity, an outlet for creativity, and a source of social stimulation. About 75 percent of workers have **jobs,** and the rest have **careers.** Occupational choice is often accidental, guided by sex, social class, proximity, apparently unrelated decisions, and luck. Vocational tests, which match a person's interests and abilities with occupations, can assist in the selection of an occupation.

OCCUPATIONAL DEVELOPMENT

An orderly career moves through a predictable pattern of stages: **crystallization, specification, implementation, establishment, consolidation, maintenence,** and **deceleration.** During the implementation stage, a **mentor** can help accelerate career development.

Work affects cognition and personality, primarily through the degree of flexibility inherent in the job. Job satisfaction is generally related to a job's challenge (which is related to its complexity) and its financial rewards, but salary is an important issue only among low-income workers. Job satisfaction increases with age, and the **job-change hypothesis** appears to explain this increased satisfaction better than does either the **grinding-down hypothesis** or the **Lordstown hypothesis.**

MALE OCCUPATIONAL PATTERNS

Men have been socialized into the role of worker, and the stages of their careers tend to parallel the stages of Levinson's theory of emotional development. However, men change occupations far more often than theories of orderly career development would predict.

FEMALE OCCUPATIONAL PATTERNS

Women's socialization for motherhood may be an important factor in their acceptance of low-paying, "helping" jobs. Single women tend to have orderly careers, but married women rarely follow the typical career plan. The **mommy track,** developed for women who place equal emphasis on family and career, has made it easier for many mothers to stay in the workforce but may also discriminate against women. Women's lower earnings may be the result of career interruptions and gender-role socialization. The problem of pay disparity in jobs of **comparable worth** is proving difficult to solve.

RETIREMENT

Job discrimination is the result of stereotypical beliefs about the capabilities of older workers, even though older workers appear to be as productive as younger workers. Unemployment among older workers often leads to reluctant retirement. An increasing number of workers are choosing to retire before the age of 65. Workers who retire very early tend to be in poor health, but once workers pass the age of 62, finances appear to be the most important consideration. Health and income are the major predictors of satisfaction in retirement. Workers who find it difficult to adjust to retirement may be mourning the loss of a useful social role.

KEY TERMS

career

comparable worth

consolidation stage

crystallization stage

deceleration stage

establishment stage

flextime

grinding-down hypothesis

implementation stage

job

job-change hypothesis

Lordstown hypothesis

maintenance stage

mentor

mommy track

specification stage

Chapter 14

♦

Leisure and Community Involvement Across Adulthood

♦

Barbara Weidmer has had as many arrests as grandchildren. A founding member of Grandmothers for Peace, she has been arrested 16 times for civil disobedience. Until 1982, Weidmer was strictly nonpolitical, devoting her energies to her husband, her children, and her grandchildren. Then she learned that 150 nuclear weapons were stored at an air force base near her home. Her anger led her to demonstrate, brandishing a sign that said "Grandmother for Peace." The publicity led to the formation of an international organization, which gives her great satisfaction, but Weidmer's efforts are not limited to the nuclear issue. "We support anything grandparents can do to help children grow up as healthy, productive citizens," she says (Taylor, 1990).

Not all older adults devote their leisure to politics. Some, like Grant Cushinberry, find their niche in charitable work. Cushinberry runs God's Little Half-Acre in Topeka, Kansas, which provides clothes, furniture, and food to those in need. For 20 years, he has been the organizer and sparkplug of the annual Topeka Thanksgiving dinner for the needy. He also sees that children have a good time. He has taken as many as 1000 children to a circus performance, and he sometimes rents the local movie theater and provides free shows. When asked why he works so hard on behalf of others, Cushinberry says, "My mother always told me, 'If you help someone you'll never regret it.' When it's a labor of love, it doesn't feel like work" (Taylor, 1990).

The hours away from work give us the opportunity to express ourselves in any way we choose. Some of our free time is spent pursuing personal interests, and we trace the pattern of leisure activities across adulthood. A sizable portion of leisure time is occupied by direct involvement with charities, political organizations, and other community institutions that create a social fabric: schools, churches, government, hospitals, and the like. In this chapter we examine some aspects of these more structured aspects of our lives, beginning with the increasing trend toward a return to formal education by adults of all ages. Next, we turn to adults' involvement in the church and their feelings about religion. The chapter closes with an exploration of political activity in adulthood, paying attention to the effects of education and gender.   ◆

LEISURE ACROSS ADULTHOOD

With retirement, the amount of free time expands enormously. But by historical standards, even fully employed adults have an incredible amount of **leisure**—time for activities they are not obligated to do. As we have seen, the average work week has dropped from 60 to 40 hours within the past century, and vacations—unheard of as late as the nineteenth century—are a standard benefit of employment. In response to the growth of free time and discretionary income, a large leisure industry has developed. This booming multibillion dollar industry produces goods and services of every description, from tennis rackets, television, and videotapes to Caribbean cruises, computers, and cookbooks.

The importance Americans give to leisure activities seems to have increased in recent years, and this increase is probably related to the emphasis most of us place on self-fulfillment. National studies indicate that about 80 percent of the population believe that life should be more than a matter of economic survival and duty and say that choice, flexibility, and freedom are important in their lives (Yankelovich, 1981).

Of course, not all the time away from work is spent in leisure activities. Family or other obligations may consume a great deal of nonworking time. The view of leisure as freely chosen means that a specific activity may be obligatory in one situation and freely chosen leisure in another. For example, a half hour spent preparing a family meal is probably an obligation, but several hours devoted to preparing an elaborate meal by a person whose hobby is gourmet cooking could be leisure. The classification of any activity seems to depend on our attitude toward it rather than the characteristics of the activity, which means that our activities are leisure only when we say they are (Cutler and Hendricks, 1990).

OBJECTIVES OF LEISURE

The objectives of leisure, according to researchers, are either relaxation, diversion, developmental pleasure, creativity, or the pursuit of sensual pleasure (Gordon, Gaitz, and Scott, 1976). Each requires a different intensity of cognitive, emotional, and physical involvement, and as intensity increases, so do the expenditure of energy, the need for focused attention, and the level of sensory stimulation. **Relaxation,** the least intense form of leisure, includes resting, daydreaming, and sleeping. **Diversion,** a medium-low form of involvement, gives us a change of pace and some relief from our routine activities of work and chores. It

Sensual pleasure is a form of leisure encompassing high-intensity activity that produces excitement or joy.

When leisure takes the form of developmental pleasure, it often enhances cognitive skills.

includes watching television or movies, light reading, most hobbies, conversation with friends, parties, games and toys, and watching athletic events.

Developmental pleasures require involvement of medium intensity, and their pursuit, though intrinsically enjoyable, often increases physical or cognitive skills. They include exercise, individual sports, serious reading, education not aimed at furthering career goals, visiting museums and art galleries, clubs and interest groups, learning to play a musical instrument, travel, "educational" games, and toys.

In **creative pleasures,** involvement increases to medium-high intensity and might be considered "useful play." Creative pleasures include obvious creative activities in artistic, literary, and music fields, altruistic activities, serious discussion, and the blending of art and play with work.

At the most intense level of involvement is the pursuit of **sensual pleasures,** which encompass sexual activity, as well as any form of leisure in which the activation of the senses provides intense pleasure, gratification, excitement, rapture, or joy. An ecstatic religious experience, intense and rhythmic dancing, or highly competitive games and sports can provide sensual pleasure. High-intensity forms of leisure are sometimes addictive (as in the use of psychoactive drugs and perhaps running) or dangerous (as in skydiving or mountain climbing).

Sometimes the objectives of leisure may blur. For example, the computer hacker who majors in computer science, gets a job programming or maintaining computers, sits in front of a terminal 16 hours a day, and sees no one except other hackers is probably functioning at the addictive level rather than blending work with play (Zimbardo, 1980). However, in our leisure activities most of us move from one level of involvement to another, pursuing either physical, cultural, social, or solitary forms of leisure.

SIMILARITY AND CHANGE IN LEISURE ACROSS ADULTHOOD

The leisure activities we find most rewarding seem to change over the life span and are influenced by gender, education, health, interests, socioeconomic level, and age. Women, for example, tend to become involved in reading, social activities, and artistic endeavors, whereas men tend to pursue team sports and outdoor activities, and join voluntary organizations (Cutler and Hendricks, 1990).

Socioeconomic levels appear to influence leisure, with people at lower levels engaging in relaxation, diversion, and sensual pleasure, and people at upper levels engaging in developmental, creative, and sensual pleasures (Gordon, Gaitz, and Scott, 1976). Some researchers explain these differences in recreational choice as the result of two seemingly contradictory factors: compensation and ''spillover'' (Burrus-Bammel and Bammel, 1985). When influenced by compensation, people may choose activities that provide satisfactions lacking in their jobs. When influenced by ''spillover,'' they generalize the qualities of their occupations to leisure. People with dull, repetitive jobs seem either to compensate radically or to let the tone of their employment spill over into leisure activities characterized by isolation, apathy, and inertia. As income and education go up, for example, the popularity of television goes down (*Gallup Reports,* 1986). An evening in front of the television is the favorite pastime of 41 percent of those who earn less than $10,000 each year, but of only 24 percent of those who earn at least $50,000 (in 1986 dollars). Whereas 44 percent of those who never graduated from high school prefer television, only 18 percent of college graduates feel that way. In fact, many college graduates would rather read than watch TV.

Among young adults, outdoor physical recreation is popular, especially among men, with swimming and walking the most popular sports (*New York Times,* 1984). Jogging has rapidly overtaken more traditional forms of recreation, with 29 percent jogging, a form of leisure that was almost never reported 20 years ago. When not participating in sports, young adults are likely to be watching them or reading about them. Ninety-six percent do so at least once a month (Vecsey, March 16, 1983). Perhaps because of their new interest in physical fitness, women are becoming more interested in spectator sports, and 41 percent follow football and baseball. Most watching takes place in front of a television, with 55 percent of both sexes ''always'' or ''usually'' interested in watching a football game and only 19 percent ''never'' interested.

Changes in leisure activities with age tend to parallel changes in the family life cycle. Married couples tend to spend their leisure time in joint activities that encourage interaction between partners and that develop shared commitment (Wilson, 1980). They may garden together, work on home projects, or spend evenings and weekends with other couples. Sexual activity is a popular pastime, with men rating it higher than women (Mancini and Orthner, 1978). Among married couples who have been married less than five years, a strong majority of husbands but less than half the wives view sexual activity as a highly desired form of recreation. Across the years of married life, the popularity of recreational sex declines, retaining the most popularity among couples who use effective contraception and have all the children they want (Udry, 1980).

Between the ages of 30 and 44, most leisure activities are centered around home and family. Watching television, visiting, gardening, working in a home workshop, hobbies, reading, walking, and such physical activities as fishing, hunting, camping, or swimming are popular (Gordon, Gaitz, and Scott, 1976). During these years participation in youth groups and school service groups peaks (Cutler and Hendricks, 1990). At this stage working mothers may find themselves with no free time at all, especially if they are divorced or have a traditional marriage.

After the age of 45, as children grow older and parents are less tied to the home, the focus of leisure activities may broaden. When children leave the nest, there are fewer constraints on recreational choices, and many child-related obligations disappear. Increased disposable income, freedom from responsibility, and additional time may lead to more evenings out, to travel, and to new interests in creative activities.

Education and income continue to influence the leisure activities of retired adults, and health may also begin to affect their choices. Active sports, such as water skiing, bicycling, downhill skiing, and tennis decline drastically in popularity with older adults, but there is only a weak relationship between age and such activities as golf, nature walks, and sightseeing (Cutler and Hendricks, 1990). Declining health may help to explain the rise in popularity of TV with age: TV is a favorite way to spend an evening among 27 percent of adults younger than 50, 40 percent of those between the ages of 50 and 64, and 47 percent of those older than 65 (*Gallup Reports*, 1986).

Although retired adults watch more TV than do college students, there is some overlap in their viewing habits. Asked about their favorite news and information programs, college students and retired adults agreed that ''60 Minutes'' was the program of choice (Mundorf and Brownell, 1990). The old (average age 72) and young (average age 20) also shared two of their five favorite programs: the ''Cosby Show'' and ''Cheers'' dominated the lists of both groups. Men of any age were more likely than women to say that they watched primarily for information, and women were more likely to say that they turned to the tube for companionship.

Despite the existence of age-related changes, there is a good deal of stability in the choice of leisure activities. High involvement in leisure before retirement predicts high involvement after retirement (Cutler and Hendricks, 1990). Researchers have found stable rates of participation in the kinds of leisure activity chosen by retired men, for example, but an increase in the amount of time they devote to these activities (Parnes et al., 1985). When researchers studied adults in Peoria, Illinois, they discovered that strenuous forms of activity (sports, exercise, and outdoor recreation) generally declined after the age of 40, but that travel, cultural, and home-based activities remained steady until the age of 75 (Kelly, Steinkamp, and Kelly, 1986). Participation in community organizations remained steady even among the oldest adults, but rates were not high at any age.

According to David Ekerdt (1986), the active life-style of many retired adults may be due in part to a ''busy ethic,'' which encourages older adults to shun relaxation for more involved forms of leisure activities. The busy ethic, which endorses an active, engaged life-style for older adults, approves leisure that is earnest, occupied, and filled with activity. By reconciling the adult obligation to work with a life of leisure, the busy ethic defines the retirement role and adapts retired life to prevailing social norms. Some researchers have even concluded that leisure may be the functional equivalent of work for retired adults, serving to organize their lives (Cutler and Hendricks, 1990).

At least for older adults, then, leisure may serve an important purpose. Leisure activities may serve, for example, to maintain people's identities and self-concepts and contribute to life satisfaction (Kelly, Steinkamp, and Kelly, 1987). Leisure in the form of travel may help maintain interactions with widely scattered friends and family members (Marshall and Longino, 1988). Finally, active leisure may promote health and well-being (Sorock et al., 1988).

Future retirees will have higher educational levels and perhaps more disposable income than today's elderly. They are also likely to be in better health (Cutler and Hendricks, 1990). Although their leisure activities will probably continue to be more sedentary than those of younger adults, many changes may occur in recreational patterns. Retirees in the twenty-first century may still enjoy listening to the records of Depeche Mode, Madonna, and the B-52s, but the frequency and intensity of their dancing is likely to diminish. Today's retirees tend to read more newspapers than anything else; tomorrow's retirees may read more books and attend more cultural activities. One form of leisure that is becoming more popular with middle-aged and older adults is education.

EDUCATION

Just as development was once believed to stop at maturity, education was reserved for childhood and adolescence. Our attitude seemed to be that education worked like a vaccine—a large dose early in life immunized us against the need for further formal learning (Birren and Woodruff, 1973). Today, however, formal education appears to be spreading across the life span, with middle-aged and older adults enrolling in traditional college programs, in special college programs devised for ''mature students,'' and in community adult education courses. Classes have been held at colleges and universities, at elementary and secondary schools, in churches, and at recreation and cultural centers. Some older adults take correspondence courses or enroll in courses given on educational television.

THE RETURN TO SCHOOL

The accelerating return of adults to educational settings has been brought about by a combination of social and historical changes (Birren and Woodruff, 1973). First, the enormous growth in the proportion of older adults, many of whom are retiring at an early age, has produced a large army of people with the leisure that gives them ample opportunity to go back to school. Second, when the last of the baby boom moved into the ''over-25'' bracket, colleges had classrooms and staff available for older adults. Third, because the more education people have, the more likely they are to be involved in a continuing education course, rising educational levels have expanded the pool of potential older students (Figure 14.1). A high school graduate is more than twice as likely to enroll in a course as a nongraduate, and a college graduate, more than twice as likely as a high school graduate (Willis, 1985).

Fourth, change seems to have accelerated in virtually every area of life. The inoculation approach to education worked fine when people noted little social change during their lifetimes, but the rapid obsolescence of today's knowledge had made life-long education common in many professions. For example, most states will not renew a license to practice medicine unless a physician has taken a prescribed number of continuing education courses. Fifth, technological obsolescence and early retirement have led to the development of new occupational patterns. Technological change forces some workers to choose between addi-

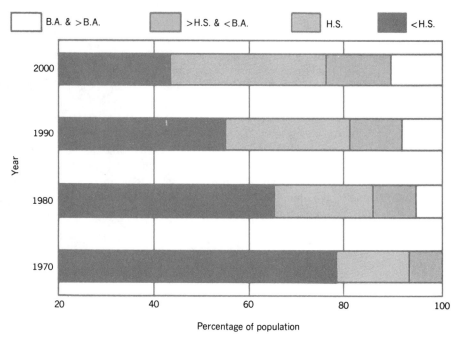

Figure 14.1   Education of older population across time.

tional training and dropping out of the labor force. Other workers are going back to school as they start second careers during middle age. For example, a retired military officer (who may be as young as 42) may enroll in business school to begin a new career in management, or a middle-aged executive may enroll in a seminary to begin a new career as a priest or minister. Finally, many middle-aged women are reentering the labor force as their child-rearing responsibilities slacken or end. Often they return to school for job training to complete their college education or to get an advanced degree. Taken together, these trends may foretell the development of a society that mixes work and study throughout life.

EDUCATION IN LATER ADULTHOOD

Although 45 percent of the current enrollment in four-year colleges consists of adults past the age of 23 (*New York Times*, October 15, 1989), the majority of these adults are in young or middle adulthood. Approximately 17 percent of adults between the ages of 35 and 54 are enrolled in college courses, and nearly 6 percent of those older than 54 have returned to school (U.S. Bureau of the Census, 1990). Researchers estimate that no more than about 4.5 percent of the elderly are enrolled at any one time (Willis, 1985).

Many gerontologists believe that continuing education could greatly improve the quality of old age. Education provides knowledge, but it is also stimulating and acts as a socializing agent, affecting attitudes, beliefs, and behavior. The goals of older students indicate that they are aware of education's value. Some older adults seek information that helps them understand and perhaps compensate for changes in their body and behavior that are the result of maturation and aging. Others seek to understand the technological and cultural change that threatens them with obsolescence. They may go on to combat the personal consequences of these changes by taking classes that minimize generational differences in knowledge and skills. Some acquire new vocational skills, perhaps to assist their entry into a second—or third—career. And some use education as a means to personal growth and satisfaction, developing meaningful retirement roles (Willis, 1985). This last goal is closely related to Erikson's (1980) theory of the life span, in which old age is a period with its own developmental tasks.

It took society some time to open the college door to older adults, in part because of our attitudes toward old age. Not too many years ago, the elderly were simply rejected. Retirement was mandatory; aging was seen as synonymous with decline, decay, and death; and no provision was made for formal schooling experiences. Absorbed with the inoculation model of education, in which schooling is preparation for the future, we regarded educating the elderly as a waste of time and money. And most people believed that older individuals were incapable of much learning.

Today, we know that older adults can profit from education. In Chapter 8, we met middle-aged and elderly adults who had earned degrees or were enrolled in college classes. The research reported in the chapters on cognition indicated that high levels of intelligence, learning, and thinking are possible far into old age—as long as secondary aging is held at bay. Few studies have been done in classroom settings, but those that are available indicate that most college students do as well as—if not better than—younger students (Kasworm, 1980). Interindividual differences are, of course, wide, with some older students outperforming most of the young and others just getting by.

When older adults return to class, they do face problems, especially if they enroll in regular college classes. Many are not interested in credentials or degrees and are not particularly motivated by tests, grades, or competition (Moody, 1986). In addition, stereotypes of the aging as incompetent, dependent, and nonproductive may weaken their self-confidence and threaten their school performance. If instructors use techniques that convince older adults of their capability, most are likely to do much better. Several methods may increase self-efficacy among older adults (Rebok and Offermann, 1983). One way is to arrange courses so that older adults experience early success, perhaps by using recognition instead of recall on initial tests. Success increases self-efficacy, because we judge our chances for future success partly on the basis of what we have done in the past. Another way to increase self-efficacy is through observing other older adults succeed (and thereby demolishing the stereotype of the incapable older person).

Verbal encouragement from instructors, family members, and other students may also help increase self-efficacy, although such social influence is probably less effective than the first two methods. Finally, perceptions of the self as ineffective or incapable in a stressful situation can lead to overarousal, which may be followed by poor performance. If older adults learn ways to reduce overarousal (for example, through relaxation techniques), this destructive condition may be minimized.

The mismatch between the degree-driven, competitive regular curriculum and the needs of older learners has been minimized by programs aimed directly at older students. One is **Elderhostel,** a network of colleges and universities that provides inexpensive, short-term courses for people past the age of 60. Founded in New Hampshire in 1975 as a summer program, Elderhostel has spread from 220 students in five colleges within the state to nearly 200,000 students in all 50 states and at sites in 40 countries (Hofmann, 1989). Elderhostel

Elderhostel classes in every state and many countries—from New Zealand to Norway and Nepal to the Netherlands—challenge older adults and expose them to new ideas.

classes are now available year round, and the subjects range from architecture, ethnic studies, genetic engineering, and computers to Shakespeare, marine ecology, transcendental meditation, and the literature of baseball. Older adults can snorkel, sail, ski, research their family trees, train in simulated spacecraft, or investigate international politics. In many Elderhostel programs, students live in dormitories and eat in college dining halls, while they take courses taught by members of the regular faculty. The courses are aimed at challenging the students and exposing them to new ideas. There are no homework, papers, or grades.

The success of Elderhostel shows clearly in the repeat enrollments. The "typical" student is 69 years old, has participated in four other programs, and has traveled from 200 to 1000 miles to reach the campus (*Elderhostel Catalog,* 1991). Some research indicates that the "older" Elderhostelers, those between the ages of 71 and 86, seem to benefit most from the programs (*AARP News Bulletin,* 1983). Louis Kousin, a 75-year-old retired fund raiser credits Elderhostel with keeping him alive. "If I didn't have this," he says, "I'd sit around and worry about my health. I take my assignments seriously and get a tremendous kick out of sharing the new experiences with my wife" (Hofmann, 1989). Kousin and his wife Cerise, 78, have been attending Elderhostel classes for the last dozen years; this year he is taking poetry while she studies painting.

Kousin is typical of the Elderhostel male: 91 percent are married. The majority of students are women (60 percent), but only 51 percent of the women are married. Elderhostelers are more likely than other older adults to be employed—at least part time. Only 67 percent are fully retired (*Elderhostel Catalog,* 1991).

Elderhostel appeals primarily to upper-middle-class adults; 53 percent have graduate study or advanced degrees, 15 percent have completed college, and another 20 percent have at least two years of college (*Elderhostel Catalog,* 1991). Clearly, Elderhostel is geared to appeal to future generations of older adults. A successful program whose participants match the present profile of U.S. population past the age of 65 is the Senior Center Humanities Program, sponsored by the National Council on Aging. The Humanities Program relies on local discussion groups conducted by voluntary leaders in neighborhood settings. The texts, which focus on such subjects as "The Remembered Past: 1914 to 1945" and "Exploring Local History," are anthologies of material from literature, philosophy, autobiography, folklore, and the arts that have been adapted to meet local interests (Moody, 1986).

Both programs, though well received and beneficial, tend to segregate older students from learners of other ages. Because the cognitive differences that develop with age are generally unimportant in classroom settings, courses that integrate students of all ages might benefit young and old alike (Birren and Woodruff, 1973). The experience of older students could help make the often abstract material presented in the classroom meaningful to the young, and contact with the young might help the old understand the rapidly changing culture. In addition to its other benefits, such integrated education might help break down age segregation in society.

RELIGIOUS INVOLVEMENT ACROSS ADULTHOOD

Although education attracts only a minority of adults, religion is important in the lives of a large majority. There have been many studies of religiosity in adulthood, but our knowledge of developmental trends is sparse. **Religiosity** refers to all kinds of religious involvement, including church attendance, personal religious practices, and the importance of religious beliefs in an individual's life. Age differences have been found in all these areas of religious involvement, but whether these trends are developmental or reflect cohort or historic time differences is not known. A post–World War II surge in church membership and attendance peaked in the mid-1960s. A subsequent decline in attendance was halted a decade later by the rise in religious fundamentalism (Chatters and Taylor, 1989). During the 1980s interest in religion apparently increased on college campuses and among the population in general (Young and Dowling, 1987). History-normative effects are not the only factors that cloud interpretations of existing research: most studies are cross-sectional in nature, and the existing longitudinal studies cover too narrow a slice of the life span to be very informative (Markides, Levin, and Ray, 1987).

Most Americans hold some sort of religious belief: 94 percent say they believe in God; 77 percent believe there is a heaven; and 76 percent think they have a good or excellent chance of getting there (Woodward, 1989). For some, like Sheila Larson, a young registered nurse, the belief is vague: "I'm not a religious fanatic," she says. "I believe in God." Her faith is uncomplicated: "It's just try to love yourself and be gentle with yourself. . . . Take care of each other. I think He would want us to take care of each other" (Bellah et al., 1985, p. 221). For Les Newman, an evangelical Baptist who recently graduated from a major business school and works as an executive, belief in traditional Christianity provides a coherent sense of self and a family-like anchor for his life. He says that his religion "has strengthened my commitment in my marriage, and it's had a great deal of impact on the way I relate to other people at work" (Bellah et al., 1985, p. 156). Older adults may see religion somewhat differently. An elderly Mexican-American woman has a simpler, less utilitarian faith: "After all, even if there has been trouble, there has been God's grace: He has helped us; He has healed us; He has enabled us to try to be worthwhile and decent people. . . . God has given each of us a soul, and it is the soul that really counts. . . . The soul finally tires of the body; it is a prison and the soul wants to leave. Words struggle to leave us, but, once spoken, they are dead. The soul leaves and lives forever. I believe it does. I hope it does (Coles, 1973, pp. 17–18).

At every age, participation in church is higher than in other voluntary organizations combined. Some 40 percent of the U.S. population attend a weekly religious service, and about 60 percent belong to some organized religious group (Bellah et al., 1985). Attendance at church functions tends to be higher for children than for young adults, but in general, attendance seems fairly stable across adulthood (Hammond, 1969). However, various factors affect church attendance, including denomination, gender, income, education, and length of residence in the community. For example, at every age, women are more likely to attend church than men, and church attendance is more prevalent among adults with high income, high education, and long-time community residence.

Once adults pass the age of 65, there is a tendency for attendance to decline with age, with poor health the major reason given by the elderly for not attending. Among blacks, however, who generally express higher levels of religiosity than do whites of the same age, the decline does not appear until the age of 75 (Chatters and Taylor, 1989). In an eight-year longitudinal study of older Mexican-Americans and Anglos, the decline in church attendance appeared only among the very old (Markides, Levin, and Ray, 1987). Among relatively healthy older Anglos, general activity levels and the strength of religious convictions were better predictors of church attendance than health (Young and Dowling, 1987). Cohort differences that affect church attendance among older adults include a preponderance of women (which tends to inflate attendance figures) and a smaller proportion of Catholics (which tends to deflate them).

Declines in church attendance among older adults are not necessarily paralleled by a waning of interest in religion. Some studies show that the drop in attendance is accompanied by an increase in private religious activities (Ainlay and Smith, 1984). Many older adults say they watch services on television or listen to religious broadcasts, which allow them to attend church without leaving their homes. Studies indicate that older adults are more likely than younger or middle-aged adults to believe in immortality and in the importance of religion, to read the Bible, and to pray in private. From 65 to 95 percent of older adults pray each day (Bearon and Koenig, 1990). Although aspects of religious belief show little age-related change in national surveys, younger adults are much less likely than middle-aged or older adults to believe that religion can provide a solution to national and world problems (Glenn, 1980a).

Older adults generally say that religion means more to them as the years go by, with cross-sectional studies indicating a steady increase in those who rate religion as ''very important''—from 64 percent among adults in their early twenties to 84 percent among those past the age of 65 (Riley and Foner, 1968). An increase in the personal meaning of religion during later adulthood is in accord with Erik Erikson's (1982) view of development. Hope, which is the basic strength of infancy, ripens to faith in old age. During this final stage of development, integrity can overcome despair only if a person finds meaning in life. Erikson is careful to point out that faith and meaning need not be embodied in a traditional religion. Among the parents of members of the California Intergenerational Studies (aged 75 to 95), some retained their life-long commitment to the church in which they had spent

Many older adults say that religion helps them handle the stresses of their life, and church attendance seems to remain high and stable as long as people are healthy and active.

their lives, but for most, theology became less important than their active concern with understanding the place of humanity in the universe (Erikson, Erikson, and Kivnick, 1986). Some were drawn to small, interdenominational congregations, whose activities became the center of their lives.

Many older adults find that religion helps them get through difficult periods and cope with stressful life changes. No matter what sort of stressful event they encountered, nearly half the adults in one group said that they handled the stress by placing their trust in God, by praying, and by obtaining help and strength from God (Koenig, George, and Siegler, 1988). In studies restricted to men, about a third said that they relied on such religious practices in time of stress (Koenig, in press).

Although religious faith or a belief in an after-life does not appear to be closely related to good adjustment in older adults, most studies have found a relation between satisfaction with life and religious activities. Religious activities and attitudes are related to life satisfaction, and the correlation gets stronger across old age. Yet some researchers question this connection. In the longitudinal study of Mexican-Americans and Anglos, the effect was confirmed among adults who remained in the study for the full eight years, but when those who subsequently dropped out were included, the connection disappeared (Markides, Levin, and Ray, 1987). Neither church attendance nor private prayer was associated with life satisfaction, suggesting that the association found in many studies may reflect the survival of an increasingly select and healthy group. This supposition is supported by the fact that only functional health and marital status were associated with life satisfaction. Age appears to affect political involvement much as it does involvement in religion: older people seem more interested in politics than are the young.

POLITICAL INVOLVEMENT ACROSS ADULTHOOD

Politics is a sphere of life where personal involvement can have an impact on the lives of others. A person's active work on behalf of a candidate, a political party, or an issue may have an influence that far exceeds the weight of a single vote. If age affects political attitudes and behavior in predictable ways, changes in the proportion of various age groups could alter a country's political course. One way to understand possible age-related changes is through their relation to the assumption of various social roles (such as student, worker, spouse, parent, and retiree). In this approach, change is stimulated by the individual's movement through the life cycle. Another way is to interpret age differences as cohort differences, looking at the exposure of various cohorts to social trends and historical events (Foner, 1972). Both approaches have been used to explain the differences that appear with age in political attitudes and behavior.

POLITICAL ATTITUDES

According to the common wisdom, we become more conservative with age. As young people, we are likely to be liberal, trying to bring society into line with our humanitarian ideals. As we pass through adulthood, we supposedly begin to resist change, becoming conservative, either because our experience and wisdom have led to more accurate perceptions of human nature (say conservatives) or because we have been successful in life and now have an economic investment in the status quo (say liberals). Looking at attitudes in connection with social roles, we could also say that the young adult's devotion to humanitarian ideals is weakened by the assumption of family responsibilities. Worries about the immediate family overshadow concern for the poor and oppressed (Glenn, 1980a). For the advantaged adult, the needs of others may give way to the demands of mortgage payments, orthodontists' bills, and tuition. In support of the general belief in a trend toward conservatism with age, we can point to older adults' tendency to be against abortion, women's roles, the use of marijuana, birth control, pornography, and homosexuality, and to take the conservative side in "law and order" issues, such as capital punishment, gun control, and protection of the rights of the accused (Hudson and Strate, 1985).

Yet a careful analysis of this age trend is likely to shake our confidence in the common wisdom. Part of the conservative trend among older people is apparently the result of lower levels of education. Well-educated people tend to be more liberal than people with less education. The rest of the difference may be due to the circumstances in which each cohort grew up. Members of a cohort are exposed at the same time and the same age to common patterns of schooling, family life, economic cycles, wars, and political events, so that the relative conservatism or liberalism of any cohort may be largely a reflection of shared experiences and perceptions. The experience of living through World War II and the cold war, for example, helps explain why older adults tend to support larger military budgets than do younger groups.

Even the terms "conservative" and "liberal" have different meanings in different cohorts. Among middle-aged adults, for example, "conservative" means a preference for free enterprise and limited government, as well as a resistance to change and new ideas. Among older adults, "conservative" means a preference for sound fiscal policies, limited spending, and a balanced budget. The middle-aged regard "liberal" as an acceptance of change, new

Most adults do not become more conservative with age; instead, shifts in their political views reflect general trends in society.

ideas, and progressive policies; older adults regard it as a preference for big government and socialism (Hudson and Strate, 1985). Some researchers believe that the social climate at the time people become voters has a powerful influence on political outlook. Those who vote for the first time when the country is in the midst of a conservative swing are always likely to be more conservative in their outlook than those who vote for the first time when the country is moving to a liberal position.

Although people tend to retain the political orientations they develop early in life, their outlooks are not set in concrete. All cohorts respond to general trends in society. As society moves in a conservative or liberal direction, each cohort is affected by the trend. Although historical influences affect all cohorts, the response is not necessarily equal. The position of a cohort in the life cycle may interact with social influence to produce an age-period effect. When an issue is connected with the perceived self-interest of a cohort, its members may be more or less susceptible to a change. For example, older adults are generally more favorably disposed than other age groups to government-supported health care and to government action that promotes employment and a good standard of living (Hudson and Strate, 1985). Similarly, adults in their late twenties and early thirties are likely to be more favorably disposed to government-supported day care than are older adults.

Older adults who have developed wisdom may find their rigid identification with either political pole lessening. Among the elderly parents in the California Intergenerational Studies, some became more tolerant of other views as they moved into their seventies and eighties (Erikson, Erikson, and Kivnick, 1986). One life-long liberal activist, for example, said that her new ability to ''see both sides'' of a question had moderated her political ideals; life-long conservatives described a similar shift toward liberal views.

Along with the support of conservative policies has gone a tendency for Republicans to outnumber Democrats among older adults. Yet there is no general switch to the Republican party with age. When individual cohorts were followed across a 12-year period, each showed fluctuation in the proportion of Republicans, apparently swayed by historical events. In 1946, for example, 58 percent of the 49 to 52 year olds were Republicans; in 1950, 60 percent were Republicans; in 1954, 58 percent; and in 1958, when they were in their early sixties, 55 percent said they were Republicans. Under cohort analysis, the "maturational" trend toward Republicanism disappeared, and the preponderance of Republicans in older cohorts seemed to be the result of socialization in the years before the Great Depression of the 1930s (Glenn, 1980a). As more educated, less conservative cohorts have moved into the ranks of older adults and as the conservative trend of the 1980s has affected all cohorts, the pattern of heavier support for Republican candidates among the elderly has begun to disappear. By the close of the decade, older Americans were more likely to consider themselves Democrats than were members of younger cohorts (Jacobs, 1990).

Social climate does not affect all members of a cohort in the same way. Differences in political orientation within each age group are generally greater than differences between age groups. Nor do cohort effects act in isolation. Personality characteristics also shape political orientation. Among adults in the California Intergenerational Studies (who were socialized during the Great Depression), those who were liberal in middle adulthood had been rated as independent, unconventional, rebellious, objective, and interested in philosophical measures during adolescence (Mussen and Haan, 1981). In contrast, from early adolescence, middle-aged conservatives had lacked independence and had tended to be submissive, in need of reassurance, and moralistic. They had spent little time in introspection and were uncomfortable with uncertainty. Researchers concluded that the child-rearing practices of their parents may have encouraged these adults to develop broad general qualities that predisposed them toward a particular political orientation. This predisposition accounts for only part of the individual differences in political attitudes and behavior. The rest can be traced to the interaction of life cycle, cohort differences, and social climate.

POLITICAL PARTICIPATION

Young adults have always been less likely to vote or to participate in political activity than other age groups, but the gap in participation between the young and older adults has been steadily widening—from 21 percentage points in 1972 to 32 percentage points in 1988. Two national studies indicate that adults between the ages of 18 and 29 have become indifferent to politics (Oreskes, 1990). The general decline in voter participation over the past two decades is confined almost entirely to adults younger than 45, with the sharpest drop found among those in their early twenties (Figure 14.2). After analyzing 50 years of public opinion data, researchers concluded that today's younger adults were no longer as well informed about political issues as were preceding cohorts at the same age. Interviews with young adults turned up indifference to all issues except interference in personal freedoms, such as access to abortion or censorship of rock recordings. According to 24-year-old Shonda Wolfe, "[Politics] just doesn't interest me at this point in my life. I'd rather be outside doing something, like taking a walk" (Oreskes, 1990, p. D21).

Just why young adults have so little interest in politics is not certain. Researchers assumed that earlier cohorts were distracted by such age-related concerns as obtaining an education, establishing a career, finding a mate, and caring for young children (Hudson and Strate, 1985). Increased geographic mobility may also have left young adults without roots in their communities. Recent additional declines in participation among the young may be the result

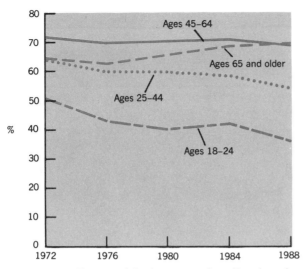

Figure 14.2 Voter participation across time. Based on the percentage of registered voters in each group who said that they voted in presidential elections, researchers have discerned a growing indifference to the political process among the young. *Source:* U.S. Bureau of the Census, 1990.

of historical factors: a post-Watergate disillusionment with politics in general or the lack of a major issue, such as civil rights or the Vietnam War, to draw them into politics.

As people grow older, their interest in politics and their tendency to vote seem to increase (Jacobs, 1990). Unconventional forms of political activity, such as political protests, are concentrated among younger adults, but other forms of political activity, such as working actively in community organizations, helping in political campaigns, and contributing money, peak during the fifties and then slowly drop off. The tendency to vote remains high until the age of 75, when it, too, declines—although adults older than 75 continue to vote at higher rates than young adults (Hudson and Strate, 1985; U.S. Senate, 1987–88) (Figure 14.3).

Older adults who have assumed positions of political leadership do not retire from the scene when they reach the age of 65. Political leaders tend to be in their fifties or older, and 50 to 70 year olds fill many of the decision-making positions in government. Historians have found that the importance of political office is linked with age, so that governors tend to be older than congressional representatives, senators older than governors, and presidents older than senators when they first assume office (Hudson and Strate, 1985). Only during times of revolutionary change are top political offices occupied by the young. This pattern appears whether we look at the United States, the Soviet Union, China, or Germany.

Older adults vote out of proportion to their numbers, as we have seen, but age alone does not determine whether an individual will vote. A detailed analysis of presidential elections showed that education is the most powerful influence on voter participation (Wolfinger and Rosenstone, 1980). At every level of income, an increase in education is matched by an increase in the probability of voting. According to Raymond Wolfinger and Steven Rosenstone (1980), education seems to affect voter participation in three ways. It gives people the skills that enable them to process political information and make political decisions; it

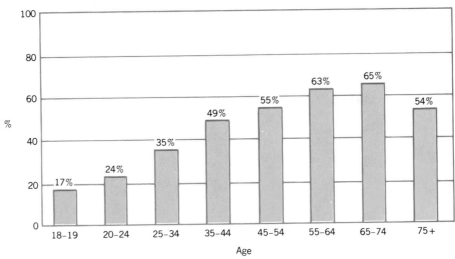

Figure 14.3   Voter participation by age, 1986 presidential election.

generally increases the sense of citizen duty, giving people more gratification from voting; and it provides the experience with such bureaucratic relationships as learning requirements for participation, filling out forms, waiting in line, and meeting deadlines so that educated people find it easier to register and then vote. The last factor may be more important than it seems at first glance. It has been speculated, for example, that farmers' experience with endless Department of Agriculture forms may be one of the factors that puts them among the occupational groups with the highest voter participation.

Sex was once a potent predictor of voting at all levels, and it is still powerful among older adults. Traditionally, men were more likely to vote than women, but the gender gap has narrowed, and by 1980 the gap had disappeared in the general population (Pear, 1983). Among young adults, women are now more likely to vote than men, but, even when education is held constant, older men are more likely to vote than older women. The major factor that depresses voter turnout among older women appears to be socialization practices. Although we take women's right to vote for granted, it was not until 1920 that the Nineteenth Amendment to the Constitution was ratified and women could vote in every state. Some of today's older women grew up believing that they were not entitled to vote at all—and all of them grew up at a time when society agreed that men should have a predominant influence in political affairs.

A second factor that depresses voter participation among older women is marital status. At every age and at every educational level, married people are more likely to vote than those who are single, separated, divorced, or widowed (Wolfinger and Rosenstone, 1980). Since most older men are married and the majority of older women are single, the difference in marital status accounts for the remaining gender gap at the polls.

Voter participation begins to decline among adults in their seventies, with the rate dropping faster and earlier for women than for men. Much of the decline is generally attributed to physical infirmities, but when education, marital status, and sex are held constant, aging does not produce a decline in turnout. Instead, it produces an increase—even in the oldest adults (Wolfinger and Rosenstone, 1980). Among the 70- to 95-year-old parents in the California Intergenerational Studies, political participation provided a way to express a concern for the country and the world at large (Erikson, Erikson, and Kivnick, 1986). Some of these oldest adults were still contributing money to political campaigns and writing letters on various issues to politicians and periodicals.

POLITICS OF AGING

Diminished participation by young adults, combined with higher levels of education, changes in the socialization of women, and longer life expectancy may increase the political influence of older Americans. In recent years, for example, the proportion of older voters in presidential and congressional elections has steadily increased (Jacobs, 1990). These demographic changes raise the question of whether older people will be politically active as "citizens" or as "old people," combining their political clout to form a pressure group that sees all issues in terms of their effect on the elderly.

Today's young-old adults are relatively healthy and have plenty of free time. Should they channel their interests and energies into "age politics," they could have an immense influence on society. A number of age-based voluntary associations have developed in the United States, and some of them have enormous memberships. Yet as late as the 1970s, their influence was sporadic at best. According to Henry Pratt (1982), during the 1960s groups such as the National Council of Senior Citizens, the Gray Panthers, and the American Association of Retired Persons (AARP) were so concerned with recruiting members and establishing their own turf that they often worked at cross-purposes. Toward the end of the 1970s, these groups began to work together to pass such bills as the Age Discrimination in Employment Act, which outlawed mandatory retirement at age 65. At about the same time, 26 organizations banded together to form the Leadership Council of Aging Organizations, a group that has been credited with blocking proposals to scale back Social Security benefits. Pratt believes that these organizations have become stable, developed a sense of purpose, acquired access to the political system, and gained a sense of legitimacy in the eyes of government policymakers.

Yet age-based organizations have not escaped criticism. Although the groups have always claimed to represent the interests of all older adults, critics say they have paid little attention to redressing the economic and social conditions of the most disadvantaged older people (Hudson and Strate, 1985; Jacobs, 1990). One of AARP's stated goals is to "help raise above the poverty line the incomes of poorer Americans of all ages" (Deets, 1990), but the needs of old adults in the middle class seem to dominate its agenda. The organization, which was a prominent and vigorous supporter of the Medicare Catastrophic Coverage Act of 1988, quickly moved for a change in its financing when the largely middle-class AARP membership expressed outrage at the progressive, income-based surcharge that accompanied the new law. After the Catastrophic Coverage Act (which covered prescription drugs and medical bills that exceed a set annual limit) was repealed, AARP put its influence behind a comprehensive national health plan that would cover all ages (*AARP Bulletin,* 1990). The Gray Panthers opposed the Catastrophic Coverage Act from the beginning on the grounds that it benefited only a small group of people and provided no care for long-standing disabilities like arthritis that grow progressively more severe (Lyman, 1988).

Despite their occasional cooperation, a merger of age-based organizations is unlikely

✦ *Adulthood in Today's World*

THE WRINKLED RADICAL

At 82, Maggie Kuhn is proud of her age. This woman who founded the Gray Panthers calls herself a "wrinkled radical," and says, "There's no disgrace or shame in growing old. We're all doing it" (Lyman, 1988, p. 29). Kuhn has led the 70,000 members of the Gray Panthers ever since she helped found the organization in 1970 after she was forced to retire because of her age.

When Kuhn was forced out of her position in the national office of the Presbyterian church, she was infuriated. She says that she cried and raged—and then got together with five other women to form the Gray Panthers. Under Kuhn's direction, the Gray Panthers has opposed compulsory retirement and pushed for a flexible, optional arrangement. The Panthers opposed the Vietnam War. In 1971 they formed a "Black House Conference on Aging" to combat what they saw as the paternalistic attitude of the White House Conference on Aging and its lack of attention to racial and economic differences. Today, Gray Panthers are working for peace, the establishment of a national health service, a restructured workplace, and a widespread use of "shared housing," to ease the problem of housing for older adults with no family (Lyman, 1988; Tannenhauser, 1987). (In Chapter 15, we will look at current shared-housing programs.)

From the beginning, Kuhn has worked arm-in-arm with the young. She still lectures on college campuses across the country, because she sees young and old as having common bonds. Both are out of the mainstream, not taken seriously by society, and have occupational problems—the young because they don't have experience and the old because their knowledge is considered obsolete (Lyman, 1988). Thirty-five percent of the people in the Gray Panthers are younger than 50. The Panthers' present goal of national health service is one that cuts across all age levels. Such a program is necessary, Kuhn says, because Medicare has so eroded that it covers less than 38 percent of older adults' health care and because a growing number of children, young, and middle-aged adults have no health insurance at all (Lyman, 1988).

Maggie Kuhn has always been a gadfly and has refused to accept what seem to her clear defects in society. Perhaps that is why she never married. Traditional marriage, like traditional society, was dominated by men. "To get along in a man's world," she says, "you had to dress like a lady, look like a schoolgirl, think like a man, and work like a horse. . . . I was engaged twice," she says, "but if I had married them, my life would have been over" (Lyman, 1988, pp. 30–31). Still restless, Kuhn already has written her tombstone inscription: Here Lies Maggie Under the Only Stone She Ever Left Unturned.

because their goals, membership, and political styles are so very different (Pratt, 1982). The largest organizations, such as the AARP and the National Council of Senior Citizens, do not depend on the delivery of political programs to sustain themselves. Most members do not join the AARP in order to pursue political goals, but instead pay their miniscule dues ($5 per year) in order to obtain access to medical insurance and discounts on travel (tours, airfare, hotels, and car rentals), prescriptions and toiletries, and other items. Thus, positions taken by the organization may not reflect member preferences (Hudson and Strate, 1985; Jacobs, 1990). The National Council of Senior Citizens tends to present the concerns of old people as an age group, but the Gray Panthers regard themselves as "transgenerational," working for the disadvantaged, no matter what their age. The Gray Panthers support legislation to help those in need and oppose drawing up programs in terms of age (see accompanying box, "The Wrinkled Radical"). Earlier groups sprang up, flourished, and died when their leaders or their issues faded. It is not yet clear whether in 2020 the Gray Panthers will be a powerful political force or an interesting relic of the twentieth century.

POLITICS OF INTERGENERATIONAL EQUITY

Will the size and political strength of older adults lead to a politics of age, setting the young against the old? The answer to this question is at the heart of debates over **intergenerational equity,** which refers to a fair distribution of the nation's resources across age groups. Some charge that inequities already exist and are slated to become larger. They note that today's older adults are in better financial shape than the country's children: about 20 percent of children, but just over 12 percent of older adults have incomes below the poverty level (Smeeding, 1990). The implication is that the voting strength of the elderly has led politicians to divert funds that should be spent on poor children (who lack voting strength) to Social Security, Medicare, and other public programs that serve older adults (Pifer, 1986). Another perceived inequity is the fact that today's retirees are getting a much higher return on payments made into the Social Security system than today's workers can hope to receive. Given the inevitable change in the old-age dependency ratio (see Chapter 1), some critics question whether baby-boom generation retirees can expect *any* support from Social Security or Medicare when the benefits must be provided by taxes on the baby-bust generation of workers (Jacobs, 1990).

Children have been neglected in recent years, but not because of any policy decision to benefit the old at the expense of the young. Factors that have influenced the apparent shift in priority probably include demographic change (an increase in older adults and a shrinkage in families with small children), racism (childhood poverty is perceived as being concentrated among minorities), political ideology (fewer social programs of any kind are being enacted), and a failure to realize the long-term consequences for society of an increasing group of malnourished, poorly educated children (Pifer, 1986). As legislators and the general public become aware that casualties among today's children translate into future costs in welfare, law enforcement, and prisons, and the loss of tax-paying workers, serious attempts to reach a new intergenerational equity may develop.

Concern over the rising old-age dependency ratio (see Chapter 1) led to a reorganization of the Social Security system in 1983. The reorganization set up a schedule to systematically increase taxes that fund the program while gradually extending the average person's working life. No matter how the system is restructured in the future, every worker who contributes will collect some kind of pension. The question as it pertains to intergenerational equity is whether young adults will collect as much in retirement as they pay in over their working lives. The system is adequately funded. In 1989 the Social Security fund had a *surplus* of more than $69 billion, but the money, invested in Treasury securities to collect interest, actually becomes part of the national debt (Martz and Thomas, 1990). The surplus that comes into the Treasury pays for current government spending, thereby obscuring the actual size of the annual budget deficit.

Despite these problems, most experts see no evidence of a looming generational conflict over equity (Jacobs, 1990). Social Security is supported by young and old alike, and political differences among older adults are at least as large as political differences among age groups. Except for specific issues that affect them directly, such as property tax relief or Social Security, older people are more likely to vote by income level than by age.

One way to ensure intergenerational equity is to base benefits on need, not age. According to Bernice Neugarten, instead of guaranteeing a minimum income for older adults, we should guarantee a minimum income for all citizens and then use the Social Security framework within that system. She advocates handling income maintenance, housing, transportation, health services, social services, and tax benefits in a similar fashion. Otherwise, she warns, a continued reliance on the criterion of age will so burden society with benefits for the young-old that it will be impossible to fund adequate programs (Neugarten and Hall, 1987). In this view, age is an inappropriate criterion for benefits in an age-irrelevant society. Older adults in the twenty-first century may be very different people from today's older adults. Perhaps, as Alan Pifer (1986) suggests, the rapid aging of the population has made some social and political structures obsolete, and the solution is to find new, more flexible structures that are capable of developing and implementing new public policies.

SUMMARY

LEISURE ACROSS ADULTHOOD

Leisure has five major objectives: **relaxation, diversion, developmental pleasure, creative pleasure,** and **sensual pleasure.** Socioeconomic level appears to affect the choice of leisure activity, perhaps because of differences in income and education. However, the differences may be due in part to compensation (seeking satisfactions that are lacking in an occupation) or spillover (generalizing the quality of an occupation to leisure). Changes in leisure activities tend to parallel changes in the family life cycle. As adults age, only strenuous leisure activities decline before the age of 75. The active, engaged life-style of many older adults may be related to the ''busy ethic,'' and leisure activities may provide a source of identity and self-concept.

EDUCATION

Adults of all ages are enrolling in formal education courses. This surge of enrollment may be the result of a change in the age structure of society, the existence of empty classrooms, rising educational levels, accelerated rates of change in all areas of life, the development of new occupational patterns, and the reentry of middle-aged women into the workforce. The goals of older students include an understanding of changes in their body and behavior, a knowledge of technological and cultural changes, a minimization of generational differences in knowledge and skills, the acquisition of new vocational skills, and personal growth and satisfaction. Because they are not motivated by grades and because the stereotypes of aging tell them that they are incompetent, some older adults may at first have trouble in the college classroom. **Elderhostel** provides inexpensive, short-term courses for older adults through a network of colleges and universities.

RELIGIOUS INVOLVEMENT ACROSS ADULTHOOD

Age differences in **religiosity** may be the result of developmental trends or of cohort or historical differences. Church attendance tends to be fairly stable until the age of 65, when a decline, which may be health-related, appears. Any decline in church attendance with age may be offset by private religious activities, and there seems to be an increase in the personal meaning of religion among the elderly.

POLITICAL INVOLVEMENT ACROSS ADULTHOOD

Most people retain the political orientation of their youth, which is modified by general trends in society. Young adults are the least likely to vote of any group. Political activity tends to peak during the fifties, but the tendency to vote remains high until about the age of 75, with older adults voting out of proportion to their number. The most powerful determinant of voting is education, although marital status also has an effect. A politics of age has not yet developed in the United States, and the influence of organizations that lobby for the elderly is sporadic. As the proportion of older adults has increased, a concern over **intergenerational equity** has developed.

KEY TERMS

creative pleasures	**leisure**
developmental pleasures	**relaxation**
diversion	**religiosity**
Elderhostel	**sensual pleasures**
intergenerational equity	

Chapter 15

◆

Social Issues and Social Support Across Adulthood

◆

Esther Fuller, 34, has spent her entire adulthood on welfare. She is a single mother with two children who lives in a deteriorating housing project in Yonkers, New York. But because of New York State's 1988 Family Support Act, which requires that welfare recipients enter government-sponsored educational and job programs, Fuller sees a bright new day dawning for her. Her county has initiated a support program known as Moms on the Move, which trains welfare mothers to fill health-care positions. Fuller attends community college, taking remedial education courses. Next year she will enter a two-year course leading to an associate degree in radiology. "It's a little scary," she says. "For so many years there was a support system. They sent you checks and everything was fine. But now all of a sudden they're trying to get you out on your own in the world" (Foderaro, 1990, p. 38). The program, which depends on federal and state funding, pays for tuition, tutoring, transportation, day care, lunches, books, and school supplies. At present 88 single parents (including a few fathers) are enrolled, aiming at jobs as dieticians, nurses, respiratory technicians, radiologists, and phlebotomists. All are considered capable of completing work at the college level. They were selected through a five-hour basic skills test, which they were required to take or lose their welfare benefits (Foderaro, 1990).

Fuller is receiving assistance from a social support system that is meant to make her self-sufficient. It is the kind of social support that most college students know little about. As long as we—and our family members—are healthy, employed, and functioning efficiently, we tend to pay little attention to social service agencies. But need, in the form of unemployment, serious illness, or emotional disturbance, can quickly teach us the importance of community services we generally take for granted.

In this chapter, we consider various forms of social supports as well as legal and economic issues that affect adults. We begin by examining the problems, starting with age discrimination against the young and the old. After looking at the economic aspects of the life course, we investigate housing, paying special attention to the housing of older adults. Finally, we consider various social supports and how they help single or poor parents rear their children, strengthen adults of all ages with physical, social, or emotional problems, and enable older adults to remain independent. Many adults have found that their—or their children's—chronological age can enlist social support on their behalf or erect barriers in their lives. ◆

LEGAL ISSUES CONCERNING AGE

Political activity, which we examined in Chapter 14, reflects a person's attempt to affect the role of government; law is the means used by government to force conformity with the social order (Weber, 1947). For thousands of years, age, law, and status have been intertwined in societies ranging from the simplest to the most complex (Eglit, 1985). Societies have found age to be the most efficient way to determine the assumption of responsibility, with different ages used for various privileges and obligations. A 12 year old may not drive a car, for example, a 17 year old may drive a car but not vote, and a 25 year old may vote but not become president of the United States. Sometimes privileges are withheld until the brink of old age. In ancient Athens, justice was administered by a group of men who had reached the age of 60.

The sword of chronological age cuts two ways; it can be used to grant status and privileges or to withdraw them. Beginning in the nineteenth century, age began to be used to withdraw adult status from the elderly, either denying them the right to employment or setting them up as a group that was unable to provide for its own basic needs (Cain, 1976). Whether age is used to withhold or withdraw privilege, it may be unfair to young or old.

In the United States, the Supreme Court has upheld laws excluding children younger than five from primary schools and barring high school students older than 18 from interscholastic sports competitions (Eglit, 1985). The major discriminatory use of age against the young, however, is in the field of housing. Few states or cities prohibit discrimination by landlords against families with children. Conditions vary from state to state. Although California courts have forbidden the barring of children from rental units and condominiums, in Florida the courts have supported the "no children allowed" rule, and Florida homeowners who buy houses in restricted developments as childless couples are served with eviction notices when they have children. Most courts have upheld zoning discrimination in housing against the "too-young," but decisions concerning retirement communities have generally noted that such discrimination is legal only when there is no shortage of housing for younger people in the surrounding area (Eglit, 1985).

According to the Department of Housing and Urban Development, 25 percent of all rental units in the United States bar children, and another 50 percent restrict the number and age of children that are allowed on the premises (Press, 1984). In the Cleveland area, for example, 37 percent of rental units prohibit children entirely. In addition, nearly all buildings with a majority of tenants past the age of 40 have some sort of restriction on the number of children per family or the proportion of units that can be occupied by families with children (Margulis and Benson, 1982). Although objections to children have generally been seen as coming from retirees, the severest restrictions in the Cleveland area occurred in buildings occupied by adults between the ages of 41 and 59. When the California Supreme Court denied the right of a landlord to exclude a family solely because it included a child, the Court stated that banning children from an apartment complex "otherwise open to the general public" was fundamentally different from communities "designed for the elderly" and their "special housing needs" (Eglit, 1985).

The old discriminate against the young in housing, but the rest of society discriminates against older adults in other ways, especially in employment. Laws protect workers from mandatory retirement, but discrimination in hiring is widespread. Employers tell older job seekers that they are "overqualified," "inflexible," or less in need of a job than younger applicants. As we saw in Chapter 13, older workers who lose their jobs often become so discouraged during job hunts that they opt for early retirement.

Until laws forbidding age discrimination by employers were passed, middle-aged workers who were not protected by seniority laws often found themselves fired for no reason other than their age. Not long ago, airline flight attendants were dismissed when they approached middle age, and some department stores periodically fired middle-aged clerks and department heads in order to maintain a youthful image for the young customers they hoped to attract. In 1967 the Age Discrimination in Employment Act (ADEA) made it unlawful for most employers to fire, demote, or reduce the salary of workers between the ages of 40 and 65 merely because of their age. In 1978 the upper limit of protection was raised to 70, and in 1986 upper age limits were abolished (Clark, 1990). Since 1970 more than 600 cases of age discrimination have been filed in federal courts. Older workers have been successful in about 35 percent of the cases (Snyder and Barrett, 1988). For the most part, the courts have relied on information regarding job performance that is framed in terms of general differences between young and old, but judges have failed to question stereotypical views presented by employers even though there are no data to substantiate them.

In 1989 it became apparent that the ADEA did not protect all aspects of employment. The U.S. Supreme Court ruled that employers may discriminate against older workers in health insurance and disability plans (Stephens, 1989). The decision came when the Court upheld an Ohio law barring public employees from retiring on disability benefits once they pass the age of 60. The law was questioned when 61-year-old June Betts, a speech pathologist on the staff of the Hampton County, Ohio, mental health agency, had to stop work because of Alzheimer's disease. Under Ohio law, Betts—who had worked for the agency for only six years—was eligible for only $158.50 per month (based on length of service) instead of $355.02 (based on disability). She lost the case solely because of her age, opening the way for employers to cut or eliminate such benefits as life or disability insurance, severance pay, sick leave, and health insurance for older workers. In fact, the decision quickly led to the dismissal of a suit by an older worker with 39 years' seniority whose award of separation pay on plant closing was reduced by the value of his pension—from $55,000 to less than $3000 (Deets, 1989). A middle-aged coworker in the same plant with 26 years' seniority received $34,500 in separation pay and on retirement can expect a company pension that is only about $150 per month less than the older worker's pension.

Credit is another area in which older adults in moderate circumstances often faced discrimination until passage of the Equal Credit Opportunity Act (ECOA), which outlawed this form of discrimination. Because of the ECOA, a Florida-based lending agency with branches in 23 states was fined $90,000 and ordered to change its practices. The Federal Trade Commission found the company had discriminated against older adults who applied

Until passage of the Equal Credit Opportunity Act (ECOA), many lending agencies discriminated against older adults who applied for loans.

for loans (*AARP News Bulletin,* 1983). Blazer Financial Services had refused loans to elderly applicants who met other financial standards, it had refused to consider pensions or public assistance as income in deciding whether to extend credit, and it had discriminated against people receiving pensions or public assistance on the grounds that they were not employed full time.

Other types of discrimination based on age exist. Some states, for example, require additional vision or driving tests after a certain age in order to renew a license. Is it discriminatory to require such tests from a 65 year old but not from a 64 year old? If, as we have seen in earlier chapters, age is a poor predictor of physical, intellectual, or social performance in later life, is it ever fair to use chronological age as an arbitrary barrier? As a group, older adults are much safer drivers than young adults, especially men in their twenties. Age discrimination can also work against those who are "not old enough." Is it discriminatory to require a 64 year old to pay full fare on a bus or to get into a movie, but not a 65 year old? (The 64 year old may be retired and living on Social Security, and the 65 year old may have an income of $100,000 a year.)

Part of the problem is that society has incompatible definitions of old age and the way that older people fit into society. According to Douglas Nelson (1982), setting the age of 65 as the "time to retire," combining disability payments in the same program as age-related Social Security payments, and establishing housing projects, senior citizen centers, and nutrition programs for older adults tends to segregate them from the rest of society and to equate old age with disability. Abolishing mandatory retirement, eliminating job discrimination, and setting up job-development programs for older workers and such programs as Foster Grandparents challenge the assumption that the old are disabled and thus combat age segregation. Nelson sees two dangers from the current situation. On the one hand, dismantling the stereotype of the old as dependent and incapacitated may be used as an excuse to eliminate or sharply restrict the income, health, and social support programs that are absolutely necessary to many of the elderly. On the other hand, an array of programs that

Programs like Foster Grandparents challenge the assumption that elderly adults are disabled.

automatically go into effect at age 65 may maintain stereotypes of aging, reinforce the segregation of the old, and encourage ageism.

One way to end the dilemma is to base programs on need, not age, a solution that was discussed earlier. A second way out of the dilemma is to redefine old age, viewing the years between 60 and 75 as an extension of middle age. For most people today, the young-old years differ little from the years after 65; it is only after they reach 75 that the frailty and vulnerability of old-old age is likely to appear. Existing standard benefit programs could be expanded to support those in the period of "extended middle age" who were truly in need.

ECONOMIC DISTRIBUTION

The need for benefit programs is linked to income, but few young adults think seriously or often about their financial situation in old age. Yet throughout life, they will make important choices—about schooling, marriage, occupation, and health practices—that will affect their life-time earnings and their economic situation in later life. When making such choices, most of us weigh present costs and benefits against costs and benefits in the future. During young adulthood, for example, some people choose to invest their resources (time and money) in education in order to reap the benefits of enhanced earnings during later life. In this instance, they shoulder current costs for the sake of future benefits, investing their resources in human capital. Some people choose to have a second (or third) child, while others limit family size, using the extra money for luxuries, to save for retirement years, or to "buy" more leisure by reducing working time (Engerman, 1978). The willingness to incur costs in money, time, or energy for the sake of future benefits is a critical factor in many decisions about health, schooling, fertility, and occupation (Fuchs, 1983). The postponement of benefits often has a powerful effect on the length and quality of our lives. As we will see, most older Americans are in much better financial shape than they were a few decades ago, but pockets of poverty exist—some of them deep.

INCOME PATTERNS ACROSS ADULTHOOD

In an industrialized society like the United States, the major source of income is wages, and the total amount received over the life course depends on productivity, the value of the job, and the length of time worked. In most cases, the more valuable or productive a worker, the shorter the time worked, whether in a shortened work year (fewer weekly hours, longer vacations) or in a shortened work life (lengthy education, early retirement) (Kreps, 1976). High productivity in the United States has allowed increases in the standard of living, the extension of education, and the support of workers in retirement.

As a general rule, when productivity increases, whether from technological advance or the worker's increased skill and experience, wages increase. For most workers, whatever their occupation, earning power rises steadily, peaking during their late forties or early fifties (Figure 15.1). Education and occupation determine just when a worker reaches that peak, and the higher the level of education or skill required in a job, the older a worker will be before attaining maximum income. The effect of early investment in schooling is especially large after the age of 45, when inequalities in health, work, and income become increasingly apparent. Almost 30 percent of this inequity is due to the fact that workers without advanced

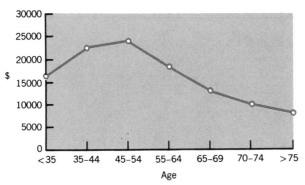

Figure 15.1 Median income by age.

schooling collected part of their life-time earnings when college graduates had no income at all but were investing their human capital in the hope of later return (Fuchs, 1983). It takes about seven years after entry into the labor market for the college graduate to reach the point at which those missed earnings are returned in the form of higher income. Although income rises steadily throughout young and middle adulthood, women's income always lags behind that of men, as we saw in Chapter 13.

Over the past 15 years, real earnings have increased at all age levels, but older adults have profited more than younger adults from the trend. Families headed by older adults have had a 33 percent increase in real earnings, but families headed by adults younger than 65 have had only a 16 percent increase (U.S. Senate, 1987–88). For many younger families the increase has come because the majority of families now have two wage-earners. The shift to a service economy has reduced the number of jobs with middle-class wages and changed American socioeconomic brackets. Between 1970 and 1985 the middle class shrank from 65.1 percent of American families to 58.2 percent. Some of the two-salary families moved into the upper class, which increased from 13 percent to 18.3 percent of American families, but others slipped into the lower class, which rose from 21.9 percent of families in 1970 to 23.5 percent in 1985 (Koepp, 1986).

The financial position of older adults *as a group* has improved dramatically in the past few decades. One reason for their rising economic status is the change in the nature of people entering old age. Those who turn 65 in any year have, on the average, higher incomes (and more education) and greater net worth than those older adults who die (Smeeding, 1990). Changes in society also account for the rising income of older adults. Social Security benefits increased sharply over these years; private pension programs expanded; public health programs were instituted; property tax relief laws were passed in all states; food stamp programs were established to fill the needs of low-income people of all ages; and a supplemental program ensured that older Americans would receive a minimum payment even if they had little or no Social Security coverage. In 1959, 35.2 percent of adults past the age of 65 had incomes below the poverty level; in 1988, the proportion had dropped to 12.6 percent (Smeeding, 1990). When assistance of various kinds—food, housing, and medical care—is included, the proportion drops even lower, to 6.4 percent.

For the first time, the majority of older Americans can look forward to a comfortable life after retirement. As a group, they have more assets than young adults, although adults

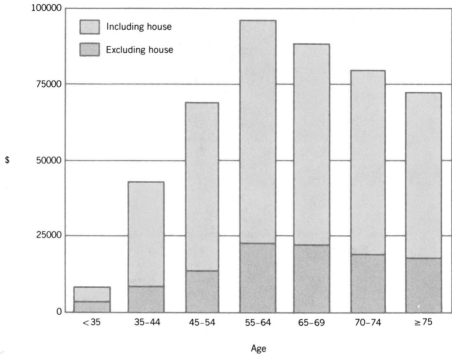

Figure 15.2   Median assets by age.

between the ages of 55 and 64 actually have the highest net worth (Figure 15.2). The middle-class, college-educated Englers are planning to live the good life. Mr. Engler, a 62-year-old retired corporation executive, has a retirement income of $26,000, made up of Social Security, private pension, and savings. The Englers have just moved to a retirement community in the Southwest (Kart, Longino, and Ullmann, 1989). Their pattern may become more prevalent among tomorrow's older adults, the cohorts born during the 1930s. Many of today's poor elderly are immigrants without education who worked at unskilled jobs, a very different group from typical elderly in 2000 (Neugarten and Hall, 1987).

   Yet the attainment of health, wealth, and time to enjoy them still eludes a sizable minority of older Americans. In particular, the new affluence has eluded many of the old-old, especially women without partners (Smeeding, 1990). In 1984 one older household out of seven had a net worth of less than $5000 in 1984 dollars (U.S. Senate, Special Committee on Aging, 1988–89). What many people do not realize is that the poverty line drawn for older adults is lower than the line that determines poverty for those younger than 65 (about $500 less per year for single adults and $775 for couples). If the same poverty line were used for both groups, an additional 700,000 "near poor" older Americans would fall below it (Margolis, 1990). In fact, 11 percent of the elderly have incomes that are no more than 25 percent above the poverty line of $5447 for single adults and $6872 for couples (Table 15.1). Whether an older person belongs to the comfortable majority or the afflicted minority depends on the interaction of public policies, a lifetime of individual decisions, and luck (Walther, 1983).

Table 15.1 **POVERTY AMONG OLDER AMERICANS, 1988**

	All >65	*65–74*	*75–84*	*85 +*
Total	12.6%	10.6%	15.5%	18.8%
Men	8.5%	7.5%	9.2%	16.6%
Married men	5.9%	5.5%	6.1%	9.7%
Women	15.6%	13.0%	19.2%	19.7%
Married women	6.1%	5.5%	7.6%	10.7%
Widows	21.3%	19.8%	20.3%	23.4%

Source: U.S. House of Representatives, Ways and Means Committee (as reported in Smeeding, 1990).

CONSUMPTION PATTERNS ACROSS ADULTHOOD

As adults age, their buying patterns change, in part because of reduced income and in part because of changing needs. Younger adults are establishing households and rearing children. They are buying houses and furnishing them, and many are spending money on child-rearing. According to the Urban Institute, it will cost $95,000 (in constant dollars) to rear a baby born in 1986 to the age of 18, and when parents also put aside money for college, the tab increases to $135,000 (*Newsweek,* September 1, 1986). Adults who do not marry may also be buying and furnishing homes, but they are likely to be heavy spenders in recreational areas as well. They have more disposable income for travel, electronic gear, sports cars, athletic equipment, and restaurant meals.

Older individuals generally spend a greater proportion of their income on food, health care, and utilities, with a significantly smaller proportion going to clothing, transportation, pension and life insurance, and entertainment. The young-old spend a smaller proportion of their income (20 percent) on shelter and furnishings than do the young (23 percent), but the old-old spend slightly more (24 percent). Even when spending a proportionately greater amount, older adults spend fewer dollars because of their smaller incomes. In only one area do the old outspend the young: health care. The old spend more dollars each year on medical services, health insurance, prescription drugs, and medical supplies than does any other age group (U.S. Senate, 1987–88).

As the figures for shelter and furnishings indicate, considering all older adults in a single group may skew our picture of consumption patterns. Some older individuals continue to work, and those who do spend significantly larger shares of their income on automobiles and restaurant meals, and slightly more on gifts and contributions. Expenditures such as vacations, recreation, clothing, personal care, and household furnishings make up a similar proportion of the elderly household budget, whether individuals are retired or employed (McConnel and Deljavan, 1983). Among the retired families in this study, most appeared to be spending slightly less than they received, and there was little indication that they drew on their savings to meet their expenses.

When they first retire, most older adults find that they spend more than they receive from various sources. Research indicates that they soon learn to adjust their consumption patterns so that their disposable income exceeds their expenses. Members of the American Associ-ation of Retired Persons, for example, share the methods they have developed to make dollars go further (*Modern Maturity,* 1983). They clip coupons, build their meals around supermarket specials, forego prepared foods, buy vegetables in season, form car pools, and pay cash for the cheapest gasoline. Contrary to most assumptions, most older adults do not gradually deplete their assets; instead, they continue to save—and save a higher proportion of their income than adults in other age groups. Older adults say they continue to save because they fear skyrocketing medical costs for disability or a terminal illness, and they are worried about becoming a burden on their adult children (Stoller and Stoller, 1987). Of course, the values and the spending and savings patterns of today's older adults were strongly influenced by the depression experience of their youth. It is difficult to predict the patterns that are likely to develop in future cohorts.

ECONOMICS OF RETIREMENT

Once people retire, their income drops considerably. Of course, many expenses probably decrease as well. A retired couple no longer has to shoulder child-rearing expenses or the costs involved in working (commuting, meals away from home, extra clothing), and some couples find their housing costs reduced as the mortgages on their homes are paid off. Other expenses may also be smaller.

How retired adults feel about their financial situation may have little relationship to their actual income level. More important may be the comparison between their present situation and their preretirement circumstances. A drastic drop, especially if it is unexpected, can lead to a feeling of relative deprivation. An analysis of six national samples indicated that a sense of relative deprivation had a stronger influence on feelings of financial well-being than social status or current income (Espenshade and Braun, 1983). A discrepancy with their own previous situation was more likely to produce feelings of deprivation than discrepancy with the situation of others.

Consider the case of Laura and J. G. Puchi, both of whom took early retirement from Lockheed Corporation in 1976. Within five years inflation had eroded their $944 monthly combined company pension to the extent that even with J. G.'s Social Security benefits, the Puchis could not maintain their standard of living. They had to give up vacation trips, restaurant meals, even Christmas gifts for their grandchildren. Their savings were depleted, and J. G. had to take a part-time job as a school janitor. The situation eased somewhat when Laura became eligible for Social Security benefits, but they said that—given another chance—they would never choose early retirement (Sheils et al., 1981). The problem is that, although Social Security payments rise regularly to keep pace with inflation, 75 percent of company pensions do not (Uchitelle, 1990). By 1990 only 7 percent of retired people could depend on company-financed pensions for half their income.

In the past, older adults seemed content with life at a subsistence level. Many lived with deprivation during the Great Depression, and all grew up in a society that made no provision for old age. Any guaranteed pension or benefits more than met their expectations. Today retirement is seen as an earned right, and when adults retire, they are unlikely to be satisfied with a drastic reduction in living standards. Although increased productivity generally leads to higher standards of living, unless provisions are made in retirement laws, the retired person gets no benefit from society's progress. When a lengthy period of retirement is paralleled by sustained economic growth, the relative position of retired people may worsen, with their standard of living becoming unacceptable in the eyes of society. For example, living without television, telephone, or electricity is no longer acceptable, although all were once considered luxuries.

After retirement, the shrinkage in expenditures often does not equal the decline in income. After age 65, the median income drops from $21,906 to $11,854 for men, and from $7445 to $6734 for women. However, these figures make no allowance for race and do not distinguish between the employed elderly and the retired elderly. As the median income for fully employed workers past 65 is $19,178 for women and $29,715 for men, the income of the typical retired person is considerably less. In fact, among those past 65, 17 percent of the men and 43 percent of the women had incomes of less than $6000 per year, and 6 percent of the men and 20 percent of the women had incomes of less than $4000 per year (U.S. Bureau of the Census, 1989) (Table 15.1).

Women make up 72 percent of older adults in poverty, and these poor women are likely to be alone, black, or Hispanic. Women are at a disadvantage because most social policies and programs are designed with the aging male worker in mind (Rodeheaver, 1987). Women, who have been seen primarily as dependents, amass no Social Security credits for work as homemakers. The rising incidence of divorce also puts women's later income in jeopardy. Those who remain married for ten years or longer are entitled to a spouse's benefit when they retire (a sum equal to half of their husband's benefit), but present laws do not consider the possibility of multiple marriages. As we saw in Chapter 13, women who work outside the home often move in and out of the labor market, a practice that reduces their own eventual Social Security benefits and often keeps them from qualifying for a private pension. (On retirement, a woman is entitled to her own earned Social Security benefits or her benefits as a spouse—whichever is higher.) The case of Mary Fremont, a 77-year-old widow who has lived alone for 20 years, is typical of women mired in poverty (Kart, Longino, and Ullmann, 1989). Fremont rents an apartment in a midwestern city, and her yearly income in 1985 was $2016 in Social Security payments—at a time when the poverty line was drawn at $5156.

Because women have traditionally been paid less than men, even those who have spent their entire lives working are unlikely to receive as large a pension as men. As women become more committed to their occupations, the problem may lessen for future cohorts, but the evidence is mixed. The gap between women's and men's Social Security income has shrunk somewhat over the past 20 years, but the disparity in private pension income has increased greatly (McLeod, 1990). In 1970 women's Social Security income was 70 percent of men's; today it is 73 percent. In 1970 women's average income from private pensions was 73 percent of men's; today it is only 54 percent.

When older adults first fall into poverty, they have better than even chances of escaping it. A longitudinal Michigan study indicates that about 42 percent of the elderly who become poor make their way above the poverty line within a year; those who are poor for two years have about one chance in four of putting poverty behind them (Coe, 1988). But once an older adult has been poor for three years, the hope of ever escaping becomes exceedingly dim, although in the much larger Retirement History Study, more than 80 percent of poor widows and almost 88 percent of poor couples were no longer poor after six years (Holden, Burkhauser, and Myers, 1987). The chances of putting poverty behind them are about the same for all races, but men are more likely to escape its grip than women (Coe, 1988). Researchers are not certain what events are most likely to precipitate the slide into poverty, but undoubtedly the nature of the triggering event affects the length of the stay.

The sobering side of these findings is that the chances that any older adult will experience poverty at some time during the latter years are considerably higher than the poverty rate among the elderly. Those who are most vulnerable to shifting economic fortunes are older adults who rely on Social Security for at least 65 percent of their retirement income, rely entirely on Medicare to cover their medical expenses, or rent their living quarters at full market value (Smeeding, 1990). Since 30 percent of elderly households (including single households) depend on Social Security for at least 80 percent of their income, the economic vulnerability of many older adults is apparent (U.S. Senate, 1987–88).

Among older Americans, Social Security benefits are the major source of income, followed by interest and dividends, earnings from employment, other pensions, and public assistance. Adults whose income is below a certain minimum level are entitled to **Supplemental Security Income (SSI)** if their "countable assets" (which do not include homeownership) are less than $1900 for individuals or $2850 for couples. In April 1988 the average monthly SSI payment was $187; however, economists believe that only about 55 percent of the eligible elderly are enrolled in this program (Clark, 1990). Money goes somewhat further among older adults because of tax breaks, assets, and **in-kind income** (goods and services that require no expenditure). For example, under regulations that took effect in 1984, Social Security benefits are not taxed among people whose income (including Social Security) is less than $25,000. Individuals who make more than $25,000 pay taxes on one-half of their Social Security benefits. Property taxes are reduced, but only when taxes exceed a certain portion of annual income, generally from 3 to 7 percent, depending on the state. In addition, elderly homeowners escape taxes on the first $125,000 in capital gains should they decide to sell their homes and move into a smaller house or apartment.

Most older adults (75 percent) own their own homes, and 83 percent have paid off their mortgages. Such assets are not easily converted into income, but if property taxes and maintenance are less than rent, homeownership increases income. In some states it is also possible to obtain a **reverse annuity mortgage (RAM),** in which the homeowner sells equity to a lending agency in return for a fixed monthly payment. When the house is sold, the lending agency receives the total of its loan plus interest.

Savings, in the form of stocks, bonds, money market accounts, mutual funds, and passbook savings, provide another source of income for some elderly. For most, however, the amount is negligible. Approximately 40 percent of older Americans' net worth is the equity in their home, so that many of the elderly are "house rich" and "cash poor." Nearly 25 percent of older adults with incomes below the poverty line have at least $50,000 in home equity, and once home equity is excluded, more than 40 percent of *all* older households have less than $10,000 in financial assets (U.S. Senate, 1987–88).

Health services are a major form of in-kind income for all elderly, with Medicare (for all) and Medicaid (for low-income elderly) picking up about two-thirds of their medical expenses. Among younger individuals, only about one-fourth of medical expenses are covered. However, the cost of medical care has risen so sharply that, after adjusting for inflation, the average older American spends more for medical care today than in 1965—when Medicare did not exist (Kane and Kane, 1990). Medical expenses remain a major problem for many older adults, who risk depleting all their assets if they or a spouse requires long-term care (Clark, 1990). When the Medicare Catastrophic Coverage Act was repealed in 1989, legislators retained two provisions that help older adults with low incomes. One protects people from impoverishment after their spouse enters a nursing home, and the other requires states to pay all Medicare premiums, deductibles, and copayments for older adults with incomes below the poverty line who cannot qualify for Medicaid.

Other kinds of in-kind income are also available. Low-income elderly are eligible for food stamps. Public transportation systems generally have reduced fares for older adults, no matter what their income level, as do most airlines and many movie theaters. Some businesses give discounts on purchases to older adults—generally about 10 percent.

In order to maintain their previous standard of living, single older adults in retirement need from 51 to 79 percent of their former income, and married couples need from 55 to 86 percent (Espenshade and Braun, 1983). (The higher the preretirement income, the lower the required proportion of income in retirement.) By itself, in 1974 Social Security replaced more than 60 percent of earned income for only 5 out of 100 single men and 21 out of 100 couples in which the wife drew dependent's benefits (an additional sum equal to half her husband's Social Security). The median replacement rate for single men was 39 percent, and for couples, 49 percent (Fox, 1979).

HOUSING

Most Americans live in houses or apartments, although some live in mobile homes or hotels and a few live on boats. A majority live in single-family housing, and 63.5 percent of all year-round dwelling units are occupied by the person who owns them (U.S. Bureau of the Census, 1989). Homeownership steadily increases until old age, jumping from 40 percent of all families headed by people younger than 35 to 77 percent of those headed by adults between the ages of 45 and 64, then dropping slightly to 75 percent among older Americans (Kendig, 1990; U.S. Senate, 1987–88). Both long-term and periodic economic events appear to affect the composition of households.

MOBILITY ACROSS ADULTHOOD

Americans have always been a highly mobile population, with the tendency to move closely associated with developmental tasks (Longino, 1990). Moving peaks during the early twenties, then declines relatively steeply until about the age of 35, followed by further, but slower, declines until the retirement years, when a series of smaller peaks in mobility appear.

Mobility and Housing in Young and Middle Adulthood

More than one-third of adults in their early twenties move at least once during a two-year period (Longino, 1990). Such moves take place in connection with employment, and the greater the education, the more likely people are to move. Migration across state lines appears to be high during the implementation and establishment stages of career development, and then slows during the consolidation period (see Chapter 13). Although it is commonly believed that frequent moves are highly stressful and may lead to illness, depression, ruptured marriages, and unhappy children, researchers are beginning to find positive aspects of executive transfers. When mobile executives are compared with those who do not move, the movers (both husband and wife) feel that they are more capable and that their lives are more interesting (Brett, 1980). The movers also have higher levels of marital satisfaction. However, mobile executives (but not their spouses) complain more about their health, and both partners are less satisfied with their social relationships.

Changing economic times have had a striking effect on the housing of young adults, with good times hastening the flight from the nest and economic turndowns either delaying the departure or bringing adult children back home. During the 1950s and early 1960s, unmarried adults in their twenties either lived with their parents or moved in with relatives or friends. Few single adults lived alone, because establishing individual households was expensive. But as real income climbed during the 1960s and 1970s, an increasing portion of single men and women could afford the luxury of privacy and autonomy. In 1950 only 4 percent of the men and 6 percent of the women between the ages of 25 and 34 lived by themselves. About 30 years later, 29 percent of single men and women in that same age group lived alone (Michael, Fuchs, and Scott, 1980).

The 1980s ushered in a new economic situation. The recession of 1981 made it increasingly difficult for the young to leave home. In fact, some who left during the late 1970s returned when the recession cost them their jobs. Others who kept their positions found that inflation had whisked independence out of their grasp, at least temporarily. By 1987 housing costs had escalated and the relative incomes of 25 to 34 year olds had shrunk—from 86 percent of that earned by people a decade older to only 77 percent (Cowan, March 12, 1989). An increasing number of young adults found it difficult to duplicate their parents' standard of living. By 1988 the proportion of adults in their twenties who lived with their parents had climbed back near the levels of the mid-1950s, and the rate was highest in households with annual incomes that exceeded $50,000.

Some who have never left home are attending college; nearly 30 percent of college students live at home. Others, like 25-year-old Todd Miller who runs a limousine business from his parents' home, see no reason to leave rent-free quarters with free laundry and maid service. Even though Miller's parents have offered to lend him enough for a downpayment on a house, he refuses to leave. "I grew up here," he says. "You're throwing me out of my own house" (Woodward, 1990, p. 54). Among the "boomerang kids," many have returned after divorce or separation, and sometimes the return is the result of personal problems with drugs or alcohol. But often it is simply the high cost of living quarters.

That is why 32-year-old Bill Kane, an engineer with IBM, and his wife Teresa, a dental hygienist, moved into the home of Kane's widowed mother. They pay all household food bills and the additional utilities caused by their presence while they save money to buy a house. "It seemed the only way we would ever be able to buy anything," said Bill Kane (Brooks, 1986, p. C6).

Young adults who can afford it buy their own homes, with a sizable minority using cash from relatives for the downpayment. Most people buy their first houses when they are nearly 30 years old, up from the age of 28 during the early 1980s. Economic cycles affect such trends, because good times increase the basic cost of housing and interest rates affect monthly payments. Between 1975 and 1982 mortgage interest rates climbed from 8.75 percent to more than 15 percent before edging down. By 1990 interest rates were hovering around 10 percent. Until the last quarter of the twentieth century, homeownership was virtually limited to married adults. Traditionally, single men and women lived in rented quarters, in part because socialization had led most to view homeownership as inappropriate for the unwed. As more and more people postponed marriage or decided to remain single, a trend in homeownership by single adults grew, perhaps encouraged by the popularity of condominiums and co-ops. Federal and state income tax laws have played some part in this trend, with the deduction of mortgage interest and real estate taxes decreasing the cost of homeownership.

Mobility and Housing among Older Adults

Most older adults are reluctant to move at all and prefer to age ''in place,'' remaining in their own homes. No matter where they live, their choice reflects a balance struck between the conflicting goals of autonomy and security (Parmelee and Lawton, 1990). Autonomy represents freedom to pursue goals on their own, with little or no need to call on others, and security represents physical safety and psychological peace, which may limit freedom and require the assistance of others. Homes within the community provide the maximum amount of autonomy and security, and up to 88 percent of older adults live in this fashion. Single, divorced, and widowed older adults prefer to live alone, and those who can afford it do so. Homeownership increases the proportion of the old who live by themselves—especially among women (Krivo and Mutchler, 1989). Older adults tend to reside in metropolitan areas, especially in the suburbs (Golant, 1990a). Just over 42 percent of adults older than 65 live in the suburbs, and nearly 32 percent live in central cities. Only 26 percent of the elderly now reside in small towns and rural areas.

Older adults tend to be satisfied with their housing and are less likely than the young to complain about inadequacies. In 1983 only 8 percent of older Americans were living in units considered ''physically deficient,'' and the proportion of low-quality housing is about the same across all age groups (Kendig, 1990). Among older adults in small Kansas towns, housing satisfaction was a predictor of mental health, more important than marital status and second only to activity—a measure composed of activity, functional health, and mobility (Scheidt and Windley, 1983).

Although older adults tend to move less frequently than do the young, researchers have detected a developmental pattern to their moves. According to Charles Longino (1990), contemporary society has produced pressures on older adults to make three basic types of moves: amenity migration, which comes at retirement; kinship migration, which comes when they experience moderate disabilities; and assistance migration, which comes when they develop major, chronic disabilities.

Amenity migration, a change of residence in order to improve life-style or to maintain a network of friends, is frequent among the 3.4 percent of the 55 to 64 year olds and some of the 2.3 percent of 65 to 74 year olds who move each year (U.S. Bureau of the Census, 1989). This kind of move is most common among relatively healthy couples with enough income to allow them free choice in relocation. Often the move is to a place where the couple has vacationed in the past and where they already have friends, typically in the Sun Belt states of the Pacific Coast and South Atlantic regions (Longino, 1990). Some of the young-old do not actually pull up their roots but become ''snowbirds,'' wintering in the same southern states each year and returning home in the spring to stay until the cold weather returns. Since 1980 the stream of older adults from the Northeast to western and southern states has slowed somewhat, and the proportion of local movers (excluding those who enter institutions) has dropped considerably (Golant, 1990b). Movers who cross state lines tend to be more affluent than older adults who do not move, whereas those who make local moves tend to be worse off (Longino, 1990). Many local movers are tenants, who are forced out of their houses or apartments by rising rents, evictions, condominium conversions, or redevelopment (Kendig, 1990).

Older adults tend to migrate to areas with high levels of unemployment—a pattern that is just the opposite of interstate migration among the young, who tend to move to areas with high earnings and low unemployment (Serow, 1987). Both young and old tend to be pushed from states with high crime rates, and the old also tend to be pushed out by cold weather. Rising crime rates, congestion, and increased living costs in southern states may be responsible for slowing the stream of elderly adults into the South (Golant, 1990b). Such patterns are important, because the arrival of older adults represents an economic bonanza for the affected regions. Retired emigrants bring their income and assets with them, which stimulates development; they draw Medicare and Medigap funds, which attract new physicians and stimulate the health-care industry; and federal funds received by the states for many programs are determined by the number of their permanent residents past the age of 60.

Kinship migration, in which older adults move to areas inhabited by their children or other close relatives, usually occurs when one or both of the partners develop some chronic disability or one of the partners dies (Longino, 1990). These migrants can live at home if they have access to services provided by their children. Kinship migration is likely to be most prominent among some of the 65 to 74 year olds and more of the 1.9 percent of the over 75 year olds who move each year (U.S. Bureau of the Census, 1989). Some of these movers were once part of the amenity migration stream, but now in their seventies, poor and widowed, they return to their home states as they move into the ranks of the old-old.

Assistance migration, the final form of move, occurs among old-old adults who have no family to depend on for services or whose disabilities become so severe that family services can no longer maintain them in their homes. The assistance migration is a move from exclusive care by family members to an institution. Most assistance migrations are local moves and may be the only move made by many older adults. The poor health of these local movers may help explain why local moves tend to have a negative impact. In one study, moving from one house to another within the same community was followed by increased illness and hospitalization, even when the adults moved out of choice and were satisfied with their new housing (Aday and Miles, 1982). But when moves are to improved housing or when the person has a confidant with whom to share worries, the impact of the move is cushioned and declines tend to be slight.

Another explanation for the negative effect of many moves becomes apparent when we consider the function of homeownership—or even a lengthy residence in the same rented house or apartment (Lawton, 1985). To adults who have lost their status as worker, homeownership provides a boost in self-esteem. To all adults who have spent decades in the same residence, their home is a familiar setting that allows them to move about confidently, coping with the environment on sensory, cognitive, and affective levels. They may have a profound psychological attachment to their home, which is pervaded by many years of memories. The house may reflect their lives or even be seen as part of the self, so that losing it is highly disruptive (Rubinstein, 1989).

Even when housing and the surrounding neighborhood are deteriorating, older people may be reluctant to move. An 84-year-old woman who lived in a dying Appalachian town described her husband's attachment to their home:

This spring my son talked. He says, "Now, Mom, you just can't stay in this house forever. You got to get a smaller place and live someplace where you can be on the level." And he took us, just by force almost, to look at mobile homes and trailers. . . . And we almost bought one. They were so beautiful. And I said, "Well, are we going to sign?" And Pop said, "Well, let's think about it till morning." So we come home, and he just sit down and started to cry. "I can't do it," he said. He lived in this house 57 or 8 years. And he said, "I just can't do it. We'll stay here" (Rowles, 1980, pp. 157–158).

AGE SEGREGATION IN HOUSING

In addition to occupying houses and apartments scattered throughout the community, non-institutionalized older adults also live in hotels, mobile homes, and various forms of age-segregated housing. Some older people, mostly men, live in **single-room occupancy (SRO)** hotels, which are often inexpensive, central-city hotels with barely adequate facilities. SRO hotels cater to retired adults, welfare clients, and discharged mental patients. They provide privacy, a toleration for personal deviation, and a modest amount of social integration (Lawton, 1985). More conventional residence hotels house as many women as men, who tend to be either widowed or married. Many residents of these hotels have relatively high incomes.

Mobile-home parks may be age-integrated or limited to older adults. Most mobile homes (92 percent) are owner occupied, and they provide homes to about 5 percent of older adults (Lawton, 1985). Mobile homes have become increasingly popular with older adults, apparently because they are inexpensive compared with other housing, and the parks provide a small, homogeneous community where residents feel secure. Many amenity moves are made to mobile-home parks.

Resident hotels and mobile-home parks may not be planned as age-segregated communities, but public housing, retirement communities, congregate housing, continuing-care communities, and board-and-care facilities are specifically designed for older adults. Whether age-segregated housing is a curse or a blessing has never been settled. Segregating old people into public housing and retirement villages reduces their contact with the young and may keep the social stereotypes of old age from crumbling under the impact of mingling with the healthy young-old. It deprives the young of benefits that might come from more experience with the wisdom of older people. And it deprives the old, eliminating the stimulation of new ideas that might come from the young and hastening their obsolescence. Against these drawbacks to society are the feelings of older people. Studies indicate that most individuals who live in age-segregated housing love it—even those who were uncertain about the arrangement before they moved in (Lawton, 1985). They say they are no longer bothered by noise or the boisterous behavior of the young. They feel more secure, and they have less fear of crime. The interaction with age peers that accompanies age-segregated housing seems to increase well-being, morale, social activity, and housing satisfaction. Yet no studies have been conducted of the effect of age-segregated living on older adults who prefer to mix with people of all ages.

Public housing for the elderly is open to adults who are at least 62 years old, along with their spouses, and to handicapped people of any age. Between 3 and 5 percent of older Americans live in these units (Kendig, 1990), and the majority are women (78 percent)—

overwhelmingly single, widowed, or divorced (Lawton, 1985, 1980). Tenants are eager to enter these units, and life in one of them can be highly beneficial. Older adults who moved into Victoria Plaza, a housing project for the elderly in San Antonio, Texas, showed marked improvements in several aspects of their lives that did not appear in applicants who were rejected (Carp, 1976). Their health improved, their mortality dropped, their housing satisfaction and social activity increased, they liked the neighborhood better, they needed fewer outside services, and they had more positive self-concepts. Although the screening process may have tended to select residents who would be most likely to thrive in the new environment, most researchers believe that moving from substandard community housing into good public housing leads to modest improvements (Lawton, 1985).

Congregate housing, in which tenants have their own apartments but eat in a common dining room, is popular with people who have mild, early impairments. The arrangement, which generally includes housekeeping services, provides security with only a mild restriction on autonomy. One such facility is described in the accompanying box, ''Upscale Congregate Care.'' It encourages socialization among residents and permits older adults to remain independent, although they may be too frail to care for themselves in isolated apartments. Many of these developments provide high-quality care, and older people who do not actually require such a service-rich environment are entering them—a trend that has caused some concern (Lawton, 1985). The environmental press in congregate housing may be so low that it may lead to deterioration and reduced competence among otherwise competent older adults (see Chapter 5).

Continuing care communities provide care at increasingly supportive levels and are generally expensive—so expensive that between 50 and 80 percent of the residents have annual incomes in excess of $50,000 (Cohen et al., 1988). After a large initial payment, a monthly maintenance fee covers food, rent, utilities, maid service, and nursing care. In some communities, residents can be as independent as they like, cooking their own meals or eating in a common dining room. The community includes full nursing-home facilities for residents who grow too frail to live in apartments, so that it serves as a long-term care insurance policy and provides varying levels of autonomy and security, depending on a resident's capacities. Residents of continuing care communities tend to enter during their late seventies, and they tend to be unmarried and childless, as well as highly educated and affluent (Parmelee and Lawton, 1990).

Retirement villages are inhabited by middle-income retirees, who purchase houses or condominiums built by the developers. A warm climate makes Florida, Arizona, and California the favorite sites for these communities, which tend to be walled cities that provide so many facilities that their residents rarely go outside the gates. Recreation facilities (golf, tennis, shuffleboard, swimming), shops, churches, service clubs, restaurants, and an array of interest clubs and activities are available. Retirement villages tend to be inhabited by the young-old. In most, residents may be as young as 50 but may not have children younger than 18. Living in a retirement village is generally a positive experience. A comparison of retired men who had moved to Arizona indicated that those who lived in retirement villages were more satisfied with their lives than men who lived in age-integrated communities, even after researchers controlled for health and socioeconomic status (Kasl and Rosenfield, 1980).

Shared housing, in which unrelated older adults share a house or in which older homeowners share their house with younger people, has become popular, especially with older adults who need a low-cost alternative to retirement facilities. Share-a-Home, for example,

♦ *Adulthood in Today's World*

UPSCALE CONGREGATE CARE

Vincent and Elizabeth Confer paid $128,000 to enter their 1100-square-foot, two-bedroom apartment at the Quadrangle, a Marriott congregate-care facility for affluent older adults. Each month they pay an additional $2300, which gives them three meals each day, fresh linen, weekly maid service, and routine medical care. Marriott also provides transportation services and recreational facilities. Should the Confers decide to leave, 90 percent of their entry fee will be refunded, and when they die, the same amount will be paid into their estate. Vincent Confer, a retired history professor, says that their only extra monthly cost is for their telephone. The Confers brought their furniture with them, and—like other residents—they have contributed ornaments to the common areas, which include a library and a living room for socializing. The Quadrangle, located near universities and colleges like Villanova, Haverford, and Swarthmore, seems an ideal environment to the Confers, who wanted a place that would offer them intellectual stimulation (Peterson, 1989).

The Quadrangle, located on a 77-acre estate in Philadelphia's Main Line suburbs, is Marriott Corporation's response to the burgeoning population of comfortably fixed retired adults. Marriott is not the only chain to notice this opportunity. Hyatt International is also building congregate-care facilities that both chains believe can be afforded by 40 to 50 percent of older adults. The hotel chains' move into the congregate-care market has been aggressive, with Hyatt building residence centers in Nevada, New Jersey, Texas, and Maryland, and Marriott opening centers in Pennsylvania, Virginia, Maryland, Washington, D.C., California, and Illinois (Peterson, 1989).

Marriott provides both congregate care (which it calls "independent full service") and continuing care (which it calls "catered living") facilities, and plans to construct more traditional nursing homes as well. One of its congregate-care facilities caters to alumni of the University of Virginia and another to retired air force officers. Marriott and Hyatt expect their developments to be highly successful because their corporate names are familiar to the affluent elderly, and their prominence eases the fears of many older adults that a center will fail and take the entrance fees with it. These fears may be grounded in reality. During the double-digit inflation of the late 1970s, a number of congregate- and continuing-care facilities did fail. When these facilities were sold to large corporations, the residents found themselves faced with new contracts that required additional investment and higher monthly payments.

brings together moderately independent adults who live in separate bedrooms but share the rest of the house (Lawton, 1985). In Vermont, Project SHARE (Shared Housing Alternatives for Rural Elders) finds adults of any age who need a place to live and matches them with older homeowners. For example, a 77-year-old widower with a seven-bedroom farmhouse was matched with a middle-aged couple, an older farm worker, and a college student (Givens, 1989). The older homeowner gives up some privacy in return for additional income and security.

INSTITUTIONALIZATION

When health fails, adults may find themselves no longer able to adapt to their familiar surroundings. The same environment creates a higher level of press (see Chapter 5), and formerly comfortable surroundings can become a burden, if not an impossible situation.

Altering the environment slightly can sometimes reduce press and extend a person's independence for months or even years. Grab bars in the bathroom, for example, higher toilet seats, handrails, nightlights, and phones with memory dialing can be added to homes and apartments, making life easier for many older people. The increasing proportion of elderly has led to the manufacture of many small gadgets, such as phone amplifiers, remote controls for lighting and appliances, levers that replace doorknobs, and knob turners that allow arthritic hands to operate stoves, faucets, television sets, and appliances. The demand has grown so large that mail-order businesses that specialize in ''aids for easier living'' have developed.

Eventually, however, the press of the altered environment may itself become too great to handle, and the old-old find themselves forced to make an assistance migration. Some of the old-old move in with a child, some manage with a home health-care worker, and the rest move to an institution. Those who are severely disabled but in otherwise good health may go into a **board-and-care home,** in which attendants provide nonmedical personal care and protective oversight but little or no nursing care. Most board-and-care facilities are in private homes; although states license some of these facilities, others are unlicensed. The quality of board-and-care homes is unpredictable, with abuse and neglect prevalent in some homes and a family-like atmosphere prevailing in others. Among board-and-care homes in the Cleveland area, the average facility cared for 3.4 older adults, and the typical resident was a 78-year-old white widow with a high school education or less whose major (or only) source of income was Supplementary Security Income (Namazi et al., 1989).

Nursing homes are the typical institution for adults who require extensive care. Residents tend to be the oldest of the old: nearly half are older than 85 (U.S. Senate, 1987–88). The majority of residents are white women, usually widows. The typical resident is also so impaired that independent living is either extremely difficult or impossible. Nearly two-thirds are disoriented or have memory impairments, and almost half have some form of organic brain disorder. For the isolated adult, institutionalization may come before it is absolutely necessary, but for the adult with spouse or living children, it usually comes only after all other possibilities have been exhausted. Because institutions are costly and seen as undesirable by older adults and gerontologists alike, an array of supporting services has grown up to extend independent living.

Although only 5 percent of older adults live in nursing homes, the chances of spending some time there are relatively high. The figure rises from 1 percent among adults between the ages of 65 and 74 to about 22 percent of those older than 85. About half of women and about a third of men will be admitted to a nursing home at some time in their lives (Kane and Kane, 1990). Nearly three-quarters of all admissions come from hospitals, and most stays are short; the typical resident either dies or is discharged within three months, with about one-third returning to the community.

Most nursing home residents are widows who can no longer care for themselves.

Impact of Institutionalization

The move to an institution or from one institution to another is often followed by decline or even death in the elderly. Because people who enter nursing homes are already seriously incapacitated, the subsequent decline may be due to their previous condition. Or deterioration may result from being thrust into a world whose total security often requires a surrender of autonomy. Institutions are dominated by rules, regulations, and arbitrary schedules, and provide an unstimulating environment. Few people move into them voluntarily. According to Ellen Langer and her colleagues (Langer, 1985; Piper and Langer, 1986), these factors, together with other aspects of life in a nursing home, lead to psychological deterioration. The routine of health-care workers tends to take away many of the decisions and responsibilities of the older person, and staff attitudes may convey the idea that the residents are sick and helpless. Their sense of control erodes, and the unstimulating environment leads to hyperhabituation. Residents become psychologically and physically dependent on the staff and may eventually function in a ''mindless,'' automatic fashion.

The process may be accelerated by staff members' tendency to reward residents for their dependency. Observational research by Margaret Baltes and her colleagues (Baltes et al., 1987) demonstrated that nursing-home residents are reinforced with attention and approval when they ask for help in dressing, using the toilet, or eating, or when they comply with suggestions from the staff. When they act in a competent, autonomous manner, however, staff members tend to end interactions and go on to another patient.

Importance of Control

Life in such a setting could easily erode any sense of autonomy and control and foster the development of learned helplessness, which was discussed in Chapter 5. As the sense of control seeps away, stress increases and health deteriorates (Rodin, 1986). The effects of learned helplessness may explain why one of older adults' most successful strategies for dealing with an institutional move is to develop a feeling of mastery and control over their lives (Lieberman and Tobin, 1983). Rearranging the environment to foster this sense of control has led to improvements in nursing-home residents. In a now-classic experiment (Rodin and Langer, 1977), researchers allowed each of the residents in one group to choose a potted plant, which they expected to care for themselves, and to select the night they would attend a movie. Members of the other group were given a plant and told the staff would care for it; they also saw a movie each week, but had no say in the night it would be shown. Within three weeks, residents who had been encouraged to take control of their environment were happier and more active than residents who had been encouraged to depend on the staff. Within 18 months, 15 percent of the group that had taken responsibility were dead, compared with 30 percent of the dependent group. (The normal death rate in the nursing home was 25 percent.) Researchers warn that intervention programs will not induce permanent change unless the residents continue to feel some control over their lives. When responsibility is given and then taken away, the residents' subsequent deterioration may leave them much worse off than they were before the intervention began (Rodin, 1986).

People vary according to the amount of control they can handle. When given responsibility, some older adults become ridden with anxiety, especially if they lack the information they need to handle a situation (Rodin, 1986). According to the person-environment or **P-E fit approach,** how successfully older adults adapt to institutionalization may depend on how well the individual's life-style or personality (including the amount of control they feel they must have) matches the characteristics and demands of the nursing home (Kahana, 1982). Individual needs vary so widely that some individuals will flourish in an environment that leads to deterioration in another. Research indicates that when the change in environment results in a highly incongruent mismatch, when there is a sharp discontinuity between the old and new environments, or when the new environment is much poorer in quality than the old, deterioration becomes probable (Lieberman and Tobin, 1983). Older adults, who are alone, poor, and unable to care for themselves, and for whom security, not autonomy, is paramount, may find the nursing home an improvement over their previous environment.

SOCIAL SERVICES

At some time in our lives, nearly all of us will need help from a community social service. Although families generally do a good job of taking care of their frail or ill members, the burden often overwhelms available resources. Moreover, some individuals may be alone in the world, with no family to turn to. Some services are completely tax-supported, some are completely staffed by volunteers, but even many of the volunteer programs rely on government aid.

Social services may be needed at any stage of the life cycle. Certain services are used by people of all income and educational levels. Crisis hot lines provide sympathy, counseling, and comfort to alcoholics, individuals with drug problems, rape victims, battered women, runaway children, gamblers, and people who fear they may commit suicide. Ad-

Older adults give more time to volunteer work than younger age groups; some, like the residents of this geriatric center, tutor high school students.

ditional services provide more extensive counseling and material aid to people with such problems. Unwed mothers are assisted throughout pregnancy.

Not all community programs are crisis-related. Many provide services for the disabled, the elderly, the temporarily unemployed, or the poor. Some of these programs are staffed by individual volunteers, some by groups organized by employers, and others by religious organization, which provide 20 percent of all volunteer social services (Kantrowitz, 1989). Among the population at large, 45 percent of adults performed some kind of volunteer service in 1987, with older adults (ages 65 to 74) giving the most time—six hours per week. Some community programs are started by individuals and then assisted by corporations. The Corporate Angel Network (CAN) is such a program. It matches cancer patients traveling for treatment to one of the 27 U.S. comprehensive cancer centers with empty seats in corporate planes. The program was started in 1981 by Priscilla Blum, herself a private pilot, when she was a 56-year-old breast cancer patient who felt that being able to travel to New York's Memorial Sloan-Kettering Cancer Center allowed her to receive the treatment she needed (Tannenhauser, 1987). Another program spearheaded by an individual is Rosie's Place, a "women's drop-in center/emergency shelter" in Boston that was started by Kip Tiernan in 1974. Providing a week's food and lodging in the form of a "social club where poor women could come to get fed, have fun, love, and be loved," Rosie's Place is funded by corporate (20 percent) and individual (80 percent) donations (Tannenhauser, 1987).

Most programs are more institutionalized than CAN and Rosie's place, and most of them have general public support. The majority of them compete for tax dollars. When choices have to be made, suggests Fay Cook (1982), people appear to use four standards as a guide: (1) whether the group in need of assistance has an alternative source of help; (2) whether the program fills essential needs; (3) whether the program will increase an individual's independence, making him or her less dependent on others; and (4) whether the person in need causes the condition himself or herself. She described a survey of Chicagoans that summed up such sentiment; agreement was general across social class, gender, and racial groups. When specific types of aid were discussed, the elderly received priority in matters of income and nutrition, the disabled in transportation programs, and children and adults younger than 65 for educational aid.

There is general public support for programs that assist the elderly, especially those who are in need. In national surveys, strong approval has consistently been shown for such tax-financed programs as medical care, Social Security, and "helping the elderly." The sentiment seems solid for maintaining existing programs, but when asked about new programs, most favor them but feel that they should aid only older adults who are in need. Not mentioned, but also factors in support for these social programs, are the facts that younger taxpayers often have older relatives who need aid and the realization that age is an inevitable, universal condition.

SOCIAL SUPPORT FOR YOUNG AND MIDDLE-AGED ADULTS

Some social supports available to young and middle-aged adults are used by people at every socioeconomic level, but are especially popular among the middle class. Self-help groups have expanded so rapidly that there is now an International Network for Mutual Support Centers that serves in an advisory capacity to the Surgeon General. The network encompasses 108 clearing houses in the United States, Canada, Western Europe, and Australia (Westchester Self-Help Clearing House, 1989). In Westchester County, New York, alone, more than 200 different self-help groups meet regularly. Groups focus on every conceivable physical, sexual, social, or emotional problem in the fields of addictive behavior, mental health, parenting, and relationships. There are groups for compulsive eaters, compulsive buyers (Debtors Anonymous), and compulsive gamblers; groups for those addicted to alcohol or to other drugs; groups for people who are grieving, have disabilities, specific health problems, or mental disorders; groups for single parents, stepparents, grandparents, foster parents, and parents of twins; groups for couples with fertility problems or those hoping to become parents through adoption.

Most self-help groups have several things in common. They are generally led by peers. They center around a situation that is shared by all members. They are free, except for a nominal fee to cover postage and refreshments. Most important, they provide support in an understanding atmosphere that encourages creative problem-solving.

Self-help groups require little more than advice and a place to meet. Communities provide more substantial support to young adults who need assistance with their families. Family planning clinics serve millions of girls and women each year, and most states have initiated special health, education, and training programs directed at preventing adolescent pregnancies and providing nutrition, counseling, child-care, and transportation services for teenage mothers (Tolchin, 1990). For mothers of any age, the Special Supplementary Program for Women, Infants, and Children (WIC) supplies special foods and nutritional information to low-income women who are pregnant, postpartum, or lactating, and to their children who are younger than five years old. Child health services provide infants and young children with preventive health care, physical examinations, and immunization. Additional programs are available in the field of nutrition, transportation, housing, and medical care. Medicaid, for example, not only picks up hospital and physician's bills, but also provides low-income families with visiting nurse services, homemakers and personal care aides, hospital supplies and equipment, and prescriptions. Legal Aid furnishes free or inexpensive help for all kinds of legal problems. Other programs provide for education, unemployment compensation, and aid to dependent children.

SOCIAL SUPPORT FOR OLDER ADULTS

Older adults who live alone are sometimes socially isolated. To meet their needs, various kinds of visitation programs have been developed. Some programs supply "friends"; others provide help with household chores or home repairs that elderly adults may not have the financial resources or dexterity to manage. A typical friendly visitor program, the Village Visiting Neighbors, sends volunteers to provide companionship and do small services, such as reading mail or paying bills for their "neighbor" (Alexander, 1983). They may also act as escorts if the neighbor would like to go shopping, visit a museum, or take some other outing that seems formidable to a lone, older adult. For example, three or four times a week Susan Dinio brings her two young sons to visit an 89-year-old widower. The widower, who has no children of his own, has become a substitute grandparent to the boys, whose own grandfather lives far away.

The Adopt-a-Grandparent program provides social support to the elderly by bringing together adolescents and adults in their seventies and eighties (Larronde, 1983). The teenagers get school credit for the program, which carefully matches the personality of young and old. Two adolescents are assigned to each adult, and the youngsters often continue their visits long after their "class" is over. This sort of program not only benefits the elderly, but also provides the young with an important opportunity to get to know older individuals. The interaction and resulting friendship may dispel some of the myths and stereotypes young people often have about aging.

The diversified physical, social, and cultural activities provided by senior centers enlarge the social world of older adults, especially those who live alone.

Older adults who are not confined to their home may attend a senior center, which provides a broad array of services and activities. Senior centers offer recreation, classes, and cultural activities, and they either provide most of the material services discussed in the next section or else put older adults in contact with providers of such services. Adults who attend senior centers tend to live alone and have low incomes but high levels of social interaction, compared with adults who do not use the centers (Krout, Cutler, and Coward, 1990). They are most likely to be between the ages of 70 and 85 and in relatively good, but not excellent, health.

Older women and men who need more assistance may attend one of the growing number of adult day-care centers, some of which cater to older adults with organic brain syndromes (see Chapter 6). Day-care centers run by rehabilitation hospitals and nursing homes tend to have more disabled participants than those run by general hospitals or social service agencies (Weissart et al., 1989). Many day-care participants require extensive help in the activities of daily living, and 40 percent suffer from some mental disorder. Centers provide social interaction, exercise, a hot noontime meal, and nursing observation and supervision. Without adult day care, most would have to have special home care, and some would have to enter a nursing home.

FINANCIAL SUPPORT FOR OLDER ADULTS

From the time they retire, most older adults receive some sort of financial support. As we have seen, Social Security provides the bulk of direct income for older adults, with Medicare the major source of in-kind income. Medicaid, food stamps, rent supplements, and SSI provide additional assistance to low-income elderly. Other special services that serve as in-kind income have emerged in the area of housekeeping, health, nutrition, transportation, and legal assistance. Such programs enable many older adults who would otherwise be institutionalized to remain at home.

Many financial support programs bring services directly into the home. For example, Medicare has certified nearly 4000 home health-care agencies. These agencies, run by hospitals, physicians, businesses, or nurses, make house calls to homebound elderly. Some home health-care agencies have been too expensive to be useful to many of the elderly, but others have been extremely effective. A service in upstate New York run by two registered nurses reduced the cost of medical care from $210 (for an ambulance visit to a hospital emergency room) to $20 (directly in the home) (Freudenheim, 1983). The team works with physicians, who step in when more extensive medical care is required. Another approach to health care has been developed in Michigan, where outreach clinics have opened in several high-rise apartment buildings for low-income elderly and handicapped adults of any age (Morris and Dexter, 1989). The clinics are staffed by a nurse who provides primary health care and a social worker who helps residents cope with death, loss, and changes in their health status.

Nutrition is another problem among older persons, especially those living alone. More than 35 years ago, after high levels of malnutrition and dehydration were found among isolated elderly, voluntary organizations developed "meals on wheels" programs, in which a hot meal is brought into the home each day. The congregate meal service, in which older adults are transported to central dining facilities for a hot meal, is another popular nutrition program. Older adults are more likely to know about meal service programs than any other form of social service.

Congregate meals programs require access service, because many of the elderly either do not have cars (especially in urban areas) or are no longer capable of driving. Many older adults live too far from bus stops to use public transportation or are physically unable to get on and off a bus or subway car. The fear of crime keeps many other older adults from using public transportation. A survey of nearly 3000 older adults in Washington State indicated that fear was highest in those who had experienced crime themselves or who had acquaintances with such experience (Lee, 1983). Healthy, well-educated adults showed the least fear of crime, perhaps because they have greater control over their lives.

An increasing number of communities now provide transportation services for older adults. Some provide door-to-door transportation on call, some use fixed routes on a regular schedule, and a few use commercial taxi companies, reimbursing the company for its services. In a Chicago program called Seniors on the Move, where vans operated on both fixed schedules and door-to-door calls, about 80 percent of trips were for shopping and about 15 percent were for health care (Cohen, 1980).

Legal services are another form of in-kind aid. Legal-aid offices set up to serve low-income people can help some of the elderly, but often individuals have too much income to be eligible for aid but not enough to pay a lawyer. Retired attorneys, volunteers from the local bar association, and paralegals who are supervised by attorneys assist older people

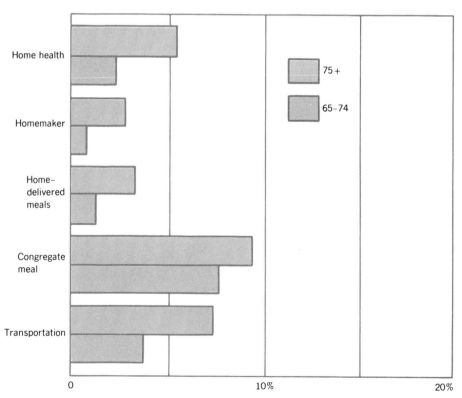

Figure 15.3 Use of community services by people age 65 and older, 1984. *Source:* Kane and Kane, 1990, p. 425.

with government forms, tax and pension problems, wills, and other legal problems. The AARP provides a volunteer program that assists older adults with their tax forms.

Another sort of legal service is the protective service, in which older adults who become mentally or emotionally impaired and unable to act in their own best interests are helped with their personal affairs. The purpose of such services, which usually involve the appointment of a guardian by the court, is to see that the older person's rights are not violated and to protect his or her well-being, safety, and assets—from salespeople, collection agencies, family members, or other individuals who may be exerting pressure.

When family, medical professionals, and social workers agree on the need for guardianship, the procedure is usually swift—especially when the older adult does not protest. A court-appointed attorney, known as the **guardian ad litem,** investigates the guardianship petition, informs the potential ward of his or her rights, and determines whether a guardian is actually needed. Sometimes the process is drawn out, especially when conflicting family

Table 15.2 **OLDER ADULTS' AWARENESS OF COMMUNITY SERVICES**

Program	Aware of Its Existence
Home-delivered meals	79%
Transportation	69%
Congregate meals	59%
Education	54%
Legal assistance	52%
Emergency energy assistance	52%
Health screening	51%
Home health aide	49%
Library	49%
Crime prevention	45%
Adult day care	45%
Volunteer services	44%
Food bank	43%
In-home visits	42%
Hearing impaired	40%
Home repair	40%
Homemaker	39%
Employment services	34%
Emergency home monitoring	33%
Telephone reassurance	30%
Financial management	29%
Housing assistance (counsel)	27%
Dental	25%
Vision	22%
Chore	21%
Counseling/long-term care	19%
Assessment and referral	14%
Complaints long-term care	10%

Source: Adapted from Chapleski, 1989, p. 541.

interests are involved. In such cases, the argument is likely to concern the selection of a guardian rather than the need for one (Iris, 1988). Often the procedure involves commitment to a nursing home. Guardianship is considered a step of last resort, because it deprives the person of autonomy.

Only a small proportion of the elderly make use of available social services, in part because they do not know about them (Figure 15.3). Those who are especially frail, poor, and isolated are the least likely to have heard of various services, and they are generally those who need them most. Among a representative sample of Michigan residents who were at least 60 years old, the average adult was aware of the existence of 7 of 28 available programs (Chapleski, 1989) (Table 15.2). **Outreach services,** a program that locates older people and informs them of the array of available social services, attempt to remedy this situation. Publicity in the media reaches some of the elderly, but other contacts are more often effective. Informal communication systems (such as churches, clubs, and extended families), people whose employment brings them in contact with older adults (such as grocers, pharmacists, delivery people, and mail carriers), and door-to-door canvassing may be required to find older adults. Once older adults are located, the outreach worker describes available services, assesses needs, and helps individuals take whatever steps are required to obtain the appropriate services. In the next chapter, we will investigate aging in other countries and special ethnic groups to get a new perspective on American policies and practices.

SUMMARY

LEGAL ISSUES CONCERNING AGE

Age can be used to grant status and privileges or to withdraw them. Discrimination against the young is most common in housing, whereas discrimination against the old is most common in employment. Because age is no longer a good predictor of capability or need, some have suggested that (1) all social programs be based on need, not age; or that (2) the marker of old age be moved to 75.

ECONOMIC DISTRIBUTION

The major source of income in the United States is wages, and earning power tends to rise steadily through young and middle adulthood. Income generally drops after retirement, but many expenses also tend to decrease—although usually not enough to offset the drop in income. Because of Social Security and pension regulations, older women are disadvantaged in comparison with men, and many rely on **Supplementary Security Income (SSI).** Assets (including homeownership), tax breaks, and **in-kind income** usually help retired adults stretch their money. ''House rich'' elderly can increase their income through the use of a **reverse annuity mortgage (RAM).** Consumption patterns change across adulthood as needs and income change. The satisfaction of retired adults with their financial situation seems to be primarily determined by the comparison between their present situation and the pretirement circumstance, with a drastic drop leading to feelings of deprivation.

HOUSING

The flight from the nest is affected by economics, with the proportion of young, single adults who live by themselves rising in good times and the proportion of young adults who live at home—or return to the nest—increasing during economic downturns. Mobility peaks during the early twenties and then slowly declines until retirement years, when a series of small peaks appear. The moves of older adults tend to follow a developmental pattern, with **amenity migration** found primarily among the young-old, **kinship migration** found among adults with slight or moderate disability, and **assistance migration** found among the old-old. Interstate moves tend to be amenity migrations, whereas local moves tend to be assistance migrations. The sort of residence selected by older adults may represent a balance struck between the conflicting goals of autonomy and security. Although only a minority of older adults live in age-segregated housing, those who do tend to be satisfied. Some older people, mostly men, live in **single-room occupancy (SRO)** hotels; others live in public housing, **congregate housing,** which is popular with the mildly disabled, **continuing care communities,** which provide a wide range of care, and **retirement villages.**

Institutionalization sometimes takes the form of **board-and-care homes,** whose residents tend to be less impaired than residents of **nursing homes.** Several factors may contribute to the declines that often follow nursing-home admissions, including the already poor health of residents, the unstimulating nature of the environment, and loss of control which may lead to learned helplessness. Studies have shown that returning some control to residents may lessen stress, improving health and satisfaction. The **P-E fit** of personality, life-style, and environment may determine how successfully older adults adapt to institutionalization.

SOCIAL SERVICES

Social programs tend to be supported by the public when the group in need of assistance has no alternative source of help, when the program fills essential needs, when the program makes an individual less dependent on others, and when the person in need did not cause the condition. Different social-support programs are designed to meet the various needs of different age groups. When older adults become emotionally impaired, the need for guardianship may develop. A court-appointed **guardian ad litem** investigates guardianship petitions, informs the potential ward of his or her rights, and determines whether a guardian is actually needed. **Outreach services** attempt to locate older people and inform them of various support programs.

KEY TERMS

amenity migration	continuing care community
assistance migration	guardian ad litem
board-and-care home	in-kind income
congregate housing	kinship migration

nursing home

outreach services

P-E fit approach

retirement village

reverse annuity mortgage (RAM)

shared housing

single-room occupancy (SRO) hotel

Supplementary Security Income (SSI)

Chapter 16

Cross-Cultural Perspectives on Adulthood and Aging

Nearly 30 years ago, anthropologist Colin Turnbull (1972) studied the Ik, a hunting tribe in the mountains of northeastern Uganda, and what he found makes us look at our own society in a new way. Instead of using bows and arrows or throwing spears at game, the Ik had always hunted in a cooperative manner. Community members spread out a large net and held it up while other members drove game into it. Almost overnight, life changed for the Ik.

Concerned about the preservation of various animal species, the central government made the Iks' traditional hunting grounds into a game preserve. The Ik were no longer permitted to hunt but were expected to become farmers. The loss of their hunting grounds demolished the basis of Ik culture. Shared social assumptions were invalidated in the eyes of tribal members. With group pride and the concept of community destroyed, life became nasty and brutish. Altruism vanished, and it was each Ik for himself or herself. The mother–child bond was destroyed, and children were left to fend for themselves from the time they were three years old. Whether a three year old was eaten by a leopard, fell into a fire, or starved to death was of no concern to the child's parents. Thrown on their own devices, children survived by forming juvenile bands that foraged for food. One Ik helped another only if there was a clear and immediate reward for doing so. The other end of the life cycle became a horror, for no one respected or cared for the old. When adults were too feeble to support themselves, they were left to die. Turnbull believes that the experience of the Ik demonstrates that human values are impossible without society and that the loss of a social tradition is almost synonymous with the loss of humanity.

The Ik are an extreme case, but the thoroughness of their destruction illustrates how heavily our experience of the life cycle is influenced by the shared beliefs of society. **Culture** consists of these shared understandings that underlie a way of life and give meaning to various aspects of shared social life. In this chapter, we examine various cultural and ethnic patterns in the hope of gaining perspective on our own lives. We begin with a look at the different ways in which cultures mark the onset of adulthood and old age. After exploring the experience of life and aging in traditional societies, we consider the effect that industrialization has on these societies. Narrowing our focus from the world to the nation, we examine ethnic differences within the United States noting how a variety of family relationships can alter the experience of the life span within the same society. We close with a brief appraisal of the problems involved in providing social services for ethnic groups within a larger society.   ◆

CULTURAL VIEWS OF THE LIFE CYCLE

Each society has its own standards and goals for various stages of the life cycle. As we saw in Chapter 1, societies divide the cycle in various ways. The standard of full adult responsibility also varies from one society to another, as does the way of reckoning age and the timing of old age.

THE MARK OF ADULTHOOD

In a high-tech society like that of the United States, the mark of adulthood is earning a living—taking a full share of economic responsibility. In many societies, adulthood is marked by marriage. Among the Mbuti hunter-gatherers of northeastern Zaire, for example, a youth is not permitted to own a hunting net until he marries, and in the eyes of the culture, marriage is dedicated to the good of society. The unmarried person is seen as not truly adult, apparently because he or she has not assumed this community responsibility.

Colin Turnbull (1983), who studied the Mbuti, reports that they reacted with surprise and disbelief to the news that he was unmarried and childless. The members of this African tribe regarded him as socially irresponsible, asking if he had no feelings about his family and his country. The ancient Chinese held a somewhat similar attitude. According to Confucian doctrine, a man became an adult on his twentieth birthday, but he was not considered a fully participating member of society until he was married and a parent (Tu, 1978).

There are good reasons for different standards of adult responsibility. In the traditional society, the family is the economic unit, controlling both production and consumption. Disease takes a heavy toll among the young in most traditional societies, and the death rate may be so high that continuation of the culture depends on encouraging the fertility of its members. In a technological society like that of the United States, the family has no direct economic function, and marriage is not required for the assumption of a full economic role. Because most children live to maturity, there is no need to encourage procreation; in fact, overpopulation becomes a concern in most industrialized societies.

THE MEASURE OF AGE

Although the biological course of development is similar in all cultures, the social experience varies around the world. Even age is calculated in different ways. In Western societies, a person's date of birth is socially important. Without official certification of birth, it is extremely difficult for an American to get a passport, a marriage or driver's license, or a Social Security card. Age is unimportant in most traditional societies, and many cultures did not count years at all until after their contact with colonial powers (Keith, 1990). Generational status is more important than age, and status is often determined by membership in an **age set**, a group of individuals born within a certain span of years (usually from 7 to 15) who move together through the life cycle. Most age sets are male; only a few societies have female age sets, and where they exist, the culture assigns them fewer rituals and ceremonies and less significant roles (Keith, 1990).

Among the Masai herding society of Kenya and Tanzania, for example, age sets cover a 15-year span, and at any time male society is organized into five male age sets: *uninitiated children,* who are younger than 15; *initiated warriors,* generally between the ages of 15 and 30; *junior elders,* generally between the ages of 30 and 45, whose sphere is procreation and domestic affairs; *senior elders,* between the ages of 45 and 60, whose sphere is public affairs; and *old men,* who are retired (van den Berghe, 1983). Masai culture is distinctive because members of a male age set move through life in lockstep. Warriors live together in a bachelor village. These age sets organize the public domain, because political and social roles accompany membership. A Masai male may not marry, own cattle, or have his own home until his age set achieves junior-elder status. Although Masai women also belong to an age set, they are virtually excluded from public life, and their roles are limited to those of wife and mother. Yet Masai women reach adulthood earlier than men, for they marry a man from an older age set, while men of their own age are still warriors, single, and without responsibility (Fry, 1980).

THE MARK OF OLD AGE

The onset of old age varies from society to society. In the United States, people are generally considered old when they reach the age of 65, whether they are single or married, poets or plumbers, robust or feeble, primarily because the initial requirements of the Social Security system set eligibility at that age. In contrast to our focus on chronological age, traditional societies may define old age in generational or functional terms. Anthropologists have concluded that the relinquishment of social responsibility bears so little connection to chronological age that it is incorrect to say that many traditional societies even have such a category as "the old" (Fry, 1985; Keith, 1990). Some societies connect aging to role changes that accompany generational events in the life cycle. In India, for example, a person crosses the threshold into old age when his or her children marry (Vatuk, 1980). Because Indians tend to marry young, an Indian man or woman may reach old age during the forties. The Masai mark old age by social roles, promoting an age set into "retirement," so that a man may be as young as 60 or as old as 75 when he "retires" (van den Berghe, 1983). As respected elders, these men have no ritual or public role; their function is limited to that of consultant in traditional matters.

Other societies define age in functional terms, so that an old person is one who can no longer carry out the major roles of adulthood. This distinction may lead to the arrival of old age at a later time for one gender than for the other. Among the Inuit Eskimo, for example, a man generally becomes old at about the age of 50, when he no longer has strength to hunt during the winter, but old age tends to come about a decade later for women, whose roles are less strenuous (Guemple, 1983). Among the Black Carib of Belize, however, women become old before men. These Central American villagers consider menopause the marker of old age in women and impotence the marker of old age in men. Thus, a woman may be old at 50, but a man of 65 could still be considered middle-aged (Kerns, 1980).

Whether or not they reach old age "first," women seem to meet the physical and psychological challenges of aging more easily than do men (Fry, 1985). Anthropologists have suggested that several factors in women's lives may be responsible. Women's lives center around home and family, which makes the transition to old age less disruptive and builds the kind of strong emotional ties with children and grandchildren that can enhance emotional and physical well-being. Lives spent adjusting to the bodily constraints of pregnancy, lactation, and menstruation make adjustments to bodily changes of age less burdensome. Finally, the social position and power of women often increase with age. As we saw in Chapter 10, as the parental imperative eases, women tend to become more autonomous at a time when men are relinquishing their occupational power and responsibilities.

Just as each culture has its own definition of old age, so the status and treatment of the old differ from one society to the next. Most of us have heard that in "the good old days" aged men and women were always held in high esteem and were consulted on community matters. In some societies this was true, but the actual situation of the elderly was neither so consistent nor so simple.

AGING IN TRADITIONAL SOCIETIES

In most traditional or "preindustrial" societies, the appearance of respect for the elderly prevails, and they receive public marks of deference. Yet many older adults in the same societies are treated badly. The fate of the old often depends on whether they are "intact" or "decrepit"—a division that is roughly equivalent to that between the young-old and the old-old (Keith, 1985).

The young-old are often active in political or religious roles. The Mbuti, for example, place the responsibility of governing the tribe in the hands of adults who are too old to hunt (Turnbull, 1983). Among the Israeli Druze, old people have special social roles based on their expertise in Hindu rituals (Keith, 1990). An association with religious rites and beliefs may be the most important contribution to the prestige of the old in traditional societies (Gutmann, 1980). The old may sometimes be seen as witches or wizards—and with good reason. Where disease and accident drastically shorten life expectancy, survival into old age indicates favor from the gods, supernatural power, or keen intelligence. Among the Kagwahiv in the Amazonian areas of Brazil, for example, the old are objects of awe, respected for their knowledge and for the spiritual strength seen as necessary for a long life. They are believed to have supernatural power and so much spiritual strength that they can safely violate food taboos (Gutmann, 1980).

Among the Hopi, the young-old may trade one set of responsibilities for another. When old men can no longer follow the flocks or work in the fields, they card wool, spin, knit, and make sandals. Old women care for children, mind the house, grind corn, make clay pots and bowls, and weave baskets (Simmons, 1945). Each person who is not bedridden has a vital role to play in society.

In hunting societies, some older adults retain vital religious roles, like this shaman who chants a ritual song to guarantee a successful whale hunt and the safety of hunters at sea.

In a society without writing, the old are the only repository of information, and their role as the tribal memory enhances their prestige. They know the "right way" of doing things, the words and the movements of rituals, the places where water can be found in times of drought. As the Bakongo of lower Zaire say, "Only the old ones can unravel the knots in a net" (Fry, 1985). Their knowledge of story, myth, and legend makes older adults entertainers as well as historians, resolvers of conflict as well as teachers, administrators as well as councillors (Goody, 1976).

Despite their avowed reverence for age, many societies treat the old-old with contempt, if not cruelty. In various cultures they are referred to as the "overaged," in the "useless state," the "sleeping period," or belonging to the "age grade of the dying" (Keith, 1985). Among traditional societies studied, 84 percent accord "nonsupportive" treatment to the old-old, with 19 percent on occasion killing, abandoning, or forsaking them (Glascock and Feinman, 1981). Societies in which the old-old are encouraged or "helped" to die are generally subsistence societies located in harsh environments, where decrepit members are a serious drain on the economy. Among the Inuit Eskimos, for example, who depend on hunting, the old-old often cooperate in their own abandonment or strangulation (Guemple, 1983). The Inuit belief that people do not really die, but are reborn to experience the life cycle again and again, makes the act ethical, if not customary.

Family resources and offspring are also important factors in the treatment of the old-old. In a survey of 95 societies, contempt was expressed primarily toward the old who had no living children (Keith, 1985). Another important influence on the status of the old is their control of material resources. In agricultural or herding societies, ownership of lands or flocks allows older adults to retain power after they can no longer labor in the field—even after they join the ranks of the old-old (Goody, 1976). If property is handed over to a son or daughter at the time of marriage, the parent may keep control over the land or else retain certain rights such as food, shelter, or a portion of the harvest.

THE EFFECT OF INDUSTRIALIZATION

Around the world, traditional societies are rapidly disappearing. As members of modern societies have carried technology into remote societies and electronic media have blanketed the globe with radio and television broadcasts, few cultures have escaped the effect of industrialization. Some formerly traditional societies have become highly developed, whereas others are just beginning to feel the effect of plentiful power, technology, highly segmented economic roles, and an emphasis on efficiency and progress. As development progresses, the proportion of older adults in a society at first remains fairly steady because fertility remains high, and infant mortality is sharply reduced. But as fertility declines, the proportion of older adults steadily increases (Meyers, 1990) (Figure 16.1).

At one time sociologists and anthropologists agreed on the premises of the **modernization theory,** which stated that changes accompanying industrialization inevitably diminished the status of the old (Cowgill, 1974). As modern medicine and sanitation improved life expectancy, the proportion of elderly in the society grew, forcing them to compete with the young for jobs or else retire and thus lose status. As industrialization progressed, the family ceased to function as the basic economic unit, and the skills of the elderly became obsolete. As the young left home for the cities, the extended family broke up, ending any control by

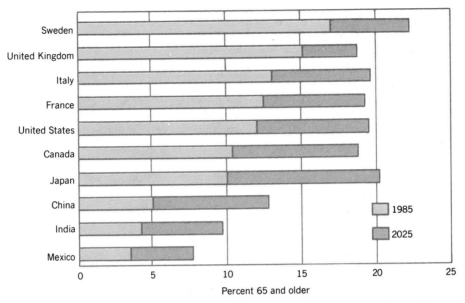

Figure 16.1 World-wide trends in longevity. The percent of the population that is 65 and older is growing in most countries, with the most dramatic increases in high-technology societies. *Source:* Torrey, Kinsella, and Taueber, forthcoming.

the old and cutting off their source of support. Finally, as literacy and the mass media provided reliable information, the cultural justification for the power of the old was destroyed.

Studies by anthropologists indicate that the effect of industrialization is not as predictable as social scientists had once believed. According to Jennie Keith (1990), the best we can do is to define the conditions under which ''some old people do better in some societies and during certain types of social change.'' Modernization has its severest effects when it undermines control of resources by the old or disrupts the strategies they have used to accumulate wealth (Fry, 1985). Among the Tonga of Zambia, for example, the coming of cheap power destroyed the status of the old (Colson and Scudder, 1981). Resettlement required by a hydroelectric dam wiped out the inherited holdings of the elders, who lacked the physical strength to clear new lands.

In a similar fashion, modernization demolished the status of the old among farming communities in western Ireland. Traditionally, aged parents had wielded economic power through their ownership of the land and had been venerated for their knowledge of the ancient Celtic tradition. But as farms became unproductive and the young emigrated, the traditional culture broke down (Scheper-Hughes, 1983). The young scorned the Celtic language, viewed the old with pity and contempt, and often ridiculed them. The extended family deteriorated, and the childless old and the unmarried elderly found themselves in old-age homes, nursing homes, or mental institutions. Men, whose relationship with their children had been based on authority, duty, and respect instead of love, suffered most.

Among Hindu families in Nepal, the extended family has survived modernization, but living in the same household with their married sons no longer assures the economic security of the elderly (Goldstein, Schuler, and Ross, 1983). The shift from farming to salaried jobs in the city of Kathmandu led to unemployment, low wages, and inflation. With the agricultural family unit no longer the basis of the economy, power passed from the landholding parent to the employed son, removing any vestige of parental control. Education not only made sons employable but also gave them new values and attitudes. The customary obedience, respect, and deference of sons gave way to individualism, independence, secularism, and democratic values. Low wages made it difficult for sons to support their families.

Without exception, elderly men and women in Kathmandu said it was essential for old people to have their own income. One woman who lived with her married son summed up the general attitude by saying, "These days money is love" (Goldstein, Schuler, and Ross, 1983, p. 716); and a 70-year-old man said, "In our society . . . sons are with you if you have property. If not, parents are left as fleas leave a dead dog" (p. 721). In a majority of households with older adults, the elderly were responsible for all or most of the household expenses, with the money obtained by renting out rooms, leasing farm land, or drawing on government pensions or savings. Away from the city, in traditional Hindu villages, older adults were economically secure but full of emotional and psychological insecurity.

Modernization has had little effect on the status of the old in some cultures. In American Samoa, for example, elderly men and women retain traditional household roles, and most live in extended families (Holmes and Rhoads, 1983). Although Samoans have begun to accept a chronological definition of old age, they do not retire but switch to less strenuous jobs. Traditionally, elders have been responsible for tedious but important jobs, such as braiding coconut twine and weaving, on the grounds that they have more patience than the young. When interviewed, the old said that the young obeyed and respected them, and researchers could see no sign that their status was threatened. The only dark cloud was the high migration rate in some areas, which could affect the future position of the elderly by drastically reducing the proportion of young people.

When older people have what society needs, change can bring benefits (Fry, 1985). On the northwest coast of the United States, for example, Coast Salish elders experienced a recent increase in status. With the growth of cultural awareness, younger members of the tribe began to search out their roots, and elders' knowledge of old rituals, old ways, and traditional culture raised their esteem in the eyes of the young (Amoss, 1981).

Modernization in the People's Republic of China also indicates that industrialization need not weaken the position of older adults. In China, addressing an older person as "Lao," which means "old," is a mark of respect and indicates that the person is wise. Thus, middle-aged men are often called "old" instead of "Mr." (Green, 1983). Perhaps unintentionally, government policies have improved the economic security of old people in China and helped to maintain them in a favorable position (Davis-Friedmann, 1983). Although early Communist Party proclamations seemed to strike at the position of the old, in practice the elderly have retained much of their former status. The party certainly subordinates the family to the state, but its need to lessen welfare burdens and reduce the demand for new housing has led it to encourage multigenerational households. The policy of allowing a retiring worker to designate which child will assume his or her job gives adults who are nearing retirement a measure of family power.

In urban areas, Chinese women retire between the ages of 50 and 55; Chinese men work until they are 60. Pensions are from 60 to 90 percent of their salaries, depending on their occupations, job performance, and past service to the country. Health care is free. Grown

In rural China, older adults either work in the fields or care for children and household, freeing young adults for field work.

children are legally responsible for their aging parents, and children who neglect their parents may be imprisoned for as long as seven years. In most cases, however, prison is not necessary. When neglect is apparent, a visit from the neighborhood committee, factory work unit, or local communist cell straightens out the situation (Green, 1983).

In rural China, where most adults are engaged in manual agricultural labor, the family remains the unit of production. Here the traditional pattern of living with a son remains firmly entrenched. Childless adults or those who have only daughters may live alone, but they stay within the community and are supplied with food, shelter, and medical care at a subsistence level. Older adults continue to work as long as they are able, either in the fields or at home. Older adults often release the young for field work by maintaining the household (Davis–Friedmann, 1983).

The results of modernization in Turkey remind us that considering ''the old'' as a single group can be misleading. In Turkey, modernization has lowered the status of elderly men within the family and the larger society, although it has not disturbed the shared values of obedience to parents and the duty of sons to support their aged parents (Gilleard and Gurkan, 1987). The reduction in status seems to parallel an area's degree of industrialization, with fewer older men retaining the traditional role of ''head of household'' and an increasing proportion becoming dependent on their sons. Yet the most modernized areas of Turkey also have the largest proportion of educated elders in professions with high status.

Although the status of the old does decline in some—but by no means all—societies after industrialization, the decline appears to be only temporary. The status of the old appears to follow a cyclical pattern: relatively low in many subsistence societies, rising to a peak in stable agricultural societies, declining with modernization, then rising again as society reaches the highest level of modernization (Fry, 1985). This view was put forth by Erdan

Palmore (1976), who proposed that, as the importance of agricultural labor diminishes, unemployment and retirement rise among older adults, probably helping to account for the decline in their status. As societies develop, change is rapid: life expectancy is extended, productivity increases, incomes rise, educational levels climb, and shifts from rural to urban settings accelerate. These rapid rates of change temporarily depress the status of the old. When modernization is complete, the rate of change slows, and the relative position of the old begins to rise. The United States reached this point in about 1967, says Palmore, and since then the status of the old has been improving in this country, in good part as a result of social programs. Eventually, he believes, society approaches a state of equality in which the status of young and old becomes virtually equal.

AGING IN ETHNIC GROUPS

Membership in an ethnic group within a society also imposes cultural expectations that affect the way individuals experience the life cycle, expectations that may differ from those of the larger culture. As a result, conclusions about the course of adult development reached on the basis of studies with middle-class groups, drawn primarily from the majority culture, may not provide an adequate understanding of development within ethnic groups. An **ethnic group** may be distinguished by race, religion, or national identity. It has its own attitudes, traditions, values, and beliefs, as well as its own expectations about sex roles, child-rearing, the family, and aging. A person's **ethnic identity,** which is based on a group's shared values and behavior, may affect a person's self-concept, self-esteem, and life-style. Because of their small representation in the power structure of the larger society, some ethnic groups are also considered **minorities,** a term that refers to any group that suffers discrimination or subordination in society because of physical or cultural characteristics (Markides, Liang, and Jackson, 1990). Although members of some white ethnic groups may face subtle discrimination, their position differs considerably from that of other minorities.

AGING AND THE FAMILY IN WHITE ETHNIC GROUPS

The dominant American culture is basically a white Anglo-Saxon Protestant (WASP) culture that was originally English but that came to include Scottish, Scotch-Irish, Welsh, and other Northern European groups that soon blended into the majority culture. At the beginning of the twentieth century, most social scientists assumed that American society was a "melting pot," that immigrants would adapt themselves to the majority culture, and that a single "American" culture would prevail. Melting pots can be produced by the process of **assimilation,** in which cultural traits from two or more distinct groups are merged, and by **acculturation,** in which new groups adopt the cultural traits or patterns of the host group. By 1940 it became clear that this melting of cultures had not taken place, primarily because immigrants tended to cluster in specific regions, allowing them to pass on their culture to new generations (Gelfand, 1982). Canada's experience shows that melting may not occur for centuries—if ever. In the Canadian province of Quebec, descendants of French immigrants have retained their language, rejected either acculturation or assimilation, and proposed independence from English-speaking areas. Similarly, the Basques of Spain have refused to melt into the majority culture. Within the Soviet Union, states like Azerbaijan that are predominantly inhabited by a single ethnic group have begun demanding a degree of independence.

Since the eighteenth century, as each ethnic group entered the United States in great numbers, it faced prejudice and discrimination. Most immigrants arrived with limited skills, little money, and less English. Even a highly skilled immigrant who spoke no English generally discovered that only low-paying jobs were available. With time, however, most white ethnic groups were assimilated to the extent that they could thrive in American society, and social assimilation generally followed economic success. Whether a group was fully assimilated, to the extent that members no longer identified with their culture of origin, depended in good part on whether they intermarried with the dominant group (Gelfand, 1982).

An ethnic community that establishes itself within American society may be different in many ways from the culture of origin. The transplanted group may preserve customs and values that existed at the time it left, so that changes in the "old country" are not reflected in the ethnic subculture. Contact with American society may change the transplanted culture in other ways. Distinctive cultural patterns that the group itself considers "traditional" may actually be patterns that have emerged in response to the challenge of living in the new

Over the past 200 years, white ethnic groups have been gradually assimilated into the dominant U.S. culture, first economically, and then socially.

host culture (Markides, Liang, and Jackson, 1990). An ethnic group sometimes resists full assimilation, despite a move into the middle class, relocation from the city to the suburbs, and a measure of intermarriage with the dominant culture. By looking at a group of Italian-Americans studied by Colleen Johnson (1983), we can see how an ethnic group maintains its cultural values.

Among these Italian-Americans in the Syracuse, New York, area, nearly all families had come from southern Italy. In this region of Italy, the family is paramount, and members are expected to subjugate their own interest to the good of the family, sacrifice for the family, avoid bringing any shame on the family, respect their parents, and support male authority. When they arrived in the United States, immigrants clustered together, and because entire families did not always emigrate together, it became customary to create substitute kin out of other immigrants. Some anthropologists believe that the especially strong Italian-American extended family has developed because of the challenges faced by new immigrants (Markides, Liang, and Jackson, 1990).

In 1980 more than half of the elderly members of the Syracuse Italian-American community had been born in Italy. Among these older Italians, 20 percent were illiterate, and 70 percent had less than eight years of schooling. Nearly all the men had retired from blue-collar jobs. The majority of their middle-aged offspring had graduated from high school, and more than 40 percent were in white-collar occupations. Intermarriage was high among the second generation, with half of the middle-aged adults married to non-Italians. Friendships and occupational relationships also included non-Italians, but the group maintained ethnic cohesiveness by living close to one another.

The family of these Italian-Americans was distinctive in several ways. Relationships among family members were interdependent, a factor that seemed to create intimacy, satisfy needs, and strengthen group allegiance. Authority and power were vested in the old as compared with the young and in the males as compared with the females. This hierarchy

The interdependence of Italian-American families ensures support and respect for the elderly.

was supported by a strong sense of respect. Authority enforced social conformity to family goals, but among the young this conformity often conflicted with the American need to pursue personal interests. Members expressed their emotions fully, and when conflicts arose, the freedom to vent feelings tended to keep behavior in line with family goals.

Compared with a control group of Protestant non-Italians, older Italian-Americans clearly had an elevated position within the family. Family interaction was virtually nonstop: 76 percent of the elderly had contact with their children daily; 39 percent saw a grandchild daily, and 89 percent saw one weekly; 61 percent saw a sibling weekly; and 66 percent saw other relatives weekly. Intermarriage did have some effect on family values; as Table 16.1 indicates, marrying a non-Italian diminished social involvement with aging parents.

The centrality of the family means that older Italians in Syracuse do not feel a deep loss of roles. Women continue their maternal and domestic roles, and, because family has always taken precedence over employment, men seem to regard retirement as an opportunity to intensify their involvement with the family. Respect for the elderly seems thoroughly ingrained among children and grandchildren, and the tradition of interdependence and help ensures continuity of social support in old age.

Whether third-generation grandchildren will form as cohesive a group as the second-generation parents is unknown. For this group, proximity seems to outweigh most of the disintegrating effects of intermarriage and ensures the retention of ethnic identity. It seems probable that as long as intense interaction and interdependence continue, family values will be passed on, and the old will retain their status.

ETHNIC MINORITIES

Most ethnic minorities are visible and identifiable by skin color or facial features. They confront barriers in almost every area of life: housing, employment, education, medical care, recreation, clubs, and churches. Discriminated against since their first contacts outside the family, members of minority groups may become self-conscious or uncertain about their own status, always wondering whether the news that an apartment is already rented, a job is already filled, a promotion has gone to a coworker, or a loan application has been turned down is the result of chance, fair application of standards, or their minority status (Moriwaki and Kobata, 1983).

Table 16.1 **FAMILY CENTRALITY OF MIDDLE-AGED CHILDREN**[a]

	In-Married Italians *(n = 76)*	*Out-Married Italians* *(n = 98)*	*Protestant Non-Italians* *(n = 56)*
Usually incorporate parents in leisure activities	36%	18%	7%
Unqualified rejection of nursing home	44%	41%	6%
High amount of aid to parents	38%	23%	15%

Source: Johnson, 1983, p. 97.

[a]Marrying a non-Italian increased the tendency to exclude parents from leisure activities but had little effect on family values.

In the face of discrimination, the minority family has had to develop special strengths. Whether because of socioeconomic differences, immigration patterns, or cultural preferences and values, minority families are more likely than white families to include several generations (Jackson, Antonucci, and Gibson, 1990). Perhaps a look at several different minority family systems will give us a clearer understanding of how the life cycle may be experienced in minority groups. We will then be able to consider whether being a minority member places an additional burden on the aged.

Aging and the Black Family

Over the years, social scientists have looked at the black family in three different ways. Early research adopted the **pathological approach,** in which black families were compared to white middle-class families, and any differences (one-parent families, poverty, low-income) were marked as characteristic deficits in the family structure. During the 1960s, the **adaptive approach** became dominant, in which the results of white middle-class/black comparisons were regarded as adaptations forced on black families by oppressive social conditions. Researchers blamed the situation instead of the family. During the 1970s, the **cultural approach,** which looked at black families within their own cultural tradition, emerged. Researchers who use this approach assume that (1) black culture emerged from an African heritage that is expressed within an American context; (2) black cultural values and beliefs are distinct from those of the white majority; and (3) black family structures vary with the situation (Wilson, 1986).

The black American experience was dominated first by slavery and afterward by segregation. From West Africa, slaves brought the values of cooperation, interdependence, and the collective rather than the individual good (Tate, 1983). They also developed an extended family system organized around adult siblings of the same sex, their spouses and children, and at times divorced siblings of the other sex (Sudarkasa, 1981). Obligations to parents (especially mothers), siblings, and other close kin tended to take precedence over obligations to spouses. Under slavery, blacks were not permitted to marry, and so a family system developed that tended to deemphasize legal marriage, tolerate premarital sexuality, and accept illegitimate births (Ladner, 1971). In 1988 nearly 75 percent of first-time black mothers between the ages of 15 and 29 were unmarried, compared with about 31 percent of Hispanic first-time mothers and 20 percent of white first-time mothers (Schmid, 1989).

The African extended family, as well as the values of cooperation and independence, led to the development of strong kinship bonds, and family often included extra relatives—both adults and children—and sometimes unrelated children. For these reasons, researchers who follow the cultural approach have adopted the *extended family* instead of the *nuclear family* as the model for studies of black Americans (Wilson, 1986). During the life of an extended family, additional members may be added as an unattached adult marries, an adolescent mother gives birth, a recently divorced family member returns, or a dependent adult or child (who may or may not be related) is absorbed (Wilson, 1986). Instead of beginning with the marriage of a couple, new extended families evolve gradually from old extended families.

Although the cultural approach has given us insights into the black family, some social scientists believe that socioeconomic pressures are at least as responsible as cultural traditions for differences between white and black families. The extended family is concentrated among low-income blacks, and those who are solidly middle class tend to have families that resemble the nuclear structure of white families (Markides, Liang, and Jackson, 1990), as does the family described in the accompanying box, "A Black Couple Retires." The poverty rate for black families (31 percent) is about three times as high as it is for white families (9 percent). By living together and sharing resources, family members alleviate the rigors of poverty. As an increasing number of white families are headed by single parents (usually women) who often rely on the extended family, differences between white and black families may be narrowing (Wilson, 1986).

Yet, even among middle-class blacks, families at all socioeconomic levels share certain cultural patterns. Among them are strong reliance on the family, a strong sense of movement and religiosity, an active involvement of both parents in child rearing and decision making, and the continual defense against discrimination (McAdoo, 1982).

The proportion of black families with children that are headed by women has grown steadily since 1960, reaching 42.8 percent by 1988 and accounting for 51.1 percent of the children (U.S. Bureau of the Census, 1990) (Table 16.2). This practice threatens to increase the economic burden of black families because female-headed families are twice as likely as two-parent families to be poor. One reason for the growth in female-headed families is the dismal economic prospects of the black male. When an unmarried black woman becomes pregnant, marriage to an unemployed man only increases the immediate economic burden she faces. Divorce also increases the number of female-headed households, although divorced mothers and their children are often reabsorbed into the extended family—which may itself be headed by a woman.

The custom of absorbing children into older families strengthens the bonds between young and old. The extended family provides fundamental support and guidance for the old, and older blacks are more likely than whites to have contact with extended kin, such as nieces and nephews or cousins. Such practices are likely to decrease any feelings of loneliness or isolation (Tate, 1983).

Among all age groups, today's middle-aged blacks may find developmental tasks the most difficult (Gibson, 1986). Because they entered the labor market when few of them had the chance to advance, their accomplishments fall shorter of their expectations than those of any other age group. In addition, their socioeconomic status is generally lower than that

Table 16.2 **THE CHANGING AFRICAN-AMERICAN FAMILY**

Both parents present	38.6%
Only father present	3.0%
Neither parent present	7.4%
Only mother present	51.1%
Divorced	8.4%
Spouse absent	12.1%
Widowed	2.5%
Never married	28.2%

Source: U.S. Bureau of the Census, 1990.

[a] Since 1960, the proportion of African-American children growing up with only their mothers in the home more than doubled. The largest rise was in families headed by unmarried women.

◆ *Adulthood in Today's World*

A BLACK COUPLE RETIRES

Too often, descriptions of black families focus on families below the poverty line, which tends to make us forget that the majority (56 percent) of black families have moved into the middle class, where they hold a wide spectrum of white-collar jobs, from bank clerk to engineer (Gelman, 1988). In suburban Detroit, the lives of Vivian and Tom Russell provide a striking contrast to stereotypes that fill the media (Kotre and Hall, 1990). Vivian, 60, has recently retired from her job as a drug-abuse counselor and Tom, 64, from a supervisory position with the U.S. Postal Service. Both spent their childhood in the segregated South, where Vivian's father was a janitor and Tom's father a laborer. Tom says he came from a "poor sharecropping family." He feels that army service in World War II provided his escape from poverty, and he used the GI bill to attend college. Vivian came up the hard way, working in a defense plant as a high school dropout, cleaning houses, and then returning to school to train as a licensed practical nurse.

By 1954 Tom was working for the post office. He and Vivian took courses at local colleges and sometimes worked at two jobs. Yet for seven years, the Russells lived in a single room, saving every extra penny for the future. "Doing without" at last paid off, making them one of the youngest couples to buy a home in a new Detroit subdivision. That is where they raised their three daughters, and while the girls were small, Vivian worked the hospital night shift so that she would be home during the day.

Both Tom and Vivian look back on their lives with pride. "I consider myself a success," says Tom, "because of the humble background I came from to where I am now. And it

of either younger blacks or their middle-aged white counterparts. Perhaps this discrepancy helps explain why middle-aged blacks feel more stress, have more personal and emotional problems, and are more likely to die from stress-related diseases than are blacks past the age of 65 (Gibson, 1986).

Yet, in the face of economic and social discrimination, even middle-aged blacks seem hopeful and optimistic. When black and white adults were asked about their eventual death, middle-aged and elderly blacks said they expected to live longer than did whites. What is more, they also *wanted* to live longer (Kalish and Reynolds, 1976). The comparatively poor health and short life expectancy of blacks make such replies mystifying to researchers, although one gerontologist (Tate, 1983) has suggested that age is less of a stigma among blacks than among whites and that older adults are held in higher esteem in the black community. Another factor that might influence attitudes is the availability of role models. As we saw in Chapter 3, when blacks live past the age of 75, they tend to be in better health and to live longer than do whites. Researchers have found that physical limitations

just didn't happen. I didn't hit a lottery. I didn't get a million-dollar sweepstake. I was a hardworkin', honest guy that saved his money and had priorities'' (Kotre and Hall, 1990, p. 346). Vivian sees their success in human terms: ''For me, success is having my children grow to adulthood without any disasters and seeing them choose what they want to do with their lives. I've accomplished that'' (p. 347).

As they enter retirement, Tom and Vivian have moved to a smaller house on an acre of land in suburban Detroit. They look forward to a good life of gardening and grandchildren. They are active in a grandparents' rights organization, and they help one of their daughters, who is a divorced single parent, care for her son. But their plans go far beyond their extended family. In their retirement, the young-old Russells are expressing generativity by serving others.

Tom spends much of his time as a volunteer in a ministry that takes the message of Christian love and guidance into a federal prison. The work, he says, ''gives me a good warm inner feeling. And that's the kinda thing you can't buy, the kinda feeling I need more than anything else. It makes me feel that I'm really doing somethin' worthwhile'' (Kotre and Hall, 1990, p. 347). Vivian is also doing something worthwhile. She gives volunteer nursing care to dying patients at a local hospice: ''I have patients who are completely helpless. I have a sense of how they feel if I turn them over and I give them a backrub to stimulate the circulation, make the sheets cool and dry, and then turn them in a different position. I feel how they feel. And I think that it's important for everybody to feel that someone cares. That's an emotion that I don't think we ever outgrow.'' The work, says Vivian, helps her feel useful: ''I need to feel that I'm doing something constructive. . . . You don't just be on this earth to take up space. It's important to make some kind of contribution'' (Kotre and Hall, 1990, p. 348).

are concentrated among those younger than 75, and those older than 75 not only are more able than those who are younger, but are also more likely to have effective and helpful informal networks of social support (Jackson, Antonucci, and Gibson, 1990).

Aging and the Mexican-American Family

The nearly 20 million Hispanic Americans are a widely varied group, and each subgroup has distinctive cultural elements (U.S. Bureau of the Census, 1990). If present trends continue, Americans of Hispanic ancestry will soon become the largest ethnic minority in the United States (Torres-Gil, 1986). About 65 percent are Mexican-Americans, or Chicanos, who make up the largest subgroup; the rest are mostly Cuban or Puerto Rican, although many Hispanics have come from other Central or South American countries. Mexican-American culture is a fusion of Spanish and Indian heritage, whereas Puerto Rican culture is a fusion of African, Taino Indian, Corsican, and Spanish elements (Garcia–Preto, 1982).

The majority of Mexican-Americans are either first- or second-generation, and their numbers may be much greater than official statistics indicate because of the large number of illegal Mexican immigrants.

In recent years Hispanic poverty rates have been climbing, and by the close of the 1980s the proportion of Hispanic families below the poverty line (29 percent) was almost as high as that among blacks (31 percent) (*New York Times,* September 4, 1986). Among the major Hispanic groups, Puerto Ricans are generally the least advantaged (lowest incomes, highest unemployment rates, and least education) and Cubans the most advantaged (highest incomes, lowest unemployment rates, and most education). Mexican-Americans fall between the other groups (Torres–Gil, 1986).

In Mexican-American culture, children validate a marriage, and romantic love between husband and wife is secondary to the preservation of marriage and the family. The prevalence of large families, the generally late departure of children from the home, and the close relationship between most parents and adult children tend to prolong the period of parenthood and emphasize parental functions (Falicov, 1982).

In addition to the centrality of the family, Mexican-American culture traditionally has stressed male leadership, the extended family, mutual aid within the family, and respect for age. These characteristics have led to a close relationship between family membership and identity, to male dominance, to the belief that the needs of the family unit are more important than the needs of any one member, to the expectation that children will care for their aging parents, to an increase in status with age, and to multigenerational families in which parents, married sons, and their families make up the household. In practice, as David Maldonado (1979) has pointed out, many of the cultural values have been impossible to implement. As the family became urban instead of rural, the extended family began to disappear, and it became increasingly difficult for children to provide for their elderly parents. Older men, who had been valued for their expert agricultural skills, and older women, who had been valued for their continued assistance in child-rearing, began to lose their functional roles and some of their traditional authority. However, the importance of the extended family continues, as does the expectation for mutual aid and respect for the elderly.

These changes may be making aging more difficult for Mexican-Americans than it was for their parents. Mexican-Americans tend to have relatively few social contacts outside the extended kin network. Although their contacts with kin are extremely high, their expectations may be even higher. As a result, the Mexican-American elderly are more likely than the elderly of other groups to be dissatisfied with the frequency of their children's and grandchildren's visits (Bengston and Morgan, 1983). Studies indicate that older couples in rural areas have significantly higher levels of morale and kin interaction than city dwellers and that only the urban elderly who manage to substitute interaction with neighbors for family contacts have high levels of morale (Becerra, 1983).

The expectation of being supported in old age may be changing, as Rosina Becerra (1983) found in a review of existing studies. Nearly two decades ago, 95 percent of elderly Mexican-Americans in the Denver area expected their relatives to care for them, but in studies conducted some years later, less than 35 percent expected to move in with their adult children if they became unable to care for themselves. Even the belief that children have the responsibility for their aged parents appears to have declined among city dwellers, with 61 percent of the adults in a southern California study saying that the young had no responsibility to care for the old. The results of a Texas study indicate that youth, urban residence, higher socioeconomic status, and third-generational status are related to such beliefs.

In at least one area, elderly Mexican-Americans have responded to the destruction of the extended family by developing their own subculture. In East Los Angeles, older individuals have formed their own voluntary organizations, in which they can function in terms of their previous identities, demonstrating their social competence and maintaining their status and pride (Cuellar, 1978). Perhaps such clubs can substitute for the loss of traditional roles that may follow the erosion of cultural values and traditions.

Aging and the Native American Family

Information about Native Americans is sparse, and much is believed to be inaccurate. Government figures are unreliable because census takers are unable to speak various tribal languages; figures from the Bureau of Indian Affairs apply only to Native Americans eligible for services; and from one study to the next, the criteria for establishing that a person is Native American change. Although information about elderly Native Americans is even scarcer, their proportion is increasing. From 1970 to 1980, while the general population of older adults increased by 27 percent, researchers estimate that the group of older Native Americans increased by 71 percent (Jackson, 1985).

Native Americans comprise more than 400 different tribal groups, speaking more than 250 languages (Edwards, 1983). Today they form four different major groups: reservation Native Americans, rural Native Americans, migrant Native Americans, and urban Native Americans. Each group has a different life-style that interacts with particular tribal values, so that generalizations about Native Americans are generally misleading (Block, 1979). For Native Americans the fruits of European settlement in what is now the United States have been the shortest life expectancy, the poorest health, and the least money of any group in this country. A decade ago, half of older Native Americans lived in poverty (Jackson, Antonucci, and Gibson, 1990).

Aging in Native American societies generally followed the pattern for traditional societies described earlier in this chapter. As economic and social changes have transformed their societies, the old have lost their position of esteem in some tribes. Where they have been able to make economic or cultural contributions, older people have managed to retain their former position. Among the rural Oto-Missouri and Iowa, two former agricultural, bison-hunting Plains tribes, roles within the extended kin network and at the tribal level gave many of the old both power and prestige (Schweitzer, 1983). Their position as specialists in ritual and religion and as repositories of language and tradition has been strengthened as tribal members who had once rejected traditional ways have been seeking to reestablish them. Speaking of her husband, a woman in her late seventies said, ''People come to him and ask him things—how to do things in the old way. [In tribal government] there is a lot of paper work and we give that to the educated ones. . . . But for lots of other things people come to the old people to find out how to do things'' (Schweitzer, 1983, p. 173).

Within the family, older members of Oto-Missouri and Iowa tribes continue to be active in child-rearing, and the traditionally close grandparent–grandchild relationship is still strong. According to the National Indian Council on Aging, 26 percent of all Native American elderly care for at least one grandchild (Edwards, 1983). When the old have landholdings or receive lease money, they also wield economic power. Some families follow an extended nuclear family pattern in which several related households are located close together. The extended kin network provides additional support for the old. Migration has weakened kinship ties, but the young who leave sometimes return to be near aging relatives or come back years later to spend their old age within the tribal community.

Unemployment is high among nonreservation Native Americans, even in times of general prosperity. Their consistently precarious economic situation has led younger Native Americans to rely on those among the elderly who have retirement benefits, Social Security, or veterans' pensions. In some cases, these benefits are the only steady sources of income within an extended kin group. Thus, older Native Americans have retained their role of caring for the young, but with cash instead of—or in addition to—their traditional role of child-rearing (Williams, 1980).

Nonreservation Native Americans in Oklahoma include many tribes, including the Cherokee, Choctaw, Creek, Chickasaw, and Seminole nations. Among these peoples—whether urban or rural—age continues to be defined in functional terms, and there is no segregation of the elderly. The traditional view that the elderly are respected lingers, but many Native Americans say that lack of respect is growing, primarily because education in white schools, the adoption of Christianity, and the influence of white values have led to a conflict between the generations. The old have given up their leadership role but continue to be consulted about cultural traditions (Williams, 1980).

Older Native Americans tend to be in poor health; 71 percent of them have difficulty performing the tasks of daily life (Manson, 1989). A majority of older Native Americans live on reservations, where serious illness creates additional stress, because few reservations have adequate medical facilities or nursing homes. When aged tribal members must enter an institution, they arc taken from the reservation, rupturing the kinship network. The emotional shock of sudden isolation from tribal members combined with an immersion into the dominant culture, with its strange diet and activity patterns, often worsens health problems (Manson, 1989). A Native American who has aged ''successfully'' within his or her own culture may be unable to survive without the customary cultural support.

Aging and the Asian-American Family

The U.S. Census Bureau classifies as Asian-American nearly 2 million people from Japan, China, Taiwan, the Philippines, Hong Kong, India, Indonesia, Korea, Pacific Oceania, Thailand, and Vietnam (Jackson, 1985). Although early Asian immigrants came to work as contract laborers, more recent immigrants have been refugees or professionals. For the past 20 years Asia has been the major foreign provider of trained professionals in U.S. society, and more than 20 percent of Asian immigrants hold professional degrees (Lum, 1983). Once they have become naturalized citizens, these immigrants send for their families.

For many years, Asian-Americans were a ''silent minority'' in the United States. Because they appeared to be a model minority, whose members had achieved socioeconomic success and needed no public assistance, few social scientists studied them. Because of immigration laws, almost no Asians entered the United States between 1924 and 1952 (Montero, 1979). This gap in immigration helps explain why the proportion of elderly grew more than 110 percent between 1970 and 1980 (Jackson, 1985).

Older Asian-Americans tend to be healthier than other groups in this society. They have fewer functional disabilities, fewer limitations on their activities due to chronic illness and disease, and lower age-adjusted death rates than the general population (Jackson, Antonucci, and Gibson, 1990). Researchers believe that cultural differences in smoking, drinking, and other high-risk behavior play a major part in the generally good health of older Asian-Americans (Yu et al., 1985).

The elderly in most Asian-American groups tend to be part of a tightly knit community in which members know one another (Montero, 1979). This is less likely to be true for older Korean-Americans, who have few well-established ethnic communities that can absorb immigrants. Recent immigrants, who have come to the United States in order to maintain family ties, tend to be under severe psychosocial stress for several years (Kiefer et al., 1985). Koreans who adapt best tend to have at least a junior high school education, apparently because they manage better socially, financially, and psychologically, and because they have less trouble learning English than immigrants with less education. Life in the new culture is also easier for immigrants who live in two- and three-generation households, even though such families tend to live in crowded quarters, their members are overworked, and their social relationships are strained.

Like Hispanics and African-Americans, older Asian-Americans have close, supportive relationships with their children (Markides, Liang, and Jackson, 1990). The traditional Asian family was a close social unit that provided support, security, and a sense of meaning for its members. The generations lived together in an extended family, and the old held a lofty status and were consulted on major decisions because of their experience, knowledge, and authority (Lum, 1983). The belief that older family members belong at home has been strengthened among Asian-Americans by the cultural value of "filial piety," the principle that parents should suffer neither want nor sorrow (Gelfand, 1982; Wu, 1975). The majority of elderly Chinese- and Japanese-Americans in the San Diego area, for example, told researchers they would call on their families if they could not manage by themselves (Gelfand, 1982).

In recent years, however, the traditional obligations to elderly parents may have diminished. Many elderly bachelors, widows, widowers, and couples live in ethnic enclaves within central cities, where they rely on nonrelatives for sociocultural support. Grown children return from the suburbs on weekends for visits, but the obligation to support elderly parents has weakened among members of the second and third generations (Lum, 1983). Increased life spans, mobility, and reliance on public responsibility, weakened family ties, and the lack of role models who practice filial piety have combined to erode this principle. The norm has eroded even among the elderly. Researchers have found evidence among Japanese-Americans, for example, that first-generation older adults who had been born in Japan expected less in the way of filial piety from their American-born and acculturated children than would have been the case in Japan (Markides, Liang, and Jackson, 1990).

The Question of Double Jeopardy

The effect of minority status on the aging process is not clear, and a new field called **ethnogerontology** has emerged to explore the question (Jackson, 1985). Because aging is a cultural as well as a biological process, as we have seen in previous sections, it appears that membership in a particular ethnic or minority group affects the experience of growing old. One view is that minority status and age combine to place an individual in double jeopardy. According to the reasoning behind the **double jeopardy hypothesis,** older adults form a highly visible group that is often stereotyped and discriminated against on the basis of age, which makes them a minority. If they also belong to an ethnic minority, they receive a double dose of discrimination. Age and minority status presumably interact, so that aging is more negative for minorities than for whites, and older minority group members will have poorer health and show more psychological stress than older whites (Ferraro, 1989).

Some researchers have objected to this view on the grounds that the experience of aging is so powerful that all old people face similar problems. According to the **age-as-a-leveler hypothesis,** all elderly, no matter what their ethnic background, encounter the same biological changes and face economic and social discrimination (Kent, 1971). Age becomes a leveler that diminishes the differences among ethnic groups, although it does not eradicate them.

No one denies that differences exist. As a group, minority elderly have less education, are poorer and less healthy, and live in worse housing than elderly whites. They tend to perceive themselves as ''old'' at earlier ages than members of other groups (Markides, 1983). If double jeopardy is real, say some researchers, then the quality of life in old age will be worse than in earlier stages of the life cycle, and the disparity between minority and white elderly will be greater than that between younger members of minority and white groups (Dowd and Bengston, 1978).

Proving the double jeopardy hypothesis has been difficult. Although studies of Los Angeles minority aged (blacks and Mexican-Americans) found double jeopardy in both income and health, other research based on a national sample found no sign of double jeopardy. Some studies showed that differences in health and income narrow with age between blacks and whites but remain about the same between Mexican-Americans and whites (Markides, Liang, and Jackson, 1990). There is, in fact, no evidence that life expectancy among Hispanics is less than it is among whites (Pifer, 1986). As for psychological well-being, which is sometimes used as a marker of ''successful aging,'' researchers have been unable to demonstrate that either minority or ethnic status has any effect other than what might be expected from differences in socioeconomic status (Markides, Liang, and Jackson, 1990).

The double jeopardy hypothesis has not been completely rejected. Nearly all the research has been cross-sectional, which does not adequately test the concept because it provides information on age differences rather than on age changes (Jackson, 1985). The apparent leveling of health differences may be due in part to the earlier poor health and mortality among blacks (Markides, Liang, and Jackson, 1990). As we saw in Chapter 3, a crossover in mortality occurs late in life, so that blacks who live into their eighties then have longer life expectancies than do whites.

Cohort and historical factors may also mask or exaggerate the effects of double jeopardy. Many of today's older blacks grew up under strictly enforced segregation. Although discrimination is still a burden, today's minorities have opportunities that did not exist in the pre–civil rights era. Pension status may be one historical factor that affects the income gap between older blacks and whites. Many of today's retired blacks worked in agriculture, nondurable manufacturing in the South, or other jobs that were not covered by private pensions. As a result, they are only half as likely as retired whites to receive pension benefits. As employment has opened up to minority members, their prospects as older adults have improved. More are covered by Social Security, civil service, and private pensions, and by the year 2000 the income gap may narrow sharply (Snyder, 1979).

Another change with possible effects on future cohorts of the elderly is in the area of health. Health insurance coverage, unknown when today's retirees were young, has raised the level of medical care among minority members in the working and middle classes and perhaps will lead to improved health in old age. If health care becomes more nearly equal, then the gap in general life expectancy between white and minority groups may shrink, and the proportion of older minority group members may grow (Figure 16.2).

Discussions of double jeopardy usually revolve around disparities in income, health, housing, and the like. Studies of minority aging have often concentrated on such socioeconomic factors and tended to neglect cultural features (Holzberg, 1982). As ethnogerontologists consider the effects of customs, life-style, and the role of the elderly in their community, they may find that in some ways, aging is easier in minority groups. Older Japanese-Americans, for example, are members of a tightly knit community, which the discrimination of the larger society does not enter (Montero, 1979). Among Japanese- and Mexican-Americans, the role of the aged also appears to be more highly valued than that in society at large. Among blacks, the strength of the extended kin network and the central role of the church may provide older adults with support that is lacking in the general community. For this reason, the effect of a weakened ethnic community on older adults arouses the same

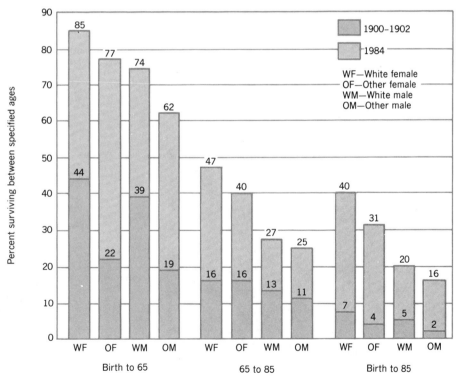

Figure 16.2 Increases in longevity by sex and race (percent). Although longevity has increased among all racial groups, it remains higher among white men and women than among other races (black, Native American, and Asian) combined.

Source: National Center for Health Statistics, 1987.

concern about minorities as exists for white ethnic groups. If ethnic social and religious traditions crumble, any extra strength that supports the economic position, identity, or self-esteem of the elderly may be lost. For Chinese-American and Mexican-American elderly, who believe that it is important that their friends belong to their own ethnic group, the erosion of the ethnic community may be slowed (Jackson, 1985). Yet their immersion in their own culture may sometimes prevent minority elderly from taking advantage of support offered by community service organizations.

COMMUNITY SERVICES FOR ETHNIC MINORITIES

Most social services appear to be aimed at ethnic groups that have undergone virtually complete acculturation. People who are the best educated and socially aware are most likely to know about the existence of various services and to be best equipped to deal with whatever bureaucracy dispenses them. They are also least likely to need these services.

If a person cannot speak English, cannot read, and is isolated from the larger community, he or she is likely to be unaware of programs that might alleviate financial or medical problems. Whether the service is medical services for young children, family planning for young adults, nutrition for pregnant women, or home meals for the elderly, the barriers are the same. Lack of proficiency in English can be responsible for the failure to use a service, for its misuse, and for duplication of care. In 1983, for example, David Tom, an elderly Chinese immigrant, was released after 31 years in a mental hospital, when someone finally discovered that he had been committed to the hospital because no one understood his dialect of Chinese (*New York Times*, 1983).

Language is not the only barrier to services. Members of the most cohesive ethnic communities are likely to know little about disease, to be skeptical about medical care, and to

In order to meet the needs of ethnic minorities, agencies need to be located within the minority community and provide multilingual assistance.

be dependent when they are ill (Wesley–King, 1983). The area of Spanish Harlem in Manhattan, for example, contains many health facilities, but cultural and linguistic barriers keep most of the Puerto Rican elderly from using them (Zambrana, Merino, and Santana, 1979). When they are ill, Puerto Ricans (who often do not speak English) go to *espiritistas,* or folk healers. These healers prescribe herbal remedies, warm baths, and massage to alleviate symptoms. When older Puerto Ricans attempt to get assistance from the medical system, the ridicule they encounter because of their use of *espiritistas* often alienates them, and they never return.

According to Donald Gelfand (1982), those who plan, implement, and operate social services need to take six factors into account. In order to reach ethnic groups, especially recent immigrants and the elderly, programs must be sensitive to group members' (1) lack of knowledge about the majority culture; (2) lack of knowledge about available services; (3) reluctance to use available services in the belief that they are accepting charity; (4) unwillingness to travel beyond neighborhood boundaries and lack of adequate transportation; (5) low expectations of services; and (6) strong preference for the maintenance of their ethnic culture, which leads them to see nonethnic service personnel as a threat to their way of doing things. Several steps might alleviate these problems: locating services within neighborhoods, using ethnic—or at least multilingual—personnel, and carrying on extensive education programs, which may have to be cast in other languages. Standing in the way of the last two steps are their cost and the possible promotion of racial or ethnic segregation in federally funded programs (Jackson, 1985).

No one knows how long the factors that inhibit ethnic participation will be important, but they will probably linger as long as ethnic neighborhoods exist. In the final analysis, however, it is not culture but jobs and political power that provide the basis for ethnic cohesion. As Gelfand (1982) points out, ethnicity will not disappear when the present generation of elderly is gone. Yet the way people view their ethnic heritage and its effect on social relations may change.

SUMMARY

CULTURAL VIEWS OF THE LIFE CYCLE

The shared beliefs of society heavily influence an individual's experience of the life cycle. In the United States, where the family has no economic function, earning a living is the mark of adulthood. In traditional societies, where the family is the economic unit, marriage generally signals the assumption of adult responsibility. In traditional societies, age is rarely reckoned in chronological terms, and in some cultures, membership in an **age set** determines one's generational status. Old age may be defined in terms of role changes that accompany generational events or in functional terms.

AGING IN TRADITIONAL SOCIETIES

Although most traditional societies proclaim respect for the old, the old-old may be treated harshly. The old-old receive the worst treatment in subsistence societies located in harsh environments. Among the factors that affect the status and treatment of the old are their political or religious roles, their informational role, and their control of material resources.

THE EFFECT OF INDUSTRIALIZATION

According to **modernization theory,** the status of the elderly declines as modern medicine, technologically based economies, urbanization, and widespread literacy pervade the culture. This decline in status does not always take place, however, and when it does, the decline may be only temporary. Once modernization is complete and the rate of change in the culture slows, the position of the old may rise, as it has in the United States since the late 1960s.

AGING IN ETHNIC GROUPS

As a result of different expectations, values, and behavior within an **ethnic group,** its members may experience the life cycle in a different way from the majority culture. **Ethnic identity** affects self-concept, self-esteem, and life-style. Once white ethnic groups achieve economic success in the United States, they may be absorbed into the dominant culture by the processes of **assimilation** and **acculturation.** However, when immigrant groups cluster in an area, they often retain their ethnic identity even though they move into the middle class and intermarry.

Ethnic minorities have not been absorbed into the dominant culture; instead they face discrimination, which has led them to develop special family strengths. Early studies of the black family emphasized the **pathological approach,** which gave way to the **adaptive approach** and then to the **cultural approach.** The black family has been shaped by African tradition as well as by economic and social pressures, and it tends to deemphasize legal marriage, tolerate premarital sexuality, and accept illegitimate births. Although the middle class tends to organize the family around the couple (nuclear family), low-income blacks tend to develop extended families. The extended family provides support and guidance for the old, which may decrease feelings of loneliness or isolation.

In Mexican-American culture, the family is central, and the culture stresses male leadership, mutual aid within the family, respect for age, and the extended family. Although the culture values multigenerational families, urbanization has made them difficult to maintain; and the change, together with the lack of social contacts outside the kin network, has led to dissatisfaction among the urban elderly.

Native American families may be affected by whether the families are in reservation, rural, migrant, or urban groups. These various life-styles interact with values of a particular tribe to alter the experience of the life cycle. In some tribes, economic and social changes have caused the old to lose their position of esteem, whereas in others ritual roles or economic power bring them respect.

Most Asian-American groups have closely knit ethnic communities in the cities, although second- and third-generation Asian Americans tend to move to the suburbs. Although acculturation has diminished the strength of filial piety, this value continues to strengthen the family position of older Asian-Americans.

Research into the effect of minority status on the aging process is known as **ethnogerontology.** According to the **double jeopardy hypothesis,** belonging to an ethnic group intensifies discrimination among the old, but according to the **age-as-a-leveler hypothesis,** all elderly, no matter what their ethnic group, suffer the same sort of discrimination. Studies of the double jeopardy hypothesis have been inconclusive, in part because most research has been cross-sectional. Rising standards of medical care and the extension of Social Security and pension coverage may result in improved minority health and narrowing income gaps between minority and white elderly.

COMMUNITY SERVICES FOR ETHNIC MINORITIES

Members of ethnic minorities are often unaware of available social services or fail to use the services they need. Gerontologists have suggested that, in order to reach ethnic groups, programs must be sensitive to any lack of knowledge about the majority culture, lack of knowledge about the services, a reluctance to depend on ''charity,'' transportation problems, low expectations, and a perception of the services as a threat to the minority culture.

KEY TERMS

acculturation	**double jeopardy hypothesis**
adaptive approach	**ethnic group**
age-as-a-leveler hypothesis	**ethnic identity**
age set	**ethnogerontology**
assimilation	**minorities**
cultural approach	**modernization theory**
culture	**pathological approach**

Glossary

———— ◆ ————

accommodation ability of the eye to change its shape in order to focus properly

acculturation process by which new groups within a culture adopt the traits or patterns of the dominant group

acuity clarity of vision

acute brain dysfunction reversible brain disorder characterized by disturbed metabolism throughout the brain; also known as delirium

acute illness physical disorder with a limited duration

adaptive approach view that most differences between black and white families in the United States are the result of black adaptation to oppressive social conditions

adulthood portion of the life span after maturity

age-as-a-leveler hypothesis proposal that the biological changes of aging diminish differences among ethnic groups

age-normative influence influence that affects almost every person in a particular society at about the same point in the life span

age set group of individuals born within a certain span of years who move together through the life cycle

age stratification sociological model of aging in which people are viewed as living through a sequence of age-related positions or roles

alcoholism addictive disorder in which dependence on alcohol interferes with health, personal relationships, occupation, and social functioning

Alzheimer's disease major cause of chronic brain dysfunction, characterized by progressively worsening memory loss and deterioration of attention, judgment, and personality

amenity migration change of residence in order to improve life-style or maintain network of friends

androgyny high levels of both male and female traits

angina pectoris severe, but temporary, pain following exertion or stress; caused by ischemic heart disease

appropriate death the sort of death a person might choose if allowed to do so

arteriosclerosis thickening and stiffening of arterial walls

assimilation process in which cultural traits from two or more distinct ethnic groups merge

assistance migration change of residence to institution after person can no longer be maintained in own home

atherosclerosis thickening and stiffening of arterial walls, accompanied by deposit of hard, yellow, fatty plaques that can choke off the supply of blood

autonomous mothering style of maternal relationship in which the mother sees children as individuals rather than as an extension of herself

autonomy feeling of self-control and self-determination

average life span mean age of survival for members of any species

beanpole family family structure in which there are few members in each generation but four or more living generations

bereavement grief that follows the death of a loved one

blending phase first year of marriage, when a couple learns to live together and to think of themselves as part of an interdependent pair

board-and-care home institution, usually in a private home, that provides nonmedical personal care and protective oversight but little or no nursing care

canalization channeling of development in a genetically programmed direction that is difficult to deflect and that is expressed in any natural human environment

career occupation characterized by interrelated training and work experience, in which a person moves upward through a series of increasingly remunerative positions requiring additional responsibility

cataracts age-related visual disorder, in which the lens becomes opaque so that light cannot penetrate it

cellular garbage theory theory of aging that assumes aging results from the accumulation of the byproducts of metabolism within the cell

changing-environment hypothesis view that age-related declines in cognition are the result of cohort differences in the physical or social environment

chronic brain dysfunction irreversible organic brain disorder that ends in death after a long decline; *see also* **Alzheimer's disease; multi-infarct dementia**

chronic illness long-standing health problem that cannot be cured and that tends to get worse with time

chronological age elapsed time since birth

classical conditioning simple form of learning in which an emotional or muscular response is transferred to a new stimulus

climacteric gradual decline in ovarian function known as "change of life" that culminates in menopause

cofigurative culture society in which elder peers set standards for cultural transmission

cognitive generativity conscious, intentional processing of experience, a self-generated process that is responsible for developmental change

cohabitation arrangement in which couples live together without legal marriage

cohort generation of people born at the same time

common-law marriage form of marriage, legal in some states, in which the state treats a cohabiting couple's declaration of marriage as a legally contracted marriage

companionate grandparent grandparent who has an affectionate, informal relationship with grandchild

companionate love tranquil, stable love characterized by intimacy and commitment

companionate marriage marriage held together by close emotional bonds, in which the partners like, admire, and respect each other and enjoy each other's company

comparable worth view that occupations primarily filled by one sex should receive the same level of pay as occupations primarily filled by the other sex, as long as the two occupations require approximately the same level of skills and responsibility

competence person's ability to respond to the demands of the environment

component efficiency hypothesis view that age-related declines in cognition are the result of reduced efficiency or effectiveness in one or more basic cognitive mechanisms

congregate housing arrangement in which residents live in their own apartments but eat in a common dining room

consolidation stage career stage, spanning the years between 35 and 45, when an experienced person advances as far as possible

continuing care community housing that provides varying levels of care, and in which residents pay a monthly maintenance fee that covers food, rent, utilities, maid service, and nursing care

contrast sensitivity ability to detect targets of varying contrast (light and dark) and width

cochlear implant hearing aid that uses an implanted receiver that sends vibrations to electrodes implanted in the cochlea

coping managing the demands of stressful situation with thoughts and acts

coupled mothering style of relationship in which mother sees children as an extension of herself

creative pleasures leisure activities of medium-high intensity; ''useful play''

creativity novel response that brings together previously unconnected elements in a new, unusual, and adaptive way

critical flicker frequency point at which a flickering light can be detected as such

cross-linkage theory theory of aging that assumes aging results from the accumulation of cross-links between molecules, produced as a byproduct of metabolism

cross-sectional design research design in which two or more age groups, each from a different cohort, are studied one at a time

crystallization stage career stage in which adolescents explore various fields, matching needs, interests, and values with opportunities

crystallized intelligence acquired knowledge and developed intellectual skills, which reflect the application of fluid intelligence to cultural content

cultural approach view that the black family structure can be understood only in terms of values and beliefs derived from the African heritage expressed within an American context

culture shared understandings that underlie a way of life

deceleration stage career stage, beginning at about age 60, when retirement is near and workers begin to reorder their priorities

declarative memory knowledge about the world, which includes episodic memories and semantic memories; ''knowing that''

delirium *see* **acute brain dysfunction**

delusional disorder functional mental disorder in which the person has either a grandiose delusion or delusions of persecution; also known as **paranoia**

dementia *see* **chronic brain dysfunction**

depression mood disorder in which a continuing despondent mood is accompanied by pessimism, low self-esteem, and feelings of foreboding

development any age-related change in body or behavior from conception to death

developmental pleasures leisure activities of medium intensity that increase physical or cognitive skills

developmental stake extent to which the parent–child relationship advances a person's developmental goals

dialectical approach view of development in which people are assumed to interact with a continuously changing environment, so that each generation presumably reaches a new level of functioning

dialectical thinking postformal thought in which contradictions are integrated into an overriding whole

discriminant validity extent to which measures correlate with the construct being measured while not correlating with other constructs

disengagement gradual withdrawal from social roles and decreased involvement with others that some sociologists believed was typical of older adults

disuse hypothesis view that age-related declines in cognition reflect older adults' failure to exercise cognitive skills

diversion leisure activities of medium-low involvement that provide a change of pace and relief from routine activities

diverticulosis condition marked by development of irregular pouches along the walls of the large intestine, often becoming obstructed, infected, and painfully inflamed

DNA-repair theory theory of aging that assumes aging occurs when accumulated DNA damage destroys the ability of cells to function

double jeopardy hypothesis view that older members of minority groups face additional discrimination because of age-based discrimination

Down syndrome genetic disorder marked by characteristic facial features, some degree of mental retardation, and premature aging

dual-process model model of intelligence as consisting of mechanics (basic cognitive processes) and pragmatics (world knowledge, expertise, metacognition)

dying trajectory emotional states that one passes through during the process of dying

early adulthood first portion of adulthood; in this book, arbitrarily set at the years from 18 to 30

ego integrity ego strength of old age in Erikson's theory; sense of coherence and wholeness to one's life

elder abuse physical violence, verbal aggression, or neglect directed toward aging parents or grandparents

Elderhostel inexpensive, short-term, residential courses for older adults that (1) have no grades or tests and (2) are held at educational institutions around the world

emphysema lung disorder in which the walls separating the alveoli are destroyed, reducing the respiratory lung surface

empty nest syndrome psychopathological reaction to the departure of children from the home

endocrine theory theory of aging that assumes aging occurs in response to programmed signals from the hypothalamus

environmental habituation recording of experience and developing automatic responses, an environmentally generated process that is responsible for developmental change

environmental press demands of the environment that motivate the individual

episodic memories memory record of events in which each memory is linked with a time and place

error-catastrophe theory theory of aging that as-

sumes aging results from the accumulation of errors in protein synthesis within the cells

establishment stage career stage, occupying approximately the years from 25 to 35, when workers settle down and establish themselves in a specific field

ethnic group group with shared values and behavior that is distinguished by race, religion, or national identity

ethnic identity identity based on shared values and behavior accompanying group membership

ethnogerontology study of the effect of minority status on the aging process

external validity extent to which information produced by research or testing can be applied in another situation

factor analysis statistical technique by which researchers examine people's performance on a variety of tasks, looking for relationships between them

five-factor model view of personality as best described by five broad dimensions of personality that underlie most personality traits

flextime flexible working schedule, which allows workers to meet family needs without missing work

fluid intelligence basic cognitive processes that are required to identify and understand relationships and to draw inferences on the basis of that understanding

formal operational thought logical, abstract thought that can be applied to hypothetical situations; in Piaget's system, characterizes the most advanced form of intelligence

free-radical theory theory of aging that assumes aging occurs when free radicals bond to other molecules within cells

functional mental disorder mental disorder that is unrelated to brain deterioration and has no organic basis

generalized slowing hypothesis view that age-related declines in cognition are the result of slowed processing throughout the brain

generativity ego strength of middle age in Erikson's theory; made up of procreativity, productivity, and creativity

geriatrics branch of medicine concerned with the study and treatment of disease among older adults

gerontology scientific study of older adults and the process of aging

glaucoma visual disorder in which a steady increase in pressure develops within the eye because fluid is unable to leave by the normal channel

grinding-down hypothesis proposal that higher levels of satisfaction among older workers results from declining expectations

guardian ad litem court-appointed attorney who determines whether a person is so mentally or emotionally impaired as to require a guardian

Hayflick limit approximate boundary to the cell's ability to divide, which is about 50 times in human fetal tissue

high-density lipoproteins (HDLs) cholesterol-protein compound that helps rid the body of excess cholesterol

history-normative influence influence that results from circumstances that exist at a particular historical moment

hospice institutions or hospital wards where the dying receive relief from pain, attention, and affection, but no technology is used to extend life

hypertension high blood pressure

hypochondriasis somatoform disorder, characterized by physical symptoms that have no organic basis and by an exaggerated fear of disease

identity ego strength of adolescence in Erikson's theory; stable sense of self that reflects one's roles and is confirmed by experience

immunological theory programmed theory of aging that assumes aging occurs when the immune system loses its ability to recognize foreign substances and abnormal cells and begins to attack the body

implementation stage career stage in which a young person makes an initial commitment to a vocation and takes an entry-level position

incontinence involuntary release of urine or feces

inefficient strategies hypothesis view that age-related declines in cognition are caused by older adults' use of less effective processing strategies

information processing view of human cognition as a system that manipulates, stores, classifies, and retrieves information

in-kind income goods and services received without cost

institutional marriage marriage held together by material concerns instead of emotional bonds

intelligence mental operations that enhance the ability to function effectively in the environment

intergenerational equity fair distribution of the nation's resources across age groups

interindividual differences differences in patterns of change across individuals

intimacy ego strength of young adulthood in Erikson's theory; ability to commit oneself to relationship involving sacrifice and compromise without losing own identity

intraindividual differences changes within the individual

involved grandparent grandparent who has a parentlike relationship with a grandchild

ischemic heart disease age-related condition in which the heart muscle is starved for oxygen, apparently as a result of atherosclerosis

job occupation with limited upward advancement

job-change hypothesis proposal that higher satisfaction among older workers is the result of better, more fulfilling jobs among older workers

kinship migration move to be near children or other relatives, usually because of chronic disability or death of a spouse

Korsakoff's syndrome an organic brain disorder found in alcoholics that is caused by long-term vitamin B deficiencies

later adulthood third portion of adulthood; in this book, arbitrarily set at the years from 50 to 65

learned helplessness condition in which a person has repeatedly failed to cope with environmental stress and, feeling powerless, has ceased all attempts to cope

leisure time for freely chosen activities, which

means that an activity that is leisure for one person is work for another

life-cycle squeeze   economic or emotional stress caused by the interaction of basic life-cycle patterns associated with work and family, as when the care of an aging parent and responsibility for children overlap

life expectancy   number of years the average person can expect to live

life review   a structured survey and reflection on one's life that may provide insight into the past and resolve old conflicts, thereby enabling a person to develop integrity

life structure   underlying pattern of a person's life

lipofuscin   inert brown pigment that accumulates in body cells and is associated with the aging process

living will   a document that requests that no measures be used to prolong life artificially in situations of physical or mental incapacity

locus of control   perception of control over one's life; individuals with an internal locus of control believe they control what happens to them; those with an external locus of control believe that chance, luck, or powerful others control what happens to them

loneliness   subjective experience in which the person perceives an unpleasant lack in the quality of social relationships

longevity   length, or duration, of life

longitudinal design   research design in which a group from a single cohort is studied at several ages

long-term memory   unlimited capacity system, containing all the information that could possibly be available

Lordstown hypothesis   proposal that the higher satisfaction of older workers is a cohort effect

low-density lipoproteins (LDLs)   cholesterol-protein compound that forms plaques, clogging arteries

macular degeneration   eye disorder in which the central portion of the retina deteriorates

maintaining phase   period of marriage, beginning in the fourth year, when family traditions are established and stress declines

maintenance stage   transitional career stage spanning the years in which workers have either met their goals or realize that they are unattainable

maximum life span   oldest age to which any individual in a species survives

mechanistic model   view of development in which people are seen as being like machines, so that development follows regular laws

Meissner corpuscles   sensory receptors concentrated on hairless areas of the body, which respond to light touch and vibration

memory capacities   basic mechanisms and strategies of memory system

memory contents   knowledge stored in memory system

menopause   cessation of menstruation, usually around the age of 50

mentor   established sponsor who takes a personal interest in a young worker, providing guidance, advice, and contacts

metacognition   understanding of the way cognitive processes work

metamemory   understanding of the way the memory system works

middle adulthood   second portion of adulthood; in this book, arbitrarily set at the years from 30 to 50

midlife crisis   physical and psychological distress that develops when the tasks of middle age threaten to overwhelm a person's internal resources and systems of support

minority   group that suffers discrimination or subordination because of physical or cultural characteristics

modernization theory   hypothesis that changes accompanying industrialization diminish the status of old people

modified extended family   typical form of contemporary American family in which the generations live apart but are linked by mutual aid and affection

mommy track   occupational schedule of women who place equal emphasis on children and career

multi-infarct dementia   chronic organic brain disorder apparently caused by repeated interruptions of blood supply to the brain

multiple intelligences   model of intelligence as composed of seven broad forms of intelligence that interact with and build on one another

myocardial infarction   heart attack, caused when blockage of coronary artery cuts off blood supply

nesting phase   second and third years of marriage, when partners explore the limits of compatibility

neurofibrillary tangle   bundles of paired, helical filaments that appear in small numbers in the normal aged brain, but heavily infest the diseased brain

nocturnal myoclonus   sleep disorder in which the sleeper's leg muscles twitch or jerk

nonnormative influence   influence that is specific to an individual and does not affect all members of society or all members of any cohort

normative stability   type of constancy in which a person's individual characteristic may change but remains at the same rank in comparison with other members of his or her own cohort

nursing home   institution for adults who require extensive care (but not skilled nursing) because of mental impairment or severe physical disability

old-age dependency ratio   number of people over 65 in society divided by the number between 20 and 64

old-old age   final portion of the life span; in this book, arbitrarily set at the years past 80

operant conditioning   form of learning in which behavior changes as a result of reinforcement

organic brain disorder   mental and emotional disruptions caused by physical changes within the brain

organismic model   view of development in which people are seen as active organisms whose changes are due to interaction with the environment

osteoarthritis   painful inflammation of the joints apparently caused by the rubbing together of bone ends

osteoporosis   pronounced loss of calcium that produces porous, brittle bones that fracture easily

outreach services   program that locates older adults and informs them of available social services

pacinian corpuscles   sensory receptors in the skin that respond to deep pressure and vibration

paranoia   *see* **delusional disorder**

paraphrenia   mild form of schizophrenia that makes its first appearance in older adults; a term applied by some gerontologists to delusional disorders of late life

parental imperative   pivotal and controlling influence of parenthood on personality across adulthood

Parkinson's disease   chronic organic brain disorder, accompanied by a tremor and a distinctive posture and walk, which often leads to severe mental impairment

passionate love   intense emotional attachment characterized by high levels of sexual passion

pathological approach   view that any differences in black families were characteristic deficits in their structure

P-E fit approach   view that older adults' adaptation to institutionalization depends on how well the individual's life-style or personality match the institution's characteristics and demands

personality   consistency of thinking, feeling, and reacting that accounts for similarities in a person's behavior

physical ontogeny   biologically initiated process that is responsible for developmental changes in physiology

postfigurative culture   society in which culture is transmitted through traditions of earlier generations

postformal thought   advanced form of thought that may develop during middle adulthood and characterized by relativistic and dialectical thinking and the realization that contradiction is a basic aspect of reality

postpartum depression   temporary depression that develops in some women following childbirth

prefigurative culture   society in which neither the past nor the present serves as a guide for cultural transmission

presbycusis progressive, age-related loss of the ability to hear high-frequency sounds

presbyopia inability to focus the eyes at short range; farsightedness

primary aging inevitable, gradual age-related changes that can be observed in all members of a species; also called normal aging

primary mental abilities factors of intelligence as proposed by Thurstone and consisting of verbal comprehension, number, space, perceptual speed, memory, reasoning, and word fluency

proactive interference disruption in learning caused when old material interferes with new material to be learned

procedural memory memory for practiced, automatic skills; "knowing how"

production deficiency failure to use a skill or capacity that a person possesses

progeria extremely rare disease that causes extreme aging in young children

programmed senescence theory theory of aging that assumes that the aging process begins when a genetic program is activated

psychometry field of mental testing

psychosis functional brain disorder in which normal mental activity is severely impaired and the person's perception of reality is drastically distorted

psychosocial moratorium period between childhood and adulthood when life choices can be worked on but no commitment must be made

random sample sample in which every member of a group that will be studied has an equal chance of being selected

reality orientation program based on repetition that attempts to keep patients with organic brain dysfunction in touch with reality

relaxation the least intense form of leisure, including resting, daydreaming, and sleeping

reliability extent to which a test measures something consistently

religiosity religious involvement, including church attendance, personal religious practices, and the importance of religious beliefs in one's life

remote grandparent grandparent who has a formal, reserved relationship with grandchild

resource-reduction hypothesis view that age-related decline in cognition is the result of a reduced quantity of one or more essential cognitive resources

retirement village development consisting of houses and/or condominiums that are restricted to adults who are at least 50 years old

retroactive interference disruption in learning caused when newly learned material interferes with material learned at an earlier date

reverse annuity mortgage (RAM) mortgage in which the lending agency pays the homeowner a fixed monthly sum against the owner's equity, and when the house is sold, the lending agency receives the total paid out plus interest

sample group of people who are selected for study and represent a larger group

schizophrenia most common psychosis, characterized by disturbed thought, perception, and emotion and often accompanied by delusions and hallucinations

secondary aging age-related changes that are caused by abuse, disuse, and disease, but that are neither universal nor inevitable

self-concept organized, coherent, and integrated pattern of perceptions relating to the self; encompasses self-esteem and self-image

self-efficacy person's judgment of his or her own competence in a particular situation

semantic memory organized knowledge about the world and about rules for manipulating other knowledge

senile miosis age-related decrease in the size of the pupil, so that less light enters the eye

senile plaque patch of debris sometimes found in cell bodies of the brain

sensual pleasures the most intense form of leisure activities, in which the activation of the senses provides intense pleasure, gratification, excitement, rapture, or joy

sequential design research design that combines elements of cross-sectional, longitudinal, and time-lag designs

shared housing   arrangement in which unrelated older adults live together or an older homeowner shares his or her house with younger people

short-term memory   limited capacity system that keeps information in consciousness

single-room occupancy (SRO) hotel   inexpensive residence hotel, usually in the central city

six-factor model   view of personality as best described by six broad dimensions of personality that underlie most personality traits

sleep apnea   sleep disorder in which the sleeper stops breathing for at least 10 seconds

social cognitive theory   version of mechanistic models in which development is lawful, but the individual is seen as active, using consequences of own and others' behavior as basis for beliefs about self, goals, and plans

socialization   process by which people absorb the attitudes, values, and beliefs of their society

somasthetic senses   senses of touch and pain

specification stage   transitional career stage in which a young person undergoes job training and makes reality-based occupational decisions

speed hypothesis   view that age-related declines in cognition are the result of slowed sensory or motor processes

stimulus persistence   slowed recovery from stimulation in the nervous system, believed to be age-related

stress   physiological and psychological responses to unpleasant or threatening events

stressor   unpleasant or threatening stimulus that evokes physiological and psychological responses

Supplementary Security Income (SSI)   monthly payment from Social Security Administration to adults whose incomes fall below a specified minimum

synergistic   combined action or effect that is greater than the sum of the separate actions or effects

terminal drop   distinct drop in IQ scores that occurs a few years before death, no matter what a person's age

tertiary aging   final, rapid deterioration that comes at the close of life

test-retest reliability   extent to which results are the same from repeated administration of a measure

three-tier model   integrative model of intelligence in which intelligence is composed of three increasingly complex levels: processing, knowing, and thinking

time-lag design   research design in which groups from several different cohorts are studied, but the studies are spaced so that each group is assessed at the same age

tinnitus   persistent ringing, roaring, or buzzing in the ears

trait   characteristic of personality; enduring disposition of thoughts, feelings, and behavior

triangular theory of love   view that love is composed of intimacy, passion, and commitment, which may be found in any combination

triarchic model   model of intelligence in which intelligence is composed of three parts: componential (basic processes), contextual (application of processes to environment), and experiential (effectiveness of application to novel tasks and effortless processing)

Type A personality   highly competitive, impatient, angry, hostile person who constantly feels pressure from time

Type B personality   relaxed, nonhostile, noncompetitive person who feels no pressure from time

validity   the extent to which a study measures what it sets out to measure

Werner syndrome   genetic disorder that causes premature aging, beginning in the teens or early twenties

young-old age   fourth portion of adulthood; in this book, arbitrarily set at the years from 65 to 80

zone of proximal development   range of performance that is not typically expressed in behavior but that may be reached with instruction

References

AARP Bulletin. (March 1990). A fairer system, *31,* 1. (chap. 14)

AARP News Bulletin. (May 1983). Heavy skills lift Californian high above her competition, *24,* 3. (chap. 5)

AARP News Bulletin. (June 1983a). Firm accepts fine, conditions in initial aging bias credit case. *23,* 3. (chap. 15)

AARP News Bulletin. (June 1983b). Tossing, turning don't faze longtime pilot. *24,* 1 +. (chap. 7)

AARP News Bulletin. (July/August 1983). Study concludes less educated get more from college classes, *24,* 3. (chap. 14)

AARP News Bulletin. (May 1986). *27,* 2. (chap. 5)

AARP News Bulletin. (January 1989). New study finds older drivers "capable, safe." *30,* 14. (chap. 7)

AARP Pharmacy Service. (October/November 1989). *Health Letter, 1,* 1. (chap. 7)

Abeles, R. P., L. Steel, and L. L. Wise. (1980). Patterns and implications of life-course organization: Studies from Project TALENT. In P. B. Baltes and O. G. Brim, Jr. (eds.), *Life-span development and behavior.* Vol. 3. New York: Academic Press. (chap. 13)

Abrahams, G., S. S. Feldman, and S. C. Nash. (1978). Sex role self-concept and sex-role attitudes: Enduring personality characteristics or adaptations to changing life situations? *Developmental Psychology, 14,* 393–400. (chap. 10)

Abrahamson, L. Y., M.E.P. Seligman, and J. D. Teasdale. (1978). Learned helplessness in humans: Critique and reformulation. *Journal of Abnormal Psychology, 87,* 49–74. (chap. 5)

Adams, R. G. (1987). Patterns of network change: A longitudinal study of friendships of elderly women. *Gerontologist, 27,* 222–227. (chap. 11)

Adams, R. G., and R. Blieszner. (1989). *Perspectives on later life friendships.* Beverly Hills, CA: Sage. (chap. 11)

Aday, R. H., and L. A. Miles. (1982). Long-term impacts of rural migration of the elderly: Implications for research. *Gerontologist, 22,* 331–336. (chap. 15)

Adelman, R. C. (1988). The importance of basic biological science to gerontology. *Journal of Gerontology: Biological Sciences, 43,* B1–2. (chap. 3)

Adelman, R. C. (1989). Myths and realities of biological aging. In D. S. Carlson (ed.), *Monograph 22, Craniofacial Growth Series.* Center for Human Growth and Development, University of Michigan, Ann Arbor. (chaps. 3, 4)

Adelson, J. (1985). Adolescence for clinicians. In G. Stricker and R. Keisner (eds.), *From research to clinical practice.* New York: Plenum. (chap. 6)

Ainlay, S. C., and D. R. Smith. (1984). Aging and religious participation. *Journal of Gerontology, 39,* 357–363. (chap. 14)

Aizenberg, R., and J. Treas. (1985). The family in late life: Psychosocial and demographic considerations. In J. E. Birren and K. W. Schaie (eds.), *Handbook of the psychology of aging.* 2nd ed. New York: Van Nostrand Reinhold. (chap. 11)

Aldwin, C. M., A. Spiro III, M. R. Levenson, and Raymond Bossé. (1989). Longitudinal findings from the Normative Aging Study: 1. Does mental health change with age? *Psychology and Aging, 4,* 295–306. (chap. 6)

Alexander, F., and R. W. Duff. (1988). Social interaction and alcohol use in retirement communities. *Gerontologist, 28,* 632–636. (chaps. 5, 6)

Alexander, R. (November 28, 1983). The Village Volunteers make a gift of friendship. *New York Times,* B10. (chap. 15)

Allport, G. W., and H. S. Odbert. (1936). Trait-names: A psycho-lexical study. *Psychological Monographs, 47,* No. 211. (chap. 10)

Alpert, J. L., and M. S. Richardson. (1980). Parenting. In L. P. Poon (ed.), *Aging in the 1980s: Psychological issues.* Washington, DC: American Psychological Association. (chap. 12)

American Psychiatric Association. (1987). *Diagnostic and statistical manual of mental disorders (DSM–III–R).* 3rd ed., rev. Washington, DC: American Psychiatric Association. (chap. 6)

Amoss, P. T. (1981). Cultural centrality and prestige for the elders: The Coast Salish case. In C. L. Fry (ed.), *Dimensions: Aging, culture and health.* New York: Praeger. (chap. 16)

Anastasi, A. (1976). *Psychological testing.* 4th ed. New York: Macmillan. (chaps. 9, 10, 13)

Ancoli–Israel, S., D. F. Kripke, W. Mason, and O. J. Kaplan. (1985). Sleep apnea and period movements in an aging sample. *Journal of Gerontology, 40,* 419–425. (chap. 4)

Ancoli–Israel, S., D. F. Kripke, W. Mason, and S. Messin. (1981). Sleep apnea and nocturnal myoclonus in a senior population. *Sleep, 4,* 349–358. (chap. 4)

Anders, T. R., J. L. Fozard, and T. D. Lillyquist. (1972). Effects of age upon retrieval from short-term memory, from 20–68 years of age. *Developmental Psychology, 6,* 214–217. (chap. 8)

Anderson, B., and E. Palmore. (1974). Longitudinal evaluation of ocular function. In E. Palmore (ed.), *Normal aging.* Durham, NC: Duke University Press. (chap. 7)

Anderson, E. W., R. J. Andelman, J. M. Strauch, N. J. Fortuin, and J. H. Knelson. (1973). Effect of low-level carbon monoxide exposure on onset and duration of angina pectoris. *Annals of Internal Medicine, 79,* 46–50. (chap. 5)

Anderson, J. W., L. Story, B. Sieling, W.–J. L. Chen, M. S. Petro, and J. Story. (1984). Hypocholesterolemic effects of oat-bran or bean intake for hypercholesterolemic men. *American Journal of Clinical Nutrition, 40,* 1146–1155. (chap. 5)

Andres, R., and J. D. Tobin. (1977). Endocrine system. In C. E. Finch and L. Hayflick (eds.), *Handbook of the biology of aging.* New York: Van Nostrand Reinhold. (chap. 4)

Angier, N. (April 17, 1990). Diet offers tantalizing clues to long life. *New York Times,* C1–2. (chap. 3)

Ankarloo, B. (1978). Marriage and family formation. In T. K. Hareven (ed.), *Transitions: The family and the life course in historical perspective.* New York: Academic Press. (chap. 11)

Angres, S. (1975). Intergenerational relations and value congruence between young adults and their mothers. Doctoral dissertation, University of Chicago. (chap. 12)

Antonucci, T. C. (1990). Social supports and social relationships. In R. H. Binstock and L. K. George (eds.), *Handbook of aging and the social sciences.* 3rd ed. San Diego, CA: Academic Press. (chap. 11)

Arenberg, D., and E. A. Robertson–Tchabo. (1977). Learning and aging. In J. E. Birren and K. W. Schaie (eds.), *Handbook of the psychology of aging.* New York: Van Nostrand Reinhold. (chap. 8)

Arnheim, R. (in press). On the late style. In M. Perlmutter (ed.), *Late-life potential.* Washington, DC: Gerontological Society of America. (chap. 9)

Avorn, J. L. (Winter 1986). Medicine, health, and the geriatric transformation. *Daedalus, 115,* 211–225. (chap. 3)

Baddeley, A. (1986). *Working memory.* Oxford: Clarendon Press. (chap. 8)

Bailey, M. B., P. W. Haberman, and H. Alksne. (1965). The epidemiology of alcoholism in an urban residential area. *Quarterly Journal of Studies in Alcoholism, 26,* 19–40. (chap. 6)

Baker, H., O. Frank, S. Thind, J. P. Jaslow, and D. B. Louria. (1979). Vitamin profiles in elderly persons living at home or in nursing homes versus profiles in healthy young subjects. *Journal of American Geriatric Society, 27,* 444–450. (chap. 3)

Balota, D. A., J. M. Duchek, and R. Paulin. (1989). Age-related differences in the impact of spacing, lag, and retention interval. *Psychology and Aging, 4,* 3–9. (chap. 8)

Baltes, M. M. (1987). Successful aging: The product of biological factors, environmental quality, and behavioral competence. Unpublished paper. Free University of Berlin. (chap. 1)

Baltes, M. M., T. Kindermann, R. Reisenzein, and U. Schmid. (1987). Further observational data on the behavioral and social world of institutions for the aged. *Psychology and Aging, 2,* 390–403. (chap. 15)

Baltes, P. B. (1987). Theoretical propositions of life-span developmental psychology: On the dynamics between growth and decline. *Developmental Psychology, 23,* 611–626. (chap. 1)

Baltes, P. B., F. Dittmann–Kohli, and R. A. Dixon. (1984). New perspectives on the development of intelligence in adulthood: Toward a dual-process conception and a model of selective optimization with compensation. In P. B. Baltes and O. G. Brim, Jr. (eds.), *Life-span development and behavior.* (Vol. 6). New York: Academic Press. (chap. 9)

Baltes, P. B., and L. R. Goulet. (1970). Status and issues of a life-span developmental psychology. In L. R. Goulet and P. B. Baltes (eds.), *Life-span developmental psychology: Research and theory.* New York: Academic Press. (chap. 1)

Baltes, P. B., and R. Kliegel. (1986). On the dynamics between growth and decline in the aging of intelligence and memory. In K. Poeck, H.-J. Freund, and H. Gänshirt (eds.), *Neurology.* Heidelberg: Springer–Verlag. (chap. 1)

Baltes, P. B., and H. W. Reese. (1984). The life-span perspective in developmental psychology. In M. H. Bornstein and M. E. Lamb (eds.), *Developmental psychology.* Hillsdale, N.J.: Lawrence Erlbaum Associates. (chap. 1)

Baltes, P. B., H. W. Reese, and L. P. Lipsitt. (1980). Life-span developmental psychology, *Annual Review of Psychology, 31,* 65–110. (chaps. 1, 2)

Baltes, P. B., H. W. Reese, and J. R. Nesselroade. (1977). *Life-span developmental psychology: Introduction to research methods.* Monterey, Calif.: Brooks/Cole. (chap. 2)

Baltes, P. B., J. Smith, U. M. Staudinger, and D. Sowarka. (in press). Wisdom: One facet of successful aging? In M. Perlmutter (ed.), *Late-life potential.* Washington, DC: Gerontological Society of America. (chap. 9)

Baltes, P. B., D. Sowarka, and R. Kliegl. (1989). Cognitive training research on fluid intelligence in old age: What can older adults achieve by themselves? *Psychology and Aging, 4,* 217–221. (chap. 9)

Baltes, P. B., and S. L. Willis. (1977). Toward psychological theories of aging and development. In J. E. Birren and K. W. Schaie (eds.), *Handbook of the psychology of aging.* New York: Van Nostrand Reinhold. (chap. 2)

Bandura, A. (1986). *Social foundations of thought and action: A social cognitive theory.* Englewood Cliffs, NJ: Prentice–Hall. (chaps. 2, 5, 10)

Bandura, A. (1989). Regulation of cognitive processes through perceived self-efficacy. *Developmental Psychology, 25,* 729–735. (chap. 8)

Bank, S., and M. D. Kahn. (1982). Intense sibling loyalties. In M. E. Lamb and B. Sutton-Smith. (eds.), *Sibling relationships.* Hillsdale, NJ: Lawrence Erlbaum Associates. (chap. 11)

Barasch, M. (1983). *Breaking 100: Americans who*

have lived over a century. New York: Quill. (chaps. 5, 7)

Barron, F. (1969). *Creative person and creative process.* New York: Holt, Rinehart & Winston. (chap. 9)

Bartoshuk, L. M., B. Rifkin, L. E. Marks, and P. Bars. (1986). Taste and aging. *Journal of Gerontology, 41,* 51–57. (chap. 7)

Bartoshuk, L. M., and J. M. Weiffenbach. (1990). Chemical senses and aging. In E. L. Schneider and J. W. Rowe (eds.), *Handbook of the biology of aging.* 3rd ed. San Diego: Academic Press. (chap. 7)

Baruch, G., R. Barnett, and C. Rivers. (1983). *Life prints: New patterns of love and work for today's women.* New York: McGraw–Hill. (chaps. 10, 12)

Basseches, M. (1984). *Dialectical thinking.* Norwood, NJ: Ablex. (chap. 9)

Baylor, A. M., and W. W. Spirduso. (1988). Systematic aerobic exercise and components of reaction time in older women. *Journal of Gerontology, 43,* P121–126. (chap. 5)

Bearon, L. B. (1989). No great expectations: The underpinnings of life satisfaction for older women. *Gerontologist, 29,* 772–778. (chap. 10)

Bearon, L. B., and H. G. Koenig. (1990). Religious cognitions and use of prayer in health and illness. *Gerontologist, 30,* 249–253. (chap. 14)

Becerra, R. M. (1983). The Mexican-American: Aging in a changing culture. In R. L. McNeely and J. L. Cohen (eds.), *Aging in minority groups.* Beverly Hills, CA: Sage. (chap. 16)

Beck, S. H. (1982). Adjustment to and satisfaction with retirement. *Journal of Gerontology, 37,* 616–624. (chap. 13)

Bell, A. P., and M. S. Weinberg. (1978). *Homosexualities: A study of diversity among men and women.* New York: Simon & Schuster. (chap. 11)

Bellah, R. N., R. Madsen, W. M. Sullivan, A. Swidler, and S. M. Tipton. (1985). *Habits of the heart.* Berkeley, CA: University of California Press. (chap. 14)

Belt, E. (1952). Leonardo da Vinci's study of the aging process. *Geriatrics, 7,* 205–210. (chap. 4)

Bengston, V. L., N. E. Cutler, D. J. Mangen, and V. W. Marshall. (1985). Generations, cohorts,

and relations between age groups. In R. H. Binstock and E. Shanas (eds.), *Handbook of aging and the social sciences.* 2nd ed. New York: Van Nostrand Reinhold. (chap. 12)

Bengston, V. L., and L. A. Morgan. (1983). Ethnicity and aging: A comparison of three ethnic groups. In J. Sokolovsky (ed.), *Growing old in different societies.* Belmont, CA: Wadsworth. (chap. 16)

Bengston, V. L., M. N. Reedy, and C. Gordon. (1985). Aging and self-conceptions: Personality processes and social contexts. In J. E. Birren and K. W. Schaie (eds.), *Handbook of the psychology of aging.* 2nd ed. New York: Van Nostrand Reinhold. (chap. 10)

Bengston, V. L., C. Rosenthal, and L. Burton. (1990). Families and aging: Diversity and heterogeneity. In R. H. Binstock and L. K. George (eds.), *Handbook of aging and the social sciences.* 3rd ed. San Diego, CA: Academic Press. (chaps. 11, 12)

Bengston, V. L., and J. Treas. (1980). The changing family context of mental health and aging. In J. E. Birren and R. B. Sloane (eds.), *Handbook of mental health and aging.* Englewood Cliffs, NJ: Prentice–Hall. (chap. 12)

Bennett, W. I. (January 10, 1988). The drink-a-day lore. *New York Times Magazine,* 55. (chap. 5)

Berg, C. A., and R. J. Sternberg. (1985). A triarchic theory of intellectual development during adulthood. *Developmental Review, 5,* 334–370. (chap. 9)

Berke, R. L. (June 22, 1989). Late childbirth is found on rise. *New York Times,* A16. (chap. 12)

Berry, R. E., and F. L. Williams. (1987). Assessing the relationship between quality of life and marital and income satisfaction: A path analytic approach. *Journal of Marriage and the Family, 49,* 107–116. (chap. 11)

Bhanthumnavin, K., and M. M. Schuster. (1977). Aging and gastrointestinal function. In C. E. Finch and L. Hayflick (eds.), *Handbook of the biology of aging.* New York: Van Nostrand Reinhold. (chap. 4)

Bielby, D. D., and W. T. Bielby. (1988). She works hard for the money: Household responsibilities and the allocation of work effort. *American Journal of Sociology, 93,* 1031–1059. (chap. 13)

Bierman, E. L. (1985). Arteriosclerosis and aging. In C. E. Finch and E. L. Schneider (eds.), *Handbook of the biology of aging.* 2nd ed. New York: Van Nostrand Reinhold. (chaps. 4, 5)

Binet, A., and T. Simon. (1905). Méthodes nouvelles pour le diagnostic du niveau intellectuel des arnormaux. *Annee Psychologique, 11,* 191–244. (chap. 9)

Birren, J. E. (1988). A contribution to the theory of the psychology of aging: As a counterpart of development. In J. E. Birren and V. L. Bengston (eds.), *Emergent theories of aging.* New York: Springer. (chap. 3)

Birren, J. E., and W. R. Cunningham. (1985). Research on the psychology of aging. In J. E. Birren and K. Warner Schaie (eds.), *Handbook of the psychology of aging.* 2nd ed. New York: Van Nostrand Reinhold. (chap. 3)

Birren, J. E., and D. S. Woodruff. (1973). Human development over the life span through education. In P. B. Baltes and K. W. Schaie (eds.), *Life-span developmental psychology: Personality and socialization.* New York: Academic Press. (chap. 14)

Bishop, J. E. (February 24, 1983). Medical science helps prolong the life span and the active years. *Wall Street Journal,* (chap. 5)

Bishop, K. (May 31, 1989). San Francisco grants recognition to partnerships of single people. *New York Times,* A17. (chap. 11)

Blackburn, J. A., D. Papalia–Finlay, B. F. Foye, and R. C. Serlin. (1988). Modifiability of figural relations performance among elderly adults. *Journal of Gerontology: Psychological Sciences, 43,* P87–89. (chap. 9)

Blair, S. N., H. W. Kohl, R. S. Paffenbarger, D. G. Clark, K. H. Cooper, and L. W. Gibbons. (1989). Physical fitness and all–cause mortality. *New England Journal of Medicine, 262,* 2395–2401. (chap. 5)

Blakeslee, S. (January 1, 1989a). Cynicism and mistrust tied to early death. *New York Times.* (chap. 5)

Blakeslee, S. (May 2, 1989b). In careful test, Parkinson's patient shows gain after fetal implant. *New York Times,* C3. (chap. 6)

Blanchard–Fields, F. (1986). Reasoning on social dilemmas varying in emotional saliency. *Psychology and Aging, 1,* 325–333. (chap. 9)

Blau, Z. S. (1973). *Old age in a changing society.* New York: New Viewpoints. (chap. 11)

Block, M. R. (1979). Exiled Americans: The plight of the Indian aged in the United States. In D. E. Gelfand and A. J. Kutzik (eds.), *Ethnicity and aging: Theory, research, and policy.* New York: Springer. (chap. 16)

Block, R., M. DeVoe, B. Stanley, M. Stanley, and N. Pomara. (1985). Memory performance in individuals with primary degenerative dementia: Its similarity to diazepam-induced impairments. *Experimental Aging Research, 11,* 151–155. (chap. 8)

Blumstein, P., and P. Schwartz. (1983). *American couples: Money, work, sex.* New York: Morrow. (chap. 11)

Blythe, R. (1979). *The view in winter.* New York: Harcourt Brace Jovanovich. (chaps. 9, 11)

Bogin, B. (1988). *Patterns of human growth.* New York: Cambridge University Press. (chap. 1)

Bondareff, W. (1985). The neural basis of aging. In J. E. Birren and K. W. Schaie (eds.), *Handbook of the psychology of aging.* 2nd ed. New York: Van Nostrand Reinhold. (chap. 4)

Booth-Kewley, S., and H. S. Friedman. (1987). Psychological predictors of heart disease: A quantitative review. *Psychological Bulletin, 101,* 343–362. (chap. 5)

Bootzin, R. R., and J. R. Acocella. (1988). *Abnormal psychology.* 5th ed. New York: Random House. (chap. 6)

Borkan, G. A., D. E. Hults, S. G. Gerzof, A. H. Robbins, and C. K. Silbert. (1983). Age changes in body composition revealed by computed tomography. *Journal of Gerontology, 38,* 673–677. (chap. 4)

Botwinick, J. (1978). *Aging and behavior.* 2nd ed. New York: Springer. (chap. 7)

Boyer, J. L., and F. W. Kasch. (1970). Exercise therapy in hypertensive men. *Journal of*

American Medical Association, 21, 1668–1671. (chap. 5)

Brant, J. (1989). Spry energy. *Runner's World,* May 31–32. (chap. 4)

Bray, D. W., and A. Howard. (1983). The AT&T longitudinal studies of managers. In K. W. Schaie (ed.), *Longitudinal studies of adult psychological development.* New York: Guilford Press. (chap. 13)

Brenson, M. (October 29, 1990). Titian and his sublime works of inevitability and freedom. *New York Times,* C13–14. (chap. 9)

Brett, J. (1980). In C. Cooper and R. Payne (eds.), *Current concerns in occupational stress.* (chap. 15)

Brim, O. G., Jr., and J. Kagan. (1980). Constancy and change: A view of the issues. In O. G. Brim, Jr., and J. Kagan (eds.), *Constancy and change in human development.* Cambridge, Mass.: Harvard University Press. (chap. 1)

Brim, O. G., Jr., and C. D. Ryff. (1980). On the properties of life events. In P. B. Baltes and O. G. Brim, Jr. (eds.), *Life-span development and behavior.* Vol. 3. New York: Academic Press. (chap. 5)

Brody, E. M., M. H. Kleban, P. T. Johnsen, C. Hoffman, and C. B. Schoonover. (1987). Work status and parent care: A comparison of four groups of women. *Gerontologist, 27,* 201–208. (chap. 12)

Brody, J. E. (1982). *The New York Times Guide to Personal Health.* New York: Times Books. (chaps. 5, 7)

Brody, J. E. (May 11, 1983a). Depression may follow the elation of childbirth. *New York Times,* C6. (chap. 12)

Brody, J. E. (December 13, 1983b). Divorce's stress exacts long-term health toll. *New York Times,* C1, C5. (chap. 11)

Brody, J. E. (February 17, 1987). Dozens of factors critical in bone loss among elderly. *New York Times,* C1, C5. (chap. 4)

Brody, J. E. (May 12, 1988). Personal health. *New York Times,* B6.

Brody, J. E. (November 2, 1989). Personal health. *New York Times,* B20. (chap. 5)

Brooks, A. (September 4, 1986). The empty nest is refeathered—temporarily. *New York Times,* C1, C6. (chap. 15)

Brown, P. L. (September 14, 1987). Studying seasons of a woman's life. *New York Times,* C23. (chap. 10)

Brown, W. V., and W. Karmally. (1985). Coronary heart disease and the consumption of diets high in wheat and other grains. *American Journal of Clinical Nutrition, 41,* 1163–1171. (chap. 5)

Bruner, J. S. (1964). The course of cognitive growth. *American Psychologist, 19,* 1–15. (chap. 3)

Buchholz, M., and J. E. Bynum, (1982). Newspaper presentation of America's aged: A content analysis of image and role. *Gerontologist, 22,* 83–88. (chap. 1)

Bulcke, J. A., J.-L. Termote, Y. Palmers, and D. Crolla. (1979). Computed tomography of the human skeletal muscular system. *Neuroradiology, 17,* 127–136. (chap. 4)

Bumpass, L., and T. Castro–Martin. (1989). Recent trends in marital disruption. *Demography, 26,* 37–51. (chap. 11)

Burger, M. C., J. Botwinick, and M. Storandt. (1987). Aging, alcoholism, and performance on the Luria–Nebraska Neuropsychological Battery. *Journal of Gerontology, 42,* 69–72. (chap. 6)

Burkitt, D. P. (December 1978). The link between low-fiber diets and disease. *Human Nature, 1,* 34–41. (chap. 5)

Burnside, I. M. (August 1979). Alzheimer's disease: An overview. *Journal of Gerontological Nursing, 5,* 14–20. (chap. 6)

Burrus–Bammel, L. L., and G. Bammel. (1985). Leisure and recreation. In J. E. Birren and K. W. Schaie (eds.), *Handbook of the psychology of aging.* 2nd ed. New York: Van Nostrand Reinhold. (chaps. 5, 11, 14)

Burton, L. M., and V. L. Bengston. (1985). Black grandmothers: Issues of timing and continuity of roles. In V. L. Bengston and J. F. Robertson (eds.), *Grandparenthood.* Beverly Hills, CA: Sage. (chap. 12)

Buskirk, E. R. (1985). Health maintenance and longevity: Exercise. In C. E. Finch and E. L. Schneider (eds.), *Handbook of the biology of aging*. 2nd ed. New York: Van Nostrand Reinhold. (chap. 5)

Buss, A. R. (1979). Dialectics, history, and development: The historical roots of the individual-society dialectic. In P. B. Baltes (ed.), *Life-span development and behavior*. Vol. 1. New York: Academic Press. (chaps. 2, 10)

Busse, E. W., and C. Eisdorfer. (1970). Two thousand years of married life. In E. Palmore (ed.), *Normal aging: Reports from the Duke longitudinal study, 1955–1969*. Durham, NC: Duke University Press. (chap. 11)

Butler, R. N. (1975). *Why survive? Being old in America*. New York: Harper & Row. (chap. 10)

Butler, R. N., and M. I. Lewis. (1982). *Aging and mental health*. 3rd ed. St. Louis: C. V. Mosby.

Butt, D. S., and M. Beiser. (1987). Successful aging: A theme for international psychology. *Psychology and Aging, 2*, 87–94. (chap. 10)

Byrne, G. (1988). Surgeon general takes aim at saturated fats. *Science, 241*, 651. (chap. 5)

Cain, L. D. (1976). Aging and the law. In R. H. Binstock and E. Shanas (eds.), *Handbook of aging and the social sciences*. New York: Van Nostrand Reinhold. (chap. 15)

Caldwell, M. A., and L. A. Peplau. (1982). Sex differences in same-sex friendship. *Sex Roles, 8*, 721–732. (chap. 11)

Calearo, C., and A. Lazzaroni. (1957). Speech intelligibility in relationship to the speed of the message. *Laryngoscope, 67*, 410–419. (chap. 7)

Callahan, J. J., Jr. (1988). Elder abuse: Some questions for policymakers. *Gerontologist, 28*, 453–458. (chap. 12)

Cameron, P. (1975). Mood as an indicant of happiness: Age, sex, social class, and situational differences. *Journal of Gerontology, 30*, 216–224 (chap. 10)

Cameron, P., D. Robertson, and J. Zaks. (1972). Sound pollution, noise pollution, and health: Community parameters. *Journal of Applied Psychology, 56*, 67–74. (chap. 5)

Campbell, A. (1979). *The sense of well-being in America: Recent patterns and trends*. New York: McGraw–Hill. (chap. 5)

Campbell, D. P. (1974). *Handbook for the Strong–Campbell Interest Inventory*. Stanford, CA: Stanford University Press. (chap. 13)

Canestrari, R. (1963). Paced and self-paced learning in young and elderly adults. *Journal of Gerontology, 18*, 165–168. (chap. 8)

Card, J. J., and L. L. Wise. (1978). Teenage mothers and teenager fathers: The impact of early childbearing on the parents' personal and professional lives. *Family Planning Perspectives, 10*, 199–204. (chap. 13)

Cargan, L, and M. Melko. (1982). *Singles: Myths and realities*. Beverly Hills, CA: Sage. (chap. 11)

Carlson, E. (June/July 1986). Join the wellness revolution! *Modern Maturity, 29*, 36–39, 89–98. (chap. 5)

Carp, F. M. (1976). Housing and living environments of older people. In R. H. Binstock and E. Shanas (eds.), *Handbook of aging and the social sciences*. New York: Van Nostrand Reinhold. (chaps. 2, 15)

Caspi, A., G. H. Elder, Jr., and D. J. Bem. (1987). Moving against the world: Life-course patterns of explosive children. *Developmental Psychology, 23*, 308–313.

Cattell, R. B. (1971). *Abilities: Their structure, growth and action*. Boston: Houghton Mifflin. (chap. 9)

Cavanaugh, J. C. (1983). Comprehension and retention of television programs by 20- and 60-year-olds. *Journal of Gerontology, 38*, 190–196. (chap. 2)

Cavanaugh, J. C., J. G. Grady, and M. Perlmutter. (1981). Forgetting and use of memory aids in 20- to 70-year-olds' everyday life. *International Journal of Aging and Human Development, 17*, 113–122. (chap. 8)

Cavanaugh, J. C., and L. W. Poon. (1989). Metamemorial predictors of memory performance in young and older adults. *Psychology and Aging, 4*, 365–368. (chap. 8)

Ceci, S. J., and J. K. Liker. (1987). Academic and nonacademic intelligence: An experimental separation. In R. J. Sternberg and R. K. Wagner (eds.), *Practical intelligence*. New York: Cambridge University Press. (chap. 9)

Cerella, J. (1990). Aging and information-processing rate. In J. E. Birren and K. W. Schaie (eds.), *Handbook of the psychology of aging.* 3rd ed. San Diego, CA: Academic Press. (chap. 8)

Chance, J., T. Overcast, and S. J. Dollinger. (1978). Aging and cognitive regression: Contrary findings. *Journal of Psychology, 98,* 177–183. (chap. 9)

Chapleski, E. (1989). Determinants of knowledge of services to the elderly: Are strong ties enabling or inhibiting? *Gerontologist, 29,* 539–545. (chap. 15)

Chappell, N. L. (1990). Aging and social care. In R. H. Binstock and L. K. George (eds.), *Handbook of aging and the social sciences.* 3rd ed. San Diego, CA: Academic Press. (chap. 12)

Chatters, L. M., and R. J. Taylor. (1989). Age differences in religious participation among black adults. *Journal of Gerontology, 44,* S183–189. (chap. 14)

Cherlin, A. (1983). A sense of history: Recent research on aging and the family. In M. W. Riley, B. B. Hess, and K. Bond (eds.), *Aging in society.* Hillsdale, NJ: Lawrence Erlbaum Associates. (chap. 12)

Cherlin, A. J., and F. F. Furstenberg, Jr. (1986). *The new American grandparent.* New York: Basic Books. (chap. 12)

Child Trends, Inc. (1989). *U.S. children and their families: Current conditions and recent trends.* Washington, DC: U.S. Government Printing Office. (chap. 12)

Chiriboga, D., and L. Cutler. (1980). Stress and adaptation: Life-span perspectives. In L. W. Poon (ed.), *Aging in the 1980s: Psychological issues.* Washington, D.C.: American Psychological Association. (chap. 5)

Cicirelli, V. G. (1982). Sibling influence throughout the lifespan. In M. E. Lamb and B. Sutton-Smith (eds.), *Sibling relationships.* Hillsdale, NJ: Lawrence Erlbaum Associates. (chap. 11)

Cicirelli, V. G. (1989). Feelings of attachment to siblings and well-being in later life. *Psychology and Aging, 4,* 211–216. (chap. 11)

Clark, M. (December 3, 1984). A slow death of the mind. *Newsweek,* 56–62. (chap. 6)

Clark, M. (February 8, 1988). What you should know about heart attacks. *Newsweek,* 50–54. (chap. 4)

Clark, M., and R. Henkoff. (October 20, 1980). A strange sort of therapy. *Newsweek,* 65–66. (chap. 5)

Clark, R. L. (1990). Income maintenance policies. In R. H. Binstock and L. K. George (eds.), *Handbook of aging and the social sciences.* 3rd ed. San Diego, CA: Academic Press. (chap. 15)

Clark, R. W. (1976). *The life of Bertrand Russell.* New York: Knopf. (chap. 9)

Clark, W. C., and L. Mehl. (1971). Thermal pain: A sensory decision theory analysis of the effect of age and sex of d', various response criteria, and 50 percent pain threshold. *Journal of Abnormal Psychology, 78,* 202–212. (chap. 7)

Clarke–Stewart, K. A. (1989). Infant day care: Maligned or malignant? *American Psychologist, 44,* 266–273. (chap. 12)

Clarkson–Smith, L., and A. A. Hartley. (1989). Relationships between physical exercise and cognitive ability in older adults. *Psychology and Aging, 4,* 183–189. (chaps. 5, 7)

Clausen, J. A. (1981). Men's occupational careers in the middle years. In D. H. Eichorn, J. A. Clausen, N. Haan, M. P. Honzik, and P. Mussen (eds.), *Present and past in middle life.* New York: Academic Press. (chaps. 10, 13)

Clayton, V. P., and J. E. Birren. (1980). The development of wisdom across the life span: A reexamination of an ancient topic. In P. B. Baltes and O. G. Brim, Jr. (eds.), *Life-span development and behavior.* Vol. 3. New York: Academic Press. (chap. 9)

Cleek, M. B., and T. A. Pearson. (1985). Perceived causes of divorce: An analysis of interrelationships. *Journal of Marriage and the Family, 47,* 179–191. (chap. 11)

Clendinen, D. (October 27, 1983). Testing the waters before retirement. *New York Times,* C1+. (chap. 13)

Clingempeel, W. G. (1981). Quasi-kin relationships and marital quality in stepfather families. *Journal of Personality and Social Psychology, 41,* 890–901. (chap. 12)

Clingempeel, W. G., and S. Segal. (1986). Stepparent–stepchild relationships and the psychological adjustment of children in stepmother and stepfather families. *Child Development, 57,* 474–484. (chap. 12)

Coe, R. D. (1988). A longitudinal examination of poverty in the elderly years. *Gerontologist, 28,* 540–544. (chap. 15)

Cohen, C. I., D. Cook, and H. Rajkowski. (1980). What's in a friend? Paper presented at the 33rd Annual Scientific Meeting of the Gerontological Society. San Diego, CA, November. (chap. 11)

Cohen, G. D. (1990). Psychopathology and mental health in the mature and elderly adult. In J. E. Birren and K. W. Schaie (eds.), *Handbook of the psychology of aging.* 3rd ed. San Diego, CA: Academic Press. (chap. 6)

Cohen, M. A., E. J. Tell, H. L. Batten, and M. J. Larson. (1988). Attitudes toward joining continuing care retirement communities. *Gerontologist, 28,* 637–643. (chap. 15)

Cohen, S. H. (1980). Multiple impacts and determinants in human service delivery systems. In R. R. Turner and H. W. Reese (eds.), *Life-span developmental psychology: Intervention.* New York: Academic Press. (chap. 15)

Cohn, B. (August 1, 1988). A glimpse of the ''flex'' future. *Newsweek,* 38–39. (chap. 13)

Coles, R. (1973). *The old ones of New Mexico.* Albuquerque: University of New Mexico Press. (chap. 14)

Coles, R. (1978). Work and self-respect. In E. H. Erikson (ed.), *Adulthood.* New York: Norton. (chap. 13)

Collins, C. (December 29, 1983). Long distance care of elderly relatives a growing problem. *New York Times,* A1+. (chap. 12)

Colson, E., and T. Scudder. (1981). Old age in Guemb District, Zambia. In P. T. Amoss and S. Harrell (eds.), *Other ways of growing old.* Stanford, CA: Stanford University Press. (chap. 16)

Colvez, A., and M. Blanchet. (1981). Disability trends in the United States population 1966–76: Analysis of reported causes. *American Journal of Public Health, 464,* 71. (chap. 5)

Comfort, A. (1980). Sexuality in later life. In J. E. Birren and R. B. Sloane (eds.), *Handbook of mental health and aging.* Englewood Cliffs, NJ: Prentice–Hall. (chaps. 4, 11)

Cook, F. L. (Fall 1982). Public support for services to older people. *National Forum, 62,* 223–225. (chap. 15)

Coomb, L. C., R. Freedman, J. Friedman, and W. F. Pratt. (1970). Premarital pregnancy and status before and after marriage. *American Journal of Sociology, 75,* 800–820. (chap. 11)

Cooney, T. M., K. W. Schaie, and S. L. Willis. (1988). The relationship between prior functioning on cognitive and personality dimensions and subject attrition in longitudinal research. *Journal of Gerontology: Psychological Sciences, 43,* P12–17. (chap. 9)

Cooper, K. H. (1988). *Dr. Kenneth H. Cooper's preventive medicine program: Controlling cholesterol.* New York: Bantam Books. (chap. 5)

Cooper, K. L., and D. L. Gutmann. (1987). Gender identity and ego mastery style in middle-aged, pre- and post-empty nest women. *Gerontologist, 27,* 347–352. (chap. 12)

Corby, N., and R. L. Solnick. (1980). Psychosocial and physiological influences on sexuality in the older adult. In J. E. Birren and R. B. Sloane (eds.), *Handbook of mental health and aging.* Englewood Cliffs, NJ: Prentice–Hall. (chap. 4)

Corby, N., and J. M. Zarit. (1983). Old and alone: The unmarried in later life. In R. B. Weg (ed.), *Sexuality in the later years.* New York: Academic Press. (chap. 11)

Cornelius, S. W., and A. Caspi. (1987). Everyday problem solving in adulthood and old age. *Psychology and Aging, 2,* 144–153. (chap. 9)

Corso, J. F. (1981). *Aging sensory systems and perception.* New York: Praeger. (chap. 7)

Corso, J. F. (1990). Sensory-perceptual processes and aging. In K. W. Schaie and C. Eisdorfer (eds.), *Annual Review of Gerontology,* Vol. 7. New York: Springer. (chap. 7)

Costa, P. T., Jr., and R. R. McCrae. (1988). Personality in adulthood: A six-year longitudinal study of self-reports and spouse ratings on the NEO Personality Inventory. *Journal of Personality and Social Psychology, 54,* 853–863. (chap. 10)

Costa, P. T., Jr., and R. R. McCrae. (1989). Personality continuity and the changes of adult life. *APA Master Lectures.* Washington, DC: American Psychological Association. (chap. 10)

Costa, P. T., Jr., R. R. McCrae, and J. L. Holland. (1984). Personality and vocational interests in an adult sample. *Journal of Applied Psychology, 42,* 390–400. (chap. 13)

Costa, P. T., Jr., R. R. McCrae, A. B. Zonderman, H. E. Barbano, B. Lebowitz, and D. M. Larson. (1986). Cross-sectional studies of personality in a national sample: 2. Stability in neuroticism, extraversion, and openness. *Psychology and Aging, 1,* 144–149. (chap. 10)

Cotman, C. W. (1990). Synaptic plasticity, neurotrophic factors, and transplantation in the aged brain. In E. L. Schneider and J. W. Rowe (eds.), *Handbook of the biology of aging.* 3rd ed. San Diego, CA: Academic Press. (chap. 4)

Cowan, A. L. (March 12, 1989). ''Parenthood II'': The nest won't stay empty. *New York Times,* 1, 30. (chap. 15)

Cowan, A. L. (August 21, 1989). Women's gains on the job: Not without a heavy toll. *New York Times,* A1, 14. (chap. 13)

Cowan, P., C. Cowan, J. Coie, and L. Coie. (1978). In L. Newman and W. Miller (eds.), *The first child and family formation.* Durham, NC: University of North Carolina Press. (chap. 12)

Coward, R. T., S. J. Cutler, and F. E. Schmidt. (1989). Differences in household composition of elders by age, gender, and area of residence. *Gerontologist, 29,* 814–821. (chap. 12)

Cowgill, D. O. (1974). Aging and modernization: A revision of the theory. In J. F. Gubrium (ed.), *Late life: Communities and environmental policy.* Springfield, IL: Charles Thomas. (chap. 16)

Cowley, M. (1980). *The View from 80.* New York: Viking. (chap. 1)

Cowley, M. (May 26, 1985). Being old old. *New York Times Magazine,* 58. (chap. 1)

Cox, M. J., M. T. Owen, J. M. Lewis, and V. K. Henderson. (1989). Marriage, adult adjustment, and early parenting. *Child Development, 60,* 1015–1024. (chap. 12)

Coyle, J. T., D. L. Price, and M. R. DeLong. (1983).

Alzheimer's disease: A disorder of cortical cholinergic innervation. *Science, 219,* 1184–1190. (chap. 6)

Craik, F.I.M., and E. Simon. (1980). Age differences in memory: The roles of attention and depth of processing. In L. W. Poon, J. L. Fozard, L. S. Cermak, D. Arenberg, and L. W. Thompson (eds.), *New directions in memory and aging.* Hillsdale, NJ: Lawrence Erlbaum Associates. (chap. 8)

Crook, M. A., and F. J. Langdon. (1974). The effects of aircraft noise in schools around London airport. *Journal of Sound and Vibration, 34,* 222–232. (chap. 5)

Crosson, C. W., and E. A. Robertson–Tchabo. (1983). Age and preference for complexity among manifestly creative women. *Human Development, 26,* 149–155. (chap. 9)

Crouter, A. C. (1984). Participative work as an influence on human development. *Journal of Applied Developmental Psychology, 5,* 71–90. (chap. 13)

Cuellar, J. (1978). El Senor Citizen Club: The older Mexican-American in the voluntary association. In B. Myerhoff and A. Simic (eds.), *Life's career-aging: Cultural variations on growing old.* Beverly Hills, CA: Sage. (chap. 16)

Cumming, E., and W. E. Henry. (1961). *Growing old: The process of disengagement.* New York: Basic Books. (chaps. 2, 10)

Cunningham, W. R. (1989). Intellectual abilities, speed of response, and aging. In V. L. Bengston and K. W. Schaie. *The course of late life: Research and reflections.* New York: Springer. (chap. 8)

Cutler, R. G. (1981). Life-span extension. In J. L. McGaugh and S. B. Kiesler (eds.), *Aging: Biology and behavior.* New York: Academic Press. (chap. 3)

Cutler, S. J., and A. E. Grams. (1988). Correlates of self-reported everyday memory problems. *Journal of Gerontology: Social Sciences, 43,* S82–90. (chap. 8)

Cutler, S. J., and J. Hendricks. (1990). Leisure and time use across the life course. In R. H. Binstock and L. K. George (eds.), *Handbook of aging and the social sciences.* 3rd ed. San Diego, CA: Academic Press. (chap. 14)

Cytrynbaum, S., L. Blum, R. Patrick, J. Stein, D. Wadner, and C. Wilk. (1980). Midlife development: A personality and social systems perspective. In L. W. Poon (ed.), *Aging in the 1980s: Psychological issues.* Washington, DC: American Psychological Association. (chap. 10)

Dalderup, L. M., and M.L.C. Fredericks. (1969). Colour sensitivity in old age. *Journal of the American Geriatric Society, 17,* 388–390. (chap. 7)

Dannefer, D. (1988). What's in a name? An account of the neglect of variability in the study of aging. In J. E. Birren and V. L. Bengston (eds.), *Emergent theories of aging.* New York: Springer. (chap. 1)

Dannefer, D., and M. Perlmutter. (1990). Development as a multidimensional process: Individual and social constituents. *Human Development, 33,* 108–137. (chap. 1)

Dapcich–Miura, E., and M. F. Hovell. (1979). Contingency management of adherence to a complex medical regimen in an elderly heart patient. *Behavior Therapy, 10,* 193–201. (chap. 8)

Darby, W. J. (November 1978). The benefits of drink. *Human Nature, 1,* 30–37. (chap. 5)

Davies, D. R., and P. R. Sparrow. (1985). Age and work behaviour. In N. Charness (ed.), *Aging and human performance.* New York: Wiley. (chaps. 8, 13)

Davis, J. M., N. L. Segal, and G. K. Spring. (1983). Biological and genetic aspects of depression in the elderly. In L. R. Breslau and M. R. Haug (eds.), *Depression and aging.* New York: Springer. (chap. 6)

Davis, K. (Winter, 1986). Aging and the health-care system: Economic and social issues. *Daedalus, 115,* 227–246. (chap. 3)

Davis, M. A., and E. Randall. (1983). Social change and food habits of the elderly. In M. W. Riley, B. B. Hess, and K. Bond (eds.), *Aging in society: Selected reviews of recent research.* Hillsdale, NJ: Lawrence Erlbaum Associates. (chap. 5)

Davis–Friedmann, D. (1983). *Long lives: Chinese elderly and the Communist revolution.* Cambridge, MA: Harvard University Press. (chap. 16)

Deets, H. B. (September 1989). High court deals blow to older employees. *AARP Bulletin, 30,* 3. (chap. 15)

Deets, H. B. (January 1990). AARP has a unique role to play in shaping future. *AARP Bulletin, 31,* 3. (chap. 14)

de Jong–Gierveld, J. (1987). Developing and testing a model of loneliness. *Journal of Personality and Social Psychology, 53,* 119–128. (chap. 11)

Dement, W., G. Richardson, P. Prinz, M. Carskadon, D. Kripke, and C. Czeisler. Changes of sleep and wakefulness with age. (1985). In C. E. Finch and E. L. Schneider (eds.), *Handbook of the biology of aging.* 2nd ed. New York: Van Nostrand Reinhold. (chap. 4)

Denney, N. W., and S. M. Heidrich. (1990). Training effects on Raven's Progressive Matrices in young, middle-aged, and elderly adults. *5,* 144–145. (chap. 9)

deVries, H. A. (1983). Physiology of exercise and aging. In D. S. Woodruff and J. E. Birren (eds.), *Aging: Scientific perspectives and social issues.* 2nd ed. Monterey, CA: Brooks/Cole. (chaps. 3, 5)

Dickstein, S., and R. D. Parke. (1988). Social referencing in infancy: A glance at fathers and marriage. *Child Development, 59,* 506–511. (chap. 12)

Dieckmann, L., S. H. Zarit, J. M. Zarit, and M. Gatz. (1988). The Alzheimer's disease knowledge test. *Gerontologist, 28,* 402–407. (chap. 6)

Dionne, E. J., Jr. (August 22, 1989). Struggle for work and family fueling women's movement. *New York Times,* A1, 18. (chap. 13)

Dixon, R. A., and P. B. Baltes. (1986). Toward life-span research on the functions and pragmatics of intelligence. In R. J. Sternberg and R. K. Wagner (eds.), *Practical intelligence.* New York: Cambridge University Press. (chap. 1)

Dobbs, A. R., and B. G. Rule. (1989). Adult age differences in working memory. *Psychology and Aging, 4,* 500–503. (chap. 8)

Doka, K. J., and M. E. Mertz. (1988). The meaning

and significance of great-grandparenthood. *Gerontologist, 28,* 192–197. (chap. 12)

Donosky, L. (November 1, 1982). Keeping your work clothes on. *Newsweek,* 58. (chap. 5)

Doty, R. L., D. A. Deems, and S. Stellar. (1988). Olfactory dysfunction in Parkinsonism: A general deficit unrelated to neurologic signs, disease stage, or disease duration. *Neurology, 38,* 1237–1244. (chap. 7)

Doty, R. L., and J. B. Snow. (1986). In F. Margois and T. Getchell (eds.), *Molecular neurobiology of the olfactory system.* New York: Plenum. (chap. 7)

Dowd, J. J., and V. L. Bengston. (1978). Aging in minority populations: An examination of the double jeopardy hypothesis. *Journal of Gerontology, 33,* 427–436. (chap. 16)

Duara, R., E. D. London, and S. I. Rapoport. (1985). Changes in structure and energy metabolism of the aging brain. In C. E. Finch and E. L. Schneider (eds.), *Handbook of the biology of aging.* 2nd ed. New York: Van Nostrand Reinhold. (chaps. 3, 4)

Dullea, G. (October 31, 1983). When parents work on different shifts. *New York Times,* B12. (chap. 12)

Eccles, J. S., and L. W. Hoffman. (1984). Sex roles, socialization, and occupational behavior. In H. W. Stevenson and A. E. Sigel (eds.), *Child development research and social policy.* Chicago: University of Chicago Press. (chap. 13)

Eckholm, E. (June 10, 1986). Aging: Studies point toward ways to slow it. *New York Times,* C1, C3. (chap. 3)

Edwards, E. D. (1983). Native-American elders: Current social issues and social policy implications. In R. L. McNeely and J. L. Cohen (eds.), *Aging in minority groups.* Beverly Hills, CA: Sage. (chap. 16)

Eglit, H. (1985). Age and the law. In R. H. Binstock and E. Shanas (eds.), *Handbook of aging and the social sciences.* 2nd ed. New York: Van Nostrand Reinhold. (chap. 15)

Eichorn, D. H., J. A. Clausen, N. Haan, M. P. Honzik, and P. H. Mussen. (1981). *Present and past in middle life.* New York: Academic Press. (chaps. 5, 9)

Eichorn, D. H., J. V. Hunt, and M. P. Honzik. (1981). Experience, personality, and IQ: Adolescence to middle age. In D. H. Eichorn, J. A. Clausen, N. Haan, M. P. Honzik, and P. H. Mussen (eds.), *Present and past in middle life.* New York: Academic Press. (chap. 9)

Eisdorfer, C. (1983). Conceptual modes of aging: The challenge of a new frontier. *American Psychologist, 38,* 197–202. (chap. 1)

Eisdorfer, C., and B. A. Stotsky. (1977). Intervention, treatment, and rehabilitation of psychiatric disorders. In J. E. Birren and K. W. Schaie (eds.), *Handbook of the psychology of aging.* New York: Van Nostrand Reinhold. (chap. 6)

Eisdorfer, C., and F. Wilkie. (1977). Stress, disease, aging, and behavior. In J. E. Birren and K. W. Schaie (eds.), *Handbook of the psychology of aging.* New York: Van Nostrand Reinhold. (chap. 5)

Ekerdt, D. J. (1986). The busy ethic: Moral continuity between work and retirement. *Gerontologist, 26,* 239–244. (chap. 14)

Elahi, V. K., D. Elahi, R. Andres, J. D. Tobin, M. G. Butler, and A. H. Norris. (1983). A longitudinal study of nutritional intake in men. *Journal of Gerontology, 38,* 162–180. (chap. 5)

Elder, G. H., Jr. (1974). *Children of the great depression.* Chicago: University of Chicago Press. (chap. 1)

Elder, G. H., Jr. (1978). Family history and the life course. In T. K. Hareven (ed.), *Transitions: The family and the life course in historical perspective.* New York: Academic Press. (chap. 12)

Elder, G. H., Jr. (1986). Military times and turning points in men's lives. *Developmental Psychology, 22,* 233–245. (chap. 9)

Elder, J. (February 9, 1989). Working overtime: A bind for parents. *New York Times,* C1, 10. (chap. 12)

Elderhostel Catalog. (January–March, 1991). Portrait of an Elderhosteler, 5. (chap. 14)

Elias, P. K., M. F. Elias, M. A. Robbins, and P. Gage. (1987). Acquisition of word-processing skills by younger, middle-aged, and older adults. *Psychology and Aging, 2,* 340–348. (chap. 8)

Elsayed, M., A. H. Ismail, and R. S. Young. (1980). Intellectual differences of adult men related to age and physical fitness before and after an exercise program. *Journal of Gerontology, 35,* 383–387. (chap. 8)

Engen, T. (1974). Method and theory in the study of odor preferences. In A. Turk, J. W. Johnston, and D. G. Moulton (eds.), *Human responses to environmental odors.* New York: Academic Press. (chap. 7)

Engen, T. (1977). Taste and smell. In J. E. Birren and K. W. Schaie (eds.), *Handbook of the psychology of aging.* New York: Van Nostrand Reinhold. (chap. 7)

Engerman, S. (1978). Economic perspectives on the life course. In T. K. Hareven (ed.), *Transitions: The family and the life course in perspective.* New York: Academic Press. (chap. 15)

Entwisle, D. R., and S. G. Doering. (1981). *The first birth.* Baltimore, MD: Johns Hopkins University Press. (chap. 12)

Epstein, S. (1979). Traits are alive and well. In D. Magnusson and N. S. Endler (eds.), *Personality at the crossroads.* Hillsdale, NJ: Erlbaum. (chap. 10)

Erikson, E. H. (1962). *Young man Luther.* New York: Norton. (chap. 10)

Erikson, E. H. (1968). *Identity: Youth and crisis.* New York: Norton. (chap. 13)

Erikson, E. H. (1969). *Gandhi's truth.* New York: Norton. (chap. 10)

Erikson, E. H. (1980). *Identity and the life cycle.* New York: Norton. (chaps. 1, 10, 14)

Erikson, E. H. (1982). *The life cycle completed.* New York: Norton. (chaps. 9, 10, 14)

Erikson, E. H., and J. M. Erikson. (1981). On generativity and identity: From a conversation with Erik and Joan Erikson. *Harvard Educational Review, 51,* 249–269. (chap. 10)

Erikson, E. H., J. M. Erikson, and H. Q. Kivnick. (1986). *Vital involvement in old age.* New York: Norton. (chaps. 11, 14)

Erikson, E. H., interviewed by E. Hall. (1987). Erik Erikson: The father of the identity crisis. In E. Hall, *Growing and changing.* New York: Random House. (chaps. 1, 10, 11)

Espenshade, T. J., and R. E. Braun. (1983). Economic aspects of an aging population and the material well-being of older persons. In M. W. Riley, B. B. Hess, and K. Bond (eds.), *Aging in society.* Hillsdale, NJ: Lawrence Erlbaum Associates. (chap. 15)

Evans, M. D., and E. O. Laumann. (1983). Professional commitment: Myth or reality? In D. J. Treiman and R. V. Robinson (eds.), *Research in social stratification and mobility: A research annual.* Vol. 2. Greenwich, CT: JAI Press. (chap. 13)

Everitt, A. V., and C. Y. Huang. (1980). The hypothalamus, neuroendocrine, and autonomic nervous systems in aging. In J. E. Birren and R. B. Sloane (eds.), *Handbook of mental health and aging.* Englewood Cliffs, NJ: Prentice–Hall. (chap. 4)

Exton-Smith, A. N. (1985). Mineral metabolism. In C. E. Finch and E. L. Schneider (eds.), *Handbook of the biology of aging.* 2nd ed. New York: Van Nostrand Reinhold. (chap. 4)

Fabrikant, G. (March 6, 1990). How major studios missed a hit. *New York Times,* D1, 5. (chap. 9)

Falek, A., F. J. Kallmann, I. Lorge, and L. F. Jarvik. (1960). Longevity and intellectual variation in a sensescent twin population. *Journal of Gerontology, 15,* 305–309. (chap. 3)

Falicov, C. J. (1982). Mexican families. In M. McGoldrick, J. K. Pearce, and J. Giordano (eds.), *Ethnicity and family therapy.* New York: Guilford. (chap. 16)

Fanning, D. (April 1, 1990). How to retire and stay alive, too. *New York Times,* F25. (chap. 13)

Featherman, D. L. (1981). The life-span perspective in social science research. Prepared for the Social Science Research Council. Unpublished paper. University of Wisconsin. (chap. 2)

Feinson, M. J. (1986). Aging widows and widowers: Are there mental health differences? *International Journal of Aging and Human Development, 23,* 241–255. (chap. 11)

Feldman, R. M., and S. N. Reger. (1967). Relations

among hearing, reaction time, and age. *Journal of Speech and Hearing Research, 10,* 479–495. (chap. 7)

Feldman, S. S., and B. Aschenbrenner. (1983). Impact of parenthood on various aspects of masculinity and femininity: A short-term longitudinal study. *Developmental Psychology, 19,* 278–289. (chap. 10)

Feldman, S. S., Z. C. Biringen, and S. C. Nash. (1981). Fluctuations of sex-related self-attributions as a function of stage of the family life cycle. *Developmental Psychology, 17,* 24–35. (chap. 10)

Ferraro, K. F. (1983). The health consequences of relocation among the aged in the community. *Journal of Gerontology, 38,* 90–96. (chap. 2)

Ferraro, K. F. (1989). Reexamining the double jeopardy to health thesis. *Journal of Gerontology, 44,* S14–16. (chap. 16)

Field, D., and M. Minkler. (1988). Continuity and change in social support between young-old and old-old or very-old age. *Journal of Gerontology, 43,* P100–106. (chap. 11)

Finch, C. E. (1988). Aging in the female reproductive system: A model system for analysis of complex interactions during aging. In J. E. Birren and V. L. Bengston (eds.), *Emergent theories of aging.* New York: Springer. (chap. 4)

Fischer, R. (1988). La difference? *Science, 240,* 130. (chap. 3)

Fiske, M. (1980). Tasks and crises of the second half of life: The interrelationship of commitment, coping, and adaptation. In J. E. Birren and R. B. Sloane (eds.), *Handbook of mental health and aging.* Englewood Cliffs, NJ: Prentice–Hall. (chap. 5)

Flavell, J. H. (1985). *Cognitive development.* 2nd ed. Englewood Cliffs, NJ: Prentice–Hall. (chap. 1)

Fleming, A. S., D. N. Ruble, G. L. Flett, and V. van Wagner. (1990). Adjustment in first-time mothers: Changes in mood and mood content during the early postpartum months. *Developmental Psychology, 26,* 137–143. (chap. 12)

Foderaro, L. W. (September 16, 1990). Leaving welfare behind by degrees. *New York Times,* 38. (chap. 15)

Folkman, S., R. S. Lazarus, S. Pimley, and J. Novacek. (1987). Age differences in stress and coping procedures. *Psychology and Aging, 2,* 171–184. (chap. 5)

Foner, A. (1972). The polity. In M. W. Riley, M. Johnson, and A. Foner (eds.), *Aging and society.* Vol. 3: *A sociology of age stratification.* New York: Russell Sage Foundation.

Foner, A., and K. Schwab. (1981). *Aging and retirement.* Monterey, CA: Brooks/Cole. (chap. 13)

Foos, P. W. (1989). Adult age differences in working memory. *Psychology and Aging, 4,* 269–275. (chap. 8)

Fox, A. (January 1979). Earnings replacement rates of retired couples: Findings from the retirement history study. *Social Security Bulletin, 42,* 17–39. (chap. 15)

Fox, M., M. Gibbs, and D. Auerbach. (1985). Age and gender dimensions of friendship. *Psychology of Women Quarterly, 9,* 489–502. (chap. 11)

Fozard, J. L. (1990). Vision and hearing in aging. In J. E. Birren and K. W. Schaie (eds.), *Handbook of the psychology of aging.* 3rd ed. San Diego, CA: Academic Press. (chap. 7)

Francher, J. S., and J. Henkin. (1973). The menopausal queen: Adjustment to aging and the male homosexual. *American Journal of Orthopsychiatry, 43,* 670–674. (chap. 11)

Freed, C. R. et al. (1990). Transplantation of human fetal dopamine cells for Parkinson's disease. Results at 1 year. *Archives of Neurology, 47,* 5.

Freeman, J. T. (1982). The old, old, very old Charlie Smith. *Gerontologist, 22,* 532–536. (chap. 3)

Freemon, F. R. (1976). Evaluation of patients with progressive intellectual deterioration. *Arch. neurol, 33,.658–659.* (chap. 6)

Freud, S. (1924). On psychotherapy. *Collected papers of Sigmund Freud.* Vol. 1. London: Hogarth Press. (chap. 6)

Freudenheim, M. (November 10, 1983). Home health unit thrives upstate. *New York Times,* B2. (chap. 15)

Fries, J. F. (1984). The compression of morbidity: Miscellaneous comments about a theme. *The Gerontologist, 24,* 354–359. (chap. 1)

Fries, J. F., and L. M. Crapo. (1981). *Vitality and aging.* San Francisco: W. H. Freeman. (chap. 3)

Frieze, I. H., J. E. Parsons, P. B. Johnson, D. N. Ruble, and G. L. Zellman. (1978). *Women and sex roles: A social psychological perspective.* New York: Norton. (chap. 10)

Fry, C. L. (1980). Cultural dimensions of age: A multidimensional scaling analysis. In C. L. Fry (ed.), *Aging in culture and society.* New York: Praeger. (chap. 16)

Fry, C. L. (1985). Culture, behavior, and aging in the comparative perspective. In J. E. Birren and K. W. Schaie (eds.), *Handbook of the psychology of aging.* 2nd ed. New York: Van Nostrand Reinhold. (chaps. 2, 16)

Fuchs, V. (1983). *How we live.* Cambridge, MA: Harvard University Press. (chaps. 13, 15)

Furstenberg, F. F., Jr. (1982). Conjugal succession: Reentering marriage after divorce. In P. B. Baltes and O. G. Brim, Jr. (eds.), *Life-span development and behavior.* Vol. 4. New York: Academic Press. (chap. 11)

Gabriel, T. (November 15, 1987). Why wed? The ambivalent American bachelor. *New York Times Magazine,* 24–34, 60. (chap. 11)

Gagnon, J. H. (March, 1979). Review of *Homosexualities: A study of diversity among men and women. Human Nature, 2,* 20–24. (chap. 11)

Gallagher, D., J. Rose, P. Rivera, S. Lovett, and L. W. Thompson. (1989). Prevalence of depression in family caregivers. *Gerontologist, 29,* 449–456. (chap. 6)

Gallup Reports. (May 1986). Favorite pastimes, Report no. 248. (chap. 14)

Garcia–Preto, N. (1982). Puerto Rican families. In M.. McGoldrick, J. K. Pearce, and J. Giordano (eds.), *Ethnicity and family therapy.* New York: Guilford. (chap. 16)

Gardner, H. (1983). *Frames of mind: The theory of multiple intelligences.* New York: Basic Books. (chap. 9)

Garfinkel, R. (1982). By the sweat of your brow. In T. M. Field, A. Huston, H. C. Quay, L. Troll, and G. E. Finley (eds.), *Review of human development.* New York: Wiley-Interscience. (chap. 13)

Gatz, M., V. L. Bengston, and M. J. Blum. (1990). Caregiving families. In J. E. Birren and K. W. Schaie (eds.), *Handbook of the psychology of aging.* 3rd ed. San Diego, CA: Academic Press. (chap. 12)

Gatz, M., S. J. Popkin, C. D. Pino, and G. R. VandenBos. (1985). Psychological interventions with older adults. In J. E. Birren and K. W. Schaie (eds.), *Handbook of the psychology of aging.* 2nd ed. New York: Van Nostrand Reinhold. (chap. 6)

Gebhard, P. H. (1970). Postmarital coitus among widows and divorcees. In P. Bohannon (ed.), *Divorce and after.* Garden City, NY: Doubleday. (chap. 11)

Gelfand, D. E. (1982). *Aging: The ethnic factor.* Boston: Little, Brown. (chap. 16)

Gelfand, S. (1964). The relationship of experimental pain tolerance to pain threshold. *Canadian Journal of Psychology, 18,* 36–42. (chap. 7)

Gelman, D. (March 7, 1988). Black and white in America. *Newsweek,* 18–23. (chap. 16)

Gentry, M., and A. D. Shulman. (1988). Remarriage as a coping response for widowhood. *Psychology and Aging, 3,* 191–196. (chap. 11)

George, L. K., G. G. Fillenbaum, and E. Palmore. (1984). Sex differences in the antecedents and consequences of retirement. *Journal of Gerontology, 39,* 364–371. (chap. 13)

Georgakas, D. (1980). *The Methuselah factor: Strategies for a long and vigorous life.* New York: Simon & Schuster. (chap. 3)

Geyer, R. F. (1972). *Bibliography alienation.* 2nd ed. Amsterdam: Netherlands Universities' Joint Social Research Centre. (chap. 13)

Giambra, L. M., and R. E. Quilter. (1985). Sustained attention during adulthood: A longitudinal and multicohort analysis using the Mackworth clock test. Paper presented at the annual meeting of the Gerontological Society of America, New Orleans. (chap. 8)

Gibson, R. C. (Winter 1986). Blacks in an aging society. *Daedalus, 115,* 349–371. (chap. 16)

Gies, F., and J. Gies. (1987). *Marriage and the family in the middle ages.* New York: Harper & Row. (chap. 2)

Gilford, R., and V. L. Bengston. (1979). Measuring marital satisfaction in three generations: Positive and negative dimensions. *Journal of Marriage and the Family, 41,* 387–398. (chap. 11)

Gilleard, C. J., and A. A. Gurkan. (1987). Socioeconomic development and the status of elderly men in Turkey: A test of modernization theory. *Journal of Gerontology, 42,* 353–357. (chap. 16)

Gilligan, C. (1982). *In a different voice.* Cambridge, MA: Harvard University Press. (chap. 10)

Givens, R. (March 20, 1989). Sharing a house of one's own. *Newsweek,* 74. (chap. 15)

Glascock, A., and S. Feinman. (1981). Social asset or social burden: An analysis of the treatment for the aged in nonindustrial societies. In C. L. Fry (ed.), *Dimensions: Aging, culture and health.* New York: Praeger. (chap. 16)

Glaser, B. G., and A. L. Stauss. (1968). *Time for dying.* Chicago: Aldine. (chap. 5)

Glenn, N. D. (1980a). Values, attitudes, and beliefs. In O. G. Brim, Jr., and J. Kagan (eds.), *Constancy and change in human development.* Cambridge, MA: Harvard University Press.

Glenn, N. D. (1980b). Psychological well-being in the postparental stage: Some evidence from national surveys. *Journal of Marriage and the Family, 37,* 105–110. (chap. 1)

Glenn, N. D., and M. Supanic. (1984). The social and demographic correlates of divorce and separation in the United States: An update and reconsideration. *Journal of Marriage and the Family, 46,* 563–575. (chap. 11)

Glick, P. C. (1980). Remarriage: Some recent changes and variations. *Journal of Family Issues, 1,* 455–478. (chap. 11)

Glick, P. C. (1984). Marriage, divorce, and living arrangements. *Journal of Family Issues, 5,* 7–26. (chap. 12)

Glick, P. C., and S.-L. Lin. (1986). Recent changes in divorce and remarriage. *Journal of Marriage and the Family, 48,* 737–748. (chap. 11)

Golant, S. M. (1990a). The metropolitanization and suburbanization of the U.S. elderly population: 1970–1988. *Gerontologist, 30,* 80–85. (chap. 15)

Golant, S. M. (1990b). Post–1980 regional migration patterns of the U.S. elderly population. *Journal of Gerontology: Social Sciences, 45,* S135–140. (chap. 15)

Goldberg, E. L., G. W. Comstock, and S. D. Harlow. (1988). Emotional problems and widowhood. *Journal of Gerontology: Social Sciences, 43,* S206–208. (chap. 11)

Goldman–Rakic, P. S. (1987). Development of cortical circuitry and cognitive function. *Child Development, 58,* 601–622. (chap. 1)

Goldstein, M. C., S. Schuler, and J. L. Ross. (1983). Social and economic forces affecting intergenerational relations in extended families in a third world country: A cautionary tale from South Asia. *Journal of Gerontology, 38,* 716–724. (chap. 16)

Goodwin, J. S., J. M. Goodwin, and P. J. Garry. (1983). Association between nutritional status and cognitive functioning in a healthy elderly population. *Journal of the American Medical Association, 249,* 2917–2921. (chap. 8)

Goody, J. (1976). Aging in nonindustrial societies. In R. H. Binstock and E. Shanas (eds.), *Handbook of aging and the social sciences.* New York: Van Nostrand Reinhold. (chap. 16)

Gordon, C., C. M. Gaitz, and J. Scott. (1976). Leisure and lives: Personal expressivity across the life span. In R. H. Binstock and E. Shanas (eds.), *Handbook of aging and the social sciences.* New York: Van Nostrand Reinhold. (chap. 14)

Gottschalk, E. C., Jr. (July 30, 1986). After years of decline, suicide rate is rising among elderly in U.S. *Wall Street Journal,* 1, 16. (chap. 6)

Gould, R. L. (February 1975). Adult life stages: Growth toward self-tolerance. *Psychology Today, 8,* 74–78. (chap. 10)

Gould, R. L. (1978). *Transformations: Growth and change in adult life.* New York: Simon & Schuster. (chap. 10)

Green, P. S. (August/September 1983). Growing old in China. *Modern Maturity, 26,* 58–59. (chap. 16)

Grossman, F. K., L. S. Eichler, and S. A. Winickoff. (1980). *Pregnancy, birth, and parenthood.* San Francisco: Jossey–Bass. (chap. 12)

Grove, G. L., and A. M. Kligman. (1983). Age-associated changes in human epidermal cell renewal. *Journal of Gerontology, 38,* 137–142. (chaps. 2, 4)

Guemple, L. (1983). Growing old in Inuit society.

In J. Sokolovsky (ed.), *Growing old in different societies*. Belmont, CA: Wadsworth. (chap. 16)

Guigoz, Y., and H. N. Munro. (1985). Nutrition and aging. In C. E. Finch and E. L. Schneider (eds.), *Handbook of the biology of aging*. 2nd ed. New York: Van Nostrand Reinhold. (chaps. 3, 5)

Guilford, J. P. (1973). Theories of intelligence. In B. B. Wolman (eds.), *Handbook of general psychology*. Englewood Cliffs, NJ: Prentice–Hall. (chap. 9)

Gutmann, D. (1980). Observations on culture and mental health in later life. In J. E. Birren and R. B. Sloane (eds.), *Handbook of mental health and aging*. Englewood Cliffs, NJ: Prentice–Hall. (chap. 16)

Gutmann, D. (1987). *Reclaimed powers*. New York: Basic Books. (chaps. 1, 3, 10)

Haan, N. (1981). Common dimensions of personality development: Early adolescence to middle life. In D. H. Eichorn, J. A. Clausen, N. Haan, M. P. Honzik, and P. H. Mussen (eds.), *Present and past in middle life*. New York: Academic Press. (chap. 10)

Haan, N., R. Millsap, and E. Hartka. (1986). As time goes by: Change and stability in personality over fifty years. *Psychology and Aging, 1*, 220–232. (chap. 10)

Hacker, A. (August 14, 1988). Women at work. *New York Review of Books, 33*, 13, 26–32. (chap. 13)

Hacker, H. M. (1981). Blabbermouths and clams: Sex differences in self-disclosure in same-sex and cross-sex friendship dyads. *Sex Roles, 5*, 385–401. (chap. 11)

Hagestad, G. O. (1981). Problems and promises in the social psychology of intergenerational relationships. In R. W. Fogel, E. Hatfield, S. B. Kiesler, and E. Shanas (eds.), *Aging*. Vol. 3: *Stability and change in the family*. New York: Academic Press. (chap. 12)

Hagestad, G. O. (1984). The continuous bond. In M. Perlmutter (ed.), *Minnesota symposia on child psychology*. Vol. 17. Hillsdale, NJ: Lawrence Erlbaum Associates. (chap. 12)

Hagestad, G. O. (Winter 1986). The aging society and family life. *Daedalus, 115*, 119–139. (chap. 12)

Hagestad, G. O. (1988). Demographic changes and the life course: Some emerging trends in the family realm. *Family Relations, 37*, 405–410. (chap. 12)

Haight, B. K. (1988). The therapeutic role of a structured life review process in homebound elderly subjects. *Journal of Gerontology: Psychological Sciences, 43*, P40–44. (chap. 10)

Haley, W. E. (1989). Group intervention for dementia family caregivers: A longitudinal perspective. *Gerontologist, 29*, 478–480. (chap. 6)

Hall, E., M. Lamb, and M. Perlmutter. (1986). *Child psychology today*. 2nd ed. New York: Random House. (chap. 9)

Hall, T. (March 15, 1989). A new temperance is taking root in America. *New York Times*, A1, C6. (chap. 5)

Hallfrisch, J., J. D. Tobin, D. C. Muller, and R. Andres. (1988). Fiber intake, age, and other coronary risk factors in men of the Baltimore Longitudinal Study (1959–1975). *Journal of Gerontology, 43*, M64–68. (chap. 5)

Hamilton, J. O'C. (February 8, 1988). Delivering what makeup only promises. *Business Week*, 63–34. (chap. 4)

Hammond, E. C., L. Garfinkel, and H. Seidman. (1971). Longevity of parents and grandparents in relation to coronary heart disease associated variables. *Circulation, 43*, 31–44. (chap. 3)

Hammond, P. E. (1969). Aging and the ministry. In M. W. Riley, J. W. Riley, Jr., and M. E. Johnson (eds.), *Aging and Society*. Vol. 2: *Aging and the professions*. New York: Russell Sage Foundation. (chap. 14)

Hanley–Dunn, P., and J. L. McIntosh. (1984). Meaningfulness and recall of names by young and old adults. *Journal of Gerontology, 39*, 583–585. (chap. 8)

Hareven, T. K. (1978). The last stage: Historical adulthood and old age. In E. H. Erikson (ed.), *Adulthood*. New York: Norton. (chap. 13)

Harman, D. (1968). Free radical theory of aging: Effect of free radical reaction inhibitors on the mortality rate of male LAF[1] mice. *Journal of Gerontology, 23,* 476–482. (chap. 3)

Harman, S. M., and G. B. Talbert. (1985). Reproductive aging. In C. E. Finch and E. L. Schneider (eds.), *Handbook of the biology of aging.* 2nd ed. New York: Van Nostrand Reinhold. (chaps. 3, 4)

Harris, D. B. (ed.). (1957). *The concept of development.* Minneapolis: University of Minnesota Press. (chap. 1)

Harrison, D. E. (1985). Cell and tissue transplantation: A means of studying the aging process. In C. E. Finch and E. L. Schneider (eds.), *Handbook of the biology of aging.* 2nd ed. New York: Van Nostrand Reinhold. (chap. 3)

Hartley, A. A., J. M. Kieley, and C. A. McKenzie. (1987). Aging and the allocation of visual attention. Paper presented at the National Institute on Aging Conference on Aging and Attention. Washington, DC, November. (chap. 8)

Hasher, L., and R. T. Zacks. (1988). Working memory, comprehension, and aging: A review and a new view. In G. H. Bower (ed.), *The psychology of learning and motivation.* Vol. 22. San Diego, CA: Academic Press. (chap. 8)

Hatfield, E., D. Greenberger, J. Traupmann, and P. Lambert. (1982). Equity and sexual satisfaction in recently married couples. *Journal of Sex Research, 18,* 18–32. (chap. 11)

Hatfield, E., and G. W. Walster. (1978). *A new look at love.* Reading, MA: Addison–Wesley. (chap. 11)

Hausman, P. B., and M. E. Weksler. (1985). Changes in the immune response with age. In C. E. Finch and E. L. Schneider (eds.), *Handbook of the biology of aging.* 2nd ed. New York: Van Nostrand Reinhold. (chap. 4)

Hayflick, L. (1977). The cellular basis for biological aging. In C. E. Finch and L. Hayflick (eds.), *Handbook of the biology of aging.* New York: Van Nostrand Reinhold. (chap. 3)

Heinemann, A. W., A. Colorez, S. Frank, and D. Taylor. (1988). Leisure activity participation of elderly individuals with low vision. *Journal of Gerontology, 28,* 181–184. (chap. 7)

Heise, D. R. (1987). Sociocultural determination of mental aging. In C. Schooler and K. W. Schaie (eds.), *Cognitive functioning and social structure over the life course.* New York: Ablex. (chap. 8)

Helson, R., and G. Moane. (1987). Personality change in women from college to midlife. *Journal of Personality and Social Psychology, 53,* 176–186. (chap. 10)

Hennig, M. (1970). Career development of women executives. Doctoral dissertation. Harvard Business School. (chap. 13)

Hennig, M., and A. Jardim. (January 1977). Women executives in the old-boy network. *Psychology Today, 10,* 76–81. (chap. 13)

Hertzog, C., D. F. Hultsch, and R. A. Dixon. (1989). Evidence for the convergent validity of two self-report metamemory questionnaires. *Developmental Psychology, 25,* 687–700. (chap. 8)

Heston, L. L., and J. A. White. (1983). *Dementia: A practical guide to Alzheimer's disease.* San Francisco, CA: W. H. Freeman. (chap. 6)

Hickey, T. (1980). *Health and aging.* Monterey, CA: Brooks/Cole. (chaps. 3, 5)

Hill, R., N. Foote, J. Aldous, R. Carlson, and R. Macdonald. (1970). *Family development in three generations.* Cambridge, MA: Schenkman. (chap. 11)

Hill, R., and P. Mattessich. (1979). Family development theory and life-span development. In P. B. Baltes and O. G. Brim, Jr. (eds.), *Life-span development and behavior.* Vol. 2. New York: Academic Press. (chap. 12)

Hilts, P. J. (August 29, 1989a). Doctors find key diabetes molecule. *New York Times,* C3. (chap. 4)

Hilts, P. J. (November 3, 1989b). Exercise and longevity: A little goes a long way. *New York Times,* A1, D19. (chap. 5)

Hirsch, B. B. (1976). *Living together: A guide to the law for unmarried couples.* Boston: Houghton Mifflin. (chap. 11)

Hochschild, A. (1989). *The second shift: Working parents and the revolution at home.* New York: Viking. (chap. 12)

Hock, E., and D. K. DeMeis. (1990). Depression in mothers of infants: The role of maternal employment. *Developmental Psychology, 26,* 285–291. (chap. 12)

Hoffman, L. W. (1986). Work, family, and the children. In M. S. Pallak and R. O. Perloff (eds.), *Psychology and work.* Washington, DC: American Psychological Association. (chap. 12)

Hoffman, L. W. (1989). Effects of maternal employment in the two-parent family. *American Psychologist, 44,* 283–292. (chap. 12)

Hoffman, L. W., K. A. McManus, and Y. Brackbill. In press. The value of children to young and elderly parents. *International Journal of Aging and Human Development.* (chap. 12)

Hofmann, D. (May 21, 1989). Elderhostel: Learning as you go. *New York Times,* 21, 42. (chap. 14)

Holahan, C. (1988). Relation of life goals at age 70 to activity participation and health and psychological well-being among Terman's gifted men and women. *Psychology and Aging, 3,* 286–291.

Holahan, C. J. (1982). *Environmental psychology.* New York: Random House. (chap. 5)

Holahan, C. K., and C. J. Holahan. (1987). Self-efficacy, social support, and depression in aging: A longitudinal analysis. *Journal of Gerontology, 42,* 65–68. (chap. 6)

Holden, C. (1987). Why do women live longer than men? *Science, 238,* 158–160. (chap. 3)

Holden, K. C., R. V. Burkhauser, and D. A. Myers. (1986). Income transitions at older stages of life: The dynamics of poverty. *Gerontologist, 26,* 292–297. (chap. 15)

Holland, J. L. (1985). *Making vocational choices: A theory of vocational personalities and work environments.* Englewood Cliffs, NJ: Prentice-Hall. (chap. 13)

Holliday, S. G., and M. J. Chandler. (1986). *Wisdom: Explorations in adult competence. Contributions to human development:* Vol. 17. Basel: Karger. (chap. 9)

Holloszy, J. O. (1988). Minireview: Exercise and longevity: Studies with rats. *Journal of Gerontology, 43,* B149–151. (chap. 3)

Holmes, L., and E. Rhoads. (1983). Aging and change in Samoa. In J. Sokolovsky (ed.), *Growing old in different societies.* Belmont, CA: Wadsworth, 1983. (chap. 16)

Holmes, O. W. (1858/1955). *The autocrat at the breakfast table.* New York: Heritage Press. (chap. 5)

Holzberg, C. S. (1982). Ethnicity and aging: Anthropological perspectives on more than just minority elderly. *Gerontologist, 22,* 249–257. (chap. 16)

Hoopes, R. (June/July 1988). Turning out the light. *Modern Maturity, 31,* 28–33, 88–94. (chap. 5)

Horn, J. L. (1982). The theory of fluid and crystallized intelligence in relation to the concepts of cognitive psychology and aging in adulthood. In F. I. M. Craik and S. Trehub (eds.), *Aging and cognitive processes.* New York: Plenum. (chap. 9)

House, J. S., and C. Robbins. (1983). Age, psychosocial stress, and health. In M. W. Riley, B. B. Hess, and K. Bond (eds.), *Aging in society: Selected reviews of recent research.* Hillsdale, NJ: Lawrence Erlbaum Associates. (chap. 5)

Houser, B. B., and L. J. Beckman. (1980). Background characteristics and women's dual-role attitudes. *Sex Roles, 6,* 335–366. (chap. 12)

Howard, A. (August 1984). Cool at the top: Personality characteristics of successful managers. Paper presented at annual meeting of the American Psychological Association. Montreal. (chap. 13)

Howell, S. C. (1980). Environments as hypotheses in human aging. In L. W. Poon (ed.), *Aging in the 1980s: Psychological Issues.* Washington, DC: American Psychological Association. (chap. 5)

Hoyenga, K. B., and K. T. Hoyenga. (1979). *The question of sex differences: Psychological, cultural, and biological issues.* Boston: Little, Brown. (chap. 10)

Hoyer, W. J. (1987). Acquisition of knowledge and the decentralization of *g* in adult intellectual development. In C. Schooler and K. W. Schaie (eds.), *Cognitive functioning and social structure over the life course.* New York: Ablex. (chap. 8)

Hudson, R. B., and J. Strate. (1985). Aging and political systems. In R. H. Binstock and E. Shanas (eds.), *Handbook of aging and the social sciences.* 2nd ed. New York: Van Nostrand Reinhold. (chap. 14)

Hultsch, D. F., and R. A. Dixon. (1990). Learning and memory and aging. In J. E. Birren and K. W. Schaie (eds.), *Handbook of the psychology of aging.* 3rd ed. San Diego, CA: Academic Press. (chap. 8)

Hultsch, D. F., C. Hertzog, and R. A. Dixon. (1984). Text recall in adulthood: The role of intellectual abilities. *Developmental Psychology, 20,* 1193–1211.

Hultsch, D. F., C. Hertzog, and R. A. Dixon. (1990). Ability correlates of memory performance in adulthood and aging. *Psychology and Aging, 5,* 356–368. (chap. 8)

Hunt, M. (1974). *Sexual behavior in the 1970's.* New York: Dell. (chap. 11)

Hurley, D. (May 1988). The mentor mystique. *Psychology Today,* 38–43. (chap. 13)

Hutchinson, K. M. (1989). Influence of sentence context on speech perception in young and older adults. *Journal of Gerontology: Psychological Sciences, 44,* P36–44. (chap. 7)

Huyck, M. H. (1982). From gregariousness to intimacy: Marriage and friendship over the adult years. In T. M. Field, A. Huston, H. C. Quay, L. Troll, and G. E. Finley (eds.), *Review of human development.* New York: Wiley-Interscience. (chap. 11)

Huyck, M. H. (1990). Gender differences in aging. In J. E. Birren and K. W. Schaie (eds.), *Handbook of the psychology of aging.* 3rd ed. San Diego: Academic Press. (chap. 10)

Hyman, B. T., G. N. Van Hoesen, A. R. Damasio, and C. L. Barnes. (1984). Alzheimer's disease. *Science, 225,* 1168–1170. (chap. 6)

Iris, M. A. (1988). Guardianship and the elderly: A multi-perspective view of the decision-making process. *Gerontologist, 28,* 39–45. (chap. 15)

Jacewicz, M. M., and A. A. Hartley. (1987). Age differences in the speed of cognitive operations: Resolution of inconsistent findings. *Journal of Gerontology, 42,* 86–88. (chap. 8)

Jackson, J. J. (1985). Race, national origin, ethnicity, and aging. In R. H. Binstock and E. Shanas (eds.), *Handbook of aging and the social sci-*

ences. 2nd ed. New York: Van Nostrand Reinhold. (chap. 16)

Jackson, J. S., T. C. Antonucci, and R. C. Gibson. (1990). Cultural, racial, and ethnic minority influences on aging. In J. E. Birren and K. W. Schaie (eds.), *Handbook of the psychology of aging.* 3rd ed. San Diego, CA: Academic Press. (chap. 16)

Jacobs, B. (1990). Aging and politics. In R. H. Binstock and L. K. George (eds.), *Handbook of aging and the social sciences.* 3rd ed. San Diego, CA: Academic Press. (chap. 14)

Jacobs, J. (1983). Industrial sector and career mobility reconsidered. *American Sociological Review, 48,* 415–420. (chap. 13)

Jarvik, L. F. (1973). Discussion: Patterns of intellectual functioning in the later years. In L. F. Jarvik, C. Eisdorfer, and J. E. Blum (eds.), *Intellectual functioning in adults: Psychological and biological influences.* New York: Springer. (chap. 9)

Jarvik, L. F. (1983). The impact of immediate life situations on depression: Illnesses and losses. In L. D. Breslau and M. R. Haug (eds.), *Depression and aging.* New York: Springer. (chap. 6)

Jarvik, L. F., and J. E. Blum. (1971). Cognitive decline as predictors of mortality in twin pairs: A twenty-year longitudinal study of aging. In E. Palmore and F. C. Jeffers (eds.), *Prediction of life span.* Lexington, MA: Heath Lexington. (chap. 3)

Joachim, C. L., and D. J. Selkoe. (1989). Minireview: Amyloid protein in Alzheimer's disease. *Journal of Gerontology, 44,* B77–82. (chap. 6)

Johansson, B., and S. Berg. (1989). The robustness of the terminal decline phenomenon: Longitudinal data from the digit-span memory test. *Journal of Gerontology: Psychological Sciences, 44,* P184–186. (chap. 9)

Johnson, C. L. (1983). Interdependence and aging in Italian families. In J. Sokolovsky (ed.), *Growing old in different societies.* Belmont, CA: Wadsworth. (chap. 16)

Johnson, T. E. (1988). Minireview: Genetic specifications of life span: Processes, problems, and potentials. *Journal of Gerontology, 43,* B87–92. (chap. 3)

Johnston, L., and S. H. Anderson. (June 9, 1983). New York day by day: A sense of history. *New York Times,* B1. (chap. 8)

Jones, L. Y. 1980. *Great expectations: America and the baby boom generation.* New York: Coward, McCann & Geoghegan. (chap. 1)

Jordan, W. D. (1978). Searching for adulthood in America. In E. H. Erikson (eds.), *Adulthood.* New York: Norton. (chap. 2)

Jung, C. G. (1969). *The structure and dynamics of the psyche.* Princeton, NJ: Princeton University Press. (chap. 10)

Kahana, E. (1982). A congruence model of person-environment interaction. In M. P. Lawton, P. G. Windley, and T. O. Byerts (eds.), *Aging and the environment: Theoretical approaches.* New York: Springer. (chap. 15)

Kalish, R. A. (1985). The social context of death and dying. In R. H. Binstock and E. Shanas (eds.), *Handbook of aging and the social sciences.* 2nd ed. New York: Van Nostrand Reinhold. (chap. 11)

Kalish, R. A., and D. K. Reynolds. (1976). *Death and ethnicity: A psycho-cultural study.* Los Angeles: University of Southern California Press. (chap. 16)

Kane, R. L., and R. A. Kane. (1990). Health care for older people: Organizational and policy issues. In R. H. Binstock and L. K. George (eds.), *Handbook of aging and the social sciences.* 3rd ed. San Diego, CA: Academic Press. (chap. 15)

Kannel, W. B. (1985). Hypertension and aging. In C. E. Finch and E. L. Schneider (eds.), *Handbook of the biology of aging.* 2nd ed. New York: Van Nostrand Reinhold. (chaps. 4, 5)

Kanter, R. M. (May 1976). Why bosses turn bitchy. *Psychology Today, 9,* 56–59 + . (chap. 13)

Kantrowitz, B. (August 15, 1988). Moms move to part-time careers. *Newsweek,* 64. (chap. 12)

Kantrowitz, B. (July 10, 1989). The new volunteers. *Newsweek,* 36–38. (chap. 15)

Kantrowitz, B., and P. Wingert. (1990). Step by step. *Newsweek: Special Edition—The 21st century family,* 24–34. (chaps. 11, 12)

Kaplan, G., V. Barell, and A. Lusky. (1988). Sub-

jective state of health and survival in elderly adults. *Journal of Gerontology, 43,* S114–120. (chap. 5)

Kaplan, M. (1983). The issue of sex bias in DSM-III: Comments on the articles by Spitzer, Williams, and Kass. *American Psychologist, 38,* 802–803. (chap. 5)

Kart, C. S., C. F. Longino, and S. G. Ullmann. (1989). Comparing the economically advantaged and the pension elite: 1980 census profiles. *Gerontologist, 29,* 745–749. (chap. 15)

Kasl, S. V., and S. Rosenfield. (1980). The residential environment and its impact on the mental health of the aged. In J. E. Birren and R. B. Sloane (eds.), *Handbook of mental health and aging.* Englewood Cliffs, NJ: Prentice-Hall. (chap. 15)

Kastenbaum, R. (1981). *Death, society, and human experience.* 2nd ed. St. Louis: Mosby. (chap. 5)

Kastenbaum, R. (1985). Dying and death: A life-span approach. In J. E. Birren and K. W. Schaie (eds.), *Handbook of the psychology of aging.* 2nd ed. New York: Van Nostrand Reinhold. (chap. 5)

Kasworm, C. E. (1980). The older student as undergraduate. *Adult Education, 31,* 30–47. (chap. 15)

Kausler, D. H. (1990). Motivation, human aging, and cognitive performance. In J. H. Birren and K. W. Schaie (eds.), *Handbook of the psychology of aging.* 3rd ed. San Diego: Academic Press. (chap. 8)

Kay, B., and J. N. Neelley. (1982). Sexuality and the aging: A review of current literature. *Sexuality and Disability, 5,* 38–46. (chap. 4)

Keating, N., and B. Jeffrey. (1983). Work careers of ever married and never married women. *Gerontologist, 23,* 416-421. (chap. 13)

Keith, J. (1985). Age in anthropological research. In R. H. Binstock and E. Shanas (eds.), *Handbook of aging and the social sciences.* 2nd ed. New York: Van Nostrand Reinhold. (chap. 16)

Keith, J. (1990). Age in social and cultural context. In R. H. Binstock and L. K. George (eds.), *Handbook of aging and the social sciences.* 3rd ed. San Diego, CA: Academic Press. (chap. 16)

Kelly, J. R., M. W. Steinkamp, and J. R. Kelly.

(1986). Later-life leisure: How they play in Peoria. *Gerontologist, 26,* 531–537. (chap. 14)

Kelly, J. R., M. W. Steinkamp, and J. R. Kelly. (1987). Later-life satisfaction: Does leisure contribute? *Leisure Sciences, 9,* 189–200. (chap. 14)

Kendig, H. L. (1990). Housing, aging, and social structure. In R. H. Binstock and L. K. George (eds.), *Handbook of aging and the social sciences.* 3rd ed. San Diego, CA: Academic Press. (chap. 15)

Kennedy, G. E. (1990). College students' expectations of grandparent and grandchild role behaviors. *Gerontologist, 30,* 43–48. (chap. 12)

Kenshalo, D. R. (1977). Age changes in touch, vibration, temperature, kinesthesis, and pain sensitivity. In J. E. Birren and K. W. Schaie (eds.), *Handbook of the psychology of aging.* New York: Van Nostrand Reinhold. (chap. 7)

Kent, D. P. (1971). The Negro aged. *Gerontologist, 11,* 48–51. (chap. 16)

Kenyon, G. M. (1988). Basic assumptions in theories of human aging. In J. E. Birren and V. L. Bengston (eds.), *Emergent theories of aging.* New York: Springer. (chap. 1)

Kercher, K., K. D. Kosloski, and J. B. Normoyle. (1988). Reconsideration of fear of personal aging and subjective well-being in later life. *Journal of Gerontology: Psychological Sciences, 43,* P170–172. (chap. 10)

Kerns, V. (1980). Aging and mutual support among the Black Carib. In C. L. Fry (ed.), *Aging in culture and society.* New York: Praeger. (chap. 16)

Keshet, H. F., and K. M. Rosenthal. (1978). Fathering after marital separation. *Social Work, 23,* 11–18. (chap. 12)

Kiefer, C.W., S. Kim, K. Choi, L. Kim, B.-L. Kim, S. Shon, and T. Kim. (1985). Adjustment problems of Korean American elderly. *Gerontologist, 25,* 477–487. (chap. 16)

Kilborn, P. T. (May 31, 1990). Wage gap between sexes is cut in test, but at a price. *New York Times,* A1, D22. (chap. 13)

Kimmel, D. C. (1978). Adult development and aging: A gay perspective. *Journal of Social Issues, 34,* 113–130. (chap. 11)

Kimmel, D. C., K. F. Price, and J. W. Walker. (1978). Retirement choice and retirement satisfaction. *Journal of Gerontology, 33,* 575–585. (chap. 13)

Kinsey, A. C., W. B. Pomeroy, C. E. Martin, and P. H. Gebhard. (1953). *Sexual behavior in the human female.* Philadelphia: Saunders. (chap. 11)

Kirkwood, T.B.L. (1981). Repair and its evolution; survival versus reproduction. In C. R. Townsend and P. Calow (eds.), *Physiological ecology.* Oxford: Blackwell. (chap. 3)

Kirkwood, T.B.L. (1985). Comparative and evolutionary aspects of longevity. In C. E. Finch and E. L. Schneider (eds.), *Handbook of the biology of aging.* 2nd ed. New York: Van Nostrand Reinhold. (chap. 3)

Kirsch, B. (October 8, 1989). Breaking the sound barrier. *The New York Times Magazine: Good Health,* 64–70. (chap. 7)

Kite, M. E., and B. T. Johnson. (1988). Attitudes toward older and younger adults: A meta-analysis. *Psychology and Aging, 3,* 233–244. (chap. 1)

Kivnick, H. Q. (1982). Grandparenthood: An overview of meaning and moral health. *Gerontologist, 22,* 59–66. (chap. 12)

Kleemeier, R. W. (1962). Intellectual change in the senium. *Proceedings of the Social Statistics Section of the American Statistical Association,* 290–295. (chap. 9)

Klerman, G. L. (1983). Problems in the definition and diagnosis of depression in the elderly. In L. D. Breslau and M. R. Haug (eds.), *Depression and aging.* New York: Springer. (chap. 6)

Kliegl, R., and P. B. Baltes. (1987). Theory-guided analysis of mechanisms of development and aging through testing-the-limits and research on expertise. In C. Schooler and K. W. Schaie (eds.), *Cognitive functioning and social structure over the life course.* Norwood, NJ: Ablex. (chap. 8)

Kligman, A. M., G. L. Grove, and A. K. Balin. (1985). Aging of human skin. In C. E. Finch and E. L. Schneider (eds.), *Handbook of the biology of aging.* 2nd ed. New York: Van Nostrand Reinhold. (chaps. 4, 7)

Kline, D. W., D. M. Ikeda, and F. J. Schieber. (1982). Age and temporal resolution in color vision: When do red and green make yellow? *Journal of Gerontology, 37,* 705–709. (chap. 7)

Kline, D. W., and F. Schieber. (1985). Vision and aging. In J. E. Birren , and K. W. Schaie (eds.), *Handbook of the psychology of aging.* 2nd ed. New York: Van Nostrand Reinhold. (chap. 7)

Kline, D. W., F. J. Schieber, L. C. Abusamra, and A. C. Coyne. (1983). Age, the eye, and the visual channels: Contrast sensitivity and response speed. *Journal of Gerontology, 38,* 211–216. (chap. 7)

Knight, B. (1988). Factors influencing therapist-rated change in older adults. *Journal of Gerontology, 43,* P111–112. (chap. 6)

Knopf, M., and E. Neidhardt. (1989). Aging and memory for action events: The role of familiarity. *Developmental Psychology, 5,* 780–786. (chap. 8)

Koenig, H. G. (in press). Religious beliefs and mental health. In H. G. Koenig, L. M. Smiley, and J. Gonzales (eds.), *Religion, health, and aging.* Westport, CT: Greenwood Press. (chap. 14)

Koenig, H. G., L. K. George, and I. C. Siegler. (1988). The use of religion and other emotion-regulating coping strategies among older adults. *Gerontologist, 28,* 303–310. (chap. 14)

Koepp, S. (November 3, 1986). Is the middle class shrinking? *Newsweek,* 54–56. (chap. 15)

Kogan, N. (1990). Personality and aging. In J. E. Birren and K. W. Schaie (eds.), *Handbook of the psychology of aging.* 3rd ed. San Diego, CA: Academic Press. (chap. 10)

Kohn, A. (September 1987). Art for art's sake: Profile of Teresa Amabile. *Psychology Today, 21,* 52–57. (chap. 9)

Kohn, M. L. (1980). Job complexity and adult personality. In N. J. Smelser and E. H. Erikson (eds.), *Themes of work and love in adulthood.* Cambridge, MA: Harvard University Press. (chap. 13)

Kohn, M. L., and C. Schooler. (1982). Job conditions and personality: A longitudinal assessment of their reciprocal effects. *American Journal of Sociology, 87,* 1257–1286. (chap. 13)

Kohn, M. L., and C. Schooler. (1983). *Work and personality: An inquiry into the impact of social stratification.* Norwood, NJ: Ablex. (chap. 13)

Kohn, R. R. (1977). Heart and cardiovascular sys-

tem. In C. E. Finch and L. Hayflick (eds.), *Handbook of the biology of aging.* New York: Van Nostrand Reinhold. (chap. 4)

Kolata, G. B. (1984). Lowered cholesterol decreases heart disease. *Science, 223,* 381–382. (chap. 5)

Kolata, G. B. (November 10, 1987a). Alcoholism: Genetic links grow clearer. *New York Times,* C1–2. (chap. 6)

Kolata, G. B. (1987b). Diabetics should lose weight, avoid fad diets. *Science, 235,* 163–164. (chap. 5)

Kolata, G. B. (1987c). Panel urges dementia be diagnosed with care. *Science, 237,* 725. (chap. 6)

Kolata, G. B. (September 26, 1989). Major study aims to learn who should lower cholesterol. *New York Times,* C1, C11. (chap. 5)

Kosik, K. S. (1989). Minireview: The molecular and cellular pathology of Alzheimer neurofibrillary lesions. *Journal of Gerontology, 41,* B55–58. (chap. 6)

Koss, E., J. M. Weiffenbach, J. V. Haxby, and R. P. Friedland. (1988). Olfactory detection and identification performance are dissociated in early Alzheimer's disease. *Neurology, 38,* 1228–1232. (chap. 7)

Kotre, J., and E. Hall. (1990) *Seasons of life.* Boston: Little, Brown. (chaps. 3, 11, 12, 13, 16)

Kozma, A., and M. J. Stones. (1990). Decrements in habitual and maximal physical performance with age. In M. Perlmutter (ed.), *Late life potential.* New York: Springer (chap. 4)

Kram, K. E. (1985). *Mentoring processes at work: Developmental relationships in organizational life.* Glenview, IL: Scott, Foresman. (chap. 13)

Kramer, D. A. (1983). Post-formal operations? A need for further conceptualization. *Human Development, 26,* 91–105. (chap. 9)

Kramer, D. A., and D. Woodruff. (in press). Relativistic and dialectical thought in three adult age groups. *Human Development.* (chap. 9)

Krause, N. (1986). Stress and coping: Reconceptualizing the role of locus of control beliefs. *Journal of Gerontology, 41,* 617–622. (chaps. 5, 9)

Kreppner, K., S. Paulsen, and Y. Schuetze. (1982). Infant and family development: From triads to tetrads. *Human Development, 25,* 373–391. (chap. 12)

Kreps, J. M. (1976). The economy and the aged. In R. H. Binstock and E. Shanas (eds.), *Handbook of aging and the social sciences*. New York: Van Nostrand Reinhold. (chap. 15)

Krivo, L. J., and J. E. Mutchler. (1990). Elderly persons living alone: The effect of community context on living arrangements. *Journal of Gerontology: Social Sciences, 44,* S54–62. (chap. 15)

Krout, J. A. (1988). Rural versus urban differences in elderly parents' contact with their children. *Gerontologist, 28,* 198–203. (chap. 12)

Krout, J. A., S. J. Cutler, and R. T. Coward. (1990). Correlates of senior center participation: A national analysis. *Gerontologist, 30,* 72–79. (chap. 15)

Kübler-Ross, E. (1969). *On death and dying.* New York: Macmillan. (chap. 5)

Kurdek, L. A., and J. P. Schmitt. (1986). Early development of relationship quality in heterosexual married, heterosexual cohabiting, gay, and lesbian couples. *Developmental Psychology, 22,* 305–309. (chap. 11)

Labouvie–Vief, G. (1985). Intelligence and cognition. In J. E. Birren and K. W. Schaie (eds.), *Handbook of the psychology of aging.* 2nd ed. New York: Van Nostrand Reinhold. (chap. 9)

Labouvie–Vief, G. (in preparation). Modes of knowledge and the organization of behavior. In M. L. Commons, C. Armon, F. A. Richards, and J. Sinnott (eds.), *Beyond formal operations.* Vol. 2: *The development of adolescent and adult thinking and perception.* (chap. 9)

Labouvie–Vief, G. V., and M. J. Chandler. (1978). Cognitive development and life-span developmental theory: Idealistic versus contextual perspectives. In P. B. Baltes (ed.), *Life-span development and behavior.* Vol. 1. New York: Academic Press. (chap. 2)

Lachman, J. L., and R. Lachman. (1980). Age and the actualization of world knowledge. In L. W. Poon, J. L. Fozard, L. S. Cermak, D. Arenberg, and L. W. Thompson (eds.), *New directions in memory and aging.* Hillsdale, NJ: Lawrence Erlbaum Associates. (chap. 8)

Ladner, J. L. (1971). *Tomorrow's tomorrow: The black woman.* New York: Doubleday. (chap. 16)

La Greca, A. J., R. L. Akers, and J. W. Dwyer. (1988). Life events and alcohol behavior among older adults *Gerontologist, 28,* 552–558. (chap. 6)

Lair, C. V., W. H. Moon, and D. H. Kausler. (1969). Associative interference in the paired-associate learning of middle-aged and old subjects. *Developmental Psychology, 1,* 548–552. (chap. 8)

Lakatta, E. G. (1985). Heart and circulation. In C. E. Finch and E. L. Schneider (eds.), *Handbook of the biology of aging.* 2nd ed. New York: Van Nostrand Reinhold. (chaps. 3, 4)

Lakatta, E. G. (1990). Heart and circulation. In E. L. Schneider and J. W. Rowe (eds.), *Handbook of the biology of aging.* 3rd ed. San Diego, CA: Academic Press. (chap. 3)

Langer, E. J. (1985). Playing the middle against both ends: The usefulness of older adult cognitive activity as a model for cognitive activity in childhood and old age. In S. Yussen (ed.), *The growth of reflection in children.* New York: Academic Press. (chap. 15)

Langway, L. (November 1, 1982). Growing old, feeling young. *Newsweek,* 56–65. (chap. 5)

LaPorte, R. E., R. Black-Sandler, J. A. Cauley, M. Link, C. Bayles, and B. Marks. (1983). The assessment of physical activity in older women: Analysis of the interrelationship and reliability of activity monitoring, activity surveys, and caloric intake. *Journal of Gerontology, 38,* 385–393. (chap. 5)

Larronde, S. (August/September 1983). Adopt-a-grandparent. *Modern Maturity, 26,* 50–51. (chap. 15)

Larson, R., R. Mannell, and J. Zuzanek. (1986). Daily well-being of older adults with friends and families. *Psychology and Aging, 1,* 117–126. (chap. 11)

La Rue, A., C. Dessonville, and L. F. Jarvik. (1985). Aging and mental disorders. In J. E. Birren and K. W. Schaie (eds.), *Handbook of the psychology of aging.* 2nd ed. New York: Van Nostrand Reinhold. (chap. 6)

Laslett, P. (1972). Mean household size in England

since the sixteenth century. In P. Laslett (ed.), *Household and family in past time.* Cambridge: Cambridge University Press. (chap. 2)

Laudenslager, M. L., S. M. Ryan, R. C. Drugan, R. L. Hudson, and S. F. Maier. (1983). Coping and immunosuppression: Inescapable but not escapable shock suppresses lymphocyte production. *Science, 221,* 568–570. (chap. 5)

Laurence, L. T. (1982). *Couple constancy: Conversations with today's happily married people.* Ann Arbor, MI: UMI Research Press. (chap. 11)

LaVoie, J. C. (1976). Ego identity formation in middle adolescence. *Journal of Youth and Adolescence, 5,* 371–385. (chap. 10)

Laws, J. L., and P. Schwartz. (1977). *Sexual scripts: The social construction of female sexuality.* Hinsdale, IL: Dryden Press. (chap. 12)

Lawson, C. (June 1, 1989). With job sharing, time for the family. *New York Times,* C1, 6. (chap. 13)

Lawton, M. P. (1977). Impact of the environment on aging and behavior. In J. E. Birren and K. W. Schaie (eds.), *Handbook of the psychology of aging.* New York: Van Nostrand Reinhold. (chap. 5)

Lawton, M. P. (1980). *Environment and aging.* Monterey, CA: Brooks/Cole. (chap. 15)

Lawton, M. P. (1985). Housing and living environments of older people. In R. H. Binstock and E. Shanas (eds.), *Handbook of aging and the social sciences.* 2nd ed. New York: Van Nostrand Reinhold. (chap. 15)

Lawton, M. P., E. M. Brody, and A. R. Saperstein. (1989). A controlled study of respite service for caregivers of Alzheimer's patients. *Gerontologist, 29,* 8–16. (chap. 6)

Layde, P. M., H. W. Ory, and J. J. Schlesselman. (1982). The risk of myocardial infarction in former users of oral contraceptives. *Family Planning Perspectives, 14,* 78–80. (chap. 5)

Lazarus, R. S., and A. DeLongis. (1983). Psychological stress and coping in aging. *American Psychologist, 38,* 245–256. (chap. 5)

Leaf, A. (1982). Long-lived populations: Extreme old age. *Journal of the American Geriatric Society, 30,* 485–487. (chap. 3)

Lee, G. R. (1983). Social integration and fear of crime among older persons. *Journal of Gerontology, 38,* 745–750. (chap. 15)

Leech, S., and K. L. Witte. (1971). Paired associate learning in elderly adults as related to pacing and incentive conditions. *Developmental Psychology, 5,* 1980. (chap. 8)

LeMoyne, J. (April 8, 1990). Everglades sentinel on watch at 100. *New York Times,* 20. (chap. 1)

Lerner, R. M. (1978). Nature, nurture, and dynamic interactionism. *Human Development, 21,* 1–20. (chap. 2)

LeVine, R. (1982). Culture, context, and the concept of development. In W. A. Collins (ed.), *Minnesota symposia on child psychology.* Vol. 15. *The concept of development.* Hillsdale, NJ: Lawrence Erlbaum Associates. (chap. 2)

Levinson, D. J., C. N. Darrow, E. B. Klein, M. H. Levinson, and B. McKee. (1978). *The seasons of a man's life.* New York: Knopf. (chaps. 10, 11, 13)

Levkoff, S. E., P. D. Cleary, and T. Wetle. (1987). Differences in the appraisal of health between aged and middle-aged adults. *Journal of Gerontology, 42,* 114–120. (chap. 5)

Levy, R. I., and J. Moskowitz. (1982). Cardiovascular research: Decades of progress, a decade of promise. *Science, 217,* 121–129. (chap. 5)

Lewin, R. (1987). More clues to the cause of Parkinson's disease. *Science, 237,* 978. (chap. 6)

Lewin, T. (April 22, 1990). When or whether to retire: New ways to handle strain. *New York Times,* A1, 26. (chap. 13)

Lewin, T. (September 21, 1990). Suit over death benefits asks, What is a family? *New York Times,* B7. (chap. 11)

Lewine, R.R.J. (1981). Sex differences in schizophrenia: Timing or subtype? *Psychological Bulletin, 90,* 432–444. (chap. 6)

Lewis, J., and B. Meredith. (1988). Daughters caring for mothers. *Ageing and Society, 8,* 1–21. (chap. 12)

Lewis, R. (June 26, 1989). Americans marrying more, enjoying it less. *Ann Arbor News.* (chap. 11)

Lieberman, M. A. (1983). Social contexts of depression. In L. D. Breslau and M. R. Haug (eds.),

Depression and aging. New York: Springer. (chap. 6)

Lieberman, M. A., and S. Tobin. (1983). *The experience of old age.* New York: Basic Books. (chaps. 10, 15)

Lieblum, S., G. Bachmann, K. Kemmann, D. Colburn, and L. Swartzman. (1983). Vaginal atrophy in the post-menopausal woman: The importance of sexual activity and hormones. *Journal of the American Medical Association, 249,* 2195–2198. (chap. 4)

Liebman, B. (1984). Drink for your health? *Nutrition Action, 3,* March, 10–13. (chap. 5)

Light, L. L. (1990). Interactions between memory and language in old age. In J. E. Birren and K. W. Schaie (eds.), *Handbook of the psychology of aging.* 3rd ed. San Diego, Calif.: Academic Press. (chap. 8)

Lindemann, E. (1944). Symptomatology and management of acute grief. *American Journal of Psychiatry, 101,* 141–148. (chap. 11)

Lindvall, O., P. Brundin, H. Widner, S. Rehncrona, B. Gustavii, R. Frackowiak, K. L. Leenders, G. Sawle, J. C. Rothwell, C. D. Marsden, and A. Bjorklund. (1990). Grafts of fetal dopamine neurons survive and improve motor function in Parkinson's disease. *Science, 247,* 574–577. (chap. 6)

Litwack, E. (1960). Reference group theory, bureaucratic career and neighborhood primary group cohesion. *Sociometry, 23,* 72–84. (chap. 12)

Livson, F. B. (1981). Paths to psychological health in the middle years: Sex differences. In D. H. Eichorn, J. A. Clausen, N. Haan, M. P. Honzik, and P. H. Mussen (eds.), *Present and past in middle life.* New York: Academic Press. (chap. 10)

Lockshin, R. A., and Z. F. Zakeri. (1990). Programmed cell death: New thoughts and relevance to aging. *Journal of Gerontology: Biological Sciences, 45,* B135–140. (chap. 3)

Loftus, E. (1980). *Memory.* Reading, MA: Addison–Wesley. (chap. 8)

Longino, C. F., Jr. (1990). Geographical distribution and migration. In R. H. Binstock and L. K. George (eds.), *Handbook of aging and the social sciences.* 3rd ed. San Diego, CA: Academic Press. (chap. 15)

Lopata, H. Z. (1973). *Widowhood in an American City.* Cambridge, MA: Schenkman. (chap. 11)

Lopata, H. Z. (1975). Widowhood: Societal factors in life-span disruption and alternatives. In N. Datan and L. H. Ginsberg (eds.), *Life-span developmental psychology: Normative life crises.* New York: Academic Press. (chap. 11)

Lopata, H. Z. (1980). The widowed family member. In N. Datan and N. Lohmann (eds.), *Transitions of aging.* New York: Academic Press. (chap. 11)

Love, D. O., and W. D. Torrence. (1989). The impact of worker age on unemployment and earnings after plant closings. *Journal of Gerontology, 44,* S190–195. (chap. 13)

Lowenthal, M. F. (1977). Toward a sociopsychological theory of change in adulthood and old age. In J. E. Birren and K. W. Schaie (eds.), *Handbook of the psychology of aging.* New York: Van Nostrand Reinhold. (chap. 2)

Lowenthal M. F., and D. Chiriboga. (1972). Transition to the empty nest: Crisis, challenge, or relief? *Archives of General Psychiatry, 26,* 8–14. (chap. 12)

Lum, P. K. H. (1983). Demography of the Asian-Pacific elderly. In R. L McNeely and J. L. Cohen (eds.), *Aging in minority groups.* Beverly Hills, CA: Sage. (chap. 16)

Lyman, F. (January 1988). Maggie Kuhn: A wrinkled radical's crusade. *The Progressive,* 29–31. (chap. 14)

Maccoby, E. E. (1980). Commentary and reply. In G. R. Patterson, *Mothers: The unacknowledged victims, Monographs of the Society for Research in Child Development, 45,* No. 186, 56–63. (chap. 12)

Macklin, E. D. (1978). Review of research on non-marital cohabitation in the United States. In B. I. Murstein (ed.), *Exploring intimate life styles.* New York: Springer. (chap. 11)

Maddox, G. I. (1970). Persistence of life style among the elderly. In E. Palmore (ed.), *Normal aging.* Durham, NC: Duke University Press. (chap. 10)

Maddox, G. L., and E. B. Douglass. (1974). Self-assessment of health. In E. Palmore (ed.), *Normal Aging II*. Durham, NC: Duke University Press. (chap. 5)

Maiden, R. J. (1987). Learned helplessness and depression: A test of the reformulated model. *Journal of Gerontology, 42*, 60–64. (chap. 6)

Maldonado, D., Jr. (1979). Aging in the Chicano context. In D. E. Gelfand and A. J. Kutzik (eds.), *Ethnicity and aging: Theory, research, and policy*. New York: Springer. (chap. 16)

Mancini, J. A., and D. K. Orthner. (1978). Recreational sexual preference among middle-class husbands and wives. *Journal of Sex Research, 14*, 96–106. (chap. 14)

Manning, R., and J. McCormick. (June 4, 1984). The blue-collar blues. *Newsweek*, 52–55. (chap. 13)

Manson, S. M. (1989). Long-term care in American Indian communities: Issues for planning and research. *Gerontologist, 29*, 38–44. (chap. 16)

Manton, K. G. (1988). A longitudinal study of functional change and mortality in the United States. *Journal of Gerontology, 43*, S153–161. (chap. 5)

Margolis, R. J. (April/May 1990). When ''poor'' is not poor enough. *The Aging Connection, 11*, 5. (chap. 15)

Margulis, H. L., and V. M. Benson. (1982). Age-segregation and discrimination against families with children in rental housing. *Gerontologist, 22*, 505–512. (chap. 15)

Mark, M. E. (August 27, 1989). Victories of the spirit. *New York Times Magazine*, 29–31. (chap. 5)

Markides, K. S. (1983). Minority aging. In M. W. Riley, B. B. Hess, and K. Bond (eds.), *Aging in society*. Hillsdale, NJ: Lawrence Erlbaum Associates. (chap. 16)

Markides, K. S., J. S. Levin, and L. A. Ray. (1987). Religion, aging, and life satisfaction: An eight-year, three-wave longitudinal study. *Gerontologist, 27*, 660–665. (chap. 14)

Markides, K. S., J. Liang, and J. S. Jackson. (1990). Race, ethnicity and aging: Conceptual and methodological issues. In R. H. Binstock and L. K. George (eds.), *Handbook of aging and the social sciences*. 3rd ed. San Diego, CA: Academic Press. (chap. 16)

Marklein, M. B. (November 1989). Wired for sound. *AARP Bulletin, 30*, 10–12. (chap. 7)

Marklein, M. B. (September 1990). Against the grain. *AARP Bulletin, 31*, 1, 4–5. (chap. 13)

Marks, L. E., and J. C. Stevens. (1980). Measuring sensation in the aged. In L. W. Poon (ed.), *Aging in the 1980s: Psychological Issues*. Washington, D.C.: American Psychological Association. (chap. 7)

Marsh, G. R., and L. W. Thompson. (1977). Psychophysiology of aging. In J. E. Birren and K. W. Schaie (eds.), *Handbook of the psychology of aging*. New York: Van Nostrand Reinhold. (chap. 4)

Marshall, V. W. (1980). *Last chapters: A sociology of aging and dying*. Monterey, CA: Brooks/Cole. (chap. 10)

Marshall, V. W., and J. A. Levy. (1990). Aging and dying. In R. H. Binstock and L. K. George (eds.), *Handbook of aging and the social sciences*. 3rd ed. San Diego, CA: Academic Press. (chap. 11)

Marshall, V. W., and C. F. Longino, Jr. (1988). Older Canadians in Florida: The social networks of international seasonal migrants. *Comprehensive Gerontology, 2*, 63–68. (chap. 14)

Martin, D. (March 25, 1989). Parents in terror: Could my child be my killer? *New York Times*, 29. (chap. 12)

Martocchio, J. J. (1989). Age-related differences in employee absenteeism: A meta-analysis. *Psychology and Aging, 4*, 409–414. (chap. 13)

Martz, L., and R. Thomas. (May 7, 1990). Fixing Social Security. *Newsweek*, 54–57. (chap. 14)

Marx, J. L. (1979). Hormones and their effects in the aging body. *Science, 206*, 805–806. (chap. 4)

Marx, J. L. (1980). Osteoporosis: New help for thinning bones. *Science, 207*, 628–630. (chap. 4)

Marx, J. L. (1987a). Alzheimer's drug trial put on hold. *Science, 238*, 1041–1042. (chap. 6)

Marx, J. L. (1987b). Oxygen free radicals linked to many diseases. *Science, 235*, 529–531. (chap. 3)

Marx, J. L. (1990a). NGF and Alzheimer's: Hopes and fears. *Science, 247*, 408–410.

Marx, J. L. (1990b). Alzheimer's pathology explored. *Science, 249,* 984–986. (chap. 6)

Masoro, E. J. (1988). Minireview: Food restriction in rodents: An evaluation of its role in the study of aging. *Journal of Gerontology, 43,* B59–64. (chap. 3)

Matthews, S. H., and J. Sprey (1985). Adolescents' relationships with grandparents. *Journal of Gerontology, 40,* 621–626. (chap. 12)

Mazess, R. B., and S. H. Forman. (1979). Longevity and age exaggeration in Vilacabamba, Ecuador. *Journal of Gerontology, 34,* 94–98. (chap. 3)

McAdoo, H. P. (October 1982). Stress absorbing systems in black families. *Family Relations, 31,* 479–488. (chap. 16)

McConnel, C. E., and F. Deljavan. (1983). Consumption patterns of the retired household. *Journal of Gerontology, 38,* 400-490. (chap. 15)

McConnell, S. R. (1983). Retirement and employment. In D. S. Woodruff and J. E. Birren (eds.), *Aging: Scientific perspectives and social issues.* 2nd ed. Monterey, CA: Brooks/Cole. (chap. 13)

McCrae, R. R., D. Arenberg, and P. T. Costa, Jr. (1987). Declines in divergent thinking with age: Cross-sectional, longitudinal, and cross-sequential analyses. *Psychology and Aging, 2,* 130–137. (chap. 9)

McCrae, R. R., and P. T. Costa, Jr. (1982). Aging, the life course, and models of personality. In T. M. Field, A. Huston, H. C. Quay, L. Troll, and G. E. Finley (eds.), *Review of human development.* New York: Wiley-Interscience. (chap. 10)

McCrae, R. R., and P. T. Costa, Jr. (1983). Psychological maturity and subjective well-being: Toward a new synthesis. *Developmental Psychology, 19,* 243–248. (chap. 10)

McCrae, R. R., and P. T. Costa, Jr. (1984). *Emerging lives, enduring dispositions.* Boston: Little, Brown. (chaps. 1, 10)

McCrae, R. R., and P. T. Costa, Jr. (1988). Age, personality, and the spontaneous self-concept. *Journal of Gerontology: Social Sciences, 43,* S177–185. (chap. 10)

McCrae, R. R., P. T. Costa, Jr., and C. M. Busch. (1986). Evaluating comprehensiveness of personality systems: The California Q-sort and the five-factor model. *Journal of Personality, 54,* 430–446. (chap. 10)

McDowd, J. M., and J. E. Birren. (1990). Aging and attentional processes. In J. E. Birren and K. W. Schaie (eds.), *Handbook of the psychology of aging.* 3rd ed. San Diego, CA: Academic Press. (chap. 8)

McDowell, E. (January 12, 1984). Happy end for novelist's 50-year effort. *New York Times,* A1, C20. (chap. 9)

McEvoy, C. L., and R. L. Patterson. (1986). Behavioral treatment of deficit skills in dementia patients. *Gerontologist, 26,* 475–478. (chap. 6)

McGuinness, D. (1985). *When children don't learn.* New York: Basic Books. (chap. 9)

McKoewn, T. (April 1978). Determinants of health. *Human Nature, 1,* 60–67. (chap. 3)

McLeod, D. (July/August 1990). Retirement far from a golden pond for women in a pension crunch. *AARP Bulletin, 31,* 1, 9. (chap. 15)

Meacham, J. A. (1983). Wisdom and the context of knowledge: Knowing that one doesn't know. In D. Kuhn and J. A. Meacham (eds.), *On the development of developmental psychology.* Basel: Karger. (chaps. 1, 9)

Mead, M. (1978). *Culture and commitment.* Rev. ed. Garden City, NY: Anchor Books. (chap. 12)

Medvedev, Z. A. (1974). Caucasus and Altay longevity: A biological or social problem. *Gerontologist, 14,* 381–387. (chap. 3)

Mellins, C., S. Boyd, and M. Gatz. (1988). Caregiving as a family network event. Paper presented at the annual meeting of the Gerontological Society of America. San Francisco, November. (chap. 12)

Melvin, T. (October 22, 1983). Ruling awaited on paternity leave. *New York Times,* WC6. (chap. 12)

Melzack. R., and P. D. Wall. (1982). *The challenge of pain.* Harmondsworth. (chap. 7)

Michael, R.T., V. R. Fuchs, and S. R. Scott. (February 1980). Changes in the propensity to live alone: 1950–1976. *Demography, 17,* 39–56. (chap. 15)

Midlarsky, E., and M. E. Hannah. (1989). The generous elderly: Naturalistic studies of donations across the life span. *Psychology and Aging, 4,* 346–351. (chap. 10)

Miernyk, W. H. (1975). The changing life cycle of work. In N. Datan and L. H. Ginsberg (eds.), *Life-span developmental psychology: Normative life crises.* New York: Academic Press. (chap. 13)

Migdal, S., R. P. Abeles, and L. R. Sherrod. (1981). *An inventory of longitudinal studies of middle and old age.* New York: Social Science Research Council (chap. 2)

Miller, B. D., and D. Olson. (1978). Typology of marital interaction and contextual characteristics: Cluster analysis of the I.M.C. Unpublished paper available from D. Olsen, Minnesota Family Study Center, University of Minnesota. (chap. 11)

Miller, F. T. (1980). Measurement and monitoring of stress in communities. In L. W. Poon (ed.), *Aging in the 1980s: Psychological issues.* Washington, DC: American Psychological Association. (chap. 5)

Miller, G. A. (1956). The magical number seven, plus or minus two: Some limits on our capacity to process information. *Psychological Review, 63,* 81–97. (chap. 8)

Miller, I. J., Jr. (1988). Human taste bud density across adult age groups. *Journal of Gerontology: Biological Sciences, 43,* B26–30. (chap. 7)

Miller, J., C. Schooler, M. L. Kohn, and K. A. Miller. (1979). Women and work: The psychological effects of occupational conditions. *American Journal of Sociology, 85,* 66–94. (chap. 13)

Miller, J., K. M. Slomczynski, and M. L. Kohn. (1987). Continuity of learning-generalization through the life span: The effect of job on men's intellectual process in the United States and Poland. In C. Schooler and K. W. Schaie (eds.), *Cognitive functioning and social structure over the life course.* New York: Ablex. (chap. 8)

Miller, K. A., and M. L. Kohn. (1983). The reciprocal effects of job conditions and the intellectuality of leisure-time activities. In M. L. Kohn and C. Schooler (eds.), *Work and personality.* Norwood, NJ: Ablex. (chap. 13)

Miller, M. (1978). Geriatric suicide: The Arizona study. *Gerontologist, 18,* 488–496. (chap. 6)

Miller, P. Y., and W. Simon. (1980). The develop-ment of sexuality in adolescence. In J. Adelson (ed.), *Handbook of adolescent psychology.* New York: Wiley-Interscience. (chap. 1)

Minaker, K. L., G. S. Meneilly, and J. W. Rowe. (1985). Endocrine systems. In C. E. Finch and E. L. Schneider (eds.), *Handbook of the biology of aging.* 2nd ed. New York: Van Nostrand Reinhold. (chap. 4)

Mischel, W. (1981). *Introduction to personality.* 3rd ed. New York: Holt, Rinehart & Winston. (chap. 10)

Mitchell, D. B., and M. Perlmutter. (1986). Semantic activation and episodic memory. *Developmental Psychology, 22,* 86–94. (chap. 8)

Modern Maturity. (June/July 1983). They show how to live on less. *26,* 94. (chap. 15)

Mohs, R. C., J.C.S. Breitner, J. M. Silverman, and K. L. Davis. (1987). Alzheimer's disease morbid risk among first-degree relatives approximates 50% by ninety years of age. *Archives of General Psychiatry, 44,* 405–408. (chap. 6)

Money, J. (1977). The American heritage of three traditions of pair-bonding: Mediterranean, Nordic, and Slave. In J. Money and H. Musaph (eds.), *Handbook of sexology.* New York: Elsevier/North Holland Biomedical Press. (chap. 11)

Monge, R., and D. Hultsch. (1971). Paired associate learning as a function of adult age and the length of anticipation and inspection intervals. *Journal of Gerontology, 26,* 157–162. (chap. 8)

Monmaney, T. (February 8, 1988). The cholesterol connection. *Newsweek,* 56–58. (chap. 5)

Montero, D. (1979). Disengagement and aging among the Issei. In D. E. Gelfand and A. J. Kutzik (eds.), *Ethnicity and aging: Theory, research, and policy.* New York: Springer. (chap. 16)

Moody, H. R. (Winter 1986). Education in an aging society. *Daedalus, 115,* 191–210. (chap. 14)

Moore, L. M., C. R. Nielsen, and C. M. Mistretta. (1982). Sucrose taste thresholds: Age-related differences. *Journal of Gerontology, 37,* 64–69. (chap. 7)

Morgan, L. A. (1986). The financial experience of widowed women: Evidence from the LRHS. *Gerontologist, 26,* 663–668. (chap. 11)

Moriwaki, S. Y., and F. S. Kobata. (1983). Ethnic

minority aging. In D. S. Woodruff and J. S. Birren (eds.), *Aging: Scientific perspectives and social issues*. Monterey, CA: Brooks/Cole. (chap. 16)

Morris, C. L., and E. B. Dexter. (1989). Taking the clinic to the clients: Geriatric health care in a residential setting. *Gerontologist, 29,* 822–825. (chap. 15)

Morrison, A. M., R. P. White, and E. Van Velsor. (1987). *Breaking the glass ceiling: Can women reach the top of America's largest corporations?* Reading, MA: Addison–Wesley. (chap. 13)

Morrison, M. H. (Winter 1986). Work and retirement in an aging society. *Daedalus, 115,* 269–293. (chap. 13)

Morrow, P. C., and J. C. McElroy (1987). Work commitment and job satisfaction over three career stages. *Journal of Vocational Behavior, 30,* 330–346. (chap. 13)

Morrow, R. S., and S. Morrow. (1973). The measurement of intelligence. In B. Wolman (ed.), *Handbook of general psychology*. Englewood Cliffs, NJ: Prentice–Hall. (chap. 9)

Mortimer, J. T., M. D. Finch, and D. Kumka. (1982). Persistence and change in development: The multidimensional self-concept. In P. B. Baltes and O. G. Brim, Jr. (eds.), *Life-span development and behavior*. Vol. 4. New York: Academic Press. (chap. 10)

Moss, H. A., and E. J. Sussman. (1980). Longitudinal study of personality development. In O. G. Brim, Jr., and J. Kagan (eds.), *Constancy and change in human development*. Cambridge, MA: Harvard University Press. (chap. 1)

Moss, M. S., S. Z. Moss, and E. L. Moles. (1985). The quality of relationships between elderly parents and their out-of-town children. *Gerontologist, 25,* 134–140. (chap. 12)

Mundorf, N., and W. Brownell. (1990). Media preferences of older and younger adults. *Gerontologist, 30,* 685–691. (chap. 14)

Murphy, C. (1983). Age-related effects on the threshold, psychophysical function, and pleasantness of menthol. *Journal of Gerontology, 38,* 217–222. (chap. 7)

Murphy, G. E., and E. Robins. (1968). The communication of suicidal ideas. In H.L.P. Resnik (ed.), *Suicidal behavior*. Boston, MA: Little, Brown. (chap. 6)

Murstein, B. I. (1980). Mate selection in the 1970s. *Journal of Marriage and the Family, 42,* 777–792. (chap. 11)

Murstein, B. I. (1985). *Paths to marriage*. Beverly Hills, CA: Sage. (chap. 11)

Mussen, P. H., and N. Haan. (1981). A longitudinal study of patterns of personality and political ideologies. In D. H. Eichorn, J. A. Clausen, N. Haan, M. P. Honzik, and P. H. Mussen (eds.), *Present and past in middle life*. New York: Academic Press. (chap. 14)

Myer, B. J. F., and G. E. Rice. (1989). Prose processing in adulthood: The text, the reader, and the task. In L. W. Poon, D. C. Rubin, and B. Wilson (eds.), *Everyday cognition in adulthood and late life*. Cambridge: Cambridge University Press. (chap. 8)

Myers, G. C. (1990). Demography of aging. In R. H. Binstock and L. K. George (eds.), *Handbook of aging and the social sciences*. 3rd ed. San Diego, CA: Academic Press. (chaps. 3, 16)

Nahemow, L., and M. P. Lawton. 1976. Toward an ecological theory of adaptation and aging. In H. M. Proshansky, W. H. Ittelson, and L. G. Rivlin (eds.), *Environmental psychology: People and their physical setting*. 2nd ed. New York: Holt, Rinehart and Winston. (chap. 5)

Namazi, K. H., J. K. Eckert, E. Kahana, and S. M. Lyon. (1989). Psychological well-being of elderly board and care home residents. *Gerontologist, 29,* 511–516. (chap. 15)

National Advisory Eye Council. (1983). *Vision research: A national plan*. Washington, DC: U.S. Department of Health and Human Services. (chap. 7)

National Center for Health Statistics. (1986). *Health, United States, 1986*. DHHS Pub. No. (PHS)87–1232. Washington, DC: Department of Health and Human Services. (chap. 3)

National Center for Health Statistics. (October 1987). Current estimates from the National Health Interview Survey, United States, 1986.

Vital and Health Statistics, Series 10, No. 164. (chap. 5)

National Center for Health Statistics. (March 1987). *Vital statistics of the United States, 1984*. Vol. II, Section 6 (Lifetables). (chap. 16)

Neisser, U. (1976). Academic and artifical intelligence. In L. B. Resnik (ed.), *The nature of intelligence.* Hillsdale, NJ: Lawrence Erlbaum Associates. (chap. 9)

Nelson, D. (Fall 1982). The meanings of old age for public policy. *National Forum, 62,* 27–30. (chap. 15)

Nesselroade, J. R., and E. W. Labouvie. (1985). Experimental design in research on aging. In J. E. Birren and K. W. Schaie (eds.), *Handbook of the psychology of aging,* pp. 35–60. 2nd ed. New York: Van Nostrand Reinhold. (chap. 2)

Neugarten, B. L. (1970). Adaptation and the life cycle. *Journal of Geriatric Psychiatry, 4,* 71–87. (chap. 12)

Neugarten, B. L. (1973). Personality change in later life: A developmental perspective. In C. Eisdorfer and M. P. Lawson (eds.), *The psychology of adult development and aging.* Washington, DC: American Psychological Association. (chap. 10)

Neugarten, B. L. (1975). The future and the young-old. *Gerontologist, 15,* 4–9. (chap. 1)

Neugarten, B. L. (1979). Time, age, and the life cycle. *American Journal of Psychiatry, 136,* 887–894 (chap. 10)

Neugarten, B. L., interviewed by E. Hall. (1987). Acting one's age: New rules for old. In E. Hall, *Growing and changing.* New York: Random House. (chaps. 1, 14, 15)

Neugarten, B. L., and D. A. Neugarten. (Winter 1986). Age in the aging society. *Daedalus, 115,* 31–49. (chaps. 1, 12)

Neugarten, B. L., and K. Weinstein. (1964). The changing American grandparent. *Journal of Marriage and the Family, 26,* 199–204. (chap. 12)

Newmann, J. P. (1989). Aging and depression. *Psychology and Aging, 4,* 150–165. (chap. 6)

Newsweek. (March 3, 1986). Transition. 71. (chap. 3)

Newsweek. (September 1, 1986). Crib to college. 71. (chap. 15)

Newsweek. (July 17, 1989). Homosexual families and the law. 48. (chap. 11)

Newton, N., and C. Modahl. (March 1978). Pregnancy: The closest human relationship. *Human Nature, 1,* 40–49. (chap. 12)

New York Times. (December 30, 1983). Man who spent 31 years in hospital is freed. A10. (chap. 16)

New York Times. (April 29, 1984). Swimming and walking top activities in poll. 38. (chap. 14)

New York Times. (March 1, 1986). Antidote for aging: The active life. 52. (chap. 8)

New York Times. (August 21, 1986). How children affect a woman's earnings. C11. (chap. 13)

New York Times. (September 4, 1986). Hispanic poverty rate nears that of blacks. A14. (chap. 13)

New York Times. (July 25, 1989a). A.M.A. describes tanning hazards. (chap. 4)

New York Times. (September 14, 1989b). Smoking of cigarettes is linked for first time to a form of cataracts. B15. (chap. 5)

New York Times. (October 15, 1989). ''College age'' means almost any age. B7. (chap. 14)

New York Times. (March 23, 1990). U.S. health gap is widening between whites and blacks. A17. (chap. 3)

New York Times. (August 8, 1990). Laughing in face of death, B. F. Skinner defends his theory of life. (chap. 8)

Nicak, A. (1971). Changes in sensitivity to pain in relation to postnatal development in the rat. *Experimental Gerontology, 6,* 111–114. (chap. 7)

Nichols, M., and S. R. Lieblum. (1983). Lesbianism as personal identity and social role: Conceptual and clinical issues. Unpublished paper. Rutgers University. (chap. 11)

Norris, F. H., and S. A. Murrell. (1990). Social support, life events, and stress as modifiers of adjustment to bereavement by older adults. *Psychology and Aging, 5,* 429–436. (chap. 11)

Norwood, T. H., and J. R. Smith. (1985). The cultured fibroblast-like cell as a model for the study of aging. In C. E. Finch and E. L. Schneider (eds.), *Handbook of the biology of aging.* 2nd ed. New York: Van Nostrand Reinhold. (chap. 3)

Nunnally, J. C. (1973). Research strategies and measurement methods for investigating human development. In J. R. Nesselroade and H. W. Reese (eds.), *Life-span developmental psychology: Methodological issues.* New York: Academic Press. (chap. 2)

O'Bryant, S. L., and L. A. Morgan. (1989). Financial experience and well-being among mature widowed women. *Gerontologist, 29,* 245–251. (chap. 11)

Ogilvie, D. M. (1987). Life satisfaction and identity structure in late middle-aged men and women. *Psychology and Aging, 2,* 217–224. (chap. 10)

O'Hara, M. W., J. V. Hinrichs, F. J. Kohout, R. B. Wallace, and J. H. Lemke. (1986). Memory complaint and memory performance in the depressed elderly. *Psychology and Aging, 1,* 208–214. (chap. 8)

Ohlsson, M. (1976). Information processing related to physical fitness in elderly people. *Reports from the Institute of Applied Psychology, 71,* 1–12. (chap. 8)

Ohta, R. J., M. F. Carlin, and B. M. Harmon. (1981). Auditory acuity and performance on the mental health status questionnaire in the elderly. *Journal of the American Geriatrics Society, 29,* 476–478. (chap. 7)

Okudaira, N., H. Fukuda, K. Nishihara, K. Ohtani, S. Endo, and S. Torii. (1983). Sleep apnea and nocturnal myoclonus in elderly persons in Vilcabamba, Ecuador. *Journal of Gerontology, 38,* 436–438. (chap. 4)

Okun, M., W. A. Stock, M. J. Haring, and R. A. Witter. (1984). The social activity / subjective well-being relation: A quantitative synthesis. *Research on Aging, 6,* 45–64. (chap. 10)

Olsho, L. W., S. W. Harkins, and M. L. Lenhardt. (1985). Aging and the auditory system. In J. E. Birren and K. W. Schaie (eds.), *Handbook of the psychology of aging.* 2nd ed. New York: Van Nostrand Reinhold. (chap. 7)

Omenn, G. S. (1977). Behavior genetics. In J. E. Birren and K. W. Schaie (eds.), *Handbook of the psychology of aging.* New York: Van Nostrand Reinhold. (chap. 3)

Oreskes, M. (June 28, 1990). Profile of today's youth: They couldn't care less. *New York Times,* A1, D21. (chap. 14)

Orwoll, L., and M. Perlmutter. (1990). The study of wise persons: Integrating a personality perspective. In R. Sternberg (ed.), *Wisdom: Its nature, origins, and development.* New York: Cambridge University Press. (chaps. 1, 9)

Osofsky, J. D., and H. J. Osofsky. (1984). Psychological and developmental perspectives on expectant and new parenthood. In R. D. Parke (ed.), *Review of child development research.* Vol. 7: *The Family.* Chicago: University of Chicago Press. (chap. 12)

Ostrow, A. C. (1980). Physical activity as it relates to the health of the aged. In N. Datan and N. Lohmann (eds.), *Transitions of aging.* New York: Academic Press. (chap. 5)

Overton, W. F., and V. Clayton. (1976). The role of formal operational thought in the aging process. Unpublished manuscript. State University of New York, Buffalo. (chap. 9)

Paffenbarger, R. S., R. T. Hyde, A. L. Wing, and C. C. Hsieh. 1986. Physical activity, all-cause mortality, and longevity of college alumni. *New England Journal of Medicine, 314,* 605–613. (chap. 5)

Painter, C. (1985). *Gifts of age.* San Francisco, CA: Chronicle Books. (chap. 10)

Palmer, J. L., and S. G. Gould. (Winter 1986). The economic consequences of an aging society. *Daedalus, 115,* 295–323. (chap. 1)

Palmore, E. B. (1974). Health practices and illnesses. In E. Palmore (ed.), *Normal aging II.* Durham, NC: Duke University Press. (chap. 5)

Palmore, E. B. (1976). The future status of the aged. *Gerontologist, 16,* 297–302. (chap. 16)

Palmore, E. B., L. K. George, and G. G. Fillenbaum. (1982). Predictors of retirement. *Journal of Gerontology, 34,* 733–742. (chap. 13)

Papalia, D. (1972). The status of several conservation abilities across the life span. *Human Development, 15,* 229–243. (chap. 9)

Parker, E. S., and E. P. Noble. (1977). Alcohol consumption and cognitive functioning in social drinkers. *Journal of Studies on Alcohol, 38,* 1224–1232. (chap. 8)

Parkes, C. M. (1972). *Bereavement: Studies of grief in adult life*. New York: International Universities Press. (chap. 11)

Parkes, C. M., and R. S. Weiss. (1983). *Recovery from bereavement*. New York: Basic Books. (chap. 11)

Parmelee, P.A., and M. P. Lawton. (1990). The design of special environments for the aged. In J. E. Birren and K. W. Schaie (eds.), *Handbook of the psychology of aging*. 3rd ed. San Diego, CA: Academic Press. (chaps. 5, 15)

Parnes, H. S. (1981). *Work and retirement*. Cambridge, MA: MIT Press. (chap. 13)

Parnes, H. S., J. E. Crowley, R. J. Haurin, L. J. Less, W. R. Morgan, F. L. Mott, and G. Nestel. (1985). *Retirement among American men*. Lexington, MA: Heath. (chap. 13)

Passuth, P. M., and V. L. Bengston. (1988). Sociological theories of aging: Current perspectives and future directions. In J. E. Birren and V. L. Bengston (eds.), *Emergent theories of aging*. New York: Springer. (chap. 2)

Pastalan, L. A., R. K. Mautz, and J. Merrill. (1973). The simulation of age-related sensory losses: A new approach to the study of environmental barriers. In W.F.E. Preiser (ed.), *Environmental design research*. Stroudsberg, PA: Dowden, Hutchinson & Ross. (chap. 7)

Pear, R. (November 22, 1983). Census Bureau finds turnout in federal elections is rising. *New York Times*, A23. (chap. 14)

Pear, R. (August 21, 1985). Some new inequalities in the pay of women. *New York Times*, 15–17. (chap. 13)

Pederson, N. L., R. Plomin, G. E. McClearn, and L. Friberg. (1988). Neuroticism, extraversion, and related traits in adult twins reared apart and reared together. *Journal of Personality and Social Psychology, 55,* 950–957. (chap. 10)

Peplau, L. A. (March 1981). What homosexuals want in relationships. *Psychology Today, 15,* 28–38. (chap. 11)

Perlmutter, M. (1983). Learning and memory through adulthood. In M. W. Riley, B. B. Hess, and K. Bond (eds.), *Aging in society: Selected reviews of recent research*. Hillsdale, NJ: Lawrence Erlbaum Associates. (chap. 8)

Perlmutter, M. (1986). A life-span view of memory. In P. B. Baltes and D. Featherman (eds.), *Life-span development and behavior*. Vol. 7. San Diego, CA: Academic Press. (chap. 8)

Perlmutter, M. (1988a). Cognitive development in life-span perspective: From description of differences to explanation of changes. In M. Hetherington, R. Lerner, and M. Perlmutter (eds.), *Child development in a life-span perspective*. Hillsdale, NJ: Lawrence Erlbaum Associates. (chaps. 8, 9)

Perlmutter, M. (1988b). Cognitive potential throughout life. In J. E. Birren and V. L. Bengston (eds.), *Emergent theories of aging*. New York: Springer. (chaps. 1, 2, 9)

Perlmutter, M., C. Adams, J. Berry, M. Kaplan, D. Person, and F. Verdonik. (1987). Aging and memory. *Annual Review of Gerontology and Geriatrics, 7,* 57–92. (chap. 8)

Perlmutter, M., and L. Nyquist. (1990) Relationship between self-reported physical and mental health and intelligence performance across adulthood. *Journal of Gerontology: Psychological Sciences, 45,* P145–155.

Perlmutter, M., L. Nyquist, and C. Adams–Price. (1989). Activity and cognitive performance across adulthood. Unpublished paper. University of Michigan. (chap. 8)

Perone, M., and A. Baron. (1982). Age-related effects of pacing on acquisition and performance of response sequences: An operant analysis. *Journal of Gerontology, 37,* 443–449. (chap. 8)

Peterson, I. (July 30, 1989). Hotel chains plunge into life-care field. *New York Times*, R1, R11. (chap. 15)

Pfeiffer, E. (1977). Psychopathology and social pathology. In J. E. Birren and K. W. Schaie (eds.), *Handbook of the psychology of aging*. New York: Van Nostrand Reinhold. (chap. 6)

Piaget, J. (1983). Piaget's theory. In P. H. Mussen (ed.), *Handbook of child psychology*. 4th ed. Vol. 1. W. Kessen (ed.), *History, theory, and methods*. New York: Wiley. (chap. 9)

Piaget, J., and B. Inhelder. (1969). *The psychology of the child*. New York: Basic Books. (chap. 9)

Pifer, A. (Winter 1986). The public policy response to population aging. *Daedalus, 115,* 373–395. (chaps. 14, 16)

Pillemer, K., and D. Finkelhor. (1988). The prevalence of elder abuse: A random survey. *Gerontologist, 28,* 51–57. (chap. 12)

Piper, A. I., and E. J. Langer. (1986). Aging and mindful control. In M. M. Baltes and P. B. Baltes (eds.), *The psychology of control and aging.* Hillsdale, NJ: Lawrence Erlbaum Associates. (chap. 15)

Pleck, J. H. (1985). *Working wives, working husbands.* Beverly Hills, CA: Sage Publications. (chap. 12)

Plomin, R., N. L. Pederson, G. E. McClearn, J. R. Nesselroade, and C. S. Bergeman. (1988). EAS temperaments during the last half of the life span: Twins reared apart and twins reared together. *Psychology and Aging, 3,* 43–50. (chap. 10)

Plude, D. J., and J. A. Doussard–Roosevelt. (1989). Aging, selective attention, and feature integration. *Psychology and Aging, 4,* 98–105. (chap. 8)

Ponds, R.W.H.M., W. H. Brouwer, and P. C. van Wolffelaar. (1988). Age differences in divided attention in a simulated driving task. *Journal of Gerontology: Psychological Sciences, 43,* P151–156. (chap. 8)

Pool, R. (1988). Caution continues over transplants. *Science, 242,* 1379. (chap. 6)

Poon, L. W. (1985). Differences in human memory with aging: Nature, causes, and clinical implications. In J. E. Birren and K. W. Schaie (eds.), *Handbook of the psychology of aging.* 2nd ed., pp. 427–462. New York: Van Nostrand Reinhold. (chaps. 2, 8)

Post, F. (1980). Paranoid, schizophrenia-like, and schizophrenic states in the aged. In J. E. Birren and R. B. Sloane (eds.), *Handbook of mental health and aging.* Englewood Cliffs, NJ: Prentice–Hall. (chaps. 6, 7)

Pratt, H. J. (Fall 1982). The ''gray lobby'' revisited. *National Forum, 62,* 31–33. (chap. 14)

Press, A. (January 2, 1984). Suffer the little children. *Newsweek,* 47. (chap. 15)

Prial, F. J. (November 15, 1982). More women work at traditional male roles. *New York Times,* 1 +. (chap. 13)

Quayhagen, M. P., and M. Quayhagen. (1989). Differential effects of family-based strategies on Alzheimer's disease. *Gerontologist, 29,* 150–155. (chap. 6)

Quinn, J. F., and R. V. Burkhauser. (1990). Work and retirement. In R. H. Binstock and L. K. George (eds.), *Handbook of aging and the social sciences.* 3rd ed. San Diego, CA: Academic Press. (chap. 13)

Quinn, J. F., R. V. Burkhauser, and D. C. Myers. (1990). Passing the torch: The influence of economic incentives on work and retirement. Kalamazoo, MI: Upjohn Institute for Employment Research. (chap. 13)

Ragozin, A. S., R. B. Basham, K. A. Crnic, M. T. Greenberg, and N. M. Robinson. (1982). Effects of maternal age on parenting role. *Developmental Psychology, 18,* 627–634. (chap. 12)

Rebok, G. W., and L. J. Balcerak. (1989). Memory self-efficacy and performance differences in young and old adults: The effect of mnemonic training. *Developmental Psychology, 25,* 714–721. (chap. 8)

Rebok, G. W., and L. R. Offermann. (1983). Behavioral competences of older college students: A self-efficacy approach. *Gerontologist, 23,* 428–432. (chap. 14)

Reedy, M. N. (1983). Personality and aging. In D. S. Woodruff and J. E. Birren (eds.), *Aging: Scientific perspectives and social issues.* 2nd ed. Monterey, CA: Brooks/Cole. (chap. 10)

Reff, M. E. (1985). RNA and protein metabolism. In C. E. Finch and E. L. Schneider (eds.), *Handbook of the biology of aging.* 2nd ed. New York: Van Nostrand Reinhold. (chap. 3)

Reich, J. W., A. J. Zautra, and J. Hill. (1987). Activity, event transactions, and quality of life in older adults. *Psychology and Aging, 2,* 116–124. (chap. 10)

Reid, G. (1972). Job-search and effectiveness of job-finding measures. *Industrial and Labor Relations Review, 25,* 479–495. (chap. 13)

Reisman, J. M. (1988). An indirect measure of the

value of friendship for aging men. *Journal of Gerontology: Psychological Sciences, 43,* P109–110. (chap. 11)

Reker, G. T., and P.T.P. Wong. (1988). Aging as an individual process: Toward a theory of personal meaning. In J. E. Birren and V. L. Bengston (eds.), *Emergent theories of aging.* New York: Springer. (chap. 10)

Renner, V. J., and J. E. Birren. (1980). Stress: Physiological and psychological mechanisms. In J. E. Birren and R. B. Sloane (eds.), *Handbook of mental health and aging.* Englewood Cliffs, NJ: Prentice–Hall. (chap. 5)

Reporter Dispatch. (July 26, 1989a). Woman recognized as world's oldest living person dies at 112. A13. (chap. 3)

Reporter Dispatch. (July 28, 1989b). Lung cancer deaths in women still on rise. A11. (chap. 5)

Reporter Dispatch. (May 3, 1990a). Study: Parkinson's patient improves after transplant of fetal tissue. (chap. 6)

Reporter Dispatch. (May 8, 1990b). Baby boomlet. A1. (chap. 12)

Rhine, S. H. (1984). *Managing older workers: Company policies and attitudes.* New York: Conference Board. (chap. 13)

Rich, S. (January 18, 1987). Marriage prospects not so bad for women past 30. *Ann Arbor News.* (chap. 11)

Richardson, G. S. (1990). Circadian rhythms and aging. In E. L. Schneider and J. W. Rowe (eds.), *Handbook of the biology of aging.* 3rd ed. San Diego, CA: Academic Press. (chap. 4)

Riegel, K. F. (1975). Toward a dialectical theory of development. *Human Development, 18,* 50–64. (chap. 2)

Riegel, K. F. (1977). History of psychological gerontology. In J. E. Birren and K. W. Schaie (eds.), *Handbook of the psychology of aging.* New York: Van Nostrand Reinhold. (chap. 10)

Riegel, P. S. (1981). Athletic records and human endurance. *American Scientist, 69,* 285–290. (chap. 4)

Rikli, R., and Busch, S. (1986). Motor performance of women as a function of age and physical activity level. *Journal of Gerontology, 41,* 645–649. (chap. 5)

Riley, M. W., and K. Bond. (1981). Beyond ageism: Postponing the onset of disability. In M. W. Riley, B. B. Hess, and K. Bond (eds.), *Aging in society: Selected reviews of recent research.* Hillsdale, NJ: Lawrence Erlbaum. (chap. 5)

Riley, M. W., and A. Foner. (1968). *Aging and society.* Vol. 1: *An inventory of research findings.* New York: Russell Sage Foundation. (chap. 13)

Riley, M. W., M. Johnson, and A. Foner (Eds.). (1972). *Aging and society.* Vol. 3. *A sociology of age stratification.* New York: Russell Sage Foundation. (chaps. 2, 14)

Rinke, C. L., J. J. Williams, K. E. Lloyd, and W. Smith-Scott. (1978). The effects of prompting and reinforcement on self-bathing by elderly residents of a nursing home. *Behavior Therapy, 9,* 873–881. (chap. 8)

Rippe, J. M. (May 1989). CEO fitness: The performance plus. *Psychology Today,* 50–53. (chap. 5)

Roach, M. (January 16, 1983). Another name for madness. *The New York Times Magazine,* 22–31. (chap. 6)

Roberts, M. J., and T G. Harris. (May 1989). Wellness at work. *Psychology Today,* 54–58. (chap. 5)

Roberts, P., and P. M. Newton. (1987). Levinsonian studies of women's adult development. *Psychology and Aging, 2,* 154–163. (chap. 10)

Robins, L. N., J. E. Helzer, M. M. Weissman, H. Orraschel, E. Gruenberg, J. D. Burke, and D. A. Regier. (1984). Lifetime prevalence of specific psychiatric disorders in three sites. *Archives of General Psychiatry, 41,* 949–958. (chap. 6)

Robinson, P. K., S. Coberly, and C. E. Paul. (1985). Work and retirement. In R. H. Binstock and E. Shanas (eds.), *Handbook of aging and the social sciences.* 2nd ed. New York: Van Nostrand Reinhold. (chap. 13)

Rockstein, M., J. Chesky, and M. Sussman. (1977). Comparative biology and evolution of aging. In C. E. Finch and L. Hayflick (eds.), *Handbook of the biology of aging.* New York: Van Nostrand Reinhold. (chap. 3)

Rockstein, M., and M. Sussman. (1979). *Biology of aging.* Belmont, CA: Wadsworth. (chaps. 3, 4, 7)

Rockwell, J. (February 4, 1990). Beating time (Father, that is). *The New York Times,* Section 2, 1, 32. (chap. 9)

Rodeheaver, D. (1987). When old age became a social problem, women were left behind. *Gerontologist, 27,* 741–746. (chap. 15)

Rodin, J. (1986). Aging and health: The effects of the sense of control. *Science, 233,* 1271–1276. (chaps. 3, 5, 15)

Rodin, J., and E. J. Langer. (1977). Long-term effects of a control-relevant intervention with the institutionalized aged. *Journal of Personality and Social Psychology, 35,* 879–902. (chap. 15)

Rodin, J., G. McAvay, and C. Timko. (1988). A longitudinal study of depressed mood and sleep disturbances in elderly adults. *Journal of Gerontology, 43,* P45–53. (chap. 4)

Rogers, J., and F. E. Bloom. (1985). Neurotransmitter metabolism and function in the aging central nervous system. In C. E. Finch and E. L. Schneider (eds.), *Handbook of the biology of aging.* 2nd ed. New York: Van Nostrand Reinhold. (chap. 4)

Rohlen, T. P. (1978). The promise of adulthood in Japanese spiritualism. In E. H. Erikson (ed.), *Adulthood.* New York: Norton. (chap. 2)

Rollins, B.C., and R. Galligan. (1978). The developing child and marital satisfaction of parents. In R. M. Lerner and G. B. Spanier (eds.), *Child influences on marital and family interaction.* New York: Academic Press. (chap. 12)

Romalis, C. (1981). Taking care of the little woman: Father-physician relations during pregnancy and childbirth. In S. Romalis (ed.), *Childbirth: Alternative to medical control.* Austin: University of Texas Press. (chap. 12)

Rose, M. R., and B. Charlesworth. (1980). A test of evolutionary theories of senescence. *Nature, 287,* 141–142. (chap. 3)

Rose, M. R., and J. L. Graves, Jr. (1989). Minireview: What evolutionary biology can do for gerontology. *Journal of Gerontology, 44,* 27–29. (chap. 3)

Rosen, R. C., and E. Hall. (1984). *Sexuality.* New York: Random House. (chap. 11)

Rosenberg, M. B., T. Friedmann, R. C. Robertson, M. Tuszynski, J. A. Wolff, X. O. Breakefield, and F. H. Gage. (1988). Grafting genetically modified cells to the damaged brain: Restorative effects of NGF expression. *Science, 242,* 1575–1578. (chap. 6)

Rosenman, R. H. (1974). The role of behavior patterns and neurogenic factors in the pathogenesis of coronary heart disease. In R. S. Eliot (ed.), *Stress and the heart.* New York: Futura. (chap. 5)

Rosenman, R. H., R. J. Brand, C. D. Jenkins, M. Friedman, R. Straus, and M. Wurm. (1975). Coronary heart disease in the Western Collaborative Group study: Final follow-up experience of 8 1/2 years. *Journal of the American Medical Association, 8,* 872–877. (chap. 5)

Rosenthal, C. J. (1985). Kin-keeping in the familial division of labor. *Journal of Marriage and the Family, 45,* 509–521. (chap. 11)

Rossman, I. (1977). Anatomic and body composition changes with aging. In C. E. Finch and L. Hayflick (eds.), *Handbook of the biology of aging.* New York: Van Nostrand Reinhold. (chap. 4)

Rovee, C. K., R. Y. Cohen, and W. Shlapack. (1975). Life span stability in olfactory sensitivity. *Developmental Psychology, 11,* 311–318. (chap. 7)

Rowe, J. W., and R. L. Kahn. (1987). Human aging: Usual and successful. *Science, 237,* 143–149. (chap. 3)

Rowe, J. W., and K. L. Minaker. (1985). Geriatric medicine. In C. E. Finch and E. L. Schneider (eds.), *Handbook of the biology of aging.* 2nd ed. New York: Van Nostrand Reinhold. (chaps. 4, 5)

Rowles, G. D. (1980). Growing old ''inside'': Aging and attachment to place in an Appalachian community. In N. Datan and N. Lohmann (eds.), *Transitions of aging.* New York: Academic Press. (chap. 15)

Rubenstein, C., P. Shaver, and L. A. Peplau. (February 1979). Loneliness. *Human Nature, 2,* 58–65. (chap. 11)

Rubin, L. (1979). *Women of a certain age: The mid-life search for self.* New York: Harper & Row. (chaps. 11, 12)

Rubin, Z. (1973). *Liking and loving.* New York: Holt, Rinehart & Winston. (chap. 11)

Rubinstein, R. L. (1987). Never married elderly as a social type: Re-evaluating some images. *Gerontologist, 27,* 108–113. (chap. 11)

Rubinstein, R. L. (1989). The home environments of older people: A description of the psychosocial processes linking person to place. *Journal of Gerontology: Social Sciences, 44,* S45–53. (chap. 15)

Rubner, M. (1908). Probleme des Wachstums unter der Lebensdauer. In *Geschellschaft fur Innere Medizine und Kinderheilkunde.* Vol. 7. Vienna: Mitteilungen, Beiblat. (chap. 3)

Rudman, D., A. G. Feller, and H. S. Nagra. 1990. Effects of human growth hormone in men over 60 years old. (1990). *New England Journal of Medicine, 323,* 1–6.

Rybash, J. M., W. J. Hoyer, and P. A. Roodin. (1986). *Adult cognition and aging.* New York: Pergamon. (chap. 9)

Ryff, C. D. (1989). In the eye of the beholder: Views of psychological well-being among middle-aged and older adults. *Psychology and Aging, 4,* 195–210. (chap. 10)

Sabatini, P., and G. Labouvie–Vief. (1979). Age and professional specialization: Formal reasoning. Paper presented at the annual meeting of the Gerontological Society. Washington, DC, November. (chap. 9)

Sacher, G. A. (1977). Life table modification and life prolongation. In C. E. Finch and L. Hayflick (eds.), *Handbook of the biology of aging.* New York: Van Nostrand Reinhold. (chap. 3)

St. George–Hyslop, P. H., R. E. Tanzi, R. J. Polinsky, J. L. Haines, L. Nee, P. C. Watkins, R. H. Myers, R. G. Feldman, D. Pollen, D. Drachman, J. Growdon, A. Bruni, J.-F. Foncin, D. Salmon, P. Frommelt, L. Amaducci, S. Sorbi, S. Piacentini, G. D. Stewart, W. J. Hobbs, P. M. Conneally, and J. F. Gusella. (1987). The genetic defect causing familial Alzheimer's disease maps on Chromosome 21. *Science, 235,* 885–886. (chap. 6)

Salholz, E. (June 2, 1986). Too late for Prince Charming? *Newsweek,* 54–61. (chap. 11)

Salthouse, T. A. (1982). *Adult cognition.* New York: Springer-Verlag. (chap. 8)

Salthouse, T. A. (1984). Effects of age and skill in typing. *Journal of Experimental Psychology: General, 113,* 343–371. (chap. 1)

Salthouse, T. A. (1987). Age, experience, and compensation. In C. Schooler and K. W. Schaie (eds.), *Cognitive functioning and social structure over the life course.* New York: Ablex. (chap. 8)

Salthouse, T. A. (1988). Resource-reduction interpretations of cognitive aging. *Developmental Review, 8,* 238–272. (chap. 8)

Salthouse, T. A. (1989). Age-related changes in basic cognitive processes. In APA Master Lectures, *The adult years: Continuity and change.* Washington, DC: American Psychological Association. (chap. 8)

Salthouse, T. A., D. H. Kausler, and J. S. Saults. (1988). Utilization of path-analytic procedures to investigate the role of processing resources in cognitive aging. *Psychology and Aging, 3,* 158–166. (chap. 8)

Saltin, B., G. Blomquist, J. H. Mitchell, R. L. Johnson, K. Wildenthal, and C. B. Chapman. (1968). Response to exercise after bed rest and after training. *American Heart Association Monograph.* No. 23. New York: American Heart Association. (chap. 5)

Sanadi, D. R. (1977). Metabolic changes and their significance in aging. In C. E. Finch and L. Hayflick (eds.), *Handbook of the biology of aging.* New York: Van Nostrand Reinhold. (chap. 3)

Sands, L. P., H. Terry, and W. Meredith. (1989). Change and stability in adult intellectual functioning assessed by Wechsler item responses. *Psychology and Aging, 4,* 79–87. (chap. 9)

Scarr, S. (1981). *Race, social class, and individual differences in I.Q.* Hillsdale, NJ: Lawrence Erlbaum Associates. (chap. 1)

Schafer, W. R., R. Kim, R. Sterne, J. Thorner, S.-H. Kim, and J. Rine. (1989). Genetic and pharmacological suppression of oncogenic mutations in RAS genes of yeast and humans. *Science, 245,* 379–385. (chap. 5)

Schaie, K. W. (1973). Methodological problems in descriptive developmental research on adulthood and aging. In J. R. Nesselroade and H. W. Reese (eds.), *Life-span developmental psychology: Methodological issues.* New York: Academic Press. (chap. 2)

Schaie, K. W. (1979). The Primary Mental Abilities in adulthood: An exploration in the development of psychometric intelligence. In P. B. Baltes and O. G. Brim, Jr. (eds.), *Life-span development and behavior.* Vol. 2. New York: Academic Press. (chap. 9)

Schaie, K. W. (1983). Age changes in adult intelligence. In D. S. Woodruff and J. E. Birren (eds.), *Aging: Scientific perspectives and social issues.* 2nd ed. Monterey, CA: Brooks/Cole. (chap. 9)

Schaie, K. W. (1987). Applications of psychometric intelligence to the prediction of everyday competence in the elderly. In C. Schooler and K. W. Schaie (eds.), *Cognitive functioning and social structure over the life course.* New York: Ablex. (chap. 8)

Schaie, K. W. (1989a). Individual differences in rate of cognitive change in adulthood. In V. L. Bengston and K. W. Schaie (eds.), *The course of later life: Research and reflections.* New York: Springer. (chap. 9)

Schaie, K. W. (1989b). Perceptual speed in adulthood: Cross-sectional and longitudinal studies. *Psychology and Aging, 4,* 443–453. (chap. 8)

Schaie, K. W. (1990). Intellectual development in adulthood. In J. E. Birren and K. W. Schaie (eds.), *Handbook of the psychology of aging.* 3rd ed. San Diego, CA: Academic Press. (chap. 9)

Schaie, K. W. (in press). Late life potential and cohort differences in mental abilities. In M. Perlmutter (ed.), *Late life potentials.* Washington, DC: Gerontological Society of America. (chap. 9)

Schaie, K. W., and C. Hertzog. (1982). Longitudinal methods. In B. B. Wolman (ed.), *Handbook of developmental psychology.* Englewood Cliffs, NJ: Prentice–Hall. (chap. 2)

Schaie, K. W., and C. Hertzog (1985). Measurement in the psychology of adulthood and aging. In J. E. Birren and K. W. Schaie (eds.), *Handbook of the psychology of aging.* 2nd ed. New York: Van Nostrand Reinhold. (chap. 2)

Schaie, K. W., and I. A. Parham. (1976). Stability of adult personality: Fact or fable? *Journal of Personality and Social Psychology, 36,* 146–158. (chap. 10)

Schaie, K. W., and S. L. Willis. (1986). Can declines in adult intellectual functioning be reversed? *Developmental Psychology, 22,* 223–232. (chaps. 1, 9)

Scheidt, R. J., and P. G. Windley. (1983). The mental health of small-town rural elderly residents: An expanded ecological model. *Journal of Gerontology, 38,* 472–479. (chap. 15)

Scheidt, R. J., and P. G. Windley. (1985). The ecology of aging. In J. E. Birren and K. W. Schaie (eds.), *Handbook of the psychology of aging.* 2nd ed. New York: Van Nostrand Reinhold. (chap. 5)

Schellenberg, G. D., T. D. Bird, E. M. Wijsman, D. K. Moore, M. Boehnke, E. M. Bryant, T. H. Lampe, D. Nochlin, S. M. Sumi, S. S. Deeb, K. Beyreuther, and G. M. Martin. (1988). Absence of linkage of Chromosome 21q21 markers to familial Alzheimer's disease. *Science, 241,* 1507–1510. (chap. 6)

Scheper-Hughes, N. (1983). Deposed kings: The demise of the rural Irish gerontocracy. In J. Sokolovsky (ed.), *Growing old in different societies.* Belmont, CA: Wadsworth. (chap. 16)

Schmid, R. E. (June 22, 1989). Motherhood in America. *Reporter Dispatch,* A1, A10. (chap. 16)

Schmidt, D. F., and S. M. Boland. (1986). Structure of perceptions of older adults: Evidence for multiple stereotypes. *Psychology and Aging, 1,* 255–260. (chap. 1)

Schneider, J. E., and G. N. Wade. (June 16, 1989). Availability of metabolic fuels controls estrous cyclicity of Syrian hamsters. *Science, 244,* 1326–1328. (chap. 2)

Schonfield, A.E.D., H. Davidson, and H. Jones. (1983). An example of age-associated interference in memory. *Journal of Gerontology, 38,* 204–210. (chap. 8)

Schrank, H. T., and J. M. Waring. (1983). Aging and work organizations. In M. W. Riley, B. B.

Hess, and K. Bond (eds.), *Aging in society.* Hillsdale, NJ: Lawrence Erlbaum Associates. (chap. 13)

Schroedel, J. R. (1986). *Alone in a crowd.* Philadelphia: Temple University Press. (chap. 13)

Schulz, R. (1982). Emotionality and aging: A theoretical and empirical analysis. *Journal of Gerontology, 37,* 42–51. (chap. 10)

Schulz, R., and C. Curnow. (1988). Peak performance and age among superathletes: Track and field, swimming, baseball, tennis, and golf. *Journal of Gerontology, 43,* P113–120. (chap. 4)

Schweitzer, M. M. (1983). The elders: Cultural dimensions of aging in two American Indian communities. In J. Sokolovsky (ed.), *Growing old in different societies.* Belmont, CA: Wadsworth. (chap. 16)

Scialfa, C. T., and D. W. Kline. (1988). Effects of noise type and retinal eccentricity on age differences in identification and location. *Journal of Gerontology, 43,* P91–99. (chap. 7)

Scott-Maxwell, F. (1979). *The measure of my days.* New York: Penguin. (chap. 10)

Sears, P. S., and A. H. Barbee. (1978). Career and life satisfaction among Terman's gifted women. In *The gifted and the creative: Fifty-year perspective.* Baltimore: Johns Hopkins University Press. (chap. 10)

Sears, R. R. (1977). Sources of life satisfaction of the Terman gifted men. *American Psychologist, 32,* 119–128. (chap. 10)

Seashore, S. E., and J. T. Barnowe. (August 1972). Collar color doesn't count. *Psychology Today, 6,* 53–54 +. (chap. 13)

Sekuler, R., and R. Blake. (1985). *Perception.* New York: Random House. (chap. 7)

Sekuler, R., and R. Blake. (December 1987). Sensory underload. *Psychology Today, 21,* 48–51. (chap. 7)

Self, P. A. (1975). The further evolution of the parental imperative. In N. Datan and L. H. Ginsberg (eds.), *Life-span developmental psychology: Normative life crises.* New York: Academic Press. (chap. 10)

Seligman, M.E.P. (October 1988). Boomer blues. *Psychology Today,* 50–55. (chap. 6)

Seligmann, J. (November 25, 1985). Women smokers: The risk factor. *Newsweek,* 76–78. (chap. 5)

Seligmann, J. (Winter/Spring 1990). Variations on a theme, *The 21st century family, Newsweek,* 38–46. (chap. 12)

Selmanowitz, V. J., R. I. Rizer, and N. Orentreich. (1977). Aging of the skin and its appendages. In C. E. Finch and L. Hayflick (eds.), *Handbook of the biology of aging.* New York: Van Nostrand Reinhold. (chap. 4)

Serow, W. J. (1987). Determinants of interstate migration: Differences between elderly and nonelderly movers. *Journal of Gerontology, 42,* 95–100. (chap. 15)

Shah, I. (1979). *World tales.* New York: Harcourt Brace Jovanovich. (chap. 2)

Shanan, J., and R. Sagiv. (1982). Sex differences in intellectual performance during middle age. *Human Development, 25,* 24–33. (chap. 9)

Shanas, E. (1979). Social myth as hypothesis: The case of the family relations of old people. *Gerontologist, 19,* 3–9. (chap. 12)

Shanas, E., and G. Heinemann. (1982). *National survey of the aged.* DHHS Publication No. (OHDS)83–20425. Washington, DC: Department of Health and Human Services. (chap. 11)

Sheehy, G. (1976). *Passages.* New York: Dutton. (chap. 10)

Sheils, M., M. Hager, C. Leslie, and D. Foote. (June 1, 1981). Can you afford to retire? *Newsweek,* 24–34. (chap. 15)

Shneidman, E. S. (1980). *Death: Current perspectives.* 2nd ed. Palo Alto, CA: Mayfield. (chap. 5)

Shneidman, E. S., and N. L. Farberow. (1970). Attempted and completed suicide. In E. S. Shneidman, N. L. Farberow, and R. E. Litman (eds.), *The psychology of suicide.* New York: Science House. (chap. 6)

Shock, N. W. (1977). Biological theories of aging. In J. E. Birren and K. W. Schaie (eds.), *Handbook of the psychology of aging.* New York: Van Nostrand Reinhold. (chap. 2)

Shock, N. W. (1985). Longitudinal studies of aging in humans. In C. E. Finch and E. L. Schneider (eds.), *Handbook of the biology of aging.* 2nd ed. New York: Van Nostrand Reinhold. (chap. 2)

Siegel, J. S., and C. M. Taeuber. (Winter 1986). Demographic perspectives on the long-lived society. *Daedalus, 115,* 77–117. (chap. 1)

Siegler, I. C., and P. T. Costa, Jr. (1985). Health behavior relationships. In J. E. Birren and K. W. Schaie (eds.), *Handbook of the psychology of aging.* 2nd ed. New York: Van Nostrand. (chap. 5)

Siegler, I. C., L. K. George, and M. A. Okun. (1979). Cross-sequential analysis of adult personality. *Developmental Psychology, 15,* 350–351. (chap. 9)

Siegler, I. C., S. M. McCarty, and P. E. Logue. (1982). Wechsler Memory Scale scores, selective attrition, and distance from death. *Journal of Gerontology, 37,* 176–181. (chap. 9)

Simmons, L. W. (1945). *The role of the aged in primitive society.* New Haven, CT: Yale University Press. (chap. 16)

Simon, A. (1980). The neuroses, personality disorders, alcoholism, drug use and misuse, and crime in the aged. In J. E. Birren and R. B. Sloane (eds.), *Handbook of mental health and aging.* Englewood Cliffs, NJ: Prentice–Hall. (chap. 6)

Simon, E. W., R. A. Dixon, C. A. Nowak, and D. F. Hultsch. (1982). Orienting task effects on text-recall in adulthood. *Journal of Gerontology, 37,* 575–580. (chap. 8)

Simonton, D. K. (1988). Age and outstanding achievement: What do we know after a century of research? *Psychological Bulletin, 104,* 251–267. (chap. 9)

Simonton, D. K. (1989). The swan-song phenomenon: Last-works effects for 172 classical composers. *Psychology and Aging, 4,* 42–47. (chap. 9)

Simonton, D. K. (1990). Creativity and wisdom in aging. In J. E. Birren and K. W. Schaie (eds.), *Handbook of the psychology of aging.* 3rd ed. San Diego, CA: Academic Press. (chap. 9)

Simonton, D. K. (in press). Does creativity decline in the later years? Definition, data, and theory. In M. Perlmutter (ed.), *Late-life potential.* Washington, DC: Gerontological Society of America. (chap. 9)

Simpson, J. B. (1988). *Simpson's contemporary quotations.* Boston, MA: Houghton Mifflin. (chap. 10)

Sinnott, J. D. (1986). Sex roles and aging: Theory and research from a systems perspective. *Contributions to human development:* Vol. 15. New York: Karger. (chap. 10)

Sivak, M., P. L. Olson, and L. A. Pastalan. (1981). Effect of driver's age on nighttime legibility of signs. *Human Factors, 23,* 59–64. (chap. 7)

Skinner, B. F. (1983). Intellectual self-management in old age. *American Psychologist, 38,* 239–244. (chap. 8)

Skodol, A. E., and R. L. Spitzer. (1983). Depression in the elderly: Clinical criteria. In L. D. Breslau and M. R. Haug (eds.), *Depression and aging.* New York: Springer. (chap. 6)

Skolnick, A. (1981). Married lives: Longitudinal perspective on marriage. In D. H. Eichorn, J. A. Clausen, N. Haan, M. P. Honzik, and P. H. Mussen (eds.), *Present and past in middle life.* New York: Academic Press. (chap. 11)

Skre, H. (1972). Neurological signs in a normal population. *Acta Neurologica Scandinavia, 48,* 575–606. (chap. 7)

Sloane, R. B. (1980). Organic brain syndrome. In J. E. Birren and R. B. Sloane (eds.), *Handbook of mental health and aging.* Englewood Cliffs, NJ: Prentice–Hall. (chap. 6)

Smeeding, T. M. (1990). Economic status of the elderly. In R. H. Binstock and E. Shanas (eds.), *Handbook of aging and the social sciences.* 3rd ed. San Diego, CA: Academic Press. (chaps. 14, 15)

Smith, E. L., and C. Gilligan. (1983). Physical activity prescription for the older adult. *The Physician and Sports Medicine, 11,* 91–101. (chap. 4)

Smyer, M. A., S. H. Zarit, and S. H. Qualls. (1990). Psychological intervention with the aging individual. In J. E. Birren and K. W. Schaie (eds.), *Handbook of the psychology of aging.* 3rd ed. San Diego, CA: Academic Press. (chap. 6)

Snyder, C. J., and G. V. Barrett. (1988). The Age Discrimination in Employment Act: A review of court decisions. *Experimental Aging Research, 14,* 3–47. (chap. 15)

Snyder, P. C. (1979). Future pension status of the

black elderly. In D. E. Gelfand and A. J. Kutzik (eds.), *Ethnicity and aging: Theory, research, and policy.* New York: Springer. (chap. 16)

Sobel, D. (August 20, 1990). B. F. Skinner is dead at 86; Pioneer of behavior studies. *New York Times,* A1, B10. (chap. 8)

Solnick, R. L., and J. E. Birren. (1977). Age and male erectile responsiveness. *Archives of Sexual Behavior, 6,* 1–9. (chap. 4)

Solomon, P. R., D. Pomerleau, L. Bennett, J. James, and D. L. Morse. (1989). Acquisition of the classically conditioned eyeblink response in humans over the life span. *Psychology and Aging, 4,* 34–41. (chap. 8)

Sorock, G. S., T. L. Bush, A. L. Golden, L. P. Fried, B. Breuer, and W. E. Hale. (1988). Physical activity and fracture risk in a free-living elderly cohort. *Journal of Gerontology, 43,* M134–139. (chaps. 5, 14)

Spanier, G. B., and R. A. Lewis. (1980). Marital quality: A review of the seventies. *Journal of Marriage and the Family, 42,* 825–839. (chap. 11)

Sparrow, P. R., and D. R. Davies. (1988). Effects of age, tenure, training, and job complexity on technical performance. *Psychology and Aging, 3,* 307–314. (chap. 13)

Spearman, C. (1927). *The abilities of man.* New York: Macmillan. (chap. 9)

Spence, A. P. (1989). *Biology of human aging.* Englewood Cliffs, NJ: Prentice–Hall. (chaps. 3, 4, 5, 6, 7)

Spence, J. T. (1979). Traits, roles, and the concept of androgyny. In J. E. Gullahorn (ed.), *Psychology and women: In transition.* New York: Wiley. (chap. 10)

Spencer, G. (May 1984). Projections of the population of the United States by age, sex, and race: 1983 to 2080. U.S. Bureau of the Census, *Current Population Reports,* Series P–25. (chap. 3)

Spencer, R. F. (1957). Evolution and development: A view of anthropology. In D. B. Harris (ed.), *The concept of development.* Minneapolis: University of Minneapolis Press. (chap. 2)

Spitzer, M. E. (1988). Taste acuity in institutional-ized and noninstitutionalized elderly men. *Journal of Gerontology, 43,* P71–74. (chap. 7)

Starr, B. D., and M. B. Weiner. (1981). *The Starr–Weiner report on sex and sexuality in the mature years.* New York: Stein & Day. (chap. 11)

Stenback, A. (1980). Depression and suicidal behavior in old age. In J. E. Birren and R. B. Sloane (eds.), *Handbook of mental health and aging.* Englewood Cliffs, NJ: Prentice–Hall. (chap. 6)

Stephens, R. (September 1989). Older workers: Out in the rain. *AARP Bulletin, 30,* 2. (chap. 15)

Sternberg, R. J. (1985). *Beyond IQ: A triarchic theory of human intelligence.* New York: Cambridge University Press. (chap. 9)

Sternberg, R. J. (1986). A triangular theory of love. *Psychological Review, 93,* 119–135. (chap. 11)

Sternberg, R. J., and C. A. Berg. (1987). What are theories of intellectual development theories of? In C. Schooler and K. W. Schaie (eds.), *Cognitive functioning and social structure over the life course.* New York: Ablex. (chap. 9)

Sternberg, R. J., and R. K. Wagner (eds.). (1986). *Practical intelligence.* New York: Cambridge University Press. (chap. 1)

Sterns, H. L., G. V. Barrett, and R. A. Alexander. (1985). Accidents and the aging individual. In J. E. Birren and K. W. Schaie (eds.), *Handbook of the psychology of aging.* 2nd ed. New York: Van Nostrand Reinhold. (chap. 7)

Stevens, D. P., and C. V. Truss. (1985). Stability and change in adult personality over 12 and 20 years. *Developmental Psychology, 21,* 568–584. (chap. 10)

Stockton, W. (November 28, 1988). Can exercise alter the aging process? *New York Times.* (chap. 5)

Stoller, E. P., and M. A. Stoller. (1987). The propensity to save among the elderly. *Gerontologist, 27,* 314–320. (chap. 15)

Storck, P., W. Looft, and F. H. Hooper. (1972). Interrelationships among Piagetian tasks and traditional measures of cognitive abilities in mature and aged adults. *Journal of Gerontology, 27,* 461–465. (chap. 9)

Streissguth, A. P., H. M. Barr, and D. C. Martin. (1983). Maternal alcohol use and neonatal habituation assessed with the Brazelton Scale. *Child Development, 54,* 1109–1118. (chap. 5)

Streissguth, A. P., D. C. Martin, H. M. Barr, B. M. Sandman, G. L. Kirchner, and B. L. Darby. (1984). Intrauterine alcohol and nicotine exposure. *Developmental Psychology, 20,* 533–541. (chap. 5)

Stuckey, M. F., P. E. McGhee, and N. J. Bell. (1982). Parent–child interaction: The influence of maternal employment. *Developmental Psychology, 18,* 635–644. (chap. 12)

Sudarkasa, N. (1981). Interpreting the African heritage in Afro-American family organization. In H. McAdoo (ed.), *Black families.* Beverly Hills, CA: Sage. (chap. 16)

Sunderland, A., K. Watts, A. D. Baddeley, and J. E. Harris. (1986). Subjective memory assessment and test performance in elderly adults. *Journal of Gerontology, 41,* 376–384. (chap. 8)

Super, D. E. (1957). *The psychology of careers.* New York: Harper & Row. (chap. 13)

Super, D. E. (1980). A life span, life space approach to career development. *Journal of Vocational Behavior, 16,* 282–298. (chap. 13)

Super, D. E. (1985). Coming of age in Middletown: Careers in the making. *American Psychologist, 40,* 405–414. (chap. 13)

Sweet, J. A., and L. L. Bumpass. (1987). *American families and households.* New York: Russell Sage Foundation. (chap. 11)

Swensen, C. H. (1983). A respectable old age. *American Psychologist, 38,* 327–334. (chap. 13)

Takeda, S., and T. Matsuzawa. (1985). Age-related brain atrophy. *Journal of Gerontology, 40,* 159–163. (chap. 4)

Tannenhauser, C. (January 20, 1987). Women with a cause. *Woman's Day,* 96–97, 147–148, 150. (chaps. 14, 15)

Tate, N. (1983). The black aging experience. In R. L. McNeely and J. L. Cohen (eds.), *Aging in minority groups.* Beverly Hills, CA: Sage. (chap. 16)

Tavris, C. A., and C. Offir. (1977). *The longest war: Sex differences in perspective.* New York: Harcourt Brace Jovanovich. (chap. 10)

Taylor, R. N. (1975). Age and experience as determinants of managerial information processing and decision-making performance. *Academy of Management Journal, 18,* 74–84. (chap. 13)

Taylor, S. C. (June/July 1990). Everyday heroes. *Modern Maturity, 33,* 40–45. (chap. 14)

Terkel, S. (1974). *Working.* New York: Pantheon. (chap. 13)

Terry, R. D. and colleagues of UCSD School of Medicine. Described in *Psychology Today,* December 1988, p. 22. (chap. 4)

Tetrud, J. W., and J. W. Langston. (1989). The effect of deprenyl (selegiline) on the natural history of Parkinson's disease. *Science, 245,* 519–522. (chap. 6)

Thomae, H. (1979). The concept of development and life-span developmental psychology. In P. B. Baltes and O. G. Brim, Jr. (eds.), *Life-span development and behavior.* Vol. 2. New York: Academic Press. (chap. 1)

Thomae, H. (1980). Personality and adjustment in aging. In J. E. Birren and R. B. Sloane (eds.), *Handbook of mental health and aging.* Englewood Cliffs, NJ: Prentice–Hall. (chap. 10)

Thomas, P. D., W. C. Hunt, P. J. Garry, R. B. Hood, J. M. Godwin, and J. S. Goodwin. (1983). Hearing acuity in a healthy elderly population: Effects on emotional, cognitive, and social status. *Journal of Gerontology, 38,* 321–325. (chap. 7)

Thurstone, L. L. (1935). *Vectors of mind.* Chicago: University of Chicago Press. (chap. 9)

Tice, R. R., and R. B. Setlow. (1985). DNA repair and replication in aging organisms and cells. In C. E. Finch and E. L. Schneider (eds.), *Handbook of the biology of aging.* 2nd ed. New York: Van Nostrand Reinhold. (chap. 3)

Tinsley, B. R., and R. D. Parke. (1984). Grandparents as support and socialization agents. In M. Lewis (ed.), *Beyond the dyad.* New York: Plenum Press. (chap. 1)

Tolchin, M. (April 16, 1989). 23% in a study feel they retired too early. *New York Times,* 27. (chap. 13)

Tolchin, M. (June 17, 1990). More states trying to curb teen-age pregnancies. *New York Times,* A24. (chap. 15)

Tonna, E. A. (1977). Aging of skeletal-dental systems and supporting tissue. In C. E. Finch and L. Hayflick (eds.), *Handbook of the biology of aging.* New York: Van Nostrand Reinhold. (chap. 4)

Torres–Gil, F. (Winter 1986). Hispanics in an aging society. *Daedalus, 115,* 325–248. (chap. 16)

Torrey, B. B., K. G. Kinsella, and C. M. Taueber. (forthcoming). In U.S. Bureau of the Census, *An aging world.* Washington, DC: U.S. Government Printing Office. (chap. 16)

Toseland, R. W., and C. M. Rossiter. (1989). Group intervention to support family caregivers. *Gerontologist, 29,* 438–448. (chap. 6)

Tracy, N. M. (July 10, 1983). Woman, 27, deals with isolating horror of progeria. *Minneapolis Tribune,* 1F + . (chap. 3)

Traupmann, J., E. Eckels, and E. Hatfield.. (1982). Intimacy in older women's lives. *Gerontologist, 22,* 493–498. (chap. 11)

Treiman, D. J. (1985). The work histories of women and men: What we know and what we need to find out. In A. Rossi (ed.), *Gender and the life course.* New York: Aldine. (chap. 13)

Trimikas, K., and R. C. Nicholay. (1974). Self-concept and altruism in old age. *Journal of Gerontology, 29,* 434–439. (chap. 10)

Troll, L. E., S. J. Miller, and R. C. Atchley. (1979). *Families in later life.* Belmont, CA: Wadsworth. (chap. 12)

Tu Wei–Ming. (1978). The Confucian perception of adulthood. In E. H. Erikson (ed.), *Adulthood.* New York: Norton. (chap. 16)

Turkington, C. (January 1987). Alzheimer's & aluminum. *APA Monitor,* 1. (chap. 6)

Turnbull, C. M. (1972). *The mountain people.* New York: Simon & Schuster. (chap. 16)

Turnbull, C. M. (1983). *The human cycle.* New York: Simon & Schuster. (chap. 16)

Turner, B. (1979). The self concept of older women. *Research on Aging, 1,* 464–480. (chap. 10)

Twain, M. [1876] (1936). *The adventures of Tom Sawyer.* New York: Heritage Press. (chap. 13)

Uchitelle, L. (May 29, 1990). Company-financed pensions are failing to fulfill promise. *New York Times,* Al, D5. (chap. 15)

Udry, J. R. (1980). Changes in the frequency of marital intercourse from panel data. *Archives of Sexual Behavior, 9,* 319–325. (chap. 14)

Uhlenberg, P., T. Cooney, and R. Boyd. (1990). Divorce for women after midlife. *Journal of Gerontology: Social Sciences, 45,* S3–11. (chap. 11)

Uhlmann, R. F., R. A. Pearlman, and K. C. Cain. (1988). Physicians' and spouses' predictions of elderly patients' resuscitation preferences. *Journal of Gerontology: Medical Sciences, 43,* M115–121. (chap. 5)

U.S. Bureau of the Census. (1983). *Estimates of the population of the United States, by age, sex, and race: 1980–82,* P–25, No. 929. Washington, DC: U.S. Government Printing Office. (chap. 3)

U.S. Bureau of the Census. (1989). *Statistical abstract of the United States.* 109th ed. Washington, DC: U.S. Government Printing Office. (chaps. 1, 11, 12, 13)

U.S. Bureau of the Census. (1990). *Statistical abstract of the United States.* 110th ed. Washington, DC: U.S. Government Printing Office. (chaps. 5, 6, 12, 13, 16)

U. S. Bureau of Labor Statistics. (February 1986). *Monthly Labor Review.* (chap. 12)

U.S. Public Health Service. (1979). *Healthy people: The surgeon general's report on health promotion and disease prevention.* DHEW Pub. No. 79–55071. Washington, DC: U.S. Government Printing Office. (chap. 5)

U.S. Senate. Special Committee on Aging. (1987–1988). *Aging America: Trends and Projections.* Washington, DC: U.S. Department of Health and Human Services. (chaps. 1, 3, 5, 6, 14, 15)

Uttal, D. H., and M. Perlmutter. (1989). Toward a broader conceptualization of development: The role of gains and losses across the life span. *Developmental Review, 9,* 101–132. (chap. 1)

Vailliant, G. E. (1977). *Adaptation to life.* Boston: Little, Brown. (chaps. 10, 13)

Vaillant, G. E., and E. Milofsky. (1980). Natural history of male psychological health: IX. Empirical evidence for Erikson's model of the life cycle. *American Journal of Psychiatry, 137,* 1348–1359. (chap. 10)

van den Berghe, P. (1983). Age differentiation in human societies. In J. Sokolovsky (ed.), *Growing old in different societies.* Belmont, CA: Wadsworth. (chap. 16)

Vatuk, S. (1980). Withdrawal and disengagement as a cultural-response to aging in India. In C. L. Fry (ed.), *Aging in culture and society.* New York: Praeger. (chap. 16)

Vecsey, G. (March 16, 1983). Survey discloses a nation of fans. *New York Times,* 25. (chap. 14)

Vecsey, G. (June 28, 1983). Mrs. King in a familiar spot. New York Times, A25. (chap. 4)

Verrillo, R. T., and V. Verrillo. (1985). Sensory and perceptual performance. In N. Charness (ed.), *Aging and human performance.* New York: Wiley. (chap. 7)

Vestal, R. E., and G. W. Dawson. (1985). Pharmacology and aging. In C. E. Finch and E. L. Schneider (eds.), *Handbook of the biology of aging.* 2nd ed. New York: Van Nostrand Reinhold. (chap. 4)

Visintainer, M. A., J. R. Volpicelli, and M.E.P. Seligman. (1982). Tumor rejection in rats after inescapable or escapable shock. *Science, 216,* 437–439. (chap. 5)

Voda, A., M. Dinnerstein, and S. O'Donnell (eds.). (1982). *Changing perspectives on menopause.* Austin: University of Texas Press. (chap. 4)

Vygotsky, L. S. (1978). *Mind in society.* Cambridge, MA: Harvard University Press. (chap. 1)

Waldman, D. A., and B. J. Avolio. (1986). A meta-analysis of age-differences in job performance. *Journal of Applied Psychology, 71,* 33–38. (chap. 13)

Walford, R. L. (1983). *Maximum life span.* New York: Norton. (chaps. 3, 4)

Walford, R. L. (1986). *The 120-year-diet.* New York: Simon & Schuster. (chap. 3)

Wallerstein, J. S., and S. Blakeslee. (1989). *Second chances.* New York: Ticknor & Fields. (chaps. 11, 12)

Wall Street Journal. (June 14, 1988). Soon, most people may have "lived in sin." 37. (chap. 11)

Walsh, D. A. (1982). The development of visual processes in adulthood and old age. In F.I.M. Craik and S. Trehub (eds.), *Aging and cognitive processes.* New York: Plenum. (chap. 7)

Walters, J. (1987). Lasting intimacy. *Longevity, 1,* no. 5, 37–38. (chap. 11)

Walther, R. J. (1983). Economics of aging. In D. S. Woodruff and J. E. Birren (eds.), *Aging: Scientific perspectives and social issues.* 2nd ed. Monterey, CA: Brooks/Cole. (chap. 15)

Wang, H. S., and E. W. Busse. (1969). EEG of healthy old persons—A longitudinal study: I. Dominant background activity and occipital rhythm. *Journal of Gerontology, 24,* 419–426. (chap. 4)

Wang, H. S., W. D. Obrist, and E. W. Busse. (1970). Neurophysiological correlates of the intellectual function of elderly persons living in the community. *American Journal of Psychiatry, 126,* 1204–1212. (chap. 4)

Wanner, R. A., and L. McDonald. (1983). Ageism in the labor market: Estimating earnings discrimination against older workers. *Journal of Gerontology, 38,* 738–745. (chap. 13)

Wantz, M. S., and J. E. Gay. (1981). *The aging process: A health perspective.* Cambridge, Mass.: Winthrop. (chaps. 4, 5, 7)

Ward, R. A. (1984). *The aging experience.* New York: Harper & Row. (chap. 13)

Warren, L. R., R. W. Butler, C. R. Katholi, and J. H. Halsey, Jr. (1985). Age differences in cerebral blood flow during rest and during mental activation with and without monetary incentive. *Journal of Gerontology, 40,* 53–59. (chap. 8)

Washburn, S. L. (1981). Longevity in primates. In J. L. McGaugh and S. B. Kiesler (eds.), *Aging: Biology and Behavior.* New York: Academic Press. (chap. 3)

Waterman, A. S. (1982). Identity development from adolescence to adulthood: An extension of theory and a review of research. *Developmental Psychology, 18,* 341–358. (chap. 10)

Weber, F., R. J. Barnard, and D. Roy. (1983). Effects of a high-complex-carbohydrate, low-fat diet and daily exercise on individuals 70 years of age and older. *Journal of Gerontology, 38,* 155–161. (chap. 3)

Weber, M. (1947). *The theory of social and economic organizations.* New York: Oxford University Press. (chap. 15)

Weg, R. B. (1983). Changing physiology of aging: Normal and pathological. In D. S. Woodruff and J. E. Birren (eds.), *Aging: Scientific perspectives and social issues.* 2nd ed. Monterey, CA: Brooks/Cole. (chaps. 1, 4)

Weindruch, R., and R. L. Walford. (1988). *The retardation of aging and disease by dietary restriction.* Springfield, IL: Charles C. Thomas. (chaps. 3, 5)

Weingartner, H., J. Grafman, W. Boutelle, W. Kaye, and P. R. Martin. (1983). Forms of memory failure. *Science, 221,* 380–382. (chap. 6)

Weir, M. W. (1964). Developmental changes in problem-solving strategies. *Psychological Review, 71,* 473–490. (chap. 1)

Weishaus, S., and D. Field. (1988). A half century of marriage: Continuity or change? *Journal of Marriage and the Family, 50,* 763–774. (chap. 11)

Weisman, A. D. (1972). *On dying and denying: A psychiatric study of terminality.* New York: Behavioral Publications. (chap. 5)

Weiss, R. S. (1979). *Going it alone: The family life and social situation of the single parent.* New York: Basic Books. (chap. 12)

Weissart, W. G., J. M. Elston, E. J. Bolda, C. M. Cready, W. N. Zelman, P. D. Sloane, W. D. Kalsbeek, E. Mutran, T. H. Rice, and G. G. Koch. (1989). Models of adult day care: Findings from a national survey. *Gerontologist, 29,* 640–649. (chap. 15)

Weissman, M. M. (1979). The myth of involutional melancholia. *Journal of the American Medical Association, 242,* 742–744. (chap. 6)

Weitzman, L. J. (1985). *The divorce revolution.* New York: Free Press. (chap. 11)

Weizsacker, C. F. von. (1980). Ageing as a process of evolution. In *Conference on structural pathology in DNA and the biology of aging.* Bonn: Deutsche Forschungsgemeinschaft. (chap. 3)

Wender, P. H., S. S. Kety, D. Rosenthal, F. Schulsinger, J.. Ortmann, and I. Lunde. (1986). Psychiatric disorders in the biological and adoptive studies of adopted individuals with affective disorders. *Archives of General Psychiatry, 43,* 923–929. (chap. 6)

Wentowski, G. J. (1985). Older women's perceptions of great-grandmotherhood. *Gerontologist, 25,* 593–596. (chap. 12)

Wesley–King, S. (1983). Service utilization and the minority elderly. In R. L. McNeely and J. L. Cohen (eds.), *Aging in minority groups.* Beverly Hills, CA: Sage. (chap. 16)

West, R. L. (August 1984). An analysis of prospective everyday memory. Paper presented at the annual meeting of the American Psychological Society. Toronto. (chap. 8)

Westchester Self-Help Clearing House. (1989). *Directory of self-help groups in Westchester County.* 7th ed. Valhalla, NY: Westchester Self–Help Clearing House. (chap. 15)

Whitbourne, S. (1985). *The aging body: Physiological changes and psychological consequences.* New York: Springer–Verlag. (chap. 7)

White, A. T., and P. E. Spector. (1987). An investigation of age-related factors in the age-job-satisfaction relationship. *Psychology and Aging, 2,* 261–265. (chap. 13)

White, N., and W. R. Cunningham. (1988). Is terminal drop pervasive or specific? *Journal of Gerontology: Psychological Sciences, 43,* P141–144. (chap. 9)

White, S. E., and K. Reamy. (1982). Sexuality and pregnancy: A review. *Archives of Sexual Behavior, 11,* 429–443. (chap. 12)

Williams, G. C. (1957). Pleiotropy, natural selection and the evolution of senescence. *Evolution, 11,* 398–411. (chap. 3)

Williams, G. C. (1980). Warriors no more: A study of the American Indian elderly. In C. L. Fry (ed.), *Aging in culture and society.* New York: Praeger. (chap. 16)

Willis, L., P. Thomas, P. J. Garry, and J. S. Goodwin. (1987). A prospective study of response to stressful life events in initially healthy elders. *Journal of Gerontology, 42,* 627–630. (chap. 5)

Willis, S. L. (1985). Towards an educational psychology of the older adult learner: Intellectual and cognitive bases. In J. E. Birren and K. W. Schaie (eds.), *Handbook of the psychology of aging.* 2nd ed. New York: Van Nostrand Reinhold. (chap. 14)

Willis, S. L. (in press). Contributions of cognitive training research to understanding late life potential. In M. Perlmutter (ed.), *Late-life potential.* Washington, DC: Gerontological Society of America. (chaps. 8, 9)

Willits, F. K., and D. M. Crider. (1988). Health rating and life satisfaction in the later middle years. *Journal of Gerontology: Social Sciences, 43,* S172–176. (chap. 10)

Wilson, J. (1980). Sociology of leisure. *Annual Review of Sociology, 6,* 21–40. (chap. 14)

Wilson, M. N. (1986). The black extended family: An analytical consideration. *Developmental Psychology, 22,* 246–258. (chap. 16)

Windley, P. G., and J. R. Scheidt. (1980). Person-environment dialectics: Implications for competent functioning in old age. In L. W. Poon (ed.), *Aging in the 1980s: Psychological issues.* Washington, DC: American Psychological Association. (chap. 5)

Wing, S., K. G. Manton, E. Stallard, C. G. Hames, and H. A. Tryoler. (1985). The black/white mortality crossover. *Journal of Gerontology, 40,* 78–84. (chap. 3)

Wister, A. V., and L. Strain. (1986). Social support and well-being: A comparison of older widows and widowers. *Canadian Journal on Aging, 5,* 205–220. (chap. 11)

Wolfinger, R. E., and S. J. Rosenstone. (1980). *Who votes?* New Haven, CT: Yale University Press. (chap. 14)

Woodruff, D. S. (1983). Physiology and behavior relationships in aging. In D. S. Woodruff and J. E. Birren (eds.), *Aging: Scientific perspectives and social issues.* 2nd ed. Monterey, CA: Brooks/Cole. (chap. 7)

Woodruff, D. S., and J. E. Birren. (1972). Age changes and cohort differences in personality. *Developmental Psychology, 6,* 252–259. (chaps. 2, 10)

Woodruff–Pak, D. S. (1987). Personal communication. Temple University. (chap. 3)

Woodruff–Pak, D. S. (1990). Mammalian models of learning, memory and aging. In J. E. Birren and K. W. Schaie (eds.), *Handbook of the psychology of aging.* 3rd ed. San Diego, CA: Academic Press. (chap. 8)

Woodward, K. L. (March 27, 1989). Heaven. *Newsweek,* 52–55. (chap. 14)

Woodward, K. L. (Winter/Spring 1990). Young beyond their years. *Newsweek: The Family,* 54–60. (chap. 15)

Wright, P. H. (1982). Men's friendships, women's friendships, and the alleged inferiority of the latter. *Sex Roles, 8,* 1–20. (chap. 11)

Wu, F. (1975). Mandarin-speaking Chinese in the Los Angeles area. *Gerontologist, 15,* 271–275. (chap. 16)

Yankelovich, D. (1981). *New rules.* New York: Random House. (chaps. 11, 12, 14)

Yarrow, A. L. (January 12, 1987). Divorce at a young age: The troubled 20's. *New York Times,* A19. (chap. 11)

Yerkes, R. M. (1921). Psychological examining in the United States Army. *Memoirs of the National Academy of Sciences, 15,* 1–890. (chap. 9)

Yesavage, J. A., T. L. Rose, and G. H. Bower. (1983). Interactive imagery and affective judgments improve face-name learning in the elderly. *Journal of Gerontology, 38,* 197–203. (chap. 8)

Young, G., and W. Dowling. (1987). Dimensions of religiosity in old age: Accounting for variation in types of participation. *Journal of Gerontology, 42,* 376–380. (chap. 14)

Yu, B. P., E. J. Masoro, and C. A. McMahan. (1985). Nutritional influences on aging of Fischer 344 rats. I. Physical, metabolic and longevity characteristics. *Journal of Gerontology, 40,* 657–670. (chap. 3)

Yu, E.S.H., C. Chang, W. T. Liu, and S. H. Kan. (1985). Asian-white mortality differences: Are there excess deaths? In Department of Health and Human Services (ed.), *Black and minority health.* Vol. III: *Cross-cutting issues in minority health.*

Washington, DC: U.S. Department of Health and Human Services. (chap. 16)

Zabarsky, M. (November 1, 1982). The patriarch of a commune. *Newsweek*, 62. (chap. 11)

Zacks, R. T. (1982). Encoding strategies used by young and elderly adults in a keeping track task. *Journal of Gerontology, 37*, 203–211. (chap. 8)

Zaks, P. M., and G. Labouvie–Vief. (1980). Spatial perspective taking and referential communication skills in the elderly: A training study. *Journal of Gerontology, 37*, 203–211. (chap. 8)

Zambrana, R. E., R.. Merino, and S. Santana. (1979). Health services and the Puerto Rican elderly. In D. E. Gelfand and A. J. Kutzik (eds.), *Ethnicity and aging: Theory, research, and policy.* New York: Springer. (chap. 16)

Zarit, S. H. (1980). *Aging and mental disorders.* New York: Free Press. (chaps. 5, 6)

Zarit, S. H., J. M. Zarit, and K. E. Reever. (1982). Memory training for severe memory loss: Effects on senile dementia patients and their families. *Gerontologist, 22*, 373–377. (chap. 6)

Zatz, L. M., T. L. Jernigan, and A. J. Ahumada. (1982). Changes on computed cranial tomography with aging: Intracranial fluid volume. *American Journal of Neurological Research, 3*, 1–11. (chap. 4)

Zick, C. D., and K. R. Smith. (1986). Immediate and delayed effects of widowhood on poverty: Patterns from the 1970s. *Gerontologist, 26*, 669–675. (chap. 11)

Zimbardo, P. G. (August 1980). The age of indifference. *Psychology Today, 14*, 71–76. (chap. 14)

Zimbardo, P. G., S. M. Andersen, and L. G. Kabat. (1981). Induced hearing deficit generates experimental paranoia. *Science, 212*, 1529–1531. (chap. 7)

Zimberg, S. (1985). Treatment of the elderly alcoholic. In E. Gottheil, K. Druley, J. Skoloda, and H. Waxman (eds.), *The combined problems of alcoholism, drug addiction, and aging.* Springfield, IL: Charles C. Thomas. (chap. 6)

Zivian, M. T., and R. W. Darjes. (1983). Free recall by in-school and out-of-school adults: Performance and metamemory. *Developmental Psychology, 19*, 513–520. (chap. 8)

Zubin, J. (1973). Foundations of gerontology—History, training, and methodology. In C. Eisdorfer and M. P. Lawton (eds.), *The psychology of adult development and aging.* Washington, DC: American Psychological Association. (chap. 1)

♦ *Photo Credits*

Chapter 1 Opener: Chester Higgins Jr./Photo Researchers. Page 6: Joel Gordon. Page 15: Dan Budnick/Woodfin Camp & Associates. Page 22 (top): Topham/The Image Works. Page 22 (bottom): Joel Gordon. Page 24: J. Pickerell/Camerique.

Chapter 2 Opener: Ulrike Welsch. Page 35: Lionel Delevigne/Stock, Boston. Page 38: Charles Harbutt/Actuality. Page 43: Lora E. Askinazi/The Picture Cube.

Chapter 3 Opener: Elizabeth Crews/The Image Works. Page 65: Courtesy Mrs. Ruth Oberholtzer. Page 68: Jaye R. Phillips/The Picture Cube. Page 72: Bill Bachman/Photo Researchers. Page 74: Alan Carey/The Image Works.

Chapter 4 Opener: Jean-Claude Lejeune/Stock, Boston. Page 84: Frank Siteman/Jeroboam. Page 85: Spencer Grant/Stock, Boston. Page 105: Mark Sherman/Bruce Coleman. Page 115: Mimi Forsyth/Monkmeyer Press.

Chapter 5 Opener: Janice Fullman/The Picture Cube. Page 126: Hunter/The Image Works. Page 136: Howard Dratch/The Image Works. Page 139: Dion Ogust/The Image Works. Page 146: Ulrike Welsch. Page 151: Evan Johnson/Jeroboam.

Chapter 6 Opener: Ilka Hartmann/Jeroboam. Page 161: Mimi Forsyth/Monkmeyer Press. Page 165: Courtesy Dr. Curt Freed, University of Colorado Health Sciences Center. Page 169: Dion Ogust/The Image Works. Page 173: Ulrike Welsch/Photo Researchers. Page 175: J. Berndt/The Picture Cube. Page 177: Bill Aron/Photo Researchers.

Chapter 7 Opener: Michael Rothstein/Jeroboam. Page 185: Bob Daemmrich/The Image Works. Page 196: Robert V. Eckert, Jr./Stock, Boston. Page 203: Irene Bayer/Monkmeyer Press. Page 205: Frank Siteman/The Picture Cube.

Chapter 8 Opener: Abigail Heyman/Archive Pictures. Page 219: Robert Kalman/The Image Works. Pages 221 and 224: Alan Carey/The Image Works. Page 233: Paul Conklin/Monkmeyer Press. Page 238: Bill Aron/Photo Researchers.

Chapter 9 Opener: Les Mahon/Monkmeyer. Page 245: Robert Kalman/The Image Works. Page 249: Rhoda Sidney/The Image Works. Page 251: Karen Preuss/Jeroboam. Page 263: Jim Harrison/Stock, Boston. Page 267: Scala/Art Resource, NY.

Chapter 10 Opener: Photo by Patricia Valois from *Gifts of Age,* © 1987 by Charlotte Painter, Chronicle Books. Page 280: Laima Druskis/Jeroboam. Page 283: Shelly Gazin/The Image Works. Page 293: Roberta Hershenson/Photo Researchers. Page 308: Joel Gordon.

Chapter 11 Opener: Hazel Hankin. Page 317: Joel Gordon. Page 329: Bob Daemmrich/The Image Works. Page 331: Alan Carey/The Image Works. Page 337: Suzanne Arms/Jeroboam. Page 339: Michael Hayman/Stock, Boston.

Permission Source Notes

Chapter 1 Figure 1.5 D. Dannefer. ''Development as a multidimensional process: Individual and social constituents.'' *Human Development,* Vol. 33, 108–137. Copyright © 1990 with permission from D. Dannefer. Figure 1.6 P. B. Baltes, H. W. Reese, and L. P. Lipsitt. ''Life-Span Developmental Psychology.'' Reprinted from the *Annual Review of Psychology,* Vol. 31. © 1980 with permission from P. B. Baltes and Annual Reviews, Inc.

Chapter 4 Figures 4.1, 4.2, 4.4, 4.5, 4.6, 4.7, 4.9, 4.10, and 4.11 G. E. Nelson. *Biological Principles with Human Perspectives.* By John Wiley & Sons, Inc. Copyright © 1980, 1984. Reprinted by permission of John Wiley & Sons, Inc.

Chapter 5 Figure 5.2 G. Kaplan, V. Barell & A. Lusky. ''Subjective state of health and survival in elderly adults.'' *Journal of Gerontology,* Vol. 43, 1988. Copyright © 1988. Figure 5.3 Living Will. Copyright by the Society for the Right to Die. Reprinted by permission of the Society for the Right to Die, 250 West 57th Street, New York, NY 10107. Figure 5.4 ''Cardiovascular Research: Decades of Progress: A Decade of Promises,'' Levy, R. I. and Moskowitz, J., *Science,* Vol. 217, pp. 121–129, Fig. 2, 9 July 1982. Copyright 1982 by the AAAS. Figure 5.6 M. P. Lawton. *Environment and Aging.* Copyright © 1980 by American Psychological Association. Reprinted by permission of M. Powell Lawton.

Chapter 7 Figure 7.2 C. Owsley, R. Sekuler & D. Siemsen. ''Contrast Sensitivity throughout Adulthood.'' *Vision Research,* Vol. 23, 1983. By Vision Research—Pergamon Press. Copyright © 1983. Reprinted by permission of C. Owsley. Figure 7.3 G. E. Nelson. *Biological Principles with Human Perspectives.* By John Wiley & Sons, Inc. Copyright © 1980, 1984. Reprinted by permission of John Wiley & Sons, Inc.

Chapter 8 Figure 8.1 P. R. Solomon, D. Pomerleau, L. Bennett, J. James, and D. L. Morse. ''Acquisition of the classically conditioned eyeblink response in humans over the life span.'' *Psychology and Aging,* Vol. 4. Copyright © 1989 by American Psychological Association. Reprinted by permission of P. R. Solomon.

Chapter 9 Figure 9.1 ''Three-tier model of cognition,'' is reproduced from Cognitive Potential Throughout Life, J. E. Birren and V. L. Bengston (eds.), p. 257. Copyright © 1989 by Springer Publishing Company, Inc., New York 10012. Used by permission of Springer Publishing Company, Inc. Figure 9.2 S. W. Cornelius & A. Caspi. ''Everyday problem solving in adulthood and old age.'' *Psychology and Aging.* Vol. 2. By American Psychological Association. Copyright © 1987. Reprinted by permission of S. W. Cornelius. Figure 9.4 K. W. Schaie. ''Stability of intelligence.'' In J. E. Birren and K. W. Schaie (eds.), *Handbook of the Psychology of Aging.* 3rd Ed. By Academic Press. Copyright © 1990, p. 297. Reprinted by permission of K. W. Schaie and Academic Press. Figure 9.5 K. W. Schaie. ''Cohort differences in cognitive abilities,'' Figure 9.6 S. L. Willis. ''Training effects for three cohorts,'' Excerpts from The View in Winter, copyright © 1979 by Ronald Blythe, reprinted by permission of Harcourt Brace Jovanovich, Inc.

Chapter 10 Figure 10.1 D. Coleman. ''1,528 little geniuses and how they grew,'' *Psychology Today,* 13, February 1980, p. 40. Copyright © 1980. Reprinted from *Psychology Today* Magazine. Figure 10.2 P. T. Costa et al. ''Stablity of personality.'' *Psychology and Aging,* Vol. 1. By American Psychological Association. Copyright © 1986. Table 10.1 R. R. McCrae & P. T. Costa. ''Five-factor model of personality.'' *American Psychologist,* September 1986. Copyright © 1986, p. 1002. Reprinted by permission of R. R. McCrae. Table 10.3 ''Psychosocial Crises'' is reproduced from The Life Cycle Completed, A Review, by Erik H. Erikson, by permission of W. W. Norton & Company, Inc. Copyright © 1982 by Rikan Enterprises, Ltd. Figure 10.4 From The Seasons of a Man's Life, by Daniel J. Levinson et al. Copyright © 1978 by Daniel J. Levinson. Reprinted by permission of Alfred A. Knopf, Inc. Excerpts from F. Scott-Maxwell. The Measure of My Days. Copyright © 1968 by Alfred A. Knopf, Inc. Reprinted by permission of Alfred A. Knopf, Inc. Excerpts from C. Painter. Gifts of Age. Copyright © 1985 Chronicle Books. Reprinted by permission of Chronicle Books.

Chapter 11 Table 11.1 R. J. Sternberg. (1986) ''A triangular theory of love.'' *Psychology Review,* Vol. 93, No. 2. Copyright © 1986 by American Psychological Association. Reprinted by R. J. Sternberg. Table 11.5 M. Gentry & A. D. Shulman. ''Remarriage as a coping response for widowhood.'' Psychology and Aging, Vol. 3. Copyright © 1988 by American Psychological Association. Reprinted by permission of M. Gentry. Table 11.7 H. M. Hacker. ''Blabbermouths and Clams: Sex Differences in Self-Disclosure in Same-Sex and Cross-Sex Friendship Dyads,'' Psychology of Women Quarterly, Vol. 5, No. 3. Copyright © 1981, 393, Table 2. Excerpts from *American Couples* by Philip Blumstein and Pepper Schwartz. Copyright © 1983 by Philip Blumstein and Pepper Schwartz. By permission of William Morrow and Co., Inc.

Chapter 12 Figure 12.1 A. S. Fleming, D. N. Ruble, G. L. Flett & V. van Wagner. ''Adjustment in first-time mothers: Changes in mood and mood content during the early postpartum months.'' *Developmental Psychology,* Vol. 26. Copyright © 1990 by American Psychological Association. Reprinted by permission of Alison S. Fleming. Figure 12.2 A. S. Ragozin, R. B. Basham, K. A. Crinic, M. T. Greenberg, and N. M. Robinson. ''Effects of Maternal Age on Parenting Role.'' *Developmental Psychology,* 18 (1982), p. 631. Copyright © 1982 by the American Psychological Association. Reproduced by permission of Keith A. Crinic. Figure 12.4 M. Gatz, V. L. Bengston and M. J. Blum. ''Caregiver Stress and Coping.'' In J. E. Birren and K. W. Schaie (eds.), *Handbook of*

◆ Author Index

♦ Subject Index